UNIVERSALS OF HUMAN LANGUAGE

VOLUME 4

Syntax

CONTRIBUTORS

Eve V. Clark
Bruce T. Downing
Talmy Givón
Helga Harries-Delisle
Laurence R. Horn
Edith A. Moravcsik
Gerald A. Sanders
Susan Steele
Leonard Talmy
Russell Ultan

Universals of Human Language

Edited by Joseph H. Greenberg

Associate Editors:
Charles A. Ferguson & Edith A. Moravcsik

VOLUME 4

Syntax

Stanford University Press, Stanford, California
1978

Several of the papers in this volume were published originally in *Working Papers on Language Universals,* published for limited distribution by the Language Universals Project at Stanford University in sixteen numbers, 1970-76, as indicated in the opening footnotes to the individual papers. Most have been modified to some extent for publication here. Number 8 in this volume, by Givón, is ©1975 Leland Stanford Junior University.

Preface

The mainspring of the contemporary interest in language universals is the conviction that linguistics as a science must develop broader goals than the description of the structures of the thousands of individual languages which exist in the present or of which we have records from the past. It must be broader even than a body of generalizing theory concerning how such descriptions can be carried out.

Theory of this latter type already existed by the early 1950's, although many defects have since become apparent. As compared with other human sciences of the time, it seemed to possess an evident superiority in methodological sophistication and rigor. Yet a thoughtful and alert observer could raise fundamental problems not evident to the practical purveyor who took for granted the tacit premises of his science.

It fell to the lot of one of the present writers, as a participant in the seminar on psycholinguistics sponsored by the Social Science Research Council in the summer of 1951 at Bloomington, to give an exposition of linguistics for the psychologists present. The task was undertaken with a sense of pride in the accomplishments of the linguistics of the period. One of the psychologists, Charles Osgood, was suitably impressed. He commented, however, to the effect that while linguistics had an admirable and well worked out method, it was being applied merely to the description of individual languages. Could the linguists present tell him anything about all languages? That would be of the highest interest to psychologists. To this the linguistics of the period had no real answer.

The stimulating quality of these remarks and of the other discussions that followed bore fruit in the work of the Social Science Research Council, leading ultimately to the Dobbs Ferry conference on Language Universals in 1961. This meeting played an essential part in inaugurating a period of renewed interest in this topic.

While there were several papers at that conference which stated tentative generalizations of universal scope regarding several aspects of language, it was realized that to extend such studies from these modest beginnings was an enormous task requiring relevant data regarding numerous other aspects of language to be

drawn from adequately large samples of languages. Hence arose
the notion of a research project in which scholars would undertake
concrete research of this sort on a large variety of linguistic
topics.

This took shape at Stanford where the Project on Language
Universals was organized. It began its activities in October 1967
and brought them to an end in August 1976. During its entire nine-
year period it was directed by Charles A. Ferguson and Joseph H.
Greenberg, both professors at Stanford University, as principal
investigators. Its main source of financial support was the National
Science Foundation, which, over the years, contributed slightly
below $1,000,000. In addition to the two principal investigators,
the Project staff included altogether thirty-two part-time or full-
time linguists, some of whom held short-term visiting positions
not spanning more than a few months, while others were with the
Project up to several years. The names of these linguists are as
follows: Rebecca Agheyisi, Alan Bell, D.N.S. Bhat, Jean Braine,
Richard Carter, Eve Clark, Harold Clumeck, John Crothers,
Gilles Delisle, Talmy Givón, Victor Girard, Mary Ellen Greenlee,
Helga Harries-Delisle, Laurence Horn, Charles Jennings, Joan
Kahr, Dorothea Kaschube, Ian Maddieson, James Michael Moore,
Edith Moravcsik, Chris O'Sullivan, Andrew Rindsberg, Merritt
Ruhlen, Gerald Sanders, Philip Sedlak, Susan Steele, Leonard
Talmy, Russell Ultan, Marilyn Vihman, Krystyna Wachowicz,
Werner Winter, and Karl Zimmer. The staff also included Nicholas
Zirpolo on a short-term bibliographer appointment, and Dal
Dresser, Vicky Shu, and Vicki Fahrenholz as successive secretary-
bibliographers for the Project; budgetary questions were attended
to throughout by Jean Beeson. In addition to those mentioned here,
from time to time visiting scholars with outside funding collabor-
ated with the Project for varying periods. Among these was
Hansjakob Seiler.

The original goals of the Project were stated by Greenberg in
his introductory words to the first issue of Working Papers in
Language Universals (WPLU) in November 1969. They were to
formulate cross-linguistic and, if possible, universally valid
empirical generalizations about language structure; generalizations,
that is, which hold true for some significant universe of languages
and which at the same time are capable of being refuted by actual
language data. The fact that such generalizations cannot be verified without reliable cross-linguistic data justifies the other original objective of the Project, which was to collect data from various languages of the world and store them in precise and comparable form. These two objectives were seen as not in themselves

sufficient but nonetheless necessary parts of the long-range goal
of accounting for similarities and differences among human language
in terms of increasingly general laws overarching various apparently unrelated aspects of language structure.

The particular format chosen for the realization of these two
initially conceived goals of the Project was the following. At any
one time the staff consisted of the two directors, a secretary-
bibliographer, and three or four researchers. Although the selection of staff linguists reflected adherence to the basic goals of the
Project, once on the staff, linguists were free to follow their own
philosophies and methodologies regarding research on typology
and universals. The papers in WPLU indeed reflect the resulting
theoretical and methodological diversity. The choice of topics was
similarly left up to the individual investigator, subject in principle
to the veto of the directors -- a power, however, which was never
actually exercised. Middle-range projects were encouraged,
requiring not more and possibly less than half a year to complete.
The rich linguistic resources of the Stanford University library,
as well as Ferguson's and Greenberg's private libraries, provided
most of the basic data. For some studies linguistic informants
from Stanford and the surrounding area were also utilized. Frequent biweekly or weekly meetings of the Project, attended at
times by other linguists from Stanford and from neighboring universities and by scholars visiting the area, provided opportunities for
reporting on and criticizing ongoing or completed work. The working paper series of the Project ensured informal and rapid dissem-
ination of results to wider circles.

It is in accordance with this mode of organization that the Project progressed toward the realization of its two goals. As far as
data collection is concerned, almost every one of the sixty-eight
working papers that were published in the twenty issues of WPLU
presented data from a variety of languages in comparable terms.[1]
In addition to the actual data, efforts were also made to provide
guidelines for data collection. This was done by "check lists" or
sets of parameters related to specific aspects of language data and
of use both to linguistic fieldworkers and to cross-linguistic re-

---

[1]This includes all full-size working papers published in the series, whether written by Project members (54) or contributed by
linguists not associated with the Project (14). The number does not
include the survey papers and shorter notes contained in WPLU.

searchers. After several years of the operation of the Project,
attempts to archive data on phonetics and phonology, an area which
seemed particularly promising in this respect, took the shape of
an independent research endeavor, the Phonology Archiving Project. This group was also Stanford-based, had the same directors
as the Language Universals Project, and received funding from the
same source. A still ongoing enterprise, the Phonology Archiving
Project has to date computer-stored the phonetic segment inventory of about two hundred languages, as well as phonological rule
information on some of them.[2] Although tentative plans for a
similar large-scale computer archiving project with respect to
grammatical information were made, their realization is still a
matter for the future.

As far as the other aim is concerned, the establishment of
cross-linguistically valid generalizations about language structures,
we believe that substantial progress has been made, as the papers
in WPLU attest, making allowances for the inevitable future revis-
ions and even the abandonment of certain generalizations in the
light of further investigation. It seems reasonable to conclude that
a substantial portion of this work will prove, in the long run, to have
contributed substantially to our understanding of human language.

As the Project's end drew nearer, it was felt that a publication
that is both more formal and also more widely available than the
WPLU series should stand as a summary of our activities.[3] Thus

---

[2]For access to this material, write to Phonology Archiving Project, Department of Linguistics, Stanford University, Stanford,
California 94305.

[3]Copies of issues 11-20 of WPLU nonetheless remain available
at $2.00 apiece. Write to Working Papers on Language Universals,
Department of Linguistics, Stanford University, Stanford, California 94305. A bibliographical list including all references cited in
WPLU papers (about 2,000) arranged according to languages (about
750) is also available from the same address (under the name
"Bibliography") for $1.00 a copy; and so are the proceedings of a
conference on nasals and nasalization held in 1974 at Stanford,
entitled Nasalfest, for $6.50 a copy. Xerox and microfiche copies
of individual papers contained in any of the twenty issues of WPLU
are also available from ERIC clearinghouse in Languages and Linguistics, Center for Applied Linguistics, 1611 North Kent Street,
Arlington, Virginia 22209.

the idea of the present book was conceived. The original intention
of simply summarizing what we have done was then complemented
by the desire to answer the very patent need in the present linguistic literature for a comprehensive statement on where exactly we
are in our knowledge about cross-linguistically recurrent structural properties of language. The "we" in the latter part of this
sentence is not confined to Project members. In the past few years
endeavors to establish and test similar generalizations have been
increasingly initiated by individual scholars and organized projects
in other countries as well as in Western Europe and the Soviet
Union. In addition, even those whose basic methodology and
approach are quite different from that employed for the most part
in the Project have taken note of its results and have felt the need
of accounting for them by incorporating them within their own
theoretical framework, or even modifying that framework to
account for them.

In accordance with these aims, we have sought to make these
volumes as comprehensive as possible, consistent with the current
stage of research and the particular interests and competences of
those scholars who were either active in or basically sympathetic
with our enterprise.

These volumes consist of forty-six papers. Roughly corresponding
to three fundamental aspects of language structure, the data-
oriented papers have been grouped into three classes: those mostly pertaining to phonology, those mostly dealing with morphological
and lexical properties of the word-unit, and those primarily involved with syntactic and related semantic problems. The second,
third, and fourth volumes of the book each contain one of these
three groups of papers. The first volume presents the general
papers which discuss questions of the theory and methodology of
typological and universals research. Each paper in the book is
preceded by an abstract and followed by its own list of references.
At the end of each volume is an author index and a language index
specific to papers in that volume.

Of the forty-six studies included in the book, thirty-five appear
here for the first time. These have been written in part by scholars
who were either members of or associated with the Stanford Project on Language Universals, in part by scholars not formally
associated with the Project who have been invited by the editors to
deal with a specific topic. Among the latter are Elaine Andersen,
Dwight Bolinger, Bruce Downing, Thomas Gamkrelidze, Brian

Head, Larry Hyman, Hans-Heinrich Lieb, Adam Makkai, Yakov Malkiel, and Elizabeth Closs Traugott. The remaining thirteen papers are original or revised versions of working papers that were previously published informally. They were written by members of this group as part of their work for the Project.

In general, the arrangement is topical; it reflects the manner in which research was actually carried out under the aegis of the Project and of the typical product as seen in the Working Papers. This approach has some advantages. In general, it selects areas of research comprehensive enough not to be trivial and, on the other hand, not so all-encompassing as to be impractical. It leads to numerous concrete and testable generalizations. We are also keenly aware of certain inevitable defects. Since, to begin with, we did not provide a comprehensive a priori scheme and did not impose particular topics on investigators, there are necessarily major omissions. There is also the danger that a somewhat ad hoc and piecemeal approach will lead to the neglect of topics that do not easily fall within present classificatory rubrics, as reflected in the overall organization of this work. For example, there is much to be learned from the phenomenon of word accent as it relates to morphological systems. However, this topic does not easily fall within conventional classifications.

The other defect is more closely tied into the basically, but not exclusively, inductive nature of this approach. Interconnections based on the presence of similar general psychological or other principles, or of even more specific factual relevance, may be overlooked through compartmentalization. Still, as an initial strategy, we believe it to be defensible in terms of its immediate fruitfulness. This is, however, something for the linguistic community as a whole to judge. Moreover, many of our investigations, it can be claimed, have already involved at least an adumbration of more comprehensive principles -- for example, of marking theory.

In behalf of the authors of the papers included in this work and in our own behalf, we would like to express our deep gratitude to all of those who made the appearance of the books possible. Thus, we would first like to thank Vicky Shu for the competence and genuine care she brought to the editing and typing of the final camera-ready version of the manuscript. We are furthermore grateful to Stanford Press and to William Carver in particular for their guidance in our endeavor to produce a book that is pleasing to the eye. Our most sincere thanks should go to Stanford University,

especially to the Department of Linguistics and its current chair-
person, Clara Bush, for being such an understanding host to the
Language Universals Project in the past nine years, and to Deans
Halsey Royden and W. Bliss Carnochan, and Provost William
Miller for their generous financial support toward the preparation
of the manuscript in final form.   Finally, we thank the National
Science Foundation for its continuing support of the work of the
project.

J.H.G.
C.A.F.
E.A.M.

Contents

Contributors

Eve V. Clark is Associate Professor in the Department of Linguistics at Stanford University. In 1969-70, she was a Research Associate with the Stanford Project on Language Universals.

Bruce T. Downing is Associate Professor and Chairman of the Department of Linguistics at the University of Minnesota, Twin Cities.

Talmy Givón is Associate Professor of Linguistics at the University of California, Los Angeles, and director of the Ute Language Project, Southern Ute Tribe, Ignacio, Colorado. In 1975-76, he worked with the Stanford Project on Language Universals.

Helga Harries-Delisle is in the Department of Foreign Languages at New Mexico State University in Las Cruces. She was a member of the Stanford Project on Language Universals in 1972-73.

Laurence R. Horn is in the Department of Linguistics at the University of Wisconsin -- Madison. He was a member of the Stanford Project on Language Universals in 1973-75.

Edith A. Moravcsik is a Visiting Assistant Professor of Linguistics at the University of Wisconsin in Milwaukee. She was a member of the Stanford Project on Language Universals in 1968-72 and again in 1975-76. She is Associate Editor of these volumes and was the editor of Working Papers on Language Universals.

Gerald A. Sanders is Professor in Linguistics at the University of Minnesota, Twin Cities. He joined the Stanford Project on Language Universals for the summer of 1971.

Susan Steele is Assistant Professor of Linguistics at the University of Arizona. In 1975-76, she was associated with the Stanford Project on Language Universals.

Leonard Talmy is presently a researcher on child language disorders at the Neuropsychiatric Institute, University of California, Los Angeles. He was a member of the Stanford Project on Language Universals from late 1972 to early 1975.

Russell Ultan is an American Council of Learned Societies postdoctoral fellow conducting research in Turku, Finland. His association with the Stanford Project on Language Universals, longer than any other Project member, spanned the years 1968-74.

UNIVERSALS OF HUMAN LANGUAGE

VOLUME 4

Syntax

Introduction

EDITH A. MORAVCSIK

This is the last of the four volumes of Universals of Human Languages. As stated in the Preface, the purpose of the work is to provide a comprehensive statement on the current state of language-typological and language-universals research. Since the grammars of all human languages include three types of generalizations -- rules about sound patterns, rules about syntactic patterns, and rules about lexical patterns — we were able to divide our material into three fairly natural parts. Volume II includes papers about phonology, volume III presents papers mostly about morphemes and words, and volume IV are mostly about syntax. The first volume in the series is simply an introduction to the others — a collection of studies on the theory and methodology of typological and universals research in linguistics.

The most general goal of these volumes is the advancement of linguistic research -- that is to say, the advancement of our understanding of the structure of human linguistic utterances and their spatial-temporal distribution in the world. Advances in this field, as in others, are facilitated by a definition of the total extent of the undertaking and by an assessment of how much has already been achieved and how much remains. Thus, what I would like to do in these introductory remarks to the syntax volume is to attempt an informal delimitation of the total range of questions that make up the domain of syntactic typological and universals research, to show which of the total set of relevant questions have been answered or have begun to be answered by the papers included in this volume (or by others not included here), and to point to some of those areas of syntax that are yet to be investigated from this point of view.

Let us assume that the grammar of a language is a set of generalizations such that each of them makes some contribution to the process of converting a meaning into a sound string, or a sound string into a meaning, and such that the statements included in the grammar are jointly sufficient to effect such conversions for all sentences of the language. Grammatical statements, in other words, will be taken to be those necessary and sufficient tools in terms of which questions of two types can be answered:

1. What is the expression of the meaning M in language L (where M is any sentence-size meaning expressible in language L)?

2. What is the meaning of the sound string S in language L
(where S is any sentence-size sound string that is meaningful in language L)?

The particular subset of these grammatical statements that effect
the conversion of the meanings of sentences into the sequences of
morpheme-size meaning units that their expression consists of
(i.e. that mediate between their "semantic representation" and
"surface syntactic representation") will be called syntactic rules.

Given this concept of syntax, there are altogether three logically
possible basic types of syntactic rules: ordering rules, addition
rules, and deletion rules. In all human language grammars, the
presence of ordering rules -- rules, that is, that provide for the
temporal arrangement of the information conveyed by the sentence
-- is logically necessary, because the meaning structure of a sentence is not a temporally structured object, whereas syntactic
surface structures consist of temporal sequences of morpheme-
size meaning units. It follows from this, therefore, that the process of converting thoughts into sentences must involve some
decision-making on the part of the speaker concerning the temporal
sequencing of the bits of thoughts to be expressed. Thus, if I say
Cats like rats., the expression of this sentence includes a particular
ordering of the five morphemes cat, s, like, rat, s, even though
the meaning of the sentence is characterizable without any reference to this temporal sequence of the meaning elements, by simply
saying that what it involves is a liking whose experiencers are cats
and whose objects are rats.

The two other logically possible basic types of syntactic rules
cannot be shown to be logically necessary, but both appear to occur
in all human language grammars. These two rule types are additions and
deletions. The positing of deletion rules, on the one hand, is ne-
cessitated by the fact that there are sentences in perhaps all human
languages with elements of meaning that are understood to be part
of the total meaning but that nonetheless have no morphemic expression. The positing of addition rules, on the other hand, is neces-
sitated by the fact that some sentences of human languages include
some morphemes in their expression that, however, are not carriers
of any meaning that is part of the meaning of the sentence, An example of such "understood meaning" is provided by the sentence Jim
called me but Jack did not. Here it is understood that Jack did not
call me, even though the expression Jack did not call me is not part
of the sentence. Thus, the meaning of call me as associated with
Jack did not can appropriately be said to have been deleted in the

course of the meaning-sound conversion process. An example of
"empty morphemes" is provided by the sentence <u>There is a cat on
the roof</u>. Here the morpheme <u>there</u> is heard as part of the form
of the sentence, but it makes no contribution to the meaning of the
sentence, as shown by the fact that <u>A cat is on the roof</u>., which
lacks the morpheme <u>there</u>, means the same thing. The content of
the morpheme <u>there</u> can thus appropriately be said to have been
added in the course of the meaning-sound conversion process. It
is in this sense, therefore, that we can classify the rules of syntax
into three types: ordering, addition, and deletion.[1]

Given this view of the concepts "syntax" and "syntactic rule,"
and given that our interest is in comparing the syntaxes of various
languages and making universal and subuniversal generalizations
about their similarities and differences, there appear to be three
natural ways of defining subfields, or "research topics," within
syntactic typological and universals research.

First, one can choose as a basis the above-outlined formal classification of syntactic rule types and investigate one of them separately from the others. In other words, principled subdomains
of research could be focused on questions such as these:

a. How do languages resemble and differ from each other with
respect to the temporal organization of sentence meanings?

b. How do languages resemble and differ from each other with
respect to what meaning elements they allow to be deleted?

c. How do languages resemble and differ from each other with
respect to what semantically empty morphemes they include
in sentence expressions?

---

[1] Strictly speaking, ordering rules are instances of addition,
since they effect the addition of a relation. Both addition and deletion rules can furthermore be regarded as subtypes of one single
logically elementary statement type characterized by the fact that,
of the "input" and "output" structures that they make reference to,
both contain some elements that the other also does, and one contains some elements that the other does not. Substitution rules --
the only other logically possible grammatical rule type -- are not
a basic type, since they can be analyzed into conflation of addition
and deletion.

Second, one can focus one's research on a meaning type, rather than a rule type, and ask questions such as these:

a. How do languages resemble and differ from each other in the expression of definiteness?

b. How do languages resemble and differ from each other in the expression of possession?

An all-inclusive, semantically based comparative investigation of human language syntaxes would involve comparing alternative expressions in various languages of at least the following meaning types:

1. Simple terms:
    1.1 predicate types with respect to:
    a. tense (present, past, etc.)
    b. aspect (imperfect, perfect, etc.)
    c. mood (declarative, interrogative, imperative, etc.)
    d. polarity (affirmative, negative)
    e. valence (intransitive, transitive, bitransitive, etc.)
    f. communicative function (asserted, presupposed, etc.)
    g. other semantic properties (stative, nonstative, etc.)
    1.2 argument types with respect to:
    a. semantic case function (agent, patient, causer, experiencer, etc.)
    b. communicative function (topic, focus, etc.)
    c. other semantic properties (noun, pronoun, sentence, animate, etc.)

2. complex terms:
    2.1 modification   a. of arguments
                          b. of predicates
    2.2 quantification   a. of arguments
                          b. of predicates
    2.3 determination   a. of arguments
                          b. of predicates

Third, one can define natural research topics in syntactic typology and universals research by making reference both to meaning types and to rule types. Thus, we can ask questions such as these:

a. How do languages resemble and differ from each other with respect to the temporal ordering of noun modifiers?

b. How do languages resemble and differ from each other with
respect to the deletability of predicates?

The 14 papers included in this volume provide a partial, rather
than complete, coverage of the field of syntactic typology and universals and, with respect to the choice of criterion that defines
their subject matter, they are heterogeneous, in the sense that
whereas the topics of most of them are semantically delimited,
there are some with topics defined by joint reference to meaning
type and rule type. In 11 of the papers, the topic is definable in
more or less purely semantic terms; in the other three, in semantic-
and-formal terms.

Types of meanings whose alternative expressions in various
languages are investigated in the 11 semantically based studies
are the following:

```
simple terms:
    predicate types:
        mood - questions
        polarity - negation
        communicative function - foregrounding-backgrounding
        other semantic properties - existential, locative, and
                                      possessive predications
    argument types:
        semantic case function - patients
        communicative function - contrast; foregrounding-
                                  backgrounding
complex terms:
    modification:  of arguments - by (relative) clause
                               - by possessor
                   of predicates - by adverb
    determination:  of arguments
```

Each expression underlined above describes the topic of one or
more papers in the volume. Thus, interrogative constructions
constitute the topic of one of Ultan's contributions, in which he
compares the ways in which various languages use intonation, constituent order, and morphological marking for the expression of
information questions and yes-no questions of various kinds. Horn's
extensive study deals with the alternative ways in which languages
formulate expressions of negation. Talmy's two papers deal with
the ways in which languages resemble and differ from each other
in the expression of foregrounded versus backgrounded information.

Clark's paper studies the translation equivalents of ENGLISH existential, locative, and possessive sentences such as There is a book
on the table., The book is on the table., Tom has a book., and
The book is Tom's.   She shows certain similarities in the expression of such meanings in various languages in relation to the
choice of verbs, the case-marking of the nouns, and constituent
order.   Moravcsik's study on objects investigates crosslinguistic
convergences mainly in respect to the case-marking -- with some
passing remarks on the agreement, order, and stress properties --
of patient (i.e. non-agentive, non-dative) arguments.   Harries-
Delisle discusses in one of her papers the ways in which contrastive
emphasis of noun phrases is signaled in human languages.   Downing's
paper investigates similarities among languages in the expression
of relative clause constructions.   Ultan's second study is about
possessively modified nouns and also about possessive sentences,
thus overlapping in part with Clark's topic.   Sanders examines
adverbially modified verbs and arrives at some crosslinguistic
generalizations concerning the form of such expressions.   Finally,
Givón studies various manifestations of definiteness and, in general,
of referentiality, in human languages.

Of the other three studies, Steele's paper is about ordering rules,
Harries-Delisle's is about deletions, and Moravcsik's is about addition rules.   The scope of each of the three papers is further delimited.   The Steele study is concerned in particular with the ordering
of major sentence constituents such as verb, subject, object, and
other verb complements, and she attempts to discover constraints
that govern permitted variations of these orderings in any one particular language.   Harries-Delisle is concerned with deletion rules
as they apply to coordinated sentences with some identical constituents.   Moravcsik's paper is about a particular kind of addition
rule -- the kind that provides for the redundant duplication of some
argument properties on other constituents, such as verbs or adjectives, associated with that argument.

As mentioned earlier, the 14 papers of this volume jointly constitute a sizable but nonetheless only partial coverage of the field
of syntactic typology and universals research.   Not all syntactic
construction types are investigated.   Thus, in terms of a meaning-
based classification of syntactic constructions, the volume does not
consider expressions of various tenses, aspects, moods other than
interrogative (e.g. imperative), noun-phrase expressions corresponding to various semantic case functions (other than patient) and
to various communicative functions such as topic, as well as many
types of predicate and argument modification, quantification, and
determination.

Some of these constructions are investigated in other recent crosslinguistic studies, especially the following:

On tense, mood, and aspect: see Steele's paper on the auxiliary and Ultan's paper on the future tense in volume III of this book; also Edward L. Blansitt, Jr., "Progressive Aspect," Working Papers on Language Universals 18, October 1975; and Bernard Comrie, Aspect (Cambridge University Press), 1976.

On grammatical relations: for the passive in particular, see Fred R. Eckman, "Agentive and Agentless Passives," Working Papers on Language Universals 14, August 1974; and Edward L. Keenan, "Some Universals of Passive in Relational Grammar," Papers from the Eleventh Regional Meeting of the Chicago Linguistic Society, 1975, pp. 340-52; for causatives, see Krystyna Wachowicz, "Some Universal Properties of Morphological Causatives," Working Papers on Language Universals 20, August 1976; A.A. Kholodovich, "Tipologiia kauzativnykh konstrukcii," Morfologicheski kausativ (Leningrad), 1969; and Masayoshi Shibatani (editor), "The Grammar of Causative Constructions," Syntax and Semantics, volume 6 (New York), 1976; and, in general, see I.I. Meščaninov (editor), Ergativnaja konstrukcija v jazykax različnyx tipov (Leningrad), 1967; Charles N. Li (editor), Subject and Topic (New York), 1976; Peter Cole and Jerrold M. Sadock (editors), Grammatical Relations, Syntax and Semantics, volume 8 (New York), 1977.

On complement clauses: see Claudia Corum, T. Cedric Smith-Stark, and Ann Weiser (editors), You Take the High Node and I'll Take the Low Node (Chicago), 1973.

On comparative constructions: see Russell Ultan, "Some Features of Basic Comparative Constructions," Working Papers on Language Universals 9, November 1972.

On argument quantification: see Joseph Greenberg's paper on numeral systems in volume III of this book; also Greenberg, "Numeral Classifiers and Substantival Number: Problems in the Genesis of a Linguistic Type," Working Papers on Language Universals 9, November 1972; and Mary Sanches, "Numeral Classifiers and Plural Marking: an Implicational Universal," Working Papers on Language Universals 11, April 1973.

On deixis, as well as on a large number of other syntactic constructions discussed or not discussed in the present volume, see Arbeiten der Kölner Universalien-Projekts, pp. 1-27, 1973-77, and the ongoing work of the Language Typology and Syntactic Fieldwork

Project, directed by S. Anderson, T. Givón, E. Keenan, S. Thompson, and R. Troike.

Similarly, from the point of view of a form-based classification of syntactic constructions, a number of deletion, addition, and ordering-rule types have not been discussed here. Some recent crosslinguistic investigations on these topics are the following:

On ordering: see Edward L. Blansitt, Jr., "Bitransitive Clauses," Working Papers on Language Universals 13, December 1973; Philip A. Sedlak, "Direct/Indirect Object Word Order: a Crosslinguistic Analysis," Working Papers on Language Universals 18, October 1975; Joseph H. Greenberg, "Some Universals of Grammar with Particular Reference to the Order of Meaningful Elements," in Greenberg (editor), Universals of Language (Cambridge), 1966; Charles Li (editor), Word Order and Word Order Change (Austin), 1975; and Talmy Givón, "Word Order Typology" (a working paper of the Language Typology and Syntactic Fieldwork Project, 1977).

On addition: see Greenberg's paper on noun classifications in volume III of this work.

On deletion: see Ingram's and Head's papers on pronouns in volume III of this work.

There are three other reasons why the present collection leaves room for further studies in the field of syntactic typology and universals. The first of these has to do with language coverage. Since our field is still lacking a comprehensive data bank where grammatical information on sizable samples of languages could be readily obtained, data-collection for crosslinguistic studies involves painstaking research. Thus, by necessity, most of the studies included here were limited to a relatively small sample of languages. All the generalizations proposed in these papers as tentative universals would have to be further tested against more language data.

The second reason has to do with the predictive power of the generalizations arrived at. Whereas many of the generalizations permit the prediction of the presence of a certain structural property in a language because the generalization clearly states that that property is present in all human languages or in all members of a particular subclass of human languages, other generalizations do not enable us to make such predictions. Generalizations not permitting such predictions are statements asserting the occurrence of some syntactic property in <u>some</u> human languages, where the relevant class of languages is qualitatively unspecified. Thus, for example, concerning the distribution of question particles, all that can be said is that some languages have them and others do not; but we do not know which do and which do not (cf. Ultan's paper on interrogative constructions). Similarly, concerning the presence of a head-coreferential personal pronoun in relative clauses, all that can be said is that there is a strong tendency for such a pronoun not to occur if the relative clause includes an initial relative pronoun (cf. Downing's paper on relative clauses). Although statements of this kind are significant and suggestive, they fall short of being useful typological and universal statements, since they do not provide a basis of predicting the presence or absence of a structural property in a language. Further research is thus needed to find the conditions that correlate with the presence of the structural property they refer to, so that prediction might become possible.

There is, finally, a third reason why the collection of typological and universal generalizations included in this volume cannot be considered definitive. Although each universal proffered is explanatory with respect to some set of facts, each elicits a further why-question. Thus, for instance, Clark suggests two ordering rules, according to one of which definite nouns precede indefinite ones, and according to the other of which animate nouns precede inanimate nouns. Though these statements serve to explain, for instance, why any one instance of a definite noun precedes another particular instance of an indefinite noun, they are also explanada themselves: we want to know why just these temporal precedence patterns exist, as opposed to their contraries. Similarly, Sanders finds that case affixes are always suffixed (i.e. never prefixed). This statement is useful because it serves to predict -- and thus also to explain, to some extent -- the position of all case affixes in all human languages. At the same time, it is an observation that is itself in need of a further explanation.

It is the hope of both the authors and the editors of this volume that the studies included here will serve both to satisfy some of the queries with which the reader has approached the volume and to stimulate further progress toward crosslinguistic generalizations of increased scope and increased predictive and explanatory power.

Toward a Typology
of Substantival Possession

RUSSELL ULTAN

ABSTRACT

Possessive constructions contain a possessor and a possessee identified by one or more morphosyntactic features: the possessor by person, third person, genitive, and possessor class referents, and the possessee by possessee class referent. Or possessor and possessee may be identified solely on the basis of their respective phrase-internal ordering. Of these, genitive and/or third person, along with ordering, constitute the basic features requisite to formulating a typology of possessive constructions, which in turn leads to certain generalizations concerning co-occurrence patterns of the various features within constructions (see Sec. 7).

Pronominal possessors may be divided into two classes formally marked for identity or nonidentity with the subject. Possessee (occasionally possessor) may show a dichotomy between greater and lesser intimacy of possession.

Possessive substantives are formed by either eliding the possessee or replacing it with a determination marker.

Genitives are equated with: topics of subject or object genitive constructions, objects of pre- or postpositional locative phrases, wholes of partitive constructions, proper names of proper-common name constructions, and standards in comparative and superlative constructions.

In most HAVE-constructions, the actual possessor, usually object-marked, is equated with the predicate of the sentence and the possessee with the subject.

This is a corrected and somewhat revised version of a paper of the same title that appeared in Working Papers on Language Universals 3, June 1970, P1-P27.

12 Russell Ultan

CONTENTS

1. Introduction

The primary purpose of this paper is to work out a typology of substantival possessive constructions based on an examination of data from 75 languages, reasonably randomly chosen (in terms of genetic affiliation and geographical distribution). By "substantival possessive constructions" I refer to the general class of attributive constructions in which the head represents a possessee (or possessed item) and the pronominal or nominal attribute represents the possessor of the possessee. Specifically excluded from consideration here will be secondary possessive constructions like my father's house or such monsters as George's friend's sister's dog's bone for two reasons: first, such constructions can be viewed as recursive in probably all languages and will thus be accounted for by a basic typology; second, little descriptive matter is available on these constructions (although they certainly exist in all languages). Order correlations between pronominally and nominally possessed constructions will also be considered in this first section.

As to the method used to elaborate the typology, I feel that a strictly or even primarily formal feature approach would lead to a fragmented and not particularly significant picture of how possessive systems are structured. I have therefore attempted to isolate the ultimate semantic components involved and the configurations into which they enter in the various types of construction encountered. This is not to say that formal considerations are ignored, merely that the role they play is in general of secondary importance. Thus, for example, whether a language uses a genitive preposition or postposition is usually determined by factors not directly connected with the formation of genitive constructions in the language.

In addition to the basic typology, a number of other possessive features and constructions of fairly widespread distribution in languages round the world, some more common than others, will be examined and discussed. One of these deals with specialized possessor and possessee subclasses such as the distinction in some languages between alienably and inalienably possessed nouns. Another concerns possessive substantives like mine or John's (as predicate). Still others include various nonpossessive (in most cases superficially so) functions of formal markers of possession: topic genitives (e.g. LATIN "subject" and "object" genitives), locative-governed genitives (largely prepositions and postpositions governing genitive constructions), partitive genitives, proper names in the genitive, and comparative and superlative genitives.

Finally, I will investigate another common device for indicating possession, HAVE-constructions,[1] often not formally designated by the usual possessive markers and constituting complete predications rather than possessive phrases (e.g. RUSSIAN u menjá kníga 'at me book' = 'I have a book.').

2. Basic Typology of Substantival Possession

2.1 Possession relationals

Discounting for the moment elliptical constructions like most predicative or independent possessive substantives, all possessive constructions must consist of at least two constituents, one denoting the possessor (G) and the other the possessee (N).

Logically, one might expect a third constituent denoting the relationship of possession linking the first two constituents; perhaps, in one sense, such a constituent is always present in any possessive construction. So, for example, even when neither possessor nor possessee is overtly marked (morphosyntactically), they and the relationship between them are marked by their relative ordering with respect to each other. Similarly, when the possessor is marked by a genitive affix or particle, it may be maintained that the genitive identifies the possessor positively and the possessee negatively, but also the relationship which exists between the two. Yet, in another sense, we may just as well say that its presence is conjectural, since there is really no specific and overt marker of the possessive relationship in either of these (and other) constructions. Nevertheless, some instances of morphosyntactic markers in the present sample would appear, at least at first glance, to qualify as overt indicators of the relationship itself. If such a third constituent exists, it must, of course, be included in any possessive typology, in which case the resultant typology will be considerably more complex than one based on two constituents only. I feel that an examination of what I had originally taken to be third constituent markers will show that these actually mark either possessor or possessee.

In ACOMA a "possessive prefix" occurs with ambivalent themes (which may be nominal or verbal). In verbal themes it denotes active (vs. passive) possession by the subject, e.g. hadyûunigú 'she will have pottery' (n- expective, qa- possessive, dyûuni 'pottery,' -gú 3rd sg. aux.); in nominal themes, e.g. k̓adyûuni 'her

---

[1]This term also appears in Bach 1967: 478.

pottery' (k̲a- < g̲- 3rd sg. + q̲a-), its function is unspecified. It
apparently occurs only with pronominally possessed alienable
themes and, as such exactly parallels the normal nominally possessed theme which is accompanied by the third person prefix in
cross reference to the possessor noun. Thus, it is clear that the
possessive prefix defines a specific class of possessors in both
nominal and verbal themes; in the former the pronominal possessor of an alienable noun.

   COCOPA forms possessive pronouns used to possess alienable
nouns by adding the subject pronoun prefix to a verb base meaning
'have, own,' as in nᵞqʷál ma?ís 'your front dress' (m̲- 2nd pers.,
a̲?í 'do' + -s̲ distrib. obj. pl. = 'have, own'). In essence, the
construction is a verb phrase (object + verb) functioning as a noun
phrase; here the verb base would appear to be a possession relational were it not for one thing — at least in this context it is
actually the distributive object form of an anaphoric demonstrative
glossed as 'have.' Demonstrative bases accompanied by personal
affixes to form possessive (and other) pronouns are not uncommon
(cf. the independent possessive pronoun in BERBER consisting of
demonstrative base + personal suffix) and are certainly not analyzable as containing a marker of possession relationship in terms of
the present typology.

   While most possessive constructions in MALAY have unmarked
constituents or possessee tagged for third person, one type might
be interpreted as containing a third constituent: it is employed
when the possessor is a kinship term or, occasionally, some other
personal substantive. Here the possessee is followed by a noun
glossed 'Besitz, Eigentum,' described as apposite to the possessee[2]
then followed by the possessor, e.g. bapa oléh perempuan itu 'that
woman's father' (note oléh 'possession' precedes the possessor,
functioning just as a preposition would in MALAY). If Kähler's
interpretation is correct, this noun seems to function as a sort of
specialized classifier, generically identifying the possessee but
defining by its privilege of occurrence a restricted class of possessors (kinship and some personal terms). It is therefore to be
regarded as a possessor class marker rather than a possession
relational, gloss notwithstanding.

   A strikingly similar situation exists in KHASI, where an element
which may function as a genitive preposition or a noun (as defined

---

[2]See Kähler 1965, but Hannes Kniffka (personal communication)
is of the opinion that, at least in COLLOQUIAL MALAY, this "noun"
functions rather as a genitive preposition.

by co-occurrence with the article) apparently is in apposite relationship with the possessee and is glossed 'possession, ownership,
the possessed.' This element often occurs in both functions simultaneously in possessive phrases, e.g. la ka joŋ ka jiŋbuonkam joŋ
ʔii 'his own business' (first joŋ noun in apposition with possessee;
second joŋ genitive preposition). However, since its occurrence
as a noun, unlike MALAY, places no restrictions on the possessor,
it must be taken as a generic classifier of the possessee. This
somewhat curious construction in KHASI, and probably also its
congener in MALAY, is reminiscent of the PIDGIN ENGLISH use
of belong as a genitive preposition or particle, e.g. table belong
me = my table. It would be interesting to know more about the
historical implications of such cases, but unfortunately these are
the only two which appear in this sample.

Given the above, I believe there is adequate justification for not
positing the existence of a possession relationship marker, at least
in accounting for all the possessive constructions found in the languages examined.

2.2 Basic constituents and possession features

Possessor and possessee may be identified by their positions
relative to one another when neither constituent is otherwise
marked, as in JAMAICAN CREOLE Rabat miizl 'Robert's measles,'
or either or both basic constituents may be marked for reference
to possessor (g) or to possessee (n), resulting in the following
simplex (no more than one marker per constituent) types:

Table 1

G	N	G	N
g	∅	∅	n
g	g	n	∅
g	n	n	g
∅	g	n	n

All these occur in our sample. However, the gross features g, n,
and ∅ are in themselves insufficiently elaborated to account for all
the types which are actually found. On the basis of constituent
referent, these features may be subdivided as follows:

Morphosyntactic Features

Possessor referent:
1. Person (per) denotes first, second, or third (and others, e.g.
   fourth, where applicable) person possessor when all are in

the same construction. One exception to this is SHONA (see below) where person refers to possessee.

2. Third person (3) denotes third person possessor when it does not contrast with first and second person in the same construction.
3. Genitive (gen)[3] identifies possessor as such (i.e. as agent of possession).
4. Possessor class (G) denotes nonpersonal agreement (e.g. number, gender, case, etc.) with possessor or special class of possessor.

Possessee referent:
Possessee class (N) denotes agreement with possessee or special class of possessee.

Order Features

Unmarked (∅): Neither possessor nor possessee is morphosyntactically marked in any way; they are identified by their relative order of occurrence in the construction, i.e. NG or GN.

Formally, there are several different types of markers (hyphens indicate pertinent morpheme boundaries; possessive features underlined):

1. Person
    a. root- or inherently marked, e.g. possessive adjective in ENGLISH my book, personal pronoun in genitive in CHAGATAY mäniñg köñglüm 'my heart.'
    b. affix-marked, e.g. prefix in ACOMA s-aṁásdí 'my hand,' suffix in ARAMAIC xalunta-x 'your (f. sg.) sister.'
    c. marked by a noun phrase, e.g. prepositional in KHASI kpaa joŋ ŋa 'my father,' postpositional in HINDI us kā bhāī 'his brother.' This feature may occur in constituency with possessor, possessee, or with both.

2. Third person
    a. root-marked, e.g. possessive pronoun in EWE lã wó afɔ (GN) 'the animal's foot' (lit. 'the animal its foot').

3This term, as used here to label a basic typological feature, is not to be confused with its common, far less restrictive usage by most grammarians to cover a general functional relationship between two substantives which indicates possession, attribution, dependency, etc. Some nonpossessive uses of genitives in the ordinary sense of the word are discussed in Sec. 5 of the present paper.

b. affix-marked, e.g. prefix in TUNICA táčɔhak ʔú-rĩhč 'the
chief's house' (lit. 'the chief his-house), suffix in TURKISH
kadının doktor-u 'the woman's doctor' (lit. 'the woman her-doctor').
Ordinarily, this feature occurs only in constituency with the
possessee, but SHONA has a peculiar construction in which it
figures with the possessor: ini wenyu (< wa-inyu 'his your')
'your me,' wa being the 3rd sg. human possessive concord prefix which may also occur with cross-reference to a first (as
here) or second person, perhaps indicating that it should be
interpreted as a possessee class rather than a third person
marker. In ARANDA the postposed third person pronoun assumes the genitive suffix of the possessor noun, the whole
functioning as a definite article in constituency with the latter,
e.g. ínṇa ekúra kántjala 'on top of the tree.' This could be
regarded as an instance of possessor class marker (the article)
rather than third person. If we thus eliminate the ARANDA
and SHONA cases from consideration as examples of third
person markers, the only occurrences of 3-markers in conjunction with possessors are always accompanied by identically
marked possessees, an observation which can be restated as:
A possessor marked for third person implies a possessee so
marked in the same construction.

3. Genitive
   a. affix-marked, e.g. prefix in AMHARIC yɛ-nɛggādēw bēt
   'the merchant's house,' suffix in BASQUE alkatear-en beya
   'the mayor's cow.'
   b. particle-marked, e.g. preposition in SYRIAN ARABIC
   š-šrūš tabaɛ haššažara 'the roots of that tree,' proclitic in
   BERBER afus n-əmmi 'my son's hand,' postposition in MANDA-
   RIN shiang de byitz 'elephant's trunk,' which also appears as
   a suffix with a pronominal possessor, e.g. woo-de shu 'my
   book.' Genitive may occur with either possessor or possessee,
   or with both. However, genitives appear more frequently with
   two kinds of constituents: possessors and constituents of nominally possessed constructions. Whenever a language marks
   the possessee with a genitive, that language also marks the
   possessor with it, although not necessarily in the same phrase.
   The sole apparent exception to this statement is PERSIAN. But
   what I have dubbed "genitive" for this language is actually the
   "izafet" suffix added to the heads of all attributive constructions,
   including those which are purely possessive; thus, the term
   genitive as used here encompasses more in the way of function
   than ordinarily. Further, whereas languages with genitive-
   marked constituents in nominally possessed phrases do not
   always have genitive-marked constituents in pronominally

possessed phrases (not necessarily the equivalent phrases),
the converse is not so. FULA is perhaps an exception because
possessive pronouns differ from personal pronouns in part by
by addition of prefixes or suffixes which I have classified as
genitives. These are apparently unique, and no functional genitive is used elsewhere in the language. Subject to the possible
exceptions noted, we may summarize the situation as follows:
1) Possessee marked for genitive implies a construction in
which possessor is so marked (not necessarily the same construction). 2) A genitive-marked constituent in a pronominally
possessed construction implies genitive marking of the corresponding constituent in a nominal construction (not necessarily
the parallel of the pronominally possessed construction).

4. Possessor class
   a. root-marked, e.g. reflexive adjective in LATIN su̅-um
   patrem vi̅dit 'he saw his (own) father' (contrasted with eius
   patrem vi̅dit 'he saw his [someone else's] father').
   b. affix-marked, e.g. prefix in ACOMA sḱahа́azа́ṅi (< s-ǫa-
   hа́azа́ṅi) 'one's hair' (ǫa- marks pronominally possessed alienable noun stem), suffix in CHAMORRO i sinanan-ñı̅ha i manamko
   'the sayings of the old people' (-ñı̅ha 3rd pl. agrees with pl.
   possessor manamko).
   c. particle-marked, e.g. preposition in TAGALOG kaibigan ni
   Arthur 'a friend of Arthur' (ni identifies personal name possessor; prep. ng is used for other possessors).

5. Possessee class
   a. affix-marked, e.g. prefix in TUNICA ʔu-hk-ʔı́yutɛ ku 'his
   hog' (hk- marks alienable possessee), suffix in RUSSIAN ot
   vа́š-evo do̅ma 'from your house' (-evo m. sg. gen. agrees with
   possessee).
   b. particle-marked, e.g. preposition in MAORI te tupuna oo
   pita 'Peter's ancestor' (oo inherited possessee; compare aa
   acquired possessee), article in FRENCH il lui a cassé le bras
   (le, which here functionally replaces the possessive adjective
   son, agrees with the possessee, bras).
   c. root-marked, e.g. noun (in apposition) in MALAY bapa olе́h
   perempuan itu 'that woman's father' (olе́h 'possession,' apposite to bapa 'father'), pronoun (base) in MAORI t-oo-na huritau
   'his birthday.' Possessor and possessee class markers may
   occur with either or both constituents.

6. Unmarked
   a. NG, e.g. MALAY buku gurukah 'a book of the teacher's,'
   b. GN, e.g. TAMIL kollan ve̅lai '(the) smith's craft.'

2.3 Possessive construction types

Having discussed the particular semantic features used to identify
possessor and possessee in possessive constructions, as well as
some of the ways in which they are formally represented, we now
go on to examine their co-occurrence patterns in possessive phrases.
While occurrence of any of these features in constituency with possessor or possessee is possible, certain combinations are extremely
rare (see especially third person above). They sometimes occur in
quite redundant complexes as can be seen by a glance at Tables 2
and 3 below listing all the types uncovered in this sample (/separates
two features represented by different formal entities, e.g. per/gen;
symbols for features represented by portmanteaus are simply juxtaposed, e.g. 3N; Ø indicates an unmarked constituent).

Table 2

Pronominal Possession

G	N	No. of languages	Analog	
per	per	6	Ø	3
per	gen	3	Ø	gen
per	N	2	Ø	Ø
per	NG	1	Ø	Ø
per	Ø	19	Ø	Ø
*Ø	per	31	Ø	Ø
*Ø	per/G	1	Ø	Ø
*Ø	per/N	2	Ø	Ø
per	gen/gen	1	Ø	gen/gen
per/gen	Ø	37	gen	Ø
per/gen	per	4	gen	3
per/N	G	2	Ø	Ø
per/N	Ø	3	Ø	Ø
per/N	N	5	Ø	Ø
per/gen	per N	1	gen	3
per/gen/N	Ø	2	gen	Ø
per/gen/N	N	4	gen	Ø
per/gen/gen	Ø	1	gen/gen	Ø
per/gen/3N	per	1	gen/3	Ø
per/gen/NG	N	1	gen	Ø

*G does not exist as a free entity in these constructions. Per
is affixed to N.

Table 3

Nominal Possession

G	N	No. of languages	Analog	
Ø	Ø	22	Ø	Ø
Ø	gen 3	1	Ø	gen/3
Ø	gen	6	Ø	gen
Ø	3	14	Ø	3
Ø	3G	2	Ø	3
Ø	3N	1	Ø	3
Ø	G	1	Ø	Ø
Ø	N	1	Ø	Ø
G	Ø	1	Ø	Ø
G	N	1	Ø	Ø
N	Ø	2	Ø	Ø
N	G	1	Ø	Ø
gen/gen	Ø	3	gen/gen	Ø
gen/3	Ø	1	gen/3	Ø
gen/3G	3 NG	1	gen/3	3
gen/G	Ø	1	gen	Ø
gen	Ø	41	gen	Ø
gen	gen	2	gen	gen
gen	3	8	gen	3
gen	N	1	gen	Ø
gen/N	Ø	2	gen	Ø
gen/N	N	4	gen	Ø
gen/NG	N	1	gen	Ø

The commonest intersections (more than four examples) between
pronominal and nominal types occurring in the same language,
listed in descending order of frequency, are:

Table 4

Pronominal		Nominal		No. of lang.	Analog	
G	N	G	N		Pronominal	Nominal
per/gen	Ø	gen	Ø	26	gen-Ø	gen-Ø
Ø	per	gen	Ø	13	Ø - Ø	gen-Ø
Ø	per	Ø	Ø	13	Ø - Ø	Ø - Ø
per	Ø	gen	Ø	12 + 1?	Ø - Ø	gen-Ø
Ø	per	Ø	3	11	Ø - Ø	Ø - 3
per/gen	Ø	Ø	Ø	9 + 1?	gen-Ø	Ø - Ø
per	Ø	Ø	Ø	8 + 1?	Ø - Ø	Ø - Ø
per/gen	Ø	Ø	3	5	gen-Ø	Ø - 3
per	Ø	Ø	gen	4 + 1?	Ø - Ø	Ø-gen
Ø	per	Ø	gen	4 + 1?	Ø - Ø	Ø-gen

2.4 Typological considerations

If we consider the morphosyntactic markers in an effort to
determine which ones are genuinely relevant, it becomes apparent
that, in all cases, possessor and possessee class markers (G
and N) are secondary and redundant, often irrelevant in terms of
possessive function.   Thus in HINDI laṛkē kī bahnẽ 'the boy's
sisters,' the postposition ka in itself marks the preceding noun as
the possessor, but also agrees with the following possessee in
gender, number and case, which parallels the normal situation
for other nonpossessive attribute-head constructions.

In GOLA concord markers in possessive phrases serve a linkage function. Nouns occur with class-number affixes as follows:
without affix, indefinite; with prefix or suffix, definite; with both
prefix and suffix, definite and emphatic.   Further, when both
prefix and suffix are present in noun + noun phrases, the phrase is
treated as a compound, i.e. the prefix must occur on the first
noun and the suffix on the second. In possessive phrases, both
constituent orders (GN and NG) are acceptable. Where both concord prefix and suffix are present, four degrees of linkage, expressed simultaneously in two ways, are possible: GN constituent
order is more bound than NG, and cross-affixing of the two constituents (possessor marked for N-class, possessee marked for G-
class) is more bound than parallel-affixing.[4] Furthermore, as
shown in Tables 2, 3 and 4, G- and N-class markers do not figure
at all in any of the high-frequency construction types.

The feature of person in pronominal constructions appears to
equate generally with an unmarked possessor in corresponding
nominal constructions. That is, an unmarked nominal possessor
is the functional equivalent of an unmarked pronominal possessor,
the sole difference between the two being the inherent marking of
the pronominal possessor for person.

Thus, schematically substituting Ø for the features of person,
possessor class, and possessee class, we are left with structural

---

[4]Compare Westermann's comment on this: "Den wirklichen
zusammengesetzten Hw [Hauptwort/Hauptwörter] scheinen solche
Verbindungen näher zu stehen, in denen das Präfix des regierenden
Hw vor das regierte Hw tritt und dadurch die beiden Hw noch näher
aneinanderrückt; aber auch das ist nur scheinbar, die engere Ver-
bindung ist nur eine lautliche, nicht eine dem Sinne nach." (emphasis
mine).

analogs of the actual construction types, a procedure which enables
us to reduce the welter of different types to a small number of basic
or underlying types as a prerequisite to formulating a typology.
For pronominal constructions the highest frequency types are ∅-
per and per/gen-∅, followed by per-∅. But since the first and last
actually constitute the same type, differing only as to affixed
(∅-per) vs. independent (per-∅) pronoun (see note, Table 2), they
can be combined, resulting in a highest-frequency analog ∅ - ∅,
followed by gen-∅.

The most commonly occurring nominal construction type is
gen-∅, followed by ∅ - ∅. This appears to be a reversal of favored
types vis-à-vis pronominal constructions, but in a number of languages the feature of person in pronominal constructions is actually
analogous to genitive in nominal constructions, e.g. YURAK with
a pronominal construction type ∅ -per (= per-∅) equivalent to the
nominal construction gen-∅, and given the fact that person serves
basically to identify the possessor and almost never denotes possessee (but compare the SHONA example above), then genitive
rather than -- or at least in addition to -- ∅ might be posited as the
nominal analog of person. If this is so, gen-∅ would clearly emerge
as the dominant basic type for all substantival possessive constructions. Furthermore, by far the commonest intersection of nominal
and pronominal types shows a basic gen-∅ for both constructions.

Based on the two most commonly occurring archtypes, gen-∅
and ∅ - ∅, and subordinating to these any remaining redundant
markers (e.g. double genitives, third person), we can set up the
following typologies for pronominal and nominal types:

Table 5

Pronominal	Nominal
A. gen-∅	A. gen-∅
1. gen/3-∅	1. gen/3-∅
2. gen-3	2. gen-3
3. gen/gen-∅	3. gen/3-3
	4. gen/gen-∅
B. ∅ - ∅	B. ∅ - ∅
1. ∅ - 3	1. ∅ - 3
C. ∅-gen	C. ∅-gen
1. ∅-gen/gen	1. ∅-gen/3
	D. gen-gen

These can be further reduced to a single typology by adding
∅-gen/gen to the nominal set above and allowing for the addition of
more subtypes as needed. It is now clear that all substantival
possessive constructions may be subsumed under four basic types
which, in descending order of frequency of occurrence, are: gen-∅,
∅ - ∅, ∅-gen and gen-gen.

2.5 Constituent order correlations

One type of correlation between pronominally possessed and
nominally possessed constructions which has not yet been touched
upon concerns the basic constituent orders for both constructions
in a given language. Many languages make use of possessive pronouns or adjectives rather than pronominal affixes (although a
number have both) to indicate the possessor in possessive phrases.
Often, as one would expect, the constituent order in pronominally
possessed constructions parallels that of nominally possessed
constructions in the same language; but in some languages the two
orders differ. When this happens the pronominally possessed
order is always GN as opposed to NG for the corresponding nominally possessed order. The only possible exception to this rule
may be ASSINIBOINE, with a normal nominal order of GN vs. a
pronominal order of NG. But this language has four sets of pronominal possessors, three of which are prefixed to the possessee.
The fourth set is composed of free forms which function as possessive predicates or, apparently (this is not always clear from
the examples cited), as attributes. We may therefore at least
tentatively propose the following: GN constituent order in nominal
possessor constructions implies the same order in pronominal
(attributive, nonaffixal) possessor constructions.

3. Specialized Possessee and Possessor Classes

3.1 Semantic types of possession classes

The basic constituents of possessive constructions are sometimes
formally subdivided into two or more classes. Excluding gender,
number, and case distinctions which, as noted above (Section 2.4),
are not strictly relevant, there appear to be two semantic types of
possession classes:

1. The pronominal possessor is formally distinguished for
   identity (i.e. is reflexive) or nonidentity with the subject
   (of the sentence) referent. LATIN suus vs. eius exem-
   plifies this type, broadly represented in the present sample,
   which of course pertains only to possessor class.

2. The possessee, or more rarely the possessor, is marked
for a semantic field of greater intimacy of possession by
or of persons, animals, or objects of primary human or
cultural importance as opposed to one of lesser intimacy.

Thus in KONKOW all kinship terms and a few personal nouns are
inalienably possessed (obligatory pronominal possessor), e.g.
ník-nè 'my mother,' and the rest alienably possessed, e.g. niḱi
má· 'my hand.' In MALTESE nouns may be pronominally possessed by means of a personal suffix or a genitive preposition plus
personal suffix (= possessive pronoun). Historically, most nouns
are from SEMITIC or ROMANCE. SEMITIC nouns are possessed
by the personal suffix, ROMANCE nouns by the possessive pronoun.
However, ROMANCE kinship nouns may take the suffix as in kujin-
u·h 'his cousin' vs. non-kin iljlekk tieɣ-u 'his jacket' with the
possessive pronoun. Here, although the pronominal possessor is
not obligatory, the situation is parallel to that in languages like
KONKOW having an alienable-inalienable dichotomy.

3.2 Possessor classes

Some languages distinguish between similar semantic classes
of possessor, like TAGALOG where the two different genitive
prepositions are used to distinguish between personal name and
all other possessors: bahay ni David 'David's house' vs. bahay ng
titser 'teacher's house.' In PIRO possessors other than kinship
terms and personal pronouns are normally marked with a genitive
suffix, whereas the latter class is unmarked. Other types of G-
class markers appearing in MALAY and ACOMA have already
been discussed in Sec. 2.1.

3.3 Possessee classes

The pronominal possessor may take the form of an independent
pronoun (or personal adjective) or a pronominal affix. The "less
intimate" form may be the same as the "more intimate" form or
it may differ from it in terms of allomorphy or derivation. The
last-named factor appears to be of particular importance for
pronominal affixes. That is, where the two are partially identical
in form, the less intimate affix or pronoun is always derived from
the more intimate by the addition of another affix, e.g. TUNICA
ʔuhk-ʔíyutɛku 'his hog' but ʔú-gači 'his mother.'

Sometimes, the difference between less and more intimate
possessor forms is in part or wholly expressed by the type of
linkage. When this is the case, the degree of intimacy of the

relationship is mirrored by the degree of linkage; that is, the
less intimate is the free form and the more intimate is the dependent (affix, clitic, prepound, etc.), as in the KONKOW example
cited above. In short, a morphologically derived form for a less
intimate possessor implies its derivation from the more intimate
possessor form (or base); and a free, less intimate possessor
may imply a bound, more intimate possessor, but not the converse.

In connection with alienable and inalienable possessors, some
languages make use of a device for "alienizing" otherwise inalienable noun stems when the absence of a specific or definite possessor is emphasized, as in SAKER which distinguishes between
alienable and inalienable (kinship terms, body parts, and parts of
wholes) nouns, but employs the prefix ka- when no possessor is
indicated: ya i -nen 'my mother' (both personal pronoun and
personal prefix are used), but ka-nen 'mother.' Thus, the alienable
stem is derived from the inalienable.

There is also a partial correlation between affix and constituent
order. An examination of the 12 languages in the sample having
inalienable pronominal prefixes shows that all have a GN constituent
order in possessive constructions; in most cases it is either the
unique or the preferred order. In other words, a prefix implies a
constituent order of GN in cases of inalienable possession by pronominal affix. Unfortunately, only one language, BERBER, has
inalienable suffixes, but it does have a preferred NG constituent
order. If what is true of BERBER is also true of all other languages with inalienable suffixes, the historical implication is clear:
such affixes in all probability evolved from presumably deaccentuated
independent pronouns, preposed to the possessee in the case of
present-day prefixes and postposed in the case of suffixes. The
above statement is further confirmed by the fact that all the languages sampled with pronominal prefixes (i.e. including not only
inalienable prefixes) have GN orders. While a sizable number of
languages have pronominal suffixes (other than inalienable), the
expected inverse correlation with an NG order is lacking. We can,
however, expand the original statement into a more general one:
personal possessive prefixes always imply a constituent order of
GN (usually favored); for personal possessive suffixes there is no
such rule.

Another constant, albeit negative, seems to be associated with
inalienable noun stems. In some languages, e.g. HUICHOL and
KONKOW, the obligatory co-occurrence feature for inalienable
stems is sometimes suspended. To my knowledge this happens

only when the noun is used as a vocative (or is accompanied by an
alienizer — see above). Compare, for example, KONKOW né!
'mother!' otherwise ník-nè, etc. 'my, etc. mother.' This being
so, we may posit the following: an inalienably possessed vocative
noun implies an inalienably possessed nonvocative but the converse
is not necessarily true.

In addition to the formal devices used to identify inalienably
possessed nouns (generally shorter forms of pronominal affixes
or different allomorphs of affix or pronoun), nonobligatory possessee classes may be marked in other ways. In ARANDA, for example,
the comitative postposition takes two different forms; one is used
with nouns referring to possessions personally held or naturally
inseparable from the possessor, the other with all remaining possessees. In EWE when the possessee refers to kin, to (certain)
locative notions, to individual or tribal names, the possessor
(noun or pronoun) is unmarked, in contrast with the norm for other
possessive constructions in which a genitive postposition follows
the possessor. The semantic classes of nonobligatory possessees,
however, are essentially the same as those of obligatory possessees.

4. Possessive Substantives

No discussion of possessive constructions would be complete
without some mention of possessive substantives, i.e. nonattribu-
tive, independent possessive pronouns or nouns. Such constructions
differ from ordinary possessive phrases by the manner in which
the possessee is represented. All possessive substantives appear
to be subsumable under one or the other of two basic types in this
respect:

1. There is no formal indication of the possessee (N-ellipsis),
as in ENGLISH yours, John's (as predicate).

2. Both possessor and possessee are overt, but substituted for
the latter is some sort of determiner, definiteness or concord marker, e.g. a demonstrative in GREBO na nenɔ 'mine,'
a definite article in MALAGASY ny azy 'his,' a concord suffix
agreeing with possessee in gender and number in ITALIAN
la tua 'yours' (f. sg. for, e.g., la giacca 'jacket').

In some languages two or more of these devices may be combined
in the same construction, as in the ITALIAN example just cited
(both definiteness and concord markers). Type 1. substantives

are most commonly marked for genitive. The only nongenitive
example found was in EWE which makes use of a G-class marker,
basically a noun meaning 'owner, master' prefixed to some personal pronouns and postposed to the others and possessor nouns.
Although this is not the ordinary genitive marker, it functions as
such in possessive substantive constructions and also to mark the
standard of comparison in some comparative constructions (see
Sec. 5.6). While both basic types appear to be randomly distributed geographically and in terms of genetic affiliation and of
possessive and basic order types, type 1. is somewhat more
common than type 2.

Under N-ellipsis we might also consider cases like FRENCH
je suis allé chez lui 'I went to his house/place/home/etc.' Historically, of course, there is no question of ellipsis, but synchronically there may be. However, because this construction
and others like it in a number of languages are more properly
viewed as constituting a kind of locative possession, they will be
discussed under that rubric (see Sec. 5.3).

As for G-ellipsis, either this is to be considered a rare phenomenon or it is simply not treated in most grammars. One such
type would be GERMAN ich gehe nach Hause 'I am going home
(i.e. to my house),' where the possessor, absent in the prepositional
phrase, is present in the subject of the sentence. Another might
be FRENCH je lui ai cassé le bras 'I broke his arm,' in which the
actual possessor is present in the form of the indirect object lui.
However, this could also be interpreted as G substitution, i.e.
replacement of *son bras by le bras (see also Sec. 6).

5. Some Nonpossessive Functions of Genitive and Personal
    Possession Markers

In addition to denoting strict possession or ownership in substantival phrases, genitive and personal possession markers
characteristically occur in all languages in at least some of the
following functions as identifiers of: the topic (subject, object, or
complement) of a verb, usually in the form of a verbal noun, but
sometimes as the verb of a subordinate clause; the heads of certain
locative constructions; the whole in partitive and partitive-like
constructions; and the standard of comparison in a number of comparative and superlative constructions. In all these instances, the
formal evidence of possessive markers affords us some rather
interesting insights into the extent and nature of the semantics of
possession in language.

5.1 Topic genitives

In many languages when verb phrases or entire clauses are
nominalized, the resultant noun phrase is often formally a possessive construction. Thus in ENGLISH we have phrases like the
burning of the house from *(they) burned the house or the dog's
barking from *the dog barked. In the first of these phrases the
genitive phrase refers to the underlying object of the source sentence; in the second, to the subject. In GREBO not only subject
and object genitives are possible, but also complement genitives,
e.g. London a mue 'going to London' (lit. 'London's going'). In
MANDARIN when a second object (personal) is added to certain
phrases consisting of verb plus object, the second object is marked
by the genitive postposition de: bang ren de mang 'helps people'
(lit. 'helps people's being busy' from bang-mang 'help in getting
busy'). In TIBETAN the subordination of entire clauses to other
clauses or to main sentence constituents by means of the genitive
suffix is used on an even more extensive scale: (1) When the subject
of the main clause follows the verb of the subordinate clause, it
may take the genitive suffix as in klu'i gdon-las bsruŋ-na sŋags-
kyi mgo-la bzlas-so 'If one wishes to protect oneself from capture
by snakes, a mantra should be uttered over one's head.' (2) The
direct object of a subordinate verb may take the genitive, e.g.
khyod-rnams ŋa'i mi ñan-to 'you, not having listened to me' (lit.
'you my not listen'). (3) When the subjects of coordinate clauses
are identical, the clauses are linked by the genitive suffix (normally
affixed to the verb of the first clause), e.g. sbyin-pa gtoŋ-gi ser-
sna mi byed 'he who gives alms is not a miser' (lit. 'alms-giving's
miser not do').

In all these examples and in the many others culled from the
present sample one point is clear: the genitive-marked constituent
or possessor is always an underlying topic, usually subject or
object (largely dependent on whether the original clause was transitive or not), and the possessee is the underlying comment, verb
or predicate. Undoubtedly related to this is the fact that most
specialized possessive pronouns or adjectives (i.e. differing formally from other personal pronouns) are either formally identical
with object (much more frequently) or subject pronouns, or are
morphologically derived from them. This applies to both free and
bound pronominal forms.

5.2 Locative-governed genitives

Probably all languages have substantival phrases consisting
basically of a locative or directional element and an element marked

as the possessor would be in an ordinary possessive phrase. Compare, for example, FINNISH minu-n taakse 'behind me,' composed of a possessive pronoun (personal pronoun plus genitive suffix) followed by a local postposition governing the genitive. The locative element in such constructions is almost always a preposition or postposition, historically a noun[5] whose distribution has been relatively narrowly restricted (presumably for semantic reasons) and whose inflection, if any, is frozen or limited to one form. In many cases these have evolved from body-part terms. Compare, for example, the so-called compound prepositions in ENGLISH: at the mouth of the river, in back of the house, etc. While the ENGLISH examples may not be totally convincing as to whether a genitive is actually present (my back does not equal in back of me and of does not function only as a marker of possession), there can be hardly any doubt in the case of FINNISH (see above) or MALTESE bey niet-na 'between ourselves' (-na personal possessive suffix) or LITHUANIAN põ tav-ę̃s 'after you (sg.)' (-ę̃s genitive suffix). In languages with nominal case systems, prepositions or postpositions usually govern specific cases. In most instances the case governed by the majority of prepositions or postpositions is the genitive (i.e. a case which includes as a major function the denotation of the possessor in possessive phrases) or possessive. All this leads us to conclude that most locative phrases involving genitives are in reality petrified possessive phrases in which the role of head of construction has shifted from the locative to the original possessor (except in the case of personal affixes).

5.3 CHEZ-constructions

Another kind of locative construction is usually composed of a generalized locative element and a possessive construction as in ENGLISH at John's or SYRIAN ARABIC ɣand-ak 'at your place.' Although, formally, FRENCH chez moi does not appear to contain a genitive, it should probably be included here inasmuch as the parallel construction à moi (il y a ...) or (il est) à moi denote possessors in precisely the same fashion (cf. chez moi il y a ...). Because of their referential meaning, such constructions are generally regarded as instances of N-ellipsis, the covert possessee being something like 'house, home, place,' but in essence they are very much like the locative-governed genitive constructions, with

---

[5]It is interesting to note that, in EWE the genitive postposition ɸé means 'place' and in JAMAICAN CREOLE the local preposition a 'at, to' is formally identical with the genitive preposition.

the exception that the locative elements involved do not ordinarily govern genitives (i.e. outside these constructions).

5.4 Partitive and partitive-like genitives

In a large number of languages constructions expressing the relationship of a part to its whole, a unit or a given quantity to its total mass, an object to its source material, a member to its class, a numerator to its denominator, a day to its month, etc. are formally genitives. Thus in CANARESE we have marad-a kombe 'branch of a tree' (part to its whole); in PASHTO də kand dva ɣáʈi 'two pieces of sugar' (units to their mass); in BENGALI loha-r cabi 'iron key, key of iron' (object to its source material); in LITHUANIAN jū̃ kas '(some)one of them' (jū̃ gen. pl. of 3rd pers. pron., member to its class); in GREBO kia sõ a kae 'the second house' (lit. 'house two's house,' ordinal construction: one unit to a specified number of units); in KHALKHA MONGOLIAN gurwan-ī nege xuwi 'one-third' (lit. 'one part of three,' numerator to its denominator); in BASQUE Bagilar-en bostean 'the fifth of June,' (day to its month).

In all such and related constructions the term designating the whole, the mass or collectivity, the class of items, the source material, the denominator, the month, etc. is a genitive. Both semantically and formally then, it would appear that the intimate relationship between a part and its whole in any of its varied manifestations is often closely interwoven with that of a possessee to its possessor. Indeed, one might say that the whole "possesses" its part. Another bit of evidence linking partitive and possessive functions is found in FINNISH, a language with a relatively large number of postpositions but few prepositions, in which most postpositions govern the genitive, but the remaining ones and all prepositions govern the partitive.

Probably related to the partitive function of the genitive is the genitive of negation found in a number of languages (RUSSIAN, POLISH, LITHUANIAN, GOTHIC and others). In such instances a negative governs a genitive complement, subject, or predicate, as in RUSSIAN ya ne čitáju gazét-y 'I'm not reading the newspaper' (ne negative and -y genitive, marking object here, vs. the corresponding affirmative with an accusative object ja čitáju gazét-u). In this kind of construction negative would seem to indicate choice from an unknown or indefinite number or class of complements (hence the use of the genitive), with ellipsis of the particular (and actual) complement. Thus, the sentence underlying the

example given might be something like *I'm not reading any of the
newspapers.

5.5 Proper name genitives

Another fairly widespread use of genitives is in phrases containing individual proper names and their appropriate common or
group names. Some languages employ apposition to express the
relationship between the two constituents, like ENGLISH Attila
the Hun; others use genitives to identify the individual proper
name, like CHAMORRO i huēs na si Peres 'Judge Perez' (na
genitive prep.) and MALTESE Toni tad-Dobbu 'Tony belonging to
the Dobbu family, Tony of the Dobbu.' Compare also some examples of other semantic categories commonly involved in such use
of genitives: names of cities in ITALIAN (and ENGLISH) la città
di Roma 'the city of Rome; ' names of peoples and languages in
FINNISH Suome-n-kansa 'the Finnish people' and Suome-n-kieli
'the Finnish language;' names of topographical features in KHAL-
KHA MONGOLIAN oŋg-ĭŋ gol 'the Ong River' or LITHUANIAN
Báltij-os jūra 'the Baltic Sea;' names of months in FRENCH (and
ENGLISH) le mois de mai 'the month of may;' book titles in PER-
SIAN ketab-e šahname 'the book Šahname.' This type of construction may be considered semantically analogous to the partitive
functions of the genitive. Here the proper noun in the genitive or
an equivalent relation as in the PERSIAN example represents the
entire class of referents bearing the name while the accompanying
common noun identifies a particular subclass of the former. This
is the case even when the proper noun has an apparently unique
referent as with Roma since the latter may refer not only to the
city of that name but also to the culture, the Rome of Caesar, the
government of present-day Italy, and so on.

5.6 Comparative genitives

Comparative and superlative relationships are often expressed
by genitive markers or by a combination of degree and genitive
markers. Logically, any comparative or superlative construction
must include a compared item, a standard (item) of the same
general class as the compared item, and a means for expressing
the degree and quality of comparison. While among languages in
general a number of different formal devices are used to mark
the degree or the standard, I will discuss only some of those entailing genitive constructions. In PASHTO, for example, adjectival comparison may be rendered by preposing the genitive də
to the standard and adding to it the postposition tsəxá denoting

origin: vror də xor tsəxá məš̌r dəy 'the brother is older than
the sister.' In KHALKHA the superlative is expressed by adding
the genitive suffix to the standard: ünegen-ī xara '(he is) the
blackest of the foxes;' the adjective is unmarked as to degree.
Somewhat more common are those constructions in which the
means of comparison is marked for degree and the standard for
genitive, as with one type of adjectival comparison in RUSSIAN:
okeán ból'š-e mórj-a 'the ocean is bigger than the sea' (-e comparative suffix, -a genitive suffix) or in TAGALOG superlatives
si Linda ang pinaka-maganda sa mga bata 'Linda is the prettiest
of the children' (pinaka-superlative prefix, sa genitive preposition).
Another type marks the standard with an affix or particle whose
primary function is not to indicate possession, although occasionally used in that capacity, e.g. TAJIK rūyaš̌ az barf safyed (tar)
ast 'her face is whiter than snow' (az preposition indicative of
origin, source, -tar optional comparative suffix) and vay az hama
naγz(tar) ast 'he is the best of all.' From these and all other
examples with formal genitives in comparative and superlative
constructions found among the languages sampled, it is readily
apparent that the standard is always genitive-marked, never the
compared item. This usage of the genitive is most probably to
be equated with the partitive function. That is, in the case of
superlatives the compared item with its qualitative descriptor is
regarded as one member of the class represented by the standard
of comparison. Note also that in most languages the standard in
superlative constructions is the quantifier 'all,' i.e., the most
inclusive class. With comparatives the descriptor marks a relative degree of the quality attributed to the compared item as contrasted with the implied quality as a whole represented by the
standard.

6. HAVE-Constructions

Certainly most, perhaps all, languages employ some kind of
equational sentence consisting of subject and predicate with or
without an accompanying existential copula to express possession.
Such sentences are typically translatable (at least in ENGLISH
into 'A has B' as, for example, with TAMIL ena-kku oru nalla
nāy (irukkiratu) 'I have a good dog' (lit. 'to me a good dog is,'
-kku dative suffix, irukkiratu copula, nāy subject) or FRENCH
le livre est à moi 'I have the book' or 'the book is mine,' where
the preposition à and the oblique form of the pronoun mark it as
the indirect object. While this kind of construction has virtually
disappeared from modern ENGLISH (but compare such relics as
woe is me!), it was more common in older forms of ENGLISH .

Although there is considerable diversity in the forms used to identify the real possessor in different or sometimes the same languages, these may be subsumed under two, possibly three, broad types and a small number of subtypes. By far the commonest of these is the one in which the possessor equals the predicate and the possessee equals the subject, as in the examples just cited. In descending order of frequency (this applies of course to the present sample and could conceivably be subject to some revision for a larger sample), this type can be roughly broken down into what might be termed:

Object-designated — the possessor is marked for indirect object (dative or benefactive), direct object or ergative. See the TAMIL example above for a dative-marked possessor. In SANGO the preposition na performs a number of oblique functions, one of which is benefactive: bongó aɛkɛ na lo 'he has a garment' (lit. 'garment is for/to him;' note subject concord a- on the copula ɛkɛ in agreement with possessee bongó). CLASSICAL TAJIK made use of a direct object postposition ro to indicate possessor, e.g. ū-ro yak pisar bul 'he had one son.' CHAMORRO identifies the pronominal possessor by selecting the ergative (i.e. subject of intransitive equals object of transitive verb) pronoun rather than the possessive, transitive subject or predicative pronoun, e.g. gwaha jo leblo 'I have books.' Also to be included here are cases like AMHARIC in which the pronominal possessor (and the possessee by concord) is included in the existential copula: lām 'all -č-əw 'he has a cow' (-əw 3rd sg. m. obj., -č 3rd sg. f. subj. agreeing with the possessee lām).

Locative-designated — the possessor is marked for any of a number of essentially locative categories, e.g. adessive in FINNISH Sinu-lla on koira 'you have a dog,' instrumental in OLD IRISH œit l-eu 'they have envy' (lit. 'envy with/by them,' optional copula), locative in PANJABI món kol emb si 'Mohan had a mango' (postposition kol 'near,' possessor món in the oblique case), locative possession in MALTESE ɤand-kom ziemel 'you have a horse' (lit. 'at/with [=FRENCH chez] you horse,' no copula).

Possessor-designated — the possessor is marked with a genitive. Note that this is not the same as a genitive attribute. In all HAVE-constructions, the possessor is a predicate or an incorporated predicate when affixed to the copula as in AMHARIC above. In LITHUANIAN the possessor may be in the dative or in the genitive as in lazd-õs dù galaĩ 'the staff has two ends' (-õs genitive suffix, copula usually omitted in the present tense as with the similar construction in RUSSIAN).

The second type is the mirror image of the first, that is, the possessor equals the subject and the possessee equals the predicate. This type appears to be fairly rare and is restricted to one kind of predicate, comitative or comitative-instrumental as in KHALKHA xür daxa-<u>tai</u> 'the man has a fur' (possessee <u>daxa</u> with comitative suffix and possessor in the nominative, no copula, lit. 'man with fur;' cf. ENGLISH she is <u>with</u> child) or SHONA <u>ndino-musoro</u> 'I have a (sore) head' (a verb: <u>ndi</u>- subj. + <u>na</u>- comitative + <u>umosoro</u> denominative verb 'head').

As noted above the dominant basic type of HAVE-construction is the one in which the possessor equals the predicate. Furthermore, within this type the most important (in terms of frequency of occurrence) is the object-designated group, followed fairly closely by the locative-designated group. In conjunction with this, the formal identity or near-identity of many personal possessives with object pronoun forms cannot be viewed as purely coincidental. As Allen (1964: 342) has suggested, after discussing a number of languages in which there is formal identity between pronominal forms for the subjects and indirect objects of transitive verbs and the personal possessives: "With transitive verbs the indirect object can hardly be said to indicate a state of possession; but it does in most cases indicate a process of 'receiving' or 'acquisition,' i.e. of 'coming into possession'." After all, the situation might just as well be reversed, i.e. a construction of the general type *<u>I am to</u> (or the like) <u>it</u> = <u>I have it</u> might be just as common as -- or even more so -- the object-designated possessor type. Or object pronouns, rather than subject or other kinds, might be less likely to resemble possessive pronouns; but this is simply not so.

7. Summary and Conclusions

Summarizing the most important of our findings:

Attributive possessive constructions consist of two constituents, a possessor and a possessee, marked by various combinations of the superficial semantic features: person, third person, genitive, and possessor class for possessor referent; possessee class for possessee referent; and a feature of relative constituent order (when the construction is otherwise unmarked) simultaneously identifying both possessor and possessee. The ultimately relevant or underlying semantic features appear to be genitive and third person (Sec. 2.4). The four most common basic types of attributive possessive constructions viewed in terms of possessive feature marking with an arbitrary constituent order of GN are, in descending order of frequency of occurrence: gen-∅, ∅-∅, ∅-gen, and gen-gen (Sec. 2.4). Furthermore, the following general statements are in order:

1. A genitive-marked constituent in a pronominally possessed construction implies genitive marking of the corresponding constituent in a nominally possessed construction (Sec. 2.2).

2. GN constituent order in a nominally possessed construction implies the same order in a pronominal (nonaffixal) construction (Sec. 2.5).

3. A possessee marked for genitive implies a construction in which the possessor is so marked (Sec. 2.2).

4. A possessor marked for third person implies a possessee so marked in the same construction (Sec. 2.2).

Specialized possessor and possessee classes belong to one of two semantic types: identity vs. nonidentity of possessor and subject, or more vs. less intimate possessor or possessee (Sec. 3.1). Also:

5. A morphologically derived form for a less intimate possessor implies its derivation from the more intimate form (Sec. 3.3).

6. A free, less intimate possessor form may imply a bound, more intimate form, but not the converse (Sec. 3.3).

7. Personal possessive prefixes always imply a GN order, but not the converse; for personal possessive suffixes there is no such rule (Sec. 3.3).

8. An inalienably possessed, nonvocative noun does not necessarily imply that the corresponding vocative noun is inalienably possessed (Sec. 3.3).

Possessive substantives fall into one or the other of two formal classes: the possessee is elided, almost always genitive-marked, or both possessor and possessee are present, but the latter is a determiner, definiteness, or concord marker (Sec. 4).

Most possessive pronouns or adjectives are formally identical or similar to object pronouns, and:

9. In possessive constructions derived from topic-comment (no specific order implied) constructions, the possessor corresponds to the topic (subject, object, etc.) and the possessee to the comment (verb, predicate, etc.) (Sec. 5.1).

Most locative-governed and CHEZ-constructions have evolved historically from attributive possessive constructions (Sec. 5.2).

10. In partitive and partitive-like constructions, the possessor corresponds to the whole and the possessee to the part (Sec. 5.4).

Proper name genitives are generally equatable with partitive constructions with the proper noun in the genitive representing the whole and the common noun the part or subclass of the whole.

Comparative genitives are viewed as extensions of partitive genitives, and:

11. In comparative and superlative genitive constructions, the genitive-marked constituent is always the standard of comparison (Sec. 5.6).

HAVE-constructions are found in two basic types: a dominant one in which the possessor is the predicate and the possessee the subject, the former formally object-, locative-, or possessor-designated; or one in which the possessor is the subject and the possessee the predicate, the latter formally comitative-designated (Sec. 6). Furthermore:

12. The subject-marked possessor of a HAVE-construction implies a comitative-marked possessee (Sec. 6).

APPENDIX I

Summary of Basic Types by Language

For detailed source information, see Bibliography. For basic attributive possessive typology code references, see Sec. 2.4. Under Subst. (Substantive Possessive Type) the symbols refer to the basic types proposed in Sec. 4: gen = Type 1 or N-ellipsis and genitive-marked possessor; N = Type 2 or no N-ellipsis, with N-subtypes dem = demonstrative, def = definiteness marker, and con = concord marker. Under HAVE the symbols refer to the basic types proposed in Sec. 6: obj, loc, gen are respectively object-, locative-, and possessor-designated, all subtypes of Type 1; sub is subject-designated, or Type 2.

Language	Location	Affiliation	==⇒
Acoma	New Mexico	Keresan	
Albanian	Albania	Indo-European	
Amharic	Ethiopia	Semitic	
Arabic, Egyptian	Egypt	Semitic	
Arabic, Syrian	Syria	Semitic	
Aramaic	Azerbaijan	Semitic	
Aranda	C Australia	?	
Asmat	SW New Guinea	Papuan	
Assiniboine	NC U.S. and Canada	Siouan	
Basque	Spain, France	isolate	
Bengali	E India	Indic	
Berber	Algeria	Afro-Asiatic	
Burushaski	Afghanistan	?	
Canarese	S India	Dravidian	
Cayuvava	Bolivia	?	
*Celtic	Ireland	Indo-European	
Chagatay	Turkestan	Turkic	
Chamorro	Guam	Indonesian	
Chinese, Mandarin	NE China	Sino-Tibetan	
Chontal	S Oaxaca	Tequistlatecan	
Cocopa	Arizona, California	Yuman	
Dani	W New Guinea	?	
English	U.S.A.	W Germanic	
Ewe	Ghana, Togo	Kwa	
Finnish	Finland	Finno-Ugric	
French	France	Romance	
Fula	C and W Africa	West Atlantic	
Georgian	Georgia (Cauc.)	Other Cauc. langs.	
Gola	Liberia	West Atlantic	
Grebo	Liberia	Kwa	
Greek, Modern	Greece	Indo-European	
Guaraní	Paraguay	Tupian	
Hebrew	Israel	Semitic	
Hindi	India	Indic	
Huichol	WC Mexico	Coran (Uto-Aztecan)	
Italian	Italy	Romance	
Jamaican Creole	Jamaica	Germanic	
Japanese	Japan	isolate	
Jaqaru	E Peru	Quechuan	

*Mainly Old Irish

Data Source	Basic Types			
	Pronom.	Nominal	Subst.	HAVE
Miller	B	B.1		
Newmark, Pekmezi	B	B.1		
Klingenheben	B	A, B, C	gen	obj
Hanna	B	B		
Cowell	A, B	A, B	gen	
Garbell	B	C, D	gen	
Strehlow	A	A, A.1, A.4, D		
Voorhoeve	B	B		
Levin	B	B	gen?	
Zamarripa	A	A	Ndem	
Ray	A	A	gen	obj
Basset	B	A, A.2	Ndem	
Lorimer	A	A	gen	obj
Spencer	A	A	gen	obj, loc
Key	B	B	Ndem	
Lewis, Pokorny	B?	A, A.2		loc
Eckmann	A.2, B	A, B.1		obj
Costenoble	A, B	A, B.1, C		obj
Chao	A, B	A	gen	
Waterhouse	B			
Crawford	B, B.1	B, B.1		
Van der Stap	A, B			
Bach, C.S. Smith	A, A.3, B	A, A.4	gen	obj, gen, sub
Westermann	A, B.1	A, B, B.1, C.1	gen?	obj
Peters	A, A.2, B	A, A.2	gen	loc
Langacker	A, B	A	Ndef	obj, loc
Westermann	A	B	Ndem	obj
Marr	A, B	A	gen	obj
Westermann	B	B		
Innes	A	A	Ndem	
Householder, Thumb	A	A	Ndem	
Gregores	B			
Rosen, Steuernagel	B	A, A.2, B		obj
Bender	A	A	gen	gen, loc
Grimes	B, B.1	B.1		
Young	B	A	Ndef	
Bailey	A, B	A, B	gen	
Chew, Harada, Jinushi	A	A	gen	
Hardman	B	A.2		

Language	Location	Affiliation == →
Karok	California	Hokan
Khasi	N Assam	Mon-Khmer
Konkow	California	Maiduan (Penutian)
Korean	Korea	isolate
Kūrkū	NE India, Burma	Munda
Lithuanian	Lithuania	Baltic
Malagasy	Madagascar	Malayan
Malay	Malaya, Indonesia	Malayan
Maltese	Malta	Semitic
Maori	New Zealand	Polynesian
Miwok, S Sierra	California	Miwokan (Penutian)
Mongolian, Khalkha	E Asia	Altaic
Ossetic	C Caucasus	Indo-Iranian
Panjabi	NC India	Indic
Pashto	Afghanistan	Iranian
Persian	Iran	Iranian
Piro	E Peru	Arawakan
Russian	U.S.S.R.	Slavic
Saker	NE New Guinea	?
Sango	C African Rep.	Adamawa-Eastern
Sentani	NC New Guinea	?
Shona	Mozambique	Bantu
Tagalog	Philippines	Malayo-Polynesian
Tajik	C Asia	Indo-Iranian
Tamil	S India	Dravidian
Tasmanian	Tasmania	?
Tibetan	Tibet	Sino-Tibetan
Tunica	Louisiana	Macro-Algonkian?
Turkish	Turkey	Turkic
Vietnamese	Vietnam	Thai languages
Western Desert	W Australia	?
Wiyot	California	Ritwan (Algonkian)
Yakut	E Siberia	Turkic
Yurak	NW Siberia	Samoyed (Uralic)
Yurok	California	Ritwan (Algonkian)

Data Source	Basic Types			
	Pronom.	Nominal	Subst.	HAVE
Bright	B	B.1		
Rabel	A	A		
Ultan	A, B	A		
Ramstedt	A	A, B		obj
Drake	A	A		obj, gen
Senn	A	A	Ncon	obj, gen, sub
Malzac	B	B, B.1, C?	Ndef	
Kähler	B	A, B	Ncon	
Aquilina	A, B	A, B	gen	loc
Hohepa	B	B	Ncon	gen
Broadbent	A.2	A.3		
Poppe	A, B	A	gen	sub
Abaev	A	A, A.2		
Gill	A?	A		loc
Shafeev	A, B	A		
Rastorgueva	B, C, C.1	C	Ndem	*gen
Matteson	B, C	A, B, C	Ncon	
Potapova	B	A	gen	loc
Z'graggen	A, B	A, B.1		
Samarin	A	A		obj, sub
Cowan	A, B	A, B, B.1		
Fortune	A, A.1, B	A	Ncon	sub
Bowen	A	A	gen	gen
Rastorgueva	A, A.2, B, C	A, A.2, C		obj
Beythan	A	A, B	gen	obj
Schmidt	B	B		
Lalou	A	A	gen	
Haas	B	B.1		
Swift	A, A.2, B	A.2, B.1		loc
Thompson	A, B	A, B?	gen	
Douglas	A	A, B		
Teeter	B	B.1		
Krueger	A, B	B.1		
Décsy	B	A		
Robins	B, B.1	B, B.1		gen

*Dative-genitive in Old Persian

APPENDIX II

Distribution of Languages by Basic Attributive Possessive Type*

Pronominally possessed:

A.   Arabic, Syrian   Georgian   Panjabi(?)
      Aranda   Grebo   Pashto
      Basque   Greek   Saker
      Bengali   Hindi   Sango
      Burushaski   Jamaican Creole   Sentani
      Canarese   Japanese   Shona
      Chamorro   Khasi   Tagalog
      Chinese (Mandarin)   Konkow   Tajik
      Dani   Korean   Tamil
      English   Kūrkū   Tibetan
      Ewe   Lithuanian   Turkish
      Finnish   Maltese   Vietnamese
      French   Mongolian (Khalkha)   Western Desert
      Fula   Ossetic   Yakut

A.1   Shona

A.2   Chagatay   Finnish   Miwok   Tajik   Turkish

A.3   English

B.   Acoma   Finnish   Pashto
      Albanian   French   Persian
      Amharic   Georgian   Piro
      Arabic, Egypt./Syrian   Gola   Russian
      Aramaic   Guaraní   Saker
      Asmat   Hebrew   Sentani
      Assiniboine   Huichol   Shona
      Berber   Italian   Tajik
      Cayuvava   Jamaican   Tasmanian
      Celtic (?)   Jaqaru   Tunica
      Chagatay   Karok   Turkish
      Chamorro   Konkow   Vietnamese
      Chinese   Malagasy   Wiyot
      Chontal   Malay   Yakut
      Cocopa   Maltese   Yurak
      Dani   Maori   Yurok
                                 Mongolian

*See Table 5 for code references.

B. 1   Cocopa   Ewe   Huichol   Yurok

C.   Persian   Piro   Tajik

C.1   Persian

Nominally possessed:

A.   Amharic   English   Khasi   Russian
       Arabic, Syrian Ewe   Konkow   Saker
       Aranda   Finnish   Korean   Sango
       Basque   French   Kūrkū   Sentani
       Bengali   Georgian   Lithuanian   Shona
       Berber   Grebo   Malay   Tagalog
       Burushaski   Greek   Maltese   Tajik
       Canarese   Hebrew   Mongolian   Tamil
       Celtic   Hindi   Ossetic   Tibetan
       Chagatay   Italian   Panjabi   Vietnamese
       Chamorro   Jamaican   Pashto   Western Desert
       Chinese   Japanese   Piro   Yurak

A.1   Aranda

A.2   Berber   Finnish   Jaqaru   Tajik
       Celtic   Hebrew   Ossetic   Turkish

A.3   Miwok

A.4   Aranda   English

B.   Amharic   Cocopa   Korean   Sentani
       Arabic,   Ewe   Malagasy   Tamil
         Egypt./Syrian Fula   Malay   Tasmanian
       Asmat   Gola   Maltese   Vietnamese (?)
       Assiniboine   Hebrew   Maori   Western Desert
       Cayuvava   Jamaican   Piro   Yurok

B.1   Acoma   Cocopa   Malagasy   Turkish
       Albanian   Ewe   Saker   Wiyot
       Chagatay   Huichol   Sentani   Yakut
       Chamorro   Karok   Tunica   Yurok

C.   Amharic   Chamorro   Persian   Tajik
       Aramaic   Malagasy (?) Piro
C.1   Ewe
D.   Aramaic   Aranda

BIBLIOGRAPHY

Abaev, V.I. 1964. A grammatical sketch of Ossetic. IJAL Pub. 35.

Allen, W. Sidney. 1964. Transitivity and possession. Lg 40. 337-43.

Aquilina, Joseph. 1959. The structure of Maltese. Royal Univ.
of Malta.

Bach, Emmon. 1967. 'Have' and 'be' in English syntax. Lg 43.
462-85.

Bailey, Beryl L. 1966. Jamaican Creole syntax, a transformational approach. London: Cambridge University Press.

Basset, André and André Picard. 1948. Éléments de grammaire
berbère (Kabylie-Irjen). Alger.

Bender, Ernest. 1967. Hindi grammar and reader. Philadelphia:
University of Pennsylvania Press.

Beythan, Hermann. 1943. Praktische Grammatik der Tamilsprache.
Leipzig: Harrassowitz.

Bloch, Jules. 1954. The grammatical structure of Dravidian
languages. Translated by Ramkrishna Ganesh Harshé. Deccan
College Handbook Series No. 3. Poona.

Bowen, J. Donald (ed.) 1965. Beginning Tagalog. Berkeley:
University of California Press.

Bréal, Michel. 1964. Semantics: studies in the science of meaning. Translated by Mrs. Henry Cust, Essai de sémantique
was first published in London in 1900. New York: Dover.

Bright, William. 1958. An outline of colloquial Kannada. Deccan
College Monograph Series No. 22. Poona.

_____. 1957. The Karok language. UCPL 13.

Broadbent, Sylvia. 1964. The Southern Sierra Miwok language.
UCPL 38.

Chao, Y.R. 1965. A grammar of spoken Chinese. Berkeley:
University of California Press.

Chew, John J., Jr. 1961. A transformational analysis of Modern
Colloquial Japanese. Yale University Ph.D. dissertation.

Costenoble, H. 1940. Die Chamoro Sprache. Koninklijk Instituut
voor Taal-, Land-, en Volkenkunde van Nederlandsch-Indië.
Den Haag: Nijhoff.

Cowan, H.K.J. 1965. Grammar of the Sentani language. Verhandelingen van het Instituut voor Taal-, Land-, en Volkenkunde
47. 's-Gravenhage: Nijhoff.

Cowell, Mark W. 1964. A reference grammar of Syrian Arabic
(Damascus dialect). Washington, D.C.: Georgetown Univ. Press.

Crawford, James M. 1966. The Cocopa language. Doctoral dissertation, University of California, Berkeley.

Décsy, G. 1966. Yurak chrestomathy. Indiana University Publications, Uralic and Altaic Series 50. Bloomington.

Douglas, W.H. 1958. An introduction to the Western Desert
language of Australia. Oceania Linguistic Monographs 4.
Sydney: University of Sydney.

Drake, J. 1903. A grammar of the Kurku language. Calcutta.

Eckmann, J. 1966. Chagatay manual. Indiana University Publications, Uralic and Altaic Series 60. Bloomington.

Fortune, G. 1955. An analytical grammar of Shona. London:
Longmans, Green.

Garbell, Irene. 1965. The Jewish Neo-Aramaic dialect of Persian
Azerbaijan. Janua Linguarum, series practica 3. The Hague:
Mouton.

Gill, Harjeet Singh and H.A. Gleason, Jr. 1963. A reference
grammar of Panjabi. Hartford Studies in Linguistics 3. Hartford: Hartford Seminary Foundation.

Greenberg, J.H. (ed.) 1966a. Universals of language. Cambridge,
Mass.: M.I.T. Press (2nd ed.) 98-100, 273.

_____. 1966b. Language universals. Current trends in lin-
guistics, III: Theoretical foundations, ed. by T.A. Sebeok,
61-112. The Hague: Mouton.

Gregores, Emma and Jorge A. Suarez. 1967. A description of Colloquial Guaraní. Janua Linguarum, series practica 27. The Hague: Mouton.

Grimes, Joseph E. 1964. Huichol syntax. Janua Linguarum, series practica 11. The Hague: Mouton.

Haas, Mary R. 1941. Tunica. Handbook of American Indian Languages, Part 4. 1-143. New York: J.J. Augustin.

Hanna, H. Morcos. 1967. The phrase structure of Egyptian Colloquial Arabic. Janua Linguarum, series practica 35. The Hague: Mouton.

Harada, Tetsuo. 1966. Outlines of Modern Japanese linguistics. Tokyo: Nihon University.

Hardman, M.J. 1966. Jaqaru: Outline of phonological and morphological structure. Janua Linguarum, series practica 22. The Hague: Mouton.

Hohepa, Patrick W. 1967. A profile generative grammar of Maori. IJAL 28.2, Pub. 20.

Householder, Fred W.Jr., Kostas Kazazis and Andreas Koutsoudas. 1964. Reference grammar of Literary Dhimotiki. IJAL 30.2, Pub. 31.

Innes, Gordon. 1966. An introduction to Grebo. School of Oriental and African Studies, University of London. The Hague.

Jespersen, Otto. 1965 (orig. pub. 1924). The philosophy of grammar. New York.

Jinushi, Toshiko Susuki. 1963. The structure of Japanese. Doctoral dissertation, State University of New York.

Kähler, Hans. 1965. Grammatik der Bahasa-Indonésia. Wiesbaden.

Key, Harold H. 1967. Morphology of Cayuvava. Janua Linguarum, series practica 53. The Hague: Mouton.

Klingenheben, August. 1966. Deutsch-Amharischer Sprachführer. Wiesbaden.

Krueger, John R. 1962. Yakut manual. Indiana University Publications, Uralic and Altaic Series 21. Bloomington.

Lalou, Marcelle. 1950. Manuel élémentaire de tibétan classique. Paris: Maisonneuve.

Langacker, Ronald W. 1968. Observations on French possessives. Lg 44. 51-75.

Levin, Norman Balfour. 1964. The Assiniboine language. IJAL 30.3, Pub. 32.

Lewis, Henry and Holger Pedersen. 1961. A concise comparative Celtic grammar. Göttingen.

Lorimer, D. L. R. 1935. The Burushaski language, I: Introduction and grammar. Institutet for Sammenlignende Kulturforskning. Oslo.

Malzac, R. P. 1950. Grammaire malgache. 3rd ed. Paris.

Marr, N. and M. Brière. 1931. La langue géorgienne. Paris.

Matteson, Esther. 1965. The Piro (Arawakan) language. Univ. of California Publications in Linguistics [UCPL] 42. Berkeley and Los Angeles.

Miller, Wick R. 1965. Acoma grammar and texts. UCPL 40.

Newmark, Leonard. 1957. Structural grammar of Albanian. IJAL 23.4, Pub. 4.

Pekmezi, G. 1908. Grammatik der albanesischen Sprache, Laut- und Formenlehre. Wien.

Peters, Ludwig and Aappo Heikkinen. 1940. 30 Stunden Finnisch. 4th ed. Berlin: Schöneberg.

Pokorny, Julius. 1914. A concise Old Irish grammar and reader. Dublin: Halle.

Poppe, Nicholas. 1951. Khalkha-mongolische Grammatik. Akademie der Wissenschaften und der Literatur. Wiesbaden: Steiner.

Potapova, Nina. 1947. Le russe, manuel de la langue russe à
l'usage des français, 2nd ed. Moscow.

Rabel, Lili. 1961. Khasi, a language of Assam. Louisiana State
University Studies, Humanities Series 10. Baton Rouge: Louisiana State University Press.

Ramstedt, G.J. 1939. A Korean grammar. Mémoires de la
Société Finno-ougrienne 82. Helsinki.

Rastorgueva, V.S. 1964. A short sketch of the grammar of Persian. IJAL 30.1, Pub. 29.

Ray, P.S., M. Hai and L. Ray. 1966. Bengali language handbook.
Center for Applied Linguistics. Washington, D.C.

Robins, R.H. 1958. The Yurok language. UCPL 15.

_____. 1962. The third person pronominal prefix in Yurok.
IJAL 28.14-18.

Rosén, Haim B. 1962, 1966. A textbook of Israeli Hebrew.
Chicago: University of Chicago Press.

Samarin, William J. 1967. A grammar of Sango. Janua Linguarum,
series practica. The Hague: Mouton.

Schmidt, Wilhelm. 1952. Die tasmanischen Sprachen. Comité
International de Linguistes. Commission d'Enquête Linguistique
5. Utrecht and Anvers: Spectrum.

Senn, Alfred. 1966. Handbuch der litauischen Sprache. Heidelberg.

Shafeev, D.A. 1964. A short grammatical outline of Pashto.
IJAL 30.3, Pub. 33.

Smith, Carlota S. 1964. Determiners and relative clauses in a
generative grammar of English. Lg 40.37-52.

Spencer, Harold. 1914. A Kanarese grammar. Mysore.

Steuernagel, Carl. 1962. Hebräische Grammatik. Lehrbücher
für das Studium der orientalischen Sprachen 5. Leipzig:
Verlag Enzyklopädie.

Strehlow, T.G.H. 1942-1944. Aranda phonetics and grammar. Sydney.

Swift, Lloyd B. 1963. A reference grammar of Modern Turkish. Indiana University Publications, Uralic and Altaic Series 19.

Teeter, Karl V. 1964. The Wiyot language. UCPL 37.

Thompson, Laurence C. 1965. A Vietnamese grammar. Seattle: University of Washington Press.

Thumb, Albert. 1964 (orig. pub. 1910). A handbook of the Modern Greek language, translated by S. Angus. Chicago: Argonaut.

Ultan, Russell. 1967. Konkow grammar. Doctoral dissertation, University of California, Berkeley.

Van der Stap, P.A.M. 1966. Outline of Dani morphology. Verhandelingen van het Koninklijk Instituut voor Taal-, Land-, en Volkenkunde 48. 's-Gravenhage.

Voorhoeve, C.L. 1965. The Flamingo Bay dialect of the Asmat language. 's-Gravenhage.

Ward, Ida C. 1936. An introduction to the Ibo language. Cambridge.

Waterhouse, Viola. 1962. The grammatical structure of Oaxaca Chontal. IJAL 28.2, Pub. 19.

Westermann, Dietrich. 1909. Handbuch der Ful-Sprache. Berlin.

_____. 1921. Die Gola-Sprache in Liberia. Hamburgische niversitat, Abhandlung aus dem Gebiet der Auslandskunde 6. Hamburg.

_____. 1930. A study of the Ewe language. London: Oxford Univ. Press.

Young, Ruth E. and M. Cantarella. 1943. Corso d'Italiano. New York.

Zamarripa y Uraga, P. 1955. Gramática Vasca. 7th ed. Bilbao.

Z'graggen, J.A. 1965. Possessor-possessed relationship in the Saker language, northeastern New Guinea. Oceania Linguistic Monographs 4.119-26.

Adverbial Constructions

GERALD A. SANDERS

ABSTRACT

The semantic, syntactic, and morphological properties of adverbial constructions are investigated in a basic sample of twenty-three languages with diverse geographical, genetic, and typological characteristics. A number of generalizations that hold for these languages are proposed as tentative observational universals about the nature and range of variation of adverbial constructions in all natural languages. Prerequisites for the principled explanation of these universals are discussed, and a schematic general theory of adverbial constructions is presented which appears to satisfy these prerequisites.

Reprinted from Working Papers on Language Universals, 10. December 1972, 93-129. This paper was prepared during the summer of 1971 when I had the pleasure of participating in the work of the Language Universals Project at Stanford. I am grateful to all of the members of the Project for their suggestions and encouragement and for the body of relevant data that they brought to my attention. I am especially indebted for such assistance to Charles Ferguson, Joseph Greenberg, and Edith Moravcsik. I, alone, however, am responsible for all errors of fact or interpretation that may be found here.

The data upon which this paper is based were drawn primarily from the set of languages listed in Appendix I, which includes for each of these languages a specification of my chief sources of information about it. (Transcriptions and translations are presented as given in the sources, except that tone markings are omitted from all transcriptions of CHINESE.)

CONTENTS

1. Introduction

All languages have certain superficial grammatical constructions which are used to express predicational relations between a
nominal or clausal argument and a predicate of temporal or spatial
location, function, direction, etc. Such constructions are most
commonly referred to as adverbials, or, where the predicate constituent is an uninflected word or clitic, as prepositional or postpositional phrases. It is well-known that the structure of these
adverbial constructions differs from language to language, both
with respect to the morphological complexity of their predicative
constituents and with respect to their order and closeness of syntactic and phonological attachment relative to the nominal constituent of the construction and its head noun. Our purpose here will
be to consider some of the observed similarities and differences
between the adverbial constructions of different languages, and
some of the possible universal principles of grammar which might
serve to explain their common properties and restricted range of
variation.

2. Predicational Characteristics

There are a number of semantic and syntactic reasons for considering case particles, prepositions, and postpositions to be more
fundamentally predicative than nominal in character. [1] Thus, if we
consider their relations to verbs, adjectives, and other clearly
predicative constituents on the one hand, and indefinite pronouns
and other clearly non-predicative constituents on the other, we find
for all languages apparently that their case markers, prepositions,
or postpositions share a greater number of significant properties

---

[1] I am assuming here, along with many other linguists and philosophers, that the only primitive categories in the semantic representations of natural language sentences are the categories Predicate,
Nominal or Argument, Quantifier, and (possibly) Proposition and
Propositional Connective. Thus, for example, if the ENGLISH
preposition in is associated with any semantic category at all in
the semantic representation of John was walking in the garden, then
it must be associated with some category out of this particular
highly-restricted set. The underlying predicative character of
instrumental, negative, and various other types of adverbial constructions has been noted and most extensively argued by George
Lakoff (1965, 1968). Important supporting evidence from CHINESE
has been presented by James Tai (1971).

with the class of predicate constituents than with the class of non-predicate, or argument, constituents.

2.1 Semantic predicational characteristics

Considering the question of predicative meaning first, it is reasonably clear, for prepositions and postpositions at least, that these generally express relations between arguments in precisely the same sense as any two-place verbal predicate. Thus, for example, compare the following verbal and prepositional predications of ENGLISH:

1. a. Symmetric
        Verbal: John resembles Bill.
        Prepositional: John is like Bill.

    b. Non-symmetric
        Verbal: Jack loves Jill.
        Prepositional: Jack is in front of Jill.

    c. Asymmetric
        Verbal: Arthur plays tennis.
        Prepositional: The book is under the table.
                       This present is for Arthur.

    d. Converse
        Verbal: Richard sold a car to Frank :
                       Frank bought a car from Richard.

        Prepositional: The hawk is over the snake :
                       The snake is under the hawk.

A fundamental relationship between verbal and prepositional predications is also suggested by the existence of paraphrase or near-paraphrase relations of the sort illustrated by 1. a. or by pairs of sentences like

2. a. Tom followed Bill : Tom went/came after Bill.
    b. The walls enclose the town : The walls are around the town.
    c. The tree separates the house and the barn :
        The tree is between the house and the barn.

However, while it appears to be the case, for some languages at least, that there are prepositional counterparts for all relationally-defined types of verbal predication, there also appear to be significant

differences in the relative normality or unmarkedness of the corresponding types. Thus, while the majority of two-place verbal
predicates are apparently non-symmetric (e. g. ENGLISH: love,
hit, see, wash), the majority of two-place prepositional predicates
are either symmetric (e. g. near, beside, like, with (comitative))
or even more frequently antisymmetric (e. g. under, over, with
(instrumental), in(side), after). Also, if we exclude active-passive
converses such as X hit Y : Y was hit by X, there seem to be very
few two-place verbal converses (e. g. X likes Y : Y pleases X, X
rides Y : Y carries X?) but a great many two-place prepositional
converses (e. g. X is over Y : Y is under X, X is before Y : Y is
after X, etc.). Moreover, while there are three-place non-conjunc-
tive verbal converses, such as X buys Y from Z : Z sells Y to X,
as well as conjunctive converse like X separates Y and Z : X
separates Z and Y, it appears that the only three-place prepositional predicates which occur at all are conjunctive converses like
X is between Y and Z : X is between Z and Y.

If it is correct that the ENGLISH prepositions in, on, and for
have the semantic function of two-place predicates in the sentences
of 3. , then it follows from the synonymy relations between these
sentences and the corresponding FINNISH sentences of 4. (Lehtinen
1964 : 121-22) that the FINNISH case suffixes for inessive, adessive,
and allative must have exactly the same predicative functions here.

3. a. Matti is in school.
   b. The coffee is on the table.
   c. This package is for you.

4. a. Matti on koulu-ssa
      "Matti be school-inessive"
   b. Kahvi on pöydä-llä
      "coffee be table-adessive"
   c. Tämä paketti on tei-lle
      "this package be you-allative"

The same relation of functional equivalence holds also between the
prepositionally-expressed predicate of the ENGLISH sentence

5.   It is on the table.

and the postpositionally-expressed predicate of the synonymous
ENGA sentence

6.   tóko kisá silyámo
      "table on be-pre-3sg. "

It is thus necessary to assume that for at least some adverbial expressions the formal distinction between the affixal, prepositional, and postpositional representation of their non-nominal constituents is due only to language-variable differences in the syntactic and lexical principles which determine the mapping relation between language-invariable predicative constructions and the particular phonological representation of these constructions in particular languages.

In general, adverbial predicates appear to be either 1) one-place predicates taking sentential or propositional arguments; 2) two-place predicates taking either 2a) a sentential argument and a nominal argument or 2b) two nominal arguments; or 3) n-place predicates, where n is greater than two and all arguments are nominal.

These types are illustrated by the following examples from ENGLISH:

Type 1: John <u>certainly</u> won't fail. (cf. That John won't fail is certain; It is certain that John won't fail.)

John <u>won't</u> fail. (cf. That John will fail is false/not true; It is false/not true that John won't fail.)

Type 2: John left <u>on</u> Monday. (cf. John's leaving/departure was on Monday.) (but cf. also: The day on which John left was Monday.)

John played the guitar <u>in</u> the garden. (cf. John's guitar-playing was in the garden.) (but cf. also: The place in which John played the guitar was the garden.)

Type 2b: The book was <u>on</u> the table.
The party was <u>on</u> Monday.

Type 3:[2] The barn is <u>between</u> the house and the road.
The house is <u>among</u> the trees. (cf. *The house is among the pine tree, the apple tree, the elm tree, and the oak tree.)

---

[2]There are also instances of Type 3 in which one of the arguments might possibly be interpreted as an eventive (but not factive) clause, rather than a simple non-clausal nominal. An example of this might be John walked between the house and the road. -- but compare The place where John walked was between the house and the road.

This predicational classification of adverbials is very rough and
tentative, of course, and it is possible not only that some of the
proposed types are not significantly distinct but also that there are
some significantly distinct adverbial types which are not differentiated by the proposed classificatory criteria. Thus, for example,
it is possible that Type 2b (e.g. The party was on Monday) may be
most appropriately viewed as only one of the many superficially
variant subtypes of Type 2a (e.g. The party started and finished
on Monday). It is also not clear how manner adverbs, for example,
are to be characterized in terms of the suggested predicational criteria. Thus it is not clear which (if any) of the following paraphrases
of John ran slowly most adequately reflects its underlying predicational structure: John's running was slow (cf. Type 1), John's running was like slow running/like something slow (cf. Types 2a and
2b), John was like a slow runner/like something slow in his running, John's running was like the running of a slow runner/ of
something slow.

Similar classificatory problems arise with respect to most other
types of adverbial expressions too. The proposed schema is thus
most appropriately viewed simply as a rough conceptual framework
or expository base for the investigation of the more specific semantic
and formal properties of the various adverbial expressions of different languages.

2.2 Syntactic predicational characteristics

Many of the syntactic parallels between the prepositions, postpositions, and case particles of adverbial constructions and the
verbs, adjectives, and predicate nominals of other predicational
constructions will be apparent from the survey of adverbial constituency and constituent-ordering in section 3. Here it will be
sufficient to merely mention two of the most striking of these
parallels:

7. The constituency and ordering relations between transitive
    verbs and their non-subject arguments in a given language
    are nearly always the same as those which hold in that lan-
    guage between prepositions or postpositions and their overt
    (and always non-subject) arguments (see Greenberg 1963,
    Universals 3 and 4):

e.g. TURKISH: kuz - u yerim   'I eat lamb.'
                  "lamb-of I-eat"
                  $\underline{N + P}$ ⌞_____⌟
                    N + P

TURKISH: postan   - ye   yakin   'near the postoffice'
         "postoffice-to   near"

$$\underbrace{\underbrace{N\ +\ P}_{N}\ +\ \underbrace{}_{P}}$$

ENGLISH: I $\underbrace{\text{eat}}\ \underbrace{\text{lamb}}$
           P + N

$$\underbrace{\text{near}},\ \underbrace{\text{the postoffice}}$$
$$\ \ P\ +\ \ \ \ \ \ \ N$$

8. In languages where transitive verbs have suffixes agreeing
   in definiteness or in person-gender-number with their direct
   objects, prepositions also have suffixes that agree with their
   objects in the same categories.

   e.g. EGYPTIAN COLLOQUIAL ARABIC:

   il-walad il-bint ḍarab -t - u
   "the-boy the-girl hit-she-him"
   'The girl hit the boy.'

   il - sitt   il-bint ḍarab-ti-ha
   "the-woman the-girl hit-she-her"
   'The girl hit the woman.'

   id-duláab   taḫt - u   tráab
   "the-cupboard under-it dust"
   'There's dust under the cupboard.'

   da btáaɛ - u   huwwa, múš bitaɛ -ak   inta
   "that belong-to-3.sg.masc. him, not belong-to-2.sg.masc.you"
   'That's his, not yours.'

There are also, of course, a number of obvious systematic differences between the superficial syntactic properties of the verbal
and adverbial predicates of any language. The most important of
these are perhaps the following:

9. Verbs may have tense or aspect or superficial-subject-
   agreement affixes, while prepositions and postpositions
   never have such affixes.

10. Prepositions and postpositions sometimes occur in embedded
    constituents of one of their arguments, while this is very
    rarely or never the case for verbs.

e. g.   That John didn't do it was (<u>like</u>) (something) <u>certain</u>.
John <u>certain-ly</u> didn't do it.

The happy boy <u>kissed</u> the sad girl.
*The <u>kissed</u> happy boy the sad girl.
*The happy boy the sad <u>kissed</u> girl.

These and other consistent differences between the verbal and adverbial predications of natural languages should ideally be explained
by means of the same set of universal principles which account for
their significant similarities.

3. <u>Superficial Constituency</u>

Adverbial constructions generally include an overt superficial
manifestation of their predicative constituents, either in the form
of a preposed or postposed word or clitic, or in the form of an
affix bound to one or more of the constituents of the construction,
or in the form of some combination of words, clitics, and affixes.
There are exceptions to this, however, in many languages, and it
is appropriate before proceeding to the more general case to consider some of the cases in which adverbial predicates are most
commonly not overtly expressed.

3. 1 <u>Reduced adverbial constructions</u>

In many (and possibly all) languages, there are certain temporal
adverbial predications which invariably occur without overt predicate
constituents. Exemplifying such reduced constructions is the ENG-
LISH temporal adverbial <u>yesterday</u>:

11.   The party was yesterday.
   Cf.   *The party was $\begin{Bmatrix} \text{in} \\ \text{on} \\ \text{at} \end{Bmatrix}$ yesterday.
   The party was $\begin{Bmatrix} \text{in the morning} \\ \text{on Friday} \\ \text{at six o'clock} \end{Bmatrix}$.

Parallel to <u>yesterday</u> here are the typically temporal arguments
<u>tomorrow</u>, <u>last week</u>, <u>Friday</u>, <u>last Friday</u>, <u>last month</u>, <u>next week</u>,
<u>next Monday</u>, <u>next year</u>, etc. and the anaphoric or deictic temporal
arguments <u>then</u> and <u>now</u>. Similar cases of temporal constructions
with non-overt predicates are found in other languages, e. g.

12.   AMHARIC
   <u>naga</u>   nā   balaw
   "tomorrow come say-to-him"
   'Tell him to come <u>tomorrow</u>.'

<u>āsrā sost kan</u> takammata
"thirteen day he-stayed"
'He stayed <u>thirteen days</u>.'

Cf. non-reduced:
saw <u>ba-mātā</u>   yigabāl
"man at-evening he-will-arrive"
'The man will arrive <u>in the evening</u>.'

13. ENGA:
     <u>kuáka</u> baá álo pyaó púpyá
     "yesterday he quickly he-went"
     'He went quickly <u>yesterday</u>.'

14. HUNGARIAN:
     A   parti   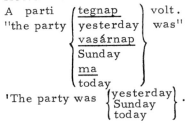   volt.
     "the party   was"

     'The party was {yesterday
                      Sunday
                      today } .

     Cf. non-reduced:
     A parti   ⎛ <u>hétfő-n</u>   ⎞ volt.
               ⎜ Monday-on   ⎟
               ⎨ <u>három-kor</u>   ⎬
               ⎜ three-time   ⎟
               ⎜   marker   ⎟
               ⎝ <u>1964-ben</u>   ⎠
                        in
     'The party was ⎧ on Monday   ⎫ .
                     ⎨ at three o'clock ⎬
                     ⎩ in 1964   ⎭

15. TURKISH
     Ali <u>bu gün</u> yapacak.
     "Ali this day is-going-to-do-[it]"
     'Ali is going to do it today.'

     <u>Bu akşam</u> altıda   başlarım.
     "this evening at-six I-will-begin"
     'I'll begin this evening at six.'

     Overt predicate constituents are also lacking from certain loca-
tive or directive expressions which occur with superficial copulas

or verbs of motion. In ENGLISH this appears to be restricted to expressions that include either the anaphoric and deictic locatives <u>there</u> and <u>here</u> or the deictic or quasi-deictic argument <u>home</u> (= "at/in specified subject's own home").[3] Compare:

16. He's there now. (*at there)
    He's here now. (*at here)
    He's home now. (= at his home)

He $\left\{\begin{array}{l}\text{went}\\\text{came}\\\text{left}\\\text{got}\\\text{stayed}\\\text{walked}\\\text{ran}\end{array}\right\}$ $\left\{\begin{array}{l}\text{there}\\\text{here}\\\text{home}\end{array}\right\}$.

    *He's school now.
    *He came (his) house.
    *He went garden.
    *He played home.

Similar constructions with arguments meaning 'there,' 'here,' or 'home' occur in certain other languages, e. g.

17. MANDARIN
    ta daw-le   jia
    "he arrived home"
    'He arrived home.'

However, while it may be the case that all languages have at least some reduced temporal adverbials (particularly for such deictic temporal arguments as <u>now</u>, <u>this morning</u>, <u>yesterday</u>, <u>last month</u>), this is not the case for locative adverbials, where predicate suppletion is often non-existent even for the deictic arguments '(at) this place' and '(at) that place,' or the quasi-deictic '(at) subject's home.' Thus, for example, THAI contrasts with ENGLISH in having no predicate reduction in the normal or unmarked expressions for deictic and anaphoric locatives.

---

[3]ENGLISH also has other monolexical adverbial expressions like <u>aboard</u>, <u>ashore</u>, <u>overseas</u>, <u>inside</u>, and <u>outside</u>. There appear to be some reasons, however, for considering these to be only special cases of the standard non-reduced adverbial type [P & NP], with <u>a</u>-, <u>over</u>-, <u>in</u>-, and <u>out</u>- as their (idiomatically proclitic) predicative constituents.

18. khǎw jù: thî nî: khǎw cà paj thî nân
     "he is-located at this"   "he will go at that"
     'He is/lives here.'   'He will go there.'

but does not exclude such reduction categorically:

19. khǎw cà paj nâ:n
     'He will go there.'

20. khǎw cà klàp bâ:n
     "he will return house"
     'He will return home.'

In TURKISH (Swift 1961), on the other hand, there appears to be
no locative reduction at all:

21. Bú - ra - da   kalacağım.
     "this-place-at I'm-going-to-stay"
     'I'm going to stay here.'

     ev - é   giderek
     "house--to going"
     'going home'

     Şúra - ya   gitmelíydi.
     "over there-to he-had-to-go"
     'He had to go over there.'

Some languages also have adverbial or adverbial-like constructions in which the only superficial constituent is one which functions
in other constructions as a predicative constituent and never as an
argument. Examples of such argument-reduced constructions are
found quite extensively in ENGLISH both for locative expressions
(22.) and for temporal ones (23.):

22. John took the dog out(side).
     (Cf. John took the dog out(side) of that place.)
     Helen walked away.
     (Cf. Helen walked away from there.)
     Dr. Brown isn't in now.
     (Cf. Dr. Brown isn't in his office now.)
     Please take off your hat.
     (Cf. Please take your hat off (of) your head.)
     You're falling behind.
     (Cf. You're falling behind the rest of us.)

23. I had never been there <u>before</u>.
    (Cf. I had never been there <u>before last Monday</u>.)
    They lived happily ever <u>after</u>.
    (Cf. They lived happily <u>after that time</u>.)

Argument-reduction of this sort appears to be quite rare, though, in natural languages as a whole, and most languages that I have investigated thus far seem to have no clear cases of this type of adverbial expression at all.

If the semantic structure underlying all adverbial constructions is that of a predication whose arguments are either propositions or nominals, then there is also another very common class of adverbial expressions which is superficially reductive in the same sense as the previous classes of predicateless and argumentless constructions. This is the class of adverbials -- typically adverbs of manner -- whose overt constituents are a predicate constituent and an adjectival constituent. Such constructions are exemplified by the following sentences from ENGLISH:

24. Grace ate the grapes <u>greedily</u>.
    (Cf. Grace ate the grapes <u>like someone greedy</u>/<u>like a greedy person</u>.)

    John ran very <u>slowly</u>.
    (Cf. John ran <u>like a very slow runner</u>,
    John ran <u>in a very slow way</u>.)

Such constructions also occur in many other languages. For example:

25. FRENCH: Jean a couru très <u>lentement</u>.
                "Jean has run very slowly"
                'Jean ran very <u>slowly</u>.'

    LATVIAN: man   iet   <u>lab-i</u>
                "to-me it-goes good-ly"
                'It's going <u>well</u> for me; I'm O.K.'

    SINHALESE: lámaya <u>honda-ṭa</u> pota kiyavanavā
                "boy   good-ly book reads"
                'The boy reads the book <u>well</u>.'

    XHOSA: ɓavuma <u>ka-mnandi</u>   Cf.: ukutya oku-mnandi
                "they-sing ly-sweet"   "food agr.-sweet"
                'They sing <u>sweetly</u>.'   'nice food'

We thus find three basic types of adverbial constructions which may be considered reductive in the sense that they have either no overt predicate constituent or no overt argument constituent, or an argument constituent without any overt nominal head. Since only the last of these can have subtypes differentiated by constituent-ordering, there are four observed reduced adverbial types in all:

1. [N] (predicate-reduced)
   John went <u>home.</u>　　　　　(locative argument)
   The party was <u>yesterday.</u> (temporal argument)

2. [P] (argument-reduced)
   John went <u>out.</u>　　　　　　(locative predicative)
   He had never danced <u>before.</u> (temporal predicate)

3. [p, adj.] (nominal-reduced)
   3a.　[p + adj.]
   　　　XHOSA: bavuma　<u>ka-mnandi</u>
   　　　　　　　　"they-sing p adj."
   　　　　　　　　'They sing sweetly.'

   3b.　[adj. + p]
   　　　They sing <u>sweet-ly.</u>
   　　　　　　　(adj. p)

The facts known to me about such reduced constructions would appear to justify the assumption of the following more or less tentative existential universals:

U.1　All languages have non-reduced adverbial constructions.

U.2　If a language has reduced adverbials, these are always more restricted in their privileges of occurrence than its non-reduced averbials.

U.3　If a language has argument-reduced adverbials, it will also have predicate-reduced adverbials. (This is more tentative than U.1 and U.2, and the truth or falsity of its converse is unknown.)

U.4　If a language has predicate-reduced adverbials, then at least some of these will have temporal arguments. Thus, if reductions with locative arguments occur in some language, reductions with temporal arguments will also occur in that language.

U.5 Both predicate-reduced and argument-reduced adverbials are typically (possibly always?) anaphoric or deictic in character, and they are seldom (possibly never?) ambiguous with respect to their non-overt argument or predicate, given the deictic and referential bases of the discourse in which they occur.

Thus, for example, I arrived yesterday is unambiguously understood to mean "The speaker of this sentence arrived on the day that immediately preceded the day on which he uttered this sentence." It cannot mean that he arrived before the preceding day, or after it, or on any day other than the day preceding his utterance of the sentence. Similarly, John went home can only mean "John went to his own home;" it cannot be interpreted as meaning that he went by his home, or from it, or around it, or that he went to someone else's home. Likewise, John has never eaten octopus before means that John has never eaten octopus before now, i.e. before the time at which this sentence is uttered. It cannot mean that John wasn't an octopus-eater before last Thursday, or before March 4, 1969, etc. The situation with respect to nominal-reduced constructions is unclear, however, although it would seem that these constructions typically are ambiguous with respect to the set (always finite, apparently, and quite small) of possible appropriate nominal arguments for their similarity predicates. Thus, for example, That elephant is running slowly could apparently be understood to mean either "That elephant is running like a slow elephant (runs)," or "That elephant is running like a slow runner (runs)."

All of these tentative universals suggest what has already been suggested by the use of the term "reduction" here and by the initial general characterization of adverbial constructions as expressions of predications: namely, that all adverbial constructions that lack superficial predicate or argument constituents are derivational reductions of fully specified non-superficial constructions each consisting of a particular n-place predicate and exactly n appropriate nominal or propositional arguments. It will be shown subsequently that all of the adverbial constructions that we are calling "non-reduced" can also be appropriately viewed as derivational reductions of more fully specified non-superficial constructions. Here it is sufficient to note with respect to the particular class of reductions that we have referred to as "reduced" that the general non-ambiguity of such constructions (or, in the case of nominal-reductions, their very restricted range of ambiguity) can be explained by the reduction hypothesis as a necessary consequence of the general independently motivated identity constraint on the adjunction or deletion of any

constituent that is not an ultimate constituent. (Cf. the related
general identity constraint on deletions proposed by Chomsky (1965),
which is often referred to as the principle of "recoverability of
deletions.") The general character of the adverbial reductive processes that might be assumed here will be taken up subsequently,
after considering some of the basic facts about the observed range
of "non-reduced" adverbial constructions in natural languages.

3.2 Non-reduced adverbial constructions

Non-reduced adverbial constructions are defined by the presence
of at least one predicate constituent and at least one nominal argument constituent with an overt noun or pronoun head. The predicate
constituent may be either simplex (monomorphemic) or complex
(multimorphemic). Simplex predicates may be relatively free, or
lexical, in character, or they may be relatively bound, either as
clitics of nominal arguments or as affixes of their noun or pronoun
heads.

(Simplex lexical predicates will be represented here by the symbol P, and simplex affixal or enclitic predicates will be represented
by the symbol p. There is often no clear basis in the available source
materials for determining whether a given adverbial predicate is a
P or a p, and many of the classifications made here are thus relatively arbitrary and entirely tentative. Wherever possible, however,
I have assigned p classifications only to those predicates which
satisfy at least one of the following criteria: 1) occurrence in medial positions of nominal expressions; 2) occurrence with minimal
stress and pitch contour and with reduced, maximally unmarked or
null syllabic segments; 3) occurrence as a set of morphophonemi-
cally alternate forms with alternations conditioned by properties of
some superficially adjacent constituent.)

Complex adverbial predicates are simplex predicates that are in
construction with a nominal argument, usually of genitival character.
(For example, ENGLISH at the back of the house, where the predicate at the back (of) is itself an adverbial construction with predicate
at and nominal argument the back; or TURKISH NP altında 'under-
neath NP,' where alt is a noun meaning 'lower part,' and where
there are suffixes in 'possessor suffix' and da 'at,' such that the
predicate altında is itself interpretable as an adverbial construction
meaning 'at the back (of something).')

Types of non-reduced adverbial constructions are differentiated
by 1) the constituents of a construction; 2) the grouping, or bracketing, relations between given constituents, and 3) the linear ordering
relations between the constituents of given bracketings. The following

outline summarizes the results to date of my investigations of the
range of non-reduced adverbial types in natural language. Major
types are defined by constituents and constituent structure, with
subtypes of each type being differentiated in terms of the possible
orderings of its constituents. (NP = nominal argument; N = noun;
P = prepositional or postpositional predicate; p = affixal or enclitic
predicate, semantically generic usually to some class of P's, typically what would generally be called a (superficial) case marker;
X(Y) = a structure Y that is a construction of the type X.)

3.2.1 Types of non-reduced adverbial constructions

4.[4] (NP, P)

    a. (P + NP)
       ENGLISH: It's on the table.

    b. (NP + P)
       ENGA: toko kisa silyamo
           "table on be-pres-3sg. "
           'It's on the table. '

5. $_{NP}(\dots(N,p)\dots)$

    a. $_{NP}(\dots(p+N)\dots)$

    No examples[5]

---

[4]Adverbial types 1(N), 2(P), and 3(p, adj.) are the reduced types
discussed in section 3.1.

[5]AMHARIC (cf. Bach 1970, Hetzron 1970, Hudson 1971) has some
constructions which might be interpreted as instances of Type 5a:

  (i)   yohannəs əndä-abbat-u gäzza-∅ (Hudson)
       "John   like-father-his ruled-he"
       'John ruled like his father. '

  (ii) kä - bet - u   mätta-∅   (Hetzron)
       "from-house-the came he"
       'He came from the house. '

  (iii) yohannəs abbat-u əndä-gäzza-∅ gäzza-∅   (Hudson)
       "John   father-his like-ruled-he ruled-he"
       'John ruled like his father ruled. '

  (iv) mäjämmriya lä-mätta - ∅ - u tämari (Hudson)
       "first   for-came-he-the student:
       'for the first student who came'

    b. $_{NP}(\ldots(N+p)\ldots)$

         LATIN: <u>reg-is</u>   'of a king'
         TURKISH: <u>ben-de</u>   'on me'

6. $_{NP}(\ldots(X,p)\ldots)$ where X is a lexical constituent determined by a precedence principle relative to the other lexical constituent of the phrase.

    a. $_{NP}(\ldots(p+X)\ldots)$

         AMHARIC: əndä - abbat-u ;   abbat-u əndä-gäzza-∅
                   "like-father-his"   "father-his like-ruled-he"
                   'like his father'   'like his father ruled'

(ftnt. 5 cont.)

    (v)   <u>əne yä - ayyä-hu-t</u> säwye <u>bä-allä - w</u> bet
        "I (REL)- saw - I -it   man   at- be - his house"
        'at the man that I saw's house'

These sentences also demonstrate, however, that the bound adverbial predicates of AMHARIC are not affixes like the case affixes of languages like LATIN, which are always in construction with nouns (and any of their attributes which are subject to noun agreement). Rather, they are essentially enclitic in character, there being only one token per nominal phrase normally, with that token being prefixed to any single constituent of the phrase subject to what appears to be the following general principle of attraction precedence: a clitic predicate is prefixed to that non-null constituent of its argument phrase which is most precedent in the ranking 1) highest predicate of the phrase (which happens in AMHARIC to also be its last predicate) 2) first word of the phrase. (See Bach 1970 and Hudson 1971 for rather different approaches to the problem of clitic placement in AMHARIC.) Sentences (iii), (iv) and (v) illustrate the precedence of highest predicates over all other constituents. The following sentences (Hetzron 1970) illustrate the precedence of first words over all other constituents of predicateless argument phrases:

    (vi) <u>kä-zzičč</u>   set   lay and mäshaf gäzzah^W (-at)
        "from-this woman on one book   bought-I (her)"
        'I bought a book from this woman.'

    (vii) <u>kä-setəyyäwa</u>   and mäshaf gäzzah^W (-at)
        "from-woman-the one book   bought-I (her)"
        'I bought a book from the woman.'

All AMHARIC adverbial constructions with bound predicates would thus appear to be most appropriately classified as instances of type 6 rather than type 5.

b. $_{NP}(\ldots(X+p)\ldots)$
No examples

7. $(NP, _p(\ldots(N, p)\ldots))$

   a. $(_p(\ldots(p+N)\ldots)+NP)$
   No examples

   b. $(_p(\ldots(N+p)\ldots)+NP)$
   No examples

   c. $(NP+_p(\ldots(p+N)\ldots))$
   No examples

   d. $(NP+_p(\ldots(N+p)\ldots)$
   HUNGARIAN: <u>a fiú elött</u>
                NP N p
              "the boy front (LOC)"
              'before the boy'
   (Cf. <u>itt</u> 'here,' <u>ott</u> 'there,' <u>Pécsett</u> 'in Pécs,' <u>eleje</u> 'the front of something')

8. $(P, _{NP}(\ldots N, p)\ldots))$

   a. $(P+_{NP}(\ldots(p+N)\ldots))$
   No examples

   b. $(P+_{NP}(\ldots(N+p)\ldots))$
   LATIN: <u>dē insulā</u>   <u>in insulam</u>
             "from island-ablative" "in island-accusative"
             'from the island'   'into the island'

   c. $(_{NP}(\ldots(p+N)\ldots)+P)$
   AMHARIC: bǎ-yohannis bet <u>wəst</u>
              "in-John house inside"
              'inside John's house"

              bǎ-meda <u>wəst</u> maṭṭa
              "in-field inside come-he"
              'He was coming into the field.'

              <u>kǎ</u>-zzičč set <u>lay</u>
              "from-this woman on"
              'from this woman'

d. $(_{NP} (...N+p)...) + P)$
   (?) JAPANESE: <u>sensō no mae</u>
                  "war of before"
                  'before the war'

9. $(_{P}(...N, p)...), _{NP}(...N, p...))$

   x. $(_{P}(...(N+p)...) + _{NP}(...(N+p)...))$
      HUNGARIAN: <u>elötte   a fiúnak</u>
                 (<u>el</u> or <u>elö</u> ='front;' <u>ott</u> or <u>tt</u> = locative
                 suffix; <u>e</u>= possessed suffix; <u>a</u> = 'the;'
                 <u>fiú</u> = 'boy;' <u>nak</u> = possessor suffix)
                 'before the boy'

   y. $(_{NP}(...N+p)...) + _{P}(...(N+p)...)$

      (?) HUNGARIAN: <u>a fiúnak elötte</u>
                     'before the boy'

<u>No examples of other subtypes of 9.</u>

10. (P, (p, NP))

    a. $(P + (p+NP))$
       (?) ENGLISH (allegro style): [nirTmayháws]
                                     'near to my house'

                                     [awTəʒəkár]
                                     'out of the car'

       (?) FRENCH: <u>près d'ici;</u>   <u>près d'la maison</u>
                   'near here'   'near to the house'

    b. $(P + (NP + p))$
       ENGLISH (genitives): I met a friend <u>of that guy over</u>
                            <u>there's</u> yesterday.

       (?) CHINESE: <u>zai fanguan li</u>
                    "(be) at restaurant in(side)"
                    'in the restaurant'

    c. $((p + NP) + P)$
       (?) CHINESE: <u>zai fanguan li</u>
                    [possibly 10b. or $(P + (NP + P))$]
                    'in the restaurant'

(?) AMHARIC: b̵-meda wəst
              possibly 10b. or 8c.
              'in the field'

d. ((NP + p) + P)
    WESTERN DESERT LANGUAGE: yapu-ngka
                              "rock-locative"
                              'on the rock'

                              yapu-ngka katu
                              "rock-loc. over"
                              'over the rock'

                              yapu pulka-ngka katu
                              "rock big- loc. over"
                              'over the big rock'

The preceding outline of observed alternations in the internal
structure of non-reduced adverbial constructions in natural languages would be consistent with the following tentative existential
universals:

U.6   No language has adverbial predicates which are expressed
      as case prefixes. (This subsumes the non-existence asser-
      tions for the unobserved but logically-possible types 5a,
      7a, 7c, 8a, and all of the unobserved subtypes of type 9.)

U.7   No language has adverbial predicates which are expressed
      as argument-internal clitics that are postposed to the con-
      stituents that they are bound to. (This subsumes the non-
      existence assertion for type 6b.)

U.8   If a language has adverbial predicates which are analyzable
      into a noun and a case affix, then any postposed arguments
      of such predicates will always include case affixes on their
      head nouns. (This subsumes the non-existence assertion
      for type 7b.)

The generalization about adverbial case affixation expressed by
U.6 would appear to be reducible to a much more general observation about the ordering of all case affixes relative to their stems:

U.6' All case affixes are suffixes.

This generalization holds for all languages that I am familiar with,

and I will thus tentatively assume that the non-occurrence of the
adverbial constructions excluded by U. 6 has nothing to do with adverbial constructions as such, but follows instead from whatever
principles serve to explain U. 6'.

It will also be observed that the examples I have cited for types
10a, 10b, and 10c. are distinctly dubious as to their proper classification, since it is not at all obvious, particularly for the examples
under 10a, that the predicative constituent labeled p is really subordinate and generic to that labeled P. Moreover, with respect to
the genitival clitics in près d'ici and of that buy over there's, it is
not even clear that there are expressions of adverbial predicates
at all. The CHINESE and AMHARIC examples in 10c. raise problems of a different and more generally significant sort. Thus for
these languages, unlike those of type 10d. exemplified by the
WESTERN DESERT LANGUAGE, the more generic of the two adverbial predicate constituents of a complex adverbial construction
appears to be superordinate rather than subordinate to the more
specific adverbial predicate. It will also be observed that in these
examples the more generic of the two adverbials (e. g. zai) precedes
rather than follows the more specific one (e. g. li). Thus if it is
really the case that zai is superordinate to li in zai fanguan li,
then the existence of CHINESE would suffice to falsify the otherwise quite well-supported generalization, first reported for nominal
anaphora by Langacker (1969), that the more specific of two anaphorically related constituents must either precede or asymmetri-
cally command the more generic constituent.

4. Superficial Syntactic Functions

The superficial syntactic functions of adverbial constructions
have not been investigated in sufficient detail to determine the nature and range of typological criteria that might be appropriate in
this respect. There are, however, a number of generalizations
about adverbial syntax which hold for all of the languages that I
have obtained data about, and I would like to put them forth here as
additional tentative universals which would presumably have to be
accounted for by any adequate general theory of adverbial constructions in natural language. Each universal will be exemplified with
respect to a representative language of each of Greenberg's (1963)
three basic types characterized by normal or unmarked order of
subject, verb, and object: I. VSO; II. SVO; III. SOV.

U. 9 All languages have sentences with sentence-initial
      adverbial constituents.

Examples:

I. IBANAG: tatadai ngaragon i pinanuntu na abbing ta mestra
"last year   hit   the child the teacher"
'Last year the child hit the teacher.'

i limana i pinanuntu na abbing ta mestra
"with his-hand hit the child the teacher"
'With his hand the child hit the teacher.'

II. ENGLISH: Last year the child hit the teacher.
In the valley, the rain was beginning to fall.

III. JAPANESE: kyonen wa denshachin ga yasukatta
"last-year topic train-fare subj. was-cheap(er)"
'Last year the train fare was cheaper.'

kyōshitsu ni seito ga sanjūnin imasu
"classroom in pupils subj. 30-men are"
'There are 30 pupils in the classroom.'

U.10. All languages have sentences with non-sentence-initial
adverbial constituents.

Examples:

I. IBANAG: nachian ta manila i abbing tatadai ngaragon
"lived in Manila the child last   year"
'The child lived in Manila last year.'

sinuntu na abbing i mestra ta limana
"hit the child the teacher with his-hand"
'The child hit the teacher with his hand.'

II. ENGLISH: The child lived in Manila last year.
The child hit the teacher with his hand.

III. JAPANESE: kare wa hikōki de kimasu
"he topic airplane by comes"
'He's coming by airplane.'

boku wa asu tōkyō e yukimasu
"I topic tomorrow Tokyo to go"
'I'll go to Tokyo tomorrow.'

U.11. For most if not all adverbial constructions in all languages,
the most "normal," most prosaic, and implicationally most

unmarked ordering for such constructions is in a non-
sentence-initial position -- following either the superficial
subject or the superficial object or both.

Examples: (See examples for U. 10)

The available data also suggest the following implicational universals.

U. 12 If a language has S(O)V ordering but not SVO orderings, then
it will have S(O)ADV V orderings, but no S(O)V ADV orderings. [6] (This is essentially only an alternative formulation
of Greenberg's Universal 7 (1963:63): "If in a language with
dominant SOV order, there is no alternative basic order, or
only OSV as the alternative, then all adverbial modifiers of
the verb likewise precede the verb.")

Examples:
JAPANESE: (a) gakusei   wa   hon   o   kaimasu
               "students topic books obj. buy"
               'The students buy books. '

           *gakusei wa kaimasu hon o

           (b) kare ga hikōki   de kimasu
                "he subj. airplane by comes"
                'He's coming by airplane. '

           *kare ga kimasu hikōki de

U. 13 If a language has either of the orderings [S ADV V X] and
[S V X ADV] , then it will have both of these orderings,
one being normal for a large majority of adverbial subtypes,
the other being normal for the remainder of adverbial subtypes.

Examples:
ENGLISH: S ADV V X normal for minority of adverbial
           subtypes:
               John never eats apples.
           */? John eats apples never.

---

[6]The non-occurrence of post-verbal objects may also imply the
non-occurrence of [S ADV O V] orderings. I have insufficient data
on such orderings, however, to determine whether or not this correlation actually holds.

S V X ADV normal for <u>majority</u> of adverbial
subtypes:
    <u>John eats apples in the garden.</u>
*/? <u>John in the garden eats apples.</u>

CHINESE: S ADV V X normal for <u>majority</u> of adverbial
subtypes:
    <u>John zuotian dale nanhaizi</u>
    "John yesterday hit boy"
    'John hit the boy yesterday. '

    *<u>John dale nanhaizi zuotian</u>

S V X ADV normal for <u>minority</u> of adverbial
subtypes:
    <u>John laile wode chia li</u>
    "John came my house inside"
    'John came to my house. '

    *<u>John wode chia li laile</u>

5. Toward a General Theory of Adverbial Constructions

   To account for the range of facts cited in the preceding sections
it is necessary to have a general theory of adverbial constructions
which is consistent both with the universally predicative semantic
function of adverbials and with the distinctive range of grouping
and ordering patterns that characterize the expressions of adverbial
constructions in natural languages. In particular, it will be necessary for any such theory to explain why the superficial internal
structure of adverbial constructions is generally if not always like
that of a verb-object construction, rather than a subject-verb construction, or a superficially complete clausal predication. It will
also be necessary to explain why the external superficial grouping
and ordering relations of adverbial constructions are like those of
the non-subject arguments of verbal predicates, rather than like
those of subject arguments, or of verbal predicates themselves.

   Although it is impossible for me to propose any such general
theory of adverbial constructions here, I would like to conclude this
survey by making certain tentative suggestions concerning some of
the basic principles of grammar which I feel would have to be included in the axiomatic basis of any adequate theory of this sort.
These suggestions will be expressed here simply as a set of schematic hypotheses, with brief comments on their possible empirical
basis and explanatory functions.

H.1 Every adverbial expression is symbolically associated with at least two distinct non-phonological representations, one consisting of an adverbial predicate in construction with one or more nominal or clausal arguments, the other consisting of a proper part of the first representation properly included in one of the arguments of the first representation.

This assumption appears to be sufficiently motivated by the fact that there is no single set of language-invariant characteristics of the superficial syntactic structures of sentences containing adverbial constructions which would permit the prediction of their meanings and meaning relations by means of any reasonably general universal principle of interpretation. By positing a semantic representation for such sentences as well as a superficial syntactic representation, it is possible to predict their meaning properties from the former representation by means of an extremely general rule of interpretation, which applies as well to all other associations of predicates and arguments. (The semantic representations of adverbial constructions are assumed like all other semantic representations to be linearly unordered and minimally bracketed; their syntactic representations are assumed to be fully ordered and much more extensively bracketed. Empirical motivation for these assumptions has been presented, for example, in Sanders 1970 and 1972.)

H.2 The correct pairings between the semantic and superficial representations of sentences containing adverbial constructions is effected by a set of universal rules justifying the phonetically-directed copying of adverbial expressions in one of their arguments and the phonetically-directed deletion of the non-penetrated argument(s) and of the non-generic constituents of the more subordinate of two identical adverbial predicates.

This hypothesis seeks to account for the universal syntactic characteristics of sentences containing adverbial expressions -- the truncation of these expressions relative to the expressions of most other predications; the frequent ordering of adverbial expressions between constituents of the construction that expresses the scope of their attribution; the general superordinateness of prepositions and postpositions relative to the nominal argument and associated generic case affixes of their constructions, signified by the marginal ordering of the former and the frequently medial ordering of the latter; the semantic genus-to-species relation that holds between case affixes and their superordinate prepositions or postpositions, and the general asymmetric predictability of case affixes from specifications of their associated prepositions or postpositions.

H. 3 All differences between languages in the forms and formal relations of their adverbial expressions are due to differences in one or more of the following:
   a. differences in lexical rules;
   b. differences in (non-universal) constraints on identity deletion;
   c. differences in (non-universal) ordering rules. [7]

Differences in lexical rules are sufficient to account for all differences of the type exemplified by the contrast between ENGLISH at home and THAI thi: ba:n, where the non-phonological representations of the given morphological segments are simply paired with different phonological representations in each language. The assumption of different constraints on identity deletion for ENGLISH, LATIN, and CHINESE, for example, would hopefully make it possible to explain the syntactic contrast between constructions like from the island, with a single superficial adverbial predicate, dē insulā 'from the island,' with a superordinate specific predicate and a subordinate generic case predicate, and zai fanguan li 'in the restaurant,' with an apparently superordinate generic predicate (zai) and a subordinate specific one (li). Thus, from a common intermediate representation of the form A the assumption of complete subordinate deletion would yield the ENGLISH-type reduction B, the assumption of subordinate Species deletion would yield the LATIN-type reduction C, and the assumption of superordinate Species deletion would yield the CHINESE-type reduction D:

A. $((PRED, GENUS_x, SPECIES_y), ((PRED, GENUS_x, SPECIES_y), (NOM)))$
B. $((PRED, GENUS_x, SPECIES_y), ((NOM)))$
C. $((PRED, GENUS_x, SPECIES_y), ((PRED, GENUS_x), (NOM)))$
D. $((PRED, GENUS_x), ((PRED, GENUS_x, SPECIES_y), (NOM)))$

Differences in ordering rules, finally, should obviously be sufficient to account for all differences between languages in the order of the constituents of their adverbial constructions and in the ordering

---

[7] Ordering rules express derivational substitution relations between the semantically-interpreted relational element for commutative grouping, or bracketing, and the phonetically-interpreted relational element for non-commutative linear ordering. For further discussion, illustration, and justification of such rules, see Sanders 1970a,b, 1972, where the nature of lexical rules is also discussed, along with some of the reasons why the process of ordering can be appropriately viewed as a special case of lexicalization.

of these constructions relative to other constituents of their superficial clauses. Thus, for example, the differences between ENGLISH
and JAPANESE in both the internal and external ordering of the
adverbial constructions in sentences like He arrives on Saturday.
and kare wa koyobi ni mairimasu "he topic Saturday on arrives"
'He arrives on Saturday.' can be fully accounted for if it is assumed
that ENGLISH has the ordering rule E and that JAPANESE has the
ordering rule J. [8]

E. $(\underline{(X)}, \underline{(V)}) = \begin{cases} 2 \ \& \ 1 \ / \ ((N), \underline{\quad}) \\ 1 \ \& \ 2 \end{cases}$ (i)
   12 (ii)

J. $(\underline{(X)}, \underline{(V)}) = 1 \ \& \ 2$
   12

These distinct ordering ordering rules are sufficient, in conjunction
with the obviously distinct lexical rules of the two languages, to determine the appropriately distinct phonetically-directed derivations
(E') and (J'):

---

[8]Slightly different versions of these rules have been presented in
Sanders 1970a, where the ordering is defined on grouped constructions of the form (N, (X)), and in Sanders 1970b, where the ordering
is defined on constructions of the form ((N), (V)). With respect to
the facts under consideration here, I know of no principled basis
thus far for making a selection out of these three alternative versions.
   It should be noted that the symbols N and V are used here in
place of the less conventional but mnemonically more appropriate
symbols ARG and PRED to represent the semantic elements that
are respectively interpreted into the observation statements "State
effecting the awareness of something to which something can be truly
attributed or predicated" and "State effecting awareness of something
which can be truly attributed or predicated of something." It should
also be noted that the constituent variable (V) in rules E and J must
stand not only for superficial verbs, adjectives, prepositions, and
postpositions, but also for all superficial verb-phrases, that is, for
all constructions consisting of verbs and their superficial objects or
complements. This interpretation of the variable (V) will be assured
if the following universal principle of analysis is assumed: For any
representation of the form (X (F) Y), (X (F) Y) stands as a variable
for any integral bracketing of elements which includes the element
F and which does not include any element F' such that F' is included
in a smaller number of bracketings than F. This principle appears
to be consistent with appropriate formulations of all known types of
empirically-defensible syntactic and phonological rules.

E'. ((N, HE, TOPIC), (((N, SATURDAY), (V, ON)), (V,
     ARRIVE))) (given by application of non-lexical syntactic
     rules)

     ((N, HE, TOPIC), ((V, ARRIVE) & ((V, ON) & (N,
     SATURDAY))))) (by rule E.i)

     ((N, HE, TOPIC) & ((V, ARRIVE) & ((V, ON) & (N,
     SATURDAY))))) (by rule E.ii)

     ((he) & ((arrives) & ((on) & (Saturday)))) (by lexical rules)

J'. ((N, HE, TOPIC), (((N, SATURDAY) & (V, ON)) & (V,
     ARRIVE))) (given by application of non-lexical syntactic
     rules)

     ((N, HE, TOPIC) & (((N, SATURDAY) & (V, ON)) & (V,
     ARRIVE))) (by rule J)

     ((kare & wa) & (((doyobi) & (ni)) & (mairimasu))) (by
     lexical rules)

The schematic hypotheses that have been suggested here obviously
constitute nothing more than a programmatic outline of one possible
general theory of adverbial constructions which might serve to explain the set of observational generalizations that have been noted
in this paper. Much work remains to be done, of course, before it
can be determined whether such a theory is in fact capable of accounting for the facts in question. Further research is also required
to determine whether the observational generalizations that have
been stated here are in fact correct for the domain of all natural
languages. Whether such research confirms or disconfirms the
generalizations and explanatory principles that have been expressed
here, it cannot help but contribute significantly to our understanding
of the nature of language.

APPENDIX I

Language and Data Sources

A. Languages explicitly cited and used for exemplification

AMHARIC   Alone, J. and D.E. Stokes 1959
                                        Bach, Emmon 1970
                                        Bender, Marvin L.(personal
                                           communication)
                                        Dawkins, C.H. 1969
                                        Hetzron, Robert 1970
                                        Hudson, Grover 1971
                                        Leslau, Wolf 1968

ARABIC (Egyptian Colloquial) Mitchell, T.F. 1962

CHINESE (Mandarin)   Chao, Y.R. 1968
                                        Tai, James H.-Y. (personal
                                           communication)

ENGA (New Guinea)   Lang, Ranier 1970

ENGLISH   (personal knowledge)

FINNISH   Lehtinen, Meri 1964

FRENCH   (personal knowledge)

HUNGARIAN   Moravcsik, Edith (personal
                                           communication)

IBANAG (Luzon, Philippines) (personal elicitation)

JAPANESE   Bleiler, Everett 1963
                                        Vaccari, O. and E.I. Vaccari 1942

LATIN   Bennett, C.E. 1963

LATVIAN   Lazdina, T.B. 1966

THAI   (personal knowledge)

TURKISH   Swift, Lloyd B. 1963

WESTERN DESERT LANG.   Douglas, W.H. 1958
   (Australia)
XHOSA   McLaren, J. 1955

APPENDIX I (cont.)

B. Other languages in the primary data base for this study

DAKOTA	(personal elicitation)
IRAQW (Tanganyika)	Whiteley, W.H. 1958
KIKUYU	Barlow, A.R. 1960 Mareka Gecaga, B. and W.H. Kirkaldy-Willis 1953
MALAY	Winstedt, Richard 1957
MASAI	Tucker, A.N. and J.T.O. Mpaayei 1955
PAPAGO	Saxton, D. and L. Saxton 1969
SAMOAN	Marsack, C.C. 1962

APPENDIX II

Preliminary Checklist for Adverbial Constructions

Abbreviations:
ADV = adverb (word or phrase)
P   = lexical adverbial predicate (= preposition or postposition)
p   = clitic or affixal adverbial predicate
NP   = nominal phrase
N   = noun
SB   = subject
OB   = object
V   = verb
S   = sentence
X(Y) = any Y that constitutes a construction of type X

Internal structure of adverbial expressions (X of ADV(X))
1.   N
2.   P
3a. p + ADJECTIVE
3b. ADJECTIVE + p
4a. P + NP
4b. NP + P

5a. NP(...(p+N)...)
5b. NP(...(N+p)...)
6a. NP(...(p+X)...) (where X ranges over lexical constituents)
6b. NP(...(X+p)...)
7a. P(...(p+N)...)+NP
7b. P(...(N+p)...)+NP
7c. NP+P(...(p+N)...)
7d. NP+P(...(N+p)...)
8a. P+NP(...(p+N)...)
8b. P+NP(...(N+p)...)
8c. NP(...(p+N)...)+P
8d. NP(...(N+p)...)+P
9x. P(...(N+p)...)+NP(...(N+p)...)
9y. (NP(...(N+p)...)+P(...(N+p)...)
10a. P+(p+NP)
10b. P+(NP+p)
10c. (p+NP)+P
10d. (NP+p)+P

Ordering of adverbial expressions
1. S(ADV+X)
2. S(X+ADV)
3. S(X+ADV+Y)
4. S(X+ADV+Y+V+Z)
5. S(X+V+Y+ADV+Z)
6. S(V+ADV+SB+OB)
7. S(V+ADV+OB+SB)
8. S(V+SB+ADV+OB)
9. S(V+OB+ADV+SB)
10. S(V+SB+OB+ADV)
11. S(V+OB+SB+ADV)
12. S(SB+ADV+V+OB)
13. S(SB+V+ADV+OB)
14. S(SB+V+OB+ADV)
15. S(SB+OB+V+ADV)
16. S(SB+ADV+OB+V)
17. S(SB+OB+ADV+V)

BIBLIOGRAPHY

Alone, J., and D.E. Stokes. 1959. The Alone-Stokes short manual of the Amharic language. 5th ed. Madras: Macmilan.

Bach, E. 1970. Is Amharic an SOV language? Journal of Ethiopian Studies 8. 1. 9-20.

Barlow, A.R. 1960. Studies in Kikuyu grammar and idiom.
Revised edition. Edinburgh: Blackwood.

Bennett, C.E. 1963. New Latin grammar. 2nd ed. New York:
Allyn and Bacon.

Bleiler, E. 1963. Essential Japanese grammar. New York: Dover.

Chao, Y.R. 1968. A grammar of spoken Chinese. Berkeley and
Los Angeles: University of California Press.

Chomsky, N. 1965. Aspects of the theory of syntax. Cambridge,
Mass.

Dawkins, C.H. 1969. The fundamentals of Amharic. Addis Ababa:
Sudan Interior Mission.

Douglas, W.H. 1958. An introduction to the Western Desert Language. Oceania Linguistic Monographs No. 4. Sydney: University of Sydney.

Greenberg, J.H. 1963. Some universals of grammar with particular
reference to the order of meaningful elements. Universals of language, ed. by J.H. Greenberg, 58-90. Cambridge: M.I.T. Press.

Hetzron, R. 1970. Toward an Amharic case-grammar. Studies
in African Linguistics 1.3. 301-54.

Hudson, G. 1971. On the possibility of a non-linear base. Manuscript, UCLA.

Lakoff, G. 1965. On the nature of syntactic irregularity. NSF
report No. 16. Cambridge: Harvard University Computation
Laboratory.

_____. 1968. Instrumental adverbs and the concept of deep
structure. Foundations of Language 4.4-29.

Lang, R. 1970. Enga questions: structural and semantic studies.
Doctoral dissertation, Australian National University.

Lazdina, T.B. 1966. Teach yourself Latvian. London: English
Universities Press.

Lehtinen, M. 1964. Basic course in Finnish. Indiana University
Uralic and Altaic Series. The Hague: Mouton.

Leslau, W. 1968. Amharic textbook. Berkeley: University of California Press.

Mareka Gecaga, B. , and W. H. Kirkaldy-Willis. 1953. A short Kikuyu grammar. London: Macmillan.

Marsack, C. C. 1962. Teach yourself Samoan. London: English Universities Press.

McLaren, J. 1955. A Xhosa grammar. Capetown: Longmans, Green.

Mitchell, T. F. 1962. Colloquial Arabic. London: English Universities Press.

Sanders, G. A. 1970a. Invariant ordering. Indiana University Linguistics Club. Revised ed. 1975. The Hague: Mouton.

_____. 1970b. Constraints on constituent ordering. Papers in Linguistics 2. 3. 460-502.

_____. 1972. Equational grammar. The Hague: Mouton.

Saxton, D. , and L. Saxton. 1969. Dictionary Papago and Pima to English. Tucson: University of Arizona Press.

Swift, L. B. 1963. A reference grammar of Modern Turkish. Bloomington: Indiana University Uralic and Altaic Series.

Tai, J. H. -Y. 1971. A derivational constraint on adverbial placement in Mandarin Chinese. Paper presented at the Winter Meeting of the Linguistic Society of America, St. Louis. Journal of Chinese Linguistics 1. 3 (1973), 397-413.

Tucker, A. N. and J. T. O. Mpaayei. 1955. A Masai grammar. London: Longmans, Green.

Vaccari, O. , and E. I. Vaccari. 1942. Complete course of Japanese conversation-grammar. New York: Ungar.

Whiteley, W. H. 1958. A short description of item categories in Iraqw. East African Linguistics Studies No. 3. Dampala, Uganda: East African Institute of Social Research.

Winstedt, R. 1957. Colloquial Malay. Singapore: Marican & Sons.

Locationals: Existential, Locative, and Possessive Constructions

EVE V. CLARK

ABSTRACT

The present paper is concerned with the general character of four constructions: There is a book on the table, The book is on the table, Tom has a book, and The book is Tom's, compared across a core sample of 30 languages. These constructions appear to be systematically related within each language in word-order, in the verbs used, and in their locative nature. The relations between them can generally be accounted for by two discourse rules. These determine the word order of each construction depending (a) on the definiteness of the non-locative nominal (book), and (b) on the animacy of the other, locative, nominal (either table or Tom).

This is a somewhat revised version of the original that appeared in Working Papers on Language Universals 3, 1970. I would like to thank all the members of Language Universals Project, as well as C. H. Kahn, J. Lyons, J. M. E. Moravcsik, and M. Vihman, for their comments on earlier versions of this paper. The research was supported by the National Science Foundation, Grant No. GS-1880.

CONTENTS

0. In this paper I plan to explore the relations between locational constructions — constructions traditionally labelled as
'existential,' 'locative,' and 'possessive' in standard grammars.
Several linguists have suggested that these constructions are
closely related to each other, in part because they are all locative in origin (e.g. Lyons 1967, 1968b, see also Verhaar 1967,
1968a, 1968b, 1969). To begin with, I will look at locational constructions in ENGLISH, and give a brief account of their properties. I will then go on to consider a more extensive sample of
languages, and will discuss the relations between existential,
locative, and possessive constructions under three headings:
word-order, definiteness, and verb agreement.

1. Locational Constructions

The constructions to be examined are the 'existential' in 1, the
'locative' in 2, the <u>have</u> possessive in 3, and the <u>be</u> possessive in 4:

1. There is a book on the table.
2. The book is on the table.
3. Tom has a book.
4. The book is Tom's.

Each of these constructions contains the same surface constituents:
both 1 and 2 contain a nominal (<u>a book</u> and <u>the book</u>) and a locative
phrase (<u>on the table</u>), but their word order is different. Both 3
and 4 contain a nominal that refers to the object possessed (<u>a book</u>
and <u>the book</u>) and a locative phrase in the form of the possessor
(<u>Tom</u>). Each of these constructions is used to describe the location of an object, either in some physical space (1 and 2) or in
someone's possession (3 and 4). The order of the Nominal and
Locative (henceforth Nom and Loc) in 1 and 2 parallels the order
of Possessed nominal (Pd) and Possessor nominal (Pr) in 3 and 4
respectively. Nom in 1 and 2 is either Definite or Indefinite, as
is Pd in 3 and 4. Loc and Pr differ in another way: in 1 and 2 Loc
is Inanimate, while in 3 and 4 (as Pr), it is Animate.

Locational constructions in FRENCH exhibit the same pattern
of word order, definiteness, and animacy:

5. Il y a un livre sur la table.
6. Le livre est sur la table.
7. Jean a un livre.
8. Le livre est à Jean.

This configuration of properties, it will be argued, is found in many other languages as well.

1.1   Word order   The word order patterns in the constructions in 1-4 and 5-8 show that the locative and the be-possessive in both ENGLISH and FRENCH have the same word order: Nom/Pd followed by Loc/Pr.   The order in the have-possessive is the reverse of this: Pr Pd, and in effect is parallel to the order in the existential construction where a copy of the Loc in 1 and 5 precedes the Nom, while the actual Loc follows it. This difference in word order that groups 1 and 3 (5 and 7) versus 2 and 4 (6 and 8) is not arbitrary: it depends on the definiteness of the Nom. Roughly speaking, whenever the Nom is definite, it occurs in initial position. When indefinite, it is normally preceded by some other constituent. There is therefore a regular alternation between the existential and the locative (-Definite to +Definite) and between the have-possessive and the be-possessive (-Definite to +Definite). The same is true of the FRENCH equivalents to these constructions (5-8).

The absence of indefinite nominals in initial position reflects a general discourse constraint in languages. The speaker uses the definite article to indicate that something has already been given in the conversation — the speaker assumes that it is already known, from context or from prior discourse, to the listener. New information is typically introduced after given information, and it may be signalled by use of the indefinite article in ENGLISH, e.g.

9. I saw a man outside. He/The man was cleaning the gutter.

In the first sentence of 9, a man follows the Definite pronoun I (Postal 1966). Once introduced, a man can be made definite, and becomes the man or he in the next utterance (Halliday 1967a, 1967b). The pro-locative there in ENGLISH has the same function as I in 9: it allows the introduction of new material in second position.

The first element in locational constructions, then, normally seems to be Definite. And this in turn suggests that the Loc is usually definite since it is the constituent that tends to be placed in initial position whenever the Nom or Pd is indefinite. Locative phrases generally seem to be definite, as in 10:

10. The cushion is on the sofa.

However, we also find sentences like 11:

11. The cushion is on a chair in the next room.

where <u>on a chair</u> is -Definite. In fact, to call the Loc +definite in locational constructions is to over-simplify. The locative phrase is actually +Specific, as in 11 where the restrictive relative clause — <u>in the next room</u> — is attached to <u>on a chair</u> (see Smith 1964). The definite article in ENGLISH is nearly always +Specific, but the indefinite one can be either +Specific or -Specific (Fillmore 1967, Perlmutter 1970). Since the precise relation between definiteness and specificity is rarely dealt with in the grammars of the languages in the sample I use, I shall talk about definiteness rather than specificity throughout this paper.

1.2 <u>Locative features</u> The recognition of the locative basis for both existential and locative constructions is not new, but the relation between them has been partly obscured by certain philosophical distinctions. The importance of the notion of existence in Western Europe derived originally from Greek philosophy which distinguished between predication and existence. Philosophers have also claimed further distinctions for uses of the verb <u>to be</u>: for instance, that it means one thing when it refers to the function symbolized by the existential quantifier in predicate calculus (e.g. <u>There are tigers in India</u>) and quite another when it represents identity (e.g <u>James is a teacher</u>). Only the first distinction, between predication and existence, has been well enough established as having any syntactic basis in natural language. Even this, though, may not have been based on a well-defined syntactic distinction in Ancient Greek (cf. Kahn 1966). Hintikka (1968, 1968-1969) has argued that for an object <u>to be</u> (i.e. to exist) normally means that it is to be found somewhere in space. He therefore claimed that one should expect concepts of existence to be expressed in locative terms in natural language. Some evidence for this argument will be appear in the present paper.

While it is obvious that 1 and 2 contain a locative phrase (<u>on the table</u>), this is not so clear in the case of 3 and 4. Yet all four constructions are being referred to as locational constructions. In effect, I argue that the possessor in the two possessive constructions is simply an animate <u>place</u>. The object possessed is located in space, just as the object designed in existential or locative sentences. In possessive constructions, the place happens to be an animate being, such that a +Animate Loc becomes a Pr.

The relations between existential and locative constructions in ENGLISH are echoed in the possessives. The possessive in 3 contains a -Definite nominal, the Pd, which follows the "place" it is located in. This type of possessive, with a -Definite Pd will be called a possessive$_1$ construction. In the other possessive construction, as in the locative one, the possessed nominal is +Definite. This possessive will be referred to as a possessive$_2$ construction.

In this paper, I will explore the hypothesis that this configuration of four constructions — the existential, the locative, the possessive$_1$ and the possessive$_2$ — is a universal one.

A certain amount of work has already been done on existential, locative, and possessive constructions, notably by Lyons (1967, 1968a, 1968b). Lyons appears to have been the first to suggest that these particular constructions are related to one another. In 1967, he put forward the hypothesis that both the existential and the possessive constructions in each language are derived from the same source, namely from the locative. He presented evidence from ENGLISH, MANDARIN CHINESE, and RUSSIAN in support of his argument. Although it is unclear in Lyons (1967) whether derivation is to be interpreted diachronically or synchronically, in a later paper (1968b), he argued that there should be some correlation between synchronic, diachronic, and even ontogenetic derivation. All three kinds of evidence, then, might provide valid support for or disconfirmation of the hypothesis. In this paper, though, the data will be limited to the synchronic relations between locational constructions in the language sample.

1.3   The language sample   The present sample consists of a core of some 30 languages distributed among a number of different language families. Additional data were also obtained for some other languages. Wherever possible, data were collected on all four locational constructions for each language, although sometimes it was only possible to find out about two or three of the four. Before discussing the data, there are several caveats about the sources I used that must be made explicit. In most work drawing on data from a number of languages, one is constrained to use whatever grammars are available. These descriptions vary considerably in quality, and they also vary enormously in the amount of syntactic information they provide. For example, many grammars give only the barest indications of 'usual word order' for a particular sentence-type, so one is forced to rely on the actual examples provided without knowing whether they are typical. The word order typologies I report, therefore, may not be entirely accurate. This does not vitiate the fact that there are consistent patterns of word order

differences in many languages for the existential-locative pair and
the possessive pair of constructions.

Another problem I encountered in many grammars was the paucity of information provided about existential constructions. Again,
the data sometimes had to be gleaned from accidental examples in
the text of the language description. Such examples have only been
used in the data where no other information was available.

It is also difficult to know how complete any grammar is in its
description of a language. In a few cases, I was able to expand
the data by using informants[1] who often both clarified and corrected
the information given in grammars. The data used in the present
study, therefore, are subject to correction, and the conclusions
based on them may eventually have to be adjusted slightly to take
into account such corrections.

2.   Word Order and Definiteness

Word order appears to vary predictably with the definiteness of
the subject nominal in existential and locative constructions across
different languages. In many languages, this is because word order
itself is the main indicator of definiteness where there is no definite
or indefinite article available. Existential constructions are usually
used to introduce new information, and they normally therefore
contain indefinite nominals. They contrast with locative constructions where the definite nominal suggests that the object referred
to is already given through previous mention (Bach 1968, Moravcsik
1969, Robbins 1968).

How is the indefiniteness of the existential nominal usually indicated? Some languages rely on word order and others on the use
of definiteness markers. ENGLISH, for example, has both a definite and an indefinite article, while many other languages have
only one definiteness marker, usually +Definite (Moravcsik 1969).
Some languages use an optional indefinite marker, usually some
form of the word for 'one' (see also Perlmutter 1970). The use of
one, though, is generally construed as emphatic, so this form of
article seldom appears in existential constructions.

---

[1] I would like to thank Charles Ferguson for obtaining data for me
from his AMHARIC informants, and I am grateful to Afia Dil,
Anwar Dil, Constancio de Castro Aguirre, Veda Charrow, Josefina
Jaime, Hannes Kniffka, Edith Moravcsik, and Olasope Oyelaran,
for providing me with additional data on their native languages.

The general preference for not placing indefinite nominals in initial position in an utterance should show up in the word order patterns for existential constructions, compared to locative constructions where no such constraint is involved. Within the language sample, there is a strong preference for the locative phrase (Loc) to precede the nominal (Nom). The position of the verb (V) appears to be relatively unimportant. The word order patterns found in the sample are listed in 12:

12. a.   Loc Nom V   13 languages
     b.   Loc V Nom   10 languages
     c.   Loc Nom   1 language
     d.   pro-loc V Nom Loc   3 languages
     e.   V Nom Loc   4 languages
     f.   Nom V Loc   6 languages
     g.   Nom Loc V   3 languages

The word orders for different languages, listed by name, are shown in Table 1. (A prime, ', following the name of the language indicates that this is also a possible, but rarer word order for that language.) In 27 of the 35 languages considered here, the Loc precedes the Nom in existential constructions. In addition, as expected, the -Definite nominal occurs in non-initial position in a total of 30 out of the 35.

Fewer than half the languages have a -Definite marker (only BASQUE, ENGLISH, FRENCH, GERMAN, HINDI, HUNGARIAN, MALAYALAM, SPANISH, and YORUBA), while 20 of the languages have no indefinite article (see Table 1). Four languages allow optional use of 'one;' I was unable to find out whether the other five allowed this. Of the languages without an indefinite article, 18 use a word order that places the Nom in either second or third position in the utterance. The word orders Loc Nom V and Loc V Nom are the most common. In only one language without an indefinite article does the Nom occur in initial position, and that is in TWI. However, TWI does have a +Definite marker. The word orders in locative constructions are usually different from those in existential ones. There are two main word order patterns:

13. a.   Nom V Loc   18 languages
     b.   Nom Loc V   14 languages

and several minor patterns:

14. a.   Nom Loc   3 languages
     b.   Loc Nom V   3 languages

TABLE 1

Word Order in Existential Constructions

Pattern	Language	[-Def] article	No article	Opt.	?
Loc Nom V (13)	Amharic			x	
	Bengali			x	
	Burmese		x		
	Chuvash		x		
	Eskimo				x
	Gujarati		x		
	Hindi	x			
	Japanese		x		
	Khalkha		x		
	Malayalam			x	
	Sumerian				x
	Swahili		x		
	Turkish		x		
Loc V Nom (10)	Syrian Arabic		x		
	Classical Chinese		x		
	Mandarin Chinese		x		
	Estonian		x		
	Finnish		x		
	German	x			
	Modern Greek		x		
	Kurukh		x		
	Panjabi		x		
	Yurok		x		
pro-Loc V Nom Loc (3)	English	x			
	French	x			
	Spanish	x			
Loc Nom (1)	Tagalog		x		
V Nom Loc (4)	Syrian Arabic'		x		
	Hebrew		x		
	Hungarian	x			
	Luiseño				x
Nom V Loc (6)	German'	x			
	Hebrew'		x		
	Hungarian'	x			
	Kashmiri			x	
	Twi		x		
	Yoruba	x			
Nom Loc V (3)	Basque	x			
	Mundari				x
	Sumerian'				x

14. c. Loc V Nom   1 language
     d. Loc Nom   1 language

The pattern for each language is shown in Table 2.

For 35 of the 40 languages listed in Table 2, the definite Nom precedes the Loc in surface word order. This contrasts very clearly with the word order pattern in existential constructions (Table 1) where the majority of languages make Nom follow Loc. Of these 35 languages, the 13 that lack a +Definite marker all have the word order pattern of Nom before Loc. Three of the five languages using the order Loc Nom have definite articles; data on the other two languages are incomplete (Table 2).

Word order is a very important device for indicating definiteness, particularly in those languages that lack articles (or their equivalent). The word order may be the only characteristic that distinguishes existential constructions from locatives. In many languages, therefore, there are regular alternations in word order between these two constructions. Where the order Loc Nom appears in existential constructions, the order Nom Loc appears in locative ones. (The position of V omitted here.) These patterns of alternation in word order are illustrated in Table 3.

Unlike the existential and locative constructions, the two possessive constructions do not usually show regular word order alternations according to the definiteness of the Nom (Pd). The dominant word order patterns found in 33 languages all have the Loc (Pr) preceding the Nom. These patterns are shown in 15:

15. a. Pr V Pd   15 languages
     b. Pr Pd V   13 languages
     c. V Pr Pd   3 languages
     d. Pr Pd   3 languages

Five languages had a different word order for possessives:

15. e. Pd V Pr   5 languages

The languages using the pattern in 15e are mainly those that use two different verbs in the two possessive constructions. The choice of verb (have versus be) depends on whether the theme of the sentence is the Loc (Pr) or the +Definite Nom (Pd). For example, compare the possessive$_1$ construction in ENGLISH with have:

16. Tom has a book.

TABLE 2

Word Order in Locative Constructions

Pattern	Language	-Def article	No article	?
Nom V Loc	Albanian	x		
(18)	Classical Arabic	x		
	Syrian Arabic	x		
	English	x		
	Estonian		x	
	Finnish		x	
	French	x		
	German	x		
	Modern Greek	x		
	Hebrew		x	
	Kashmiri		x	
	Luiseño		x	
	Shona			x
	Spanish	x		
	Temne	x		
	Twi	x		
	Yoruba	x		
	Zuni			x
Nom Loc V	Amharic	x		
(14)	Basque	x		
	Bengali	x		
	Chuvash		x	
	Eskimo			x
	Hindi		x	
	Hungarian	x		
	Japanese		x	
	Kurukh	x		
	Malayalam		x	
	Mundari	x		
	Panjabi		x	
	Sumerian			x
	Turkish		x	
Nom Loc	Mandarin Chinese		x	
(3)	Klamath			x
	Swahili		x	
Loc Nom V	Gujarati	x		
(3)	Taos			x
	Tunica	x		
Loc V Nom (1)	Gbeya			x
Loc Nom (1)	Tagalog	x		

TABLE 3

Word Order Alternations in the Hyperlocative Constructions

Language	Existential	Locative
Amharic	Loc Nom V	Nom Loc V
Bengali	Loc Nom V	Nom Loc V
Chuvash	Loc Nom V	Nom Loc V
Eskimo	Loc Nom V	Nom Loc V
Hindi	Loc Nom V	Nom Loc V
Japanese	Loc Nom V	Nom Loc V
Malayalam	Loc Nom V	Nom Loc V
Sumerian	Loc Nom V	Nom Loc V
Swahili	Loc Nom V	Nom Loc
Turkish	Loc Nom V	Nom Loc V
Syrian Arabic	Loc V Nom	Nom V Loc
Mandarin Chinese	Loc V Nom	Nom Loc
Estonian	Loc V Nom	Nom V Loc
Finnish	Loc V Nom	Nom V Loc
German	Loc V Nom	Nom V Loc
Modern Greek	Loc V Nom	Nom V Loc
Kurukh	Loc V Nom	Nom V Loc
Panjabi	Loc V Nom	Nom V Loc
English	pro-Loc V Nom Loc	Nom V Loc
French	pro-Loc V Nom Loc	Nom V Loc
Spanish	pro-Loc V Nom Loc	Nom V Loc
Hebrew	V Nom Loc	Nom V Loc
Hungarian	V Nom Loc	Nom V Loc
Luiseño	V Nom Loc	Nom V Loc

Languages that retain the same order in both constructions:

Basque	Nom Loc V
Gujarati	Loc Nom V
Kashmiri	Nom V Loc
Mundari	Nom Loc V
Tagalog	Loc Nom
Twi	Nom V Loc
Yoruba	Nom V Loc

Total number of languages with an alternation in order = 24
Total number of languages with no change in order = 7

to the possessive$_2$ construction with be:

17. The book is Tom's.

In 16, the possessor (Loc/Pr) is the sentence theme and subject, while in 17, it is the object possessed, denoted by Nom/Pd, that is the theme and subject. The Pd in 16 is normally -Definite; it can only be +Definite if the Pr carries contrastive stress, e.g.

18. Tom has the book.

However, the Pd in 17 has to be +Definite (and hence +Specific), so 19 sounds odd although 20 is alright because one is emphatic:

19. A book is Tom's.
20. One book is Tom's.

ENGLISH and a few other languages use two verbs in the possessive constructions, have in possessive$_1$ constructions with a -Definite Nom/Pd, and be in possessive$_2$ constructions with a +Definite Nom/Pd. Those languages using two verbs are marked by a prime, ', in Table 4. The majority of languages in the sample, however, used only one verb for both possessive$_1$ and possessive$_2$ constructions. As Table 4 shows, there is a strong tendency across languages to keep the Animate Pr in initial position. How, then, is the +Definite nature of the Pd indicated in those possessive$_2$ constructions equivalent to 17? In languages without a +Definite marker, this is generally done by the addition of an emphatic (or topicalization) marker to the Pd, rather than by a change in word order. For languages with at least one definiteness marker (either + or - Definite), there is no ambiguity between possessive$_1$ and possessive$_2$ constructions anyway.

To sum up, there are two main possessive word order patterns which account for practically all the languages in the sample: Pr V Pd and Pr Pd V. In each case, the Loc/Pr precedes the Nom/Pd. Of the 33 languages examined here, 32 have this word order. (KLAMATH, the one exception, appears to have the order Pd Pr only.) The other languages with Pd Pr order in one possessive construction (possessive$_2$) also have the order Pr Pd, although the reverse does not hold.

The possessive constructions differ from existential and locative constructions in word order because they do not show regular alterations

TABLE 4

Word Order in Possessive Constructions

Pattern	Language
Pr V Pd (15)	Albanian
	Mandarin Chinese
	English
	Estonian
	Finnish
	French
	German
	Modern Greek
	Hungarian
	Kashmiri
	Khalkha
	Mundari
	Temne
	Twi
	Yoruba
Pr Pd V (13)	Albanian'
	Amharic
	Basque
	Bengali
	Burmese
	Chuvash
	Hindi
	Hungarian
	Japanese
	Malayalam
	Panjabi
	Turkish
	Yurok
V Pr Pd (3)	Ancient Greek
	Hebrew
	Luiseño
Pr Pd (2)	Eskimo
	Tagalog
Pd V Pr (6)	English'
	French'
	German'
	Klamath
	Twi'
	Yurok'

depending on the definiteness of the Pd. A few languages have two
word orders for possessive constructions, but the vast majority
have only one. Does this word order resemble the word order of
either the existential or the locative construction? The Pr Pd
order, save for the animacy of the first nominal, is identical to
the Loc Nom order predominant in existential constructions. In
most possessive and existential sentences, the Loc (Pr) precedes
the Nom (Pd). In fact, all the languages for which this is true for
the existential construction have at least one possessive construction with the same order: Pr Pd. The word order patterns for
existential and possessive constructions are shown in Table 5.

Besides the languages of the sample where there are data for
at least the existential and possessive constructions, there are
a few other languages for which I have data on only one construction. In general, these data agree with the trends observed so far.
For instance, the Nom in existential constructions in CLASSICAL
ARABIC and TUNICA are non-initial. Only one language, GBEYA
— which has a +Definite marker —, has the Nom in initial position
in existential constructions (Samarin 1966). As far as possessive
constructions are concerned, the predominant order, Pr Pd, is
also found in the following languages: CLASSICAL ARMENIAN,
CELTIC, DYIRBAL (Dixon 1969), CLASSICAL GEORGIAN, AN-
CIENT GREEK, KANURI, KURDISH, LATIN, CLASSICAL MON-
GOLIAN, OLD PERSIAN, PORTUGUESE, SHONA, TEMNE, THAI,
VAI, and YUMA. Exceptions to this order appear to be BILIN
(Palmer 1965), CAMBODIAN (Martini 1956), and KLAMATH
(Barker 1964). The only recorded possessives in these sources
have the word order Pd Pr.

To summarize: word order plays an essential role in indicating
definiteness. It is therefore commonly used to differentiate between existential and locative constructions (see Table 3), especially in those languages without any definiteness markers. Word
order is also important for those languages that do have definiteness
markers because of an apparently general restriction on -Definite
nominals being introduced as the first item in an utterance. In a
number of languages, therefore, the word orders Loc Nom (existential) and Nom Loc (locative) appear in complementary distribution.

The -Definite nominal in existential constructions usually occurs
after the verb or after a definite nominal. Possessive[1] constructions have a similar word order pattern, with the +Definite Pr
preceding the -Definite Pd. Any language with the order Loc Nom
in the existential has a possessive construction with the order
Pr Pd, but the reverse does not hold (see Table 5).

TABLE 5

Existential and Possessive Word Orders

Loc Nom	Pr Pd	Pd Pr
Amharic	Amharic	---
Bengali	Bengali	---
Burmese	Burmese	---
Classical Chinese	Classical Chinese	---
Mandarin Chinese	Mandarin Chinese	---
Chuvash	Chuvash	---
Eskimo	Eskimo	---
Estonian	Estonian	---
Finnish	Finnish	---
Modern Greek	Modern Greek	---
Hindi	Hindi	---
Japanese	Japanese	---
Khalkha	Khalkha	---
Malayalam	Malayalam	---
Panjabi	Panjabi	---
Swahili	Swahili	---
Turkish	Turkish	---
Yurok	Yurok	---
English	English	English
French	French	French
German	German	German
Spanish	Spanish	Spanish
Tagalog	Tagalog	Tagalog
---	Basque	---
---	Hebrew	---
---	Hungarian	---
---	Kashmiri	---
---	Luiseño	---
---	Mundari	---
---	Twi	---
---	Yoruba	---
---		Syrian Arabic

Total languages   = 32
Total with Loc Nom = 23
Total with Pr Pd   = 31
Total with Pd Pr   = 6

Although the existential and locative constructions show regular
alternations in word order, the possessive constructions do not.
Most of the languages in the sample examined had a single word
order — Pr Pd — for both possessive$_1$ and possessive$_2$. If a
language does have the word order Pd Pr in one possessive construction, however, it normally has the other word order, Pr Pd, in
the other possessive. The predominance of the Pr Pd word order
in possessive constructions can be probably be attributed to the
preference for +Animate nominals to precede -Animate ones within
a sentence (cf. Svartvik 1966).

3. Verbs and Verb Government

The preceding section examined the relations between existentials, locatives, and possessives in terms of word order. If these
constructions are related to each other, these relations should be
reflected in the verbs used. For example, the existential and the
locative might share the same verb form, as might the two possessives. Alternatively, the verbs used might reflect some other
aspect of the relations between these four constructions. For example, the verb in the existential might be the same as the verb in
the possessive$_1$ construction rather than being the same as the verb
in the locative. And the verb in the locative might be the same as
the verb in the possessive$_2$ construction. The verbs, then, might
be affected by the word order and definiteness in several ways.
The degree to which the verbs in these constructions are related
will be examined below.

The verbs in these locational constructions are usually glossed
as 'be' in grammars. They are often irregular, and in many languages are related to the copula and auxiliary verbs. Where these
verbs have defective conjugations, other verbs may be used suppletively to make up the paradigm of different tenses, as in MUNDARI
(Langendoen 1967). The past and future tenses frequently take on
a different aspectual status, being glossed as 'become' or 'happen'
rather than as 'be.' In some languages another verb is used to
supply the past tense forms for the existential construction, e. g.
TURKISH. In addition, the future is sometimes excluded from
occurring in the existential construction even though it occurs in
the other three locationals. Besides having defective and irregular forms, the verbs in these constructions may also be set apart
from regular verb paradigms in some languages by having a special
negative verb form in place of the usual negative-marker-plus-verb
for negation.

The verb in locational constructions is, broadly speaking, governed by the Nom/Pd. This is always true for locative constructions, but the verb in the existential is sometimes an invariable form that marks tense but not number agreement. For example, FRENCH uses il y a whether the Nom is singular or plural; ENGLISH, in contrast, uses there is or there are depending on the number of the following Nom. In possessive constructions, either the Pd or the Pr may govern the verb. The latter (Pr) is rare; it generally occurs only in those languages with two different verbs in possessive constructions. Although the verb in possessive constructions is usually governed by the Pd, the surface word order in these constructions is usually Pr followed by Pd. In other words, the animacy of the possessor appears to take precedence over the subject in many languages that put the subject first. A few languages use an invariable third person verb that marks tense but not number in the possessive constructions as well as in the existential, e.g. ESTONIAN, FINNISH (Lehtinen 1963). Most languages, however, use verbs that mark both tense and number, and even person when the Pr governs the verb.

The verbs used in the existential and locative constructions of the sample languages are shown in Table 6. In these two constructions, 25 of the 40 languages use the same verb in the existential and the locative. A few languages, like AMHARIC and MALAYALAM, allow optional use of the existential verb in locative constructions even though the latter normally contain a separate verb form. The verb in the locative, for some languages, is optional in the present tense (see Table 6). If negated, however, the optional verb becomes obligatory, e.g. MANDARIN CHINESE.

Although most of the verbs are glossed as 'be' in the grammars and descriptions consulted, a number of languages use what might be called inherently locative verbs, e.g. ARABIC and HEBREW 'to be found,' GBEYA 'to stand,' TUNICA 'to lie,' 'to sit,' 'to dwell,' TWI 'to be at' (see Section 4 for further discussion of these).

The verbs used in possessive constructions are listed in Table 7. Over half the languages (15 of the 26) use the same verb in both possessive constructions. Where possessive$_2$ uses a different verb from possessive$_1$, there is usually a word order difference between the two as well (see Table 5). The verb in possessive$_2$ constructions in such cases is usually the same as the verb in the locative construction provided the locative and existential use different verbs. If they use the same verb, the verb used in the possessive$_2$ construction is

TABLE 6

Verbs Used in the Existential and Locative Constructions*

Language	Existential	Locative
Amharic	allä	nắw (allä)
Classical Arabic	yūjadu 'be found', kāna	yūjadu
Syrian Arabic	fī 'at' (prep.)	kān
Basque	izan	izan
Bengali	ač	ač
Bilin	waṅna	waṅna
Burmese	ʃiˊ	ʃiˊ
Classical Chinese	you	tsai
Mandarin Chinese	you	∅, shi**
Chuvash	pur	pur
English	be	be
Eskimo	qar	-it- (-qar- 'place where'), ípoq
Estonian	olema	olema
Finnish	olla	olla
French	avoir 'have'	être
Gbeya	yor 'to stand'	ɔ, ya
German	sein	sein
Modern Greek	ékhei 'have'	eînai
Gujarati	chẹ	chẹ
Hebrew	yeš	∅, ni^{y}mtsa 'be found'
Hindi	hōnā	hōnā
Hungarian	van	van
Japanese	iru [+Animate]	iru
	aru [-Animate]	
Kannada	iru	iru
Kashmiri	a:sun	a:sun
Khalkha	bai	bol
Kurukh	raʔna	raʔna
Luiseño	mi·~mi·x	mi·~mi·x
Malayalam	uṇṭə	aaṇə (uṇṭə)
Mundari	menaq	menaq
Panjabi	hae	e
Shona	-ri-po	-ri
Spanish	hay < 'have'	estar
Sumerian	gál	gál
Tagalog	may, mayroon	∅
Tunica	ʔuˊhki	ʔuˊra 'lie,' ʔuˊna 'sit, dwell'
Turkish	var	∅, var
Twi	wɔ	hyɛ 'be at, ' yɛ
Yoruba	wã	wã
Yurok	ʔokʼ^{w}s	ʔokʼ^{w}s

*The gloss of the verb-forms is 'be' unless otherwise noted.
** ∅ indicates an optional use of third-person, singular, present tense if verb-form is also listed. Otherwise ∅ means that no verb is used.

TABLE 7

Verbs Used in the Possess$_1$ and Possess$_2$ Constructions

Language	Possess$_1$	Possess$_2$
Albanian	k'e 'have'	j'e 'be'
Amharic	allä-w	näw
Bengali	ač	ač
Burmese	ʃi′	ʃi′
Celtic (Irish)	ta	is
Mandarin Chinese	you	shi
Chuvash	pur	pur
English	have	be
Estonian	olema	olema
Finnish	olla	olla
French	avoir 'have'	être
German	haben 'have'	sein
Hebrew	yeš	(3rd sg. pronoun)
Hindi	hōnā	hōnā
Hungarian	van	van
Japanese	aru	aru
Kashmiri	a:sun	a:sun
Khalkha	bai	bai
Luiseño	mi·~mi·x [-An] a·č~aš [+An]	mi·~mi·x
Malayalam	uṇṭə	uṇṭə
Mundari	menaq	menaq
Spanish	tener 'hold, have'	ser -Alienable estar +Alienable
Tagalog	may, mayroon	nasa, kay (preps.)
Turkish	var	var
Twi	wɔ	wɔ́
Yurok	ʔok′ʷs	ʔok′ʷs

usually the copula for that language. The possessive$_1$ is usually
the same as the verb in the existential, and may be an auxiliary
verb when used elsewhere. Many grammars gloss all the verbs
in possessive constructions as 'be.'[2]

The copula and the auxiliary verbs in most of the sample languages turn up in some form in the locational constructions. For
example, the copula appears as the verb in the locative construction in 23 of the sample languages (see Table 8). The auxiliary
verb is used as the verb in the existential in 10 of the sample languages listed in Table 8. If the language is one with only one
auxiliary verb, it is usually identical in form to the existential
verb; if the language has two or more auxiliary verbs, one may
be used as the copula as well, and this form may be used in the
locative and possessive$_2$ constructions. Where the possessive$_1$
construction is the only odd man out in the verb used, and that
verb is not the copula, it turns up as an auxiliary elsewhere in the
language, e.g. ALBANIAN k'e, BASQUE euki, ENGLISH have,
GERMAN haben.

The data available on the copula and the auxiliary verbs for the
sample languages are not extensive enough to draw any real conclusions. From Table 8, it looks as though languages that use two
different verbs for the existential and locative, or for the possessive constructions, usually use both verbs as auxiliaries elsewhere
in the language. Furthermore, the verb that appears in the locative (and sometimes in the possessive$_2$ construction) also turns up
as the copula in predicate nominal constructions.

Negative verb forms appear in 17 of the languages in the sample.
They are listed in Table 9. If the verb in the locational construction is also used elsewhere as the copula, the negative form of the
verb also appears in all those constructions. The negative verb
form sometimes appears in both existential and locative constructions, even if two different verbs are used in the positive, e.g.
KHALKHA, PANJABI. Other languages have two different negative
verb forms in such cases, e.g. MALAYALAM.

---

[2] The glosses provided for the verbs in locational constructions
were often different in the grammars consulted depending on what
the construction was, e.g. Vesper 1968. Without a literal translation as well as the ENGLISH gloss, it is often hard to tell from a
standard grammar what verb is used in these four constructions.

TABLE 8

Summary of Verbs Used in Locational Constructions

Language	Existential	Locative	Possess$_1$	Possess$_2$	Cop	Aux
Albanian	(?)*	j'e	k'e	j'e	j'e	k'e, j'e
Amharic	allä	näw (allä)	allä-w	näw	näw	(?)
Syrian Arabic	fĭ	Ø, kān	fĭ/tabaɛ/ ɛando, etc.	fĭ/tabaɛ/ ɛando, etc.	Ø, kān	fĭ, kān
Basque	izan	izan	euki/ ukhan	(?)	(?)	izan, euki/ ukhan
Bengali	ač	ač	ač	ač	Ø pres. hɔoa fut. ač past	hɔoa
Burmese	ʃiˊ	ʃiˊ	ʃiˊ	ʃiˊ	(?)	(?)
Celtic (Irish)	ta-	is	ta-	is	is	(?)
Mandarin Chinese	you	Ø, shi	you	shi	shi	(?)
Chuvash	pur	pur	pur	pur	(?)	(?)
English	be	be	have	be	be	have, be
Eskimo	qar	-it-	qar	(?)	-u-	(?)
Estonian	olema	olema	olema	olema	olema	(?)
Finnish	olla	olla	olla	olla	olla	(?)
French	avoir	être	avoir	être	être	avoir, être
German	sein	sein	haben	sein	sein	haben, sein
Modern Greek	ékhein	êinai	ékhein	êinai	êinai	ékhein

TABLE 8 (continued)

Language	Existential	Locative	Possess$_1$	Possess$_2$	Cop	Aux
Gujarati	che̞	che̞	(?)	(?)	∅ pres. (?) che̞	
Hebrew	yeš	∅, 3rd pronoun	yeš	3rd pronoun	3rd pron.(?) ∅ pres. hove	
Hindi	hōnā	hōnā	hōnā	hōnā	hōnā	hōnā
Hungarian	van	van	van	van	∅ pres. (?) van	
Japanese	iru [+Animate] aru [-Animate]	iru	aru	aru motte aru	no	aru
Kashmiri	a:sun	a:sun	a:sun	a:sun	a:sun	a:sun
Khalkha	bai	bol	bai	bai	bai, bol	bai
Klamath	(?)	gi	gi	gi	gi	(?)
Kurukh	ra?na	ra?na	(?)	(?)	ra?na	(?)
Luiseño	mi·~mi·x	mi·~mi·x	mi·~mi·x	mi·~mi·x	(?)	(?)
Malayalam	uṇṭə	aaṇə (uṇṭə)	uṇṭə	uṇṭə	aaṇə	(?)
Mundari	menaq	menaq	menaq	menaq	menaq	(?)
Tagalog	may, mayroon	kay (prep.),may, sa (prep.) mayroon	nasa, kay	∅	(?)	
Turkish	var	var	var	var	dir	(?)
Twi	wɔ	hyɛ, yɛ	wɔ	wɔ́	yɛ	(?)
Yoruba	wà	wà	ní	ni	ni	(?)
Yurok	?ok'ʷa	?ok'ʷa	?ok'ʷa	?ok'ʷa	∅	(?)

* (?) means no data available.

Eve V. Clark

TABLE 9
Negative Verb Forms

Language	Positive V	Where used	Negative V	Where used
Bengali	ač	Exi, Loc, Pos_1 , Pos_2 Cop (past tense)	neĭ	Exi, Loc, Pos_1 , Pos_2 Cop (past tense)
Chuvash	pur	Exi, Loc, Pos_1, Pos_2	śuk	Exi, Loc, Pos_1, Pos_2
Eskimo	qar	Exi, Pos_1	-it-	Exi, Pos_1
Estonian	olema	Exi, Loc, Pos_1, Pos_2, Cop	pole	Exi, Loc, Pos_1, Pos_2, Cop
Finnish	olla	Exi, Loc, Pos_1, Pos_2, Cop	ei ole'	Exi, Loc, Pos_1, Pos_2, Cop
Gujarati	chẹ	Exi, Loc, Cop	nəthi	Exi, Loc, Cop
Hebrew	yeš	Exi, Pos_1	$e^y n$	Exi, Pos_1, Cop*
Hindi	hōnā	Exi, Loc, Pos_1, Pos_2, Cop	nəhĭ	Exi, Loc, Pos_1, Pos_2, Cop
Hungarian	van	Exi, Loc, Pos_1, Pos_2, Cop	nintš	Exi, Loc, Pos_1, Pos_2, Cop
Japanese	iru [+An] aru [-An]	Exi, Loc, Pos_1, Pos_2 Aux (aru)	nai	Exi, Loc, Pos_1, Pos_2
Khalkha	bai bol	Exi, Pos_1 , Pos_2 Cop, Aux Loc	alğ	Exi, Loc Pos_1, Pos_2 , Cop
Kurukh	ra?na	Exi, Loc, Cop	malka	Exi, Loc Cop (with adj.) Cop (with class names)
Malayalam	uṇṭə aanə	Exi, Pos_1, Pos_2 Loc, Cop	illa alla	Exi, Pos_1, Pos_2 Loc, Cop
Mundari	menaq	Exi, Loc Pos_1, Pos_2, Cop	bangaq	Exi, Loc Pos_1, Pos_2, Cop
Panjabi	hae e	Exi, Pos_1 Loc, Pos_2, Cop	neĩ	Exi, Loc Pos_1, Pos_2, Cop
Tagalog	may, mayroon	Exi, Pos_1	wala	Exi, Pos_1
Turkish	var	Exi, Loc, Pos_1, Pos_2		Exi, Loc, Pos_1, Pos_2

*With [-Definite] subject.

To sum up, the verb forms used in the four locational constructions also seem to reflect the relationship between these constructions. Verb use is not as clearly patterned as word order, but
the same relations emerge here too. For example, the verbs are
more often the same than different in the existential and locative
pair, and in the possessive pair. In some languages, existential
and possessive$_1$ constructions are related by the verb used as well
as by the definiteness of the nominals. This is also the case for
some locative and possessive$_2$ constructions. In no cases do the
patterns of verb use suggest other relations between these constructions; for example, the existential and possessive$_2$ never appear
as a pair. Lastly, with the exception of JAPANESE, most of the
verbs used in these constructions appear elsewhere in the language
as copula and auxiliary verbs.

The subject of the verb in existential and locative constructions
is normally the Nom. In the existential construction, though, the
verb only occurs in third person forms because the Nom is always
-Definite. (First and second person forms would require a definite
subject since I, we, and you are always +Definite (Postal 1966).)
The existential verb may agree in number with the Nom, as in
ENGLISH or ITALIAN, or it may appear in an invariable, usually
singular, third person form as in ESTONIAN, FRENCH, or MOD-
ERN GREEK. The locative construction, in contrast, always
agrees in person and number with its subject which is usually the
Nom. Languages for which Nom is usually given as the subject
of the locative are listed in Table 10.

Although the Nom is described as the usual subject of locative
constructions, some languages can make the Loc the subject instead. In ENGLISH, for example, the existential in 21 can be
transformed into 22 where the Loc proper now precedes the Nom
and a copy (on it) follows Nom:

21.   There is a book on the table.
22.   The table has a book on it.

The construction in 22 seems to be closely allied to possessive$_1$
constructions in ENGLISH: they share the same verb, have, and
both contain -Definite Noms. Compare 23:

23.   Tom has a book.

When the Loc in locative constructions is made the subject of the
verb, however, it usually requires contrastive stress on the locative phrase:

TABLE 10

Languages with Number Agreement between Verb and Nom
in the Existential and Locative

Amharic	Hebrew
Classical Arabic	Hindi
Syrian Arabic	Hungarian
Basque	Japanese
Bengali	Kashmiri
Burmese	Khalkha
Classical Chinese	Kurukh
Mandarin Chinese	Luiseño
Chuvash	Malayalam
English	Mundari
Eskimo	Panjabi
Estonian	Spanish
Finnish	Sumerian
French	Turkish
Gbeya	Twi
German	Yoruba
Modern Greek	Yurok
Gujarati	

24. The <u>table</u> has the book on it.

The stress on the Loc makes the construction in 24 resemble the possessive construction in 25 where the +Definite Nom also appears in second place:

25. <u>John</u> has the book.

When the Loc in existential and locative constructions becomes the subject, the actual verb used changes from <u>be</u> to <u>have</u>. With normal word order, the Nom appears as the subject of <u>be</u>. In the alternative forms where the Loc is subject, the verb is changed to <u>have</u>, the possessive$_1$ and auxiliary verb. Unfortunately, these relations could not be pursued further for the current sample of languages because few grammars provide information on the possible subjects of locational constructions.

The subject of the verb in both possessive constructions is usually the Pd, the nominal denoting the object possessed, as shown in Table 11. If Pr does appears as subject of the verb, it is only in possessive$_1$ constructions, not in possessive$_2$ ones. The Pd is always the subject in possessive$_2$ constructions (the data for three languages in the sample are missing), and is subject of the verb in two thirds of the sample languages' possessive$_1$ constructions as well (Table 11). In those languages where Pd is the subject of both possessive constructions, there is only one verb used in the possessive$_1$ constructions, but Pd as the subject in possessive$_2$ constructions use two different verbs, usually glossed as equivalent . to ENGLISH <u>have</u> and <u>be</u>.

Where the Pd is the subject in possessive$_1$ constructions, the verb form used is constrained in same way as the forms in the existential construction. The subject of the verb is always -Definite, so the verb is always in the third person. Except for ESTONIAN and FINNISH, the verb in the possessive usually agrees in number with the subject. The verb in possessive$_2$ constructions agrees in person and number with its +Definite subject.

Lyons (1968a, 1968b) suggested that languages with <u>have</u>-possessive constructions as well as <u>be</u>-possessives are only superficially different from the majority of languages with only <u>be</u>-possessives. He argued that the verb forms <u>have</u> and <u>be</u> are alternative forms which are transformationally introduced depending on whether the theme of the utterance is the Pd, which requires <u>be</u>, as in ENGLISH:

26. The book is Tom's.

TABLE 11

Subject of the Verb in Possessive Constructions

Language	Possess$_1$	Possess$_2$
Albanian	Pr	Pd
Amharic	Pd	Pd
Syrian Arabic	Pd	Pd
Basque	?	Pd
Bengali	Pd	Pd
Burmese	Pd	Pd
Cambodian	Pd	Pd
Chuvash	Pd	Pd
English	Pr	Pd
French	Pr	Pd
German	Pr	Pd
Modern Greek	Pr	Pd
Hebrew	Pd	Pd
Hindi	Pd	Pd
Hungarian	Pd	Pd
Japanese	Pd	Pd
Kashmiri	Pd	Pd
Khalkha	Pd	Pd
Latin	Pd*	Pd
Luiseño	Pd	Pd
Malayalam	Pd	Pd
Mundari	Pr	?
Panjabi	Pd	Pd
Shona	Pr	?
Spanish	Pr	Pd
Swahili	Pr	?
Tagalog	Pd	Pd
Turkish	Pd	Pd
Yoruba	Pr	Pd
Estonian**	Pd	Pd
Finnish**	Pd	Pd

* Later Pr.

** Verb form is third person singular and invariable
except for tense. Pd is counted as the subject here
because Pr is always in the adessive (locative) case
in Possessive constructions.

or whether the theme is the Pr, which requires have:

27. Tom has a book.

Lyons' argument rests on the assumption that both have and be are dummy verbs introduced in order to carry tense, aspect, and person markers in the surface structure. This might explain why some languages allow optional deletion of the third person singular present tense of be in certain constructions. Lyons' argument would also account for the appearance of have in 22 and 24 above.

Although the Pd is generally the subject of the verb in possessives just as the Nom is in the existential and locative, the Pr may also be chosen as the theme and be made into the subject instead, using a different verb. Some languages, however, do not make Pr into the subject when it is chosen as theme. Instead of using a different verb, they simply indicate thematization either by a change in word order (the theme is placed in initial position, for example) or by the addition of an emphatic particle to the relevant nominal. These options are also applied to the Pd when it is the theme (and subject).

To summarize: the Pd appears as the subject of both possessive constructions in most of the languages in the sample (Table 11). Both possessive$_1$ and possessive$_2$ constructions in most languages are be-type possessives. Moreover, the presence of a have-possessive in a language always implies the presence of a be-possessive in the same language, but not the reverse.

Overall, the pattern of verb use provides further evidence for the relatedness of existential and locative on the one hand, and between the two possessives on the other. At the same time, the verbs also point to the relation found between existential and possessive$_1$ constructions, and between locative and possessive$_2$ constructions.

4. Locative Properties

Both the Loc and the Pr in locational constructions have certain locative properties. The nominals in the Locative phrase typically denote objects, usually 'places,' e.g. room, field, house, chair. In many languages, this nominal is also marked by a locative case ending and by a preposition or postposition that specifies further the exact locative relation between the Nom and the place denoted by the Loc. The Loc itself will not be discussed in any detail here. Instead, the emphasis will be on the locative properties that often characterize the Pr.

The Pr, like the Loc, often carries a locative case ending, usually with the meaning of at a place or to a place. (Some languages use the same case ending for the indirect object.) Languages that rely on prepositions or postpositions rather than case endings also use locative markers for the Pr. Linguists like Hjelmslev (1935) and Anderson (1971) have argued, in fact, that all case endings and prepositions are locative in origin: language is built on a spatial metaphor. There is some evidence for this in many of the expressions used to indicate possession. Several African languages, for instance, use a copula verb together with a locative phrase meaning 'in the hand' or 'grasped in the hand' to indicate possession, e.g. EWE le 'be, be present,' le asi 'be in the hand of.' The locative nature of Pr is much less clear, though, in languages like ENGLISH.

Pr is frequently marked by a preposition or a postposition in both inflectional and non-inflectional languages. In SYRIAN ARABIC, for example, the Pr may be preceded by one of several different prepositions to which a pronoun suffix is added. This suffix agrees in number and gender with the noun in the Pr (see Cowell 1964:477). These prepositions are otherwise used to indicate location, and they are positional rather than directional in meaning. That is, they indicate a place at which rather than towards which or away from which (Lyons 1968a, Becker & Arms 1969), e.g. fī 'in, on, at,' ɛando 'at, with' (Cowell 1964:284-285). BURMESE optionally marks the Pr with the stative (non-directional) locative marker hma 'at.' This marker can only be used with words for people or people's names in possessive constructions. Hma is otherwise restricted to occurrence with -Animate nominals (Stewart 1955:12). CAMBODIAN also uses a postposition with the Pr, one with the meaning of 'with' (Martini 1956). KANURI also marks the Pr with the postposition 'with' (Lukas 1937:28f). In HINDI the Pr is marked by the genitive case together with one of three locative postpositions. These postpositions, ke, ko, and ke pas, are determined by the Pd. For example, ke is used with the Pr when the Pd is +Animate, ke pas when the Pd is +Concrete, and ko when the Pd is +Abstract (see B. Kachru 1968:34). In JAPANESE it is the postposition used to mark the dative, ni, that comes into service for the Pr. In TAGALOG the Pr is indicated by a locative preposition (either 'at' or 'near') as long as the Pd is +Definite. When the Pd is -Definite, the Pr is marked by the existential marker, may or mayroon (Bowen 1965:44f., 87f.). In TURKISH the locative postposition da 'at, in' is usually used to mark the Pr (Swift, 1963:137); otherwise the Pr may have a genitive case ending (Bach 1967). In FRENCH the Pr is usually indicated by the locative preposition à 'at, to,' otherwise used to indicate location. This listing will serve to indicate how extensively locative particles appear in possessive constructions to indicate the Pr.

The cases used most often to indicate the Pr are those usually labelled 'dative' and 'genitive.' In CLASSICAL GEORGIAN, for example, the Pr was marked by a combination of the dative case and a postposition meaning 'with.' The dative case, in many of the sample languages, is also used for location, with the meaning 'at,' 'in,' or 'to' a place. The genitive case is not used as frequently as the dative with a spatial meaning.

The dative case is used to mark the Pr in ALBANIAN (Newmark, 1957:5, the "marginal" case), BASQUE (Tovar, 1954:62), CELTIC (Benveniste 1960: 114), CLASSICAL GEORGIAN (Benveniste 1960: 121), GERMAN, ANCIENT GREEK (Allen 1964), HEBREW, HUNGARIAN (Kiefer 1968:62), JAPANESE (Makino 1968:4), KASHMIRI (B. Kachru 1968:28, 34), KHALKHA (Street, 1963:163, 198), KURDISH (Benveniste 1960:121), LATIN (Allen 1964), MALAYALAM (Asher 1968:98f.), and CLASSICAL MONGOLIAN (Poppe 1954:147).

The genitive case is used for the Pr in CLASSICAL ARMENIAN (Allen 1964), BENGALI, CHUVASH (Krueger 1961:116, 184), ENGLISH, GERMAN, HINDI (Y. Kachru 1968: 49), PANJABI, and YORUBA(Bamgboṣe 1966:65, 76f.). The other case found marking the Pr in the sample of languages is the adessive, a locative case usually translated as 'in' or 'on,' used in ESTONIAN and FINNISH (see Harms 1962:119, Lehtinen 1963:46f.). YAWELMANI uses a special possessive suffix for the Pr. This suffix is also used to express agency in passive constructions (Newman 1944:241). Finally YUMA uses the "absolute" form to indicate the Pr. This form of the noun is otherwise used for the direct object of transitive verbs (Halpern 1946).

The two cases generally used for the Pr, then, are the dative and the genitive. In many languages these are cases used to express locative relations as well (see Hjelmslev 1935). Watkins (1966) argued further that these two cases appear as possessive markers because they were used to indicate two types of possession in INDO-EUROPEAN. The dative characterized something like temporary possession, without necessarily implying ownership, while the genitive was used for true ownership. Watkins based his proposal partly on Ancient Roman Law which drew this distinction between the two kinds of possession. LATIN used both dative and genitive to express possession, e.g.

28. <u>Liber est Johanni.</u>

where the Pr, <u>Johannes,</u> is in the dative; and

29. Liber est Johannis.

where the Pr is in the genitive. (The construction in 28 was later
replaced by <u>Johannes librum habet.</u>) MODERN CELTíC (IRISH)
still appears to distinguish between the two forms of possession
where the Pr is concerned, and many speakers still use two verbs:
<u>ta</u> (in the present tense only) is used in existential and possessive$_1$
constructions with a -Definite Nom, and <u>is</u> is used in the locative
and possessive$_2$ constructions (see Greene, 1966:42). The Pr in
possessive$_1$ constructions is dative, and the Pr in possessive$_2$
constructions is genitive (Watkins 1966: 2192). If this was in fact
a widespread distinction in INDO-EUROPEAN, then most of the
languages in this family could be said to have opted for one or other
of the two cases commonly used for <u>all</u> their possessive constructions. This would account for the frequency with which the dative
and the genitive are used to mark the Pr.

To sum up, many of the languages in the sample use a locative
marker of some sort to indicate the Pr in possessive constructions.
Outside these constructions, the locative markers are normally
used only with locative nominals. In many cases, such markers
are usually only allowed to occur with -Animate nouns. The evidence from these languages suggests that in many instances, the
Pr in possessive constructions is treated explicitly as a locative
nominal. The Pr therefore has a role similar, and often identical,
to that of the Loc in existential and possessive constructions.

Many of the verbs used in locational constructions are inherently
locative. In languages that have a verb-less existential construction (in the present) like SYRIAN ARABIC, for example, the existential is marked by the preposition <u>fī</u> which is generally translated
as 'there is.' However, it is actually a locative preposition that
means 'in,' 'on' or 'at.' This preposition is also used in possessive
constructions (see Cowell 1964). In many languages, however, the
verb itself has an inherently locative meaning. In ESKIMO <u>qar</u>
'to be' is a morpheme that is always glossed as '...place where
there is...' in locative phrases (Swadesh 1944). <u>Y</u> in FRENCH
existential constructions is the locative pronoun. GBEYA uses a
stative existential <u>ai</u> which Samarin (1966: 76f.) analyzed as $\underline{\partial} + \{i\}$:
<u>i</u> is a locative demonstrative particle, strengthened by the demon-
strative suffix <u>-ε</u> that is added to the Loc in existential constructions.

GERMAN da sein (rarely used nowadays) contains the locative
pronoun da 'there,' just as FRENCH does.   In KURUKH the verb
raʔna is regularly glossed as 'be' in existential constructions, and
as 'dwell,' 'inhabit,' or 'live (in)' in locative ones (Vesper 1968).
LUISEÑO mi·~mi·x is translated by Kroeber and Grace (1960: 132)
as 'exist' in existential constructions, but as 'be there' in locatives.
PORTUGUESE há, like SPANISH hay and ITALIAN c'è, ci sono,
also contains a locative element.   Similarly, SHONA uses an existential verb, -ri-po, that contains the demonstrative pronoun po.
Elsewhere, this pronoun combined with the verb root ri- is used
to indicate location.

   Some languages use the verb 'to be found' in both existential and
locative constructions.   For example, TURKISH var 'be' is replaced in all non-present tense by bulun 'be found' (Swift 1963).
CLASSICAL ARABIC uses yūjadu 'be found' in both existentials
and locatives (Shehadi 1969).   KASHMIRI also uses a verb with
the meaning 'be found' – vɪjūːd – derived from ARABIC (B. Kachru
1968).   HEBREW likewise uses niʸmtsa 'to be found' in both existentials and locatives.   Lastly, TWI has the form wɔ ho, or wɔ
alone, in these constructions.   This verb is variously glossed as
'exists,' 'happens,' 'is found,' or 'is located' by Ellis and Boadi
(1969:54).

   Aside from the inherently locative verbs found in existential
constructions, there are a large number that occur, naturally
enough, in locative constructions.   Many of these are the 'to be
found' or 'to be placed' variety, e.g. GREEK briskomai, FRENCH
se trouver.   However, most of these verbs have a restricted role
in locational constructions as a set.   The point to be made here is
that the inherently locative verbs mentioned so far are normally
used in place of any verb 'be,' and in addition to the Loc already
in both existential and locative constructions.

   This brief survey of some of the locative features attached to the
Pr and of the inherently locative nature of the verbs used in locational constructions provide further evidence in favor of the hypothesis that the constructions identified as locationals are closely
related to each other in many languages, and probably all have a
locative basis.

5. Conclusions

   The existential, locative, and possessive constructions examined
in the present sample of languages are related to one another in word

order, in the verbs used, and in their locative characteristics. The word order relationships appear to depend primarily on the definiteness of the Nom in existentials and locatives. In most languages there is a regular alternation between the order Loc Nom in existentials -- where the Nom is -Definite -- and Nom Loc in locatives -- where the Nom is +Definite (see Table 3). In possessives, however, this alternation is usually absent even though the Pd (equivalent to Nom) is -Definite in one construction and +Definite in the other. The commonest word order in both $possessive_1$ and $possessive_2$ constructions is Pr Pd, equivalent to the order Loc Nom (see Table 4). A major difference between the existential and locative pair and the two possessives is that the locative nominal in the latter, Pr, always denotes an entity that is <u>animate</u> and (normally) human. If animacy or humanness take precedence in any way over definiteness, then this difference might explain why there is so rarely alternation in word order between $possessive_1$ and $possessive_2$ constructions.

These word order relations reveal certain implicational universals holding among these four constructions (Greenberg 1966). For example, the occurrence of the order Pd Pr in a possessive always implies the existence in that language of another possessive construction with the order Pr Pd (Table 5). Secondly, if a language has an existential construction with the word order Loc Nom, it invariably has at least one possessive construction with the order Pr Pd, but the reverse does not hold (Table 5)

The verbs used in these four constructions — existential, locative, $possessive_1$ and $possessive_2$ -- also relate these constructions in pairs. The data in Table 6, 7, and 8 show that the following pairings are the commonest:

    a. existential and locative <u>vs</u> $possessive_1$ and $possessive_2$

    b. existential and $possessive_1$ <u>vs</u> locative and $possessive_2$

The first pairing, it could be argued, is made on the basis of the animacy of the Loc/Pr nominals, and the second on the basis of the definiteness of Nom/Pd in the four constructions. Although the actual distribution of verbs in these constructions is not as consistent as the word order relations, the evidence favors the typology proposed in Section 1.

The parallels in structure between existential and locative on the one hand, and the two possessives on the other, are further emphasized

by the locative characteristics of the Pr — the nominal equivalent
to the Loc in the existential and locative. Because of these, the
principal difference between the Loc and the Pr in these constructions turns out to be that the Loc is -Animate and the Pr is +Animate.

The typology of these four constructions, as a set, appears to be
very consistent across languages. That all the sample languages
contain the four locational constructions is probably not surprising.
But the relationships between the four also shown a strong uniformity across different languages. A single structure might well have
the same typology across different languages "by accident," but a
configuration of four structures showing similarities across languages is much less likely to be accidental. The typology of locational constructions, therefore, may well be a universal one.

The word order relations in this typology depend, apparently, on
the definiteness and the animacy of certain nominals. The effect of
these properties can be expressed in the form of general <u>discourse
rules</u>. These rules can account for the main word order patterns
found in locational constructions. (They would undoubtedly apply
to many other constructions in most languages as well.)

The first of these discourse rules can be stated as follows:

I.   +Definite nominals precede -Definite nominals.

This rule, of course, applies within sentences. If <u>I</u> is applied to
existential constructions — where the Loc is nearly always +Definite
(or at least +Specific) — then the relative ordering of Nom and Loc
will be:

a.   Loc   +   Nom
     [+Definite] [-Definite]

If both the nominals in a simple sentence are +Definite, then a
second discourse rule applies:

II.   +Animate nominals precede -Animate nominals.

The word order in locative constructions, therefore, will often
depend on this second discourse rule since both nominals (the one
labelled Nom and the one labelled Loc) are already +Definite:

b.   Nom   +   Loc
     $\begin{bmatrix} +\text{Definite} \\ +\text{Animate} \end{bmatrix}$ $\begin{bmatrix} +\text{Definite} \\ -\text{Animate} \end{bmatrix}$

The Nom in locative constructions, of course, is not always +Ani-
mate, yet the word order is nearly always Nom Loc. This suggests
that nominals in prepositional phrases are usually subordinated to
other nominals, and therefore tend to follow them.

The same two rules can be applied to the two possessive constructions to produce appropriate word orders. Possessive$_1$ constructions need only rule I — the same rule that applies to the
existential:

c.   Pr   +   Pd
    [+Definite]   [-Definite]

(Notice that rule II would produce the same order, in fact, because
the Pr is normally +Animate and the Pd normally -Animate.) Pos-
sessive$_2$ constructions, like the locative, have two +Definite nominals in them, so they require rule II:

d.   Pr   +   Pd
    [+Definite]   [+Definite]
    [+Animate]   [-Animate]

Although rule II applies to both locative and possessive$_2$ constructions, the resultant word order is actually different. This is because the Pr in possessive constructions is +Animate while the Loc
in locatives is -Animate. In fact, if the locative construction contains a +Animate nominal, it will be the Nom.

Discourse rules like I and II are probably ordered. For instance,
in predicting the word orders most commonly found in locational
constructions, the definiteness rule, I, applies first whenever a
sentence contains a -Definite nominal. In effect, this rule represents a preliminary attempt to capture the generalization that
-Definite nominals do not occur in initial position in an utterance.
If there is no -Definite nominal present, then, where possible, the
animacy rule, II, applies.

Although I have called I and II rules, this is not intended to
imply that they are without exceptions in the language sample. In
fact, language-particular constraints may over-ride these general
discourse rules. For example, some languages require the subject
of the verb to stand first whatever its status as far as definiteness
or animacy is concerned compared to other nominals in the same
sentence. Discourse rules represent an attempt to capture some
of the decisions made by the speaker (Halliday 1967b, Firbas 1964).

These decisions are based in part on the patterns of how given and new information are conveyed in particular languages. The general convention that given information is marked as +Definite, for example, would account for certain differences in word order among the locational constructions considered here. At the same time, such rules are clearly not peculiar to locational constructions alone. They act on the language as a whole. The discourse rules proposed here require a great deal of refinement, and need to be integrated with other discourse rules that are just as important overall. The reason for selecting those rules that appear to be based on definiteness and animacy is that they appear to capture some of the main word order differences among locational constructions, and to account for them quite reasonably.

BIBLIOGRAPHY

The list includes many of the grammars and articles consulted,
even though they are not all referred to directly in the text.

Anderson, J. M. 1971. The grammar of case: Towards a local-
istic theory. London: Cambridge University Press.

Allen, W. S. 1964. Transitivity and possession. Language 40.
337-343.

Asher, R. E. 1968. Existential, possessive, locative and copulative sentences in Malayalam. The verb 'be' and its synonyms,
Part 2., ed. by Verhaar, 88-111.

Bach, E. 1967. 'Have' and 'be' in English syntax. Language 43.
462-485.

_____. 1968. Nouns and noun phrases. Universals in
linguistic theory, ed. by E. Bach & R. T. Harms, 91-122.
New York: Holt, Rinehart & Winston.

Bamgbose, A. 1966. A grammar of Yoruba. (West African
Language Monographs) London: Cambridge University Press.

Barker, M. A. R. 1964. Klamath grammar. (University of Calif.
Publications in Linguistics) Berkeley & Los Angeles: University
of California Press.

Becker, A. L. and D. C. Arms. 1969. Prepositions as predicates.
Papers from the Fifth Regional Meeting, Chicago Linguistic
Society, 1-11.

Bendix, E. H. 1966. Componential analysis of general vocabulary:
The semantic structure of a set of verbs in English, Hindi and
Japanese. The Hague: Mouton.

Benveniste, E. 1960. 'Etre' et 'avoir' dans leurs fonctions linguistiques. Bulletin de la Société Linguistique de Paris 55.
113-134.

Bowen, J. D. 1965. Beginning Tagalog. Berkeley & Los Angeles:
University of California Press.

Cowell, M. W. 1964. A reference grammar of Syrian Arabic.
Washington, D. C.

Dixon, R. M. W. 1972. The Dyirbal language of North Queensland.
London: Cambridge University Press.

Ellis, J. and L. Boadi. 1969. 'To be' in Twi. The verb 'be' and
its synonyms, Part 4., ed. by Verhaar, 1-71.

Fillmore, C. J. 1967. On the syntax of preverbs. Glossa, 1/2.
91 - 125.

Firbas, J. 1964. On defining theme in functional sentence analysis.
Travaux Linguistiques de Prague 1. 267-80.

Fortune, G. 1968. Predication of being in Shona. The verb 'be'
and its synonyms, Part 3., ed. by Verhaar, 110-25.

Gragg, G. 1968. The syntax of the copula in Sumerian. The verb
'be' and its synonyms, Part 3., ed. by Verhaar, 86-109.

Graham, A. C. 1967. 'Being' in Classical Chinese. The verb 'be'
and its synonyms, ed. by J. W. M. Verhaar, 1-39.

Greenberg, J. H. 1966. Some universals of grammar with particular reference to the order of meaningful elements. Universals
of language, ed. by J. H. Greenberg, 73-113. Cambridge, Mass.:
M. I. T. Press (2nd ed.).

Greene, D. 1966. The Irish language. Dublin.

Halliday, M. A. K. 1967a. Notes on transitivity and theme in
English, I. Journal of Linguistics 3. 37-81.

_____. 1967b. Notes on transitivity and theme in English, II.
Journal of Linguistics 3. 199-244.

Halpern, A. M. 1946. A grammar of the Yuma language. Linguistics structures of native America (Viking Fund Publications in
Anthropology, 6). New York.

Harms, R. T. 1964. Finnish structural sketch. Bloomington, Ind.

Hashimoto, A. Y. 1969. The verb 'to be' in Modern Chinese.
The verb 'be' and its synonyms, Part 4., ed. by Verhaar, 72-111.

Hjelmslev, L. 1935. La catégorie des cas. Acta Jutlandica 9.
Aarhus: Universitets forlaget.

Hintikka, J. 1968. Language games for quantifiers. American
    Philosophical Quarterly, Monograph Series 2: Studies in
    logical theory, 46-72. Oxford: Basil Blackwell.

_____. 1968-9. Behavioral criteria of radical translation.
    Synthese, vol. 19, 1-2, 69-81.

Kachru, B. B. 1968. Some notes on the copulative sentence in
    Kashmiri. The verb 'be' and its synonyms, Part 2., ed. by
    Verhaar, 20-43.

Kachru, Y. 1965. A transformational grammar of Hindi verbal
    syntax. Unpublished Ph. D. dissertation, University of London.

_____. 1968. The copula in Hindi. The verb 'be' and its
    synonyms, ed. by J. W. M. Verhaar, 35-59.

Kahn, C. H. 1966. The Greek verb 'to be' and the concept of being.
    Foundations of Language 2. 245-65.

Kazazis, K. 1968. The Modern Greek verbs of 'being.' The verb
    'be' and its synonyms, Part 2., ed. by Verhaar, 71-87.

Kiefer, F. 1968. A transformational approach to the verb van
    'to be' in Hungarian. The verb 'be' and its synonyms, Part 3.,
    ed. by Verhaar, 53-85.

Kroeber, A. L. and G. W. Grace. 1960. The Sparkman grammar
    of Luiseño. (University of California Publications in Linguistics)
    Berkeley and Los Angeles: University of California Press.

Krueger, J. R. 1961. Chuvash manual. (Uralic and Altaic Series)
    Bloomington, Ind.: Indiana University Press.

Langendoen, D. T. 1967. The copula in Mundari. The verb 'be'
    and its synonyms, Part 1., ed. Verhaar, 75-100.

Lehtinen, M. 1963. Basic course in Finnish. Bloomington, Ind.:
    Indiana University Press.

Lukas, J. 1937. A study of the Kanuri language. London.

Lyons, J. 1967. A note on possessive, existential, and locative
    sentences. Foundations of Language 3. 390-96.

Lyons, J. 1968a. Introduction to theoretical linguistics. London: Cambridge University Press.

_____. 1968b. Existence, location, possession and transitivity. Logic, methodology, and philosophy of science, III, ed. by B. van Rootselaar and T.F. Staal, 495-509. Amsterdam: North-Holland Publishing Co.

Makino, S. 1968. Japanese 'be.' The verb 'be' and its synonyms, Part 3., ed. by Verhaar, 1-19.

Martini, F. 1956. Les expressions d'être en siamois et en cambodien. Bulletin de la Société Linguistique de Paris 52. 289-306.

Mey, J. 1968. On the notion 'to be' in Eskimo. The verb 'be' and its synonyms, Part 2., ed. by Verhaar, 1-34.

Moravcsik, E.A. 1969. Determination. Working Papers in Language Universals 1. 64-98. Stanford University.

Newman, S. 1946. The Yawelmani dialect of Yokuts. Linguistic structure of native America (Viking Fund Publications in Anthropology, 6). New York.

_____. 1968. Zuni equivalents of English 'to be.' The verb 'be' and its synonyms, Part 2., ed. by Verhaar, 60-70.

Newmark, L. 1957. Structural grammar of Albanian. IJAL 23, 4 (Part 2).

O'Coigneallaig, M. 1968. On verbs of being in Classical Armenian. The verb 'be' and its synonyms, Part 3., ed. by Verhaar, 44-52.

Palmer, F.R. 1965. Bilin 'to be' and 'to have.' African Language Studies 6. 101-111.

Perlmutter, D. 1970. Surface structure constraints in syntax. Linguistic Inquiry 1, 2. 187-255.

Poppe, N.N. 1954. Grammar of written Mongolian. Porta Linguarum Orientalium, Neue Serie, 1. Wiesbaden.

Postal, P.M. 1966. On so-called pronouns in English. Monograph Series on Languages and Linguistics 19. 177-206.

Robbins, B. L. 1968. The definite article in English transformations. The Hague: Mouton.

Samarin, W. J. 1966. The Gbeya language. (University of California Publications in Linguistics) Berkeley and Los Angeles: University of California Press.

Shehadi, F. 1969. Arabic and 'to be.' The verb 'be' and its synonyms, Part 4., ed. by Verhaar, 112-25.

Smith, Carlotta S. 1964. Determiners and relative clauses in a generative grammar of English. Language 40. 37-52.

Stewart, J. A. 1955. Manual of colloquial Burmese. London.

Street, J. C. 1963. Khalkha structure. (Uralic and Altaic Series) Bloomington, Ind.: Indiana University Press.

Svartvik, J. 1966. On voice in the English verb. The Hague: Mouton.

Swadesh, M. H. 1946. South Greenlandic (Eskimo). Structures of native America (Viking Fund Publications in Anthropology, 6). New York.

Swift, L. B. 1963. A reference grammar of Modern Turkish. Bloomington, Ind.: Indiana University Press.

Tovar, A. 1954. La lengua vasca. Monografías Vascongados, 2. San Sebastian.

Verhaar, J. W. M. 1967. The verb 'be' and its synonyms, Part 1.
1968a. The verb 'be' and its synonyms, Part 2.
1968b. The verb 'be' and its synonyms, Part 3.
1969. The verb 'be' and its synonyms, Part 4.
Foundations of Language, Supplementary Series 1, 6, 8 and 9. Dordrecht: Reidel.

Vesper, D. R. 1968. A generative grammar of Kurukh copula. The verb 'be' and its synonyms, Part 2., ed. by Verhaar, 112-148.

Watkins, C. 1966. Remarks on the genitive. To honor Roman Jakobson, 2191 - 98. The Hague: Mouton.

Some Aspects of Negation

LAURENCE R. HORN

ABSTRACT

Negation occupies a central position in systems of communication, logical representation, and natural language. Many general
works on language and specific treatments of the function of negation
and the syntax of its realization in natural languages have merely
scratched the surface; this paper will focus on several manifestations of the functionally marked status of negative sentences. In
Section 1, a number of oppositions relevant to negation are defined
and briefly discussed and the conditions for incorporation of negation
into quantificational and modal operators are explored. Sec. 2 reveals the behavior of "negative polarity" items and the contexts
which trigger their occurrence. Multiple instances of negation
within a sentence may result in either cancellation or reinforcement
of negative force; both possible effects are discussed in Sec. 3. The
process of negative transportation, the lower-clause interpretation
of higher-clause negation, is sketched in Sec. 4, and an attempt is
made to define the semantic class of predicates which permit such
interpretations. A conspiracy against direct expression of negation
in embedded non-indicative clauses is unmasked in Sec. 5, and a
correlation is drawn between this constraint and clause structure
to shed light on the linguistic function of negation.

I am grateful to both the Project and the National Endowment for
the Humanities (Grant No. F73-313) for their support of my research,
I hereby apologize to any of the above, and to my indulgent readers,
for any errors, misinterpretations, or skewings I may have committed along the way.

CONTENTS

Tone your wants and tastes down low enough,
and make much of negatives.
-- Walt Whitman, Specimen Days

O grammar rules, O now your virtues show;
  So children still read you with awful eyes,
  As my young dove may in your precepts wise
Her grant to me, by her own virtue know.
For late with heart most high, with eyes most low,
  I crav'd the thing which ever she denies:
  She light'ning Love, displaying Venus' skies,
Least once should not be heard, twice said, No, No.
  Sing then my Muse, now Io Pean sing,
  Heav'ns envy not at my high triumphing:
But grammar's force with sweet success confirm:
  For grammar says (O this dear Stella weigh,)
  For grammar says (to grammar who says nay)
That in one speech two negatives affirm.
        -- Sir Philip Sidney, Astrophel and Stella
                              (Sonnet 63)

O me No O's
    -- Ben Jonson,
      "The case is altered"

0. Introduction

The concept of negation and the study of its expression in natural
language has engaged philosophers, linguists, and psychologists for
thousands of years. The distinction between contrary and contradictory oppositions goes back at least to Aristotle. Yet even now
many disputes central to the concerns of scholars investigating language hinge crucially on the nature and acquisition of negative constructions.

Defenders and challengers of the chimpanzee's credentials for
admittance into "the temple of language" (Linden 1975) debate whether
Washoe and Lana truly control negation as an abstract notion; dev-
elopmental psycholinguists attempt to explicate and empirically
display the asymmetry of "marked" negative and "unmarked" affirmative counterparts (as in the work of Herbert and Eve Clark);
philosophers of language find that the choice between a classical
two-valued logic and a multi-valued system with truth value gaps
hinges on the representation of the distinction between the two
readings for The King of France is not bald, and whether these readings constitute a syntactic ambiguity of scope, a lexical ambiguity
of the negation, or neither (Atlas 1974); interpretivists and generative semanticists come to theoretical blows over the tenability of
rival accounts of the phenomenon of negative transportation (cf.
Horn 1975).

Unfortunately the scope of this paper must be far narrower than
the scope of negation demands; fortunately, however, this need be
only one of a series of monographs and articles on a subject which
one assumes will continue to reward and frustrate the ambitious
inquirer. As such it will attempt more to complement and supplement than to supplant a number of other relevant works.

Jespersen's classic "Negation in English and Other Languages"
(1917), a revised and abridged form of which appears as Chapter
XXIV of Jespersen (1924), remains unsurpassed for its insight and
comprehensiveness; the material to be presented here is intended
as a revisitation and expansion of Jespersen's exposition. Other
more recent works on the topic include Klima (1964), a presentation and analysis of some of the central characteristics of ENGLISH
negation, particularly in its syntactic aspects, within the framework
of embryonic transformational grammar. Zimmer (1964) is an ex-
ploration of the logical and linguistic diversity of types of affixal
negation. Smith (1969) is an "investigation of the consequences of
adopting [generative semantics] for the analysis of certain aspects

of negation," including polarity, <u>until</u> and other adverbials, negative transportation, and the interaction of negation and quantifiers.
An approach based on interpretive semantics is explored by Jackendoff (1969) and Lasnik (1972).

While these works concentrate on ENGLISH negation (cf. Gaatone
1971 for a comprehensive account of negation in FRENCH within a
traditional descriptive framework), a broader and more pragmatically founded treatment of a wide range of data bearing on "negative speech acts" is presented in Givón's recent paper in the WPLU
series (1975). Givón emphasizes that negation cannot be understood
as a coherent process without bearing in mind the presuppositionally
marked status of negatives vis-à-vis corresponding affirmatives.
He notes that negatives typically occur "where the corresponding
affirmative has been mentioned, contemplated, or when the speaker
believes that the hearer tends toward the affirmative" (cf. Jespersen
1917, pp. 4-5: "The chief use of a negative sentence [is] to contradict and to point a contrast"), and correlates this presuppositional
markedness of negation with a number of typological regularities,
among them the greater conservatism, both morphological and syntactic, the more restricted distribution, and the greater psychological complexity of negative constructions.

This paper will attempt to continue the tradition of these and
other pioneering studies by exploring several aspects of negation
not exhausted by them (nor can they hope to be exhausted here).
The topics to be surveyed include an outline of the semantics of
negation, including its interaction with other scope-inducing operators, lexically incorporated negation, the phenomena of negative
polarity and negative transportation, multiple negation (mutually
destructive and mutually reinforcing), and the constraints on negation within embedded clauses.

1. Meaning of Negation: Interpretation and Scope

1.1 A few oppositions

The first distinction of negative types, as mentioned, is due to
Aristotle, who distinguishes contradictories (which exhaust the
range of possibilities, so that in any circumstances one member
of a contradictory opposition must be true and the other false) from
contraries (which do not exclude the middle, so that neither contrary may be true although both cannot). Thus for the quantifiers

I call an affirmation and a negation contradictory when what
one signifies universally the other signifies not universally,

e.g. 'every man is white' and 'not every man is white,'
'no man is white' and 'some man is white.' But I call the
universal affirmation and universal negation contrary opposites, e.g. 'every man is just' and 'no man is just.'
So these cannot be true together, but their [contradictory]
opposites may both be true with respect to the same thing,
e.g. 'not every man is white' and 'some man is not white.'
                (Aristotle, de Interpretatione 17b16-25 [tr. Ackrill])

Some and not every, semi-opposed terms which may both be true
(but not both false) together -- now known as subcontraries -- are,
says Aristotle, opposed in language but not in reality.

Thus also we may say that impossible and necessary are contraries
(contingent events being neither one nor the other), but impossible
and possible are contradictories (nothing can be neither possible
nor impossible). On the other hand, probable and improbable
are contraries, it being neither probable nor improbable that a
fair coin will land heads. This difference between superficially
parallel prefixal negatives will be explored below.

For a wide range of morphological (prefixal) negatives, the
opposition is clearly contrary. Thus we may have friends neither
happy nor unhappy, neither attractive nor unattractive; events
neither expected nor unexpected, neither usual nor unusual; and
so on. The prefix non-, however, and often the Greek-derived a(n)-
as well, tend to specify contradictory negation, often distinguished
from another, contrary negation of the same adjectival form:
unamerican vs. non-American, immoral vs. amoral. (Cf. Zimmer
1964, and Jespersen 1917: Chapter XIII, for discussion.)

These "derivative" negatives (Jespersen 1924: 322) attaching to
single words have been distinguished from negations operating on
full sentences, expressed in ENGLISH by not or n't within the
auxiliary: Jespersen defines these two types as special and nexal
negations respectively, while others (among them Klima 1964) prefer the terms constituent and sentential negation.

The lines, however, are not easy to draw with confident con-
sistency, and the value -- perhaps even the well-definedness -- of
this dichotomy is not as clear as for Aristotle's semantic opposition.
Correlation with morphology is incomplete, position often determining negation type. Jespersen includes as special negations which
"belong logically ... to one single idea" not only prefixal cases like
unhappy, never, disorder, but also non-overtly negative words like
fail and lack and words preceded by not, so that

1. She is not happy.

is analyzable either as special (= 'not happy') or nexal (='she isn't happy').

On the other hand, nexal negations include not only verb-attracted negative adverbs (as the contracted forms in ENGLISH) but cases in many languages "of a weak ne or similar particle placed before the verb, and sometimes amalgamated with it (cp. earlier E. nis, nill)" (1924: 329). And yet nill, which survives in willy-nilly and corresponds to LATIN nolo, had more the sense of 'refuse,' 're-ject,' or 'prevent,' a contrary negation within the scope of the verb of willing and thus a distinct type from that found in the clearly nexal do(es) not want.

For Jespersen, 2. is a nexal and 3. a special negation,

2. Many of us didn't want the war.
3. Not many of us wanted the war.
4. Many of us wanted the war.

and yet in an intuitive sense it is the latter which truly negates 4.: 3. denies the assertion made by uttering 4., while 2. is quite com-patible with it.

Klima attempts a syntactic determination of sentential negation, the criteria including acceptability of either-tags (vs. too), of nega-tive appositive tags (e.g. not even), and of positive tag questions. Thus the a. cases below are sententially negated, the b. cases not:

5. a. Mary isn't happy and John isn't happy either.
   b. *Mary is unhappy and John is unhappy either.

6. a. The attacks weren't successful, not even the last one.
   b. *The attacks were unsuccessful, not even the last one.

7. a. It isn't possible to solve that problem, is it?
   b. *It is impossible to solve that problem, is it?

These tests, however useful, prove to be insufficient for deciding the crucial cases, largely because they often give conflicting results; cf. Green (1969) and Jackendoff (1969) for related discussion.

The notion of sentential negation may well have to be treated as non-discrete (or, to borrow J.R. Ross' term, squishified). In addition, of course, Klima's operational definition is restricted in

its application to ENGLISH, and it is not obvious how to generalize
it to the majority of world languages where no corresponding litmus
tests exist.

One might plausibly insist that at least a necessary (though not
sufficient) criterion for S' to qualify as a (sentential) negation of S
is that S and S' be mutually inconsistent, i.e. that the proposition
⌜S and S'⌝ be a contradiction. By this criterion, 2. is eliminated
from contention as a putative negation of 4. So too, 9. may negate
8. but 10. does not:

8. You can leave.
9. You can't leave.
10. You can (if you choose) not leave.

In fact, many apparent constituent negations may be considered
as marked cases of sentential negation. 2. and 3. may be logically
represented as follows:

2'. (Many x)$_{x \epsilon \text{'us'}}$ ~[x wanted the war]

3'. -(Many x$_{x \epsilon \text{'us'}}$ [x wanted the war])

-- both cases of sentential negation, but of different sentences, the
"open sentence" bound by the quantifier in the first case and the
entire sentence corresponding to 4., including quantifier, in the
latter.

This will be reminiscent of another familiar opposition, due to
Russell (1905).

11. The King of France is not bald.

is claimed to be ambiguous, although both readings constitute negations of

12. The King of France is bald.

The ambiguity is representable as a scope distinction, the narrow
scope negation reading 13. and the wide scope reading 14.:

While 14. is automatically true in cases where no French king exists,
the "external" negation being contradictory, 13. cannot be. Narrow
scope ("internal") negation entails the existence of a definite subject

according to Russell (who thus considers 11. false on this reading) and presupposes existence according to Frege, Strawson, and others (for whom the internal reading is neither true nor false when its presupposition fails, the question of its truth value then not arising). On either view, the wide scope, external reading, 14., is satisfied given a French republic.

The standard view that sentences like 11. are ambiguous, lexically or syntactically (depending on the details of the analysis), is thus common to both classical (Russellian) and three-valued logicians, but it has come under recent challenge. Atlas (1974), working within the pragmatic framework favored in many recent studies by linguists and philosophers of language, argues that while sentences with negation following a universal quantifier as in

15. Everyone didn't show up.

are indeed ambiguous with respect to negative scope, the definite description case 11. is not. He provides evidence largely drawn from semantic intuitions for determining that

the difference between presuppositional and non-presuppositional understandings of [11] (or [14]) is not a difference in sense. The sentence is not ambiguous. ...It does not contain syntactical "scope ambiguities" with respect to 'not'. Nor does it contain a lexically ambiguous 'not.'

Rather, both 11. and 14. are considered general or vague; the specific inference of why the truth conditions for 12. are not satisfied is filled in contextually, in accord with such principles as those advanced by Grice (1968). Clearly, intuitions differ, along with the options taken to represent those intuitions which can be agreed upon. (Cf. also the extensive discussion of this issue in Givón 1975.)

Returning to the question of "constituent negation" per se, it is hard to see how this notion can be made semantically coherent. A common example cited is

16. The professors didn't sign the petition yesterday.

Depending on which constituent receives the intonation peak, the negative will be understood as attaching to that constituent. Thus 16. may be assigned, in addition to the neutral, sentential interpretation, any of the following readings:

17. a. It wasn't the <u>professors</u> who signed (but someone else).
     b. It wasn't the <u>petition</u> that they signed (but something else).
     c. They didn't <u>sign</u> the petition (but rather ate it for break-
         fast, etc.).
     d. It wasn't <u>yesterday</u> that they signed it (but some other time).

Rather than treat negative sentences with <u>n</u> constituents as <u>n+1</u>
ways ambiguous, however, it seems preferable to borrow a page
from Atlas's notebook: the negation in 16. is <u>semantically</u> sentential, and the apparent difference in readings (as to <u>why</u> the truth
conditions for the corresponding affirmation fail to be met) is attributable to the factor of what is pragmatically presupposed (taken
as common ground, assumed as given information) and thus not
available to be directly negated or questioned. (Cf. also the remarks against constituent negation in Cornulier 1974.)

1.2 Scalar values and the interpretation of negation

> <u>Not</u> means 'less than,' or in other words 'between the terms
> qualified and nothing.' Thus <u>not good</u> means 'inferior,' but
> does not comprise 'excellent' ... This is especially obvious
> if we consider the ordinary meaning of negatived numerals:
> He does not read three books in a year / the hill is not two
> hundred feet high/ his income is not £200 a year ... -- all
> these expressions mean less than three, etc.
>
> But the same expression may also exceptionally mean 'more
> than,' only the word following <u>not</u> then has to be strongly
> expressed..., and then the whole combination has generally
> to be followed by a more exact indication: his income is not
> <u>two</u> hundred a year, but at least three hundred / not <u>once,</u>
> but two or three times, etc.
>
>   (Jespersen 1924: 325-6; cf. Smith 1969 and
>   Horn 1972 for discussion)

Thus we find that in

18. a. Sally has three children.
     b. Sally doesn't have three children.

18.b. negates the lower bound ('at least three') of 18.a. and -- in
neutral contexts -- leaves unaffected the upper bound ('at most
three'). In fact, scalar predicates, i.e. those which can be arranged on a strength scale defined by entailment of the form
$P_1 < P_2 < ... < P_n$ (where P_n entails all P_k such that $k < n$), can

be said to assert or entail only their lower bound. <u>Three</u> therefore
<u>means</u> 'at least three,' <u>good</u> 'at least good.' The fact that 'at most
three' is often inferrable from an assertion of 18.a, or that 'good'
tends to exclude 'excellent' or 'superb,' is a consequence of Grice's
general conversational maxim of quantity: "Make your contribution
as informative as is required (for the current purposes of the exchange)" (1968: 45).

To use a weaker scalar value where a stronger value on the same
scale is known to apply and where the difference is relevant is to
mislead the addressee. Relevance is clearly a matter of pragmatics:
if I asked Sally a question like 19.a.

19.a. Do you have three children?
  b. Yes (in fact I have four).
  c. No (I have four).

she might answer with b. if she were an applicant for aid for dependent children, but c. would be an appropriate response if she
knew I were conducting a survey on the problems of middle children.
An affirmative answer to 19.a by someone with <u>two</u> children would
not be just misleading; it would be a lie.

Sentences like 18.a and questions like 19.a are thus not (contra
Smith 1969) semantically ambiguous, but open as to whether a
Gricean "implicature" of upperboundedness is contextually derivable (cf. Horn 1972:1.2 for discussion). Lower bound is asserted,
however, and thus constitutes the matter for denial in neutral negations, although, as Jespersen's second paragraph notes, the
intonation and/or continuation can signal that the implicature is
under denial instead, and the 'more than' reading emerges. In
these cases, a 'just' or 'only' is often felt to be suppressed (or in-
sertable) prior to the scalar item.

Non-scalar negation is also possible, the denier often conveying
a dissatisfaction with the appropriateness of the focussed item and
substituting an item which is neither weaker or stronger. This
might be considered not 'less than' or 'more than' negation, but
merely 'other than.' Instances of the three types of negation are

20.a. She isn't pretty.   (=less than pretty)
        It isn't warm out today.

  b. She isn't (just) pretty, she's beautiful. (=more than pretty)
        It isn't (just) warm out, it's sizzling.

  c. She isn't pretty, but she is intelligent. (=other than pretty)
        It isn't warm out, but it is sunny.
                        (cf. Horn 1972 for more details)

1.3 Interaction of negation and other logical operators

The paramount systematization of scalar values in natural language is in the system of quantification. Jespersen outlines a
"tripartition" of values arranged by negativity and degree, instantiated as follows (1917: Chap. VIII; 1924: 324-5):

21. A: all   everything everybody always   everywhere
     B: some/a   something   somebody   sometimes somewhere
     C: none/no   nothing   nobody   never   nowhere

Like the other intermediate values in the B group, some is explicitly
taken here

in the ordinary meaning it has in natural speech [='some but not
all'] and not in the meaning logicians sometimes give it, in
which it is the positive counterpart of no (nothing) and thus
includes the possibility of all.   (Jespersen 1924: 324)

Of course, the situation is analogous to that for the cardinal numbers, and we would insist instead that some does indeed have the
meaning assigned by logicians, as the positive contradictory of
no(ne), but it is not used in situations where the corresponding
A-term is known to hold. (This claim is defended and amplified
upon in Horn 1973, which includes a brief history of this contro-
versial issue.)

Modal and deontic (obligation-based) notions can be considered
"a special case of the tripartition," as Jespersen insightfully re-
cognizes, viz.:

22. A: necessity   must/need   command   must
     B: possibility   can/may   permission   may
     C: impossibility cannot   prohibition must not/
                                                may not

This observation corresponds to the Leibnizian definition of the
necessary as what is true in all possible worlds, the possible in
some possible world(s), and the impossible in none; similar correlations have been drawn by Russell and Carnap. (Cf. Horn 1972:
2.3 for related discussion.)

The key equivalence purporting to govern these categories, and
instances of each are given below:

23. a. not A = B (not all = some)

23. b.   not C = B   (LATIN <u>non-nulli</u> 'some,'
                        <u>non-numquam</u> 'sometimes')
     c.   A...not = C (necessary... not = impossible)
     d.   C...not = A (impossible not = necessary; nobody was
                        unkind; LAT. <u>non potest non amare</u> 'must
                        love')

                                (Jespersen 1924: 326-8)

Now while the equivalences in b. and d. are unobjectionable and
indeed correspond to theorems of standard modal logics, 23.a
cannot be defended as a logical equivalence, although -- for the
pragmatic reason mentioned earlier -- the B value is generally
restricted in use to situations in which the corresponding A value
is not known to apply. When knowledge is incomplete, however,
we do find such sentences as

24. a.   It's possible that he will be nominated; indeed it's
          (virtually) certain.
     b.   Some of you will follow this argument, but I'm not
          sure about the others.

In fact, by accepting Jespersen's equivalences we find that <u>not
necessary</u> = <u>possible</u> = <u>not impossible</u> (by a. and b.), and we conclude that whatever is necessary is impossible. Reducing 23.a
to a conversational rather than logical equivalence permits us to
escape this absurdity (which, curiously, Aristotle was led to as
well, basically for Jespersen's reasons; cf. Horn 1973 for elaboration).

Jespersen observes correctly that the 'A...not' configuration,
for which his formula 23.c is "logically" exact, nevertheless
often has quite a different interpretation in natural language, if
the A-term is a quantifier. Examples like

25. All that glisters is not gold.
     Thank Heaven, all scholars are not like this.
     Tout le monde n'est pas fait pour l'art.

abound, where A...not = B (or, more correctly, A...not = not A =
B...not).

Jespersen attributes this phenomenon to "the result of two tendencies, to place the subject first, and to attract the negation to
the verb" (1924: 327), so that the negative which would logically
precede the universal ('Not all that glisters...') is attracted instead to the unmarked nexal position as in 25.

This creates Carden's "NEG-Q" readings in sentences like 15., which coexist for most speakers with the more recessive (logically "correct") "NEG-V" readings, where 23.a is operative and the corresponding C-form (<u>nobody, none</u>) is denoted. As Jespersen notes, such readings emerge when the negative is attached prefixally or implied, e.g. <u>Everyone was unkind.</u> (Cf. Carden 1970 for discussion.)

A question arises, however, as to why -- given the interplay of Jespersen's two general tendencies -- a negative following a B-class quantifier doesn't have the same ambiguity, so that the prominent reading, or at least an available one, of 26.a.

26. a. Someone didn't show up.
         Something that glisters is not gold.

     b. No one showed up.
         Nothing that glisters is gold.

would be that paraphrased by 26.b. If 'A...not' = 'not A,' why not 'B...not' = 'not B' (= C)?

In fact, this reading is impossible in simple cases, although in certain "affective" environments (cf. Klima 1964 and Baker 1970) the negative may indeed have scope external to the existential. Thus note the paraphrase between

27. a. I'm surprised that something hasn't gone wrong.
     b. I'm surprised that nothing has gone wrong.

28. a. It's funny someone hasn't complained yet.
     b. It's funny no one has complained yet.

And in many verb-final languages, Alice Davison has informed me, it is the rule rather than the exception for a negative to the right of the existential (B-class) quantifier to be interpreted as outside its scope; the literal rendering of 26.a into INDO-ARYAN, DRAVIDIAN, and TURKISH tends to have the meaning of 26.b.

The fact that in ENGLISH and many other languages no such reading is available may be a consequence of a significant property of Jespersen's tripartition which he left unexplored. Notice that C-terms represent contrary and contradictory negations of the corresponding A- and B-terms respectively; but what is the contradictory of the A-term? We seem to need a fourth, "D"-value for <u>not all</u>, <u>not necessary</u>, and so on (or, alternatively, for the

equivalent <u>some...not</u> (as in 26.a), <u>possible...not</u>). The point
emerges when we compare Jespersen's tripartite division with
the quadripartite arrangement familiar to students of ancient and
medieval logic in the form of the square of opposition:

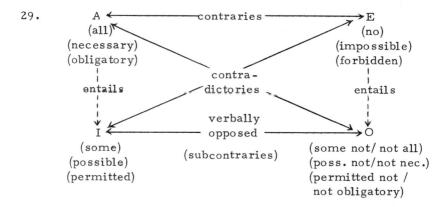

29.

A ⟵————————contraries————————→ E
(all)   (no)
(necessary)   (impossible)
(obligatory)   (forbidden)
                                    contra-
entails   dictories   entails
                              verbally
I ⟵—————— opposed ——————→ O
(some)   (subcontraries)   (some not/ not all)
(possible)   (poss. not/not nec.)
(permitted)   (permitted not /
                                                            not obligatory)

It will be observed that Jespersen's categories A, B, C map onto
the A, I, E vertices of the Aristotelian logical square, but the O
vertex goes unmated.

It is significant that Jespersen does not include a fourth, D,
category along with A, B, and C. Although his system (in which,
given 23.a, D would represent the same value as B) is untenable
and in fact logically incoherent, in the light of sentences like 24.
in which <u>some</u> does not exclude <u>all</u>, there is a good deal of insight
to Jespersen's "error."

Correlating with Jespersen's three-cornered system is a key
asymmetry in potential for lexicalization: while virtually all languages afford one-word lexical representations of the positive A
and B value quantifiers and many if not most languages lexicalize
C-type universal negatives (<u>none</u>, <u>never</u>, <u>nobody</u>; cf. Jespersen
1917: Chapter X for cross-language variants), no language to my
knowledge contains a one-word lexical expression of the negative
universal, or particular negative, quantifier or quantificational
adverb (<u>not all</u>, <u>not always</u>). This can be attributed to the pragmatic principle of which Jespersen's 23.a and resultant tripartition are merely the overstrengthening: if vertices I and O are
related in that the utterer of an I-form assertion (e.g. <u>some men</u>
<u>are mammals</u>) implicates that -- as far as he knows -- the cor-
responding O-form proposition (<u>some men are not mammals</u> or
<u>not all men are mammals</u>) holds, then it is not incumbent upon a
language, as it were, to provide simple lexicalizations for both.

Notice that although the same argument applies in the opposite direction, since articulation of an O-sentence implies the corresponding I-proposition, it is always the I form that will lexicalize, with the result that incorporated negation is always within the scope of a universal quantifier. Why the I rather than the O, granted that we don't need both? The answer, I would suggest, lies in the marked status of negative expressions; the case of the missing O is one more symptom of the asymmetry outlined in Givón (1975) and thus reinforces the analysis presented therein.

The availability of the neg-incorporated I-forms, it is not unreasonable to speculate, results in liberating the <u>all...not</u>-type configuration to serve as a needed alternative to the marked <u>not all</u> structures in conveying a sentence of type O.

The asymmetry among the quantifiers extends to the binary connectives and correlative conjunctions corresponding to them: the E vertex (Jespersen's category C) is represented by ENGLISH <u>nor</u> ('and not,' lit. 'not or') and SWAHILI <u>wala</u> (from ARABIC <u>wa</u> 'and' + <u>la</u> 'not'), but there is no item in any language lexicalizing <u>or not</u> as *<u>nand</u> would be in 30.b:

30. a. John can't come, {and Sally can't (either).}
                            {nor can Sally.   }
     b. John can't come, {or Sally can't. }
                          {*nand can Sally. }

So too with correlative <u>neither...nor</u> and preconnective <u>neither</u> ('both...not'); no lexicalization can exist for 'not both.' Schematically, we have this display:

31.		QUANTIFIER	CONNECTIVE	PRECONNECTIVE
	A:	all	and	both (...and)
	B:	some	or	either (...or)
(A~=)C:		none { all~ } { ~some }	nor { and~ } { ~or }	neither (...nor) (both~, ~either)
(B~=)D:		*nall { some~ } { ~all }	*nand { or~ } { ~and }	*noth (...nand) (one~, ~both)

This asymmetry in the logical square generalizes to the modal operators, but the facts are a bit less absolute. Thus we do find <u>unnecessary</u>, an O-type, as a lexical item in ENGLISH, but one

significantly less integrated into the language than the corresponding E-type impossible, both semantically (logically impossible vs.
*logically unnecessary) and morphologically (productive, non-
assimilating un- prefix vs. non-productive assimilating in-; absence of corresponding nominal *unnecessity alongside impossibility).
In other languages equivalents may exist of the E-type and not the
O-type; no language exhibits the reverse. Thus, to take some cognate examples,

32. FRENCH: impossible vs. *innécessaire
    LATIN: impossibile vs. *innecessarius, -a, -um

While ENGLISH provides an extensive set of lexicalizations embedding E-type modal complexes under causatives, and similarly
instantiated sets are found in other languages, the O-type tends to
be far rarer, with the 33.b. examples among the few likely candidates:

33. a. 'cause something to be / become impossible, illegal,
        immoral': ban, bar, deter, disallow, enjoin, exclude,
        forbid, inhibit, interdict, preclude, prevent, prohibit,
        proscribe, refuse, veto, withhold

    b. 'cause something to be / become unnecessary,' 'cause
        it to be possible (legal, moral) for something not to be':
        excuse (someone from something), exempt

Contraction constitutes a special case of lexicalization, and the
generalization is maintained: 'not possible'-type complexes tend
to contract, while 'possible not'-types do not. Thus while 34.a
is ambiguous (between the "liberal" position of 34.b and the
"radical" line of 34.c), the contracted form in 34.c permits
only the 'not possible' interpretation.

34. a. A good Christian can not attend church (and still be
        saved).
    b. A good Christian can ⎧even   ⎫ not go to church...
                              ⎨(or so) I'm told ⎬   [O-type]
                              ⎩if he chooses   ⎭
    c. A good Christian ⎧cannot⎫ go to church...
                         ⎩can't ⎭   [E-type]

The same distinction holds between could not and couldn't, although
no orthographic convention permits *couldnot to disambiguate the
uncontracted form as cannot does.

While the negation in the contracted forms <u>can't</u> and <u>couldn't</u> is contradictory, the contractions in 35.b are clearly contraries of their corresponding affirmatives.

35. a. You $\begin{Bmatrix} \text{should} \\ \text{ought to} \\ \text{must} \end{Bmatrix}$ marry.

    b. You $\begin{Bmatrix} \text{shouldn't} \\ \text{oughtn't to} \\ \text{mustn't} \end{Bmatrix}$ marry.

The middle is not excluded by each of these pairs as it is by <u>can</u> and <u>can't</u>: of people for whom marriage is a matter of indifference and total freedom of choice it cannot be said either that they must or mustn't marry.

The only general statement capable of encompassing both sets of permitted contractions must refer to the semantic value of the logical operators involved and not just to the juxtaposition of logical scopes; the explanation will then follow lines dictated by the Gricean quantity maxim. In Jespersen's terms, negation tends to be lexically incorporated in complexes which represent <u>contraries</u> of A-words or <u>contradictories</u> of B-words. (Matters have been misleadingly simplified; cf. for example the contractibility of <u>needn't</u> and the variability of acceptable contraction in <u>mightn't</u>. Cf. Horn 1972 for details and for additional evidence.)

Space forbids extensive discussion of the case of the midscalar values, those intermediate between A and B. As described in Horn (1972: 4.24), those values above the scalar midpoint will, like A-words, incorporate <u>contrary</u> negations (i.e. negatives <u>within</u> their scope); it will be seen below that these "A-minus"-type values help define the class of "negative transportation" predicates. An operator F is above the midpoint on its scale if and only if 'F... and F...not...' is logically inconsistent; thus since

36. *It's probable he'll win and it's probable he won't.
    *A majority of the voters preferred Schwartz and a majority of them didn't.
    *It's usual for him to agree with me and it's usual for him not to.

are contradictions, <u>probable</u> is above the midpoint (50-50 chance) on its scale and the incorporated form <u>improbable</u> is a contrary negation (='probable not') rather than a contradictory; so too with <u>minority</u> and <u>unusual</u>.

On the other hand, <u>many</u> and <u>often</u> are below the midpoints of
of their respective scales —

37.   Many arrows hit the target and many arrows didn't.
      He often agrees with me and he often doesn't.

— and, as predicted, are "B+" rather than "A-" values with respect to lexical incorporation, so that <u>few</u> (=not many) and <u>seldom</u>
(=not often) are contradictories.

As with any "conspiracy" in language, the generalizations outlined in this section vary in absoluteness not only across languages
and dialects but across grammatical categories: no O-type lexical
quantifier or connective has been instantiated, as 31. indicates,
but a sprinkling of O-type verb can be found, and a number of adjectives. It should also be noted that such exceptions can often be
shown to be more marginally integrated into the linguistic system
than the corresponding E-type form, as we saw with <u>unnecessary;</u>
equally, it is found that where no single E-type negative incorporation is available, the E-complex is often easier to express than
the O-complex.

TURKISH admits both abilitative and necessitative verbal affixes:

38.   a.   okuyabılır   'can read,' 'able to read'
           okunabılır   'can be read,' 'is readable'
      b.   okumalı   'ought to read'
           okunmalı   'ought to be read'

The contradictory of the B-word 38.a. is not only lexicalized but
realized via a morphological shape synchronically unpredictable
from the abilitative and negative affixes, surfacing as <u>-maz</u> in 39.a:

39.   a.   Ahmet kitabı okuyamaz.   'Ahmet can't read the book.'
           Kitap okunamaz.   'The book is unreadable.'
      b.   Ahmet kitabı okumamalı. 'Ahmet oughtn't to read the book.'
           Kitap okunmamalı.   'The book ought not to be read.'

While the 39.b. forms do incorporate negatives, the negations are
contraries rather than contradictories. The only way to express a contradictory negation outside the scope of <u>-malı</u> involves an analytic
two-word construction involving the non-affixal TURKISH equivalent
of <u>not</u>:

40.   oku(n)malı değil   'doesn't have to (be) read'

The morphological simplexity of 39. is not atypical for repre-
sentatives of the E-vertex (Jespersen's C-words). Note, for example, that FRENCH jamais and personne, which have developed
negative, C-word meaning in the absence of proclitic ne (cf. Gaatone
1971: 3ème partie), are not combined forms. The AMERICAN SIGN
LANGUAGE equivalent for 'can't,' 'impossible' consists of a sign
distinct from both negation and possibility; the corresponding O-
form ('doesn't have to') is a combination of signs for negation and
obligation. In BASQUE ezin 'impossible' we find the negative
morph ez but no analyzable modal element; as in TURKISH and
AMESLAN, the O-form must be expressed periphrastically.

Standard MALAGASY contains no single lexical quantifier of
either E-form or O-form, but in colloquial speech tsy misy (lit.,
'not some') is heard contracted to [tsiš]; no contraction exists for
'not all.'

ENGLISH adjectives with -able suffixes easily incorporate negation -- unable, unreadable, inevitable, incomprehensible -- and
these always have the E-form meaning 'incapable of being Ved,'
never 'capable of not being Ved.' In languages with verb-verb derivational markers for abilitatives, like TURKISH, the same scope
pattern is found. Thus the SWAHILI derivational affix -ik/-ek
marks potentiality or capability; a negative affix (ha...i) in the
same verb form always has its scope outside that of the modal:

41. a. -lika 'be edible' (< -la 'eat'):
        Maembe hayaliki.   'The mangoes are inedible.'
    b. -tendeka 'be practicable' (< -tenda 'do'):
        Haitendeki.   'It is unfeasible.'

An additional manifestation of the E/O asymmetry is provided
by FRENCH. Pouvoir 'to be able' occurs impersonally with reflexive morphology as well as with personal subjects; in either
case its sentential negation is the logically transparent contradictory type, denoting the E-type of impossibility:

42. Elle ne peut pas venir.   'She can't come.'

    Il ne se peut pas qu'elle   'It's impossible for her to
    vienne.   come.'

Negation of the impersonal necessitative verb falloir, while superficially identical to the 42. pattern, is associated with the embedded
sentence, hence a contrary negation, again resulting in the denotation of impossibility:

43. a. Il faut qu'elle vienne.
'She must come,' 'It's necessary for her to come.'

 b. Il ne faut pas qu'elle vienne.
'She mustn't come,' 'It's impossible for her to come.'

Similarly with the weaker "A-" devoir 'ought to,' 'should':

44. a. Elle ne doit pas venir.
'She shouldn't come.'

(Compare the RUSSIAN ne nado, where again the "illogical" I-reading 'impossible' forces out the syntactically transparent but pragmatically overpowered O-reading 'not necessary'.)

The contradictory negation of falloir is expressible only with formal and/or periphrastic constructions, e.g.

45. Il n'est pas besoin de venir.
'There is no need to come.'

46. Il n'est pas nécessaire qu'elle vienne.
'It's not necessary that she come.'

47. Elle n'a pas besoin de venir.
'She doesn't need to/have to come.'

48. Elle n'a pas à venir.
She doesn't need to/have to come.'

We see that even when no difference in lexicalization distinguishes E and O forms, the former is more directly and simply expressible than the communicatively peripheral latter. This point emerges, though subtly, in JAPANESE. McGloin (1976: 394) contrasts the "unmarked" I-form (49.a) with its marked O counterpart (49.b):

49. a. Minna   ik-ana-kat-ta yo.   'Nobody went.'
  b. Minna wa ik-ana-kat-ta yo.   'Not all went.'

In both cases the negative affix is incorporated into the verb, and not the quantifier minna 'all,' but note the difference in complexity: the O reading is signalled by the presence and position of the topic marker wa.

It should be clear that the regularities of the asymmetries outlined here (and in more detail in Horn 1972: Chap. 4) can be captured

only within a framework that provides an analysis of scalar predicates based on Grice's pragmatic principles and a means of distinguishing negatives from affirmatives by accounting for the
relatively marked status of the former in information content.

2. Negative Polarity

2.1 Negative strengthening and diachrony

> The history of negative expressions in various languages
> presents the following curious fluctuation: the original
> negative adverb is first weakened [to the point of procliti-
> cization], then found insufficient and therefore strengthened,
> generally through some additional word, and this in its turn
> may be felt as the negative proper and may then in the
> course of time be subject to the same development...
>
> (Jespersen 1917: 4)

As an example of this process, the development of the FRENCH
negative is cited, among others. LATIN ne dico (cf. incorporated
nescio, nequeo) is strengthened by the addition of oenum 'one
thing,' forming preverbal non (< noenum < ne-oenum), hence non
dico. Non is then weakened through gradual stages back to the
original PROTO INDO-EUROPEAN negative, giving us OF jeo ne
di. Although this form with proclitic negation survives into cor-
ners of MODERN FRENCH (je ne peux, n'importe; cf. Gaatone
1971: 69-79 for other cases), the normal form for negation has been
strengthened by the accrual of postverbal elements like mie 'a
crumb,' point 'a point,' and especially pas 'a step.'

   This last has become reanalyzed as the true autonomous negative in je ne dis pas, to the point where the proclitic ne or n' tends
to drop in colloquial speech, resulting in je dis pas (Jespersen 1917:
7; 1924: 335). The ne is retained in the standard dialect as "une
marque de redondance de la négation, une sorte de préfixe négatif...
conditionné par une autre terme qui est le principal porteur de la
valeur négative," nominal structures tending to suppress this agreement marker even in the formal language, hence une chose jamais
vue alongside je n'ai jamais vue cette chose (Gaatone 1971: 99).
Extended discussion of parallel developments in GERMANIC are
given in Jespersen 1917: 14-22.

   The word selected for this strengthening effect may be an adverbial element, either intrinsically negative (ENGLISH not < nought
'nothing,' GERMAN nicht) or originally positive, forms (like DANISH
ikke 'not' < eitt 'one' + positive -ge) which "acquired a negative

signification through constant employment in negative sentences,''
the coloring effect typical of instances of Bréal's ''contagion''
(Jespersen 1917: 8). In these GERMANIC cases, the original PIE
ne has long since disappeared.

Negatives of the first type often include those indefinites into
which a negation may be incorporated, as in the derivation of LA-
TIN non; cf. ENGLISH none and naught (< ne + wiht 'wight'), or
never (now often an emphatic negative not denoting aspect or time);
LAT. nullus and SPANISH ningun (cf. ullus, algun), etc. Other
instances of the second process, the positive-to-negative shift,
include FRENCH personne and rien (< LAT. rem 'thing') and
SPANISH nada (< LAT. (res) nata 'insignificant [lit., 'born'] thing').

But the most universally consistent class of such strengtheners
is a set of words referring to small portions, the perceptually or
psychologically indivisible atoms of any category. This set includes
such expressions as ENGLISH (not a bit/scrap/jot/iota/shred/soul
but also extends to the subclass represented by

50. ⎧I don't care a ⎫ hoot, damn, farthing, fig, hang,
    ⎨I don't give a ⎬ plugged nickel, red cent
    ⎩It's not worth a⎭
                          (not all cross-combinations are possible)

These classes of expressions are productive in ENGLISH and other
languages, as are corresponding minimal unit phrases selected by
various activity and perception verbs, as Schmerling (1970) points
out; she lists (I didn't) say a word/eat a bite/drink (or touch) a
drop/sing a note/lift a finger/move a muscle, or -- more generally
-- V (i.e. see, hear, smell, need, say,...) a thing. As Schmerling
points out (cf. also Horn 1971), intonational, semantic, and pragmatic evidence leads to the conclusion that these expressions are
intimately related to even-constructions; note for example He didn't
touch a drop, much less drain the bottle. Fauconnier (1975) presents
an insightful scalar analysis of these minimal unit phrases and their
relation to superlatives like the slightest noise, the least thing.

Jespersen's examples of devices for rendering a negative ''more
impressive, ... vivid or picturesque'' include the aforementioned
FRENCH pas and point, ITALIAN non mi batterò un fico secco
(deriving from an unsavory incident, subsequent to the unsuccessful
Milanese revolt against Frederick Barbarossa, involving a fig and
''the fundament of a mule;'' for details, see Farmer and Henley
(1891: 392), who list as derisive equivalents of far la fica FRENCH
faire la figue, GERMAN die Feigen weisen, and DUTCH de vyghe
setten), DANISH ikke spor/stygge 'not a trace/shade,' and GREEK

ouðen (< ðen), as well as LATIN and ENGLISH nil, from nihil
(< ne + hilum 'shred, trifle') (Jespersen 1917: 15 -16).

It is to be observed that these minimal unit expressions occur
either not at all or with a different, usually more literal meaning
when they occur without negation. They are thus prime candidates
for the roster of "negative polarity items" (NPIs); cf. Buyssens
(1959), Klima (1964), and Baker (1970). In SPANISH, for example,
such minimal NPIs as palabra de, gota de occur without an article;
their positive counterparts cannot (Rivero 1971). Cervantes' article-
less NPI expressions corresponding to '(not a) word, drop, insect,
fig, coin' are discussed in Haynes (1933), pp. 118-21.

Lafitte's BASQUE grammar (1962) lists such minimal NPIs as
the following (his FRENCH glosses and their ENGLISH renderings
are themselves NPIs in their extended sense):

51.   (with partitive) / (bat 'one')
   (ez)...limarrik   / limar bat   '(pas) un brin' ('bit')
          mikorik   / mikor bat   '(pas) un miette') ('crumb')
          bihirik   / bihi bat   '(pas) un grain' ('grain')
          izpirik   / izpi bat   '(pas) un bout' ('piece')
          chortik   / chorta bat   '(pas) un goutte' ('drop')

The BASQUE sentence

52. Ez dut gizon bihirik ikhusi.   'I didn't see a soul.'

has no positive counterpart, and if its literal ENGLISH equivalent
-- 'I didn't see a grain of man' -- is not idiomatic ENGLISH, it is
nevertheless readily understandable.

We also find a negative strengthening NPI (ez) deus '(not) at all;'
cf. pas du tout, gar nicht, DANISH slet ikke, and SWAHILI (si) kamwe
'(not) at all/ever.' Here we have true polarity items: while I ate
a bite (especially in I had a bite to eat) and I drank a drop (but not
e.g. I saw a soul) have developed a secondary occurrence in positive contexts (particularly those contexts in which a negative is
expected and, in the terms of Givón 1975, the "figure" and "ground"
are consequently reversed), *I saw him at all is totally impossible.

In JAPANESE we find tittomo 'not at all' (the mo characteristic of NPIs), sukosimo or ikkoo ni 'not a bit,' manziri to mo si (nai)
'(not) to sleep a wink,' and so on (McGloin 1976:397-419). Expressions

for insomnia figure plentifully among NPIs; cf. also dormir de la nuit.

Few if any languages are totally devoid of minimal or 'at all'-type negative-strengthening NPIs.

2.2 Trigger types

If NPIs are "les satellites de la négation" (Gaatone 1971), the sun around which they revolve is often obscured, partially eclipsed, or just strongly imagined, as the negative elements which function as their "triggers" may be incorporated, distant, or implied. NPIs thus serve to define the notion "negative environment."

Gaatone devotes the fourth part of his comprehensive treatise to the "contextes formellement négatifs" and "contextes formellement non-négatifs" which may trigger such NPIs as de longtemps, du tout, le moins du monde, grand-chose, grand-monde, and âme qui vive (cf. a living soul). Jespersen and countless others have also discussed non-overtly negative environments. These include, for ENGLISH (and many other languages): conditional clauses (if you see anyone) and questions (does she like him at all?), especially rhetorical questions (who would lift a finger for you?; when has he ever said a word against his mother?) -- all of which are compatible with (if not only with) the truth of the corresponding negative (cf. Borkin 1971); comparatives and equatives (better than ever; as good as anyone) which contain an implicit negative (cf. Joly 1967 and Sec. 3.2.1 below); negative-incorporated adverbs and adjectives, with or without negative morphology (never, not many, none; few, seldom, rarely; impossible, hard, tough); and time phrases with obvious paraphrases of the form 'not for X amount of time...' (it's been weeks/ages/a long time/a coon's age/*raining since I've seen anything like that; note the corresponding series of NPI expressions (not) in weeks/ for a coon's age, etc.).

Superlatives and related modifiers of uniqueness like first, last, and only (and non-universal all in that's all (*everything) he ever thinks about anymore) explicitly exclude every member of the domain but the one(s) specified from some property and consequently trigger NPIs (the first man to (so much as) move a muscle, the only one with any problems). Unless is akin to 'if not,' before to 'when not,' barely, hardly, and scarcely to 'almost not' (although the latter two appear to be more strongly negative in some environments: he has hardly any money = he has barely any (=almost none), but he's hardly a linguist ≠ he's barely a linguist), and too (as in too frightened

to say a word) to 'so much that not (possible);' all function as
polarity triggers.

Adversative or inherently negative verbs (refuse, dislike, prevent, forbid, lack) also establish negative environments (cf. Klima
(1964) who prefers the more general label "affective" environments),
as do the Kiparskys' class of emotive factives (surprised, pleased,
glad, sorry, odd, strange,...). Baker (1970) points out that this
last class involves counterexpectation; on his view (more on which
below) it is the entailment of the overtly negative b. phrase which
renders the NPI in 52.a acceptable:

52. a. I'm surprised that he said anything.
     b. I expected him not to have said anything.

In any case, it should be clear that the trigger properties of even
the least obviously negative elements result directly from the
buried negatives they semantically, if not morphologically, contain.

NPIs may precede their triggers, although the result often has
a literary or stylized flavor, as with backwards pronominalization.
Cases I have observed include

53. When his chances of ever drawing another breath seemed
     remote ... (K. Amis)
     The prospects of his ever getting loose were very dim
     indeed. (S.F. Chronicle)

Among environments cited by Jespersen as negative by implication only is the curiously widespread occurrence of expressions
with (the) devil (= 'not'). Thus we have the devil a word, the devil
a bit ('nothing'), and the deuce a man ('nobody'). Jespersen men-
tions a popular jingle (1917 : 31-2)

     When the devil was ill, the devil a monk would be
     When the devil got well, the devil a monk was he!

and Farmer and Henley (1891: 272) cull the following instance from
an 1836 novel, where inversion and scalar construction with even
make the negative force clear: "The devil a thing was there in
sight, not even a small white speck of a sail."

Similarly, we find sorrow or sorra ([sɔrə]) used as an implicit
negative in Ireland, as in sorrow a bit o' pity will you get out o' me,
again with negative-triggered inversion, and in other languages

DANISH <u>fanden</u> (Satan) and <u>djaevelen</u>, GERMAN <u>den teufel hast du</u> =
<u>gar nichts hast du</u>, etc. (Jespersen 1917: 34-5). More restricted
to ENGLISH, and probably evanescent, is the expression "I'm a
Dutchman if I do" to indicate strong refusal (cf. <u>I'm damned if I do</u>),
which Farmer and Henley (1891: 349) attribute to a long-standing
hatred between English and Dutch during the 17th century sea wars,
a hatred also responsible for <u>dutch courage</u> 'pot-valiancy,' <u>dutch-</u>
<u>bargain</u> 'a bargain all on one side,' <u>dutch medley</u> 'hubbub,' <u>dutch</u>
<u>treat</u>, <u>dutch widow</u> 'prostitute,' and <u>do a dutch</u> 'desert' (ibid., pp.
347-9).

Whether an implicit negative is enough to trigger an NPI depends
on the speaker and on the NPI. My recorded examples include

54.   A fat lot of good that ever did me.
      Small thanks you get for that, either.
      As if anyone else could do it.
      She seemed to think I might be betraying sisterhood by
         showing that it was ever any different. [L. Wolfe,
         referring to women's rôle as victim rather than
         instigator of adultery]
      I'm anything but happy with that analysis, either. [J.D.
         McCawley, lecture]
      I thought she was a friend of yours. That's why I ever
         even noticed her. [D. Parker; must be read "That's
         the only reason why..."]
      The tone [of Germaine Greer's attack on manufacturers
         of vaginal deodorants] wasn't light-hearted, which
         might have justified touching the subject at all. [C.
         McCabe, S.F. Chronicle]

and a creative example of a negative environment with backwards
triggering,

      San Francisco is beating anyone these days as often as
         the Atlantic City Seagulls beat the Harlem Globetrotters.

While many of the same categories of NPIs, particularly the
minimal unit expressions and the indefinites of the <u>ever</u>, <u>any</u> class,
recur cross-linguistically, many others are language specific.
Thus <u>much</u> has become virtually restricted in modern colloquial
ENGLISH to negative (i.e. affective) environments, although --
unlike NPIs in general -- it does occur freely before comparatives
(<u>not much good</u> vs. *<u>much good</u> but OK <u>much better</u>). The same
is not true of its FRENCH equivalent <u>beaucoup</u>, although the latter
does sport NPI synonyms, <u>grand-chose</u> and <u>grand-monde</u>.

Not surprisingly, then, Behre in a detailed study of Agatha Christie's use of negation finds that affirmative <u>much</u> is largely restricted to foreign (often FRENCH) speakers and to narration, occurring very seldom in native speakers' dialogue. Thus we have the following contrasts (Behre 1967:124):

Narrator: "...looking at him with much interest"
Dialogue: "He looked at her with a good deal of interest."

Poirot: "I have much experience in these matters."
Miss Marple: "I have quite a lot of experience in ..."

"The elegant young man said in good but slightly stilted English, 'I had much difficulty in getting away tonight.'"

Behre also points out that <u>a good deal</u>, as in the second excerpt cited, is (where <u>a great deal</u> is not) restricted to affirmative environments, with no immediately commanding negative. It is thus a <u>positive polarity item</u> (PPI). Other ENGLISH examples of PPIs include <u>would rather</u>, <u>far</u> (+comparative), <u>pretty</u> (+adj.), and members of suppletive adverbial pairs (PPI <u>still</u> alongside NPI <u>anymore</u>, <u>already</u> alongside <u>yet</u>, <u>somewhat</u> vs. <u>at all</u>). But PPIs are a more marginal phenomenon than NPIs: rarer (although extant in a wide range of languages, e.g. the JAPANESE PPI '-ka words' paralleling the NPI '-mo words' [McGloin 1976: 398ff.]), less semantically well-defined into natural classes (although often including a subset of indefinite adverbs), and less environmentally controlled (resulting from PPIs being "anti-triggered" by the absence of a negative rather than normally triggered as are NPIs, it being a consequence of the markedness of negation that most languages contain negative but not affirmative morphemes).

While positive trigger conditions can always be relaxed in direct denials (at least in ENGLISH), negative polarity trigger conditions often cannot:

55.　a.　Fred <u>would</u> (would <u>so</u>) lift a finger to help you.
　　　　? Joe <u>does</u> (does <u>so</u>) have a red cent.
　　　　*John <u>did</u> (did <u>so</u>) eat any cake.
　　　　*Mary <u>has</u> (has <u>so</u>) retired yet.
　　　　*Sally <u>did</u> (did <u>so</u>) arrive until midnight.

　　　b.　John <u>isn't</u> far taller than Bill.
　　　　? John <u>didn't</u> eat some cake.
　　　　Mary <u>hasn't</u> already arrived.
　　　　Trees <u>don't</u> still grow in Brooklyn.
　　　　I <u>wouldn't</u> rather be in Philadelphia.

Acceptability of a NPI is determined by the strength and distance
of the negative trigger (that is, negative force of a trigger tends
to vary directly with the overtness of the negative morphology and
inversely with its distance from the NPI) and by the item itself
(e.g. within the NPI time adverbial system, ever is more "liberal,"
appearing in a wider range of contexts, than yet and (standard dialect) anymore, which are in turn freer than the extremely restrictive until; for many speakers especially in rural areas, anymore
appears in non-polarity contexts as a rough paraphrase of nowadays,
as when D.H. Lawrence's Birkin proclaims "Suffering bores anymore," and can prepose to initial position: "Anymore they are"
(cf. Horn 1970 for discussion)).

The nature of predicates intervening between trigger and NPI
is often a factor as well: factives erect a strong barrier, parenthetical verbs a particularly weak one. Thus we find (where anymore is taken in its NPI use):

56. a. John didn't realize that Mary ⎧ had ever done a thing like that. ⎫
                                       ⎪ *lives in Chicago anymore.   ⎬
                                       ⎪ *has moved to Chicago yet.   ⎪
                                       ⎩ *arrived until midnight.   ⎭

     b. If Al were to ⎧ ever do a thing like that ... ⎫
                       ⎪ ? eat beans anymore...   ⎬
                       ⎪ (cf. ? If Al has left yet...)   ⎪
                       ⎩ *arrive until midnight...   ⎭

     c. Did Mary ever bake bread?
         Has Mary arrived yet?
         Does Mary live in Chicago anymore?
         *Did Mary arrive until midnight?

That strength of negative force is not strictly a formal matter
can be seen by the following contrast, the strongly negative-imply-
ing be damned if idiom contrasting with the less powerfully trig-
gereing true conditional:

57. a. I'd be surprised if he hires you ⎧ before ⎫ you get your
                                          ⎩ *until ⎭
         hair cut.

     b. I'm damned if I'll hire you until you get your hair cut.

But any full account of the behavior of NPIs must be extremely
complex, since it is not obvious that the data can even be arranged
hierarchically, as with Ross's squishes. Notice that acceptability

may depend on whether the negative is asserted, presupposed, or
entailed, as seen in the following display:

58. a. I wish I didn't know anyone here.
     b. *I wish I knew anyone here.
     c. I don't know anyone here.

58' a. *I wish I didn't know what the hell I was doing.
     b. I wish I knew what the hell I was doing.
     c. I don't know what the hell I'm doing.

NPI any appears in the overtly negative context of 58.a but not in
58.b., although the latter presupposes the acceptable 58.c. The
situation with NPI wh + the hell is precisely the reverse, acceptability apparently a factor of whether (as in 58.b) lack of relevant
knowledge can be inferred, regardless of the superficial syntax.

2.3 Polarity and "negative transportation"

It is clear, given these complexities, that one must be wary of
arguments which depend crucially on the distribution of NPIs, with
their intractable variability across triggers, individual items, and
speakers' idiosyncrasies. Unfortunately, the classical argument
(attributed by R. Lakoff (1969) to M. Kajita) for "negative transportation," the positing of a rule moving an embedded negation into
a higher clause (cf. Sec. 4 below) rests on the patterning of until,
lift a finger, and other relatively restricted NPIs. Thus compare

59. a. I $\begin{Bmatrix} \text{thought} \\ \text{claimed} \\ \text{realized} \end{Bmatrix}$ [Mary wouldn't arrive until Sunday].

     b. I didn't $\begin{Bmatrix} \text{think} \\ \text{*claim} \\ \text{*realize} \end{Bmatrix}$ [Mary would arrive until Sunday].

Non-durative occurrences of until are claimed to be restricted to
clauses containing negation; cf. *Mary will arrive until Sunday.
The ungrammatical sentences in 59.b. are thus blocked, since
main clause negation will not trigger embedded clause until (although there is an acceptable reading in which until modifies the
act of cognition or speech rather than the arrival). Think is acceptable in 59.b. without a tautoclausal negative in surface structure, so -- runs the argument -- the negative must have been in
the lower clause at the time the restriction on until is met, then

raised by negative transportation (NT), a rule applying over such predicates as think, believe, suppose, and want, but not over claim or realize.

Similar arguments can be, and have been, constructed for other restrictive polarity items — can help, sleep a wink, in years — to the extent that their triggers can be shown to have to be tauto-clausal. Indeed, the ability of a predicate to intervene between a negative and a lower-clause strict NPI is often taken as the crite-rion for its membership in the class of NT predicates.

Arguments for NT as a rule of SPANISH and FRENCH are given by Rivero (1971) and Prince (1976) respectively; these arguments hinge on the interaction of polarity and mood. Thus, corresponding to the indicative complement below verbs of belief or opinion in SPANISH (as in FRENCH) affirmative sentences, we find two pos-sibilities for the mood of the subordinate clause when the main verb is negated:

60. a. Creo que no es así.   'I believe that it's not so.'
    b. No creo que sea así. (subj.) ⎱
    c. No creo que es así. (indic.) ⎰ 'I don't believe that it's so.'

Rivero argues (contra Bolinger 1968) that the subjunctive version, 60.b, but not the indicative 60.c, paraphrases and derives from the lower negative version 60.a. Prince independently argues the same for FRENCH, and both draw consequences for NT from evi-dence based on this identification.

Rivero cites the following contrastive pairs.

61. a. Mi hermano no cree que ⎰ entiendas (subj.) ⎱palabra de
        francés.   ⎱*entiendes (indic.)⎰
        'My brother doesn't believe she understands a word of
        French.'

    b. Juan no cree que María ⎰ venga (subj.) ⎱y yo lo creo
        tambien.   ⎱*viene (indic.)⎰
    lit., 'Juan doesn't believe that Maria is coming and I believe
        it [=that she isn't] too.'

Unlike the choice of mood in 60., we find that the complement of 61.a, containing NPI (entender) palabra de (francés)'(understand) a word of (French)' which is triggered only by a tautoclausal nega-tive in deep structure (note the absence of an article, diagnostic for the polarity idiom), must appear in the subjunctive. The

indicative version, corresponding to the straightforward denial
'It is not the case that my brother believes...,' would not meet
the clausemate condition for the negative trigger of the <u>palabra de</u>
idiom and is therefore unacceptable.

61.b., with the sense 'J. doesn't think M. is coming and I don't
think so either,' argues for a pretransported source with a lower
negative which <u>lo</u> (semantically including that negative, as the
literal gloss indicates) pronominalizes. The indicative version
would be perfectly acceptable without <u>tambien,</u> on the reading '...
but as for me, I think she is;' the negation is of course not within
the pronominalized clause in this case.

While the literal gloss of 61.b. is ungrammatical in ENGLISH,
a similar pronominalization is acceptable in such sentences as 62.,
from Lindholm (1969:154):

62. I don't think Bill paid his taxes and Mary is quite sure of it.
     [=that he didn't]

Prince's arguments are in the same vein, although more fully
flushed out. The evidence is taken from the behavior of negative
polarity idioms

63. a. Je ne suppose pas qu'Armande $\begin{Bmatrix} ait \\ {*a} \end{Bmatrix}$ dormi de la nuit.
         'I don't suppose Armande slept a wink.'

     b. *Je n'ai pas oublié qu'Armande $\begin{Bmatrix} ait \\ {*a} \end{Bmatrix}$ dormi de la nuit.
         'I haven't forgotten that A. slept a wink.'

(where <u>ait</u> marks third person singular subjunctive and <u>a</u> indicative),
from the negative partitive, which contains no article

64. a. Je ne pense pas qu'Henri $\begin{Bmatrix} ait \\ {*a} \end{Bmatrix}$ d'argent.
         'I don't think Henri has any money.'

     b. Je ne me suis pas rendu compte qu'Henri $\begin{Bmatrix} {*ait} \\ a \\ a\ de\ l'argent. \end{Bmatrix}$ d'argent.
         'I didn't realize that Henri has (*any) money.'

and from the negative particles <u>personne, rien,</u> and <u>jamais.</u>

65. a. Je ne crois pas que Pierre $\begin{Bmatrix} ait \\ {*a} \end{Bmatrix}$ rien dit.
         'I don't believe Pierre said anything.'

65. b. *Je ne dis pas que Pierre {ait} rien dit.
                                 {*a }
       'I don't say P. said anything.'

In each crucial a. case, the subjunctive (diagnostic for NT in Prince's
argument as in Rivero's) is obligatory in the subordinate clause, and
the main clause predicate must be a neg-transporter.

Similar arguments are provided by McGloin (1976: 384-8) for
JAPANESE (based on NPIs <u>tittomo</u> 'at all' and <u>made</u> 'until,' "which
require the presence of the negative in the same simplex sentence
at some level of the derivation," but which may be separated from
their negative trigger by main clause opinion predicates <u>omou</u> and
<u>kangaeru</u>) and by Oh (1971: 48) for KOREAN (based on NPI <u>pakkey</u>
'only' which can occur negated or embedded under negated main
clause predicate <u>sayngkakhata</u> 'think;' in other contexts the suppletive <u>man</u> 'only' must be used).

The BASQUE NPIs listed in 51. seem to share this syntactic
trait:

66. a. Uste dut Patxi'k ogi mikorik ez duela.
        "think AUX Patxi-ERG. bread crumb(PART.) not he has"
        'I think Patxi doesn't have a crumb of bread.'

    b. Ez dut uste Patxi'k ogi mikorik baduela.
        'I don't think Patxi has a crumb of bread.'

Substitution of a non-NT predicate for <u>uste</u> results in a sentence
at best marginal. (BASQUE data are courtesy of C. Corum.)

Unfortunately, beyond the apparent circularity in an argument
which assumes (in the statement of cooccurrence restrictions on
NPIs) what it purports to explain, there seems to be a good deal
of variation in the stringency of the constraint on trigger position,
even for highly restricted items. Lindholm (1969:153-54) cites the
following sentences in which he finds NPIs <u>until</u> and <u>lift a finger</u> are
acceptable despite the unavailability of a paraphrase with the negation in the lower clause, and hence the concomitant unavailability
of a NT derivation:

67. a. It isn't clear that he'll leave until next week.
    b. I didn't claim that I'd finish the paper until Friday.
    c. I can't believe that he'd take the exam until he's ready.
    d. You can't make me believe that he lifted a finger to help.

While there may be acceptability differences among speakers, most can force a grammatical reading by devising contexts in which a negative implication is strongly suggested, e.g. 'It's quite likely he won't leave until next week' in the first case.

Cornulier (1974: 39ff.) supports Lindholm's examples with data from FRENCH [glosses mine].

67'. a. Je ne sache pas qu'il ait jamais dit cela.
          'I don't know that he's ever said that.'

      b. Je sais qu'il n'a jamais dit cela.
          'I know that he never said that.'

      c. Il n'a jamais dit cela, que je sache à ma connaissance.
          'He has never said that, that I know of [to (the best of) my knowledge].'

67'.a, with its peculiar unembedded subjunctive and its nonfactive occurrence of savoir, is an admittedly marked form, restricted to elevated style ("style soutenu"); the equivalent sentence with indicative sais was grammatical in earlier periods. In any event 67'.a does not have a source with embedded negation; its paraphrase is almost, but not quite 67'.b -- as it would have to be if savoir were in fact a true NT verb of the croire stripe -- but rather it is 67'.c, an admission of lack of positive knowledge, rather than an assertion of knowledge to the contrary. (Notice that the same point can be made for the ENGLISH glosses.) Yet apparently the suggestion of the corresponding negative 67'.c is strong enough to achieve the effect of 65.a: jamais is separated from its triggering negative by savoir, apparently vitiating Prince's argument.

R. Lakoff's tag-polarity argument (R. Lakoff 1969) for NT in such sentences as 68.a.

68. a. I don't suppose the Yankees will win, will they?
     b. I {don't know} that there's anything he can do about it,
           {can't see }
         is there?

and the parallel argument for FRENCH (cf. Prince 1976) based on si-tags and responses to the a. sentences of 63.-65. (si appearing only as an expectation-cancelling response in negative contexts) are similarly called into question by the availability of positive tags in the non-NT cases of 68.b and the acceptability (cf. Cornulier 1974: 40) of appending a si-tag to 67'.a.

Even the pronominalization argument based on sentences like
61.b and 62. appears defeasible if

69. Je ne sache pas qu'elle soit jamais venue, et tu t'en doutes
     aussi bien que moi.

-- where en pronominalizes the proposition "qu'elle n'est (ou ne soit)
jamais venue" -- is indeed as acceptable as Cornulier maintains (p. 29);
here again, as with 67'.a , there is no recourse to a deep structure with negation embedded under savoir.

On the other side of the coin, there are languages which seem
to contain NT paraphrase pairs -- cf. RUSSIAN:

70. a. Ya dumayu, čto on ne pridet.
         'I think he won't come.'

     b. Ya ne dumayu, čto on pridet.
         'I don't think he will come.'

-- yet which impose such stringent conditions on trigger placement
for NPIs (e.g. RUSS. ni duši 'not a soul') that no evidence can be
garnered from their occurrence. (I owe the RUSSIAN data to D.
Crockett.)

Indeed, many FRENCH speakers consider 65.a-type sentences
marginal at best; Paradis (1974: 8) considers

71. (*) Je ne crois pas que Marcel ait rien compris.

ungrammatical, preferring to replace rien with the non-NPI indefinite quoi que ce soit. Yet Gaatone provides many attested examples of the pattern Prince draws upon, including

72. Je ne crois pas qu'elle se serait jamais consolée.
     Je ne pense pas qu'on doive rien admirer.

The polarity tests, evidently, do not show what they claim to;
apparently we cannot conclude for any NPI that it is in truth restrictive enough to demand a tautoclausal negative trigger in deep
structure (or "at some level of the derivation" to use McGloin's
more accurate language), excluding the 'merely' implied negation
of the Lindholm and Cornulier sentences, and yet liberal enough to
permit intervening predicates in surface structure, just so long as
these predicates are in the NT class. Without such NPIs, the facts

of polarity can provide no confirmation for a syntactic rule of
negative transportation.

3. Multiple Negation

3.1 Cancellation
3.1.1 Cancellation and logical form

> Language has a logic of its own, and in this case its logic
> has something to recommend it. Whenever two negatives
> really refer to the same idea or word (as special negatives)
> the result is invariably positive; this is true of all lan-
> guages ... The two negatives, however, do not exactly
> cancel one another so that the result [of not uncommon,
> not infrequent] is identical with the simple common, fre-
> quent; the longer expression is always weaker: " this is
> not unknown to me" or "I am not ignorant of this" means
> 'I am to some extent aware of it,' etc. The psychological
> reason for this is that the détour through the two mutually
> destructive negatives weakens the mental energy of the
> listener and implies ... a hesitation which is absent from
> the blunt, outspoken common or known. In the same way
> I don't deny that he was angry is weaker than I assert ...
> (Jespersen 1924:332)

So comments Jespersen in rejecting the "logical" position that two
negations simply make an affirmation: "language is not mathematics"
(p. 331).

Indeed, a weakening of the negative force, whether or not through
overexertion is often striking: a couple in a February 1971 New
Yorker cartoon are seen hesitating before a door with a "NOT UN-
WELCOME" mat in front, the wife commenting, "See what I mean?
You're never sure just where you stand with them."

The purported universality of Jespersen's weakening process is
called into question, however, by a citation in Bach (1968: 98) from
an unpublished paper by Eugene Loos:

> In Capanahua negation of a noun is recursive and produces
> a series of increasing intensity but alternating negativity:
> he, not-he, not-not-he (=he indeed), not-not-not-he (=some-
> one else).

I have not been able to confirm this report, which if true would be
remarkable.

In any case such ENGLISH direct denials as "You shouldn't not
go to the party (just because you don't have a thing to wear)" seem
to be full force and not weakened affirmations.

The more interesting cases of logical double negation (as distinguished from the reinforcing type to be discussed in Sec. 3.2) are
those in which the two negatives do not "refer to the same idea or
word" but an affirmative is nevertheless conveyed. We saw that
Jespersen's principles (23.b,d) above correctly predict that e.g.
LATIN non-nulli ('not none') = 'some,' while nulli...non = 'all.'
These principles are in fact special cases of a general property
of pairs of words called duals. An A-word and a B-word, to use
Jespersen's labels, are duals (of each other) if and only if the following equivalences hold:

73. ~A = B~   ~B = A~
     A = ~B~   B = ~A~

It has been common knowledge for thousands of years that any
one of these equivalences will yield the other three; thus, as
Aristotle relates, possible and necessary are interdefinable, since
what is necessarily the case is impossible not to be the case, and
vice versa. So too in deontic (obligation- and permission-based)
logics, an act is permissible by definition if there is no obligation
not to perform it. The correspondents to the equivalences in 73.
found in propositional calculus are known as the laws of quantifier
negation, e.g. $\sim \forall x \sim \phi = \exists x \phi$. Other deductions based on these dual
equivalences include

74. Not everybody didn't come = Somebody came.
     Nobody didn't come = Everybody came.
     It's not certain that he didn't win = It's possible he won.
     You're required to leave = You're not permitted to stay.
                       [i.e. to not leave]
     You can't not go = You must go, You have to go.

The last example, with one negation each outside and within the
scope of a possibility (or permission) operator yielding the A-value
of the appropriate type, represents a paradigm case of double negation. Harries (1973) lists the following parallels; among others,
of ' can't not '= 'must':

75. [GERMAN] Hans kann nicht den Mann nicht hassen.
                  (=he must hate the man)
     [HUNGARIAN] John nem tudta nem szeretni öt.
                  'John couldn't not love her.'

[LATIN]   <u>Non</u> possum <u>non</u> amare
               (also in Jespersen, = 'I must love')
[RUSSIAN]   Ja <u>ne</u> mog <u>ne</u> dat' emu nagrádu
               'I couldn't not (=had to) give him a reward.'
[MANDARIN]   John <u>bu</u> néng <u>bu</u> tsanchia nàge yiènhui.
               'John can't not attend that party.'

Indeed, languages often seem to further ecology by exploiting this very principle of interdefinability. The normal expression for necessity in MALAGASY is <u>tsy maintsy</u> (lit. 'not able not') and in BASQUE is <u>ezin bertze</u> (lit. 'impossible not').

Double negatives of the logical form 'not V not' will thus result in stronger assertions than 'V' if V is the weaker (entailed) member of the dual opposition, but weaker assertions than 'V' if V is the stronger (entailing) member. We can now see that the fact that <u>I don't deny</u> is weaker than <u>I assert</u> and <u>I don't doubt</u> weaker than <u>I believe</u> (given the demonstrable empirical claim that <u>deny</u> = <u>assert that not</u> and <u>doubt</u> = <u>believe that not</u>) is a consequence not of anything as shadowy as usurpation of mental energy but rather of the fact that cancelling the two negatives will result in expressing the corresponding dual, perhaps 'I suggest' in the <u>don't deny</u> case and 'I am open to the idea (proposition) that...' for <u>don't doubt</u>. If, on the other hand, <u>believe</u> is taken as the weaker value of its dual opposition (entailed by <u>know</u>), <u>I don't doubt</u> will then convey a stronger proposition than <u>I believe</u>, perhaps something akin to <u>I am certain</u>.

3.1.2 Cancellation and polarity

If NPIs occur only within the scope of negatives and PPIs only in their absence, we might expect two cancelling negatives, whatever the logical value of the equivalent affirmative, to provide an atmosphere in which PPIs flourish and NPIs wither. Such is indeed what we find in such contrastive sets as

76. a. I ⎰*believe   ⎱ that anyone has arrived yet.
         ⎱ don't believe   ⎰
            doubt
            *don't doubt
            *have no doubt

     b. I ⎰ believe   ⎱ that someone has already arrived.
         ⎱ *don't believe ⎰
            *doubt
            don't doubt
            have no doubt

77. a. $\left\{\begin{array}{l}\text{Why} \\ \text{*Why not}\end{array}\right\}$ eat any meat. (=you shouldn't eat any)
                                              (=you should eat some)

   b. $\left\{\begin{array}{l}\text{*Why} \\ \text{Why not}\end{array}\right\}$ eat some meat.

78. a. I $\left\{\begin{array}{l}\text{*believe} \\ \text{don't believe} \\ \text{doubt} \\ \text{*don't doubt} \\ \text{*have no doubt}\end{array}\right\}$ that she has a red cent. /
                                  that she's much of a sailor.

   b. I $\left\{\begin{array}{l}\text{know} \\ \text{?believe} \\ \text{*doubt} \\ \text{have no doubt}\end{array}\right\}$ that she's a hell of a good sport.

78' a. It's $\left\{\begin{array}{l}\text{*easy} \\ \text{not easy} \\ \text{hard/impossible} \\ \text{*not hard} \\ \text{too late} \\ \text{*not too late}\end{array}\right\}$ for him to do anything much
                                                            about it.

   b. It's $\left\{\begin{array}{l}\text{easy} \\ \text{*not easy} \\ \text{*hard} \\ \text{not hard}\end{array}\right\}$ to see that she's far stronger than he is.

79. a. Max $\left\{\begin{array}{l}\text{is} \\ \text{?isn't}\end{array}\right\}$ the only one around here who was at all upset.

   b. Max $\left\{\begin{array}{l}\text{?is} \\ \text{isn't}\end{array}\right\}$ the only one around here who was somewhat
                                                            upset.

As mentioned in the previous section, PPIs are often marginally acceptable under (single) negation in contexts of direct denial; the contrasts, however, are clear: NPIs (the a. examples above) are found in explicitly or implicitly negative contexts, PPIs (the b. cases) in affirmative and doubly negated contexts -- or, more generally, doubtly "affective," even where one of the negations is inherent (79.b) or just strongly implied (77.b).

Baker (1970) considers sentences in which PPIs are acceptable under two non-contiguous negations, as in the a. sentences below;

80. a. You can't convince me that someone isn't still holed up
       in this cave.
    b. *Someone isn't still holed up in this cave.

81. a. There isn't anyone in this camp who wouldn't rather be
       in Montpelier.
    b. *He wouldn't rather be in Montpelier.

despite the fact that these sentences "contain subordinate clauses
which are not acceptable as independent sentences," viz. the singly
negated b. sentences. After examining and rejecting the analyses
of polarity in Klima 1964 and Jackendoff 1969 as failing to predict
the grammaticality of the a. sentences, Baker proposes the following account:

82. [=Baker's (47)]a. Negative-polarity items are appropriate
       in structures within the scope of negations [including
       questions, conditions, and the like, as he notes], whereas
       affirmative-polarity items [PPIs] are appropriate elsewhere.

    b. Given semantic representations P_1 and P_2 satisfying the
       following conditions:
       (A) $P_1 = X_1 Y Z_1$ and $P_2 = X_2 Y Z_2$, where Y is itself a
           well-formed semantic representation;
       (B) P_1 entails P_2;
       then the lexical representation appropriate to Y in P_2
       [by 82.a] is also appropriate to Y in P_1.

Thus 80.a "appears to entail something like [83.], though by what
principles is hard to say at present" (but cf. G. Lakoff 1970 for a
hypothesis which exploits the dual equivalences of 73. through
repeated applications).

83. I firmly believe that someone is still holed up in this cave.

Similarly, 81.a with the logical structure '~$\exists$x~ (x WOULD
RATHER be in Montepelier)' entails the corresponding universal
affirmative in which would rather is permitted:

84. Everyone in this camp would rather be in Montpelier.

It is the acceptability of PPIs in these simple affirmatives which
renders them appropriate in the doubly negative sentences entailing
those affirmatives.

Now 82.a is itself not as unexceptionable as it appears, given the vagaries of trigger-NPI conditions observed above (cf. Schmerling 1970 for additional discussion); note also that the proposal 82. does nothing to rule out unacceptable NPIs within the scope of negatives which are themselves negated, as in the b. examples of 76.-79, although it does successfully predict the acceptable PPIs in the same frames.   This is, of course, a complex matter: just as PPIs are often acceptable in direct denials of affirmatives, NPIs may be acceptable in double negative environments if they are read as direct denials of negatives, often with concomitant contrastive stress on the negation.   This may explain a Merle Haggard song title, "I'm Not Too Old to Cut the Mustard Anymore."

But it is 82.b which constitutes the seminal and insightful proposal of Baker's hypothesis, and unfortunately it too is amply counterexemplified; the entailment condition proves simply much too powerful.   Smith (1969: 3.2) points out that 85.a entails the perfect 85.b and yet is itself unacceptable.

85.   a. *Not everybody in L.A. would lift a finger to help a
          lady in distress.
      b. Somebody in L.A. wouldn't lift a finger to help a lady
          in distress.

In fact, a negative outside the scope of a universal fails to trigger even the most liberal polarity items, for most speakers: *Not all people love anybody.   On the other hand, not many in 85.a is fine, despite the greater difficulty in determining which dual quantifier it corresponds to (Smith suggests all but at most a few (not)).

Nor is the difficulty restricted to O-type logical structures:

86.   a. *It's not possible that Mary will marry anyone/
                                  lift a finger to help.
      b. It's certain that Mary won't marry anyone/
                             won't lift a finger to help.

Indeed, Baker himself admits (1970:183) that -- on the basis of the interdefinability of the duals some and all -- his proposal predicts the grammaticality of *Someone did anything much; similarly if There's nobody who doesn't love anyone is acceptable, so should be *Everyone loves anyone. And 58.b, which not only entails but presupposes the impeccable 58.c is nevertheless at best marginal for most speakers.

Even with the correct prediction for the case of 80., it is hard
to imagine a system which will account for 80.a (and Lindholm's
parallel lift a finger example in 67.) and not overgeneralize to cases
like

87. a. You ⎧*can, if you want, not⎫ convince Sally that someone
            ⎨*shouldn't   ⎬ isn't still holed up in this
            ⎩? didn't   ⎭ cave.

     b. ?? You didn't make me believe that he lifted a finger to
        help.

The crucial differentiating factor between these sentences and their
acceptable counterparts with can't is that these cannot be used to
convey an 83.-type affirmative. What seems to be required for
the government of polarity items, judging from these facts and the
Lindholm-Cornulier cases in Sec. 2.3 above, is not a logic of entailment so much as a pragmatics of relevant entailment in context,
i.e. speakers' intentions.

3.1.3 Double negation and mood

PPIs are not the only typological feature shared by affirmative
and double negative contexts. Parenthetical expressions, as observed by Wittgenstein, Urmson, Searle, and other philosophers
of their tradition(s), are devices for qualifying the force of an
assertion or other speech act (see Ross 1973, Cattell 1973, and
Hooper 1975 for discussion and references). Parenthetical clauses,
like the sentence adverbials to which they are related both semantically and distributionally, may weaken or otherwise modify the
force of the main clause but not contradict or reverse it.

Thus in 88.a. we can take the main clause parenthetically, as a
modification of the real assertion contained within the complement
rather than as an assertion of its own; the main clause subject and
verb are then syntactically parentheticalized, which in ENGLISH
results in postposability (as in 88.b) or insertion between constituents of the complement (which is now elevated to main clause
syntactically as it is the asserted clause communicatively throughout 88.).

88. a. ⎧I think   ⎫ that it will rain tomorrow.
         ⎨I claimed   ⎬
         ⎩Mary realized ⎭

88. b. It will rain tomorrow, $\begin{Bmatrix} \text{I think.} \\ \text{I claimed.} \\ \text{Mary realized.} \end{Bmatrix}$

c. It will, $\begin{Bmatrix} \text{I think,} \\ \text{I claimed,} \\ \text{Mary realized,} \end{Bmatrix}$ rain tomorrow.

In many languages, parentheticalization of a clause is marked by overt (morphological) adverbialization, but the pragmatic effect is comparable.

But now note that corresponding to 89.a we find no 89.b - type parentheticals:

89. a. Mary $\begin{Bmatrix} \text{doubts} \\ \text{doesn't think} \\ \text{denies} \end{Bmatrix}$ that it will rain tomorrow.

b. *It will rain tomorrow, Mary $\begin{Bmatrix} \text{doubts.} \\ \text{doesn't think.} \\ \text{denies.} \end{Bmatrix}$

Such parentheticals, if permitted, would reverse the assertive force of the main clause (=89.a's subordinate clause), and communication would tend to break down; languages do not seem to tolerate the illocutionary force of a sentence being made to depend upon the secondary material of a parenthetical clause, phrase, or word.

As we might predict, negated negative parentheticals are fine, and show the same distribution as positive parenthetical clauses; as 90.b illustrates, the same paradigm is displayed by the quasi-parenthetical as-clauses.

90. a. It will rain tomorrow, $\begin{Bmatrix} \text{I don't doubt.} \\ \text{I have no doubt.} \\ \text{you can't deny.} \end{Bmatrix}$

b. The earth, as everyone/*no one knows, is flat.
    The earth, as no one/*everyone denies, is flat.

Bolinger (1968) hypothesizes that constructions permitted in ENGLISH parenthetical clauses (or "postposed main phrases") are just those whose ROMANCE counterparts govern the indicative.

This restriction eliminates both verbs of coercion or valuation
(want, order, approve, demand) and negated or intrinsically negative verbs, i.e. just those constructions requiring the ROMANCE
subjunctive. But, as with parentheticals and PPIs, negated negatives govern the indicative in SPANISH:

> 91. a. Creo que es (INDIC) feliz.
>   'I believe he is happy.'
>
>   b. Dudo/No creo que sea (SUBJ) feliz.
>   'I doubt/don't believe he is happy.'
>
>   c. No dudo que $\begin{cases} es \\ *sea \end{cases}$ feliz.
>   'I don't doubt he is happy.'

The identical pattern is displayed by (no) niego 'I (don't) deny' with
respect to digo.

In CHIBEMBA, the subjunctive is also governed by verbs of coercion (='want,' 'urge,' 'allow') and negative structures, while double
negation demands the indicative (data from Givón 1971):

> 92. a. n-déé-twiishika a-inga-isa.
>   "I   doubt   he come(SUBJ)"
>   'I doubt that he'll come.'
>
>   b. n-shi-léé-twiishika $\begin{cases} *a\text{-inga-isa.} \\ ukuti\ a\text{-à-ishile.} \end{cases}$
>   "that he'll come(INDIC)"
>   'I don't doubt that he'll come.'

Similarly, the BASQUE verbs of wanting, forbidding, advising
and doubting govern the (subjunctive) -n suffix on the embedded verb,
while simple declaratives and double negatives govern the (indicative)
-la suffix (data from Lafitte 1962):

> 93. a. Uste dut egia dela.
>   'I believe that it's true.'
>
>   b. Ez dut uste harena den.
>   'I don't believe that it's his.'
>
>   Dudatzen dut ekorriko duen.
>   'I doubt that he's bringing it.'

93. c. Ez dut dudatzen etchera doa<u>l</u>a.
         'I don't doubt that he's going home.'

One more correlation can be drawn between affirmatives and double negatives. It is well known that just as interrogatives share many traits with negatives (including NPI trigger potential), negative questions are often communicatively equivalent to a positive assertion (<u>Didn't she leave</u>? ≅ <u>She left, didn't she</u>?). Indeed, in ENGLISH and other languages, formally negative questions often bear declarative or exclamatory intonation contours, despite their interrogative form: <u>Isn't it a beautiful day</u>(!)

It has also been often noted that ironic or sarcastic interpretations of positive declaratives vanish under negation; interrogatives, too, tend to be interpretable only literally. Negative questions, on the other hand, like affirmatives, can be read ironically. Thus we find

94. a. Harry's a real genius/nice guy. [ironic interpretation OK]
     b. Is Harry a real genius/nice guy? ⎫
     c. Harry isn't a real genius/nice guy.⎬ [literal only]
     d. Isn't Harry a real genius/nice guy(?) [ironic OK]

Sarcastic nasalization, which for speakers in G. Lakoff's dialect forces a nonliteral reading, is appropriate in 94.d as well as 94.a but not in b. or c.

3.2 <u>Pleonasm</u>
3.2.1 <u>Paratactic negation</u>

If the positive product of two negative integers is taken as the (imperfect) model for negative cancellation in natural language, we may find in the <u>sum</u> of negative integers a model for an even more pervasive phenomenon associated with multiple negation in language, that in which the result is not cancellation but reinforcement.

The classical cases of "illogical" double negation anathema to prescriptivists of standard ENGLISH have perfectly grammatical counterparts in the received dialects of languages throughout the world. Jespersen (1917: 64-72) cites cases of "cumulative negation" ranging from OLD, MIDDLE, and EARLY MODERN ENGLISH (e.g. Shakespeare's "I will not budge for no man") as well as dialogue purporting to represent "vulgar" speech (cf. Labov 1973 for a comprehensive account of the relation between standard and non-standard systems of negation), FRENCH, SPANISH, GREEK, SLAVIC,

HUNGARIAN, and BANTU. In these examples, negation is spread
over various items, generally indefinites, within a single clause,
much in the manner of number or gender agreement in noun phrases;
Jespersen observes that "repeated negation seems to become a
habitual phenomenon only in those languages in which the ordinary
negative element is comparatively small in regard to phonetic bulk"
(1917: 71-2) — hence the gradual disappearance of cumulative negation in EARLY MODERN ENGLISH about the time OE preverbal n(e)
was supplanted by postverbal not.

A closely related, equally significant, and functionally more
complex phenomenon is that of "paratactic negation, " in which

> a negative is placed in a clause dependent on a verb of
> negative import like 'deny, forbid, hinder, doubt.' The
> clause here is treated as an independent sentence, and
> the negative is expressed as if there had been no main
> sentence of that particular type. (Jespersen 1917: 75)

Smyth (1920) calls the use of negative mē after ANCIENT GREEK
verbs corresponding to 'deny,' 'hinder,' 'avoid,' 'lack' and their ilk
a "redundant" or "sympathetic" negation and observes it in the biblical GERMAN of Verbot Ihnen Jesus, daß sie Niemand sagen sollten
(Mark 9:9).

ENGLISH examples abound in the standard language to about 1700.
Traugott (1972: 96) relates that OE verbs tweo 'doubt,' forbead-,
forber-, geswic- 'stop,' and wiðcweð- 'refuse' regularly govern
dependent clauses with paratactic negatives. So too Chaucer (Nature defendeth and forbedeth that no man [i.e. anyone] make hym-
self riche) and Shakespeare (First he denied you had in him no [=any]
right; You may deny that you were not the meane of my Lord Hastings
late imprisonment). R. Lakoff (1968) cites Swift (He doubted it would
be impossible for me to swim ashore; if we read doubt here as 'fear,'
of course, the negative in impossible is not redundant), and Jespersen
gives an instance as recent as Darwin (It never occurred to me to
doubt that your work ... would not advance our common object).

Often cited as the classic example of redundant or pleonastic
negation is the FRENCH ne appearing (optionally) under verbs of
fearing and preventing, negated verbs of doubt and denial, and after
comparatives (cf. Gaatone 1971: 80-99), but — as Gaatone is careful
to point out — it should be remembered that this "ne explétif" is not
a full negation. We find contrasts of the following sort:

95. a. Je crains qu'elle vienne / qu'elle ne vienne.
'I'm afraid she's coming.'

b. Je crains qu'elle ne vienne pas.
'I'm afraid she isn't coming.'

After a comparative, ne again seems to carry no negative force; a
full (ne...pas) negation in this environment is as impossible in
FRENCH as in ENGLISH.

Citations involving full negations appearing paratactically in embedded clauses are given by Jespersen (1917: 75-80) for DANISH and
GERMAN; R. Lakoff's LATIN example (96.) is echoed by Lafitte's
citation for BASQUE (97.):

96. Potuisti prohibere ne fieret.
'You could have prevented it from happening.'

97. Debekatu diot ez dezan holakorik egin.
'I forbade him to do such a thing.' (lit.'...so that he not
do...')

LATIN recuso 'refuse' and deterro 'prevent' as well as negated
verbs of doubt also govern complementizers with morphological
negatives, quin and quominus:

98. Non dubitavit quin ei crederemus.   (Cicero)
'He didn't doubt that we believed him.'

Haynes attributes paratactic negation in Cervantes and his con-
temporaries, common with verbs of fearing, doubt, denial, avoiding,
preventing, and so on, to a "crossing or confusion," "contamina-
tion," or -- more charitably -- "conceptual fusion": the speaker

is aware of one or more different ways of expressing his
idea and, by reason of a subtle fusing or telescoping of
these simultaneous influences, he uses the additional
negative at the precise moment it is felt to be most
necessary.   (Haynes 1933: 44-5)

A clear case of fusion is in the expressions no poder que no [+SUBJ]
and no poder de no [+INFIN] 'to keep from': "there must have been
a struggle between the ideas cause that not and prevent, so that not,"
(Haynes 1933: 55). Jespersen's explanation of the emergence of

paratactic negation after negative-incorporating <u>too</u> in a sentence
from Austen (<u>There was none too poor or too remote not to feel an
interest</u>) is along similar lines, given that <u>too X to Y</u> = so X as to not Y.

The analysis of paratactic negation as fusions (or, to adopt
Bolinger's term, blends) may be seen as either a reply or a concession to the invective of prescriptivists like Fowler (1926: 383-4)
who excoriate the negative "evoked in a subordinate clause as a
mere unmeaning echo of an actual or virtual negative in the main
sentence" as being "wrong and often destructive of the sense."
Paratactic negatives thus draw off the surplus wrath overflowing
from that visited on the more stereotypic "illogical" double negatives of the clause-bounded, "nothing from nobody nohow" variety
mentioned earlier.

Yet the good fight seems to be a losing battle. Fowler admits
"we all know people who habitually say <u>I shouldn't wonder if it didn't
turn to snow</u> when they mean <u>if it turned</u>." Equally "illogical," and
equally frequent, are weather forecasts warning "Don't be surprised
if it doesn't rain" and friends assuring us that they miss <u>not</u> seeing
us around anymore.

This last case is particularly interesting: In the first place,
<u>miss</u> is a clear example of a verb with a semantic negative which
is too impotent to trigger even the weakest NPIs (<u>I regret not having
eaten anything last night</u> / *<u>I miss having eaten anything last night</u>),
and is thus fair game for a Jespersen-Haynes blend to reinforce the
negative import, in keeping with the obvious psychological plausi-
bility of the correlation between the degree to which a negative is
"buried" into a lexical item and the amount of strengthening it will
require. Notice that it is not clear whether someone (even if (s)he
is not within the paratactic "miss not"-dialect) can literally miss
our not being there in the sense of regretting our presence. Equally
striking is the parallel between <u>miss not</u> and a MANDARIN construction <u>chā-yīdiar</u> 'miss-a-little,' as described by Li (1975). Depending on whether <u>méi</u> is taken as a true or a paratactic negative, we
got opposed readings for 99.:

99. Tā chā-yīdiar méi zŏu   (lit. 'he miss-a-little not leave')
    a. 'He barely left.' (=just missed not leaving)
    b. 'He almost left.' (=just missed leaving)

Without a pause separating <u>chā-yīdiar</u> and the negative <u>méi</u>, the a.
reading is the unmarked; the longer the pause, the more strongly
the paratactic, blended reading is forced.

Pauses, in fact, often palliate the scorn of the prescriptivist over the tautoclausal double negative as well. No one objects, as Jespersen notes (1924: 334), to "He cannot sleep, not even after taking an opiate;" such negative appositives seem quite unobjectionable, as when a recent novelist writes, "The university would never stand for him living with a woman, not in quarters provided and paid for by the faculty." But, as Jespersen points out (ibid.), the line is often hard to draw: "does a sentence like 'I cannot goe no further' (Shakespeare) become more logical by the mere addition of a comma: 'I cannot goe, no further'?"

A particularly telling battle in what often seems a class war waged between Jespersen and his acolytes in their trenches and the prescriptive grammarians and lexicographers in theirs is the case of comparatives. Fowler (1926) and the New English Dictionary reject as illogical the construction "more than I can help." But, as Jespersen insists,

> It would certainly be unidiomatic to say, as Whately demands, more than I can not help; the idiom is caused by the fact that every comparison with than implies a negative idea (he has more than necessary implies "it is not necessary to have more," etc.) and it is on a par with the logic...in the French use of ne (plus qu'il ne faut) and in the dialectal nor for than. (Jespersen 1917: 80)

Joly (1967), quoting Jespersen's remarks approvingly, presents extensive evidence that the second clause of a comparative is inherently negative; he argues that a negative element is morphologically included not only in nor (for which he cites a wide range of dialects into which it survives as a comparative marker) but in than itself. In any case, the acceptability of other NPIs in the same frame as can help (taller than anyone; later than they (as) yet realize) and the impossibility of full negatives in the same context, in ENGLISH or FRENCH, argue persuasively for the inherent negativity of comparatives.

Attempting to account for this negativity, and its specific effect of triggering FRENCH pleonastic ne, Bourciez has in fact argued for a blend approach similar to Jespersen's. As cited by Haynes (1933: 62) in support of a similar account of comparatives in Don Quixote, the schema in Bourciez is:

100. tu es fresche plus qu'est rose ⟍ tu es plus fresche que
      tu es fresche, plus n'est rose ⟋ n'est rose

Problematical for both this hypothesis and the more complex psychological arguments on the nature of the act of comparison in Joly 1967 is the fact that equatives in ENGLISH seem to constitute negative environments, in that they trigger NPIs, and yet cannot be tenably subsumed under the argument for inequality as a source for the negative property. It may be significant, however, that only "at least"-type equatives, which are compatible with inequality, permit NPIs to follow them, while doubly-bounded equatives do not:

101. a. John is {at least / *exactly} as tall as anyone I know.

 b. Movies are {at least / *exactly} as good as ever.

3.2.2 Negative parentheticals

While space precludes an account here of some of the truly remarkable pleonastic or "dummy" negatives in ENGLISH, I will just mention the so don't I construction heard in parts of the eastern U.S. ("John can stand on his head and whistle Dixie" -- "So can't [=can] I") and the optionality of the negative in the fixed colloquialisms That'll teach you (not) to... and I could(n't) care less; cf. Lawler 1974 for discussion of these and other intriguing examples.

A more significant construction, but one apparently little extant outside ENGLISH, is the negative parenthetical. We noted above the ungrammaticality of affirmative main clauses with negative parentheticals, as in *89.b. When the main clause itself contains an overt negative, however, the parenthetical may as well -- if its verb is within the opinion class, and within the subclass permitting NT. Thus in

102. a. It won't rain, I believe.
 b. It won't rain, I don't believe.

102.a,b are virtual paraphrases, the latter perhaps less marked in conversation if either is. Notice the impossibility of substituting a non-NT verb like claim or realize for believe in 102.b, while other verbs of the assertion-weakening class -- imagine, suppose, think, reckon -- can freely occur. Indeed, we find that 103.a is acceptable to just those speakers for whom 103.b can be used, like 103.c, as an indirect or qualified assertion of 103.d.

103. a. The Cubs won't win it this year, I don't guess.
 b. I don't guess the Cubs will win it this year.

103.   c.   I guess the Cubs won't win it this year.
       d.   The Cubs won't win it this year.

Correlations such as the one governing 103. lead Ross to generate 102.b from I believe it won't rain by reanalyzing NT as a
process of copying and deletion rather than a single movement rule.
After the negative is copied into the main clause, yielding I don't
believe it won't rain (to be distinguished from the superficially
identical sentence with logical double negation), the embedded complement may be fronted or "slifted" (< S[entence]-lifted) to become
the main clause, in which event the otherwise obligatory rule deleting the rain-clause negative is blocked, and 102.b under which
the deletion rule is inapplicable (or at most optional), if the upstairs
negative is incorporated. But there is also good reason to doubt
the correctness of the slifting analysis in general and the copy-delete
reanalysis of NT in particular; cf. Cattell 1973, Cornulier 1974
and G. Lakoff 1974 for details.

In any case, whatever the theoretical justification for Ross' reanalysis, its empirical justification rests on thin ice. Most languages with clause-based postposable parentheticals (of the type of
88.b and 102.a) — among them GERMAN, SWAHILI, LATIN, and
FRENCH -- have no correspondent to the dummy negative model of
102.b. In RUSSIAN, 104.b is indeed marginally acceptable alongside the perfect 104.a,

104.   a.   On ne pridet, ya dumayu.
            'He won't come back, I think.'

       b.   ?On ne pridet; ya ne dumayu.
            'He won't come back, I don't think.'

but the tendency is to regard the putative parenthetical in b. rather
more as an afterthought or separate comment ('He won't come...
or I don't think so, anyway') than the literal gloss would suggest.

The same holds in TURKISH:

105.   a.   Geliyor, zannederim.
            'He is coming, I think.'

       a'. Gelmiyor, zannederim.
            'He isn't coming, I think.'

       b.   Gelmiyor; zannetmiyorum.
            'He isn't coming; (at least) I don't think so.'

Both the additional pause in the "negative parenthetical" sentence
(as in the RUSSIAN 104.b) and the syntax (the true parenthetical
verb in 105.a is in the aorist tense vs. the present tense of the
corresponding negative) point to the quasi- (if not totally) bisen-
tential status of the 105.b example.

The situation in ESTONIAN appears to be closer to the dummy
negative of ENGLISH. While postposed clausal parentheticals are
in general felt to be slightly peculiar, 106.c with its pleonastic
negative is no worse -- and perhaps a little less awkward -- than
its positive counterpart, 106.b :

106. a. Ma usun/väidan et ta ei tule.
          'I believe/claim that he isn't coming.'

      b. ?? Ta ei tule, ma usun/väidan.
          'He isn't coming, I believe/claim.'

      c. Ta ei tule, ma ei ? usu/*väida.
          'He isn't coming, I don't believe/claim.'

As in ENGLISH, the non-NT verb of saying cannot appear in a negative parenthetical. It is again not clear whether the second clause
in 106.c would be considered as a separate sentence. (The RUS-
SIAN, TURKISH, and ESTONIAN data are due to Dina Crockett,
Ayhan Aksu, and Marilyn Vihman, respectively, and any transcrip-
tion errors to me.)

This problematical status of the clause relations of parantheti-
calized sentences is difficult to reconcile with the account of Ross
(1973) or similar rules of complement preposing (cf. Hooper 1975).
On the other hand, it seems to be compatible with the approach of
G. Lakoff (1974), who attempts to account for parentheticals by
formalizing the notion of blends as amalgams, two or more logical
structures combining under a specified set of semantic and pragmatic conditions to result in a single sentence. Under this neo-
Jespersenian treatment, 102.b would derive from the complex
It won't rain + I believe it won't rain. The second subsentence may
undergo NT and -- as an intermediate stage -- an overt conjunction
may introduce it, indicating its qualifying or hedging nature, viz.
It won't rain; (or) at least I don't believe it will.

The RUSSIAN, TURKISH, and perhaps ESTONIAN cases might
result, then, from constraints blocking further amalgamation or
reduction of this form into a version like that for 102.b.

Cattell (1973) presents and contrasts two competing analyses of ordinary and negative parentheticals which respectively prefigure Ross' slifting and Lakoff's amalgams.   Lawler (1974) relates these constructions and the not even-type to the less frequently discussed process resulting in fragments like not then I wouldn't or not with my wife you don't. And consider, as a final curiosity, this comment by a young British war refugee in a Joyce Cary novel, in which the negative parenthetical is apparently triggered by a strongly sarcastic reading in the main clause: Girls are a lot of good, I don't think.

4. Negative Transportation

4.1 NT: The phenomenon

Negative transportation, "the strong tendency in many languages to attract to the main verb a negative which should logically belong to the dependent nexus" (Jespersen 1917: 53), is -- like pleonastic negation -- a phenomenon of natural language about which philosophers and other idealists have little interest and less patience. Quine deplores "the familiar quirk of English" whereby " 'x does not believe that p' is equated to 'x believes that not-p' rather than to 'it is not the case that x believes that p' " as "an incidental idiomatic complication" to be best left ignored; Hintikka also notes the "peculiarity" and Deutscher the "unfortunate ambiguity" between the (illogical) disbelief and (logical) non-belief readings of sentences like Jespersen's 107.a   (cf. Horn 1975 for references).   These two readings are represented as 107.b and 107.c, respectively.

107. a. I don't think he has come.
        b. I think he has not come.
        c. It is not the case that I think he has come.

Note that on the NT (b.) reading the negation is contrary; on the external (c.) reading it is contradictory.

This inconvenient "peculiarity" or "quirk" is, however, neither limited to ENGLISH nor isolated to verbs of the opinion or belief class; rather it betrays a fundamental syntactic, semantic, and pragmatic process manifested throughout divergent language families and across distinct but systematically related classes of predicates.

Jespersen (1917: 54) cites the following DANISH example (attested in Schandorff) to demonstrate that the negative ikke must be understood as "belonging" to the lower clause, given the continuation (impossible in ENGLISH, though the sense is clear):

108. Je tror ikke, at mange har læst Brand (og at færre har
                                              forstaaet den).
      "I believe not that many have read..."
      'I believe that not many have read Brand (and that (even)
      fewer have understood him).'

Much additional evidence, including the polarity argument discussed
in Sec. 2.3, has been adduced in defense of a syntactic rule of NT deriving the relevant reading of 107.a from its quasi-paraphrase
107.b; much counterevidence has also been marshalled. Some
have argued that the process resulting in the parallel understandings
of 107.a is "merely" semantic or pragmatic in nature and not the
consequence of a rule of grammar at all. Others, as Atlas disputes
the putative ambiguity of the internal/external readings assigned to
the definite description case 11. and Jerry Sadock (in unpublished
work) has questioned the notion that the universal negative structure
of 15. is truly semantically ambiguous with respect to scope (rather
than just general and pragmatically determined), have maintained
that 107.a is in fact unambiguous, having only the <u>sense</u> of the external, contradictory reading; the use of such logically contradictory
negations to convey the contrary, lower-neg reading is attributed to
a pragmatic inference from the external reading to the internal,
mirroring the semantic entailment in the opposite direction, this
pragmatic inference arising in contexts in which the subject of an
NT sentence like 107.a will be assumed to have come to some sort
of conclusion about the truth of the complement. (For a more detailed exposition and critique of this view, due to R. Bartsch and
since adopted, often independently, by others, see Horn 1975: 279-
82. and Horn to appear: Sec. 1.)

   A different sort of objection, one unfortunately difficult -- like
the parallel fusion analyses of paratactic negation by Jespersen and
Haynes -- to incorporate into a formal description, is presented by
Bolinger:

> The idea that in <u>I don't think he's coming</u> we have a negative
> element that belongs truly to the subordinate verb and that
> can be transferred, like a syntactic ping-pong ball, to
> another position without altering its logical connections,
> I think is not quite true. ...It does not merely hop from
> one [clause] to another but belongs semantically to both.
>   (Bolinger 1968: 23-4)

   I will not detail the theoretical issues here (but cf. Horn 1975
and the references therein), except to suggest my own tentative

conclusion, that NT is a syntactic rule which originates as a functional device for signalling negative force (like other illocutionary
force markers) as early as is possible within a sentence (this possibility being determined by a complex interaction of language-specific
and perceptually-based properties), and is thus a grammaticization
of functional principles -- not unlike a wide range of linguistic
phenomena including most movement rules and constraints, as
recent work by Grosu, Kuno, and Firbas, following the earlier
Prague school tradition, have attempted to demonstrate.

Whatever the syntactic evidence, pro and con, for a rule of NT,
it is dubious whether the semantic evidence, if it is to be based on
the putative paraphrase relation between 107.b and the non-external
reading of 107.a, can be seriously maintained. R. Lakoff (1969)
credits Bolinger with the observation that the negative force in the
transported reading of 107.a is perceptibly weaker than in its untransported congener, 107.b. In fact, Poutsma (1928:105) had found
that "the shifting of <u>not</u> often has the effect of softening down the
negativity of a sentence." This softening process is far from restricted to NT-related pairs; rather, as we have already had occasion to mention, it appears to be an epiphenomenon of all rules
affecting placement and morphology of the negative element. In a
paradigm like

   108'. I think she's sad.
        I think she's unhappy.
        I think she's not happy.
        I think she isn't happy.
        I doubt she's happy.
        I do not think she's happy.
        I don't think she's happy.

each version is a little weaker in negative force or commitment on
the speaker's part than the one preceding.

Nor is this principle ENGLISH-restricted. Mrisho Kivugo informs me that, in SWAHILI, 109.a -- while equivalent in meaning
to the untransported 109.b.

   109. a. Sidhani (kama) ni kweli.   'I don't think (that) it's true.'
       b. Nadhani (kama) ni kweli.   'I think (that) it isn't true.'

-- suggests a more polite form of opposition as a result of its
greater indirectness and would thus be used in different circumstances than would the harsher 109.b.

The NT predicates generally cited in discussions of the phenomenon are those of the class which occur in ENGLISH in the negative parenthetical environment of 102.b -- think, believe, suppose, imagine, expect -- but only when they have the 'hold an opinion' sense. When believe signifies 'accept the claim,' it is not a neg-transporter (Lindholm 1969), nor is imagine when it means 'form a mental image' or suppose when it corresponds to 'assume the hypothesis.'

When we examine other languages, we do indeed find belief-(or opinion-)class predicates among the neg-transporters if NT is a process in the language at all. Among a list of these verbs are included LATIN credo, FRENCH croire and imaginer, SPANISH creer and pensar, GERMAN glauben, RUSSIAN dumat', TURKISH zanned-, KOREAN mit- and sängkakh-, JAPANESE omou and kangaeru, BASQUE uste, SWAHILI kudhani, and ESTONIAN usun. A negation syntactically outside the scope of any of these predicates can be understood as weakly asserting (à la Hooper 1975) the negation of the complement clause embedded under that verb.

But not all verbs with the approximate meaning of believe will trigger NT. Thus xošev 'think' permits NT readings in HEBREW —

110.　a.　Ani xošev še-hu lo yavo.
　　　　　"I think that-he not come" 'I think that he won't come.'$\tilde{=}$

　　　b.　Ani lo xošev　še-hu yavo.　'I don't think he'll come.'

-- but maamin 'believe,' substituted into the same frame, does not. Apparently this verb, used for expressions of faith as well as opinion, is too strong to permit the sort of transparency to negative force which NT demands.

In MALAGASY, the reverse is true. Negative tsy raises to preverbal position over some difficulty with verbs glossed as 'croire' but with much greater difficulty over the equivalents of 'penser,' if the intuitions of Ed Keenan's informants are correct:

111.　a.　Tsy $\left\{\begin{array}{l}\text{inoa-ko}\\\text{believed by-me}\\\text{mino aho}\\\text{believe I}\end{array}\right\}$ fa ... $\tilde{=}$ $\left\{\begin{array}{l}\text{Inoa-ko}\\\text{Mino aho}\end{array}\right\}$ fa tsy...
　　　　　"not"　　　　　　　　　　　　"that"

　　　b.　Tsy $\left\{\begin{array}{l}\text{noheveri-ko}\\\text{thought by-me}\\\text{nihevitra aho}\\\text{thought I}\end{array}\right\}$ fa ... $\neq$ $\left\{\begin{array}{l}\text{Noheveri-ko}\\\text{Nihevitra aho}\end{array}\right\}$ fa tsy...
　　　　　"not"　　　　　　　　　　　　"that"

As in many languages, negation in MALAGASY raises more easily over want-type predicates governing the infinitive rather than the indicative clause of the above examples. This is a result of the interaction of NT and complementizer type which we shall explore in Sec. 5.1 below.

While NT predicates tend to be drawn from the same semantic classes cross-linguistically (as pointed out by R. Lakoff 1968), we find that different members of these classes fall within the subset which permits NT. Variation ranges over dialects and even idiolects as well as languages. We discover want among ENGLISH neg-transporters but not desire, or -- for some speakers -- wish; believe and suppose neg-raise for all, guess and anticipate for some, and hope (semantically approximate to 'want' + 'believe possible') for none.

When we leave our own speech communities we learn that the cognate GERMAN verb of hoping, hoffen, is a NT predicate, and we realize that the concern expressed in a Scandinavian-accented voice overheard on a bus in the Midwest, "I don't hope that you got scared," is understandable in the light of the impeccable DANISH equivalent,

112.   Jeg håber ikke, at De blev bange.

Venturing back in time, we find the following LATIN exchange in Plautus,

113.   — Te ille deseret.   'He will leave you.'
       — Non spero.   'I hope not.'

often cited as an instance of "anticipatory negation" by the traditional classical grammars. Yet espérer, the FRENCH descendant of spero, no longer permits NT, while its semantic neighbor souhaiter (perhaps intermediate between 'wish' and 'hope') does.

It is difficult to see how such variations, typical of lexical exceptions to syntactic rules (as G. Lakoff 1970b points out), could be accounted for were NT to yield to a general semantic (or, a fortiori, pragmatic) principle of interpretation.

4.2 NT predicates and natural classes: a scalar hypothesis

The classes into which NT predicates, in ENGLISH and other languages, tend to cluster or be subsumable can be instantiated as follows.

114. a. think, believe, suppose, imagine, expect,
          reckon (anticipate, guess)
      a'. seem, appear, look like, sound like, feel like...
      b. be probable, be likely, figure to
      c. want, intend, choose; be supposed to, ought to;
          be desirable; advise

But why do we find these classes and no others? Why, for example,
are factives universally excluded from the ranks of neg-transporters?
The Kiparskys attempted to account for this gap by invoking their
hypothesized fact-complement which would block both NT and other
movement rules, but their analysis has suffered too many unanswered
counterexamples to survive. A more promising proposal is that of
G. Lakoff (1970b: fn.4), who ties the non-transporting status of factives to the Poutsma-Bolinger "uncertainty principle" mentioned
above: if NT is triggered by the speaker's uncertainty about the
truth of the complement, and this very complement is presupposed
by speakers of factive sentences, NT will never be triggerable
under such predicates.

Nor will it be under implicatives either, since no more uncertainty is permitted by entailed complements than by those which are
presupposed (see Karttunen 1970 for a definition of implicative and
semi-implicative verb classes). Thus be likely is a neg-transporter,
but not (factive) be significant; intend and want are, but (implicative)
manage, venture, forget, and bother (cf. Horn 1971) are not.

On the other hand, we observe that able and possible, whose
complements are neither presupposed nor entailed, are never NP
predicates; and what of the verbs of 114.c which don't bear any
obvious connection with certainty or uncertainty? The relations
between the predicates of this class and the NT predicates of classes
a. and b. can be perceived with the aid of a strength scale on which
both epistemic (belief- and knowledge-based) and deontic (obligation-
and permission-based) predicates can be plotted, as in 115. Elements
toward the right (strong) end of the scale entail corresponding elements to their left (cf. Horn 1972 for details).

115.

be able	believe, suppose, think	know, realize
be possible	be likely, probable	be clear, evident
	figure to	be sure, certain
←WEAKER—	seem, appear, look like	be odd, significant
may, might —STRONGER→	should, ought to, better	must, have to
can, could	be supposed to	need, be necessary
allow, permit, let	be desirable, advisable	be obligatory
be allowed	be a good idea	make, cause, force
be legal	want, choose, intend, plan to	order, demand, force
	suggest, advise	

Parallel to this scale for the positive modal elements, we could construct one for their negative counterparts, where the following correspondences would be observed:

116. a. The negation of a weak value (e.g. <u>possible</u>, <u>allow</u>) will be a strong value on the corresponding negative scale (<u>impossible</u>, <u>forbid</u>).

      b. The negation of a strong scalar value (e.g. <u>certain</u>, <u>have to</u>) will be a weak value on the corresponding negative scale (<u>not certain</u>, <u>don't have to</u>).

      c. The negation of a mid-scalar value (e.g. <u>likely</u>, <u>advisable</u>) will be an intermediate value on the corresponding negative scale (e.g. <u>not likely</u>, <u>not advisable</u>) -- note that the negative-incorporating forms <u>unlikely</u> and <u>inadvisable</u> are not the contradictory negations we are concerned with here, but contrary negations derived by NT from structures embedding a lower negative.

By 'mid-scalar' in 116. we are referring with slight inaccuracy to values which are actually to the right (stronger side) of the midpoint of their respective scales, by the contradiction test defined in Sec. 1.3. Thus 'I believe he left and I believe he didn't' acknowledges, an inconsistent belief set, 'he wants to go and he wants to stay [=not-go]' reports contradictory desires, and so on. It is this position we are calling mid-scalar which harbors all neg-transporting predicates; the weaker and (with an exception we shall discuss below) stronger positions cannot. We have already seen why strong scalar epistemics exclude NT: their use presupposes or at least entails their complement -- while <u>it's likely</u> (or <u>I think</u>) Mary left leaves open the possibility that she didn't leave, <u>it's certain</u> (or <u>I'm sure</u>) Mary left explicitly rejects this possibility. Thus not only factives and implicatives but the (semi-implicative) IF-verbs of Karttunen (1970), those from which an entailment is deducible only from positive instances, are excluded as neg-raisers.

With the weak scalars, corresponding to Karttunen's ONLY-IF predicates, no entailment follows from a positive occurrence, but negated <u>able</u> and <u>possible</u> sentences do entail the negation of their complements. We must evidently examine each pair < F(S), ~F(S) > and determine if an entailment is derivable from <u>either</u> member; if so, F is scratched from the roll of potential neg-transporting predicates.

What is common to all NT predicates is the relative slimness of
the functional difference between the pre-raised form with lower
negation and the logical form with the negative taking wide scope.
It is the closeness of the external neg-readings of not likely, not
believe, not advisable to likely not, believe not, advisable not respectively which renders the negated predicates potential neg-
transporters, and the relative distance of not possible, not realize,
not obligatory from possible not, realize not, obligatory not which
removes these from contention.

Of course, no entailments are derivable with the deontics, strong
or weak, affirmative or negative. If something is obligatory (or
forbidden), it doesn't follow that it will (or won't) occur, merely
that it better (or better not), if dire consequences are to be avoided.
The deontic analogue of certainty is clear: the key is whether an
"absolute" obligation is derivable from either a deontic predicate
or its negation. Since absolutely is restricted in its distribution
to strong positive and negative scalar values, cross-cutting the
epistemic/deontic distinction (along with many others; cf. G. Lakoff
1970 and Horn 1972 for discussion), and does not peacefully coexist with either intermediate or weak scalars —

117. a. absolutely certain/obligatory/must/necessary/insist
      b. *absolutely possible/permitted/can/allow
      c. absolutely impossible/prohibited/can't/mustn't/forbid
      d. *absolutely (not) likely/(not) advisable/should(n't)/suggest

— cooccurrence of a predicate or its contradictory negation with
absolutely is thus diagnostic for non-transportability.

Assumed in this line of argumentation is the functional principle
that NT will not be condoned where it would result in the emergence
of pernicious ambiguities (where the contradictory/contrary distinction carries high functional load) and consequent breakdowns in
communication.

The ENGLISH syntactic modals in 115. are difficult to test, due
to their notoriously defective paradigm and non-support by do, but
environments like that in 118. are crucial, the modal in question
embedded under a negated verb which is itself a neg-raiser:

118. I don't think you $\begin{cases} \text{\# can, \#? may} \\ \text{should, ought to, better} \\ \text{\# ? must, \#have to} \end{cases}$ leave.

      ($\tilde{=}$ 'I think you M stay')

('#' indicates unavailability of a paraphrase with the corresponding
lower-neg version; thus, "I don't think you should leave" can convey a suggestion to stay, but "I don't think you can leave" cannot
convey permission to do so.) As expected, weak and strong scale
modals fail to raise negatives on epistemic or deontic readings;
mid-scalars succeed. This holds not only for the mid-scalars in
the above example, but for dialectal variants given in Visser's
historical syntax, as is clear in a sentence he cites from Ring
Lardner -- I don't feel as if I should ought to leave -- in which the
negative element has emerged intact from a triple jump.

   Similarly, GERMAN sollen, but not the weaker können or the
stronger müssen , tolerates NT. And it is the LATIN equivalent
of should which figures in an 11th-century investigation of NT by
St. Anselm. Anselm (as quoted in Henry 1967:193ff.) takes issue
with Paulus, a fifth-century jurist who argued: Qui facit quod facere
non debet, non videtur facere quod iussus est -- 'he who does what he
non debet seems not [note the NT over videtur 'seems'] to do what
he is commanded to do.' To which Anselm rejoins that non...omnis
qui facit quod non debet, peccat, si proprie consideretur -- 'not
everybody who does what he non debet sins, if the matter is considered strictly (proprie, suggesting 'with the (contradictory) reading
of the negation, as it appears in surface structure'). But, warns
Anselm, we tend to say non debere peccare for debere non peccare
('we ought not to sin'): non debere really means 'not to be a duty'
but we don't always sin by doing what isn't a duty. When a man does
what he non debet, on the strict (non-NT) reading, as by marrying,
he does not necessarily sin thereby. And yet, bemoans Anselm, we
can't "say" non debet ducere uxorem without interference from the
"common use" of this construction to render (via NT) debet non
ducere uxorem, an injunction to celibacy. Anselm, in focusing on
one of the rare instances in which the functional load carried by the
internal (NT)/external distinction for mid-scalar negation is a serious (not to say solemn) matter, also casts a curious light on
Quine's perception of NT as an incidental quirk of ENGLISH well
worth leaving unexamined.

   It must be admitted that, unlike weak scalar predicates of ability,
possibility, and permission, the strong deontic equivalents of have
to, must do -- like their mid-scalar 'ought' confrères -- trigger
NT in a wide variety of languages. ANCIENT GREEK (keléuo),
FRENCH (falloir), BASQUE (behar), RUSSIAN (nado, nužno, veleno),
and ESPERANTO (devas) are among those where at least one strong
deontic neg-raises; HEBREW, ESTONIAN, MALAGASY, and TUR-
KISH are not. This apparent anomaly might be attributable to the

fuzzier nature of absoluteness with respect to obligation as against
certainly (i.e. the greater psychological distance from probable to
certain than from ought to must), and to the interaction of the functional anti-ambiguity principle with the pressure for expressibility
of E-vertex as against O-vertex configurations of the square of
opposition, as discussed in Sec. 1.3 above.

The Poutsma-Bolinger uncertainty principle has its deontic
counterpart. Gaatone (1971: 54) finds the two sentences

119.   a.   Il ne faut pas que ce mariage se fasse.
       b.   Il faut que ce mariage ne se fasse pas.

appearing a page apart in a Montherlant novel. While they share
cognitive meaning (='This marriage must not take place'), the
second, culminating a series of the hero's reflections about the
upcoming event, is much the stronger in force.

It should also be noted that the principle blocking pernicious
ambiguity is maintained for the strong deontics in that the non-NT
(external) reading has been virtually eliminated in the ne pas falloir
and (RUSSIAN) ne nado constructions. Of course, even with mid-
scalars, the NT reading is generally salient, although (as for some
FRENCH speakers with falloir) the external (higher-neg) reading
does emerge in direct denial contexts. Further, only the raised,
contrary negation is incorporable into mid-scalars, as the following examples indicate:

120.   doubt = believe...not
       improbable = probable...not (cf. impossible)
       unlikely = likely...not
       inadvisable = advisable...not
       disinclined = inclined...not
       disadvantageous = advantageous...not
       shouldn't = should...not
       oughtn't = ought...not
       LATIN nolo = volo...non (cf. nequeo 'be unable')

The mid-scalar condition, while generally necessary to qualify
a predicate for membership into the NT-triggering classes, is far
from sufficient. Thus, want and intend, though not directly epistemic or deontic notions, are easily assimilable into the class of
deontics -- a desire or intention being a sort of obligation or 'should'
which one imposes on oneself -- just as the perception verbs of 114.a'
collapse with the opinion verbs, the relation between think-type and

seem-type expressions being too well-established to need elaboration here (note, e.g., methinks/meseems as assertion weakeners
in earlier ENGLISH). But verbs denoting effort, as try and attempt,
while probably mid-scalar, are universal non-neg-transporters,
as are true verbs of communication.

It is well known that the ANCIENT GREEK verb phēmi 'I say'
takes a preceding negation interpreted as within its scope -- ou
phēmi, lit. 'I don't say,' corresponds to 'I say...not,' or 'I deny'
(LAT. nego). Indeed, phēmi is often cited as a prime case of the
classicists' "anticipatory negation," e.g. by Smyth (1920: 610). But,
as Fournier (1946) points out, the "subjective" phēmi expressing
conviction of judgment is opposed to other, "objective" GREEK
verbs of saying, eipein~ erein and legein, which emphasize the
linguistic act itself. Unlike the others, it governs the infinitival
complementizer characteristic of GREEK verbs of the opinion/
belief class, and indeed is even glossed (secondarily) as 'think,'
'deem,' or 'suppose' in GREEK lexicons: "comme [phēmi] ex-
prime avant tout le jugement convaincu, la notion d'énonciation est
facultative" (Fournier 1946:13). It is not surprising, then, that it
shares with its syntactic and semantic associates of the opinion
class their ability (not visited upon other GREEK verbs of saying)
to transport negs.

Some observed occurrences of ENGLISH say similarly admit
of judgmental rather than communicative readings and likewise
trigger NT. 121.a is from a letter to Dr. Joyce Brothers (note
the sense imposed by the continuation), while 121.b is due to
Cattell (1973: 635), who notes that our intuition that the negative
arises in the lower clause is confirmed by the availability of the
corresponding negative parenthetical (121.c), diagnostic for application of NT:

    121. a. I'm not saying she actually has affairs with other men --
              at least I don't think she does.
        b. I wouldn't say Sally is pregnant.
        c. Sally isn't pregnant, I wouldn't say.

The would-modified trigger in 121.b,c tends to support the observation of Polly Jacobson that NT as a rule is easiest over stative
verb occurrences, and is echoed by a similar contrast in HEBREW,
where communication verb omer transports negatives only in a
complex with hayiti 'would':

    122. a. Ani lo omer lexa la'azov.
             'I'm not telling you to leave.' (no NT reading)

122. b. (Ani) lo hayiti omer lexa la'azov.
          'I suggest that you not leave.' (lit., 'I wouldn't tell
                                                  you to leave')

Causatives, like other IF-verbs, should not raise negs out of
their (entailed) complements; thus the causative element blocks
transportation over persuade and convince despite their incorporated NT verb (cf. Lakoff 1970) of belief (with persuade that) or
intention (with persuade to). Yet Jespersen glosses GREEK ou
sumbouleúo, lit. 'not persuade,' as 'dissuade,' i.e. 'persuade...
not' (1917: 53). The BASQUE verbal phrase buruan sarazi 'convince' (lit., 'put in the head of') also permits NT. These predicates, however, may only constitute an apparent counterexample,
since they may more accurately be said to convey advise or re-
commend, focusing more on the opinion transmitted than on the
result intended or achieved. The GREEK verb is in fact often
rendered 'advise,' as in Smyth's NT example,

123. ou sumbouleúon strateuesthai
      sumbouleúon mē strateuesthai   'advising not to march'

For discussion of other apparent counterexamples to the scalar
hypothesis, and its extension to the quantificational values, see
Horn 1975 and to appear.

Negative transportation, then, is a widespread phenomenon and,
pace Cornulier (who claims of the set of NT predicates "leur unité
est insaissable parce qu'elle n'est pas" (1974: 55-6)), a coherent
one. It is not universal, however, as many languages do not meet
the required structural conditions or establish insurmountable
barricades in the path of transporting negatives. The negative
element in AZTEC, for example, is always initial, while complementizers in PALAUAN are impermeable by any material from
the lower clause. On the other hand, in addition to the languages
mentioned in this section, Rick Wojcik and Robert Van Valin inform
me that NT is well-established in BRETON and LAKOTA, respectively, and Martin Mould has observed that although students
in UGANDA are under constant discouragement in the schools
against contaminating their GANDA with NT constructions, assumed to be a foreign import from ENGLISH, the efforts appear
to be in vain — and not surprisingly, when we learn that NT
flourishes in related inland languages like LUYIA, GUSII, and
SOGA, in the absence of any direct contact with ENGLISH
influence.

Both the epistemic mid-scalars, referring to the truth of a pro-position or the likelihood of an event, and the deontic mid-scalars, referring to the goodness or desirability of an act or event, are predicates of opinion -- opinions of the mind or of the heart. One may believe that God exists, believe in God, or believe in (the desirability of) mud baths; asked for our opinion on the election of Porky Pig, we can reply that it's a great idea.

Nor is this a property of complement-embedding mid-scalars alone. Indeed, as Cornulier (1974) insists, a comprehensive account of the phenomenon of "negative transportation" should not treat as coincidental with NT the fact that even in single-clause sentences, negation of mid-scalar (opinion) verbs and adjectives tends to be interpreted as contrary rather than contradictory: to say that one doesn't like (or doesn't want) ice cream is -- on the primary reading -- to express dislike (or rejection), although no lower-negative source is available. Whether such a comprehensive account can unite these mid-scalar phenomena and retain an ex-planation of the properties of the NT cases which seem to demand a grammatical solution (see above and Horn 1975) is a puzzle which awaits solution.

5.   Embedded Negation and Clause Structure

5.1 NT and complementizer type

The last aspect of negation to be considered in this study is the nature of a constraint against negation in non-finite embedded clauses. The first manifestation of this constraint arises in con-nection with cases in which the application of NT is mysteriously blocked or impeded when the lower negative belongs to a finite clause.

While 124. is acceptable in DANISH (Jespersen 1917: 54),

124.   Saa vil jeg aldrig ønske, at du maa blive gift.
       'Then I wish that you would never get married.'

its literal ENGLISH gloss — 'I would never wish that you would get married' -- does not permit the lower-neg reading. In general, as the contrasts in 125. and 126. indicate,

125.   a. I don't/never wish to see you again. (=wish not/never to)
       b. I don't/never wish that I will see you again. (≠ wish I won't/
                                                          never will)

126. [I've never seen a purple cow,]
    a. I never hope to see one. (=hope never to)
    b. I never hope that I will see one. (≠ hope I never do)

the lower-neg reading for negated main clause hope and wish are possible over the infinitival complementizer in the a. sentences but not over the finite clauses of their b. counterparts. (Notice in passing that while hope is not a NT predicate in ENGLISH, it does (like wish) permit "never-transportation" out of an infinitival complement.)

NT is not quite blocked by the finite fa complementizer in MALAGASY, as we observed in 111., but the raised-neg versions of 127.a,b are felt to be odd (although acceptable on the irrelevant, external reading of the negation), whereas the infinitival clauses governed by semantically related verbs freely release their negatives in 127.c,d:

127. a. Tsy mino aho [fa ___ lasy ny mpianata]
       "not believe I   that"
       'I don't believe the students left.'

    b. Tsy maniry aho [fa ___ ho strana ianao]
         "desire"   "will cure you"
       'I don't desire to cure you.'

    c. Tsy nampoisiko   [___ ho tonga ianao]
         "expected-by-me"   "come"
       'I don't expect you to come.'

    d. Tsy mikasa [___ hanao   izany   (intsony)] aho
         "intend"   "will-do that(pron.) any-longer"
       'I don't intend to do that (any longer).'

    e. {?Tia   tsy   hanao }
        { "want not will-do" } izany (intsony) aho
        { Tsy te-hanao   }
       'I don't want to do that (any longer).'

Even more strikingly, NT is not only permissible but virtually obligatory over tia 'want' which in fact tends to reduce to a proclitic and merge with the lower verb, as seen in 127.e.

A related fact is the case of ANCIENT GREEK phēmi mentioned in the previous section: the only GREEK verb of saying which governs the infinitive, rather than the finite hoti and hōs complementizers, is also the only one permitting "anticipatory negatives," as in

128. Ou phēmi ienai.
"not I-say to-go"
'I say that I'm not going/ I deny that I'm going.'

5.2 The embedded negation constraint

Many languages not only permit extraction of negatives more freely out of non-indicative clauses but come close to mandating it under those circumstances. This is often the case for subjunctives as well as infinitival complements. Martinon's 1927 FRENCH grammar observes that 129.a has taken over (accaparé) the sense of 129.b , "qui ne se dit pas."

129. a. Je ne veux pas que vous sortiez.
'I don't want you to leave.'

b. Je veux que vous ne sortiez pas.
'I want you not to leave.'

Cornulier (1973), in reporting Martinon's judgment, differs from it in degree but allows that the latter is perhaps felt as awkward to the extent that it is seen to be synonymous with the former.

A corresponding asymmetry is found in SWAHILI. Both 130.a and 130.b are grammatical, but the latter, with unraised neg, is not only "stronger" (as is its indicative counterpart in 109. above) but downright peculiar, except when uttered as a response to the query, "What do you want to do?"

130. a. Sitaki kwenda.   'I don't want to go.'
b. Nataka nisiende. 'I want not to go.' (lit., 'that I not go')

As will have already been observed in the glosses, the same constraint holds in ENGLISH. Givón includes, among other examples of "the greatly restricted distribution of negatives as embedded within various grammatical contexts" (1975: 85-90), the examples

131. a. I want (? not) to work.
b. I made him (? not) fall off the cliff.
c. He continued (? not) to work.

(Elsewhere in the paper Givón emphasizes the pragmatic nature of the principles responsible for these restrictions and their reversibility in context.)

The functional approach suggested by Martinon and Cornulier implicitly extends to the cases in 132.a, none of which have a corresponding higher-neg paraphrase and all of which are acceptable as they stand.

132. a. He tried/managed/learned/promised/preferred
              not to smoke.
       b. ? He was able not to smoke.
       b'. He didn't have to smoke.
       c. It was possible for him (not) to smoke.
       c'. It was not necessary for him to smoke.

132.b is strange in the same way as <u>He wanted not to smoke,</u> and although its neg cannot transport (<u>able</u> being a weak scalar), there is a paraphrase based on the dual equivalence discussed in Sec. 3.1.1 Perhaps in the manner of Baker's polarity hypothesis the (near) equivalence of 132.b to 132.b' renders the former otiose and therefore awkward; perhaps also a similar explanation could extend to the awkwardness of negation in 131.b, given that <u>make not</u>= <u>not let.</u> In any event, 132.c — with a similar paraphrase in 132.c' using its own dual -- is impeccable.

Worse still for this ecological approach, embedded negation allegedly tolerated only when there is no viable alternative, are the facts in 133.:

133. a. I hope {*not } to see you again.
                  { never }
       b. I persuaded him not to smoke.
       c. I advise you not to smoke.
       d. She seemed/appeared not to have heard.

133.a should presumably be good with <u>not</u> and bad with <u>never,</u> since only the latter has a raised-neg paraphrase. Yet the facts are clearly the reverse. <u>Persuade</u> permits an embedded negation, despite the (quasi-)paraphrasal relation between <u>persuade not</u> and <u>dissuade.</u> And <u>advise, seem,</u> and <u>appear,</u> all bona fide NT predicates, and all governing non-finite complement clauses, nevertheless freely embed negatives.

One generalization that might be defended (although not here, space preventing) is that the predicates manifesting the constraint against embedded negatives (ENC) are just those which have a high affixal potential cross-linguistically, affixation representing the terminal point of clausal non-independence (beyond the way-stations of subjunctive mood, infinitival complementation, and intermediate

stages of verb-raising or clause-union (cf. Aissen 1974)). These
verbs include intentionals like <u>want</u> and <u>intend</u>, causatives like
<u>make</u> and <u>let</u>, periphrastic modals like <u>able</u> and <u>have to</u>, and as-
pectuals like <u>begin</u> and <u>continue</u>.

Predicates within these classes seem to differ unpredictably in
the extent to which they are subject to the ENC. Thus with the
ENGLISH "quasi-modals" (Paul Chapin's term) of 134., we find
the following pattern:

134. a. He is apt/? supposed/*going/*about not to smoke.
      b. ? He used not to smoke.

Examples attested by Jespersen (1917: 50) with negation under in-
choative <u>get</u> --

135. I soon got not to care. (Galsworthy)
      If one were to live always among such rich colours, one
      would get not to see them.

strike at least my own modern ears as strained; the ENC is perhaps less vigorously enforced in British novels, where <u>able not</u> is
also not uncommon.

Even for the paradigm cases of ENGLISH ENC verbs, however,
the constraint is relaxed to the point of extinction when the verb
embeds a full (<u>for-to</u>) infinitival complement, or even a structure
with intervening main clause object (raised from embedded subject
position), the ENC applying only when the embedded subject is deleted by EQUI-NP (coreferential subject) deletion. Thus, while
we have seen that the ENC is responsible for the awkwardness of
such unlike-subject cases as Martinon's subjunctive construction
in 129., and is also invoked in full infinitival constructions in many
languages (e.g. BAMBARA, where -- Claudia Corum informs me --
the "for-to" <u>kɔ</u> complementizer, unlike finite <u>ko</u>, does not freely
permit negatives in embedded clauses which it introduces), we find
a sharp contrast between ENC-attributable violations in 136.a and
the acceptable sentences in the 136.b group, parallel but for the
greater "clausiness" of the complement or the degree to which it
is marked as a separate syntactic (and perceptual) entity.

136. a. ?? I want/expect/intend/mean/need not to smoke.
      b.   I want/expect/intend/mean/need (for) you not to smoke.

Correlating with the indiscernability of the biclausal structure
of the a. sentences -- the proposed source for the applicability of

the ENC -- we note that contraction of <u>want</u> + <u>to</u> > <u>wanna</u> with non-
negated complements marks the same property of clausal nondis-
creteness: such contractions are, of course, impossible in b.,
even without negation, and even when the intervening object has
been removed by relative clause, question, or topic formation.
In fact, this same inverse correlation between contractibility and
negative placement can be invoked to demonstrate that ENC, like
contraction (cf. G. Lakoff 1970a), is a global rather than superficial phenomenon:

  137. a. You are the one I want to marry.
        ≃ i.   I want to marry you.
          ii. I want you to marry.

        b. You are the one I want not to marry.

While both readings of 137.a are possible, the salient one -- and
the <u>only</u> one available under contraction to <u>wanna</u> -- is the i. gloss,
with <u>you</u> as object of <u>marry</u>. With embedded negation as in 137.b,
on the other hand, the ENC blocks this interpretation and only the
version with <u>you</u> as subject of <u>marry</u> emerges.

    It should be noted that apparent violations of the ENC like that
in 138.a might be analyzed as a type of "constituent negation" as
in the monoclausal 138.b, however that is to be handled (cf. Sec.
1.1 above):

  138. a. I want not to be pitied but to be censured.
        b. I want not the salami but the pepperoni.

By the same token, Dina Crockett informs me that RUSSIAN NT
predicate <u>dolžen</u> 'should' does not embed negatives -- except in the
contrastive structure <u>dolžen ne</u> (VP) <u>a</u> (VP') which corresponds to
138.a.

    More troublesome is the greater acceptability of negatives under
<u>want</u> when associated with relatively complex or "heavy" comple-
ment structures. Thus as against the ENC-violating 139.a, we do
not strenuously object to 139.b:

  139. a. ??I want not to mention this again.
        b.   I want not to have to mention this again.

The b. sentence tends to be read with a pause after <u>want</u>.

    Another asymmetry which may be laid at the door of the ENC
is presented by the fact that predicates like <u>lazima</u> 'it is necessary'

which govern the subjunctive in SWAHILI, as in 140.a, do not cooccur with the negative (-si-) subjunctive (140.b), at least not
without the awkwardness of the related 130.b.

140.   a. Lazima tuvisome.
           'It is necessary that we read them.'

       b. ? Lazima tusivisome.
           'It is necessary that we not read them.'

       c. Tusivisome.
           'We are not to read them / Let's not read them.'

       d. Ni marufuku tuvisome.
           'It is forbidden that we read them.'

Instead, the sense must be expressed by a monoclausal negative
subjunctive (governed, à la R. Lakoff 1968, by the abstract performative of ordering) as in 140.c or by the neg-incorporated
paraphrase of 140.d.

A parallel is found in the ENGLISH let's construction:

141.   a. Let us not go.
       b. Let's (not) go.
       c. Don't let's go; Let's don't go.

Causative (i.e. permissive) let is an ENC predicate, so that 141.a
yields only marginally the literal reading 'Allow us to stay;' it may,
however, convey the suggestion to stay, although the uncontracted
form is marked on this interpretation. Contracted let's, as in 141.b,
is only a suggestion, and freely permits embedded negation. This
idiomatic construction is perceived, like SWAHILI 140.c, as containing but one surface clause (that defined by go) and is thus not
subject to the ENC; the fact that let's is here viewed as an illocutionary force marker rather than as an autonomous verb + object
is signalled by the colloquial paraphrases in 141.c, to which
Jespersen and Bolinger have drawn attention.

5.3 ENC in causative constructions and a typology of alternatives

We have just noted that let is subject to the ENC. The fuller
paradigm in 142. bears out the correlation of the ENC and clausiness:

142.   a. I allowed/forced/ordered him not to smoke.
       b. I let/made/had him (? not) smoke.

The causatives in a. embed negatives more easily than those in b.,
since the embedded clauses in the former group are more set off
by the overt complementizer to and thus relatively more independent.

The operation of the ENC in 142.b, however, is far weaker
than in languages which display true clause-union (C-U) in causative constructions, involving the raising of the lower verb and its
attachment to the upper causative either as an integral lexical
complex (as in FRENCH and ITALIAN) or by lexical incorporation
(as in TURKISH and JAPANESE); cf. recent works by Aissen
(1974), Cole, Hyman and Zimmer and others for discussion and
argumentation.

The crucial contrast in FRENCH is that between the fully biclausal (143.a.) which can embed a negative and the effectively
monoclausal 143.b. which cannot:

143.   a. Il m'a forcé à (ne pas) venir.
           'He forced me (not) to come.'

       b. Il m'a fait (? *ne pas) venir.
           'He made me (? not) come.'

       c. Il ne m'a pas fait venir.
           'He didn't make me come.'

The entire faire venir construction may be negated, as in 143.c,
but it may not be broken up by (lower clause) negation.

The C-U nature of the 143.b case is manifested by clitic placement. In general, an underlying lower object can only cliticize
onto its own verb, as 144.a shows. With faire-causatives, however, the clitic — like the negative — may not rent the faire +
INFIN construction asunder but must instead attach to the front
of the complex, as seen in 144.b:

144.   a. Je veux/peux manger le gâteau.
           'I want to/can eat the cake.'

       a'. Je veux/peux le manger. }
           *Je le veux/peux manger. } 'I want to/can eat it[the cake].'

       b. J'ai fait manger le gâteau à Jean.
           'I had Jean eat the cake.'

144. b'. *J'ai fait le manger à Jean.⎫
           Je l'ai fait manger à Jean.⎬ 'I had Jean eat it[the cake].'

The facts in ITALIAN are similar, as is indicated by the contrast between the marginality of negation in 145.a and its un-
acceptability in the C-U example (145.b).

145. a. Maria fa si che Gino (?non) mangiare.
      b. Maria fa (?*non) mangiare Gino.

         'Maria makes Gino (not) eat.'

But the distribution of clitics is defined more squishily. Verbs like
those in 146.a, which (significantly) introduce their infinitival
clauses with prepositions, never (in at least some dialects) permit
lower object clitics to "hop" to the main clause. Intermediate
cases are those in 146.b, where hopping is optional, although
(mirroring the more complete development in FRENCH, where the
starred forms of 144.a' used to occur freely) less frequently than
in older ITALIAN; Don Giovanni's immortal "Io mi voglio divertire"
would be likely rendered <u>Voglio divertirmi</u> by his would-be modern
successors. In 146.c, a true C-U causative, hopping is obligatory.

146. a. Cerco/Spero di mangiarlo.
          (vs. *Lo cerco/spero di mangiare)
          'I try/hope to eat it.'

      b. Voglio/Posso mangiarlo. ≃ Lo voglio/posso mangiare.
          'I want to/can eat it.'

      c. *Ho fatto mangiarglielo. (but: Glielo ho fatto mangiare.)
                                        DAT+ACC
          'I had him eat it.'

Earlier periods of Italian also permitted the reduction of the
'want' verb to <u>vo</u> and its affixation to the predicate embedded under
it, as we observed in (127e) from Malagasy. As we would expect,
such reduction triggered both obligatory clitic hopping and strong
application of the ENC:

147. a. Lo vo sapere. but Voglio/*Vo saperlo.
          'I want to know it.'

      b. Voglio/*Vo non sapere.
          'I want not to know it.'

When a sentence contains both clitic and negative we find that the clitic tends not to hop when the negative remains behind: the degree of clausal non-independence required to trigger clitic-hopping is sufficient to activate the ENC. This is to some extent the case in ITALIAN (?<u>Lo voglio non sapere</u>), but even more strikingly in Osvaldo Jaeggli's dialect of SPANISH, where the following judgments are found:

148. a. (?)Quiero no comerlo. } 'I want not to eat it.'
      b. *Lo quiero no comer. }

      c.   No quiero comerlo. } 'I don't want to eat it.'
      d.   No lo quiero comer. }

The dative in 149. is symptomatic of C-U in CZECH, as Jindrich Toman has argued, and we find that negatives cannot intervene:

149. Karel nechal Petrovi (??ne) škrabat brambory.
      "Karl had Peter (+DAT) not peel   potatoes"
      'K. had P. (not) peel potatoes.'

The synonymous EQUI construction (accusative <u>Petra</u> for <u>Petrovi</u> in the above) does not involve C-U and does not trigger the imposition of the ENC; embedded negatives are at worst slightly awkward.

The violations are even clearer in languages with morphological causative markers, as in TURKISH:

150. Kasab-a   et-i   kes-tir-(me)-dik
      "butcher-DAT meat-ACC cut-CAUS-not-PAST"
      'We had (didn't have) the butcher cut the meat.' (but cf.
      discussion below)

In such languages, negation is often marked affixally as well, but generally the negative marker is restricted so as to occur outside the causative, i.e. more distant from the root, as in 150. The negative prefix (<u>ha-</u> or <u>si-</u>) or suffix (<u>-i</u>) in SWAHILI, for example, attaches to a verb stem which may be already causativized by the <u>-y</u> or <u>-iš</u>/<u>-eš</u> suffixes and is always external to the causative in scope.

KOREAN has both "clausal" and "lexical" causatives, as illustrated in 151.a and 151.b, respectively. Both permit external or wide-scope negation, but "there is no way to incorporate the negation of constituent sentences into lexical causative constructions" (Yang 1974:109-10); rather, as in 151.c, the biclausal alternative must be employed to express narrow-scope negation:

151. a. John-i Mary-lil   us - ke   (an)   ha - assta
                         "smile-COMP not CAUS-PAST"
         'John made (didn't make) Mary smile.'

    b. John-i Mary-lil (an) us -ki-assta (ki   ke +ha)
         'John made (didn't make) Mary smile.'

    c. John-i Mary-lil an us -ke ha -assta.
         'John made Mary not to smile.'[sic](e.g. by hitting her face)

We might note here that similar behavior is exhibited by the
marginal examples of C-U in ENGLISH with non-agentive let:

152. a. He let the rock (?not) go/fall.
     b. He let (*not) go (of) the rock.
     c. The rock was let (*not) go of.

153. a. He let the door (? not) open.
     b. He let (*not) open the door.
     c. The door was let (*not) open.

The status of 152.b, c as a causative related to 152.a in synchronic
grammar is brought into question by the fact, which came to my
attention through Geoff Nunberg, that one can let go of a wall but
hardly let a wall go.

How can CAUSE + NOT be expressed when it can't be done directly
with normal causative syntax (given the prevalence of C-U causatives
ensuring imposition of the ENC)? More generally, how can we express the content of V + NOT when V is an ENC predicate? As we
have seen, one option to which languages often have recourse is the
employment of a synonymous non-ENC construction, as we have
seen in examples from FRENCH, SWAHILI, ITALIAN, CZECH, and
KOREAN. With ENC verbs which are also NT triggers, as the 'want,'
'intend' class(es), the negative may be raised to the upper clause
with no cognitive meaning change.

Another course taken is to incorporate the offending negative into
either the upper verb (as in 154.b) or the lower (as in 154.c):

154. a. ? I made him not leave.
     b. I prevented him from leaving.
     c. I made him stay.

Incorporation is also illustrated by the attested LATIN sentences of
155., into a higher verb in a. and a lower quantifier in b.:

155. a. Nolo/Nego te amare.
          'I don't wish to/I deny that I love you.'

      b. Dico nihil esse pulchrius... (cf. ?*Dico non te amare)
          'I claim nothing to be more beautiful...'

There is, however, an apparently arbitrary constraint operative in
ENGLISH which blocks the co-occurrence of negative incorporation
and raising from embedded subject position, thereby ruling out the
b. sentences of 156. analogous to LATIN 155.a

156. a. {I believed him }(?not) to be a scoundrel.
          {He was claimed}

      b. *{I doubted him } to be a scoundrel.
          {He was denied}

(The extension of this constraint is explored in unpublished work
by Polly Jacobson and myself.)

One more escape route from the ENC relies on the existence of
the dual equivalences previously cited. Thus, corresponding to
the awkward 154.a we find the perfectly acceptable I didn't let him
leave; cf. the discussion of 132. above.

Some languages, however, apparently not content with the
CAUSE + NOT paraphrases at their disposal, have developed another
wrinkle. ITALIAN, to express the content of 157.a, treats the
higher-neg 157.b -- superficially identical to the unambiguously
wide-scope negation in the FRENCH 143.c -- as ambiguous, the
preferred reading being the prima facie odd one, (ii):

157. a. ?*Paola mi fa non dormire.
          'Paola makes me not sleep.'

      b. Paola non mi fa dormire.
          (i) 'P. doesn't make me sleep.'
          (ii) 'P. doesn't let me sleep.' (=157.a)

      c. Fammi dormire!
          (i) 'Make me sleep!'
          (ii) 'Let me sleep!'

Cornulier (1974) uses this lexical ambiguity of non-NT class
causative fare (or, otherwise viewed, scope ambiguity of the negation, since non fare in 157.b = non lasciare, the dual equivalent of
fare...non) as a reductio of arguments for a lexically governed

rule of NT, opting for a treatment of all putative NT cases as lexically ambiguous in the same way (weak vs. strong _croire_, _vouloir_,
etc.), but notes that the same ambiguity of _fare_ surfaces in imperative contexts as well (in 157.c), where once again context determines intended or construed meaning (the (i) reading a request for
a sleeping pill or lullaby, (ii) for a cessation of football practice in
the next room).

In general, though, the permissive or "weak" reading surfaces
only or especially under negation of the causative element. This
occurs in CZECH, where 158. — the apparent contradictory of unnegated 149. — has the narrow scope ('prevent') reading for negation preferred.

158. Karel ne nechal Petrovi škrabat brambory.
      'K. didn't let/?*make P. peel potatoes.'

This ambiguity is the rule in languages with morphological causative markers, like the Biblical HEBREW cases cited by Cornulier
(from J. Heller); negation in TURKISH 150. can thus be semantically internal, though syntactically external, to the strong causative. Similarly, Colette Craig informs me, in JACALTEC:

159. Mač^h ix tx'ah-a   xil kope wet   an
      "not she wash-FUT clothes me(DAT) 1stp."
      'She didn't let/make me wash the clothes.'

— where the unnegated equivalent (minus mač^h) is only a strong
causative. In all these cases, we find that the external reading of
the negation (='not make') is possible, perhaps even dominant, in
direct denials of a positive causative assertion.

A similar, if more complex, phenomenon is presented by Gragg
(1972: 80) for AMHARIC. The negation of the "second causative," as in

160. āl -i̱ - ās - ballā-n̄ - m   āl - u
      "not-I-CAUS-eat-me-NEG said-they"
      '(lit.) They said, I will not cause me to eat.'

— literally "to fail to cause someone to do something" — actually
signifies 'not to permit someone to do something.' Then, since
(by the rules of "semi-indirect discourse"), "I" in the above gloss
is coreferential to the 'they' subject but "me" designates the speaker,
and given the idiomatic value of "to say not to permit" as 'to prevent,' we have the conveyed meaning of 160.: 'They prevented me
from eating.'

It might be appended that this lexical (or scope) ambiguity of causatives, while it strikes a naïve ENGLISH ear as peculiar, is not without its ENGLISH reflexes: Bacall admits to Bogart in "Dark Passage," "I thought I had a good life here, but your going away doesn't make it seem good anymore." But it should not be assumed that all languages with affixal causatives permit (or force) 'prevent' readings to emerge under external negation: in SWAHILI and GUARANÍ, for example, the neg-incorporation route must be travelled.

In keeping with the E/O expressibility asymmetry of Sec. 1.3, it appears that the negation of the weak scalar value of permission never allows a 'not cause' (or 'let...not') interpretation; Paola non mi lascia dormire has only the 'prevent' sense.

Some languages -- among them ESTONIAN, TAGALOG, and GREEK -- provide a separate negation, often labelled "emphatic," for dependent non-indicative clauses, thus in effect opting out of the ENC. ESTONIAN yields the following display:

161. a. Ta ei   pea tulema.
         "he not must come"
         'He doesn't have to come.' [pea, unlike its conditional
         peaks 'should,' is not a NT-verb]

     b. Ta peab {*ei } tulema.
                { mitte}
         'He has to/must not come.'

     c. Ma usun et ta {ei   } tule.
                      {*mitte}
         'I believe that he isn't coming.'

Tedeschi (1975) notes that TAGALOG's "general negative" hindi gives way to the "special negative" huwag in "IMPERE" contexts (imperatives, hortatives, and optatives) -- whether embedded or free -- but not in embedded finite clauses. Indeed, the emergence of split infinitive negations in ENGLISH -- I want to not come -- may be viewed as an attempt to develop a strong negative like that of ESTONIAN or TAGALOG, one not subject to the ENC; not-come functions here as a quasi-predicate in its own right, the object of my desire.

Smyth (1920) points out that in ANCIENT GREEK sentence pairs like that of 123. above, "ou with the principal verb may be equivalent in sense to mē with a dependent infinitive;" the mē negation, often

termed "subjective," is a negative of rejection or refusal, contrasting with the "objective," propositional ou of main or subordinate
indicative clauses (cf. LATIN non vs. ne).

It is perhaps the persistence of suppletive negatives into MOD-
ERN GREEK (ðen having supplanted ou via intermediary ouðen:
see Jespersen 1917:16) which explains the otherwise surprising appearance of a negative intervening between a C-U causative and
lower verb in 162., due to Brian Joseph:

162. a. ðen   ekana   na   fiɣi   ton yani
        "NEG₁ I-made SUBJUNC.leave John(ACC)"
        'I didn't make John leave.'

     b. ekana   na   mi   fiɣi ton yani.
        "I-made SUBJUNC.NEG₂ leave John(ACC)"
        'I made John not leave.'

The acceptability of negation in 162.b may also be attributable to
the lesser degree of clause-unionization in the GREEK causative
as compared with, say, FRENCH: Joseph points out that while
lower object clitics do not attach to the lower verb in GREEK (any
more than in ROMANCE), they can't hop up either -- filling the
fourth hole in the paradigm defined by ITALIAN (151.a-c.).

Finally, some languages -- including those in the UTO-AZTECAN
and MAYAN groups -- permit no embedded non-finite negation what-
soever, even to the result of introducing what appear to be pernicious ambiguities.

As far as why the ENC exists, in the great majority of languages
which are subject to it: I would suggest that the function of negation
is to deny a proposition or claim, or to substitute an inverse act
for the one under consideration. The less the dependent clause
looks and acts like a sentence -- the less it seems to express a
complete proposition, thought, claim, or act -- the less negation is
admitted without corresponding discomfort, if it is admitted at all.

5.4 Concluding remarks: not to put too fine a point on it

I hope it has become clear in this necessarily brief survey to
just how great an extent the understanding of communicative intent
is essential to an understanding of the properties of negation in
natural language; nor is the converse far from the case either.
To take some random instances, the "Notes and Comment" section
from the 6/14/76 New Yorker's "Talk of the Town" (p.24) illustrates

the presuppositional markedness of negation in its discussion of
such political devices as the "Negative Boast" (Nixon's immortal
"I'm not a crook," the contemporary version of the player queen
Hamlet thought protesteth overmuch) and the "Negative Thrust"
("a candidate's denying that he is, say, a machine politician as a
way of implying that his opponent is precisely that"). Four weeks
later in the same periodical, Veronica Geng presents a nice exploi-
tation of NT, the ENC (with want), and the weakening effect of the
ensuing logical double negation in this excerpt from her piece
"More Mathematical Puzzles and Diversions" (p. 30):

> There is nothing mysterious about speech; it is merely
> a way of expressing thoughts without having to write them
> down. Yet the incredible verbal sequence known to logicians
> as the Maze of Venus quickly dispels the illusion that
> spoken language is a plausible means of communication.
> Here is the classical formulation of this sequence:
> A: I don't think you want to see me more often.
> B: That's not true.
> A: Then you do want to see me more often.
> B: I didn't say that. I just don't not want to see you
>   more often.

Or more succinctly, we could cite the adroit disclaimer due to
Marivaux: "Madame, je ne voudrais pas ne pas être votre amant."

Acknowledgment

In addition to the references cited in this paper, I would like to
express my indebtedness to the following people for their assistance
with data from the following languages: Claudia Corum for BASQUE
and BAMBARA; Jindrich Toman for CZECH; B.G. Madsen for
DANISH; Marilyn Vihman for ESTONIAN; Mark Mandel for ESPE-
RANTO; Delphine Perret for FRENCH; Brian Joseph for Greek;
Dina Crockett, Aryeh Faltz and Yael Ziv for HEBREW; Francesco
Antinucci and Larry Hyman for ITALIAN; Colette Craig for JACAL-
TEC; Ed Keenan for MALAGASY; Dina Crockett and Bill Darden for
RUSSIAN; Osvaldo Jaeggli for SPANISH and GUARANÍ; Mrisho
Kivugo and Carol Scotton for SWAHILI; and Ayhan Aksu and Jorge
Hankamer for TURKISH. I would also like to acknowledge Barbara
Abbott, Dwight Bolinger, Peter Cole, Benoît de Cornulier, Polly
Jacobson and Geoff Nunberg, along with numerous others (and
especially the members of the Language Universals Project and
of the Berkeley Summer 1975 linguistics workshops, where much
of this material was presented in embryonic form), for their useful
comments and ideas, too many of which I hope I have not ignored.

BIBLIOGRAPHY

Aissen, J. 1974. Verb raising. Linguistic Inquiry [LI] 5. 325ff.

Atlas, J. 1974. Presupposition, ambiguity, and generality; a coda to the Russell-Strawson debate on referring. Unpublished ms., Pomona.

Bach, E. 1968. Nouns and noun phrases. Universals in linguistic theory, ed. by Bach and Harms. New York.

Baker, C.L. 1970. Double negatives. LI 1. 169ff.

Behre, F. 1967. Studies in Agatha Christie's writings. Göteborg.

Bolinger, D. 1968. Postposed main phrases: an English rule for the Romance subjunctive. Canadian Journal of Linguistics [CLS] 14. 3ff.

Borkin, A. 1971. Polarity items in questions. Papers from the Seventh Regional Meeting of the Chicago Linguistic Society, 53ff.

Buyssens, E. 1959. Negative contexts. English Studies 40. 163ff.

Carden, G. 1970. A note on conflicting idiolects. LI 1. 218ff.

Cattell, R. 1973. Negative transportation and tag questions. Language 49. 612ff.

Cornulier, B. de. 1973. Sur une règle de déplacement de négation. Le Français Moderne 41. 43ff.

_____. 1974. La négation anticipée: ambiguité lexicale ou effet de sens? Unpublished ms. Marseille-Luminy.

Farmer, J.S. and W.E. Henley. 1891. Slang and its analogues, vol. II. Reprinted by Arno Press, New York, 1970.

Fauconnier, G. 1975. Pragmatic scales and logical structure. LI 6. 353ff.

Fournier, H. 1946. Les verbes "dire" en grec ancien. Paris.

Fowler, H.W. 1926. Modern English usage. Oxford.

Gaatone, D. 1971. Etude descriptive du système de la négation en français contemporain. Genève.

Givón, T. 1971. Dependent modals, performatives, Bantu subjunctives, and what not. Unpublished ms. UCLA.

_____. 1975. Negation in language: pragmatics, function, ontology. Working Papers on Language Universals [WPLU] 18. 59ff.

Gragg, G. 1972. Semi-indirect discourse and related nightmares. CLS 8. 75ff.

Greenberg, J.H. 1963. Some universals of grammar with particular reference to the order of meaningful elements. Universals of Language, ed. by J.H. Greenberg, 73-113. Cambridge, Mass.

_____. 1969. Some methods of dynamic comparison in linguistics. Substance and Structure of Language, ed. by J. Puhvel, 147-203. Berkeley and Los Angeles.

Grice, H.P. 1968. The logic of conversation. Unpublished ms., excerpted in Speech Acts/Syntax and Semantics 3, ed. by Cole and Morgan. New York, 1975.

Harries, H. 1973. A note on double negation and modals as main verbs. WPLU 11. 211ff.

Haynes, A. 1933. Negation in Don Quixote. Austin.

Henry, D. 1967. The logic of St. Anselm. Oxford.

Hooper, J. 1975. On assertive predicates. Syntax and Semantics 4 (ed. by Kimball). New York.

Horn, L. 1970. Ain't it hard (anymore). CLS 6. 318ff.

_____. 1971. Negative transportation: unsafe at any speed? CLS 7. 120ff.

_____. 1972. On the semantic properties of logical operators in English. Unpublished dissertation, UCLA. (Page references to IULC reprint, Bloomington, 1976.)

_____. 1973. Greek Grice: a brief survey of proto-conversational rules in the history of logic. CLS 9. 205ff.

_____. (to appear.) Remarks on neg-raising. Syntax and Semantics 9 (ed. by Kimball). New York.

Jackendoff, R. 1961. An interpretive theory of negation. Foundation of Language [FL] 5. 218ff.

Jespersen, O. 1917. Negation in English and other languages. Selected writings. London.

_____. 1924. The philosophy of grammar. Reprinted by Norton, New York, 1976.

Joly, A. 1967. Negation and the comparative particle in English. Québec.

Karttunen, L. 1970. On the semantics of complement sentences. CLS 6. 328ff.

Klima, E. 1964. Negation in English. The structure of language, ed. by Fodor and Katz. Englewood Cliffs, N.J.

Labov, W. 1972. Negative attraction and negative concord in English grammar. Language 48. 773ff.

Lafitte, P. 1962. Grammaire basque (Navaro-Labourdin dialect). Bayonne.

Lakoff, G. 1970. Linguistics and natural logic. Semantices of natural language, ed. by Davidson and Harman. New York, 1972.

_____. 1970a. Global rules. Language 46. 627ff.

_____. 1970b. Pronominalization, negation, and the analysis of adverbs. Readings in English transformational grammar, ed. by Jacobs and Rosenbaum. Waltham, Mass.

_____. 1974. Syntactic amalgams. CLS 10. 321ff.

Lakoff, R. 1968. Abstract syntax and Latin complementation. Cambridge, Mass.

_____. 1969. A syntactic argument for negative transportation. CLS 5.140ff.

Lasnik, H. 1972. Analyses of negation. Unpublished dissertation, M.I.T.

Lawler, J. 1974. Ample negatives. CLS 10. 357ff.

Li, C. 1975. Miss-a-little: an unexpected case of ambiguity. Paper presented at California Linguistic Association meeting, San Jose.

Linden, E. 1975. Apes, men, and language. New York.

Lindholm, J. 1969. Negative raising and sentence pronominalization. CLS 5. 148ff.

McGloin, N.H. 1976. Negation. Japanese generative grammar/ syntax and semantics (ed. by Shibatani) 5. New York.

Martinon, Philippe. 1929. Comment on parle en français. Paris.

Oh, C-K. 1971. On the negation of Korean. Language Research 7. 45ff.

Paradis, M. 1974. La place de la négation syntaxique en français. Recherches linguistiques à Montréal, vol. II.

Poutsma, H. 1928. A grammar of late modern English. Groningen.

Prince, E. 1976. The syntax and semantics of NEG-raising, with evidence from French. Language 52. 404ff.

Rivero, M-L. 1971. Mood and presupposition in Spanish. FL 7. 305ff.

Ross, J.R. 1973. Slifting. The formal analysis of natural languages, ed. by Gross, Halle and Schützenberger. The Hague.

Russell, B. 1905. On denoting. Mind 14. 479ff. (Anthologized everywhere.)

Schmerling, S. 1970. A note on negative polarity. Unpublished ms. Champaign-Urbana.

Smith, S. 1969. Meaning and negation. Doctoral dissertation, UCLA. Reprinted by Mouton, The Hague, 1975.

Smyth, H.W. 1920. A Greek grammar. New York.

Tedeschi, P. 1975. Logical operators in Tagalog. University of Michigan Papers in Linguistics 1.4.

Traugott, E.C. 1975. A history of English syntax. New York.

Yang, I-S. 1974. Two causative forms in Korean. Language Research 10. 83ff.

Zimmer, K. 1964. Affixal negation in English and other languages. Word Monograph No. 5. New York.

Some General Characteristics
of Interrogative Systems

RUSSELL ULTAN

ABSTRACT

Devices used to mark questions and certain types of tab questions
in 79 randomly chosen languages are examined in terms of features
of intonation and word accent, order and segmental elements as
well as parameters of expected response (yes-no, information,
alternative questions) and of grammatical domain (word, sentence).
Intonation in yes-no questions typically consists of a rising or higher-
pitched or -stressed terminal contour, always in prepositional languages and nearly always in postpositional. The same is true of
information questions but to a lesser extent. Question words generally tend to be marked by higher pitch or greater stress, particularly in SOV languages. Yes-no-question inversion results in VSO
constituent order. In information-question inversion question words
are almost always sentence-initial in SVO and VSO languages, while
in SOV languages there is a tendency to maintain neutral declarative
order. These favored orders reflect topicalization of the verb in
yes-no questions and of the nonverbal constituent in information
questions. Question particles are usually sentence-initial or -final,
the latter especially in SOV languages. There appear to be no
general restrictions on cooccurrence of question particles with
either interrogative inversion or question words. Most tag questions contain negative markers. The response to a confirmation-
requesting tag question generally mirrors the affirmative or negative
mode of the declarative portion of the question, thus reaffirming its
truth value.

Reprinted from Working Papers on Language Universals 1,
November 1969, 41-63.

CONTENTS

1. Introduction

Although a respectable number of illuminating studies on the role of intonation in particular languages (e.g. Bolinger 1957 or Halliday 1967) and in languages in general (see Bolinger 1962, Gantzel 1966, Hermann 1942, Lieberman 1967) have appeared in print, relatively little has been published on the subject of interrogative structures, which encompass not only intonational but also other devices employed to express interrogation: particles, question words, tags, word order, etc. A special exception to this lacuna in the literature is Bolinger's (1957) detailed analysis of ENGLISH interrogative structures. The purpose of the present paper is to begin to fill this gap by presenting the results and conclusions derived from comparing the interrogative systems of 79 languages selected as randomly as possible in terms of geographical, genetic, and typological distribution, given the available descriptive data.[1]

Starting with certain observations we have made concerning the expression of interrogative concepts, we note for example that many languages make use of a terminal rising contour to designate a yes-no question, sometimes with, sometimes without other interrogative markers such as inversion of subject or object, interrogative particles, etc. Furthermore, all languages seem to have nonintonational devices for indicating questions. Certainly, at the very least, all languages mark information questions with interrogative words such as who, what, where, etc. Many label questions -- especially yes-no questions -- with special interrogative particles or affixes. Compare, for example, FINNISH ko (enclitic) in tuliko hän kotiin? 'did he come home?' with hän tuli kotiin 'he came home' or KONKOW -de in ?àmammájdy čedejem 'did you(pl.) see that man?' with ?àmammájdyhajemo čen 'you(pl.) saw that man.' The fact that interrogative particles usually occur either at the beginning of the clause (or enclitic to the initial constituent) or at the very end leads us to suppose some relationship between the particle position and the dominant type of constituent order for a given language. Similarly, interrogative words seem to occur most commonly in sentence-initial position, which may account for inversion in some types of information questions and which is

---

[1] All subsequent statistics and percentages are of course based on the size and internal distribution of the sample, a fact which should be retained when these are used in general statements in the body of this paper.

undoubtedly related to the general increase in topical emphasis
ordinarily associated with initial position in most or even all
languages. Probably most languages append tag questions to
declarative statements to request confirmation, as FRENCH n'est-
ce pas? or RUSSIAN pravda? (or né pravda?). Is this negative
expression of these tags characteristic of such questions? Many
modern European languages make use of standard inversion patterns to signal yes-no questions, and still other patterns for some
kinds of information questions. Compare not only ENGLISH did
he come home? or FRENCH est-il rentré chez lui? but also FIN-
NISH tuliko hän kotiin? or mitä hän teki? 'what did he do?' (vs.
hän teki sitä 'he did that'). How widespread is this use of inversion among languages in general? These and other observations
have led us to the more formal examination of interrogative systems
which has resulted in the exposition which follows.

In his study (1957) Bolinger begins by dividing the identifying
characteristics of interrogative utterances into four classes:
interrogative distribution (generally occurrence before a reply);
syntax (inversion, interrogative words, interrogative tags, and
other syntactic devices); interrogative intonation (predominance of
terminal rising or high pitch); interrogative gesture (eyebrows
lifted, head inclined forward, mouth left open at end of utterance,
etc.). Of these, we will consider primarily intonation and syntax,
distribution to a lesser extent, and gesture not at all. The latter
might best be treated under the heading of kinesic phenomena, but
the principal reason for excluding it is simply that little (in most
cases, no) descriptive material on the subject exists. Similarly
for distribution, its comparative neglect in most descriptions precludes the possibility of comprehensive generalization.

While other factors such as emphasis or nuances added to the
general interrogative theme (e.g. degree of familiarity between
speaker and hearer, degree of doubt, rhetoricity of the question)
characteristically produce variations in the form of interrogative
sentences (particularly in intonation), for the most part only the
major, more or less neutral types will be discussed here. The
assumption is that if these can be accounted for in terms of a few
simple variables, the remaining types may be accounted for by
additions to or deletions from the predicated norms of other features or feature complexes. Also omitted from consideration are
echo questions, repeated questions, rhetorical questions, and a
few other types, not because they are not pertinent to the subject
under investigation but again because insufficient data are available
for general comparison.

1.1 Classification of Q-features

There are a number of possible ways to classify interrogative (Q) features. One of these, Bolinger's, has already been briefly alluded to. In order to facilitate the organization of the material and the subsequent discussion, we propose the following classification:

1. Intonation -- including sentence and tag intonation as well as particle and interrogative word accent.[2] Take as examples interrogative sentence intonation in TUNICA lóta wiwánăn 'do you want to run?' (´= stress, ˇ = rising pitch -- indicative statements end in high register ultimas, quotatives in low ultimas); tag intonation in KHASI wa phii la da san katnikatni, ʔĕem 'oh, you have grown up so much, haven't you?' (vs. falling pitch on ultima for neutral declarative statement); interrogative particle (QP) accent in JAPANESE wakarima̓sita ka˅ 'did you understand?' (⌐ ¬ = raised pitch, ˅ = slight rise in pitch without lengthening syllable vs. Q-intonation in yes-no questions without QPs which comprises rising and lengthened ultima, and falling for normal declaratives); and interrogative word (QW) accent in SYRIAN ARABIC wĕnak hal-ʔiyyām mā hada bisūfak? 'where have you been these days, that no one sees you?' (´ = main sentence stress and highest pitch, wĕn 'where').[3]

2. Order -- including main constituent inversion, positional relationships of affix to stem and of tag, QP, or QW to clause or clause constituent, e.g. inversion in MALAY datangkah bapak nanti? 'is father coming later?' (lit. 'comes father later?' vs. normal declarative SVO order); Q-suffix in ASMAT tetámčenanóm 'shall we give him?' (tetám 'give,' -an Q-suffix); sentence-final tag in TAGALOG hindi mabait ang babae, ano? 'the girl isn't nice,

---

[2] These terms are used with their more or less conventionally accepted referents: intonation includes meaningfully contrastive sentence or clause terminal contours (comprising feature complexes of pitch, stress, duration, etc.; word accent includes features of pitch and/or stress (and/or duration) used to contrast question words (QW) or particles (QP) with corresponding nonquestion words.

[3] Other interesting interrogative devices based on phonological oppositions noted by Greenberg (1969: 32-34) in several languages are use of terminal glottalization and/or voicing to mark questions vis-à-vis voicelessness in the corresponding statements, or long final vowels versus short ones.

is she?;' clause-final QP in MANDARIN <u>nii bu pah laohuu ma?</u>
'aren't you afraid of tigers?' (<u>ma</u> QP); and sentence-initial QW
in GAELIC <u>ciod è rinn thu an diugh?</u> 'what did you do today?'

3. <u>Segmental elements</u> -- including interrogative particles
(and affixes), words, tags, examples of all of which are shown
above.

Cross-cutting this classification are two others which are
relevant to the discussion. The first of these concerns the <u>type of</u>
<u>expected response</u>: <u>yes-no</u> (YN) or any questions requiring a yes
or no reply, as in <u>do you live here?</u>; <u>information</u> (IN) or a question
containing a QW and requiring a more specifically informative
reply than a simple yes or no, as in <u>what did he say</u>?; alternative
(AL), or a question that poses, either explicitly or implicitly, two
alternative answers as in MANDARIN <u>nii mierge chu. chiuh bu chu.</u>
<u>chiuh a?</u> (lit. 'are you going out not going out tomorrow?' -- both
clauses simply juxtaposed), or SANGO <u>tongana mɔ tɛ ngunzá,</u>
<u>mɔ tɛ susu mélangé na ní wala?</u> 'when you eat greens, do you eat
fish mixed with them, or not?' (with sentence-final conjunction),
or JAPANESE <u>onazi desu ka, tigáimasu ka</u> 'is it the same or is
it different?' (both clauses marked by QP).

The second classification deals with a formal division of all
Q-features into those pertaining to clause or sentence as opposed
to those pertaining to word, in essence a morphology-syntax dichotomy. Thus, sentence and tag intonation, tag, QP, and QW
order, restrictions of co-occurrence (e.g. QP and QW in the same
clause) are clause features; others are word features. Semantically, this division generally reflects a corresponding focus of
interrogation on the entire proposition (clause) as against a particular referent (word).

In addition to the above-outlined organization of data, we expect
to find some correlations between Greenberg's basic order types
(1963) and certain Q-features, particularly those relevant to
constituent order. We therefore briefly summarize these for
the reader's convenience in following the presentation, along
with their proportionate representation in our sample. Languages
unidentified as to order type are not included in the percentage
figures.

1. Preferred order of simple declarative transitive sentences
with nominal subject and object:

	Percentage of sample
VOS	2.7
VSO	18.7
SVO	34.6
SOV	44.0
(4 languages unidentified)	

2. Prepositions predominant (pr)   46.7
   Postpositions predominant (po)   53.3
   (4 languages unidentified)

3. Relative order of nominal
   possessor (G) and possessed (N):

   GN   56.4
   NG   43.6
   (1 language unidentified)

4. Relative order of attributive
   adjectives (A) and head nouns (N):

   NA   53.8
   AN   46.2
   (2 languages unidentified)

1.2 Some questions to be answered

Returning to our earlier observations on the characteristics of interrogative systems, we are now in a position to formulate a number of specific questions which we will endeavor to answer within the framework described above.

1. Is a terminal rising contour or high pitch always associated with questions vis-à-vis some other contour (usually falling) marking simple declarative statements? Do YN, IN, and tag questions differ in this respect? If so, how?

2. Do QWs, QPs, and Q-affixes tend to occur in conjunction with high or rising pitch or prominent stress?

3. Do languages which normally have terminal falling contour on YNQs have obligatory terminal rising contour on such questions when interrogation is not marked in any other way?

4. Are there any significant distributional restrictions on co-occurrence of Q-intonation and QW-accent in INQs?

5. What is the relationship between Q-intonation and YNQs or INQs?

6. Is there any correlation between inversion as an interrogative device and some basic order type(s)? In YNQs? In INQs?

7. Is there any correlation between the clause position of QWs and basic order types?

8. Is there any correlation between position of QPs with respect to clause constituents or of Q-affixes with respect to stems and the basic order types?

9. Are there any restrictions of co-occurrence between Q-markers (QPs and Q-affixes) and QWs?

10. Are there any restrictions of co-occurrence between Q-markers and inversion?

11. What is the relationship between Q-markers and negative particles or affixes?

12. What is the truth value inference[4] of the anticipated reply to negatively or positively stated questions?

13. What is the relationship between indefinite substitutes (such as ENGLISH someone, somewhere, whatever, etc.) and QWs?

14. What is the relationship between relative or subordinating conjunctions and QWs?

15. Do interrogative pronouns always exhibit a human/nonhuman or animate/inanimate dichotomy?

2. Intonation

Among clause-level Q-features, intonation holds the first rank. Throughout the history of structural linguistics it has been debated whether intonational phenomena should be regarded as extralinguistic, marginal (e.g. DeGroot 1945, Martinet 1960, Rigault 1962), or on a par with other linguistic structural domains such as phonology or syntax (e.g. Pike 1945, Gleason 1955, Faure 1962). A principal

---

[4] I am indebted to Joseph Greenberg for suggesting this apt expression.

argument for including it in the proper domain of linguistics is
based upon the widespread contrast between a terminal falling and
a terminal rising contour representing a meaningful distinction
between an attitude of finality or conclusiveness and one of suspension, incompleteness, doubt, questioning, or the like on the part
of the speaker. It can also be argued that if this is a universal
dichotomy, it is essentially a human trait and, as such, has no
place in a strictly linguistic description. Nevertheless, it seems
to us that, even if it is universal, it does consist of a formal-
semantic covariance which constitutes a linguistic structure just
as much as does an opposition like boy-boys in ENGLISH.

Furthermore, although Q-intonation is often accompanied by
some other Q-marker (e.g. inversion, QP, etc.), most languages
(perhaps all?) also have Q-utterances distinguished from their
corresponding declarative utterances solely by means of Q-intonation.[5] Compare for example RUSSIAN vy čitáete knígu (statement)
'you are reading a book' and čitáeteli vy knígu (question by subject
inversion and QP), both with falling intonation, as opposed to vy
čitáete knígu? (question) with rising intonation.

2.1 YNQ-intonation types

Up to now we have spoken of Q-intonation and terminal rising
contour as though they were synonymous. This is not quite so.
While the rising contour is certainly the most frequently occurring
type of Q-intonation, there are others. In the present sample we
found some 15 additional contours among 24 of the languages
sampled, which can be further reduced to eight more general types,
as follows:

Type:	Example
1. slight terminal rise	Diola
slight terminal rise with length	Iraqi Arabic
2. terminal acceleration	Mandarin
3. higher pitch toward end of contour:	
higher ultima	Vietnamese
higher penult	Chontal
higher pitch on last stressed vowel	Bashkir
rising toward last stressed vowel	Hebrew

---

[5] The general prevalence of rising or higher-pitched contours to
mark YNQs would appear to be directly related to early infant acquisition of this Q-feature as noted by Lewis (1936), Leopold (1953),
and others in Bellugi and Brown (1964).

Type:	Example
4. higher sentence register	Sango
higher sentence register with final drawl	Mandarin
5. higher ultima followed by falling	Aramaic
extra-high ultima falling to mid	Hausa
6. higher pitch toward beginning of contour:	
higher initial syllable	Western Desert
higher stressed vowels	Finnish
7. higher stressed vowels at any point	
within contour	Guaraní
8. terminal fall	Chitimacha, Fanti,
	Grebo

It will be noted that terminal rise for YNQs and the first seven
types, with the possible exception of type 2,[6] all share one feature:
higher pitch (register or glide) or more prominent stress at some
point in the contour, usually towards the end, as opposed to falling
or low-pitched ultima in simple declarative statements. This
leaves us with type 8, for which all examples have been given.
This YNQ-intonation is clearly incompatible with all others, especially in CHITIMACHA,[7] where falling Q-intonation contrasts
with rising declarative intonation. As for FANTI, I have no doubt
that falling Q-intonation is the norm, but I wonder if a higher sentence register type does not also exist, as has been described for
closely related TWI. While rising Q-intonation is not shown for
YNQs in GREBO, there is a tag with that intonation. Of the three
type 8 languages, FANTI and GREBO are tonal, i.e. make use of
morphological tone, belong to the same basic order typology (SVO/
po/GN/NA), and are genetically related (KWA group, Niger-Congo);
CHITIMACHA apparently does not make use of morphological tone,
but has a basic order typology similar to the other two (SOV/po/
GN/NA). Furthermore, several non-type-8 languages, such as
DIOLA, MANDARIN and VIETNAMESE, are also tonal languages.
Thus, it seems that tonal structure in itself is insufficient to account
for the deviant interrogative contour of type 8.

Of the 53 languages for which we have any information on YNQ-
intonation, 71.7% have rising, 34% have higher pitch of one sort
or another, and 5.7% have falling contour only. Another 5.7%

---

[6]MANDARIN, the only language so described, also has a standard terminal rising Q-intonation.

[7]I am grateful to Dorothea Kaschube for bringing the CHITI-
MACHA situation to my attention.

have both rising and falling types. All languages with falling Q-intonation are postpositional; languages with rising contour or higher pitch are evenly distributed typologically and otherwise.

2.2 Tag intonation types

Q-intonation on tags which, as we have noted, are principally YNQs confirms our findings. Only four languages out of 29 on which information is available do not have rising or higher pitched Q-intonation as a favored tag type.

2.3 INQ-intonation types

INQ-intonation is almost equally divided between rising or higher pitched on the one hand and falling finals on the other: 47.9% for the former and 52.1% for the latter, based on information from 36 languages (62% of those with rising or higher intonation also have falling INQ-types). While INQs are associated with a much higher incidence of rising finals than corresponding declarative statements, nothing in the typological or other distributions of languages with rising finals versus those with falling finals leads us to assume any constant relationship between certain order types and one or the other of the prevalent Q-intonations.

2.4 Q-accent and Q-intonation

Of the 17 languages for which QWs with some distinctive Q-accent were described, nine permitted co-occurrence with Q-intonation, seven did not, and information was lacking for one. Thus, no general restriction exists on co-occurrence of Q-accent and Q-intonation in the same sentence, nor of QP-accent and Q-intonation, although here the information is even more sketchy, only seven languages with QP-accent being represented.[8]

3. Inversion

An interrogative device which is somewhat less widespread than intonation is the inversion of one or more constituents of the sentence with respect to their normal declarative order. Basically, inversion is of two kinds, generally manifesting formally different patterns and usually representing different degrees of interrogative redundancy. These correspond to the YN-IN dichotomy.

---

[8]GREBO and SANGO might be added, but it is not clear whether we are dealing with particles or tags.

3.1 YNQ-inversion

On the basis of the present sample YNQ-inversion appears to
be a rather uncommon interrogative device, occurring in only
seven languages (six of which are modern European) out of 38.
An eighth, SYRIAN ARABIC (primarily a VSO language with an
alternative SVO order),[9] has an emphatic inversion of the resultant type VOS, but this is not restricted to interrogative sentences
nor does it seem to impart an element of interrogation to Q-sentences.
One often speaks of subject or object inversion with reference to
YNQs. In view of our findings, a better term might be verb inversion, since in the languages employing this device the simplest
possible statement for reordering the constituents (considering
only S, V, and O) is always: remove the verb and place it at the
beginning of the sentence.[10] These languages include SVO, SOV,
prepositional and postpositional types; thus the inverted order
will always be VSO. However, it should be noted that the sample
contains only one such SOV language, HUNGARIAN.[11] In languages
having periphrastic verbs the finite auxiliary always occupies the
V slot in inverted YNQs, the main verb always following (although
not necessarily directly) the subject. Five of the seven languages
with YN-inversion also make use of QPs in YNQs. Of these only
FRENCH est-ce que is mutually exclusive with verb inversion in
YNQs; FINNISH, HUNGARIAN, MALAY and RUSSIAN have no
such restriction.

3.2 INQ-inversion

INQ-inversion undoubtedly stems directly from the predilection
among many languages for placing QWs at the beginning of the

---

[9]Charles Ferguson views modern spoken SYRIAN ARABIC as
primarily a SVO language (p.c.), but we have classified it as VSO
on the basis of Cowell's statements on constituent order.

[10] This statement applies when S and O are nominals; when one
or both are pronominal, it may or may not be valid— compare, for
example, FRENCH l'a-t-il vu? where the order with pronominal O
is OVS.

[11] There is some question whether HUNGARIAN favors the SVO
type over SOV. As with SYRIAN ARABIC, we have accepted the
information given in the source on these matters. However,
Sauvageot's description appears to be based at least in part on
literary rather than colloquial language, which may account for
the difference in prevalent order types.

sentence, regardless of basic order type. SOV languages, however, are less prone to this tendency than other types (56.5% of 21 SOV languages vs. 74% of 46 non-SOV languages). The resultant inversion is particularly striking for virtually all languages when the QW is the object of the verb, since object in sentence-initial position is not a favored declarative type for most languages (see Greenberg 1963, especially 76-77). Beyond the preference for having QWs in initial position, there is no particular correlation between the relative ordering of the remaining non-initial sentence constituents, e.g. OSV or OVS, and the basic order types. In fact, for a number of these languages alternative orders are acceptable.

3.3 Inversion and sentence-initial position

This general tendency for most languages to favor sentence-initial QWs is essentially the same phenomenon as the earlier one on initial position of the verb in YNQ-inversions. In YNQs the whole sentence is normally subject to questioning. In most languages — probably in all -- the finite verb is the core of the simple sentence. Indeed, it and usually it alone may constitute a minimal major sentence. In INQs the QW substitutes for the item subjected to questioning. The focal point in both YNQ and INQ is what is being questioned. It is therefore no coincidence that the questioned items occupy or tend to occupy the generally emphatic initial position in the sentence. For noninterrogative examples of this emphatic position, compare him, I saw! or wilfully, he shot the policeman. One particularly striking example of this kind of emphatic shift appears in ENGLISH INQs like who from? or what with? where what is generally viewed as a strictly prepositional language exhibits postpositions.

4. Tags

Another common interrogative device which comes under the heading of clausal types is the tag question. Tags in a given language may be at least operationally defined as characterized by some or all of the following features. They are always clitic, usually enclitic, to a sentence, most often declarative. In this respect they differ from other longer Q-utterances which always may and generally do occur independently (i.e. as sentences, of course, not independent of the discourse). In a way tags may be likened to independent clauses in complex sentences. Thus, a tag question like John is married, isn't he? could just as well be paraphrased is it not so that John is married? Some tags consist of single words like you saw him, eh?, others are phrases, e.g. GERMAN nicht wahr? or clauses as in the previous ENGLISH

example. The great majority of tags, whether words, phrases or
clauses, are accompanied by intonation patterns characteristic of
YNQs. But the addition of a tag to a declarative sentence converts
the entire construction into a question, thus functioning much as a
QP does.

4.1 Binary choice tags

The tags we have investigated may be classified in several ways.
The kind of reply expected may be a binary or multiple choice.
The binary type falls into two classes: 1) a request for confirmation of the statement portion of the question, in essence a YNQ;
2) an alternative tag, in which a correlative conjunction or other
similarly functioning constituent is tacked onto the statement, as
in FANTI iríkò anée 'are you going, or [what]?' (anée 'or').

Class 1 tags   which almost always anticipate yes answers or
are meant to be taken as rhetorical may be further subdivided into
a number of semantic subclasses:

1. Negative constructions like the FRENCH prototype n'est-ce
pas? or KHASI wa phii la da san katnikatni, ʔeem? 'oh, you have
grown up so much, haven't you?' (ʔeem negative), in which the
tag consists of or includes a formal negative marker.

2. Positive constructions usually based on a copula or existential predicate like ROTUMAN fā ta pot pau, ne? 'the man is very
clever, isn't he?' (ne predicative particle), or THAI khun ca pay
Hua Hin, chây măy? 'are you going to Hua Hin?' (chây măy 'is it...?').

3. Interjections like ENGLISH eh? or HAUSA za kà tàfi, ko?
'will you leave, huh?' (ko in non-Qs is a clause introducer 'even if,
although').

4. Miscellaneous types such as RUSSIAN ty jegó slúšil, právda?
'you heard him, didn't you?' (although actually this appears to be
analogous to type 2 above, especially in view of the normal zero
copula here), or TAGALOG hindi maganda ang damig, ano? 'the
dress isn't pretty, is it?' (ano 'what') similar to Oxonian silly fellow, what? and one or two others not readily classifiable with the
three principal types noted.

The binary choice tags are almost always sentence-final. The
sole exception we have found is HEBREW (ISRAELI) halo?, a type 1
tag which occurs initially. However, HEBREW also has another

type l tag which occurs in final position. A very few languages
allow alternative tag positions, e.g. KANNADA tānē, normally
final, may follow other nonfinal constituents on which interrogative
attention focuses in nominal predications, or FRENCH n'est-ce pas
in n'est ce pas qu'il est venu hier? and le chef — n'est-ce pas — est
arrivé hier.

While information on co-occurrence patterns of positively or
negatively stated declaratives and subsequent tags and also on the
anticipated responses to such questions is not abundant, it will
be interesting to examine those cases for which we do have data.
Logically, any of the three variables in a given situation -- declarative, tag, and response -- may be stated either positively or negatively resulting in eight possible types:

Tag	Positive		Negative	
Declarative	Positive	Negative	Positive	Negative
Response P	1	2	3	4
Response N	5	6	7	8

Actually, we have data on types 1, 3, 4, 6, 7 and 8. Of these 3 is
by far the most common, followed by 1. Types 4 and 7 are ques-
tionably represented by one language each. Restated in tabular
form:

Type	Declarative	Tag	Response	Number of Languages
3	P	N	P	10 + 5 (?)
1	P	P	P	5 + 1 (?)
6	N	P	N	2 + 1 (?)
8	N	N	N	1
4	N	N	P	1 (?)
7	P	N	N	1 (?)

As to the truth value inference of the response vis-à-vis the question, these seem to fall into two general types:

1. The response reaffirms (or echoes) the truth value of the
   declarative portion directly, regardless of the value of the
   tag (types 1, 3, 6 and 8).

2. The response reaffirms the truth value of the declarative
   portion by appropriately answering the tag (types 4 and 7).

4.2 Multiple choice tags

Multiple choice tags are, at least in the present sample, entirely
limited to the how about...? type, which differs in two important
respects from binary choice tags: it is usually clause-initial and
requires a reply which is generally not restricted to two alternatives
but calls for additional information, or a yes or no followed by a
complementary statement. This kind of tag often comprises a special introductory word followed by a main clause constituent which
has been singled out for attention and removed from its normal
context, a procedure which points to a kind of emphatic displace-
ment to clause- or sentence-initial position, similar in effect to
the near-universal preference for sentence-initial QWs in INQs
(see Sec. 3.2 and 3.3). Examples of this type are FINNISH entäs...
(see above for example), AGTA á in á ya arikavwat-en O ey? 'say,
friend, what about the purse there?' or TURKISH ya in bu kadar
yetişir, diyorsun, ya yetişmezse? 'this much will be enough, you
say; and what if it isn't enough!' The TURKISH tag is particularly
interesting because it also functions as a sentence-final tag of the
confirmation-requesting n'est-ce pas? type: kösede bir fırın vár
ya? 'there's a bakery on the corner, right?'

5. Interrogative Particles

After intonation, interrogative particles are the most widespread
device for marking YN clauses or sentences, and INQs to a somewhat lesser extent. Both structurally and semantically they differ
from QWs, which are most often in constituency with words or
phrases and focus interrogatively on more particular referents.
Particles are generally in constituency with the entire clause,
thus tending to focus interrogation on the proposition as a whole,
like Q-intonation. Sentence-final QP wéndé in GBEYA geʔdéa a
wa ʔdú go wa bá hɛ̧́ ɛ̧́ wéndé? 'is it the dregs that they dish up and
give to me?' questions the entire utterance, while QW o in o á tɔ̃́ à
há mɛ̃́ ondé? 'who told you?' questions the subject referent only.
In connection with this it is worth noting that Q-affixes (not of the
information type as, for example, IRAQI ARABIC š- 'what' in
šítriid? 'what do you want?') are almost invariably appended to
verb stems or predicate words as a manifestation of their relevance
to the core of the clause or sentence. Use of the term particle here
is strictly speaking inaccurate; a few languages have Q-affixes
which perform the same function as QPs in other languages. In
some descriptions it appears likely that classification of such elements as affixes rather than particles is inexact. Compare, for
example, PIRO where the "Q-suffix" -he occurs in word-final

position and may be added to any major word class: verb, noun,
adjective, adverb. On the other hand, in a language like KONKOW
the Q-element de can be analyzed only as a modal suffix added to
the verb before the inflectional endings for number and person.
On the whole, however, Q-affixes are relatively rare. We therefore use the term particle here to refer to an uninflected word,
clitic or free, or an affix which fulfills a function similar to that
of the true particles discussed in this paper.

5.1 QPs and Q-accent

QPs sometimes occur with special pitch or stress features
analogous to Q-intonation. The LITHUANIAN QP ar̃ carries rising pitch on the vocalic r; the TURKISH enclitic mi, except after
the present tense, is preceded by a stressed syllable regardless
of where word stress would normally appear; JAPANESE ka occurs
with rising pitch in YNQs (vs. falling or level in rhetorical questions); MANDARIN ma, as it were, induces a generally higher level
of sentence intonation ending in a "slight drawl." Of the 22 languages for which we have definite information, nine have such
features and 13 do not. Distribution of these languages is quite
random. Although the evidence is not conclusive due to the small
size of the sample, there is clearly a better than chance probability
that QPs will be accompanied by some kind of Q-accent.

5.2 QP-position

While QPs may occur after almost any sentence constituent in
some languages (e.g. TURKISH), in most languages the position
is or tends to be fixed. QPs often follow or are enclitic to clause
constituents (in 42 languages plus nine with suffixes out of a total
66). Some of these normally follow the first constituent of a clause.
In quite a few cases the QP is sentence-initial and in a relatively
large number it is clause- or sentence-final. If we group those
which are enclitic to the clause-initial constituent with the clause-
initial ones, a justifiable procedure in terms of the distributional
restriction applying to enclitics, we end with an almost equal distribution of languages with initial vs. final QPs and a relatively
small residue of nine languages with QPs which occur neither
initially nor finally (but note that five of the nine also have QPs in
initial or final position). As Greenberg (1963) has already noted,[12]

---

[12] Our statement differs slightly from Greenberg's. He summarizes the situation as follows: "With well more than chance
frequency, when question particles or affixes are specified in

there is a direct relationship between the position the QP occupies
in the clause and the basic order type of the language: when the
QP is clause-initial (or enclitic to the initial constituent), the verb
almost always precedes the object in a normal declarative statement; when the QP is final, the verb may precede or follow the
object -- final QP tends to be much more common in postpositional
languages (of 36 such languages QPs are sentence-final in 61.1%,
sentence-initial in 16.7% and have other positions or are lacking
in the remainder).

5.3 QPs and INQs

Logically, one would expect to find QPs only in YNQs, since
INQs by definition already contain at least one clearly marked
interrogative device (one or more QWs). As a comment on redundancy in language it is worth noting that the odds are practically
even for this kind of situation: of 42 languages QPs occur with
INQs or YNQs in 25 languages and only with YNQs in 23 (6 languages
have both types). Furthermore, the genetic, geographic and typological distributions of both types are quite random.

5.4 Negative QPs

In our discussion of tags we noted that the negative binary choice
predominates. GAELIC, IRISH, BASHKIR, PIRO and possibly
ROTUMAN have QPs which are at least formally identical with
negatives. Such "particles" have also been described for BENGALI,
FULA and VIETNAMESE, but their distributions and functions in
these languages seem to point more toward a classification as tags.
In all cases we lack information on the anticipated response to such
questions.

6. Interrogative Words

Interrogative words are characteristic of all languages. That
is, all languages have interrogative substitutes for nouns and a

---

(ftnt. 12 cont.)
position by reference to the sentence as a whole, if initial, such
elements are found in prepositional languages and, if final, in
postpositional." This is generally in accord with our findings,
except that, of the languages sampled for this feature with QP
initial or enclitic to the sentence-initial constituent, 24% are
postpositional.

number of adverb-like words or phrases expressive of locative,
temporal, enumerative, manner, purpose and other functions. A
few languages have interrogative verb substitutes like WESTERN
DESERT ya·ltji- in wati ya·ltjinu? 'the man did what?' or MANDA-
RIN gannma in nii gannma lao ku? 'what are you crying for?;'
and a few have interrogative interjections such as TONGAN inē
'what about it?;' and a very few have QW-affixes like the prefix š-
in IRAQI ARABIC šdataakul? 'what are you eating?' or the ROTU-
MAN suffix -s with nouns as in hanues 'which country?'

6.1 Human/nonhuman in Q-pronouns

The number and kind of distinctions which QWs may or may not
reflect in terms of those existing elsewhere in a given language
vary considerably from language to language, but at least one contrast appears to be nearly universal: Q-pronouns show a human/
nonhuman or, in a few cases, an animate/inanimate dichotomy.
The only exceptions we have noted are KHASI, SANGO and LITHU-
ANIAN. In KHASI either of two allomorphs of the interrogative
base may represent 'who?' or 'what?' but there is some tendency
to prefer one, -ey, for the human substitute. In SANGO 'who?' is
normally rendered by zo wa 'what person?' but is occasionally
represented by the pronoun yɛ 'what?' Senn's (1966) description
of QWs in LITHUANIAN appears to be thorough, but apparently
no alternative grammatical device distinguishes a personal from
an impersonal Q-pronoun — only the semantics of the context.

6.2 QW-accent

Although data on QW-accent are scarce, 20 languages have fortis
stress or sentence stress, high pitch, rising contour, or a combination of stress and high pitch on the QW. These languages are
evenly distributed.

6.3 QW-position

As mentioned earlier (see Sec. 3.3) languages of all types tend
to locate the QW in sentence-initial position, although this is less
common among languages with a basic order of SOV; such was the
case in 73.4% of 53 languages. Sentence-final position as a QW-
norm is characteristic of only one language, KHASI. However, in
25% of the languages QWs apparently retain the normal position of
the constituents for which they substitute or, in a very few cases,
occupy other specialized positions in the sentence (e.g. preceding
the verb phrase only in GUJARATI).

6.4 Indefinites, relatives and QWs

Somewhat peripheral to the question of QWs but clearly related
is the connection between indefinite pronouns, adjectives, adverbs,
etc. and relatives or subordinating conjunctions on the one hand
and QWs on the other. Indefinite words are at least in part either
formally identical with or related to QWs. Thus, ENGLISH somewhat, whatever are derived from what (but something, someone
are not based on what, who). The only possible exceptions to this
statement in the present sample appear to be SAMOAN and ROTU-
MAN, both POLYNESIAN languages with highly structured definite-
indefinite systems quite distinct from the corresponding QWs.

The generally sketchy information we have on relatives (in many
instances none at all) tends to support the view that they share
a relationship with QWs similar to that of the indefinites in most
languages.

7. Summary Statements

Listed below are a number of statements that recapitulate briefly
our findings on interrogative systems. Note that they are valid for
the 79-language sample used in this study.

Intonation

1. YNQ intonation types consisting of rising terminal, higher
pitched or special stress contours are found in nearly all languages:
always in prepositional, almost always in postpositional languages.
Therefore, nonoccurrence of a rising terminal, higher pitched or
special stress YNQ-contour implies a postpositional language.

2. The presence of tag questions with nonrising (or higher
pitched or stressed) contours implies also tag questions with rising
etc. contours.

3. There is a considerably better than chance probability (a little
less than 75% in the present sample) that an INQ-intonation type
consisting of rising terminal, higher pitched or special stress contour may occur in languages of all basic order types, although this
is somewhat less likely for postpositional languages.

Word Accent

It should be noted that the following statements concerning word
accent on Q-elements are much more than any of the other summary
statements, since the evidence on which they are based is quite limited.

1. There is a slight tendency for QPs to occur with higher pitch or prominent stress in SOV languages.

2. QWs tend to occur with higher pitch or prominent stress in languages of all basic order types. This tendency is somewhat more marked in SOV languages.

3. There are no typological restrictions on the co-occurrence of QWs with Q-accent (higher pitch, etc.) and Q-intonation (rising terminal contour, etc.) in the same INQ nor on the co-occurrence of QPs with Q-accent and Q-intonation in the same question.

Order

1. The presence of YNQ-inversion implies a basic order type in which subject precedes verb.

2. YNQ-inversion implies a resultant VSO order. In periphrastic constructions the finite auxiliary always occupies the V slot of the inverted constituent order and precedes the main or non-finite verb.

3. If a language has INQ-inversion, QWs are almost always sentence initial. [13]

4. While languages of all basic order types may have INQ-inversion, SOV languages are less likely than others to have it; they tend more to retain the basic constituent order of simple declarative sentences in INQs.

5. QWs tend to occur in sentence-initial position in languages of all types; the ratio in favor of this is approximately three to one. However, the ratio in SOV languages is only about one to one. [14]

6. Further, with regard to statements 2 and 5, the emphatic nature of sentence-initial position is the key to both types of inversion. In YNQ-inversion the verb carrying the burden of emphasis is initial; in INQ-inversion the QW subject to emphasis is initial.

---

[13] This confirms Greenberg's statement (1963: 83).

[14] This is in general agreement with Greenberg (1963: 83), but we have found exceptions to the absolutely stated first part of his Universal #12: "If a language has dominant order VSO in declarative sentences, it always [emphasis mine] puts interrogative words or phrases first in interrogative word questions;" -- notably in SAMOAN and in SANGO.

7. Most QPs occur in sentence-initial (or enclitic to the initial constituent) or in sentence-final position. QPs almost always occur finally in SOV languages and show a greater tendency to occur initially in other types.

8. Q-affixes in YNQs are relatively rare. Q-suffixes are found principally in SOV languages.

9. There appears to be no general restriction on the co-occurrence of QPs and YNQ-inversions. The sole exception to this in the present sample is FRENCH in which the two devices are mutually exclusive in YNQs.

10. Binary choice tags are almost always sentence-final, multiple choice tags sentence initial.

Segmental elements

1. QWs and QPs may or may not co-occur in INQs with about equal frequency in languages of all types.

2. In nearly all languages some indefinite substitutes are formally identical with or related to the corresponding QWs. This is very likely true of relative substitutes to a slightly lesser degree (insufficient data on this at present).

3. Q-pronouns in almost all languages show a formal contrast which reflects human/nonhuman or more rarely animate/inanimate opposition.

4. QPs occur in all types of languages with roughly equal frequency.[15]

5. A Q-affix appended to a predicate word implies a YNQ; one appended to a QW implies an INQ.

6. About 75% of languages of all types use tag questions which consist of or contain negative particles or affixes.

7. Most of the available information on negatively or positively stated Q-responses is on confirmation-requesting tag questions.

---

[15] Note that Greenberg's statement (1963: 82) excluding occurrence of QPs in VSO languages is not supported by our investigation. VSO languages like AGTA, CHONTAL, DIOLA, SCOTTISH GAELIC and others do make use of QPs.

Barring doubtful types 4 and 7 noted in Sec. 4.1, we may tentatively state that the response to a confirmation-requesting tag question implies a like (in terms of negative or positive statement) declarative portion of the question, thus reaffirming the truth value of the former.

APPENDIX I

Individual language Q-feature synopsis

The chart which follows summarizes the basic Q-feature and order types for the languages sampled in this study. It does not condense all the data available to us, only what we deem to be most generally relevant. In some cases where information on a particular order type or Q-feature was not specifically described, it was possible, with varying degrees of certainty, to resolve the nature of the item on the basis of textual examples and/or by piecing together discrete bits of information included in other (non-Q) sections of the description. We have added ? in cases of considerable doubt. Additional symbols used here are:

acc	accent
aff	affix
f	1. falling (intonation); 2. sentence-final (position)
h	higher pitch or stress
i	sentence-initial or enclitic to initial constituent
int	intonation
inv	inversion
o	other (position, accent, etc.) than the predominant type(s) for a given Q-feature
p	prefix
pos	position
r	rising terminal contour
s	suffix
+	yes
-	no
/	either...or...

Generally where two of these appear under the same rubric, e.g. TAG: pos: i/f, int: r/o, the corresponding sequence is observed for both features, i.e. the language has an initially occurring tag with rising intonation and a final tag with non-rising intonation.

Language	Order	Type	Int YN	Int IN	Inv YN	Inv IN	TAG pos	TAG int	QP pos	QP acc	QP aff	QW pos	QW acc
Agta	VSO pr	NG NA			-	+	i/f	r/o	i			i	
Albanian	SVO pr	NG NA	r	r/f			i	r	i			i	
Amharic	SOV po	GN AN	r	r/f	-	+	f	r				o?	
Arabic, Iraqi	VSO pr	NG NA				+			f/o			i/o	h
Arabic, Syrian	VSO pr	NG NA	r	h	-	+	f					i	h
Aramaic, Neo-	SOV pr	NG NA	r/h	h								i/o	
Aranda	SOV po	GN NA							i?/f				
Asmat	SOV po	GN NA	h	h	-	-			f		p/s	o	h
Bashkir	SOV po	GN AN	h	h	-	-			f?			o	h
Basque	SOV po	GN NA	r?		-				f			i?	
Bengali	SOV po	GN AN	r/h	r/f			f	r	o	o		o	h
Buriat	SOV po	GN AN	h	h	-	-			f	o	s	o	h
Burmese	SOV po	GN AN							f/o			i?	
Chichewa	SVO pr	NG NA											
Chinese, Mandarin	SVO pr	GN AN	h	h	-		f		f	o		o	r
Chitimacha	SOV po	GN NA	f	f		+			f?	o			
Chontal	VSO pr	NG AN	h	f	-	+			i			i	
Diola	VSO pr	GN NA	r	r			f					o	
English	SVO pr	GN AN	r	r/f	+	+	f	r	f	o		i/f	o/h
Ewe	SVO po	GN NA											
Fanti	SVO po	GN NA	f	f			f/o	h/o	f	o			
Finnish	SVO po	GN AN	f/h	f/h	+	+	i/f	h	i	o		i	h/o
French	SVO pr	NG NA	r	r/f	+	+	i/f	h/r	i	o		i	o/r
French, Louisiana	SVO pr	NG NA	r	f	-	+			i	o		i/f	o/r
Fula	SVO pr	NG NA	r	f	+	+	f	r				i	
Gaelic, Scottish	VSO pr	NG NA	r/h	f	-	+			i			i	o
Gbeya	SVO pr	NG AN	r	r			f		f	h		i	

Language	Order Type	Int YN	Int IN	Inv YN	Inv IN	TAG pos	TAG int	QP pos	QP acc (r/o)	QP aff	QW pos	QW acc
Grebo	SVO po GN NA	f		-	+	f	r	f/*if/o	r/o		i	
Guarani	SVO po GN AN	h	h/o	-	+	f?	r	i			i	o
Gujarati	SOV po GN AN	r	f	-	-	f?	h				o	
Gunwinggu	SOV pr NG NA			-	+						i	
Hausa	SVO pr NG NA	h	h/f	-	+	f/i	h/o	i			i	
Hebrew	VSO pr NG NA	r		-	+	f/i					i	o
Hidatsa	SOV po GN NA?			-							i	
Huichol	SOV po? GN AN?										i?	
Hungarian	SOV po GN AN	h		+	+			f			i	
Irish	VSO pr NG NA			+	+			i?			i	
Jamaican Creole	SVO pr GN AN	r	f	-	+	f	r	f	r		i	
Japanese	SOV po GN AN	r	f	-	+	f	r	f/o			o	h
Jaqaru	GN AN	h	h	-				f		s	i	
Kannada	SOV po GN AN	r	f/h	-		f	r	f			i	
Karok	GN							i				
Khasi	SVO pr NG NA	r/h	r/h	-	+						f	h
Klamath	GN AN	r/f						i			i	
Konkow	SOV po GN AN	f/r	f/h	-	+			i	o	s	i	
Kurku	SOV po GN AN							f			i/o	o/h
Lithuanian	SVO pr GN AN			-	+			i	r		i	
Malagasy	VOS? pr NG NA			-	+			i/o			i	
Malay	SVO pr NG NA	r		+	+	f/i	r	o			i	
Mongolian, Khalkha	SVO po GN NA			-	-			f			o	
Nyangumata	SVO? AN	r		-		f	h				i?	h
Ojibwa	SVO po GN AN			-				i		s	i	
Ossetic	SOV po GN AN				+						i	

*discontinuous QP, part initial, part final

Language	Order Type	Int		Inv		TAG		QP			QW	
		YN	IN	YN	IN	pos	int	pos	acc	aff	pos	acc
Panjabi	SOV po GN AN	r				f	r				i?	
Persian	SOV pr NG NA										i	
Piro	SOV po GN AN	r	r/f					i			i	
Quechua	SOV po GN AN			-	+?	o	r				i	
Rotuman	SVO pr NG NA			-?	-	f		i			o	
Rumanian	SVO pr NG NA	r		+	+	f	r	i			i	h/o
Russian	SVO pr NG AN	r	f	+	+	f	r	i	o		i	o
Samoan	VSO pr NG NA	r?						i			o	
Sango	VSO pr NG NA	r/h	f	-	-	f	r	f	r		o	
Squamish	VSO pr NG AN							i			i	
Tagalog	VOS pr GN AN	r	f	-?	+	f	r	i	o		i	
Tajik	SOV pr NG NA					f	r?	i				
Telugu	SOV po GN AN	r	r	-	-	f		f	r		o	r
Tetelcingo	SVO pr NG NA	h			+			f			i	
Thai	SVO pr NG NA	r		-	-	f	r	f	h/o		o	
Tongan	VSO pr NG NA			-?	+	f					i/o	
Tunica	SOV po GN NA	r						f				
Turkish	SOV po GN AN	r	r/f			f/i		o	r		i/f	
Twi	SVO po GN NA	h	f	-?	+	f?	h	f	h			
Uzbek	SOV po GN AN	r	f			f?	h	f?	h		o	
Vietnamese	SVO pr NG NA	h		-	-	f	r/o	f				
Vogul	SOV po GN? AN							f?				
Western Desert	SOV po GN NA	r/h		-	-			o			o	h
Wolio	VSO pr NG NA	r		+?	+?	i					i	
Yakut	SOV po GN AN					f		f				
Zapotec	VSO pr NG NA	r/h			+	f	r/h	i	o	p/s	i	

APPENDIX II

Q-feature and basic order type summary

Following is a statistical summary of the information in Appendix I arranged by Q-features and their intersections with the basic order types. The figures in the matrix represent the number of languages in this sample which exhibit a particular feature, but the actual totals should be taken cum grano salis, since various kinds of sampling errors probably do exist (erroneous assignment to a basic order type, descriptive gaps in the sources, my own reinterpretation of certain features, e.g. tag for particle, and others). Nevertheless, I feel that on the whole this summary gives a reasonably correct picture of some general relationships between Q-features and the basic order types. Doubtful examples are included in the totals without special notation, but these may be verified by cross-checking the corresponding Q-feature column in Appendix I.

The figures in parentheses after each feature represent the total number of languages for which data were available on the particular feature. Figures in TOTAL column A refer to the total number of languages which reflect that feature representation; those in column B, the number of languages in column A which show alternative representations.

Symbols used here to represent the basic order types are:

VOS	verb-object-subject
VSO	verb-subject-object
SVO	subject-verb-object
SOV	subject-object-verb
pr	prepositional
po	postpositional
NG	possessed-possessor
GN	possessor-possessed
NA	head-attribute
AN	attribute-head
?	unidentified

Table: Q-FEATURES by BASIC ORDER TYPES

Q-FEATURES	?	VOS pr NG/NA	VOS GN/AN	VSO pr NG/NA	VSO pr NG/AN	VSO GN/NA	SVO pr NG/NA	SVO pr NG/AN	SVO po GN/NA	SVO po GN/AN	SOV pr NG/NA	SOV po NG/NA	SOV po GN/NA	SOV po GN/AN	TOTAL A	TOTAL B
Intonation																
YN (53) rising	2	1		6		1	9	2		2	1	3		11	38	10
higher	1			3	1		4	1	1	2	1	1		4	19	4
falling	1					1			2	1			1		6	3
IN (36) rising						1	3	1		1				5	11	8
higher	1						2	1		2	1			4	12	5
falling				3			5	2	2	2	1			9	25	11
Tag (29) rising		1		3			7	1	2	1	1			6	22	4
higher				1			2	1	2	1				1	8	4
other	1			1			2		1	1					4	2
Accent																
QP (22) rising				1					1	1				3	6	1
higher							1	1						1	3	1
other				1			3	1	3	1	1		1	3	15	2
QW (20) rising							1	1			1			1	3	1
higher				2			2	1	1	1			1	6	13	4
other							4	1	1	1				1	8	5
Order																
Inversion																
YN (38) +	1						3	1	2	1	1	4	1	1	7	
−				6	1		4	2	2	2	1		8	8	31	
IN (46) +			1	8	1		8	1	2	3	1	2	5	5	34	
−		1	1	2			2		2	2	1	6	6	6	12	

continued

continued

Q - FEATURES	?	VOS pr NG/NA	VOS pr GN/AN	VSO NG/NA	VSO pr NG/NA	VSO pr GN/AN	SVO NG/NA	SVO pr NG/NA	SVO pr GN/AN	SVO po GN/NA	SVO po GN/AN	SOV pr NG/NA	SOV NG/NA	SOV po GN/NA	SOV po GN/AN	TOTAL A	TOTAL B
Position																	
Tag (37) initial				3			4				1				1	9	7
Tag (37) final	1		1	6			8	1	3	3	2	1			8	34	8
Tag (37) other										1					1	2	1
QP (57) initial	2	1	1	6	2		4	1	1	1	3	1	1		1	25	3
QP (57) final	1			2		1	2	1	1	4			1	4	13	30	5
QP (57) other	1	1		1			1			1				1	3	9	5
Q-affix (8) prefix				1										1		2	2
Q-affix (8) suffix	1			1							1			1	5	9	2
QW (64) initial	3	1	1	9	2		7	2	3	3	3	3		1	9	47	6
QW (64) final							2		1	1						4	3
QW (64) other				4		1	4		1			1		2	7	20	5

APPENDIX III

Field worker's guide

A natural by-product of any research project is the discovery of numerous gaps or omissions of relevant information in the descriptions which serve as raw material for the particular area under investigation. This negative (and often frustrating) side of the researcher's work can, however, be turned to the advantage of the field worker when presented as a check list or memo on the kinds of information which should be elicited from informants. We can scarcely claim that the suggestions offered here exhaust the subject of interrogative systems; however, it is hoped that their application will at least result in more systematic and complete descriptions for this important part of any language.

Phonological devices

1. Terminal countours in YNQs, INQs, tags, and other questions as opposed to those found in declarative statements, e.g. rising or higher final, drawl, acceleration, etc.

2. QP, Q-affix, and QW accent as opposed to corresponding word accent in declarative statements.

3. Non-intonational or non-accentual phonological contrasts used as interrogative markers, e.g. glottalized/nonglottalized, voiced/voiceless, long/short (particularly vowels), etc.

Word Order

1. Inversion (generally of verb and subject) in YNQs and INQs, with special attention to auxiliary position in periphrastic constructions.

2. Other (nondeclarative) orders such as use of dependent clause order in YNQs in SCOTTISH GAELIC.

3. Juxtaposition of alternative Q-clauses.

Morphosyntactic devices

1. QP or Q-affix
   a. in YNQs, INQs, tags
   b. as relative or conjunction introducing 'if' or 'whether' clauses (probably QP only)

2. Hypothetical modal (e.g. dubitative, subjunctive, optative) affixes or particles used as Q-markers.

3. Tags
  a. negatively expressed
  b. positively expressed by a
    copula or existential verb   truth-value-inferential / of expected response / or rhetorical
  c. alternative by conjunction or particle, or by parataxis of
    alternative clauses
  d. additive or emphatic ('how about...?' 'and...?' etc.)

4. QW or QW-affix
  a. formal classes: pronouns, adjectives, adverbs, proverbs,
    interjections, conjunctions, etc.
  b. semantic classes: qualitative, quantitative, locative,
    temporal, manner, purpose, etc.
  c. concord classes: gender, number, person, case
  d. alternative or comparative Q-pronouns or adjectives
    ('which of two?'), particularly in languages which do not
    otherwise distinguish between dual and plural
  e. derivational classes: indefinite and relative pronouns,
    adverbs, etc. and any correlations with other substitute
    paradigms such as demonstratives or personal pronouns
  f. use of QWs in indirect questions
  g. special dependency relations between QW and clause type,
    as in BASQUE, where QWs sometimes require non-finite
    verb forms.

Furthermore, all possible co-occurrence patterns and restrictions involving the various Q-devices should be carefully investigated.

BIBLIOGRAPHY

Abramson, A.S. 1962. The vowels and tones of Standard Thai:
acoustical measurements and experiments. IJAL 28, Pub. 20.

Agard, F.B. 1958. Structural sketch of Rumanian. Language
Monograph 26.

Anceaux, J.C. 1952. The Wolio language. Verhandelingen van
het Koninklijk Instituut voor Taal-, Land-, en Volkenkunde,
deel II. 's-Gravenhage.

Bailey, Beryl Loftman. 1966. Jamaican Creole syntax: a transformational approach. London.

Barker, M.A.R. 1964. Klamath grammar. University of California Publication in Linguistics [UCPL] 32. Berkeley.

Bellugi, Ursula and Roger Brown (eds.) 1964. The acquisition of language. Monographs of the Society for Research in Child Development 291. Yellow Springs, Ohio.

Bloomfield, Leonard. 1917. Tagalog texts with grammatical analysis. University of Illinois Studies in Linguistics and Literature 3. (Reprinted in 1967 by Johnson Reprint Corp., New York.)

_____. 1956. Eastern Ojibwa. Ann Arbor: Univ. of Michigan.

Böhtlingk, O. 1964. Über die Sprache der Jakuten. Indiana Univ. Publications, Uralic and Altaic Series 35. Bloomington, Ind.

Bolinger, Dwight L. 1957. Interrogative structures of American English (the direct question). American Dialect Society Pub. 28. Univ. of Alabama Press.

_____. 1962. Intonation as a universal. Proceedings of the Ninth International Congress of Linguists, Cambridge, Mass. (Janua Linguarum, series maior XII) 833-48. The Hague: Mouton.

_____. (Isamu Abe and Tetsuya Kanekiyo, eds.) 1965. Forms of English: accent, morpheme, order. Cambridge, Mass.

Briggs, Elinor. 1961. Milta Zapotec grammar. Instituto Lingüistico de Verano. Mexico.

Bright, William. 1957. The Karok Language. UCPL 13.

_____. 1958. An outline of colloquial Kannada. Indian Linguistic Monograph series I, viii. Poona.

Campbell, Stuart and Chuan Shaweevongse. 1962. The fundamentals of the Thai language (2nd ed.). New York and Melbourne.

Cardona, G. 1964. A Gujarati reference grammar. Univ. of Pennsylvania, unpublished.

Carmody, Francis J. 1945. The interrogative system in modern Scottish Gaelic. UCPL 1/6. 215-26.

Chao, Y.R. 1965. A grammar of spoken Chinese. Berkeley.

Churchward, C. Maxwell. 1940. Rotuman grammar and dictionary. Sydney.

_____. 1953. Tongan grammar. Oxford University Press.

Churchward, Spencer. 1951. A Samoan grammar (2nd ed.). Melbourne.

Cornyn, William. 1944. Outline of Burmese grammar. Language Dissertation 38.

Cowell, Mark W. 1964. A reference grammar of Syrian Arabic (Damascus dialect). Washington, D.C.: Georgetown Univ. Press.

DeGroot, A.W. 1945. L'intonation de la phrase néerlandaise et allemande. Cahiers Ferdinand de Saussure 5. 17-31.

Douglas, W.H. 1958. An introduction to the Western Desert Language of Australia. Oceania Linguistic Monographs 4. Sydney: University of Sydney.

Drake, J. 1903. A grammar of the Kurku language (Kolarian subgroup of Munda). Calcutta.

Ellis, C. Douglas. 1961. The so-called interrogative order in Cree. IJAL 27.2. 119-24.

Erwin, Wallace M. 1963. A short reference grammar of Iraqi Arabic. Washington, D.C.: Georgetown Univ. Press.

Faure, Georges. 1962. Aspects et fonctions linguistiques des variations mélodiques dans la chaîne parlée. Proceedings of the Ninth International Congress of Linguists, Cambridge, Mass., ed. by H.G. Lunt, 72-7. The Hague: Mouton.

Forbes, Nevill. 1964. Russian grammar (2nd ed.). Melbourne.

Gantzel, Lars Holm. 1967. The meaning of terminal pitch pattern. Doctoral dissertation, Stanford University.

Garbell, Irene. 1965. The Jewish Neo-Aramaic dialect of Persian Azerbaijan. Janua Linguarum, series practica 3. The Hague.

Gill, H.S. and H.A. Gleason, Jr. 1963. A reference grammar of Panjabi. Hartford Studies in Linguistics 3.

Gleason, H.A. Jr. 1955. An introduction to descriptive linguistics. New York: Henry Holt and Co.

Gregores, Emma and Jorge A. Suarez. 1967. A description of colloquial Guaraní. Janua Linguarum, series practica 27. The Hague.

Grimes, Joseph E. 1964. Huichol syntax. Janua Linguarum, series practica 11.

Haas, Mary R. 1941. Tunica. Handbook of American Indian Languages 4. 1-143. New York: J.J. Augustin.

Hai, Muhammad Abdul and W.J. Ball. 1961. The sound structure of English and Bengali. Dacca: Dacca Univ. Press.

Halliday, M.A.K. 1967. Intonation and grammar in British English. Janua Linguarum, series practica I. The Hague.

Hardman, M.J. 1966. Jaqaru: outline of phonological and morphological structure. Janua Linguarum, series practica 22. The Hague.

Healey, Phyllis M. 1960. An Agta (Philippines) grammar. Summer Institute of Linguistics. Manila.

Hermann, E. 1942. Probleme der Frage. Nachrichten von der Akademie der Wissenschaften in Göttingen. Philologisch-Historische Klasse, Nr. 3.4.

Hòa, Nguyễn Dình. 1957. Speak Vietnamese (1st ed., later eds.: 1963, 1965). Saigon.

Hockett, Charles F. 1955. A manual of phonology. IJAL 21.4, Memoir 11.

Hodge, Carleton T. 1947. Outline of Hausa grammar. Language Dissertation 41.

Holmer, Nils M. 1942. The Irish language in Rathlin Island, County Antrim. Royal Irish Academy, Todd Lecture Series 18. Dublin: Hodges, Figgis.

Innes, Gordon. 1966. An introduction to Grebo. School of Oriental and African Studies, University of London.

Jorden, Eleanor Harz. 1955. The syntax of modern colloquial Japanese. Language Dissertation 52.

_____. 1962. Beginning Japanese, parts I, II. New Haven: Yale Univ. Press.

Juilland, Alphonse and Marilyn J. Conwell. 1963. Louisiana French grammar. Janua Linguarum, series practica 1. The Hague: Mouton.

Kähler, H. 1965. Grammatik der Bahasa-Indonesia (Malay). Wiesbaden: O. Harrassowitz.

Kálmán, B. 1965. Vogul chrestomathy. Indiana University Publication, Uralic and Altaic Series 46. Bloomington, Ind.

Kraft, Charles H. 1963. A study of Hausa syntax, I, II. Hartford Studies in Linguistics 8, 9.

Kuipers, Aert H. 1967. The Squamish language. Janua Linguarum, series practica 73. The Hague: Mouton.

Lafitte, Abbé P. 1944. Grammaire basque (Navarro-Labourdin littéraire). Bayonne.

Lehtinen, Meri. 1963. Basic course in Finnish. Indiana Univ. Publications, Uralic and Altaic Series 27. Bloomington, Ind.

Lewis, G.L. 1967. Turkish grammar. Oxford: University Press.

Lewis, Morris Michael. 1936. Infant speech: a study of the beginnings of language. New York.

_____. 1938. The beginning and early functions of questions in a child's speech. British Journal of Educational Psychology 8. 150-71.

_____. 1959. How children learn to speak. New York.

Lieberman, Philip. 1967. Intonation, perception, and language. Cambridge, Mass.: M.I.T. Press.

Lisker, Leigh. 1938. Introduction to spoken Telugu. New York: ACLS.

Malzac, R.P. 1950. Grammaire malgache (3rd ed.) Paris.

Martin, Samuel E. 1942. Morphophonemics of standard colloquial Japanese. Language Dissertation 47.

Martinet, André. 1960. Eléments de linguistique générale. Paris.

Matteson, Esther. 1965. The Piro (Arawakan) language. UCPL 42.

Matthews, G. Hubert. 1965. Hidatsa syntax. Papers on Formal Linguistics 3. The Hague.

Newmark, Leonard. 1957. Structural grammar of Albanian. IJAL 23.4, pub. 4.

Oates, L.F. 1964. A tentative description of the Gunwinggu language (of western Arnhem Land). Oceania Linguistic Monographs 10. Sydney.

Obolensky, Serge, D. Zelelie and M. Andualem. 1964. Amharic basic course. Foreign Service Institute, Washington, D.C.

O'Grady, Geoffrey N. 1964. Nyangumata grammar. Oceania Linguistic Monographs 9. University of Sydney. Sydney.

Pike, Kenneth L. 1945. The intonation of American English. Ann Arbor: University of Michigan Press.

Pittman, Richard S. 1954. A grammar of Tetelcingo (Morelos) Nahuatl. Language Dissertation 50.

Poppe, Nicholas. 1960. Buriat grammar. Indiana University publications, Uralic and Altaic Series 2. Bloomington, Ind.

_____. 1964. Bashkir manual. Indiana University Publications, Uralic and Altaic Series 36. Bloomington, Ind.

Potapova, Nina. 1947. Le Russe, manuel de la langue russe à l'usage des français (2nd ed.). Moscow.

Rabel, Lili. 1961. Khasi, a language of Assam. Louisiana State University Studies, Humanities Series 10.

Rastorgueva, V.S. 1963. A short sketch of Tajik grammar. IJAL 29.4, pub. 28.

Rastorgueva, V.S. 1964. A short sketch of the grammar of
Persian. IJAL 30.1, pub. 29.

Ray, P.S., M. Hai and L. Ray. 1966. Bengali language handbook.
Center for Applied Linguistics, Language Handbook Series.
Washington, D.C.

Redden, James E. et al. 1963. Twi basic course. Foreign Service
Institute. Washington, D.C.

Rédei, K. 1965. Northern Ostyak chrestomathy. Indiana University Publication, Uralic and Altaic Series 47. Bloomington, Ind.

Rigault, A. 1962. Réflexions sur le statut phonologique de l'intonation. Proceedings of the Ninth International Congress of
Linguists, 849-58. Cambridge, Mass.

Rosén, Haim B. 1962 and 1966. A textbook of Israeli Hebrew.
Chicago: University of Chicago Press.

Ross, Ellen M. 1963. Introduction to Ecuador Highland Quichua,
or Quichua in ten easy lessons. (Mimeographed)

Salzmann, Zdeněk. 1956. Arapaho I: phonology. IJAL 22.1.
49-56.

Samarin, William J. 1966. The Gbeya language. UCPL 44.

_____. 1967. A grammar of Sango. Janua Linguarum, series
practica 38. The Hague.

Sapir, J.D. 1965. A grammar of Diola-Fogny. West African
Language Monograph. London: Cambridge University Press.

Sauvageot, Aurélien. 1951. Esquisse de la langue hongroise. Paris.

_____. 1957. Les procédés expressifs du français contemporain.
Paris.

Senn, Alfred. 1966. Handbuch der litauischen Sprache (Band I:
Grammatik). Heidelberg.

Sjoberg, Andrée. 1962. Phonology of Standard Uzbek. Indiana
University Publication, Uralic and Altaic Series 13. Bloomington,
Ind.

Stennes, Leslie H. 1961. An introduction to Fulani syntax. Hartford Studies in Linguistics 2.

Stockwell, Robert P. 1960. The place of intonation in a generative
grammar of English. Language 36. 360-7.

Street, J.C. 1963. Khalkha structure. Indiana University Publications, Uralic and Altaic Series 24. Bloomington, Ind.

Strehlow, T.G.H. 1942-1944. Aranda phonetics and grammar.
Oceania Linguistic Monographs 7. University of Sydney, Sydney.

Swadesh, Morris. 1946. Chitimacha.   Linguistic structures of
native America, ed. by C. Osgood. Viking Fund Publications
in Anthropology 6. 312-36.

Swift, L.B. 1963. A reference grammar of modern Turkish.
Indiana University Publications, Uralic and Altaic Series 19.
Bloomington, Ind.

Togeby, Knud. 1965. Structure immanente de la langue française
contemporaine. Paris.

Ultan, Russell. 1967. Konkow grammar. Doctoral dissertation,
University of California, Berkeley.

Voorhoeve, C.L. 1965. The Flamingo Bay dialect of the Asmat
language. 's-Gravenhage.

Ward, Ida C. 1936. An introduction to the Ibo language. Cambridge
Univ. Press.

Waterhouse, Viola. 1962. The grammatical structure of Oaxaca
Chontal. IJAL 28.2, part II, pub. 19.

Watkins, Mark H. 1937. Chichewa grammar. Language Dissertation 24.

Welmers, William E. 1946. A grammar of Fanti. Language
Dissertation 39.

Yotsukura, Sayo. 1967. The Japanese tone and intonation systems.
Linguistics 35. 66-105.

On the Case Marking of Objects

EDITH A. MORAVCSIK

ABSTRACT

In some languages some non-agentive and non-dative noun phrases admit of alternative case markings. The paper is a study of the semantic conditions from which such case marking alternatives can be predicted. Four types of alternations are investigated: accusative-adverbial, accusative-partitive, accusative-nominative, and accusative-topic. The recurrence of certain semantic features conditioning such alternations, such as definiteness, affectedness and animacy, is noted and it is pointed out that the same type of semantic information is also conditional to alternative agreement, order and stress patterns of some non-agentive and non-dative noun phrases, as well as to alternative expressions of some agentive and dative ones.

This paper is an abridged version of an unpublished one entitled "On case function and sentence form" which I wrote in 1975 as part of my work for the Stanford Project on Language Universals. I am grateful for comments on the longer paper from members of this research group. I also wish to express my gratitude to Charles Li for having invited me to attend the conference on Subject and Topic held in Santa Barbara, California in March 1975, which experience contributed to my writing this paper; and to Mara Hegedeos for discussions on object case marking. Data on a number of languages in this paper come from her data file; in all such instances reference to the original source will be followed by a mention of her name.

CONTENTS

1. Introduction

All languages can provide for the formal differentiation of noun phrases that denote otherwise identical referents performing different participant functions in an event. There are, in particular, three generalizations that I believe can be safely made about the way such formal differentiation is universally provided for. First, the meanings of at least some participants can in all languages be expressed by symbolizing them separately from the event proper itself. All languages, in other words, have separately lexicalized verbs and nouns: there is no language, for instance, where the three meanings 'I saw a man,' 'I saw an elephant' and 'you saw a man' can be expressed only by three distinct sound sequences which include no subsequences identifiable as carriers of the submeanings 'saw,' 'a man,' 'an elephant,' 'I,' and 'you' and where all other such three-place predications are also expressed in this "holophrastic" manner. Second, the differentiation between functionally distinct participants is effected in all languages by means other than multiple lexicalization. No language, that is, differentiates between the two expressions of 'the man' in sentences such as The man ate the bear. and The bear ate the man. in terms of two distinct sound sequences which include no substring identifiable as corresponding to 'the man' in its case-functionally neutral sense. Third, the set of form devices that languages use to differentiate between functionally distinct participants can be simply characterized as including segmental markers, linear order and stress; where the segmental markers are either segment sequences adjacent to the noun (generally called case markers) or markers adjacent to the verb (generally called verb-agreement markers).

The correspondence relation between case-marking, verb-agreement, linear ordering, and stressing, on the one hand, and semantic case function, on the other, is not one-to-one, however; the same agreement pattern, for instance, may correspond to more than one distinct semantic case function, and the same semantic case function may be alternatively expressed by more than one distinct case marking. The concern of this present paper is this latter aspect of the complex relation between case meaning and case form. The general question being asked is this: if case-marking, verb-agreement, linear order, and stress in simple intransitive and transitive sentences are not fully predictable from semantic case function, then what are they predictable from? Since semantic case function appears necessary for predicting such form properties of sentences but it is clearly not sufficient, the question is what the additional conditions may be that would

successfully complement semantic case function specifications for
the prediction of these form properties. The actual scope of the
paper will be restricted to the consideration of (adpositional or
morphological) case-marking only (to the exclusion of verb-agreement, ordering and stressing) and in particular to the case-marking
of noun phrases whose semantic function is non-agentive and non-
dative. Such noun phrases will be called (semantic) Objects.[1]

The obvious procedure for trying to answer this question will
be that of examining sentence sets of various languages whose
noun phrases are identical in semantic case function but differ
nonetheless in case marking and attempting to establish what, if
any, semantic conditions are correlated with the different markings.
After some preliminary remarks (2.1), section 2.2 will consider
sentence pairs where the alternative case markings are accusative
versus some adverbial case; section 2.3 will be concerned with
accusative-partitive alternations; section 2.4 with accusative-
nominative alternations; and section 2.5 with accusative-topic
alternations. A summary of our findings and a brief outlook towards other aspects of the general problem will be provided in the
concluding section.

---

[1] Semantic case-function labels will be used impressionistically
throughout the paper and no attempt will be made to justify their
assignment. I will simply label a noun phrase by semantic case-
label X if it seems intuitively correct to me to say: "The referent
of this noun phrase is an X participant of the event and not a Y, Z...
participant of the event;" where "Y, Z..." comprises the total set
of case labels that I will be using, except for X. I will assume the
following set of case-labels: AGENT, DATIVE, EXPERIENCER,
INSTRUMENT, GOAL, SOURCE, NEUTRAL. As far as case-
marking labels are concerned, by the term "accusative" I will mean
a case marker whose use includes the marking of at least some
non-emphatic, animate and definite noun phrases with the semantic
function NEUTRAL (i.e. that are the passive participants of events
such as 'hitting,' 'cutting,' 'breaking,' or 'eating'), that are said to
be fully affected by the event (i.e. they undergo a change of state
in their full extent); and whose use excludes the marking of any
agentive noun phrase in simple transitive sentences. The term
"adverbial case" refers to any case marker whose use includes the
marking of either instrumental or locative noun phrases. "Partitive"
is a normally adnominal case that marks the total quantity of which
a part is designated. "Topic" is a case whose semantic range is
functionally undifferentiated and which marks semantically topical
noun phrases.

2. Case-marking Alternatives for Objects

2.1 Preliminary remarks

I would first like to point out two non-semantic conditions that
in ENGLISH, as well as in some other languages, account for
some case-marking alternatives of semantic Objects. One such
type of condition is lexical properties of the verb; the other is
properties of the internal constituent structure of the verb. Instances where it is the lexical properties of the verb that determine
the morphological case marking of case-functionally alike noun
phrases are illustrated by the following sentences of ENGLISH and
HUNGARIAN. In each sentence the semantic case function of the
post-verbal noun phrase is NEUTRAL; nevertheless, the morphological case markings as governed by the particular verb range
from accusative to various adverbial cases.

ENGLISH:
He considered the question.
He laughed at her behavior.
He insisted on the answer.
He puzzled over the problem.
He referred to the solution. (Stockwell, Schachter, Partee 1973: 36, 42f)

HUNGARIAN:

Mérlegelte a kérdés-t.	"considered-he/she the question-accus." 'He/she considered the question.'
Nevetett a magatartásá-n.	"laughed-he/she the behavior-his/her-on" 'He/she laughed at his/her behavior.'
Ragaszkodott a válasz-hoz.	"insisted-he/she the answer-to" 'He/she insisted on the answer.'
Tűnődött a probléma felett.	"mused-he/she the problem over" 'He/she mused over the problem.'
Utalt a megoldásra.	"referred-he/she the solution-onto" 'He/she referred to the solution.' (All HUNGARIAN data in the paper are my own.)

Whereas these seem to be truly idiosyncratic differences, there are
also some more systematic alternatives in case choice that depend
on the internal syntactic structure of the verb. Thus, as the following sentences illustrate, it makes a difference from the point of view
of case choice whether the verb is a lexical verb, a lexical adjective,
or a verb-noun phrase, even though the alternative verb forms are

synonymous. The generalization that these examples reveal is that whereas the adjective or the verb-noun phrase does not take the accusative, the lexical verb may.

ENGLISH:
This indicates progress.
This is indicative of progress.

He counted the apples.
He made a count of the apples.

HUNGARIAN:
Ez érdekli őt.	"this interests-him/her him/her"
	'This interests him/her.'
Ez érdekes neki.	"this interesting to-him/her"
	'This is interesting to him/her.'
Jelentette az esetet.	"reported-he/she the case-accus."
	'He/she reported the case.'
Jelentést tett az esetről.	"report-accus. made-he/she the case-from"
	'He/she made a report of the case.'

There are, however, many instances of case marking variation involving the accusative where the choice between the alternative cases cannot be seen as dependent either on lexical or structural properties of the verb since the sentences that exhibit the case variation include verbs that are alike both structurally and lexically. These are the cases we will now turn to.

2.2 Accusative and adverbial

A subset of those verbs in ENGLISH whose complements are alternatively case-marked for the accusative and some adverbial case constitutes a natural semantic class in that its members all express the notion of filling or providing or that of emptying or depriving.[2] Some examples to illustrate these verbs and their

---

[2] Not all verbs that belong to the semantic class of verbs of filling and emptying in ENGLISH also belong to the same syntactic class; verbs such as pour, fill do not tolerate freely the accusative-adverbial alternation of their complements. Thus, one can pour wine into the bottle but one cannot pour the bottle with wine; and one can, in turn, fill the bottle with wine but not fill wine into the bottle. In HUNGARIAN, however, both of these two verbs behave like other verbs of filling in that their complements do alternate in accusative-adverbial case marking.

use are the following:

John smeared paint on the wall.
John smeared the wall with paint.

John planted trees in the garden.
John planted the garden with trees.

He cleaned the fat out of the pan.
He cleaned the pan of the fat.

In ENGLISH the marking of accusative noun phrases is partly by
segmental marking, partly by position: the accusative noun phrase
is a postverbal prepositionless noun phrase. The sentence pairs
cited above thus show that either of the two non-agentive complements of these verbs may occur either in the accusative or in an
instrumental or locative case.

The accusative-adverbial alternation does not correlate in these
sentences with a semantic case-functional alternation: each of the
two noun phrases retains its semantic case function in spite of their
variation in form. Thus, the referents of the phrases paint, trees
and the fat are invariantly the things moved into or onto something
or taken out of something in both members of the pertinent sentence
pair; and referents of the phrases the wall, the garden and the pan
are similarly invariant in their functions as goals or sources of a
movement (cp. Stockwell, Schachter Partee 1973: 49). Nonetheless,
as pointed out by all linguists who have investigated such verbs of
filling and emptying in ENGLISH, and most clearly by Anderson
(1970), there is indeed a semantic difference between the alternative
constructions. The semantic difference can be appreciated through
the differential entailments of members of each pair. Thus, for
instance, smearing the wall with paint entails that something has
been done to the wall; and smearing paint on the wall entails that
something has been done with the wall. In the first instance the
entailment is that the wall has been "affected;" in the second case
there is no such entailment. Furthermore, planting the garden
with trees entails that as a result the whole garden had trees in it,
whereas planting trees in the garden does not entail this. Thus,
in the first instance involvement of the whole location is understood,
whereas in the second there is no such understanding. In general
the locative complement marked as accusative is asserted to be
affected by the event in its full extent, whereas the locative marked
as locative adverbial is not asserted to be so affected.

In addition to verbs expressing filling or emptying there are also
other verbs in ENGLISH whose semantic locative complements may

be alternatively marked as accusative or locative. The above-
proposed generalization about the correlated semantic conditions
appear to hold for these other verbs as well. Thus, as pointed out
by Anderson (1970), the first sentences in the pairs below imply
the successful completion of the action whereas the second sentences do not:

   a. John climbed the mountain.
       John climbed up the mountain.

   b. John leapt the chasm.
       John leapt over the chasm.

   c. John swam Lake Michigan.
       John swam across Lake Michigan.

   In HUNGARIAN, which is a language both genetically unrelated
and areally distinct from ENGLISH, the class of verbs expressing
filling or providing and emptying or depriving behave almost exactly
the same way as their ENGLISH translation equivalents (compare
Zsilka 1967). These HUNGARIAN verbs, too, occur in two alternative constructions that differ in form by the different case markings
of the two complements involved and that also differ in meaning in
exactly the same way the corresponding constructions in ENGLISH
do. Note, for example, the following sentences:

Other such verbs were listed and discussed by Jespersen (1954:
238ff); e.g. stab (at), kick (towards), strike (at), catch (at). In
each case the construction including an accusative locative implies
the successful execution of the action, whereas the construction
involving a prepositional locative implies merely an attempt.
There are, furthermore, also verbs whose complements alternate
between accusative and adverbial marking with the corresponding
by now familiar semantic difference, although the complements
are not semantically locative but neutral; e.g. know (about/of),
hear (about/of). There are, furthermore, verbal meanings which
are conveyed by different phonological shapes depending on the
associated semantic difference and whether they are transitive or
intransitive; e.g. weep over -bewail; feed on -consume; look at -
watch. There are, finally, also a number of verbs whose complements can be alternatively either in the accusative or in an adverbial
case; nonetheless, the two constructions have exactly the same
meaning. E.g. improve (on), check (on), forget (about).

a. János rámázolta a festéket a falra.
    "John onto-smeared-he-it the paint-accus. the wall-onto"
    'John smeared paint on the wall.'

    János bemázolta a falat festékkel.
    "John in-smeared-he-it the wall-accus. paint-with"
    'John smeared the wall with paint.'

b. János elültette a fákat a kertben.
    "John away-planted-he-them the trees-accus. the garden-in"
    'John planted the trees in the garden.'

    János beültette a kertet fákkal.
    "John in-planted-he-it the garden-accus. trees-with"
    'John planted the garden with trees.'

As these sentences illustrate, in HUNGARIAN as in ENGLISH, both
the NEUTRAL and the GOAL phrase may be alternatively marked
as accusative -- which in HUNGARIAN means a suffixed -t (except
in first and second person singular personal pronouns and possessed
nouns which may or may not take this suffix) and being agreed-with
by the verb in definiteness -- or they may occur in the instrumental
case (-val/-vel, with the v assimilated to the final consonant of the
stem) or in a locative case (-ra/-re 'onto,' -ban/-ben 'in' in the
above examples), respectively. The semantic difference between
the alternative constructions is also exactly the same as in ENGLISH
and it could be thus similarly demonstrated by showing that the alternative constructions entail different sentences.

There is only one significant difference between corresponding
constructions in the two languages which has to do with the form in
which the verb appears in the alternative constructions. Whereas
the form of the verb in the alternative ENGLISH constructions is
in most cases the same, in HUNGARIAN the two forms differ in
most cases in that their verbal prefixes differ. HUNGARIAN verbal
prefixes are similar in function to ENGLISH post-verbal particles
such as up, down, through, etc. and to the verbal prefixes in AN-
CIENT GREEK, LATIN, GERMAN and RUSSIAN in that they convey
sometimes a directional meaning, other times the meaning of completed action and again other times both. In ENGLISH, as noted by
Fraser (1971), verbal particles can cooccur only with a semantically
locative accusative and not with a semantically neutral accusative
in these constructions; see, for instance:

They loaded up the wagon with hay.
*They loaded up the hay on the wagon.

In HUNGARIAN what corresponds to this <u>up</u> that cooccurs with
locative accusative is <u>meg</u>-, a verbal prefix with no directional
but purely completive meaning; or, in some cases, <u>be</u>- 'in' as in
the above examples or <u>át</u>- 'through;' see, for instance:

Rárakta a szénát a szekérre.
"onto-put the hay-accus. the cart-onto"
'He/she put-he/she-it the hay on the cart.'

Megrakta a szekeret szénával.
"up-put-he/she-it the cart-accus. hay-with"
'He/she loaded the cart with hay.'

Belefonta a szalagot a hajába.
"into-it-wove the ribbon-accus. the hair-his/her-into"
'He/she wove a ribbon into his/her hair.'

Átfonta a haját a szalaggal.
"through-wove-he/she-it the hair-his/her-accus. the ribbon-with"
'He/she braided his/her hair with the ribbon.'

Another verbal prefix that may cooccur with an accusative locative
is <u>tele</u>- 'full;' its use corresponds to the use of <u>full of</u> in ENGLISH
which also occurs only with locative accusatives; compare

Telerakta a szekeret szénával.
"full-put-he/she-it the wagon-accus. hay-with"
'He/she loaded the cart full of hay.'

*Telerakta a szénát a szekérre.
"full-put he/she-it the hay-accus. the cart-onto"
'He/she loaded the wagon full of hay.'

In summary: the difference between the ENGLISH and HUNGAR-
IAN constructions is that whereas in ENGLISH completive verbal
particles occur only with some verbs and only if the accusative is
the semantically locative phrase, in HUNGARIAN some verbal
particles occur with any verb and with both kinds of accusative.

HUNGARIAN also resembles ENGLISH in that it has a number
of additional verbs whose complements may be either in the accusative or in some adverbial case with the same corresponding semantic
difference that obtains in ENGLISH. Compare the following:

a. Megmászta a hegyet.
   "up-climbed-he/she-it the mountain-accus."
   'He/she climbed the mountain.'

   Felmászott a hegyre.
   "up-climbed-he/she the mountain-onto"
   'He/she climbed up the mountain.'

b. Átugrotta az árkot.
   "across-leapt-he/she-it the ditch-accus."
   'He/she leapt the ditch.'

   Átugrott az árkon.
   "across-leapt-he/she the ditch-on"
   'He/she leapt across the ditch.'

c. Átúszta a tavat.
   "across-swam-he/she-it the lake-accus."
   'He/she swam the lake.'

   Átúszott a tavon.
   "across-swam-he/she the lake-on"
   'He/she swam across the lake.'

Besides ENGLISH and HUNGARIAN, there are a number of other genetically, areally and typologically disparate languages that offer examples for the correlation between accusative-adverbial case-marking variation, on the one hand, and totally versus partially affected object, on the other. I have some examples from KABARDIAN, ESKIMO, WALBIRI and AMHARIC. Both KABARDIAN and ESKIMO are ergative languages — the case of the subject of an intransitive sentence is the same as the case of the object of an intransitive sentence. The case of the direct object, however, varies in both languages depending on some semantic properties of the object:

KABARDIAN:
š'álem txəλər yež   "boy-erg. book-nom. reads"
                        'The boy is reading the (whole) book.'

š'áler txəλəm yóže   "boy-nom. book-loc. reads"
                        'The boy is reading (in) the book.'

ħam q° əpšħǎr yeʒàqe   "dog-erg. bone-nom. chews"
                        'The dog chews up the bone.'

ḫăr q°ə́psḫăm yóʒaqe   "dog-nom. bone-loc. chews"
                             'The dog is chewing (on) the bone.'
                                        (Knobloch 1952: 416)

ESKIMO:
uyaɣaq tiɣußaa   "stone-nom. he-took"
                             'He took the stone.'

uyaɣqamik tiɣusißuq   "stone-instrumental he-took"
                             'He took a stone.'
                                        (Swadesh 1946 - Hegedeos)

As these examples show, the direct object is marked adverbially in
KABARDIAN if it is partially involved in the event and in ESKIMO
if it is indefinite; and it is marked as "nominative" (which, being
the case of the definite, animate, pragmatically neutral direct
object in two-place predications, corresponds to our definition of
"accusative") if it is totally involved (in KABARDIAN) or definite
(in ESKIMO). In WALBIRI the accusative-adverbial alternation
correlates with the object of an accomplished versus of an attempted
action.

    WALBIRI:
    njuntuluḷu npatju pantuṇu ŋatju
    "you-erg. you-I spear-past I-nom."
    'You speared me.'

    njuntuluḷu npətjuḷa pantuṇu ŋatjuku
    "you-erg. you-I-? spear-past I-dative"
    'You speared me.' or 'You tried to spear me.' (Hale 1973: 336)

In AMHARIC preverbal adverbial phrases may occur either case-
marked by their appropriate adverbial case marking or case-
marked as accusatives. For some of these cases a semantic
difference was indicated in my sources; in others there was none
indicated. Examples are the following:

    AMHARIC:
    kăzzičč set lay and măṣhəf găzzah^w(at)
    "from-this woman on one book I-bought(-her)"

    yahaččən set and măṣhəf găzzah^{w}at
    "this-accus. woman one book I-bought-her"

According to Hetzron (1971: 331) both sentences mean 'I bought a book from this woman' but whereas the first simply "describes the woman as the origin of the book," the second implies that "the woman managed to give the book away, she does not own it anymore." In other words the accusatively marked source phrase appears to be described as one undergoing a change of state, whereas the adverbially marked phrase does not. Haile (1971:109) gives similar examples without any comment on the semantic difference between the two alternatives:

Almaz bəməṭrəgiyaw betun ṭərrəgəccɨbbət
"Almaz with-broom-the house-the clean-he-with-it"
'Almaz cleaned the house with the broom.'

Almaz məṭrəgiyawɨn betun tərrəgəccɨbbət
"Almaz broom-the-accusative house-the clean-he-with-it"
'Almaz cleaned the house with the broom.'

The preceding examples from ENGLISH, HUNGARIAN, KABARDIAN, ESKIMO, WALBIRI and AMHARIC are all consistent with the following generalization: if in a language the same verbal meaning is expressible either through a construction where a complement of the verb is in the accusative or through a construction where the same complement is in an adverbial case and there is a meaning difference between the two constructions, this semantic contrast will be either a contrast between a definite and an indefinite object, or a contrast between an object that is fully involved in the event and one that is partially involved, or a contrast between affected and not affected participant.

2.3 Accusative and partitive

In HUNGARIAN, as well as in a number of other languages, accusatively marked noun phrases may also alternate with partitively marked ones, with their semantic case-function remaining the same non-agentive and non-dative function. Note the following examples from HUNGARIAN:

Ette a süteményt.	"ate-he/she-it the pastry-accus."
	'He ate the pastry.'
Evett a süteményből.	"ate-he/she the pastry-from"
	'He/she ate some of the pastry.'
Olvasta a könyvet.	"read-he/she-it the book-accus."
	'He read the book.'

Olvasott a könyvből.	"read-he/she the book-from" 'He read some of the book.'

The semantic correlates of this case variation are the same as those that we have noted for the accusative-adverbial case alternation of semantically locative phrases: the accusative correlates with the meaning of the referent of the noun phrase being involved in the event in its full extent and the partitive indicates that only part of the specified extension of the object is involved.

There are two restrictions on this case-marking alternation. First, whereas non-completive verbs may occur either with an accusative or with a partitive complement, verbs that express completed action must take an accusative complement. Compare the following examples:

Ette a süteményt.	"ate-he/she-it the pastry-accus." 'He/she ate the pastry.'
Evett a süteményből.	"ate-he/she the pastry-from" 'He/she ate some of the pastry.'
Megette a süteményt.	"up-ate-he/she-it the pastry-accus." 'He ate up the pastry.'
*Megette a süteményből.	"up-ate-he/she-it the pastry-from"
*Megevett a süteményből.	"up-ate-he/she the pastry-from"
Olvasta a könyvet.	"read-he/she-it the book-accus." 'He/she read the book.'
Olvasott a könyvből.	"read-he/she the book-from" 'He/she read some of the book.'
Elolvasta a könyvet.	"away-read-he/she-it the book-accus." 'He read the book (and has finished it).'
*Elolvasta a könyvből.	"away-read-he/she-it the book-from"
*Elolvasott a könyvből.	"away-read-he/she the book-from"

The other restriction is that the accusative complement cooccurring with a completive verb must be known in its quantity – that is to say, it must be either definite or quantified, but it cannot be both non-definite and non-quantified. Compare, for instance:

Ette a süteményt.	"ate-he/she-it the pastry-accus." 'He/she ate the pastry.'
Evett tizenkét süteményt.	"ate-he/she twelve-pastry-accus." 'He ate twelve pieces of pastry.'
Evett süteményeket.	"ate-he/she pastries-accus." "He/she ate some pieces of pastry.'
Megette a süteményt.	"up-ate-he/she-it the pastry-accus." 'He/she ate up the pastry.'
Megette a tizenkét süteményt.	"up-ate-he/she-it the twelve pastries-acc." 'He/she ate up the twelve pieces of pastry.'
*Megette süteményeket.	"up-ate-he/she-it pastries-accus."
*Megevett süteményeket.	"up-ate-he/she pastries-accus."

I will next turn to considering instances of accusative-partitive case marking alternation in languages other than HUNGARIAN. We will see that these other instances of this alternation are similar to those in HUNGARIAN in that the semantic correlates are the same or similar and that the constraints on the alternation in terms of the completeness of the verb and the quantification of the object are also related. Languages of which I have relevant data mostly belong to the Baltic and Slavic subgroups of INDO-EUROPEAN (LATVIAN, LITHUANIAN; RUSSIAN, POLISH) and to the Finnic branch of FINNO-UGRIC (FINNISH, ESTONIAN) and constitute an areally coherent group in North-East Europe. An INDO-EUROPEAN language outside this areal group which also exhibits phenomena of this kind is GOTHIC; and there are also relevant data from the both areally and genetically distinct BASQUE language.

In LATVIAN and LITHUANIAN as well as in GOTHIC the case marking of objects depend on whether their verb is affirmative or negative. In GOTHIC and LATVIAN the choice is furthermore restricted to possessive sentences -- to sentences, that is, that express somebody's owning something. In both of these languages the thing possessed is the subject of such sentences and it is in the nominative case if the sentence is affirmative and it is in the genitive -- which is also the partitive case in these languages -- if the sentence is negative. Examples for the negated sentences are these:

GOTHIC:
jah ni was im barnē   "? was not ? child-gen."
                                       'They had no child.' (Wright 1899:130)

LATVIAN:
man nav naudav   "to-me not-is money-gen."
                                       'I have no money.' (Lazdina 1966:28)

In LITHUANIAN (Dambriūnas 1966) the same alternative holds for possessive sentences:

jis tùri knỹga   "he ? book-nom."
                                       'He has a book.'

jis netùri knỹgos   "he not-? book-gen."
                                       'He has no book.'

but the same alternation also holds for direct objects of transitive sentences: if the verb is affirmative, the object is in the accusative and if it is negative, the object is in the genitive (which, again, is also the partitive case in the language), e.g.:

jis nedirba slãlo   "he not-making desk-gen."
                                       'He is not making a desk.'

In POLISH objects of negated verbs are generally in the genitive (which is the partitive case of the language), whether they are subjects of an intransitive sentence (in which case they are in the nominative in affirmative sentences) or whether they are objects of a transitive sentence (in which case they are in the accusative in transitive sentences). Compare the following:

mam czas   "I have time-acc."
                                       'I have time.'

nie mam czasu   "not I-have time-gen."
                                       'I have no time.'

tu są okulary   "here are glasses-nom."
                                       'The glasses are here.'

tu nie ma okularów   "here not ? glasses-gen."
                                       'The glasses are not here.'

nie zamierzam spredać domu   "not intend-I sell-to home-gen."
                                       'I have no intention to sell the home.'
                                       (Schenker 1966:28; Damerau 1967:116)

Partitively specified objects, however, are not restricted to
negative sentences in this language: they also occur in affirmative
sentences under certain conditions. Although usage appears to be
fluctuating and the conditions are complex, including choice of verb,
choice of noun, emphasis and style, at least some subset of the
alternating sentence pairs is consistent with the following generalization: the case alternation correlates either with the definiteness
versus indefiniteness of the object or with the completedness versus
incompleteness of the action. Compare the following:

POLISH:
daj me ołówka
"give me pencil-gen."
'Give me a pencil!'

daj me ten czarny ołówek
"give me this black-nom. pencil-nom."
'Give me this black pencil!'

daj me tego czarnego ołówka na chwilę
"give me this-gen. black-gen. pencil-gen. for minute"
'Hand me this black pencil for a minute!'

The first sentence has indefinite object which is in the genitive.
The second sentence has a definite object in the nominative. The
third sentence also has a definite object but the meaning to be conveyed here is 'lending for a short time,' rather than 'giving' -- as
Brooks says (1967), in the second sentence, "there is no mention
of time and whether or not the pencil was to be returned," whereas
in the third "the black pencil is asked for a short time and will
probably be returned" -- and it is to this momentariness of the
event of lending that the genitive case corresponds even though the
object is definite. The nominative-gen. difference in the first two
sentences thus corresponds to the indefinite-definite distinction
with respect to the meaning of the object; and the nominative-gen.
distinction in the second and third sentence corresponds to the
complete versus incomplete distinction with respect to the meaning
of the verb.

In RUSSIAN objects are alternatively case-marked accusative
(nominative) or genitive both in negative and in affirmative sentences. In both sentence types there is a correlation between
definiteness of object and non-genitive marking and indefiniteness
of object and genitive marking; as well as between completedness
of action and non-genitive marking and non-completedness of action

and genitive marking. The definiteness difference as conveyed by
differential case marking in affirmative sentences can be illustrated
by the following examples:

RUSSIAN:
peredajte me xleb
"pass me bread-nom."
'Pass me the bread.' ("all the bread (the plateful, the loaf)")

peredajte me xleba
"pass me bread-gen."
'Pass me some bread.' ("some of the bread, i.e. a slice")

student otpil piva
"student drank beer-gen."
'The student had a drink of beer.'

čerez minutu on dopil pivo i ušël
"after minute he up-drank wine-nom. and left"
'A minute later he drank up the beer and left.' (Christian 1961)

cvetov narvali
"flowers-gen. picked-we"
'We picked some flowers.'

plesni-ka ešče dofejku
"pour still little-coffee-gen."
'Do pour some more coffee.'   (Crockett 1975)

ždat' avtobusa
"wait-to bus-gen."
'to wait for the bus'

ždat' p'atyj avtobus
"wait-to fifth-nom. bus-nom."
'to wait for bus number five'   (Brooks 1967)

The semantic difference between completed and not completed action
in affirmative sentences as conveyed by differential case marking is
exemplifiable by a sentence very similar to the POLISH sentence
cited earlier: according to Jakobson (1966), the sentence <u>daj mne
tvojego noža</u> "give me your-gen. knife-gen." means 'Give me your
knife (for a short time).' whereas I gather the sentence <u>daj mne tvoj</u>

nož "give me your-nom. knife-nom." would simply mean 'Give me your knife!"

Objects in negative sentences in RUSSIAN as well as in POLISH used to be always in the genitive. The development towards marking some such objects as accusative-nominative rather than genitive, which started in POLISH only recently, was in process in RUSSIAN already in the middle of the nineteenth century and has been going on ever since. Present usage, as in POLISH, is heterogeneous, conditions are complex and of diverse types as indicated by the large literature on the subject.[3] Nevertheless, the two conditions

---

[3] See, for instance, Magner 1955, Uglitsky 1956, Restan 1960, Christian 1961, Ward 1965, Davidson 1967. The conditions that enter can be roughly classified as sentence-semantic, lexical-semantic, grammatical and stylistic. First of all the choice of specific verbs and specific object nouns may be criterial. Thus, concrete nouns, proper names, animate nouns, singular nouns, singular nouns of the feminine declension are more often in the accusative than those that belong to the opposite category and body part names and the word for 'this,' eto, are generally in the genitive. If a sentence is a negative interrogative sentence with an affirmative answer expected, then the object may be in the accusative. The choice of emphatic constituent in the sentence also enters; according to Ward 1965 the two versions of the sentence 'He did not buy a machine.' answer two different questions: on ne kupil mašinu, with 'machine' in the accusative, answers the question: 'He did not do what?' and on ne kupil mašiny, with 'machine' in the genitive, answers the question 'He did not buy what?' Objects indirectly governed by a negative verb, those preceding a negative verb rather than following it, those modified, those in imperative sentences and those cooccurring with a predicate instrumental are more often in the accusative. Some of these conditions also appear to hold in POLISH (see Brooks 1967); such as the fact that indirectly governed objects or those occurring in negative questions with an affirmative answer expected or those preposed to the verb are more often in the accusative. It is interesting to note that objects in imperative sentences behave differently from objects of declarative sentences from the point of view of case-assignment not only in RUSSIAN -- where they tend to be in the accusative even if negated, rather than in the genitive -- but also in FINNISH where they are in the nominative rather than in the genitive. For the FINNISH facts see Timberlake 1975. Finally, the choice of case-marking on negated objects is also a matter of style in that there are more frequent occurrences of the accusative in colloquial than in literary style. There are also sentences where the accusative and the genitive are simply in free variation; e.g. on ne prines moju lapatu / mojej lapaty "he not brought-he my-accus. shovel-accus./my-gen. shovel-gen." 'He did not bring my shovel.'

that we have seen to be sufficient to account for at least some of
the case-marking alternations also suffice to do so in RUSSIAN.
Some sentences to illustrate the definiteness-distinguishing role
of the case alternation are the following:

ne proexalo avtomobil'a
"not went-by-it car-gen."
'Not a car went by.'

ne slyšno ptitsy
"not heard-it bird-gen."
'Not a bird is to be heard.'   (Davidson 1967)

otveta ne prišlo
"answer-gen. not came-it"
'No answer came.'

otvet ne prišol
"answer-nom. not came-it"
'The answer didn't come.'   (Jakobson 1966)

on ne ljubit eti stixi
"he not likes these-nom. verses-nom."
'He does not like these verses.'

on ne ljubit stixov
"he not likes verses-gen."
'He does not like poetry.'

ja ne vižu dna
"I not see-I bottom-gen."
'I don't see (a/the) bottom.' (as if looking down into a pail of water)

Ja ne vižu dno
"I not see-I bottom-nom."
'I don't see the bottom.' (as if looking down into a pail of water
and trying to see the bottom)   (Magner 1955)

An example suggestive of the case-marking difference being correlated with completedness difference is this:

ona nam obed ne prigatovila
"she us dinner-nom. not up-prepared-she"
'She did not prepare (completed) dinner for us.'

ona nam obeda ne gatovila
"she us dinner-gen. not prepared-she"
'She did not prepare dinner for us.'   (Magner 1955)

In ESTONIAN and in FINNISH the direct object is either in the nominative or in the genitive, or in the partitive. The conditions correlated with the choice between the nominative and the genitive will be mentioned in the next section; it is the alternation of the nominative or genitive with the partitive that is of concern now. The conditions that correspond to this choice are those that we have just seen to be included among the set of varied and complicated conditions that determine the corresponding choice in POLISH and RUSSIAN. The rule for ESTONIAN and FINNISH is this: the direct object is in the partitive if it is indefinite and/or if the action is in complete (progressive or repeated) and/or if the verb is negated. As in the Slavic and Baltic languages, the case of at least some intransitive subjects alternates under the same conditions between nominative and partitive.

The object-definiteness and action-completedness distinction as correlated with the case marking of the object can be illustrated for ESTONIAN by the following sentences:

jõin vett	"I-drank water-part." 'I drank (some) water.'
jõin vee ära	"I-drank water-gen. up" 'I drank (all) the water.'
tahan õuna süüna	"want-I apple-part. eat-to" 'I want to eat an apple.'
tahan selle õuna ära süüa	"want-I this-gen. apple-gen. up eat-to" 'I want to eat (up) this apple.'
kirjanik kirjutab uut romaani	"writer is-writing new-part. novel" 'The writer is writing a new novel.'
kijranik kirjutab uue romaani	"writer is-writing new-gen. novel" 'The writer will write a new novel.'
kijranik kirjutas uut romaani	"writer was-writing new-part. novel" 'The writer was writing a new novel.'
kirjanik kirjutas uue romaani	"writer was-writing new-gen. novel" 'The writer wrote a new novel.'
otsi endale tööd	"yourself find work-part." 'Find yourself (some) work!'

otsi endale too   "yourself find work-gen. "
                                     'Find yourself a job.'
                                     (Raun and Saareste 1965: 32-33)

An example to illustrate case-use in affirmative and negative sentence is this:

mees tǎppap naise   "man will-kill woman-gen. "
                                     'The man will kill the woman.'

mees ei tǎppa naist   "man not will-kill woman-part. "
                                     'The man will not kill the woman.'
                                          (Harms 1962: 127)

In ESTONIAN there are certain verbs expressing feelings, wishes, sensations, approval or disapproval — verbs, that is, that do not affect their objects in that no change of state is caused to them — which require a partitive object even in the affirmative. For example:

armastan seda inimest   "I-love this-part. person-part. "
                                     'I love this person.'

As pointed out by Raun and Saareste (1965: 33) the verb 'love' with a genitive complement such as in the sentence armastan selle inimese "I-love this-gen. person-gen. " "does not mean anything or may be vaguely associated with killing somebody by love." However, if these verbs cooccur with a completive adverb (such as ära 'off, away,' labi 'through, finished,' maha 'down,' üles 'together,' kinni 'closed, stick,' heaks 'well'), they require genitive or nominative rather than partitive objects; e.g.:

ma ootasin rongi   "I waited-for train-part. "
                                     'I waited for the train.'

ma ootasin ära rongi tuleku "I waited-for train-of arrival-gen. "
                                     'I waited for the train's arrival.'

ta tundis selle naist   "he knew this-part. woman-part. "
                                     'He knew this woman.'

ta tundis selle naise ära "he knew this-gen. woman-gen. up"
                                     'He recognized this woman.'

seda opilast kiidete väga "this-part. student-part. was-praised highly"
                                     'This student was praised highly.'

see plaan kiideti heaks   "this-nom. plan-nom. was-praised well"
                                     'This plan was approved.'
                                           (Oinas 1966: 224)

Illustrative sentences for similarly conditioned genitive/nomina-
tive partitive alternations for transitive objects and intransitive
subjects in FINNISH may be the following:

halvan paistia	"I-want steak-part." 'I want some steak.'
halvan paistin	"I-want steak-gen." 'I want a/the steak.'
otan kahvia kaapista	"I take coffee-part. cupboard-from" 'I take/am taking some coffee from the the cupboard.'
otan kahvin kaapista	"I-take coffee-gen. cupboard-from" 'I take the coffee from the cupboard.'
en ota' kahvia kaapista	"not will-take-I coffee-part. cupboard-from" 'I will not take coffee from the cupboard.'
pöydällä on kirja	"table-on is book-nom." 'There is a book on the table.'
pöydällä ei ole' kirjaa	"table-on not is book-partitive" 'There is no book on the table.' (Lehtinen 1963: 69f)
mies loi koiraa	"man struck dog-part." 'The man struck the dog.'
mies tappoi koiran	"man killed dog-gen." 'The man killed the dog.' (Wickman 1955: 11ff)

In BASQUE the direct object is marked partitive in contexts that
are more restricted than similar contexts in the FINNIC and SLAVIC
languages just discussed. The direct object is in the partitive in
this language if it is indefinite and the object of a negated verb.
Note the following examples (de Rijk 1972):

ijito ori ikusi degu	"gypsy-nom. that seen have-we" 'We have seen that gypsy.'
ez degu ijito ori ikusi	"not have-we gypsy-nom. that seen" 'We have not seen that gypsy.'

ijitoa ikusi degu   "gypsy-a seen have-we"
                           'We have seen a gypsy.'

ez degu ijitorik ikusi   "not have-we gypsy-part. seen"
                           'We have not seen a gypsy.'

As the first two sentences show, definite noun phrases have the same
nominative markings in affirmative and negative sentences; indefinite noun phrases, however, as the third and fourth sentences
indicate, are differently marked depending on whether the sentence
is affirmative or negative; and the marking they have in negative
sentences is partitive marking.

The sentences of GOTHIC, LATVIAN, LITHUANIAN, POLISH,
RUSSIAN, ESTONIAN, FINNISH and BASQUE show that in some
languages objects -- whether objects of transitive or subjects of
intransitive sentences -- may be alternatively marked by an accusative-nominative marker or by a partitive marker, that this
marking difference does not correlate with any difference in semantic case function, and that it correlates at least in some cases
with one or more of the following semantic properties of the verbs
or nouns involved:

   a. the definiteness-indefiniteness of the noun phrase,
   b. the extent to which the object is involved in the event,
   c. the completedness versus non-completedness of the event,
   d. whether the sentence is affirmative or negative.

Wickman (1955:14), in discussing the FINNISH case, proposes that
the correct generalization for this language is that objects of non-
resultative actions are in the partitive and those of resultative
actions in the nominative or genitive. If the attribute "resultative"
is applied to an action that does take place, that does involve a
specific thing for its non-agentive participant that is actually affected by the action and it is affected with respect to its total quantity
or extension, Wickman's proposal provides an informal but basically
correct way of capturing the semantic conditions that correlate with
the accusative/nominative-partitive case alternation in all the examples discussed above.

2.4 Accusative and nominative

In some languages there is a cross-sentential alternation between
marking an object as accusative and marking the semantic case-
functionally same object as nominative -- that is, as the subject of

a transitive sentence. There are two distinct types of sentences
in which objects appear marked as a transitive subject: in sentences
which do not also include a transitive subject and in sentences which
also include a transitive subject. The following examples illustrate
these two sentence types.

a. LATIN:
puer puellam amat   "boy-nom. girl-accus. loves"
                                                  'The boy loves the girl.'

puella a puero amatur   "girl-noml by boy-ablat. is-loved"
                                                  'The girl is loved by the boy.'

puella amatur   "girl-nom. is-loved"
                                                  'The girl is loved.'

puella beata est   "girl-nom. happy is"
                                                  'The girl is happy.'

b. SPANISH:
el chico ve la nieve   "the-nom. boy sees the-nom. snow"
                                                  'The boy sees the snow.'

el chico ve a esa chica   "the-nom. boy sees accus. this girl"
                                                  'The boy sees this girl.'

Case-functionally neutral noun phrases in these sentences are 'girl'
in the LATIN examples and 'snow' and 'girl' in the SPANISH ones.
Of the LATIN sentences the first has puella marked accusative and
the others have it marked as nominative. Of the SPANISH sentences
the first has the object – la nieve – marked nominative and the second
has it (esa chica) marked accusative. The LATIN sentences that
have the object marked as nominative do not also include another
nominative — they are passive or intransitive sentences. The first
SPANISH sentence, however, that has the object marked as nominative also includes another noun phrase that is marked nominative —
the transitive subject of the sentence.

The semantic conditions correlated with the two kinds of marking
variation of objects appear to be opposites of each other in that
nominatively marked objects of intransitive sentences have more
semantic properties in common with a "typical" transitive subject
than accusatively marked objects in such sentences; but nominatively
marked objects in transitive sentences have less in common with
"typical" transitive subjects. In the LATIN sentences cited above,

for instance, the difference between what puellam in the first sentence and puella in the other sentences stand for is the same difference that also obtains between puellam and puer in the first sentence; or between a puero and puer in the second and first sentences, respectively; namely, the difference between the topic of the sentence and what is said about it. The nominative marking of objects in passive and other intransitive sentences which they share with transitive subjects thus appears to correspond to the shared semantic property of topicality between such objects and transitive subjects. Things are different in the SPANISH case. The conditions in SPANISH with which the differential case marking of objects correlates involve the animacy and the definiteness of objects: objects that are animate and definite (such as esa chica above) are accusatively marked but objects that are not animate and definite (such as la nieve above) are nominatively marked. But to the extent that a "typical" transitive subject is animate and definite, this means that in this case objects that are unlike transitive subjects are marked as transitive subjects; whereas in the LATIN case we saw that objects that were, in some sense, like transitive subjects were marked as transitive subjects.

These generalizations about the semantic correlates of accusative-nominative case marking alternations of direct objects in LATIN and SPANISH hold for other languages as well that do exhibit such alternations. Studies by Shopen (1972) and Keenan (1975b) have suggested that passive subjects do share semantic discourse function with transitive subjects in ENGLISH and in some other languages,[4] and the correlation in transitive sentences between accusative marking and definiteness and/or animacy has been noted and illustrated for

---

[4] In FINNISH, as discussed by Timberlake (1975) and also in ESTONIAN (Raun and Saareste 1965: 32ff and Oinas 1966: 237-8), agentless passives constitute a class with two other constructions on the basis of the semantic object being marked nominative, rather than genitive as otherwise: these are imperative sentences and infinitives that are subjects of a sentence. Compare, for instance, an ordinary sentence where the object is marked genitive: mies sao kirjan "man-nom. gets book-accus." 'The man gets the book.' and an agentless passive, imperative, and infinitive-subject sentence, respectively, where the object is marked nominative: sinne viedään lahja "there will-be-taken present-nom." 'The present will be taken there;' saata tyttö kotiin "take girl-nom. home" 'Take the girl home;' (minun) täytyy tehdä se "(I -gen.) is-necessary to-do it-nom." 'It is necessary for me to do it.'

a number of languages by Blansitt (1973) and Hegedeos (1973). The interesting question, of course, is the distribution of these case-marking alternation patterns in the languages of the world. Whereas the first type of alternation may be universal -- in that perhaps all languages allow for the identical case marking of a topical object and a topical agent without at the same time also allowing for the identical marking of any other topical constituent as well -- the second type is not universal in that not all but only some languages case-mark animate and/or definite objects of transitive sentences one way and inanimate and/or indefinite ones in another way. In what follows, therefore, I will list and possibly illustrate such case alternations in all the languages where I know that it occurs.

Languages in which the conditions that correlate with the differ-ential marking of direct objects in transitive sentences include both conditions related to definiteness and also conditions related to animacy or some other type of natural gender distinctions include some INDO-EUROPEAN languages such as SPANISH, RUMANIAN, ALBANIAN, BENGALI, HINDI and OSSETIC, some FINNO-UGRIC ones such as PERMIAN, and some ALTAIC ones such as BURIAT and MONGOLIAN. The more particular semantic classes in terms of which object marking rules can be stated for these languages are these: personal pronouns, proper names, human nouns, animate nouns, definite noun phrases, singular noun phrases. In addition, in ALBANIAN the semantically not fully characterizable classes of grammatically masculine and feminine versus neuter nouns are significant in this respect. In all of these languages, with the pos-sible exception of ALBANIAN, there is free -- that is, both seman-tically and grammtically unconditioned -- variation between accusative and nominative marking within at least one of the above-mentioned semantic classes of objects. The pattern that I found most frequent in this small sample is obligatory accusative marking for definite and animate noun phrases; optional choice between accusative or nominative markings for definite and inanimate noun phrases; and nominative marking for noun phrases that are indefinite regardless of whether they are animate or not. This appears to be the rule for BENGALI, HINDI, OSSETIC and MONGOLIAN. Sentences to illus-trate this from HINDI are these:

Ram Sita ko marta hɛ	"Ram Sita accus. beat aux."
	'Ram beats Sita.'
chwri ko law	"knife accus. bring"
	'Bring the knife!'
chwri lao	"knife bring"
	'Bring a knife!'

Omission of ko in the first sentence would be ungrammatical; the
respective omission and addition of ko in the second and third
sentences would alter the meaning. In HINDI, however, two additional qualifications have to be added, one restricting the class of
contexts where the accusative marking is used and one widening it.
First, if the sentence includes a dative, then the dative receives
the accusative marking and the object does not regardless of its
definiteness and animacy status; and second, the accusative marker
can apparently also be used with indefinite inanimate objects if the
sentence would otherwise be ambiguous as to which of the two noun
phrases is the agent and which is the object; such as in the sentence
hira ʃiʃe ko kaṭta həy where ko is the accusative marker distinguishing ʃiʃe from hira as being the object and which means 'A
diamond cuts glass.'[5] The rule in BURIAT is also the same as in
BENGALI, HINDI and OSSETIC except that in this language the
accusative-nominative alternation also has to do with the completedness of the action as the following examples indicate:

modo sabšaa	"wood/tree cut-he" 'He chopped wood.'
modiiji sabšana	"wood/tree-accus. cuts-he" 'He cuts the tree.' (where it is assumed that he will get it cut)(Poppe 1960 - Hegedeos)[6]

The class of objects marked in RUMANIAN is somewhat smaller in
that the use of the accusative preposition pe is not obligatory with
all animates but only with humans and it is optional with other
non-human animates, and in that pe does not appear to be used at
all with inanimate objects even if they are definite (Seiver 1953 -
Hegedeos). The rules for PERMIAN (Wickman 1955) and SPANISH,
beyond the understanding that they involve both animacy and definiteness, are not sufficiently clear to me to enable me to compare these
languages with the ones mentioned above.

---

[5] For case-marking in HINDI see Harley 1944, Allen 1950-51,
Bender 1967, Saksena 1973. For OSSETIC see Abaev 1964 - Hegedeos;
for BENGALI see Ray, Hai and Ray 1966 - Hegedeos, and Ferguson
1970.

[6] In BURIAT the alternation is actually between the accusative
and the "oblique stem" which in most cases has the same form as
the nominative, except for a small class of nouns where the nominative has an -n suffix which, however, is dropped in the oblique
stem (Poppe 1960 - Hegedeos).

ALBANIAN is the only one of these languages where the statement of the rule must involve reference to non-semantic lexical properties of the nouns involved. In this language the direct object has the same form as a nominative except if it is definite, singular, and either masculine or feminine grammatically (Mann 1932 - Hegedeos). The three gender classes of masculine, feminine and neuter are non-semantic classes at least to the extent that the masculine and feminine classes include inanimate nouns as well. Thus, given the three nouns mal- 'mountain,' deg- 'branch,' and djath- 'cheese,' which are masculine, feminine and neuter, respectively, the forms that differ in the accusative and in the nominative are only these:

mali	'the mountain-nom.'	dega	'the branch-nom.'
malin	'the mountain-accus.'	degen	'the branch-accus.'

Otherwise accusative and nominative forms are the same: mal means 'a mountain' in both cases, malet means 'the mountains' in both cases, male means 'mountains' in both cases; degë means 'a branch' in both cases, degat means 'the branches' in both cases, dega means 'branches' in both cases; and djatht, djath, djathnat and djathna mean 'the cheese,' 'a cheese,' 'the cheeses' and 'cheeses,' respectively, in both cases. Apart from the fact that the ALBANIAN rule involves reference to non-semantic classes of nouns, it also differs from the other languages in that the conditions that correlate with the alternation of accusative-nominative marking also correlate with alternation with respect to other cases. Thus, the dative and the ablative are not distinguished for singular indefinite masculine and neuter nouns but they are distinguished for definite singular neuter nouns obligatorily and for definite singular masculine nouns optionally. In contrast with this, in all the languages mentioned so far and that will be mentioned, the alternation correlated with definiteness pertains only to the accusative marking.

The basic rule that holds for BENGALI, HINDI, OSSETIC and MONGOLIAN suggests that of the two basic types of semantic conditions -- definiteness and animacy -- definiteness is the "stronger" one in that the contexts in these languages where accusative marking may occur at all and those where it must not occur can be defined by reference to definiteness and not by reference to animacy. The contexts, that is, where accusative marking occurs at all, whether obligatorily or optionally, are the contexts of definite objects and not those of animate objects; and those where accusative marking never occurs are the contexts of indefinite objects and not those of inanimate objects. Animacy enters only to define within the class of definite noun phrases those contexts where accusative marking must occur, as opposed to those where it may or may not occur.

This precedence of the definiteness condition is further suggested
by the fact that in most of those languages where the accusative-
nominative marking distinction for direct objects depends on a set
of conditions that does not include both definiteness and animacy,
this set of conditions includes definiteness only, and that, apart
from a group of INDO-EUROPEAN languages, there are only a few
cases where the condition is animacy only. Languages in which the
choice between accusative and nominative marking correlates with
the definiteness distinction but not with the animacy distinction include a number of ALTAIC languages (BASHKIR, MANCHU, TATAR,
TURKISH), some FINNO-UGRIC languages (KAMASSIAN, LAPPISH,
MORDVIN, VOGUL), some from the INDO-EUROPEAN family
(PANJABI, PERSIAN, TAJIK, ARMENIAN), some SEMITIC languages (HEBREW, LEBANESE ARABIC, AMHARIC, TIGRE), some
CUSHITIC ones (KEMANT, BILIN), some MALAYO-POLYNESIAN
languages (MARANAO, TAGALOG, TANGOAN-SANGO, MALOESE);
furthermore GÃ and TWI of the African languages and MANDARIN.
Of these there are very few languages where the rule would simply
say: all definite direct objects of transitive sentences are marked
accusative and all indefinite ones are marked nominative. The only
languages where I do not have any reason to doubt the validity of
this simple rule are TURKISH, MANCHU, MARANAO, AMHARIC,
KEMANT and BILIN. In all the others of the listed languages only
some but not all definite nouns are marked accusative and/or some
indefinite nouns are also marked accusative. Languages where
definiteness is a necessary but not sufficient condition to predict
accusative marking of objects in transitive sentences are these:
PUNJABI, PERSIAN, TAJIK, TIGRE, TAGALOG, MANDARIN,
GÃ, and TWI. The additional conditions which, taken together with
definiteness, provide for a set of conditions that are sufficient to
predict accusative marking differ in these languages. In PUNJABI
only pronouns are obligatorily marked accusative, other definite
noun phrases only optionally (Comrie 1973). In PERSIAN and TAJIK
(Rastorgueva 1964 and Rastorgueva 1963 - Hegedeos), pronouns,
proper names and possessed nouns are obligatorily marked as
accusative and other definite noun phrases only optionally. In TIGRE
some but not all direct objects are accusative-marked again and the
conditions are not known to me (Leslau 1945). In TAGALOG, also,
definite direct objects may but they do not have to be marked for
accusative (Schachter and Otanes 1972). In MANDARIN all direct
objects that cooccur with the preposition bǎ and have thus a form
that is distinct from the form of nominative nouns are definite and
they are either objects of simple verbs that require that their (definite) object should cooccur with bǎ, such as kàn 'regard' or mèng-
dào 'dream of;' or they are (definite) objects of complex verbs such

as <u>jiā wūdǐng</u> 'add roof,' <u>bāo pí</u> 'peel skin;' or they are objects
of verbs that express a completed action; or they are focussed.
The latter two conditions are exemplified by the following:

ta sī le nèifeng xìn
"he tear aspect that letter"
'He tore up that letter.'

ta bǎ nèifeng xìn sī-diào le
"he accus. that letter tear-completion aspect"
'He tore up that letter.'

ta mài le tāde chē
"he sell aspect his car"
'He sold his car.'

ta bǎ tāde chē mài le
"he accus. his car sell aspect"
'He sold his car.' (with 'car' being the topic) (Thompson 1972)

Both in GÃ and in TWI preverbal direct objects and no postverbal
direct objects are marked and all preverbal direct objects are
definite; but not all definite objects are preverbal and thus marked
and the conditions are not clear (Trutenau 1973; Stewart 1963,
Christaller 1875).

Languages, on the other hand, where definiteness is a sufficient
but not a necessary condition to predict accusative marking are
BASHKIR, TATAR, LEBANESE ARABIC and HEBREW. In BASH-
KIR, TATAR and LEBANESE ARABIC definiteness is not a necessary condition in that in addition to all definite noun phrases,
interrogative pronouns, too, are accusatively marked which are
semantically indefinite (Poppe 1964, 1963, Koutsoudas 1967). In
HEBREW the accusative preposition occurs with all definite direct
objects but also with some indefinite ones such as indefinite and
interrogative pronouns and indefinite nouns (Cole 1975). Finally,
definiteness does not appear to be either necessary or sufficient
to predict accusative marking in KAMASSIAN, LAPPISH, MORDVIN
and VOGUL in that, according to Wickman (1955), although there is
a tendency in all of these languages to mark definite noun phrases
as accusative and indefinite ones as nominative, there are both
definite noun phrases that are marked nominative and indefinite
ones that are marked accusative, with the conditions being unclear.

The languages where, to my knowledge, the accusative-nominative
marking alternation correlates with animacy distinctions and not

with definiteness are LUISEÑO, TELUGU and some INDO-EUROPEAN
languages. In LUISEÑO the rule appears to be simple: animate nouns
have an accusative marker and inanimate ones do not; compare, for
instance, the word for 'lizard' which is <u>kasilla</u> in the nominative
and <u>kasillay</u> in the accusative and the word for 'basket' which is
<u>tukmal</u> both in the nominative and in the accusative (Hyde 1971: 35f).
In TELEGU, according to Rào (1967: 71-73), the accusative suffix
<u>ni</u>/<u>nu</u> is not used usually if the object is "a lifeless thing." In MA-
RATHI (Gupte 1975) the direct object is obligatorily marked if human,
optionally marked if animate non-human and not marked if inanimate.
Finally, in a great number of European languages such as ANCIENT
GREEK, LATIN, GERMAN and RUSSIAN, grammatically masculine
and feminine nouns, which include most naturally animate ones and
some naturally inanimate ones, are differentiated for nominative
and accusative, but grammatically neuter ones are not.

In sum: we noted that objects may be nominative-marked in
intransitive sentences if they resemble transitive subjects by functioning as topics, and that they may be nominative-marked in transitive sentences if they are unlike "typical" agentive transitive subjects
in that they are inanimate or indefinite or both. The particular categories along which the accusative-nominative alternation patterns
include the following:[7] human nouns, personal pronouns, proper
names, animate nouns, definite nouns, possessed nouns, topical
nouns, completed action. In addition other factors are lexical properties of the verb, grammatical number, grammatical gender. In
some cases the choice of the two markings depends on whether the
sentence also includes a dative phrase or not; and on whether the
sentence would be ambiguous if the object were not distinctively
marked from the nominative or not. We also noted that although

---

[7] There are also some languages for which my sources said the
use of the accusative marker was simply optional — that is, the
choice between marking or not marking an object is semantically
and otherwise unconditioned. This is the case for MALAGASY
(Keenan 1975a) where the dative-prefix can apparently be optionally
used to mark a non-dative object; compare: <u>naname vola an-sRabe</u>
<u>aho</u> "gave money accus.-Rabe I" 'I gave money to Rabe;' <u>nahita</u>
<u>an-sRabe Rakoto</u> "saw accus.-Rabe Rakoto" 'Rakoto saw Rabe.'
Optionality is claimed for the use of the object marker -<u>si</u> in KU-
NAMA as well (Tucker and Bryan 1966: 340). In LAHU the object
marker (Matisoff 1973: 155ff) and in KANURI (Lukas 1937) both subject and object markers are said to be used optionally and are
obligatory only if ambiguity would otherwise arise.

there are both languages where definiteness is the crucial semantic
property and animacy is irrelevant and also languages where animacy is critical without definiteness, in those languages where
both are relevant, definiteness is the more significant of the two
properties since the property of animacy separates only those cases
where accusative marking is obligatory from those where it is
optional, whereas definiteness separates those where accusative
marking occurs at all from those where it does not. To the extent
that definiteness and completedness of action figured among the
relevant semantic conditions, the general nature of the accusative-
nominative alternation can be seen to be similar to the general
nature of the accusative-adverbial and accusative-partitive alternation examined earlier.

2.5 Accusative and topic

The most basic shared property of all case alternations of objects
— except for one class to be mentioned presently — that we have
surveyed so far is that the intuitively felt semantic markedness
relation between the semantic classes that corresponded to the
class of accusatively marked and to the class of otherwise marked
noun phrases was always such that the semantically marked class
corresponded to the accusatively marked class, and the semantically
unmarked class correlated with the non-accusative marking. Thus,
affected and not unaffected, totally involved and not partially involved,
definite and not indefinite, and animate and not inanimate noun phrases
were accusatively marked. The class of alternations that constitutes
an exception to this generalization is the alternation of the accusative
with the nominative case in sentences which do not include a transitive subject since, as it was noted, here the non-topical (or unmarked)
objects are accusatively marked and the topical (or marked) ones
are in the nominative. The last class of case-alternations of direct
objects that I will now turn to is unlike the accusative-adverbial,
accusative-partitive and one class of the accusative-nominative alternations, and it is like this other class of accusative-nominative
alternations in that the semantic class of accusatively marked noun
phrases will be seen to be unmarked in comparison with the semantic
class of non-accusatively marked noun phrases. The case in question
whose alternation with the accusative will be discussed is the topic
case. A topic case marker is a segment sequence associated with
members of a class of noun phrases whose membership is case-
functionally unrestricted -- it may include noun phrases of any possible semantic case function -- and it is definable instead by all
members sharing the semantic property of topicality.

Languages in which such alternations are observable include
TAGALOG, SAMOAN, JAPANESE, KOREAN and LISU. In TAGA-
LOG, as mentioned earlier, indefinite objects are case-marked as
definite (but not topical) agents: by the preposition ng. Definite
objects may be preceded by the preposition sa if they are not topical; and if they are topical, they will be preceded by ang which
is the preposition introducing all other non-pronominal and non-
proper name topical noun phrases as well. Compare, for instance:

naghihintay siya ng dilubyo   "waiting he-topic ng flood"
                                'He is waiting for a flood.'

hinihintay niya ang dilubyo   "waiting he-non-topic topic flood"
                                'He is waiting for the flood.'
                                ('flood' being topical) (Bowen 1965)

Similar alternations can be observed in SAMOAN between the prepositionless accusative and the topic case marked by the preposition
o; in JAPANESE between the accusative marked by the postposition
o and the topic case marked by the postposition wa; in KOREAN
between the accusative marked by the postposition il /lil and the
topic case marked by the postposition in/nin (Park 1973); and in
LISU between the postpositionally unmarked accusative and the
topic case marked by the postposition nya (Li and Thompson 1975b).

3. Conclusions

In some languages there are pairs of sentences whose members
differ from each other in that a non-agentive non-dative noun phrase
of the same semantic case function is differently case-marked. This
study has shown that there is considerable cross-linguistic conver-
gence both as to the additional functions of those case-markings that
figure in such alternations and also as to the semantic conditions
that are associated with the alternative markings. In particular
accusative-adverbial, accusative-partitive, accusative-nominative
and accusative-topic alternations were seen to be cross-linguistically
recurrent; and the former three were seen to be recurrently associated with distinctions of definiteness, animacy and total affectedness
of the referent of the object noun phrase in sentences some of whose
verbs were, too, seen to be cross-linguistically synonymous (such
as in sentences with verbs of filling and emptying). All the data
discussed in this paper and otherwise known to me are thus consistent with the following generalizations. If in a language a particular
non-agentive and non-dative noun phrase is alternatively case-marked
in two distinct ways, the alternation will be that of an accusative and

an adverbial marking, or that of an accusative and a partitive marking, or that of an accusative and a nominative marking, or that of
an accusative and a topic marking. If there is any semantic difference between an accusative marking and either an adverbial, or a
partitive, or a nominative marking (to the exclusion of passivization),
this semantic difference will be related either to definiteness, or to
animacy, or humanness or to degree of affectedness of the Object,
with the accusative, by definition, marking the more definite (rather
than the less definite), the animate or human (rather than the inanimate or non-human), and the totally affected (rather than the unaffected) noun phrase.

As noted in the introduction, the scope of this study in the alternative expressions of case-functionally alike noun phrases was restricted in that only segmental case-marking alternation has been
considered, and this only with respect to noun phrases whose case-
function is non-agentive and non-dative. In closing, however, I
would like to briefly point at some evidence indicating that the semantic properties that are correlated with the alternative case-
markings of semantic objects are also the ones that are correlated
with at least some other types of form variation of semantic objects
and also with the case-function-preserving form-variation of noun
phrases that are agents and datives. Thus, for instance, a number
of studies noted that the occurrence and non-occurrence of verb-
object agreement is correlated in some languages (such as HUN-
GARIAN or MODERN GREEK) with the definiteness and/or animacy
of the object (cp. Haas 1973, Moravcsik 1974, Givón 1975). Similarly,
the preverbal versus postverbal ordering of the object noun phrase
is correlated with the definiteness of the object in MANDARIN (cp.
Li and Thompson 1975a); and the very alternation of lexicalizing the
object separately or co-lexicalizing it with the verb is also correlated
with referential properties such as genericity and definiteness and
with animacy in a number of languages (cp. Oates 1964: 55, 25-9 on
GUNWINGGU, Woodbury 1975 on ONONDAGA, and Sapir 1911 and
Mardirussian 1975 for a cross-linguistic account of object incorporation). That at least some case-marking variation of dative noun
phrases is also correlated with a semantic difference in "total"
versus "partial" affectedness is indicated by the use of ENGLISH
verbs such as present something to someone versus present someone
with something, pay something to someone versus pay someone, and
reply to someone versus answer someone; and their HUNGARIAN
synonyms. And there is at least one language, HINDI, which provides
examples of the case-marking of an agent noun phrase being correlated with its definiteness (cp. Ray, Hai and Ray 1966 - Hegedeos).

I hope that the data and informal generalizations presented in
this paper will be of use in constructing and testing general theories
about the correspondence relation between semantic case function
and sentence form in natural human languages.

BIBLIOGRAPHY

Abaev, V.I. 1964. A grammatical sketch of Ossetic. International
    Journal of American Linguistics [IJAL] 30.4. Part 2, Publication
    35.

Allen, W.S. 1950-51. A study in the analysis of Hindi sentence
    structure. Acta Linguistica 6. 68-87.

Anderson, W.R. 1970. A little light on the role of deep structure
    in semantic interpretation. NSF Report No. 26, Harvard Univer-
    sity, Cambridge, Mass. II.1-II.13.

Bender, E. 1967. Urdu grammar and reader. Philadelphia: Uni-
    versity of Pennsylvania Press.

Blansitt, E.L. Jr. 1973. Bitransitive sentences. Working Papers
    on Language Universals [WPLU] 13. 1-26. Stanford University.

Bowen, J.D. 1965. Beginning Tagalog. Berkeley and Los Angeles:
    University of California Press.

Brooks, Maria Zagorska. 1967. The accusative-genitive contrast
    in some Polish constructions. To honor Roman Jakobson: essays
    on the occasion of his seventieth birthday, Vol. I, 395-401. The
    Hague: Mouton.

Christaller, Rev. J.G. 1875. A grammar of the Asante and Fante
    language, called Tshi (Chwee, Twi). Basel, republished in 1964.
    Ridgewood, New Jersey: Gregg Press Inc.

Christian, R.F. 1961. Some consequences of the lack of a definite
    and indefinite article in Russian. The Slavic and East European
    Journal 5.19, no. 1, 1-12.

Cole, P. 1975. An apparent asymmetry in the formation of relative
    clauses in Modern Hebrew. Studies in the Linguistic Sciences
    5.1.1-35.

Comrie, B. 1973. The ergative: variations on a theme. Lingua
32. 239-253.

Crockett, D. 1975. Agreement in contemporary standard Russian.
To appear.

Dambriūnas, L., A. Ulimas, W.E. Schmalstieg. 1966. Introduction to Modern Lithuanian. New York.

Damerau, N. 1967. Polnische Grammatik. Berlin.

Davidson, R.M. 1967. The use of the genitive in negative constructions. Studies in the modern Russian Language 2. Cambridge.

de Rijk, R.P.G. 1974. Partitive assignment in Basque. Anuario
del Seminario de Filologia Vasca "Julio de Urquijo," 6, San
Sebastian, 130-173.

Ferguson, C.A. 1970. Grammatical categories in data collection.
WPLU 4.

Fraser, B. 1971. A note on the spray paint cases. Linguistic
Inquiry 2.4. 604-607.

Givón, T. 1975. Topic, pronoun and grammatical agreement.
Papers presented at the Conference on Subject and Topic held
in Santa Barbara, California.

Gupte, Sharad. 1975. Verb agreement in Marathi. Michigan State
University Working Papers in Language and Linguistics 1. 173-80.

Haas, O. 1973. Zum "objektanzeigenden Pronomen" der Balkan-
sprachen. Acta Linguistica Academiae Scientiarium Hungaricae 23. 1-2, 121-127.

Haile, Getatchew, 1971. The suffix pronouns in Amharic. Papers
in African Linguistics, ed. by Chin-wu Kim and H. Stahlke,
101-111. Edmonton-Champaign: Linguistic Research, Inc.

Hale, K. 1973. Person marking in Walbiri. A festschrift for
Morris Halle, ed. by S.R. Anderson and P. Kiparsky, 308-344.
New York, Chicago: Holt Rinehart and Winston, Inc.

Harley, A.H. 1944. Colloquial Hindustani. London.

Harms, R. T. 1963. Estonian grammar. Bloomington, Indiana.

Hegedeos, M. Z. 1973. Unmarked direct objects. UCLA term paper, manuscript.

Hetzron, R. 1971. Toward an Amharic case-grammar. Studies in African Linguistics 1.3. 301-354.

Hyde, V. 1971. An introduction to the Luiseño language. Banning, California.

Jakobson, R. 1966. Beitrag zur allgemeinen Kasuslehre. (Reprint) Readings in Linguistics by E.P. Hamp, F. Householder, R. Austerlitz, II. 51-89.

Jespersen, O. 1954. A Modern English grammar on historical principles, Part III. London, Copenhagen.

Keenan, E. 1975a. Remarkable subjects in Malagasy. Paper presented at the Conference on Subject and Topic held in Santa Barbara, California.

_____. 1975b. Some universals of passive in relational grammar. Papers from the Eleventh Regional Meeting, Chicago Linguistic Society (Chicago, Ill.), ed. by L.J. San, T.J. Vance, 340-352.

Knobloch, J. 1952. La voyelle thématique -e-/-o- serait-elle un indice d'objet indo-européen? Lingua 3. 407-420.

Koutsoudas, A. 1967. Doubled nominals in Lebanese. Glossa 1.1. 33-48.

Lazdina, T.B. 1966. Teach yourself Latvian. London.

Lehtinen, M. 1963. Basic course in Finnish. Bloomington, The Hague.

Leslau, W. 1945. Short grammar of Tigre. Publications of the American Oriental Society, Offprint Series No. 18.

Li, C. and S.A. Thompson. 1975a. The semantic function of word order: a case study in Mandarin. Word order and word order change, ed. by C. Li, 163-196. University of Texas Press.

_____. 1975b. Subject and topic: a new typology of language.

Paper presented at the Conference on Subject and Topic held in Santa Barbara, California.

Lukas, J. 1937. A study of the Kanuri language. Oxford University Press.

Magner, T.F. 1955. Negation and case selection in Russian. Word 11.4. 531-544.

Mann, S.E. 1932. A short Albanian grammar. London.

Mardirussian, G. 1975. Noun-incorporation in universal grammar. Papers from the eleventh regional meeting, Chicago Linguistic Society (Chicago, Ill.), ed. by R.E. Grossman, L.J. San, T.J. Vance, 383-389.

Matisoff, J.A. 1973. The grammar of Lahu. Berkeley, Los Angeles: University of California Press.

Moravcsik, E. 1974. Object-verb agreement. WPLU 15. 25-140.

Oates, L.F. 1964. A tentative description of the Gunwinggu language. Oceania Linguistic Monographs 10.

Oinas, F.J. 1966. Basic course in Estonian. Bloomington, The Hague.

Park, Byung-Soo. 1973. On the multiple subject construction in Korean. Linguistics 100. 63-76.

Poppe, N.N. 1960. Buriat grammar. Bloomington, Indiana.

_____. 1963. Tatar manual. Bloomington, Indiana.

_____. 1964. Bashkir manual. Bloomington, Indiana.

Rāo, B. Sāmbasiva. 1967. Telugu made easy. Secunderabad.

Rastorgueva, V.S. 1963. A short sketch of Tajik grammar. IJAL 29.4, Part II, Publication 28.

_____. 1964. A short sketch of the grammar of Persian. IJAL 30.1, Part II.

Raun, A. and A. Saareste. 1965. Introduction to Estonian linguistics. Wiesbaden: Otto Harrassowitz, Ural-Altaische Bibliothek 12.

Ray, P.S., M.A. Hai, L. Ray. 1966. Bengali language handbook. Center for Applied Linguistics.

Restan, Per A. 1960. The objective case in negative clauses in Russian: the genitive or the accusative. Scando-Slavica 6. 92-112.

Saksena, Radha. 1973. Handout on Hindi constituent order, UCLA.

Sapir, E. 1911. The problem of noun-incorporation. American Anthropologist 13.

Schachter, P. and Fe Otanes. 1972. Tagalog reference grammar. Berkeley and Los Angeles: Publication of the University of California.

Schenker, A.M. 1966. Beginning Polish. New Haven, London.

Seiver, G.O. 1953. Introduction to Romanian. New York.

Shopen, T. 1972. Logical equivalence is not semantic equivalence. Papers from the Eighth Regional Meeting, Chicago Linguistic Society (Chicago, Ill.), ed. by J.N. Levi, G.C. Phrase, 340-350.

Stewart, J.M. 1963. Some restrictions on objects in Twi. Journal of African Languages 2.2 145-149.

Stockwell, R.P., P. Schachter, B.H. Partee. 1973. The major syntactic structures of English. New York, Chicago: Holt, Rinehart and Winston, Inc.

Swadesh, M. 1946. South Greenlandic (Eskimo). Linguistic Structures of Native America, ed. by H. Hojjer.

Thompson, S.A. 1972. Transitivity and some problems with the ba construction in Mandarin Chinese. Studies in East Asian syntax, UCLA papers in syntax, ed. by G. Bedell, 70-86.

Timberlake, A. 1975. The nominative object in Finnish. Lingua 35. 3-4, 201-230.

Trutenau, H.M.J. 1973. The verbal status of the NP-links of Gã. Studies in African Linguistics 4.1. 71-86.

Tucker, A.N. and M.A. Bryan. 1966. Linguistic analyses: the Non-Bantu languages of North-Eastern Africa. Oxford.

Uglitsky, Z. 1956. Accusative and genitive with transitive verbs preceded by a negative in contemporary Russian. The Slavonic and East European Review 34. 83. 377ff.

Ward, D. 1965. The Russian language today: system and anomaly. Chicago.

Wickman, B. 1955. The form of the object in the Uralic languages. Uppsala.

Woodbury, H. 1975. Onondaga noun-incorporation: some notes on the interdependence of syntax and semantics. IJAL 41.1. 10-20.

Wright, J. 1899. A primer in the Gothic language. Oxford.

Zsilka, J. 1967. The system of Hungarian sentence patterns. Bloomington, Indiana.

Definiteness and Referentiality

TALMY GIVÓN

ABSTRACT

The paper discusses the typology of subsystems in grammar
which map the grammatical functions of definite-indefinite and
referential-generic. It lays down the universal semantic and pragmatic constraints which underlie these subsystems cross-linguistically, then illustrates some of the major typological variations
attested in languages, in the process also probing some of the most
common diachronic pathways which give rise to the observed typological diversity. The relationship between the grammar of definiteness and referentiality and the following other subparts of the
grammar will be discussed: pluralization, numerals, gender,
negation, the case-marking system, word order, verb typology,
deictic elements, topicalization, pronominalization and grammatical agreement. It will be shown how these related areas of the
grammar may interact with the subsystem under consideration.

CONTENTS

1. Preliminaries

This paper describes some of the more common ways in which languages map the discourse-pragmatic contrast of 'definite' vs. 'indefinite' as well as the semantic contrast of 'referential' vs. 'non-referential.' In no language is this subsystem totally isolated from other parts of the grammar, except perhaps in brand-new CREOLES close enough to their point of inception. While discussing the more common ways in which languages seem to divide the semantic-pragmatic pie of definiteness and referentiality, I will also attempt to show how other typological variables in the grammar interact -- both synchronically and diachronically -- with the subsystem under consideration. These other variables involve the following areas of the grammar:

a. Plurality, numerality and nominal gender (Secs. 2, 4, 6)
b. Negation (Sec. 3)
c. The case-marking system (Secs. 5, 6, 8.4)
d. Word order, verb typology, deixis (Sec. 6)
e. Degree of definiteness opacity (Sec. 7)
f. Topicality, pronominalization and grammatical agreement (Sec. 8)

In Sec. 1. 1 below, I will begin the discussion by outlining some of the universal semantic and pragmatic constraints which underlie our grammar of definiteness and referentiality.

1. 1 Referentiality[1]

a. In the terms used here, referentiality is a <u>semantic</u> property of nominals. It involves, roughly, the speaker's intent to 'refer to' or 'mean' a nominal expression to have non-empty references — i.e. to 'exist' -- within a particular universe of discourse.[2] Conversely, if a nominal is 'non-referential' or

---

[1] For an extensive discussion of referentiality and referential opacity, see Jackendoff 1972 and Givón 1973. The type discussed here may be also labeled as 'existential opacity' and should not be confused with 'degree of definiteness opacity' as discussed in Keenan 1972.

[2] Philosophers most often assume, I suspect erroneously, that the Universe of Discourse is somehow co-extensive with 'the real world,' but language is clearly concerned with the former, often in relative disregard of the latter. The traditional paradoxes of 'morning vs. evening star' or the unicorn tend to melt away when one acknowledges this distinction, as language seems to.

'generic,' the speaker does not have a commitment to its existence within the relevant universe of discourse. Rather, in the latter case the speaker is engaged in discussing the genus or its proper-ties, but does not commit him/herself to the existence of any spe-cific individual member of that genus. [3]

    b. The three basic sentence-scope modalities in language are FACT, POSSIBLE and NEG, with the last one being a stronger case of POSSIBLE.

    c. Some of the operators responsible for the modality POSSIBLE are sentential in scope, such as QUESTION, FUTURE, HABITUAL,[4] CONDITIONAL, PROBABILITY modals and at least one type of NEGATION ('external'). The scope of other operators responsible for this modality is VP scope, excluding the sentential subject/topic but including subject of VP-complement sentences. The most com-mon of these operators are 'internal' NEGATION, various non-implicative intensional verbs such as 'want,' 'seek,' 'order,' 'request,' inherently negative verbs such as 'lack,' 'refuse,' forbid,' 'deny,' as well as many non-factive verbs such as 'think,' 'believe,' etc.

    d. Nominals falling under the scope of a POSSIBLE or NEG modality may receive either a referential or non-referential inter-pretation. Otherwise all nominals are always interpreted refer-entially.

---

[3] By discussing the genus or its properties one may, though, commit oneself to the existence/referentiality of the genus itself within the universe of discourse. In most ordinary cases this may lead to the tacit commitment to the existence of individual members of the genus. However, the speaker using a generic expression is still not committed to 'mean' any particular individual.

[4] Under this modality I will consider both cases in which subject and predicates alike are non-referential, as in 'A unicorn is an animal with one horn,' as well as cases in which the subject is referential but the predicate is not, as in 'This unicorn is a beau-tiful animal.' Cases with a non-referential subject but a referential predicate are systematically excluded from language (see discussion in Givón 1973 and Keenan 1975).

[5] There are convincing arguments presented in both Jackendoff 1972 and Givón 1973 for assuming that in natural languages the existential quantifier is the unmarked case.

1.2 Definiteness

a. Object under the scope of the modality NEG can be either definite or non-referential, but never referential-indefinite.[6]

b. The subject nominal in most languages, particularly in the main clause, tends to be either definite or generic. In most languages this is a categorial constraint on the grammar, but in some languages the same constraint appears rather at the text-count level.[7]

c. In languages with a categorial constraint against referential-indefinite subjects, those may still appear as the subjects of existential/presentative constructions, which are marked in a number of ways.[8]

d. The object (most specifically 'accusative') nominal in sentences, on the other hand, is the one most commonly used to introduce new — referential indefinite — nominals into discourse.[9]

e. In many languages in which the notion 'subject' is viable,[10] there is a strong tendency for the subject nominal to appear first in the sentence. This reflects a more general tendency for the topic/theme ('old information') to appear before the new information. Thus, one of the most characteristic features of existential constructions — in which new referential-indefinite nominals are introduced — is the tendency to move the subject away from the sentence-initial position.

---

[6]This may be probably extended to subject nouns as well. For detailed discussion of this discourse-motivated constraint, see Givón 1975a.

[7] For details see Keenan 1975, Givón 1974, 1975b, Kirsner 1973 and Hetzron 1974.

[8] See discussion in Hetzron 1974, Givón 1974, 1975b.

[9] I will restrict the discussion here only to direct or accusative objects. For further details see Givón 1974, 1975b.

[10]For a number of works concerning the typological validity of the notion 'subject,' please consult Li and Thompson 1975a. For some interesting exception to the general tendency of 'topic goes first,' see Creider 1976.

f. The notions 'definite' and 'indefinite,' so far as <u>referential</u> nominals are concerned, are used here strictly in their discourse-pragmatic sense, i.e. 'assumed by the speaker to be uniquely identifiable to the hearer' vs. 'not so assumed,' respectively.

g. The category 'non-definite,' while seldom mentioned in the literature, stands somewhere in the middle between 'non-referential' and 'referential-indefinite,' in the sense that while logically a particular individual or individuals are taken to exist, their actual individual identity is <u>not</u> an essential part of the message.

For an informal, inductive introduction to the notions discussed above, consider the underlying nominals in the following sentences:

1. a. REF-INDEF: He bought <u>a book</u> yesterday.
   b. REF-DEF: He bought <u>the book he wanted</u> yesterday.
   c. NON-REF: <u>Humans</u> are <u>mammals</u>.
                   ('generic subject and generic predicate')
                   <u>The elephant</u> is <u>a mammal</u>.
                   (GEN subject and GEN predicate)
                   He 'is <u>a teacher</u>. (GEN predicate)
                   He didn't buy <u>any book</u>. (NON-REF object)
                   He's looking for <u>a new house</u> to buy.
                   (NON-REF object)
   d. NON-DEF:[11] He bought <u>shirts</u>.
                   He went to <u>the movies</u>.

While the discussion below will deal largely in synchronic statements about grammars, in a number of instances it is useful to view the mapping of definiteness and referentiality at least partially in <u>diachronic</u> terms, i.e. in terms of the historical source which gave rise to a particular marker. Specific comments in this regard will be made throughout.

---

[11] The category NON-DEFINITE may be viewed as a subcategory of referential-indefinite, in the sense that while the verbal expression indicates that the speaker is committed to the <u>existence</u> of <u>some</u> individual, the actual identity of that individual is left unspecified, presumably because it is of no import in that particular communication. A reasonable inference is, then, that it is the <u>genus affiliation</u> of the individual which really matters. In a number of languages NON-DEF nominals, particularly objects, tend to be incorporated into the verb.

2. The Wheel: Plurals, Numerals, Gender

The system I would like to discuss first, one which lays a number of claims to holding a unique position among languages, is that of PLANTATION CREOLES as described by Bickerton (1975a, 1975b). The unique position of these CREOLES involves the fact that their strictly categorial rules of grammar arise via a first generation of native speakers, given a chaotic, non-categorial input of a highly variable PIDGIN stage. Bickerton has noted that in each instance, whether in Africa, the Caribbeans or Hawaii, the same system of morphological marking of definiteness and referentiality arises in the CREOLE, one which may be rendered via the wheel diagram in 2. below (with the actual markers representing those of HAWAII CREOLE).

2.

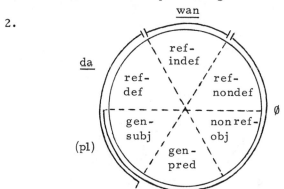

The marker /wan/ is the ENGLISH 'one,' and /da/ is the ENGLISH 'the.' To illustrate their use, consider the following sentences patterned after HAWAII CREOLE:

3. a. I see da book.   'I saw the book.' (REF-DEF)
   b. I see wan book.   'I saw a book.' (REF-INDEF)
   c. I no see book.   'I didn't see a/any book.' (NON-REF)
   d. Joe he teacher.   'Joe is a teacher.' (GEN-PRED)
   e. He see movie.   'He saw a/some movie.' (NON-DEF)

A certain overlap exists in the mapping of generic subjects, where -- somewhat as in ENGLISH -- they may be rendered either with the definite marker /da/ plus the singular, or zero plus a plural.

Bickerton (in personal communication) has observed that a number of other non-CREOLE languages may be modeled by a similar wheel, to the extent that while the mapping areas and the various markers

differ from one language to another, the markers always cover
<u>continguous</u> semantic areas of the wheel. Thus, the following dia-
gram holds for HAWAIIAN (POLYNESIAN, from Bickerton, personal
communication):

4.

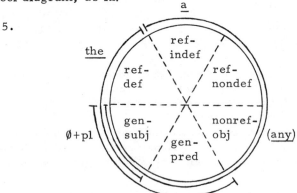

The partial or complete grouping of <u>definite</u> with <u>generic</u> subjects
is found again and again, in one guise or another, cross-linguistically. It is due to the quite universal overlapping of the notions
'subject' and 'topic' (see extensive discussion in many papers in
Li 1976), and that universally topics may be either referential-
definite or generic, but never referential-indefinite.

The referential-indefinite marker <u>kakahi</u> in HAWAIIAN is most
likely the numeral 'one,' and its limitation to this category only,
much like in CREOLE, reflects the early stage of its introduction
as an indefinite marker (see further diachronic discussion below,
as well as in Givón 1976).

The article system of ENGLISH may also be rendered via the
wheel diagram, as in:

5.

ENGLISH illustrates a situation where the ex-numeral 'one' (a(n))
has extended its coverage around the wheel all the way to generic
subjects, where it overlaps with two other possible mappings, that
of the definite /the/ and that of zero plus plural. Further, the
emphatic 'one,' 'single' /any/ is used under the scope of negation,
question and conditional (probably several other NON-FACT modalities as well), presenting often a subtle but stable semantic
contrast with /a/. Finally, the grammar of pluralization inter-
sects with the diagram in 5. at a number of points. Mapping
category generic-subject, it presents an optional choice, but for
generic-predicates it presents a semantic contrast sg./pl. Finally,
the quantifier some (de-stressed) also contrasts semantically along
the same dimension with a in the mapping of the categories referential indefinite and nondefinite.

   ROMANCE languages such as PORTUGUESE or SPANISH represent another possible variation on the wheel model. Thus, consider the wheel of SPANISH in 6. below:

6.

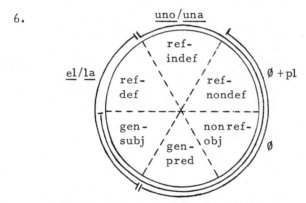

The system represents a number of complexities, some due to an
expected state of diachronic flux. To begin with, while the numerals uno/una (often reduced to the invariant un) may extend their
coverage around the wheel almost as a in ENGLISH, older usage
of zero in the non-referential and generic area still prevails.
Thus, consider the variations in:

7. a. No há dicho palabra.   'He didn't say a word.'
   b. No há dicho una palabra.   'He didn't say one word.'
   b. No há dicho ninguna palabra.   'He didn't say any word.'

A clear, though subtle, semantic contrast of emphasis still exists
between these variants. A similar contrast may also be shown in
the generic-predicate category:

8. a. Es <u>un buen amigo</u>.
      'He's a good friend.'/'It's a (specific) good friend.'

   b. Es <u>buen amigo</u>.
      'He's a good friend.'

   c. Es <u>professor de universidad</u>.
      'He's a college professor.'

   d. Es <u>un professor de universidad</u>.
      'It's a (specific) college professor.'/'He's a college professor.'

The use of the numeral/indefinite in 8.a and 8.d makes it possible
to construct a <u>referential</u> interpretation of the predicate, in addition
to the <u>generic</u> ('attributive') interpretation which is already possible.
While without the numeral, as in 8.b and 8.c, the predicate is interpreted only generically. This type of complementary distribution
cum variation is rather typical in a language that is in the middle
of extending the coverage of the numeral from <u>referential</u>-indefinite
to <u>generic</u>-indefinite as well.[12]

Other features of the SPANISH/PORTUGUESE system include
gender and number inflection for both definite and indefinite articles,
emphatic negative polarity items akin to <u>any</u>, but gender inflected
(<u>ninguno</u>, <u>ninguna</u> in SPANISH), and a wide use of the <u>zero plus
plural</u> forms in non-definite or generic contexts, where it may
overlap — and sometimes contrast — with other markers.

3. <u>From referentiality to definiteness: BANTU</u>

In this section I will describe initially the article system of
BEMBA, where the lexicon makes no provision for the definite/
indefinite distinction, but only for that of referential vs. non-referential. The VCV- form of the noun prefix marks <u>referential</u> nouns
(in the sense described in Sec. 1.1 above), while the corresponding

---

[12] Historically, the development of 'one' into an 'indefinite' marker
proceeds through two stages: the first representing a generalization from [numeral] to [ref-indef], the second from [ref-indef] to
[indefinite]. ENGLISH represents the more or less complete application of the second stage, while SPANISH and PORTUGUESE
are somewhere in the middle of undergoing the second stage. In
MANDARIN and ISRAELI HEBREW (see below), SHERPA, HUN-
GARIAN, HAWAII CREOLE and many others, only the first stage
of reanalysis has taken place. For further discussion of the universal diachronic process involved, see Givón 1976.

CV- form of the prefix marks <u>non-referential</u> ones. I will later
show how this system can evolve naturally — relying upon some of
the general rules discussed in sections 1.1 and 1.2 above — toward
one which marks a definite/indefinite contrast, as in DZAMBA,
another BANTU language.

In non-modal environments in BEMBA, one finds only VCV-
noun prefixes on either subjects or objects:

9. a.   <u>umu</u>-ana   a - à -somene <u>ici</u>-tabo
        "VCV-child he-past-read VCV-book"
        '<u>The</u> child read <u>a/the</u> book.' (DEF-subject, REF-object)

   b.   *<u>mu</u>-ana a-à-somene <u>ici</u>-tabo
        *'<u>Any</u> child read the/a book.' (*NON-REF-subject)

   c.   *<u>umu</u>-ana a-à-somene <u>ci</u>-tabo
        *'The child read any book.'   (*NON-REF-object)

The subject is obligatorily definite or generic in this language, and
aside from the use of deictics and relative modifiers, the DEF/
INDEF contrast for objects is left unmarked, as can be seen from
9.a above. Indefinite subjects may appear in existential constructions as in 10. below, but they are marked by the same VCV- prefix
characteristic of all referential nouns:

10.   pa-ali   <u>umu</u>-ana   a - à - soma   <u>ici</u>-tabo...
        "there-was VCV-child he-CONS-read VCV-book..."
        'There was <u>a</u> child who/and he read a book...'

Under the scope of a POSSIBLE modality, one finds:

11. a.   umu-ana   a - a - fwaaya <u>ici</u>-tabo
         "VCV-child he-past-want VCV-book"
         'The child wanted <u>the</u> book.'   (REF, DEF)
    or   'The child wanted <u>a specific</u> book.' (REF, INDEF)

    b.   umuana a - a - fwaaya <u>ci</u>-tabo
         "child he-past-want CV-book"
         'The child wanted <u>a</u> book <u>(be it any)</u>.' (NON-REF)

Finally, under the scope of NEG, where REFERENTIAL nouns are
obligatorily <u>definite</u>, one finds a full identification of REF = DEF
and NON-REF = INDEF. Thus, consider:

12. a. umuana t-a-à-somene ici-tabo
      "child neg-he-past-read VCV-book"
      'The child didn't read the book.'   (REF = DEF)

   b. umuana t-a-à-somene ci-tabo
      "child neg-he-past-read CV-book"
      'The child didn't read a/any book.' (NON-REF = INDEF)

The same generalization with respect to the two opacity-created
modalities in 11. and 12. above also applies to subjects of sentences
embedded under the scope of these modalities.[13]

A variation on the BEMBA system (which is most likely the older
one) may be seen in DZAMBA, where in non-modal environments --
where nouns are obligatorily referential -- the VCV/CV prefixal
contrast marks the distinction between definite and indefinite, respectively. Under the scope of negation, the same identification of
DEF = REF and INDEF = NON-REF holds as in BEMBA (see 12. above).
While under the scope of other POSSIBLE modalities the VCV-marked
nouns are referential but ambiguous with respect to definiteness
in subjects, the CV-prefix marks non-referential nouns, as in
BEMBA.[14]

In terms of diachronic development, the drift from the reference-
marking system in BEMBA toward the definiteness-marking system
of DZAMBA is clearly motivated by the general semantic-pragmatic
constraints outlined in sections 1.1 and 1.2 above. The universal
constraint against referential-indefinite subjects tends to create
the identification of DEF = REF in that position. The same is also
true under the scope of NEG. Only in two environments -- under
the scope of POSSIBLE modalities other than NEG and under FACT
outside the subject position -- are the two marking systems in actual
conflict. And out of these two environments, FACT imposes obligatory referentiality on nouns under its scope, so that the transfer

---

[13] For further discussion see Givón 1973. It may further be possible to show that NEG is not the only POSSIBLE modality which
forces the identity of the REF/NON-REF distinction with that of
DEF/INDEF, although it is certainly the strongest case of this type.
For a discussion of cases of 'semi-referentiality' under other POS-
SIBLE modalities (such as QUESTION or CONDITION), see Givón
1976.

[14] For details see Bokamba 1971, as well as discussion in Givón
1973, 1974b.

of the VCV/CV contrast from referentiality to definiteness causes
no loss in expressive power. The impact of the conflict between
the two systems — and of a change from the one to the other — is
thus confined to a relatively small corner of the nominal grammar.

In terms of the wheel diagram, BEMBA and DZAMBA may be
contrasted as follows:

13.

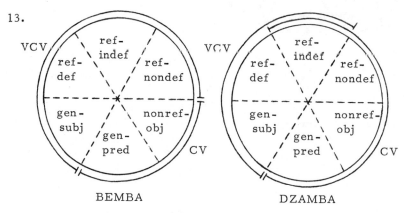

<table>
<tr><td>BEMBA</td><td>DZAMBA</td></tr>
</table>

4. The Numeral 'One' as an Indefinite Marker: ISRAELI HEBREW

The gender-inflected numeral 'one' in ISRAELI HEBREW marks
only referential indefinites, much like the CREOLE system described
in section 2. above. The actual form is reduced and destressed as
expected.[15] Thus, in subject position:

14. a. ísh-xad   bá   héna etmól   ve-
       "man-one came here yesterday and-..."
       'A man came here yesterday and...'

    b. ishá-xat   báa héna etmól   ve-
       "woman-one came here yesterday and-..."
       'A woman came here yesterday and...'

In object position the 'truly referential' indefinite is marked by 'one,'
while the 'semi-referential' non-definite is marked by zero.

---

[15] Plurals may be marked by the quantifier kamá 'some,' but the
rules here are less categorial and zero may be used just as well
for referential-indefinite plural nouns. For further discussion of
the entire situation in HEBREW, see Givón 1976.

15. a. kaníti   séfer-<u>xad</u>   etmól
         "bought-I book-one yesterday"
         'I bought a (specific) book yesterday.'

     b. kaníti séfer etmól
         "bought-I book yesterday"
         'I bought a book yesterday.'

In 15.a the specific identity of the book is potentially a germane
part of the message, while in 15.b it is not.

Non-referential nouns are marked with <u>zero</u>, and they contrast
with both referential definites and indefinites under the scope of
POSSIBLE:

16. a. aní mexapés séfer   (NON-REF)
         "I looking-for book"
         'I'm looking for a book.' (be it any)

     b. aní mexapés séfer-<u>xad</u>...   (REF-INDEF)
         "I looking-for book-one"
         'I'm looking for a (particular) book...'

     c. aní mexapés et ha-séfer...   (REF-DEF)
         "I looking-for ACC the book"
         'I'm looking for the book...'

Under the scope of NEG, indefinites cannot be referential (see Secs.
1.1 and 1.2 above), and one finds an emphatic and non-emphatic versions of the non-referential noun, the former marked with particles
akin to 'any':

17. a. ló   kaníti   séfer   (external, unemphatic)
         "NEG bought-I book"
         'I <u>didn't</u> buy a book.'/'It's <u>not true</u> that I bought a book.'

     b. ló   kaníti   áf   séfer   (internal, emphatic)
         "NEG bought-I even book"
         'I didn't buy <u>any</u> book.'

     c. áf-<u>xad</u>   ló   bá   le-shám   (external, subject position)
         "even-one NEG came to-there"
         '<u>Nobody</u> came there.'

In predicate position, -xad 'one' marks referential predicates only,
while attributive/generic ones are marked with <u>zero</u>:

18. a. hu moré   (GEN)
    "he teacher"
    'He's a teacher.'

  b. hu moré-<u>xad</u> she-pagáshti etmól (REF-INDEF)
     "he teacher-one that-met-I yesterday"
     'He's a teacher that I met yesterday.'

  c. ze moré-<u>xad</u>   she-ani makír   (cleft, REF-INDEF)
     "it teacher-one that-I know"
     'It's some teacher that I know.'

The same stage of development of the numeral 'one' as a <u>referential</u>
indefinite marker may be seen in CREOLES, SHERPA, MANDARIN,
HUNGARIAN, TURKISH and many others. In the history of RO-
MANCE and GERMANIC the entire development from quantifier to
'indefinite' via this intermediate stage may be clearly traced (see
comments in Givón 1976). SPANISH is slightly behind FRENCH on
this diachronic cline (see examples 7. and 8. above, as well as
footnote 12).

5. Definite-Accusative: ISRAELI HEBREW

   One of the most common interaction between the grammar of
definitization and the case system of the language is found in instances where the definite-accusative carries a special case-
marking. In ISRAELI HEBREW this marking comes on top of the
definite article, as in:

20.   kaniti   <u>et</u>   <u>ha</u>-sefer etmol   (DEF)
       "bought-I ACC the-book yesterday"
       'I bought the book yesterday.'

21.   kaniti sefer-<u>xad</u> etmol   (REF-INDEF)
       "bought-I book-one yesterday"
       'I bought a book yesterday.'

But the definite-accusative marker could function as a definitizer
for accusative nouns without any definite article (see a more complex example, involving also word order, in MANDARIN CHINESE,
further below). Thus, in PERSIAN, for example, the definite-
accusative suffix functions alone to serve as a marker for both:[16]

---

[16] For the data, I am indebted to Vida Samiian (personal communication).

22. a. mard-e   dar-o   boz-kart   (DEF)
       "man-NOM door-ACC open-did"
       'The man opened the door.'

    b. mard-e   ve-dar boz-kart   (INDEF-REF)
       "man-NOM a-door open-did"
       'The man opened a door.'

Other variations of the definite-accusative connection may be found
in HINDI, HUNGARIAN and probably many others. For further
discussion of similar development in URALIC and FINNO-UGRIC
languages, see Comrie 1975. The development of a special marker
for definite accusative is of course not surprising. The accusative
position is the 'most indefinite' of all major arguments of the verb,
in contrast with the subject and dative which are overwhelmingly
definite.[17]

   Further, one may note, after Comrie (1975), that in a language
with low or zero coding for definiteness (i.e. only deictic particles,
for example), the definite-accusative marking makes great sense
in terms of case-marking differentiation. The subject is almost
universally definite by general rules (see Sec. 1.2 above) and thus
needs no further specification. Indirect and oblique cases are
usually adequately marked, and their definiteness often highly predictable in discourse. The definite-accusative marker thus leaves
the unmarked accusative to be unambiguously interpreted as indefinite.

   Finally, an interaction between dative case-marking, definite
accusatives and/or the feature 'human' is found in SPANISH, LAN-
GUEDOC, AMHARIC, NEO-ARAMAIC, BIKOL (see discussion
below) and probably many others. For further discussion of universal considerations which underlie this interaction, see Givón
1975b and Comrie 1976.

6. Word Order, Verb Typology, Numeral Classifiers and
   Demonstratives: MANDARIN[18]

   Definitization in MANDARIN CHINESE represents an extremely
complex array of devices, where the system of mapping definitization is in the very midst of undergoing a number of diachronic

---

[17]See discussion in Givón 1975a, 1975b.

[18] For the MANDARIN CHINESE data, I am indebted to Charles Li
(personal com.), but see also Li and Thompson 1974, 1975a, 1975b.

changes in word order, verb morphology/syntax/semantics and the
rise of special morphemes to mark definite and indefinite nouns.
In addition, word order devices to mark definitization shade into
marked-topicalization, another universal process closely related
to definitization.

MANDARIN is one of the languages which abides absolutely by
constraint b, Sec. 1.2 above. That is, subjects in the normal
subject-first word order may only be definite (or generic):

23.   kèrén zhùo-gūng
        "guest work"
        'Guests always work.'/'A guest always works.' (GEN)
        'The guest(s) always work(s).' (DEF)

If the singular/plural distinction, as well as the generic/definite,
are to be disambiguated, the distal demonstrative 'that' may be
used. But this requires the use of noun classifiers (for both the
singular and plural), and thus the introduction of noun gender
which is not marked on the noun itself. Further, the demonstrative 'that' may lose its deictic value only in the singular, but retains it in the plural.

24. a. nèi-ge kèrén zhùo-gūng
        "that-cl. guest work"
        'That/the guest works.'

    b. nèi-xiē   kèrén zhùo-gūng
        "that-cl.pl. guest work"
        'Those guests work.'

For morphologically complex, historically transitive verbs such
as 'work' (lit. 'do-work'), the only way to indefinitize the subject
is via the existential construction using the verb 'be/exist':

25.   yŏu kèrén zhùo-gūng
        "be guest work"
        'There's a guest who works.'/
        'There're some guests who work.'   (REF-INDEF)

And to disambiguate the singular from the plural, the numeral 'one'
plus the singular/plural noun classifier may be used:

26. a. yŏu yī-ge kèrén zhùo-gūng
        "be one-cl. guest work"
        'There's a guest who works.'   (REF-INDEF)

26. b. yǒu yī-xiē   kèrén zhùo-gūng
    "be one-cl.pl. guest work"
    'There're some guests who work.'

When the verb is intransitive and morphologically simplex, existential constructions may also be used for indefinitizing the subject,
as in 18. and 19. above. But in addition one may simply reverse
the subject-verb order to verb-subject to achieve the same end,
as in:

27. a. kèrén lái le
    "guest come asp.(past)"
    'The guest(s) arrived.'   (DEF)

    b. lái kèrén le
    "come guest asp."
    'A guest/some guests arrived.'   (REF-INDEF)

Let us now turn to the mapping of definiteness and indefiniteness
in accusative objects. The first device involves the use of the erst-
while serial verb bǎ in an SOV word order. This device is preferred for morphologically complex verbs and obligatory when those
verbs also take certain manner adverbs. However, it cannot be
used when the verb is morphologically simplex. Consider first:

28. a. wǒ bǎ zhūangzi dǎ-pò   le
    "I ba window hit-broken asp."
    'I broke the window(s)."   (DEF)

    b. wǒ dǎ-pò le   zhūangzi
    "I hit-broken asp. window"
    'I broke a window/some windows.' (REF-INDEF)

To disambiguate the singular/plural indefinite, the numeral 'one'
together with a classifier may be used in the same SVO order, as in:

29. a. wǒ dǎ-pò le yī-ge zhūangzi
    'I broke a window.'

    b. wǒ dǎ-pò le yī-xiē zhūangzi
    'I broke some windows.'

Finally, using the same SVO order, one may also disambiguate the
singular/plural definite accusative by using the demonstrative 'that,'
but the deictic meaning is retained in the plural, as in:

30. a. wǒ dǎ-pò le nèi-ge zhuāngzi
        'I broke that/the window.'

   b. wǒ dǎ-pò le nèi-xiē zhuāngzi
       'I broke those windows.'

There are many verbs which cannot use the ba construction for
definitizing their objects, and in general those are verbs for which
the surface direct object is semantically not a patient/accusative,
such as 'see,' 'hear,' 'read,' 'feel,' 'write' and others. Their
objects may be definitized via the use of the demonstrative with
SVO word order, as in 30. above. Their unmarked object in the
SVO order is interpreted as indefinite as in 28.b, and the singular/
plural may be disambiguated as in 29. above. In addition one may
definitize the object via two word order devices, SOV and OSV
orders, as in:

31. a. wǒ tīng le yīnyuè (le)
        "I hear asp. music prt."
        'I listened to (some) music.'   (REF-INDEF)

   b. wǒ yīnyuè tīng le
       'I listened to the music.'   (DEF)

   c. yīnyuè wǒ tīng le
       'I listened to the music.'   (DEF)

Under the scope of POSSIBLE, with verbs that use the ba construction, one obtains definitization with the SOV word order, as in:

32.   wǒ yào tā bǎ zhuāngzi dǎ-pò   de
        "I want he ba window hit-broken prt."
        'I want(ed) him to break the window(s).'

The unmarked noun in the SVO order is opaque, yielding either the
non-referential or referential-indefinite interpretation, as in:

33.   wǒ yào tā dǎ-pò zhuāngzi
        "I want he hit-broken window"   (REF-
        'I want him to break a/some (specific) window(s).' INDEF)
        'I want him to break a/some (any) window(s).' (NON-REF)

The same ambiguity is obtained if the numeral 'one' is used together
with the classifier to disambiguate the singular from the plural in
the SVO order. Except that in the non-referential reading, the

quantifier value of 'one' is more apparent, that is, it hasn't been completely de-marked onto a bona-fide indefinite marker.

For verbs which cannot use the ba construction, one faces another problem. The SOV and OSV orders cannot be used in an embedded clause. That is, they have the same restrictions one normally finds on marked topicalization devices.[19] Thus, in the context used here, the object may be definitized only with the use of the demonstrative in an SVO order, as in:

34. a. wǒ yào tā kàn bàozhǐ
         "I want he read newspaper"
         'I want him to read a/some newspaper(s).' (NON-REF)
         '. . . . a/some (specific)newspaper(s).' (REF-INDEF)

    b. wǒ yào tā kàn yī-fèn bàozhǐ
        "I want he read one-cl. newspaper"
        'I want him to read a (specific)newspaper.' (REF-INDEF)
        'I want him to read a (any) newspaper.'   (NON-REF)

    c. wǒ yào tā kàn yī-xiē   bàozhǐ
        "I want he read one-cl.pl. newspaper"
        'I want him to read some (spec.)newspapers.'(REF-INDEF)
        'I want him to read some (any) newspapers.'(NON-REF)

    d. wǒ yào tā kàn nèi-fèn bàozhǐ
        'I want him to read that/the newspaper.'   (DEF)

    e. wǒ yào tā kàn nèi-xiē bàozhǐ
        'I want him to read those newspapers.'   (DEF)

35.   *wǒ yào tā bàozhǐ kàn (*'I want' + SOV)
      wǒ yào bàozhǐ tā kàn ('I want' + OSV)

Under the scope of NEG, with verbs using the ba construction, one obtains:

36.   wǒ méi bǎ zhuāngzi dǎ-pò
      "I NEG ba window hit-broken"
      'I didn't break the window(s).'   (DEF)

---

[19]See some discussion further below, as well as in Givón 1974. This is not a restriction due to the scope of the POSSIBLE modality per se, but rather a more general constraint pertaining to embedded clauses.

And the singular/plural may be again disambiguated by the use of 'that' with the classifiers in an SVO word order. The unmarked object in an SVO order yields only a non-referential reading, as in:

37.   wǒ méi dǎ-pò zhuāngzi
       "I NEG hit-broken window"
       "I didn't break any window(s).' (NON-REF)

However, contrary to constraint a. Sec. 1.2 above, when the numeral 'one' is used to disambiguate for singular/plural, it precipitates a <u>refer-ential</u>-<u>indefinite</u> reading, as in:

38. a. wǒ méi dǎ-pò   yī-ge zhuāngzi
       "I NEG hit-broken one-cl. window"
       'There's a window that I didn't break.'   (REF-INDEF)

   b. wǒ méi dǎ-pò   yī-xiē zhuāngzi
       "I NEG hit-broken one-cl.pl. window"
       'There are some windows that I didn't break.'(REF-INDEF)

Construction 38, while considered 'grammatical,' is nevertheless unpreferred, and the native speaker prefers to render it as the existential construction, where the referential-indefinite noun is first introduced as the subject of 'be/exist' in a VS word order:[20]

39.   yǒu yī-ge zhuāngzi wǒ méi dǎ-pò
       "be one-cl. window I NEG hit-broken"
       'There's a window that I didn't break.' (REF-INDEF)

Finally, the objects of verbs which cannot use the <u>ba</u> construction may definitize under negation via using the demonstrative plus classifier in an SVO word order, as in:

40.   wǒ méi kàn nèi-fèn bàozhǐ
       "I NEG read that-cl. newspaper"
       'I didn't read that/the newspaper.'   (DEF)

---

[20] As noted in Givón 1975a, in ENGLISH, too, there is an appar-ent violation of constraint a, Sec. 1.2, as in e.g.: 'Mary didn't read <u>a book</u> that was assigned, and as a result she flunked the exam.' While this is true at the 'grammar' or 'competence' level, text counts reveal that the frequency of occurrence of such a usage in text is <u>zero</u>, so that the universality of constraint a, Sec. 1.2 is in fact demonstrated in discourse, though not always in 'compe-tence.'

And again the plural demonstrative retains its deictic force, as in:

41.   wǒ méi kàn nèi-xiē bàozhǐ
       'I didn't read those newspapers.' (DEF)

In addition the SOV and OSV orders may be used for definitization,
if the negation is in the main clause, as in:

42. a. wǒ bàozhǐ méi kàn
        'I didn't read the newspaper(s).' (DEF, SOV)

    b. bàozhǐ wǒ méi kàn
        'I didn't read the newspaper(s).' (DEF, OSV)

The unmarked object yields again only a non-referential reading,
as in:

43.   wǒ méi kàn bàozhǐ
       'I didn't read any newspaper(s).' (NON-REF)

The marked indefinite with 'one' yields a referential-indefinite
reading, as in:

44.   wǒ méi kàn yī-fèn bàozhǐ
       'There's a newspaper that I didn't read.'

But again, an existential construction as in 45. is preferred over 44.:

45.   yǒu yī-fèn bàozhǐ   wǒ méi kàn
       "be one-cl. newspaper I NEG read"
       'There's a newspaper that I didn't read.'

As one can see, the complexity for the translator between ENG-
LISH and MANDARIN is rather staggering. In addition the ba
construction itself as a device for definitization is restricted in
its distribution almost to the same extent as the SOV and OSV word
orders, and may appear only in a number of 'that-S' type complements of assertive verbs ('say,' 'think,' but not of 'know').[21]

---

21 Both Hooper and Thompson (1973) and Hooper (1974) have
observed that the sentential complements of assertive (as against
presuppositional) predicates allow more syntactic freedom, in
particular with respect to various 'stylistic' transformations labeled 'root transformations' by Emonds (1970). For a more general discussion of this, see Givón 1974.

This raises the general question of whether the ba, SOV and OSV
devices for definitization are really that, or rather, whether they
are devices for marked-topicalization.   Their distributional restrictions strongly suggest the latter rather than the former.   Any
topic-shifting devices universally allow either generic or referen-
tial-definite nouns, which is precisely what the SOV and OSV orders
in MANDARIN allow (as well as what the subject in the SVO order
allows).   This problem will be discussed in greater detail further
below.

7.   Degree-of-Definiteness Opacity: FRISIAN and MALAGASY

The referential opacity discussed so far, which appears only
under the scope of non-FACT modalities, involves roughly the
existential quantifier, i.e. lack of the commitment of the speaker
him/herself to believing in the actual existence of an individual
about whom they make a certain proposition.   There exists another
type of referential opacity, one which I shall label here 'degree-
of-definiteness' opacity, which may appear under the scope of FACT
modalities.   It involves situations where the speaker believes in the
existence of a unique individual about whom a proposition is made,
but may not be able to actually identify that individual, i.e. he may
not know who the person actually is.[22] Let us consider the following
example;

46.   The man who killed Smith is blind.

A speaker, say Sherlock Holmes, may utter 46. in a context where
he actually knows who Smith's murderer is, or alternatively, under
the condition where he only knows that whoever it was who killed
Smith must have been blind.   Under the first reading, the restrictive relative clause functions as a definite identity operator, and
the whole subject NP may be replaced by a proper name, say 'John.'
Under the second reading, the restrictive relative clause has an
attributive function, and the entire NP may not be replaced by a
proper name.   Now, in most languages there is no lexical mapping
to resolve this type of ambiguity between the transparent (definite
identity) and opaque (attributive) interpretation.   However, Keenan
and Ebert (1973) have shown two cases in which such lexical mapping
actually exists.   The first is FRISIAN, where two articles exist,
one of which is used ambiguously as in 46. above:

---

[22] For an extensive discussion of this type of referential opacity,
see Keenan 1972.

47. John wonert ham dat di maan wat woon bisööben wiar.
"John wonder him that the man who won drunk was"
'John was surprised that the man who won was drunk.'

Sentence 47. may either mean that John knew who the man was, say
'Bill,' and that Bill's being drunk surprised him; or alternatively,
that John was surprised that a winner, whoever it be, was drunk.
The other article in FRISIAN has only the opaque reading:

48. John wonert ham dat a maan wat woon bisööbert wiar.
"John wonder him that the man who won drunk was"
'John was surprised that the man who won was drunk.'

In MALAGASY there is a definite article which allows either the
opaque or the transparent reading, as in:

49. Gaga Rakoto fa mamo ny mpandresy.
"surprised R. that drunk the winner"
'Rakoto was surprised that the winner was drunk.'

But there also exists another article which allows only the transparent reading:[23]

50. Gaga Rakoto   fa mamo ilay mpandresy.
"surprised R. that drunk the winner"
'Rakoto was surprised that the winner was drunk.'

8. Definiteness, Topicality and Pronominalization

The MANDARIN examples cited in Sec. 6 above already suggested that it is not always possible to keep definiteness apart from
other discourse-related devices used to map various situations in
which an argument is mentioned not for the first time in discourse.
In this section I will cite a number of examples in which the grammar or mapping of definiteness in language shades into other discourse devices, such as topicalization, pronominalization or
grammatical agreement, and in particular, how different languages
may choose to draw the lines which divide these discourse-mapping
device from each other at different point. I will begin by a short

---

[23] The degree of specificity in marking exhibited by FRISIAN
and MALAGASY is not common. One should also note that neither
of these two has resolved the ambiguity/vagueness completely.
Each one has only one unambiguous article, while leaving the
second reading to be covered by an ambiguous morpheme.

outline of some universal discourse situations pertaining to the
manner in which a previously-mentioned topic may be recalled
into discourse.

8.1 Complexity and recall of discourse topic

Probably the most simple and least problematic environment for
recalling a discourse topic is that in which the topic argument is
mentioned directly prior to its recall, is mentioned there alone
with no other argument which may possibly confuse the hearer,
and in an otherwise unambiguous fashion. Most languages will
recall it in this environment by the use of anaphora (simple deletion), if they have no pronominal system, or by the use of anaphoric
pronouns, if available. This should be considered the least complex,
least marked topic-recall environment, since the position (directly
prior) and nature (unambiguous) of the prior mention of the topic
makes the hearer's task of assigning coreference almost automatic.
Let us label this device simple anaphoric pronominalization, as in:

51. John worked, and then he rested.

Almost as simple a device, in terms of the hearer's task of
assigning coreference relations (or recalling the topic), is that of
simple definitization, which up to this point we have taken for
granted. This device is used in a number of non-contrastive situations where the use of pronouns will not suffice to identify the individual. This may be because a large gap exists between the prior
and subsequent mention of the topic, during which other arguments
have been discussed whose pronominal gender is not distinct; or
when it is clear that the hearer could identify the topic from
his own context, i.e. even when it has not been overtly mentioned
in previous discourse. Some of the situations here involve pragmatic considerations of dependency, quite often resulting in the
use of possessive pronouns as the definitizing markers, as well as
reliance on various cultural conventions. Why it is clear that this
is a more-marked discourse environment than anaphoric pronominalization is because it seems that the speaker assumes the hearer
will have more difficulty in identifying the coreferent, and is thus
supplying more specific information -- i.e. the entire noun -- rather
than relying only on the most generic features which characterize
the pronominal system.[24] Let us label this device definitization, as in:

---

[24] For a detailed discussion of this, see Givón 1975b. For an
extensive and enlightening discussion of marked and unmarked
thematization/topicalization, see Creider 1976.

52. Once upon a time there lived <u>a gracious king</u>. He reigned
over a lovely country, was married to a beautiful queen
and had three lovely children, a parakeet and a court
jester. Now one day <u>the king</u> ...   (large gap)

53. <u>The sun</u> is so bright today. (uniqueness)

54. <u>My wife</u> arrived yesterday. (uniqueness via cultural and
                                   pragmatic conventions)

55. <u>The rascal</u> is at it again. (uniqueness via personal experience)

The next type of an environment shares a number of the constraints on anaphoric pronominalization, except that it is <u>contrastive</u>.
<u>Two</u> (or more) topics are mentioned in <u>directly prior</u> discourse, but
they are of different pronominal genders, so that the pronominal
system of the language can handle this situation and establish unique
reference for both. This device may not be used by languages with
zero pronouns or languages with only one gender, unless further
convention of primacy hold. Since primacy conventions usually
involve, in this case, subject and object relation, a situation which
would unambiguously require contrastive pronouns is one where both
topics have the same case-function. Further, this device usually
requires stressed pronouns. Let us label it <u>contrastive pronomi-</u>
<u>nalization</u>, as in:

56. I saw <u>the queen</u> and <u>the king</u>. Shé wore black, while hé
wore red.

Quite often the use of this device involves also certain parallelism
in the grammatical structures of the sentences involved, as well
as contrastive conjunctions such as 'but,' 'while,' 'though,' etc.

The next situation, again non-contrastive, is in some sense a
further complication over simple definitization. It involves <u>topic-</u>
<u>shifting</u> to the left, most commonly with an <u>intonational break</u> and
quite commonly with a <u>pronominal reflex</u> in the main proposition.
It is quite hard to differentiate the environment for this device from
that which precipitates the use of simple definitization, short of
saying that it involves two extra, possibly interdependent considerations. One may involve such a large gap between the prior and subsequent mention of the topic that the speaker suspects the hearer
may have trouble recalling the topic, if only simple definitization
is used. However, it seems to me that this may be coupled with
another condition. Topics are normally not simply mentioned in

discourse once and then dropped. They linger on; entire stories
or paragraphs deal with them. Now, when more than one potential
topic is mentioned in prior discourse, the speaker proceeds to
deal with one of them in great length, and then he shifts back to
another one, i.e. he changes topic. At that point, it seems to me,
the use of topic-shifting becomes felicitous. The actual topic-
introducing devices may vary enormously. Thus, consider:

57. Once upon a time in a faraway land there lived a king who
     was married to a beautiful queen. The king ruled over a
     vast country; he had many slaves and servants, not to
     mention mere vassals, and frequently went to wars in
     order to increase the size of his treasury.
     a. Now the country over which he ruled was rather flat...
     b. Now, as to his country, it was rather flat...
     c. As to his kingdom, it was rather flat...
     d. Let us now speak of his kingdom. It was rather flat...

Thus, topic-shifting devices do not merely indicate that a different
topic is being mentioned, but further that a new topic has now been
picked up as the subject matter of the discourse.

Next, let us consider the device of contrastive topic-shifting.
It stands in the same relation to topic-shifting as contrastive
pronominalization to simple pronominalization, and on occasion
uses the same devices, plus additional ones. The discourse
context roughly involves topic-shifting to an argument that stands
in contrast, in terms of what the speaker says about it, to the
preceding topic argument. Thus, typically this involves pairs,
parallel constructions and, quite often, contrastive conjunctions
such as 'but,' etc. Considering 57. above, 'country' is not a very
good contrastive topic-shift vis-à-vis 'king,' since it is semantically so different so that there are relatively few properties of
the two which are likely to be constrasted. Suppose, however,
that the following discourse environment occurred, where both
'king' and 'queen' are mentioned as prior topics and then recalled
contrastively:

58. Once upon a time there lived a gracious king together with
     his lovely queen in a faraway land. They had one son, the
     young prince, who caused them no end of grief. He would
     destroy his toys, torture his pets and chop up the living-
     room furniture. Now the king, he took it all in stride,
     muttering into his beard about the sorrows of child rearing.
     But the queen, she got sadder and sadder everyday...

It is not very clear whether in all cases one ought to consider the
first member of the pair a contrastive shifted-topic, though clearly
the second one qualifies and, further, in many languages both the
first and second require the use of devices that are only characteristic of contrastive topic-shifting. Further, in many languages
there are certain topic-shifting devices which can be used only
contrastively and, most often than not, involve neither intonation
break nor recalled pronouns. Thus, consider:

> 59. a. I want to buy presents for all the members of my family.
>   For my older boy I bought a bicycle, and for my little
>   girl (I bought) a plastic paratrooper.
>
>   b. I hate almost all vegetables, especially spinach. Now
>   potatoes I like.

There are grounds to believe that this contrastive device does not
involve changing the subject of the discussion, so that in fact it is
less marked in terms of discourse environment than contrastive
topic-shifting as seen in 58. above. In other words, the discourse
device in 59. is used to contrast topics when the continuity of the
subject of discourse is not broken.

There are two universal constraints which seem to apply to topic-
shifting devices cross-linguistically. The first limits these constructions only to main clauses, with some allowances made for
'that-S' type complements of assertive predicates.[25] Though the
evidence is not unambiguous, I suspect the restriction is not as
absolute on non-shifting contrastive topicalization such as on 59.

The second universal restriction, shared by all topic-shifting
constructions, by definites, contrastive topics and by the subject
nouns of language such as MANDARIN or BEMBA, is that of definiteness. The nouns participating in these constructions may either be
definite or generic, but never referential-indefinite. This is an
obvious restriction, tagging these constructions as ones in which a
new argument cannot be introduced into discourse. With all this in
mind, let us now consider a number of examples to contrast them
with the ENGLISH data presented above.

8.2 Topic and definitization: MANDARIN

Without repeating the data presented in Sec. 6 above, one should
recall that it was left unclear whether the SOV and OSV word order

---

[25] See discussion in Sec. 6 above, as well as footnote 19.

devices for definitization were indeed 'mere definitization' or topic-shifting devices. The nouns occurring in them could be either definite or generic, which is a general restriction holding to definite NPs as well as topic-shifting. The distributional restrictions in these word order devices in MANDARIN, including the ba construction, strongly hint that they are topic-shifting rather than definitization devices. Now, since the use of demonstratives for definitization, particularly in the plural, does not rid them of their deictic force, one may argue that it is not a proper equivalent for mere definitization. If this is true, then MANDARIN shows certain gaps in expressive specificity in the area of mere definitization, particularly in embedded clauses. These gaps are, in all probability, largely illusory, since the greatest need for differentiation and elaboration, particularly with respect to discourse phenomena, lies in the main clause.[26]

8.3 Topic, pronoun and definitization: JAPANESE[27]

JAPANESE has a definite marker sono, as well as a topic case suffix -wa which is used with unstressed nouns for topic-shifting and in combination with stress for contrastive topics. The restrictions on the distribution of this device parallel those mentioned above, i.e. it may be used only in main clauses and bars referential-indefinite readings.[28] Finally, JAPANESE uses mostly zero pronouns in anaphoric situations. This presents the first 'shading' ('slicing the pie') problem for the translator, since in situations where ENGLISH can use contrastive pronouns, JAPANESE must use the full noun with -wa:

60. Simple pronominalization:

watashi-wa John-ni   at-ta   ga   Ø   aisatsu-o
"I-top.   John-dat. see-past but (Ø) greeting-acc.
shi-nak-atta
do-NEG-past"
'I saw John, but I didn't greet him.'

---

[26] See discussion in Givón 1974.

[27] For the JAPANESE data used here, I am indebted to Katsue Akiba (p.c.), but see also Kuroda 1972 and Kuno 1974.

[28] The contrastive use of -wa phrases may appear in embedded clauses, but it is not altogether clear that it is still functioning there as a topic device distinct from contrastive stress-focus, i.e. where the entire proposition is presupposed and the noun in focus is then identified in contrast to other members of a possible set.

61. Contrastive pronominalization:

    watashi-wa John-to-Maria-ni at-ta John-ni-wa aisatsu-o
    "I-top.   J-and-M-dat. see-past J-dat.-top. greeting-acc.

    shi-ta ga Maria-ni-wa aisatsu-o shi-nak-atta
    do-past but M-dat.-top. greeting-acc. do-NEG-past"

    'I saw <u>John</u> and <u>Mary</u>. I greeted h<u>i</u>m but I didn't greet h<u>e</u>r.'

Further, one could show that the use of -wa phrases in JAPANESE
shades into definitization, as in:

62. watashi-wa otoko-to-inu-ni   at-ta   otoko-wa
    "I-top.   man-and-dog-dat. see past man-top.

    aisatsu-o   shi-ta
    greeting-acc. do-past"

    'I saw the <u>man</u> and the dog (and) I greeted <u>the man</u>.'

Thus, although the definite article <u>sono</u> exists in the language, it
does not cover exactly the same discourse function as its equivalent
in ENGLISH, since part of that function seems to be covered by the
contrastive use of -wa. But that use of -wa can only be available
in main clauses, so that for the same function of definitization in
non-main clauses, one must resort to the use of the definitizer
sono, as in:

63. a. otoko-ga tagami-o   kai-ta
      "man-subj. letter-acc. write-past"
      'The man wrote the letter.'

   b. watashi-ga otoko-ni tegami-o kaku-yoo-ni   it-ta
      "I-subj. man-dat. letter-acc. write-inf-dat. say-past"
      'I told the man to write <u>a</u> letter.'

   c.*watashi-ga tegami-wa otoko-ni kaku-yoo-ni   it-ta
      "I-subj. letter-top. man-dat. write-inf.-dat. say-past"

   d. watashi-ga otoko-ni sono-tegami-o kaku-yoo-ni it-ta
      "I-subj. man-dat. the-letter-acc. write-inf.-dat. say-past"
      'I told the man to write <u>the</u> letter.'

One could argue that 'letter' could be topic-shifted with -wa over
the subject of the main clause, as in:

64. (sono)-tegami-wa watashi-ga otoko-ni kaku-yoo-ni it-ta
    "the-letter-top. I - subj.   man-dat. write-inf.-dat. say-past"
    'As to the letter, I told the man to write it.'

However, it is not entirely clear that in this case the value of the
-wa phrase remains equivalent to mere definitization, rather than
becoming topic-shifting.

There are various other complications arising from the use of
-wa as a mere definitizer. One of those involves the problem of
'surprising shift' in the discourse from the 'unmarked' or 'conventionally expected' pattern of continuation. For example, consider
the following in the context of 'once upon a time there was a beautiful
princess':

65. ohimesama-wa shiawase-deshita
    "princess-top. happy-was"
    'The princess was happy.'

    a. ohimesama-wa takusan-no tomodachi-ga arimeshita
       "princess-top. many-gen. friend-subj.   had"
       'The princess had many friends.'

    b. sono ohimesama-ga ookami-ni osow-are-ta
       "the princess-subj. wolf-by   attack-passive-past"
       'The princess was attacked by a wolf.'

The sentence 65.a continues predictably from its antecedent, i.e.
'happy' → 'have friends.' Sentence 65.b, however, if substituted
for 65.a, breaks that continuity rather rudely and unpredictably,
i.e. 'happy' → 'attacked by wolf.' And in that context -wa as a
topic marker or definitizer cannot be used, but rather the subject
case-marker -ga is used, together with the definitizer sono.

Finally, to illustrate one more consideration that is clearly
pragmatic, consider the following case, where 66.a is the discourse
context, and either 66.b or 66.c may be the continuation:

66. a. A new quarter has started.

    b. seito-tachi-$\begin{Bmatrix} \text{wa} \\ \text{*ga} \end{Bmatrix}$ atarashii hon-o kubar-are-ta
       "student-pl.-$\begin{Bmatrix} \text{top.} \\ \text{*subj.} \end{Bmatrix}$ new book-acc. distribute-pass.-past"
       'The students were given new books.'

66. c. atarashii hon-$\left\{\begin{array}{c}\underline{ga}\\ *wa\end{array}\right\}$ seito-tach-$\underline{ni}$ kubar-are-ta

"new   book-$\left\{\begin{array}{c}top.\\ *subj.\end{array}\right\}$ student-pl.-dat. distribute-pass.-past"

'<u>New books</u> were distributed to the students.

The pragmatics of 'a new quarter,' within the university context, establishes both 'books' and 'students' as potentially legitimate topics, as may be seen by the legitimacy of 66.b and 66.c in the equivalent ENGLISH discourse. But in some sense in JAPANESE, and I suspect also in ENGLISH, 'students' are considered more <u>topical</u> than 'books' in this context. That this is the case in ENGLISH may be shown by the peculiar oddity, in the very same context (66.a), of 67.b, c and d below.

67. a. The new quarter has started.
    b. ?<u>The books</u> were distributed to the students.
    c. ?<u>The new books</u> were distributed to the students.
    d. ?The students were given <u>the new books</u>.

However, notice how the anchoring of 'books' to 'students' rescues the sentence:

68.   The students were given <u>their new books</u>.

This seems, then, to be a problem related to definitization or topic recall, rather than topic-shifting <u>per se</u>.

8.4 <u>Topic, subject, dative and passivization: BIKOL</u>

In spite of the various complications seen in MANDARIN and JAPANESE above, both are typologically languages in which the notion of 'subject' is reasonably viable, if that notion is defined by a number of semantic, discourse and syntactic distributional properties.[29] In this section I will illustrate the definitization problems in a Philippine language, BIKOL, whose typological characteristics with respect to the notion 'subject' -- as distinct from 'topic' -- are of a rather different sort.[30]

---

[29] For a detailed discussion of subject properties, see Keenan 1975. For a dissenting view concerning the status of 'subject' in MANDARIN and JAPANESE, see Li and Thompson 1975b.

[30] For an extensive discussion of the notions 'subject' and 'topic' in Philippine languages, see Schachter 1975. For the BIKOL data cited here, I am indebted to Manuel Factora.

In this language one argument in the simple sentence ('main clause') is assigned a topic status marked by a prefix (?ang-), and in many ways this argument functions as the subject. It may be either definite or generic, a restriction shared by the subjects of some languages (MANDARIN, BEMBA) and by marked-topicalized constructions of all languages. The accusative ('patient') is marked, when indefinite, by another prefix (ning-). It may be definitized in three different ways, one of which involves switching the ning-prefix into the normal dative-locative prefix sa-. The other two involve promotion of the accusative to the 'topic' status, i.e. the use of the marker ?ang-. Promotions of this type involve also changing the verb-masking prefix ('focus marker'), which indicates which of the arguments of the verb is in the ?ang- case:

69. nag-pákul ?ang-babáye ning-kandíng
    "agent-hit top.-woman acc./indef.-goat"
    'The woman hit a goat.'

70. p-in-ákul kang - babáye ?ang-kandíng
    "acc. -hit agent/def. woman top. -goat"
    'The woman hit the goat.'

71. na-pákul kang-babáye ?ang-kandíng
    "acc. -hit agent-woman top. -goat"
    'The goat was hit by the woman.'

72. nag-pákul ?ang-babáye sa - kandíng
    "agent-hit top. -woman dat./def. -goat"
    'The woman hit the goat.'

Thus, while both 70. and 71. assign the topic marker to the patient, 71. is judged to be 'more like a passive,' while 70. is 'more like definite accusative.' And further, it is not quite clear how exactly to represent the difference between definitizing the accusative/patient by promotion as in 70., as against definitizing it by the dative marker as in 72. The most intelligent guess is that 71.> 70.> 72.> 69. hierarchize as to degree of topicality, with the indefinite in 69. being clearly non-topic, and the topic-marked patient in 71. being clearly the highest. Further, while the argument in the ?ang-case can only be definite (or generic),[31] once an agent is 'demoted,'

---

[31] It may be argued that generic topics are definite within the universe of types, much like non-generic ones are definite within the universe of tokens. It is less clear whether the same discourse contexts make a type into a topic as those which make an individual token into one.

it could either take the agentive kang- prefix (as in 70. and 71.
above) and be definite, or take the ning- case as indefinite, as in:

73.   p-in-ákul ning-babáye   ?ang-kandíng
        "acc.-hit indef.-woman top.-goat"
        '<u>A</u> woman hit the goat.'/'The goat was hit by <u>a</u> woman.'

74.   na-pákul ning-babáye   ?ang-kandíng
        "acc.-hit indef.-woman top.-goat"
        'The goat was hit by <u>a</u> woman.'

So far then, one may say that any constituent in the ?ang- case is
definite, and out of the ?ang-case for agents the contrast DEF/
INDEF is marked by kang-/ning-, while for patient by sa-/ning-,
respectively.

An added complication involves the dative-locative case. It is
normally marked by sa-, but for some verbs, that sa- is only to
be interpreted as definite, and for indefinites one must substitute
ning-, as in:

75. a. nag-la?úg   ?ang-kandíng sa-harúng
       "agent-enter top.-goat dat./def.-house"
       'The goat entered <u>the</u> house.'

    b. nag-la?úg   ?ang-kandíng ning-harúng
       "agent-enter top.-goat   indef.-house"
       'The goat entered <u>a</u> house.'

On the other hand, with other verbs the sa- marker is ambiguous
and can mean either DEF/INDEF, and ning- cannot be used, as in: [32]

76. a. nag-dumán ?ang-laláke sa-tindáhan
       "agent-go   top.-man   dat.-store"
       'The man went to <u>the</u>/(<u>a</u>?) store.'

    b. *nag-dumán ?ang-laláke ning-tindahán

_____

[32] It is not clear whether this is a question of the semantic properties of the verb as distinct from the pragmatics of the context in
which it is most frequently used. For example, if the verb 'put X
on Y' is normally used within the sub-universe 'house,' where 'table,'
'chair,' 'bed,' 'shelf,' etc. may be unique dependent variables of the
house or specific rooms within it, chances are that as locative goals
of 'put,' they will be definitized even without prior mention.

There are reasons to believe that even a complete lack of indefinite-marking for either locatives or datives would, at the discourse level, be a relatively small loss. Datives are mostly <u>human</u> and much more likely to be topic/definite in discourse.[33] Locatives are either conventionally/pragmatically unique, or else they usually belong to the <u>setting</u> for an action, which is normally mentioned in discourse before the action, and is thus likely to be definite when the actions/events concerning agents, patients and datives are described.

Now, when dative/locative arguments are 'promoted' to the topic case (<u>?ang</u>), they may only be definite (or generic), as in the general constraint:

77. d-<u>in</u>-uman-án kang-laláke ?ang-tindáha
     "loc.-go   agent-man   top.-store"
     'The man went to the store.'

78. <u>na</u>-duman-án kang-laláke ?ang-tindáha
     "loc.-go   agent-man top.-store"
     'The store was gone-to by the man.' [ENG. approximation]

Since locative, benefactive and instrumental arguments can be all 'promoted' to topicality (<u>?ang</u>) as in 78, these 'passivization' devices in BIKOL are not altogether analogous to the ENGLISH passive which is restricted mostly to accusative objects and some datives.

Since the 'promotion to <u>?ang</u>' process is not fully equivalent to passivization, is it then more equivalent to marked-topicalization? There is a strong piece of evidence which suggests that this could not be the case. Marked-topicalization devices, as I have shown above, are confined mostly to the main clause. However, the <u>?ang</u> NPs in BIKOL have a complete distribution in all embedded clauses. In fact, in relative clauses the equi-NP within the embedded sentence must in most Philippine languages[34] be in the topic case, otherwise relativization cannot proceed:

---

[33] See discussion in Givón 1975b.

[34] In BIKOL there are a number of exceptions to this rule, mostly involving dative/locatives, which under certain conditions may be relativized even without advancement to <u>?ang</u>-phrase status in the embedded clause.

79. a. nag-pákul áko   sa-laláke na nag-gadán ning-kandíng
       "agent-hit I(top.) def.-man that agent-kill indef.-goat"
       'I hit the man who killed a goat.'

    b.*nag-pákul áko sa-laláke na g-in-adán ?ang-kandíng
              " . . .   acc.-kill top.-goat"

    c. nag-pákul áko   sa-kandíng na g-in-andán kang-laláke
       "agent-hit I(top.) def.-goat that acc.-kill agent-man"
       'I hit the goat that was killed by the man.'/
       'I hit the goat that the man killed.'

    d.*nag-pákul áko sa-kandíng na nag-gadán ?ang-laláke
              " . . .   agent-kill top.-man"

Finally, it is not very clear whether BIKOL has the same mapping of marked-topicalization as in ENGLISH, MANDARIN, JAPA-
NESE or BANTU. The 'neutral' topic marker ?ang most likely
covers at least part of this function. And a deictic particle si,
which can appear only as a substitute of ?ang, may cover part or
most of this function, without any 'movement to the left' which is
so universally characteristic of marked topicalization.

8.5 Topic, pronoun and grammatical agreement: BANTU

In a number of languages, topicalization and its correlated anaphoric pronominalization shade into the grammar of definitization,
and sometimes into obligatory grammatical agreement. In principle, this is a highly universal process,[35] motivated by the con-
vergence of several synchronic and diachronic driving forces. In
this section I will briefly illustrate this phenomenon by examples
from two BANTU languages.

In RWANDA one may observe the following mapping of definiteness and referentiality in objects of negated verbs:

80. a. ya-boonye umugabo
       "he-saw   man"
       'He saw a man.'   (REF-INDEF)

    b. nhi-ya-boonye umugabo
       "NEG-he-saw   man"
       'He didn't see any man.' (NON-REF)

---

[35] See details in Givón 1975b.

80. c. umugabo, nhi-ya-mu-boonye
     "man   NEG-he-him-saw"
     'The man, he didn't see him.'/
     'He didn't see the man.'   (DEF, TOP)

Thus, the only way to definitize the object of a negated verb is by topic-shifting plus an obligatory anaphoric object **pronoun**. The pronoun thus becomes an integral part of the lexical marking of definiteness (in objects), and this has been further extended in the affirmative to the point where the topicalization movement is not obligatory here, and in fact there is a contrast between 'definite' --with only the pronoun, and 'topicalized' -- with both left-movement and pronoun:

81. a. umugabo, ya-mu-boonye
     'As to the man, he saw him.'   (DEF, TOP)

    b. ya-mu-boonye umugabo
      'He saw the man.'   (DEF)

The difference between 81.a and 81.b is critical, because while topic-shifted constructions such 81.a can appear only in main clauses, 81.b may appear in embedded clauses.

A further extension of this process is found in SWAHILI, where, for inanimate (or non-human) nouns, the normal definitization process of objects is via the anaphoric pronoun in both the negative and affirmative:

82. a. ni-li-ki-soma kitabu   'I read the book.'
    b. si-ku-ki-soma kitabu   'I didn't read the book.'
    c. ni-li-soma kitabu   'I read a book.'
    d. si-ku-soma kitabu chochote   'I didn't read any book.'

For human objects, however, pronominalization -- or object agreement -- has become obligatory, and definitization must be marked by other devices:

81. a. ni-li-mw-ona mtu mmoja   'I saw one person.'
    b. si-ki-mw-ona mtu yeyote   'I didn't see any one.'
    c. ni-li-mw-ona mtu yule   'I saw that man.'
    d. ni-li-mw-ona yule mtu   'I saw the man.'

As I have shown elsewhere, the progression topic/pronoun > definite > grammatical agreement represents a diachronic cline, along which a language may progress by gradual de-marking of constructions.

Thus, the interaction of grammatical agreement with topicalization and definitization in language is a rather natural phenomenon. [36]

9. Summary

I have shown how the grammar of definitization and referentiality in language shades naturally into a number of other sub-system in the grammar which are 'semantically contiguous' to it. Much of the actual marking system used in definitization in language may depend on the inventory of other syntactic and morphological devices available in the grammar as a whole, and much of that often hinges on diachronic rather than synchronic factors. This is to an extent also true of PLANTATION CREOLES, since the availability of a definite article or demonstrative in the language which serves as the lexical donor in these languages is to quite an extent a diachronic accident. It is nevertheless clear that the interaction between the definitization system and other subparts of the grammar, such as referentiality, topicality, numerals, plurality, deixis, case system and grammatical agreement, is controlled by coherent language-universal principles, the more important of which I have tried to illustrate above.

BIBLIOGRAPHY

Bickerton, D. 1975a. Creolization, linguistic universals, natural semantax and the brain. Paper read at the Conference on Pidgins and Creoles, University of Hawaii, Honolulu, January 1975 (ms).

_____. 1975b. Creoles and natural semantax. Lecture at U.C. L.A., April 1975 (ms).

Bokamba, E.G. 1971. Specificity and definiteness in Dzamba. Studies in African Linguistics 2.3. 217-238.

Comrie, B. 1975. Direct object case-marking in Uralic languages: an explanatory model. Paper read at the Fourth International Conference on Finno-Ugric Languages, Budapest, September 1975 (ms).

---

[36] For a general discussion see Givón 1975b, where similar phenomena in SPANISH, AMHARIC, GE'EZ, NEO-ARAMAIC and other languages are cited.

Comrie, B. 1976. Definite and animate: a natural class? Cambridge University (ms).

Creider, C. 1976. Thematization and word order. Paper read at the Winter LSA Meeting, 1975, University of W. Ontario (ms); another version read at the Seventh Conference on African Linguistics, University of Florida at Gainsville, April 1976.

Emonds, J. 1970. Root and structure preserving transformations. Doctoral dissertation, M.I.T.

Givón, T. 1973. Opacity and reference in language: an inquiry into the role of modalities. Syntax and semantics, ed. by J. Kimball, Vol. II. New York: Academic Press.

_____. 1974a. Toward a discourse definition of syntax. U.C. L.A. (ms).

_____. 1974b. Syntactic change in Lake-Bantu: a rejoinder. Studies in African Linguistics 5.1. 117-139.

_____. 1975a. Negation in language: pragmatics, function, ontology. Working Papers on Language Universals 18. 59-116. Stanford University.

_____. 1975b. Topic, pronoun and grammatical agreement. Subject and topic, ed. by C. Li. New York: Academic Press.

_____. 1976. The development of the numeral 'one' as an indefinite marker in Israeli Hebrew. Generative studies in Hebrew linguistics, ed. by S. Bolozky and M. Barkai. Tel Aviv: Tel Aviv University Press.

Hetzron, R. 1974. The presentative movement, or why the ideal word order is VSOP. Word order and word order change, ed. by C. Li. Austin: University of Texas Press.

Hooper, J. 1974. On assertive predicates. UCLA Papers in Syntax 5. (May 1974).

_____ and S. Thompson. 1973. On the applicability of root transformations. Linguistic Inquiry 4.4.

Jackendoff, R. 1971. Modal structure in semantic representation. Linguistic Inquiry 2.4.

Keenan, E. 1972. On semantically based grammar. Linguistic Inquiry 3.

_____. 1975. Toward a universal definition of 'subject.' Subject and topic, ed. by C. Li. New York: Academic Press.

_____ and K. Ebert. 1973. A note on marking transparency and opacity. Linguistic Inquiry 4.3.

Kirsner, R. 1973. Natural focus and agentive interpretation: on the semantics of the Dutch expletive er. Stanford Occasional Papers in Linguistics 3. 101-114.

Kuno, S. 1974. The structure of the Japanese language. Cambridge: M.I.T. Press.

Kuroda, S-Y. 1972. The categorical and thetic judgment. Foundations of Language 9.

Li, C. (ed.) 1976. Subject and topic. New York: Academic Press.

_____ and S. Thompson. 1974. The semantic function of word order. Word order and word order change, ed. by C. Li. Austin: University of Texas Press.

_____. 1975a. Topic prominent languages. Paper read at the Winter LSA Meeting (ms).

_____. 1975b. Subject and topic: a new typology of language. Subject and topic, ed. by C. Li.

Schachter, P. 1975. The subject in Philippine languages: topic, actor, actor-topic or none of the above. Subject and topic, ed. by C. Li.

Agreement

EDITH A. MORAVCSIK

ABSTRACT

With a working definition of grammatical agreement proposed
and the questions seen as pertinent to the study of agreement
phenomena listed, a crosslinguistic survey of three types of
agreement features -- gender, number, and person -- is presented followed by some crosslinguistic generalizations about
agreeing constituents. The theory according to which agreement
markers and anaphoric pronouns are grammatically derived by
the same types of rules is informally shown to be predictive of
some of the restrictions observed both in respect to agreement
features and agreeing constituents.

This is a partly abridged, partly expanded version of my paper
Agreement as it appeared in Working Papers on Language Univer-
sals, 5, 1971. I am grateful to Alan Bell, Charles A. Ferguson,
Joseph H. Greenberg, Fred W. Householder and Elizabeth C.
Traugott for comments.

CONTENTS

1. Introduction

The purpose of this paper is to present some crosslinguistically valid informal generalizations concerning grammatical agreement.

The working definition of the term "agreement" which delimits the class of phenomena to which it will be applied in the paper is the following: a grammatical constituent A will be said to agree with a grammatical constituent B in properties C in language L if C is a set of meaning-related properties of A and there is a covariance relationship between C and some phonological properties of a constituent B_1 across some subset of the sentences of language L, where constituent B_1 is adjacent to constituent B and the only meaning-related non-categorial properties of constituent B_1 are the properties C.[1]   Thus, for instance, the verb is said to agree with the subject in number and person in ENGLISH because there is a relationship of covariance between the number and person specifications of the subject noun phrase and between the phonological shape of the verbal suffix across a subset of those sentences of the language that are in the present tense in that if the subject noun phrase is singular third person, the suffix is s and if it is some other number and person, the suffix is zero. Constituents A and B — the subject noun phrase and the verb in the ENGLISH example -- will be called agreeing constituents; constituent B_1 -- the verbal suffix above — will be called agreement marker; and perperties C — number and person above -- will be called agreement features.

The above is a working definition in the sense that no theoretical naturalness is being claimed for the class of phenomena that it delimits. It will be adopted simply since the set of phenomena within its scope appear to be intuitively similar; but it is possible that a principled and complete account of the structure of all human languages would leave this class uncharacterized.

The working definition proposed excludes some things from the class of agreement (or concord) phenomena which, however, appear

---

[1] Although I have no actual example for it, it is possible that in some languages agreement is marked suprasegmentally, rather than segmentally; such as by some particular stress-pattern in the agreeing constituent. The present working definition of agreement would admit of such cases in that the suprasegmentally manifested agreement marker would nonetheless have to be prelexically represented as a constituent adjacent to the agreeing one.

to bear some similarity to agreement. Excluded is, for instance,
lexical selection since here there is no agreement marker; the
property FLUID, for instance, in which the verb <u>pour</u> and its
direct object "agree" is not represented by a separate morpheme
in either the verb or the object. Excluded are furthermore phonological assimilation phenomena since their description does not
involve reference to meaning-related properties. Stylistic, dia-
lectic, or language uniformity across the constituents of discourses
is also not characterized as a phenomenon of grammatical agreement by our working definition in that the terms included in the
definition are inapplicable to it. [2]

The definition, however, does include, first of all, various kinds
of phenomena that have traditionally also been called "agreement"
such as the agreement of quantifiers, modifiers, determiners,
verbs, and anaphoric pronouns with nouns in gender, number, person, case, and definiteness; as well as others that have not been
traditionally subsumed under this label. To this latter group belong instances of "negativity agreement" between some nouns and
verbs in HUNGARIAN (compare <u>Valamit láttam</u> "something-accus-
ative saw-I" 'I saw something,' <u>Semmit nem láttam</u> "nothing-
accusative not saw-I" 'I saw nothing'); 'genericity agreement"
between some nouns and verbs in ENGLISH (compare <u>An Englishman washes his hands before dinner</u>, *<u>An Englishman is washing
his hands before dinner</u>), "tense-agreement" and "mood-agreement"
in the cases of LATIN and ENGLISH, [3] dislocation, and government.

If we assume that the goal of linguistic research is to provide
principles of maximal cross-sentential and crosslinguistic generality whereby symbolic equivalence relations between meanings
and sounds in all human languages can be accounted for, the following questions appear to me to constitute the total set of questions
that would have to be asked and answered in order to provide a complete linguistic account of grammatical agreement:

---

[2] For some remarks on the similarity between grammatical agreement and phonological assimilation, compare Chomsky 1965:175f.
For discussions about the similarities of "style agreement" and
grammatical selection, see Gumperz 1966 and McCawley 1968:135-6.

[3] For "mood agreement" in ENGLISH, see Jespersen 1924:27ff.

1.   Given the set of those sentences in any language across which agreement is observable,

   a.   what are the meaning-related and form-related properties of those constituents that are in agreement relation with each other as opposed to those that are not?

   b.   what are the meaning-related properties of the agreement markers -- that is to say, what are the agreement features?

   c.   what are the form properties of the agreement markers?

2.   Given a language whose sentences include sentences with agreement, what, if any, are the meaning related or form-related properties of those sentences with agreement as opposed to those without it -- to the extent that these properties are distinct from properties of the constituents involved?

3.   Given the set of all languages, what are the properties -- whether in terms of structure or in terms of temporal or spatial attributes -- of those languages whose sentences do include sentences with agreement as opposed to those whose sentences do not? A complete account, in other words, would require the characterization of those languages that have agreement as opposed to those that do not; the characterization of those sentences in any agreement-language that exhibit agreement as opposed to those that do not; the characterization of those constituents in any set of agreement-sentences that participate in the phenomenon as agreeing terms as opposed to those that do not; and the characterization of those meaning-related and phonological properties that constitute agreement markers as opposed to those that do not.

Of these questions, the present study will be centrally concerned only with those under 1.a and 1.b. Nothing will be said, in other words, about which languages in the world include sentences that exhibit agreement phenomena and which do not;[4] or whether there are any properties of those sentences in a language that have agreement as opposed to those that do not -- properties, that is, that are distinct from properties of the constituents that participate in

---

[4]If the term "agreement" is taken, as in this paper, to include "dislocation," and if Sanders and Tai are correct in proposing that dislocation is a universally present structure (Sanders and Tai 1972), then agreement itself would also be a universal phenomenon. Nonetheless, languages certainly vary in what subtypes of agreement they have; for an attempt to tackle the question: which languages have agreement between the verb and its major nominal constituent complements, compare Li and Thompson 1975.

agreement; or about what the form properties of agreement markers
are. Discussion will center on these two questions only: given the
sentences of a language that has agreement, what are the meaning-
related and form-related properties of those constituents that are
in agreement relation with each other as opposed to those that are
not, and what are the properties with respect to which they agree?
The focus of discussion will actually be even more limited partly
in that only a small sample of languages will be considered, and
partly in that of the various kinds of phenomena that were listed
above as falling within the scope of our working definition of agreement, only those instances will be discussed where the agreed-with
constituent is a nominal or a noun phrase; and of these, only those
where the agreement features are features of gender, or of number,
or of person, and not those of definiteness or case.   Section 2.1
will consider the nature of these three kinds of agreement properties
and section 2.2 will discuss the constituents that participate in
agreements of these three kinds.   Section 3 will summarize the
results.

2.   Agreement features and agreeing constituents

2.1 Agreement features

2.1.1 Gender. Gender features will be understood as a set of
any non-quantificational, non-referential or deictic, and non-case-
related properties of nominals or noun phrases that are ever lexicalized separately in the language from the rest of the lexical
properties of the nominal, either as an affix adjacent to the stem
itself or as an agreement marker associated with some other constituent; or both. Gender thus includes distinctions related to
animacy, humanness, sex, or any other qualitative property of
nominal referents, as well as distinctions that are not correlated
with any such semantic property -- such as the masculine-feminine-
neuter distinction in GERMAN or other INDOEUROPEAN languages
or the semantically equally non-interpretable distinctions on which
noun classification in BANTU languages is based.

Gender agreement par excellence can be illustrated from RUS-
SIAN by the following sentences:

babuška čitala	"grandmother-feminine read-feminine"
	' The grandmother was reading.'
čelovek čital	"man-masculine read-masculine"
	' The man was reading.'

okno otkrylos'   "window-neuter opened-itself-neuter"
                    'The window opened.'

In each sentence, the verb agrees in gender with the noun.

In these sentences, the particular gender property with respect
to which agreement takes place is represented by an affix not only
on the agreeing constituent — the verb — but also on the noun itself
with which agreement takes place, in the form of the endings -∅,
-a, and -o; and, as a larger class of similar examples would show,
there is a simple one-to-one relation between nominal gender suffixes and past-verb gender suffixes. Consideration of wider range
of facts both within RUSSIAN and from other languages suggest,
however, that all of this is not always the case; that, in particular,
a nominal gender affix may be irrelevant for determining agreement.
The irrelevance of a nominal gender affix from the point of view of
determining agreement is manifested in three ways in various languages. First, it is possible that a constituent agrees in gender
with a noun phrase even though the noun has no gender affix associated with it. Second, it is possible that a noun has a gender affix;
nonetheless a constituent that in principle could agree with it does
not show any kind of gender agreement with it. Third, it is possible
that a noun has an overt gender marker but the constituent that
agrees with the noun in gender agrees with it not in the overtly
marked gender but in one that is not overtly marked on the noun.
In what follows, I will illustrate and discuss examples for each of
these cases.

That there can be agreement with a noun whose gender properties
are not overtly marked on the noun itself can be shown from RUS-
SIAN itself; compare

ty čital   "you read-masculine"
                   'You were reading.' (said of a masculine 'you')

ty čitala   "you read-feminine"
                   'You were reading.' (said of a feminine 'you')

In these sentences the verb agrees with the subject noun in gender
just like in the previously cited sentences; even though masculinity
and femininity have no overt markers on the second person pronoun whereas they do on the nouns. Similar examples can be cited
from ENGLISH; compare

The man is in the room. He is old.
The mother is in the room. She is old.
The table is in the room. It is old.

Similarly, that the presence of an overt gender marker on the noun does not insure agreement on the part of all constituents that could agree with it is also illustratable from RUSSIAN. In this language the past tense does agree in gender with the subject; but not the present tense verb. Compare

babuška čitaet   "grandmother-feminine read-third person singular"
                     ' The grandmother is reading. '

čelovek čitaet   "man-masculine read-third person singular"
                     ' The man is reading. '

okno otkryvaetsja   "window-neuter open-third person singular"
                     ' The window is opening. '

I have, however, no examples of languages where (some) nominals are marked for gender; and, nonetheless, no constituent in any sentence of the language ever shows agreement with the nominal in that gender.

These examples from RUSSIAN and ENGLISH have shown that overt gender marking of the nominal is not a necessary condition for gender agreement to take place; nor is it a sufficient condition predicting agreement to take place with respect to any constituent that in principle might agree with it. Next I would like to show that not only is overt gender marking not sufficient to guarantee the occurrence of agreement but it is not even sufficient in some cases to predict the gender of the agreement marker once gender agreement does take place in some constituent.

Whereas I have no examples of nouns that are agreed-with in terms of a gender property that is distinct from the one overtly marked on them in all sentences of the language, there are several examples of a noun being agreed with in terms of the overtly marked gender property in some sentences of the language and in terms of a gender property distinct from the one overtly marked in other sentences. A clear example to illustrate this is provided by SWA-HILI. In this language, all nouns have overt gender markers called class prefixes. Whereas the nominal gender classes definable in terms of these nominal prefixes are congruent with the nominal classes definable in terms of adjective agreement-- adjectives, that is, do agree with nouns in those genders that are marked on the noun -- this is not always the case for anaphoric pronominal agreement, in that all nouns referring to human beings (and some referring

to animals) regardless of their prefixes require anaphoric pronouns
of a uniform shape -- of a shape that otherwise occurs with nouns
belonging to the first nominal prefix class (which, by the way, includes mostly human nouns) (Lyons 1968: 284-6).

There are many other languages as well where the gender in
which there is agreement is different depending on what the agreeing constituent is. The case of LINGALA is parallel to SWAHILI.
Most nouns belong to prefix classes which are also the classes in
terms of which relative pronouns agree with them. However,
demonstrative pronouns, the word for 'other,' anaphoric pronouns,
and the verb show agreement depending on the animacy of the subject noun (Alexandre 1967). MANDJAKU (Doneux 1967) has a large
number of concord prefixes for adjectives, numerals, the word for
'other,' and for various pronouns, but the verb shows only a two-
way distinction depending on whether the subject noun is plural
human or not. In MBEMBE nouns belong to eleven classes according to their prefixes and agreement requirements. Each class
governs three sets of concord prefixes, depending on the particular
part of the sentence or discourse. Examinations of these concord markers shows four different noun classes which differ with respect to their
prefixes only, not to the concord morphemes they govern; the set
of these four classes exhausts those which contain nouns referring
to human beings (Barnwell 1969).[5] It is also interesting that per-
sonified animals take Class I agreement despite their formal membership in Class III. In LUVALE pronouns, adjectives, possessives,
and numerals agree with the noun. Nouns, according to their prefixes, belong to 14 classes, nine of which refer to animate beings.
All such animate nouns are exceptional in their agreement requirements because they take Class I agreement for all agreeing terms
(except in a genitive construction) (Horton 1949:24ff.). In TEMNE
if the noun is animate both verbs and attributive adjectives disregard
noun class membership and agree as if the noun were of Class I
(Hutchinson 1969:9-10, 103-4). In AKKADIAN some nouns are, by
form, feminine, although they refer to male beings, such as 'chief.'
Such nouns may take either female or male pronominal reference
in the verb; although data are scarce, there is some evidence that
this may apply also to attributive adjectives (von Soden 1952:186-7).

A generalization about alternative agreements depending on the
type of the agreeing constituent with which all the above-cited

---

[5]Two other pairs of classes also have identical concord morphemes and differ only in their prefixes; no explanation has been
found for this, given Barnwell's data.

evidence is the following: if there is any set of agreeing constituent
types whose members show agreement in terms of semantically
interpretable — or "natural" — gender properties, this set will include constituent types that are external to the noun phrase -- that
is to say, verbs and anaphoric pronouns. Or, putting it in another
way: the occurrence of semantic or natural gender agreement
within the noun phrase implies such agreement ouside it in the
same language.[6]

In our survey of cases where the gender of agreement is different
from the overtly marked gender of the noun we have seen a number
of languages where constituents agree differently with a noun depending on the constituent class they belong to. In addition to constituent class membership, there is also another property of
agreeing constituents which may determine variant agreement and
this is their linear order in respect to the agreed-with constituent.
This may be illustrated from MODERN ARABIC.[7]   In ARABIC

---

[6] More complicated to generalize about is agreement in GERMAN
with nouns such as Mädchen 'girl.' The noun itself has no overt
gender marking. Noun phrase internal agreement -- that is, the
agreement of articles, demonstrative adjectives, descriptive adjectives and possessive adjectives -- is in the neuter gender; but relative pronouns and anaphoric pronouns may be either in the neuter
or in the feminine gender. Compare, for instance, the following
sentences: Das schöne Mädchen, das/die du gestern sahest, ist
krank. Es/sie ist im Krankenhaus. "the-neuter pretty-neuter girl,
which-neuter/whom/feminine you yesterday saw, is sick. it/she
is in-the hospital" 'The pretty girl whom you saw yesterday is sick.
She is in the hospital.' What is interesting about it is that both feminine and neuter agreement "make sense" here in that the meaning
'girl' includes both the property 'feminine' and also the property
'small;' and in GERMAN naturally feminine nouns take feminine
agreement and diminutive nouns take neuter agreement.

[7] From the data I am familiar with, it appears undecidable whether
the agreement in gender of the participial complement of the auxiliary avoir in FRENCH with object nominals depends on whether
the object nominal is pronoun or noun or on whether the object nominal precedes the verb or follows it; since all object nominals with
which the participle shows agreement are both pronominal and preceding and all object nominals with which it shows no agreement
are both nominal and following.

the verb has to be masculine if the subject is masculine regardless of the linear order relation of the subject and the verb; but the verb may be either feminine or masculine if the indefinite subject is feminine depending on whether the subject follows or precedes the verb. Compare the following:

wálad ʔəžáani   "boy came-he-to-me"   'A boy came to me. '
ʔəžáani wálad   "came-he-to-me boy"   'A boy came to me.'
bə́nt ʔəžə́tni   "girl came-she-to-me"   'A girl came to me. '
ʔəžə́tni bə́nt   "came-she-to-me girl"   'A girl came to me. '

These sentences show that the verb may agree in gender both with masculine and with feminine subjects regardless of order relations. The next four sentences will show that whereas postposed, but not preposed, feminine subjects may take masculine agreement, masculine subjects may not take feminine agreement whether postposed or preposed: ʔəžáani bə́nt "came-he-to-me girl" 'A girl came to me. '

*bə́nt ʔəžáani   "girl came-he-to-me"
*ʔəžə́tni wálad   "came-she-to-me boy"
*wálad ʔəžə́tni   "boy came-she-to-me" (Ferguson & Rice 1951).

The significance of linear order for determining correct gender agreement is further illustrated by examples where a constituent agrees with a noun phrase that includes more than one noun conjoined with each other. Examples come from LATIN, TEMNE, and FRENCH. In LATIN the predicate adjective shows the same gender as the subject nouns conjoined by et if they are alike in gender. It is also possible to conjoin nouns which differ with respect to masculinity-femininity-neuterness: if the conjoined nouns are all animate the predicate adjective is masculine; if all are inanimate, it is neuter. The adjective modifying the entire noun phrase (all those conjoined) agrees in gender with the nearest noun. In TEMNE if inanimate nouns belonging to different gender classes are conjoined, the predicate shows the gender of the first conjoined noun. If the conjoined nouns in the set are all singular, but some are animate and others inanimate, the verb may show the animate gender (and plurality) or it may show the gender of the first conjoined noun (and singularity, in case it is inanimate). If the nouns are animate and inanimate and (some of them) are plural, the verb is in the plural animate gender or in the plural form of the gender of the first noun. [8] Proximity is also criterial in FRENCH in the

---

[8] This information about TEMNE is inferred from data that formed part of the M.A. examination problems at Indiana University in May

case of agreement with conjoined noun phrase. Compare

Le calme et la fraîcheur du vieux couvent sont si exquises.
"the-masculine calmness and the-feminine freshness of-the
old cloister are so exquisite-feminine-plural"
'The calmness and the freshness of the old cloister are so
exquisite.'

where the verb whose subject is a conjoined noun phrase consisting
of a masculine and a feminine noun is in the feminine, rather than
masculine, plural, thus following the gender of the closer conjunct
(Blinkenberg 1950: 101). These examples indicate that the factors
that determine gender agreement with conjoined noun phrases that
are heterogeneous in their overtly marked gender properties include their semantic gender (in particular, animacy) and the order
of the conjuncts.

The results of this brief survey of the conditions that determine
the occurrence versus non-occurrence of gender agreement and
the kind of gender in respect to which there is agreement may be
summarized as follows. The presence of an overt gender marking
on the noun may be neither necessary nor sufficient to guarantee
gender agreement for all constituents that could in principle agree.
Once gender agreement does take place with a noun whose gender
is overtly marked, the gender that is marked on the noun may again
be neither necessary nor sufficient to predict the particular gender
marked on the agreeing constituent. Consideration of instances of
gender agreement where different constituents agree in terms of
either the overtly marked gender of the noun or in terms of a gender not so marked led us to the question: what conditions correlate
in general with alternative gender agreements? The conditions we
established were two in kind: the membership of the agreement
constituent and linear order. With respect to the former, all evidence was compatible with the generalization according to which if
some constituents agree in terms of semantically interpretable
gender properties, these constituents will include some noun-
phrase-external constituents. With respect to linear order, we
have seen examples for the agreement-significance of constituents

---

(ftnt. 8 cont.)
1968. For additional data and discussion of gender agreement with
conjoined noun phrases of non-identical gender, see Givón 1970
(concerning BANTU languages) and Mould 1971 (about BANTU and
HEBREW).

that precede the agreeing constituent rather than follow it (ARABIC
and possibly FRENCH); examples for the agreement-significance
of constituents that are adjacent, rather than non-adjacent, to the
agreeing constituent; and examples for the agreement significance
of nouns within a set of conjoined ones that are first, rather than
non-first.

2.1.2 <u>Number</u>   The most straightforward type of number
agreement is manifested in sentences involving nominals with
overtly marked singularity or plurality and agreeing constituents
such as nominal modifiers, verbs, or pronouns that are in the
singular or plural, respectively; such as the following sentences
of ENGLISH:

> Call the girl and tell her to hurry.
> Call the girls and tell them to hurry.

where the distinction between <u>her</u> and <u>them</u> corresponds to the
overtly marked singular-plural distinction between <u>girl</u> and <u>girls</u>.
A consideration of a wider set of data, both within ENGLISH itself and in other languages, indicates that the correspondence
relation between agreeing and agreed-with constituents is not always this simple; it is not generally true that an agreeing constituent is in the singular with all and only singularly-marked nominals
and that it is in the plural with all and only plurally-marked nominals. Rather, generic plural marking of nominals may be just as
unpredictive of the number manifested in the agreeing constituent
as we have seen overt nominal gender marking to be. In what follows, I wish to illustrate this by showing that there exist both
instances where a plurally-marked nominal is agreed-with by a
singularly-marked constituent and where singularly-marked nominals are agreed-with by a plurally-marked constituent.

Nominals that are marked singular and that nonetheless take
plural agreement with some constituents in some languages are of
the following five types:

a. numerated nominals
b. conjoined nominals
c. nominals with a comitative complement
d. collective nominals
e. simple (non-numerated, non-conjoined, non-comitatively-
    complemented, and non-collective) nominals.

Anaphoric pronominal reference to numerated and conjoined
nouns, just like to overtly pluralized nouns, appears to be

universally plural if the meaning of these noun phrases involves a
set of non-correferential nominal meanings. As for verb agreement, the picture is less clear. After conjoined singular nouns,
there are examples of both singular and plural verbs in COPTIC
(Till 1961: 199) and in HUNGARIAN. After numerated nouns, either
singular or plural verb forms may be used in AMHARIC (Obolensky
et al. 1964: 311) and in OLD ASSYRIAN (von Soden 1952: 186), and
only singular verb forms in (present-day) HUNGARIAN. Apart
from these instances, however, verb agreement, too, is plural
with these types of noun phrases. The nouns themselves, however,
after a numeral, are not overtly pluralized in all languages; nor
are the noun-phrase-internal modifiers coocurring with numerated
nouns. BAKI (Fraser 1891: 76) and FIJIAN (Churchward 1941: 14-5)
have an optional nominal plural marker which is in complementary
distribution with numerals. In AMHARIC (Obolensky et al. 1964:
31), ASSYRIAN (von Soden 1952: 194), and HAUSA (Robinson 1930:
60), the singular or the plural noun form (and presumably also the
adjective and the demonstrative and possessive pronouns) may each
cooccur with a numeral. In RUSSIAN and in ARABIC (Cowell
1964: 367) some numerals cooccur with singular, others with plural
nouns. In COPTIC (Mallon 1956: 76ff.), in TURKISH, in (present-
day) HUNGARIAN, and in BALTI (Forchheimer 1953: 114), (as in
BAKI and FIJIAN mentioned above), the plural noun form must
not cooccur with numerals. In FINNISH, however, it is apparently
possible for the demonstrative pronoun and the adjective to show
plurality if they cooccur with a numerated (singular) noun, e. g. in
nuo hauskat kymmenen minuttia "these beautiful-plural ten minute"
(Mey 1960: 107). All this shows that, while it is not easy to generalize about plurality as represented within a noun phrase, the agreement properties of conjoined, numerated, and (superficially) pluralized
noun phrases tend to be the same with respect to noun phrase   external constituents such as anaphoric pronouns and verbs more than
with respect to noun phrase internal constituents.

The stipulation concerning multiple reference associated with the
generalization presented above is necessary since there are a number of languages where conjoined or numerated nouns do not take
plural agreement in some cases whereas they do in others; and
where the condition correlated with the lack of plural agreement is
that the phrase does not refer to more than one distinct thing.
FRENCH is a case in point. Blinkenberg (1950 : 29) points out that
the conjoined FRENCH noun phrase mon ami et collègue 'my friend
and colleague' takes singular verb agreement. Examples of this
sort can easily be found in other languages (for FINNISH see Mey
1960: 104). Blinkenberg also points out that a sentence which starts

with <u>Ma famille et la tienne</u> 'my family and yours' can be continued
as ... <u>est très connue dans la région</u> 'is well known in the area;'
or as ... <u>sont très connues dans la région</u> 'are well-known in the
area' with corresponding difference in meaning. That the two
superficially conjoined phrases here are not referentially noniden-
tical is evidenced by the way they are understood, and also by the
fact that they would not undergo numeration (i. e. they would not
take <u>deux hommes</u> and <u>deux familles</u> as appositions). If, for plural
agreement, referential nonidentity of the nominals within the noun
phrase is required, then it follows that not only will noun phrases
that include only referentially identical nouns not show plural agree
ment, but neither will noun phrases which lack referential marking
entirely. With this in mind, let us consider some facts of SYRIAN
ARABIC (Cowell 1964: 424):

> l-kət^əb mā bihəmmū   'The books don't interest him. '
> l-kət^əb mā b^əthəmmo   'Books don't interest him. '

The subject noun phrase, in both cases, has the definite article and
is plural. The difference is that the predicate of the first sentence
is plural, i. e. it agrees, while in the second it is (feminine) singular. The first sentence refers to specific and identified books,
the second to books in general. Compare this with the ENGLISH
sentence: <u>An Englishman never does that; he/they has/have different habits</u> which is synonymous with <u>Englishmen never do that;
they have different habits.</u> This shows that noun phrases which
refer to kinds of things rather than to specific objects are deviant
or unstable in their number and in their number agreement requirements.

Certain noun phrases, however, cannot be said to be devoid of
reference and in fact appear to refer to more than one object; and
they may still take singular verbs and pronouns. Such phrases are:
titles of books -- <u>Les Illusions Perdue a été publié</u> or <u>ont été pub-
liées en 1835 et 1843</u>; names of places -- <u>Les Cabannes est</u> or <u>sont
un village placé le long de la route</u>; references to words -- <u>'les os'
ne se prononce pas comme cela</u>; and references to quantities --
<u>Mille francs est une grosse somme</u>, <u>Deux livres lui suffira</u> (Blinken-
berg 1950: 37, 74, 52, 69); or ENGLISH <u>Ten thousand dollars isn't
much. Here is ten and ten more. Where is your two bushels? This
is only five apples. Five more two cents's and I'll have enough.</u>
(F. W. Householder's examples).

Of the five types of noun phrases that may at least in some languages not be overtly marked for plurality and may nonetheless

require plural agreement with some constituents, so far we have
discussed conjoined and numerated nouns. Let us now turn to nouns
with comitative complements and to collective nouns. Comitative
constructions requiring plural verb agreement occur in FRENCH,
such as Le pape avec le cardinal sont retournés (Blinkenberg 1950:
86). Such sentences are synonymous, at least with respect to one
of their meanings, with the corresponding coordinations (Le pape
et le cardinal ...). Words such as LATIN populus, ENGLISH
crowd or police, FRENCH la plupart, la reste are inflectionally
singular and may take singular or plural agreement in the verb
and in the anaphoric pronoun (but usually singular in the adjective
and in other noun phrase internal terms). This is true for FIN-
NISH, for ARABIC (Cowell 1964: 426) and also for AKKADIAN,
except that there the singular-plural option is available for the
attributive adjective as well (von Soden 1952:186). In COPTIC,
given a sentence where various orders of a subject noun, modifying adjective, and one or more verbs are possible, the following
rule appears to operate: whatever comes before the collective--
i.e. all or one of the verbs or the adjective -- is singular; of those
following the collective subject, the verb(s) must -- and the adjective may -- be plural (compare Mallon 1956:179). In certain languages, singular agreement can be used with conjoined noun phrases
if they are understood as constituting a unit. This is the case in
FINNISH; compare isa ja äiti on kylässä "father and mother is
village-in" 'The father and mother are in the village' (Mey 1960:
104); see also OLD BABYLONIAN (von Soden 1952:186). In ENG-
LISH, nominals such as a pair of, a couple of, are inflectionally
singular; nonetheless, if they are subjects of a present-tense verb,
the verb is in the plural.

The fifth type of case where a singularly marked noun takes plural
agreement is provided by languages where nouns are never marked
for generic plurality; pronominal reference nonetheless to plurally
understood nouns is plural; such as CHINESE.

All the above examples illustrated the fact that it is possible for
nominals that are not overtly marked for generic plurality to take
plural agreement. The irrelevance of overt number marking on
the noun for number agreement can also be shown by instances of
the opposite type: by instances, that is, where a noun that is marked
for generic plurality requires singular agreement. In ANCIENT
GREEK, for instance, plural neutral nouns take singular verb-
agreement. Similarly, in MODERN ARABIC, plural inanimate
subjects and even conjoined plural inanimate nouns if functioning
as subjects may take either singular or plural verb agreement,

although conjoined singular inanimate nouns take singular verb-
agreement (Charles Ferguson, personal communication).

Thus far, agreement with respect to only two number categories
has been considered. Descriptions of various languages, however,
make reference to additional distinctions such as those between
dual, trial, plural of paucity and plural of abundance. All of these
distinctions appear to be subdistinctions within the category "plural,"
rather than distinctions comparable with the one between "singular"
and "plural." One argument in favor of this contention is provided
by the fact that thus we can maintain a universal concept of what
plurality means; if we chose some other alternative, plurality
would have to be defined as "more than one" or "more than two,"
depending on the alternative categories of a particular language.
That the dual, for instance, is semantically part of the plural system can be shown in several other ways. Crosslinguistically,
synonymy exists between dual and plural (but not between dual and
singular) forms. Also, given a language with a dual marker in the
noun, a plural but not a singular noun phrase may be used to replace it. If a particular agreeing term lacks the category of dual,
it will be plural with respect to the verb, as in ANCIENT GREEK
or MODERN ARABIC (Cowell 1964:420) and in AKKADIAN, where
the category of dual was abandoned in the adjective earlier than in
the noun and thus plural adjectives cooccur with dual nouns (von
Soden 1952:187). HOPI is an exception where the dual nominal
subject takes singular, not plural, agreement in the predicate; for
pronouns, which have no overt dual marker, duality is expressed
by a plural pronoun plus singular predicate, and plurality requires
plural pronoun plus plural predicate (Whorf 1946: 175). Moreover,
if the meaning of the dual is extended in any direction it is toward
"more than two" rather than "one." For instance, dual nominal
forms are used in AKKADIAN not only for paired parts of the body
but also for other parts, such as "teeth" or "fingers." That the
dual in AKKADIAN may mean "more than two" is also shown by
the numerals for 20, 30, 40, 50, etc. which are dual forms of 10,
3, 4, 5, etc., respectively (von Soden 1952:74ff., 91). In OLD
ASSYRIAN the dual verb form may be used after two or more conjoined subjects (von Soden 1952:186). The same extended meaning
of the dual is evidenced in GERMAN and in HUNGARIAN where
equivalents of "a pair" usually refer to two or more than two objects.

Another argument for the dual as part of plural comes from the
morphological structure of dual forms: they often consist of the
plural marker plus something else, e.g. in OLD ENGLISH (for

more evidence and discussion of markedness distinctions in number.
see Greenberg 1963: Universals #34 and #35; 1966).

A third argument for the dual and trial as subcategories rather
than alternatives to the plural is provided by a distributional fact:
whereas the presence of plural in the nouns of a particular language always implies its presence in some pronoun, this implication does not apply to the dual and the trial. As mentioned above,
dual is a nominal but not a pronominal category in HOPI and in
spoken ARABIC; it is a category of the verb but not of the pronoun in YUROK.

The potential extension of the meaning of the dual into "more
than two" can be generalized as extending the meaning of the highest unit class in a particular language into "a few." For instance,
in FIJIAN it is the trial that is reported to stand for three or more
(Churchward 1941:25ff.). While for FIJIAN there is still some
justification for calling this form a trial, because of its morphological structure, some languages have a category of "few" and
one of "many," both formally unrelated to any unit category. Two
such non-unit plurals which are morphologically and semantically
distinct are reported for AKKADIAN, ARABIC, BAINUK, and
SENUFO. In AKKADIAN (von Soden 1952: 76-7) šarrānu is glossed as '(eine Anzahl einzelner) Könige' and šarrū is 'die Könige
(schlechthin),' ilanu is 'die (persönlichen grossen) Götter' and
ilū is 'Götter = Pantheon.' The meaning of the "paucal" plural
ending -ānu is explained as follows: "es bezeichnet eine Mehrheit,
die sich aus einer zählbaren Anzahl in sich selbständiger Einzel-
teile zusammengesetzt." In ARABIC (Cowell 1964: 369) the paucal
is said to imply paucity and individuality of objects referred to; it
may or may not be used with numerals. (When a plural of paucity
is used without a numeral between 2 and 10, it usually implies
that the things referred to are few in number and individually dis-
criminated.) This plural is formed from the unit singular form of
nouns, e.g. samake 'a fish' forms samakat 'fish (plural).' The
other plural implies abundance, must not be used with numerals,
and is formed from the collective singular form of the noun, e.g.
samak 'fish (collective)' forms ?asmak '(many or various)fish.'
In BAINUK (Sauvageot 1967: 225ff.), busumɔl means 'a snake,'
i-sumɔl means 'snakes (a counted quantity),' and ba-sumɔl means
'snakes (not counted because counting is impossible or considered
superfluous).' If the noun phrase contains a numeral, the "counted"
plural must be used. In SENUFO (Sauvageot 1967: 236), siɣ means
'tree,' siɣe means 'trees (countable),' and sir means 'trees (un-
countable).' Whorf (1946:170) reports that HOPI nouns also have

two plurals, a paucal and a multiple, but from his data I am unable
to see what is involved there.

Let us now decide how to account for the facts that have prompted
grammarians to set up these two plural categories for the languages
mentioned. First of all, which is the "real" plural? Plurals (and,
normally, duals and trials) in various languages may occur with or
without numerals. This suggests that the plural without, rather
than with, a numeral should be considered peculiar to AKKADIAN,
ARABIC, BAINUK, and SENUFO. The non-numeratable plural in
all these languages shows, in contrast with the other plural, additional common characteristics. First, its meaning is said to imply
a large number of objects. Second, it implies that this number is
unspecified or unspecifiable and that the group is undiscriminated.
But these are the two semantic properties which distinguish collectives from regular plurals, as pointed out above for ENGLISH.
Considering also that both "plural of abundance" and collective
forms (may) take "ordinary" plural agreement in pronouns and
verbs, the only distinction left between these two categories is
that the forms for "plural of abundance" are always, but for collective are not necessarily, derivable by productive inflection
from singular nouns. Leaving open the question about the significance of this difference, we tentatively conclude here that in a
grammar it is redundant to adopt the two categories as separate
ones and that their derivation should be the same for collective
and for "plural of abundance" forms. Thus it now seems that all
number distinctions come down to distinctions between numerated
and non-numerated plurals, duals, trials, and collectives — all
opposed to singular.

The preceding was simply a discussion of the number categories
relevant to number agreement and an illustration of the fact that
overt plurality marking on nouns is neither necessary nor sufficient to predict agreement in plurality. This latter observation is
the same as the one made about gender agreement before. In closing, I would like to point out three additional ways in which gender
agreement and number agreement are similar. First, both number
and gender agreement may be different depending on the agreeing
constituent in that one constituent may agree with a noun and another
not;[9] or one constituent may agree with a noun one way and another in

---

[9] It is interesting that the form of nouns as they appear in compounds is generally without both gender and number (and also without case) marking even though in other contexts nouns do have such
markings in the language. Compare GERMAN Rotköpfchen 'Little

another way. It holds both for gender and number that if any constituent
in a language show agreement in these property types, some anaphoric pronoun always does. The distinction between noun-phrase
internal and noun-phrase external agreement is significant in that
noun phrase external agreement can nearly always be predicted
in terms of "semantic gender" and "referential number," whereas
agreement with respect to various modifier-type elements shows
the same markers as the noun inflection itself, which may, but
need not, reflect underlying meaning elements. Second, number
agreement, too, may vary also with the linear order of agreeing
and agreed-with constituents; just as we have seen gender agreement to vary with it in some instances. Third, a general process
of "reification" (for some examples and discussion of this notion
see McCawley 1968:131-2) appears a reasonable way to account for
certain cases of "suspension of agreement" in both gender and
number. The apparent non-agreement with book titles, place
names, and the like was pointed out in the section on number, but
it also holds for gender. What it boils down to is that any noun
phrase can be thought of as a name for an object, such as "book,"
or for "(a) thing, in general;" then gender and number agreement
may take place with that more general name of the object or with
the semantic properties of "(a) thing." Thus, suspension of gender
agreement in the ANCIENT GREEK sentence Hōs charien est
anthrōpos hotan anthrōpos ē (Menander) 'What a nice thing is Man
when he is indeed a Man.' ("How nice(-neuter) is man(-masculine)
when man(-masculine) he-is.") and suspension of number agreement
in the ENGLISH sentence, Distinctive features is a good thing is
simply explained by the fact that all noun phrases are "singular"
and "neuter" in the sense that they refer to things taken together
as a unit; this property can be predicated, made into an apposition,
or simply "assumed," thus making it relevant for agreement.

Apart from these conditions that participate in determining both
alternatives of gender and alternatives of number agreement, the

---

(ftnt. 9 cont.)
Red Ridinghood' with rotes Köpchen, ENGLISH five-dollar bill with
five dollars, or GERMAN Haustor with das Tor des Hauses, etc.;
or see MO:RE (Canu 1967:178-9) where the first term of a compound
loses its number marking; or MAASAI where parts of compounds
lose their gender prefix (Tucker and Tompo 1955:46-7). F. Householder pointed out to me that while AMERICAN ENGLISH holds to
the rule that plurals must drop the suffix before entering a compound as first member e.g. brain trust, billiard table (but dry-
goods store), in BRITISH ENGLISH there is a recent development
such that the plural suffix is retained, e.g. brains trust, darts match

relatedness of gender and number agreement is also manifested
in phonological shape in that gender and number markings are generally either adjacent to each other or they may even constitute
an unsegmentable "portmanteau" morph; such as, for instance,
in LATIN.

2.1.3 _Person_   Person is a non-nominal category in most languages: pronouns but not nouns have person distinctions. I have
only a few examples of instances where there is verb agreement
in person with nouns that do not overtly show person distinctions
but whose referents are understood as first, or second, or third
person depending on the agreement. Examples come from SPAN-
ISH and WALBIRI.

SPANISH:
nadie lo vimos   "nobody him saw-we"
                                         'None of us saw him.'

cualquiera podríamos hacerlo   "anyone could-we do-it"
                                         'Any of us could do it.'

toda la familia fuimos   "whole the family went-we"
                                         'My whole family, including me,
                                         went.'

la gente de aquí no comemos eso "the people of here not eat-we that"
                                         'People from here (we) don't eat
                                         that.'[10]

WALBIRI:
ŋarka ka-ŋa puḷa-mi   "man present-I shout-nonpast"
                                         'I man am shouting.'

ŋarka ka-npa puḷa-mi   "man present-you shout-nonpast"
                                         'You man are shouting.'

ŋarka-tjara ka-ḷitjara puḷa-mi "man-dual present-we shout-non-
                                         past" 'We men (dual exclusive)
                                         are shouting.' (Hale 1973:317)

As Greenberg noted, "All languages have pronominal categories
involving at least three persons and two numbers." (Greenberg
1963:113, Universal #42.) Although part of what is being claimed

---

10
    For these data I am grateful to Edward L. Blansitt, Jr.

in this statement is that in all languages there will be some contexts
where number distinctions in all three persons will be significant,
this does not mean that the personal pronominal paradigm consisting of free (i. e. unbound) forms will have number distinctions
manifested in all three persons. The generalization concerning
the number distinctions in free personal pronominal forms seems
to be this: it is universally present in the first person but not in
the second and third.[11] The fact that overt plurality marking in
the first person pronoun is a universal can be, if not explained,
at least placed in a wider factual context. The following correlation holds for all languages examined: overt marking of plurality
in nonhuman (or inanimate) noun phrases implies that plurality is
overtly marked in human (or animate) noun phrases of that language.
Only animate nouns have plural marking in TELUGU and TETON
(Forchheimer 1953:101 and 85) and in TEWA (Yegerlehner 1959).
In YUROK(Robins 1958:23) only a few nouns have plural markings
and these appear to refer mainly to humans. In WUNAMBUL all
human nouns -- and only those -- have plurals (Forchheimer 1953:
35), and in MAIDU (Forchheimer 1953:44) and CHITIMACHA
(Swadesh 1946b:319) only (but not all) human nouns. This distinction is borne out in agreement as well. In UP-COUNTRY SWAHILI
the animate but not the "general" demonstrative has number distinction
(Alexandre 1967). In ARABIC, as referred to earlier, if the subject is plural inanimate, the predicate adjective may be plural or
singular (feminine), whereas plural agreement is required for animate subjects (Ferguson and Rice 1951). In ANCIENT GREEK, as
also mentioned before, plural neuter subjects take singular third

---

[11]Forchheimer (1953:12) points out that CHINESE PIDGIN ENGLISH
may be an exception to this. He also contends that "the first person
distinguishes number more readily than the second and the second
more readily than the third" (p. 6). In some languages, overt expression of (non-numerated) plurality is obligatory only for the
three personal pronouns (CHINESE) or for the first and second person pronouns (BURMESE) or for the first person pronoun only (KO-
REAN). (See Forchheimer 1953:41-2, 42-3, and 65-6, respectively.)
Subdistinctions within number may be the same as for nouns, i. e.
dual, trial, etc. It may be pointed out that although there are languages with an exclusive-inclusive distinction in the first person
plural and a dual distinction only in the inclusive but not in the exclusive form (such as SOUTHERN PAIUTE, see Forchheimer 1953:
88), and also languages with a dual form in both the exclusive and
the inclusive forms, no language has been encountered which distinguishes a dual and a plural in the exclusive but not in the inclusive
form.

person agreement in the verb. In AMHARIC conjoined animate
singular subjects require a plural verb, while conjoined inanimate
singular subjects may take a masculine singular verb (observation
supplied by C. A. Ferguson). In HUNGARIAN plural and singular
verb forms are in more or less free variation after a subject
phrase which conjoins singular nouns; but plural verb forms are
more often used after conjoined singular human nouns. Most TUR-
KIC languages have obligatory pluralization only for human noun
phrases. In TEMNE if the subject phrase is a conjunction, the
plural predicate form must be used if the first member of the conjunction is plural; if it is not, the singular or the plural predicate
form may be used if the subjects are animate (or human?), but if
they are inanimate (or nonhunan), only a singular predicate form
may be used.

   Given the fact that first person pronouns are always human and
animate, the above-demonstrated correlation between human-
animate gender and number marking would predict overt plural
marking for all first and second person pronouns in languages
which have plural marking for non-human (nonanimate) nouns.
This claim, however, is different from the statement we are trying to explain: it is, in one sense, a more general claim in that
it concerns not only the first person pronoun but both first and
second person pronouns; on the other hand, it is more restricted
in not predicting universality of overt plural marking for the first
person pronoun. In other words, the connection between overt
number marking and animacy, mysterious as it is itself, at best
only partially explains the universality of overt number marking in
the first person.

   There is some indication that, of the three persons, the first
and the second constitute a natural class as opposed to the third;
of the two classes, the one including first and second is more
marked than the one including the third; and that of the first and
second person, the second is more marked than the first. The
former point is supported by data from ATHAPASCAN languages,
from NGWE, from KANURI as well as from many other languages.
In ATHAPASCAN languages (for CHIPEWYAN, see Li 1946:411)
and for APACHEAN, see Hoijer 1945:195f.) and in KANURI the
linear order relations of pronominal affixes differ depending on
whether the affix is first or second person or whether it is third
person. In NGWE (Dunstan 1966:88), pronouns whose meanings
include reference to third person have low-high tones; all others
have either high or a complex pattern which includes high but is
distinct from low-high. Further evidence is provided by the shape
of plural pronouns: in many languages the plural form of the third

person pronoun is morphological segmentable and thus similar to nominal plurals whereas the plural of first and second person pronouns is non-segmentable and/or irregular. Compare, for instance, HUNGARIAN: én 'I,' mi 'we,' te 'you (sing.)' ti 'you (plur.),' ő 'he/she,' ők 'they,' felhő 'cloud,' felhők 'clouds.'[12]

---

[12] Aspects of inflectional irregularity form the foundations of Forchheimer's typology; he presents, discusses, and classifies many pronominal paradigms. In general, if the second person pronoun forms its plural by inflection rather than by suppletion, the third person pronoun does too; and if the first person plural is inflectional, so are the second and third person plurals. Similarly, if the (inflectional) plural of a second person pronoun is like a nominal plural, so is the plural of the third person pronoun; and if the plural of the first person pronoun is pluralized as a noun, so are the second and third person plurals. In other words, it apparently does not happen that the first (and/or the second) person pronoun has nominal-type plural, or inflectional plural in general, without the third person pronoun having the same kind. To refer to some languages not discussed in Forchheimer, TEWA (Yegerlehner 1959) and ORIYA (Tripathi 1957) provide examples of pronominal paradigms where all persons have the same inflectional pluralizer; CHITIMACHA (Swadesh 1946b: 327) is an example of the other extreme, where all plural pronominal forms differ from each other and also from nominal plurals. HUNGARIAN and RUSSIAN belong to the well-represented type where the first and second person pronouns have suppletive plurals and the third person pronoun has nominal-inflectional plural. The regularity of third person personal pronoun plurals and the irregularity of first and second person personal pronominal plurals can of course be seen as parallelled by the difference between the concept of plurality as it applies to third person versus how it applies to first and second person plurals This difference in respect to the meaning of plurality is simply that whereas "third person plural" refers to a set of individuals that are homogeneous in person -- all of them are third person -- first and second person plurals refer to sets of individuals that are heterogeneous in person. First person plural, for instance, does not refer to a set of 'I'-s, since there is only one speaker for each discourse paragraph; but it refers to a set that includes 'I' and in addition either second person(s) or third persons or both. Similarly, the second person plural, although it may perhaps involve reference to a set of hearers may also be person-wise heterogeneous if it involves reference to the hearer and at least one third person. The semantic analyzability of plural first and second person pronouns into person-wise heterogeneous sets is paralleled by some syntactic

The generalization that first and second person is more marked
than third person may be supported by the observation that is true
for all languages that I know of: that verbs agreeing with subjects
which either semantically or overtly include reference to both a
third person and a non-third person referent, will agree in the
non-third-person; 'I and he,' for instance, would take plural first,
rather than plural third, agreement; and 'you and he' will take
second person plural, rather than third person plural, agreement.
It is interesting to note that if the subject is a first and second
person, then the agreement will be first, rather than second, person plural -- a fact that could be taken to be evidence for the markedness of first person over second. There is, however, much evidence
that would indicate the inverse markedness relation between first
and second person: that second person exceeds first person in
markedness. Such evidence is the following. In ALGONQUIAN,
Bloomfield's data allow the following generalization: if the second
person is involved as either subject or object (or "actor" and
"goal," in Bloomfield's terms), the verbal prefix will be a second
person prefix. If neither is second person but one is first person,
the prefix is first person. Or, as far as QUECHUA is concerned,
Wonderly's data do not contradict the following rule: for transitive
verb forms where the verb indicates reference to the person of
both subject and object, the order of these personal suffixes is such
that if the second person is involved as either subject or object, its
reference will be word final; if it is not involved, the third person

---

(ftnt. 12 cont.)
and morphological facts; such as that in GERMAN and many other
languages as mentioned above, plural first and second person pronouns are agreed-with by the verb in the same person as the corresponding conjunctions of singular pronouns (both 'we' and 'I and
you,' when subjects, take first person plural agreement on the verb;
and both 'you (plur.)' and 'you (sing.) and he' take second person
plural agreement); and that in some languages even the phonological form of plural personal pronouns is segmentable into the forms
of the corresponding singular personal pronouns; such as in EWE,
KELE, and NKOSI (Forchheimer 1953:132f.); and in BAMILEKE
(Voorhoeve 1967:427):

bãg-jé	"we-he"	'we (I and he)'
bãg-u	"we-you (sing.)"	'we (I and you (sing.))'
bĭh-jé	"you (plur.)-he"	'you (plur.)(you (sing.)and he)'
bŏ-jé	"they-he"	'they (two)'

Notice that the order of elements in such pronouns is always first
person followed by second/third and second person followed by third,
and that the plural set always precedes.

reference will be word final. It might also be of interest that in
the CUZCO dialect of QUECHUA, the future forms are regular
except in the second person plural (Yokoyama 1951:56ff.). In
addition, the ordering of personal pronoun clitics or affixes is
across a number of many unrelated and areally distinct languages
second person preceding first person preceding third person.
This is for instance the case in SPANISH and CHIPPEWA, compare Sanders 1974.

The three person distinctions in two numbers posited by Greenberg as universally present are not the only person-number distinctions made in languages. Additional distinctions include the
distinction between first person plural "exclusive" and first person
plural "inclusive;" and that between obviative and non-obviative
in the third person. The exclusive-inclusive distinction is one
made on the basis of the membership of the plural set that includes
the first person. In ENGLISH, a language which does not make
this distinction, the pronoun we may refer both to a set consisting
of 'I,' 'you,' and, possibly, others, and also to a set consisting of
'I' and others but not 'you.' Languages having this distinction simply have two different forms depending on whether 'you' is or is
not included in the set. In QUECHUA, for instance, ñuxa means
'I,' ñuxayku means 'we not including you' -- it is therefore the
"exclusive" form -- and ñuxančik means 'we including you' -- it
is therefore the "inclusive" form (Wonderly 1952:369-370). A list
of languages having this distinction is given in Forchheimer 1953,
with no claim for exhaustiveness. His list includes the following:
ALGONQUIAN, BALTIC, BERBER, CHINOOK, COOS, DYIRRINGAN,
PIDGIN ENGLISH, EWE, FULANI, GARO, HAWAIIAN, IROQUOIAN,
KAMILAROI, KANAURI, KIOWA, KWAKIUTL, LAKOTA, MALAY,
MAYA, MELANESIAN, MIKIR, ORDOS MONGOL, MUNDARI, NO-
GOGA, NKOSI, NUBIAN, OLD NUBIAN, OTOMI, SOUTHERN PAIUTE
PAPUA (BONGU, KATE, NYUL-NYUL, SAIBALGAL) PURIK, RO-
TUMAN, SHOSHONE, SIERRA POPOLUCA, SIUSLAWAN, SOMALI,
TAGALOG, TAMIL, TELUGU, TUNGUS, WINNEBAGO, WORORA,
YOKUTS. I can add the following: BAKI, BAMENDJOU, BAMILEKE,
BANGANGTE, BIERIAN, FIJIAN, FUTUNA, GILYAK, ILOCANO,
MALEKULA, MALOESE, MARANAO, NGWE, QUECHUA, TANGOAN,
TANNA. In many instances the first person inclusive pronoun re-
sembles in form the second person singular and the first person
exclusive resembles the first person singular; and if either one of
them is segmentable, it is the exclusive, rather than the inclusive
form. Lyons suggests (1968:277) that a similar exclusive-inclusive
distinction could be made in the second person plural, distinguishing
sets only consisting of 'you'-s and sets consisting of 'you' and others.
No language, however, has been found making such a distinction.

Besides exclusive and inclusive forms, another "exotic" person
category is a subdivision of the singular third person in terms of
"obviative" and "non-obviative." Languages with this distinction
belong to the ALGONQUIAN and to the ATHAPASCAN groups of
AMERICAN INDIAN languages. For ALGONQUIAN see Bloomfield 1946:94; for POTAWATOMI, in particular, see Hockett
1948:7-9. For NAVAHO see Hoijer 1945:195ff., for CHIPE-
WYAN see Li 1946:402, for CHIRICAHUA see Hoijer 1946a:76.

Almost all descriptions agree that this is a distinction made with
respect to animate nouns, and that it is to distinguish one (third
person) noun from another (third person) noun. However, Hockett
remarks (1948:8) that obviation is also possible with respect to
inanimate subjects and intransitive verbs and Bloomfield (1946:94)
hints at CREE and OJIBWA using the obviative even if the other
person referred to in the sentence is first or second person. Nowhere is it said to be a pronominal category; only nouns and verbs
have this distinction. Number distinctions do not exist in ALGON-
QUIAN. Although descriptions leave room for choice of the particular third person animate noun in the sentence that is to be in the
obviative, if the sentence contains more than one of them, generally
it seems that the obviative is a category of the direct or indirect
object, rather than of the subject, a category of the possessed item,
rather than of the possessor, and a category of the comment, rather
than of the topic. A "farther obviative" is described for POTAWA-
TOMI and for CREE; it is used if three nouns are involved. In
POTAWATOMI, the "farther obviative" is simply marked by the
reduplication of the obviative affix. Similar to obviative is the
category of "recurrent" in ESKIMO. Some of the conditions under
which the "recurrent" in ESKIMO is used are the following: given
a third person subject, the recurrent is used for a third person
possessor in the same or in a subordinated clause, for the subject
of a subordinated clause, or for the object of a subordinated clause,
if the subject of that clause and the object of the main clause are
also identical in reference. Swadesh points out that, given these
conditions, the recurrent is also used if the subject of the main
clause is not that particular singular third person but a plural such
that it includes that third person; e.g. in the sentence "When they
arrived, he himself (i.e. one of those referred to by "they") died."
(Swadesh 1946a:40ff.).

Both obviative and recurrent markings are simply ways of differentiating between referentially identical and referentially different things and thus they are akin to the distinction made in ENGLISH
and in many other languages by former and latter, by the definite
versus indefinite marker, and by reflexive or reciprocal versus

non-reflexive and non-reciprocal pronouns.[13] Whereas recurrent
marking, just like definiteness marking, applies to referents that
are the same as the one(s) previous mentioned, the system of
obviation marks those referents that are non-identical with one(s)
previously mentioned.[14]

So far we have surveyed the kinds of pronominal distinctions
that languages make depending on whether the set of referents includes one individual or more than one; whether it includes the
Speaker or the Hearer or not; and whether the non-speaker non-
hearer referents are the same as ones mentioned before or not
the same. Besides these number and referential identity distinctions that are associated with personal pronominal forms, in a
number of languages there are also gender distinctions associated
with them. Greenberg noted about sex gender: "If a language has
gender distinctions in the first person, it always has gender distinctions in the second or third person or in both." (Greenberg
1968:Universal #44). This statement allows for languages with
the following patterns:

    a. sex gender in second person only (e.g. BASQUE)
    b. sex gender in third person only (e.g. ENGLISH)
    c. sex gender in second and third person only (e.g. HEBREW)
    d. sex gender in first and second person only
    e. sex gender in first and third person only (e.g. GUMULGAL)
    f. sex gender in first, second, and third person (e.g. KAKADU)

and excludes g.: sex gender in first person only. For some

---

[13] The assumption of a similar distinction between 'same' and
'different' referents seems to be needed in order to understand
the complex pronominal paradigm of BAMENDJOU (Tayoumo 1969).
A peculiar feature of this system is that besides "regular plurals,"
there are special forms glossed as referring to a plural set plus
an additional 'he' or additional 'others.' These pronouns all contain i ('he,' by itself) and apo (compare op 'they').

[14] Regarding possessors, in CHIPEWYAN (Li 1946:402,415) the
otherness of a third person possessor (or object) is overtly expressed, given a third person subject in the sentence. In other
languages such as RUSSIAN, HUNGARIAN, LATIN or HOPI
(Whorf 1946:170) and ESKIMO (Swadesh 1946a:40ff.), it is the
sameness of the possessor with the subject that is marked.

discussion of gender and person, see Forchheimer 1953:33-7. In searching for an explanation of why gender distinctions in the third person are present if gender distinctions are made in any other person, it seems that one might reasonably expect overt gender distinctions to be more common in constituents which have many different gender possibilities. Now, if gender includes features such as humanness and animacy, then it is clear that some aspects of gender are redundant for first and second person pronouns, but not for third person. In particular, a proper account of verb selection, for instance, requires that first and second person pronouns be marked as human and animate. Third person pronouns, on the other hand, are viewed here as reduced noun phrases which may therefore refer to anything. In other words, the fact that some gender distinctions in the third person are never made in the first and second person is a simple corollary of the fact that speech can occur <u>between</u> humans only but <u>about</u> anything human or nonhuman.

This reasoning accounts for the absence of animacy and humanness distinctions but not for the infrequency of overt sex specifications in first and second person pronouns. Although no explanation can be offered, it should be pointed out that even if inflection does not generally signal sex in these pronouns, they are required to be specified in some way for sex gender for proper agreement in languages where the predicate agrees in gender (e.g. FRENCH <u>tu es venu</u> and <u>tu es venue</u>); and for proper selection in all languages (e.g. <u>you (fem.) are pregnant</u> but *<u>you (masc.) are pregnant</u>).

Having surveyed person distinctions in various languages and various distinctions within persons related to referential sameness-otherness, number, and gender, let us now turn to agreement in person. First of all, since person is generally a pronominal and not a nominal category, the agreed-with constituent in person agreement will always be a pronoun, rather than a noun (but see the SPANISH and WALBIRI examples above). Second, the agreeing constituents are always noun phrase external, rather than noun phrase internal. Part but not all of this observation simply follows from the fact that those noun phrase internal constituents that could agree with the head of the noun phrase -- quantifiers, modifiers, and determiners -- simply do not cooccur with a personal pronominal head in a noun phrase: personal pronouns cannot be modified or determined and they cannot be adjectivally quantified;[15] witness

---

[15]For quantifying personal pronouns, a possessive construction is used in ENGLISH, GERMAN, HUNGARIAN, and KEBU (Wolf 1907: 796).

the ungrammaticality in ENGLISH of *the pretty she, *the two
he-s/they, *the I. What is not accounted for is the fact that relative pronouns apparently do not agree in person, either, even though
they do cooccur with personal pronouns within the same noun phrases;
e. g. I who came from the country.... Non-modifiability (except by
a relative clause) and non-determinability makes personal pronouns
appear to be related to proper names and to definitely marked noun
phrases in general. Indeed, a lot of additional facts indicate that
personal pronouns are treated as definite noun phrases in various
languages (for ENGLISH, see Postal 1966). Personal pronouns
have an object marker in TURKISH (Lyons 1968:276) just as demonstratives, possessed nouns etc. do. In FIJIAN the verb has
a special suffix if the object is a proper name, the pronoun 'whom?'
or a personal pronoun (Churchward 1941: 17ff.). In NORTHERN
PEKINGESE the word order rules that apply to definite noun phrases
also apply to personal pronouns (Mullie 1932:58). [16]

With respect to noun-phrase-external -- in particular, predicate --
agreement with personal pronouns, I can make two remarks. First,
as was pointed out above, there appears to be a universally valid
principle whereby predicate agreement with conjoined subjects of
different persons is determined. The principle simply says that
if one of the conjuncts is first person, the predicate will also be
first person; and if one of the conjuncts is second person and none
are first person, then the predicate, too, will be in the second
person. Second, agreement properties of personal pronouns are
mostly but not always the same regardless of whether they are
used in their proper sense or in some extended sense such as used
as polite pronouns or as generic pronouns. Examples of the "polite"
use of personal pronouns where agreement is different from when
they are used in their deictic sense come from FINNISH, where the
plural second person can be used to refer to a singular second person, and the predicate then may be in the singular (Mey 1960:105ff.);
from FRENCH where vous when referring to singular takes singular
predicate adjective although the verb is plural (C. A. Ferguson's
observation), and from ANCIENT GREEK where if a woman in a
tragedy uses the plural first person when speaking about herself,
an agreeing adjective or participle may be in the singular (Smyth
1956:271). Polite or less intimate forms of referring to the Addressee can all be characterized by increased paradigmatic remoteness

---

[16] A curious case is presented by HUNGARIAN, however, where
the transitive verb shows the "indefinite inflectional paradigm" if
its object is a first person or second person pronoun, instead of
showing the paradigm that goes with definite objects.

from the first person. That is to say, these forms, if identifiable
at all, are either third person or some plural forms. The following chart provides some examples:

| | Persons used to refer to Addressee less intimately: | | | |
	Singular 3rd	Plural 2nd	Plural 3rd	Special Pronoun
LANGUAGES	HUNGARIAN (reflexive)	FIJIAN (Churchward 1941:25ff.)	GERMAN	AMHARIC (Obolensky, Zelelie, Andualem 1964:23-4)
	GILYAK (Austerlitz 1959)	FRENCH	ITALIAN	TIGRINYA (Forchheimer 1953:30)
		ITALIAN		ORIYA (similar to reflexive) (Tripathi 1957:81)
		GILYAK (Austerlitz 1959)		

In polite or reverential reference to the third person, the plural
third person is used in FIJIAN (Churchward 1941:25ff.); the obviative in CHIRICAHUA (Hoijer 1946a:76) and a special form in NA-
VAHO (Hoijer 1945:197). Polite style pervades the entire pronominal
system in CAMBODIAN: all three persons have alternatives according to this style (Gorgoniyev 1966:72). All types of predicate constituents do not agree alike with polite plural pronoun subjects; if
the referent of the polite, formally plural pronoun is singular and
any predicate type shows plural agreement with it in the language,
it will be the verb; and if any predicate type shows singular agreement with, it will be the predicate noun as Comrie pointed out
(Comrie 1975).

Similarly, agreement properties of personal pronouns are generally the same when they are used in an indefinite or "generic"
sense. In ENGLISH for instance, many personal pronouns ($\underline{I}$, $\underline{you}_s$,
$\underline{we}$, $\underline{you}_p$, $\underline{they}$) may be used, under certain conditions, with no
deictic connotation, just to represent 'one' or 'people.' This
extension of meaning stems of course from the representation of
all personal pronouns as including the meaning element 'any human
being.' Notice, however, that in YUROK, where the second person
plural is used for 'general subject,' the prefix of such verbs may

be in the third person singular,   while the suffix would signal
second plural (Robins 1958: 35-6, 50).

In sum: this was a survey of the person distinctions of various
languages and of agreement in person. We have seen that the tripartite distinction between Speaker, Hearer and Third person is
universal in languages. Additional categories arise by marking
same and different third persons (cp. "obviative," "recurrent")
and by marking various semantically plural sets depending on the
persons of the individuals they include (cp. first person plural
exclusive and inclusive, second person plural, third person plural).
About the expression of number, we noted that the singular-plural
distinction is universal in free personal pronouns in the first person; about gender distinctions we noted that if they appear in any
person, it will be the third person. Some crosslinguistically valid
observations were offered about the agreement of predicates with
conjoined personal pronouns and politely or generically used personal pronouns.

2.2 Agreeing constituents

So far we have been concerned with the question: what are the
properties in terms of which constituents agree with nominals?
Next, we will turn to the question of just which are those constituents that may agree with nominals. There are actually three
domains within which the set of agreeing constituents could be
defined: within the total set of all sentences of all languages;
within the sentences of any one language; and within one sentence
of a language. In other words, the question are the following:

  a. What is the total set of constituent types whose members
      may ever agree with a nominal, whether within the same
      language or not, and whether within the same sentence or
      not?
  b. What is the total set of constituents whose members may
      ever agree with a nominal in the sentences of any one
      language?
  c. What is the total set of constituents whose members may
      ever agree within the same sentence of a language?

In what follows, I would like to propose some generalizations in
respect to each of these three questions.

First of all, there is one generalization that holds for all constituents that agree with nominals whether in the same language or

not and whether in the same sentence or not: that all such constituents are understood as including reference to the nominal. The
particular content of this claim is that in no sentence of any language is there a constituent that agrees with a nominal such that
that constituent includes reference to a nominal other than the one
it agrees with or that does not include reference to any nominal
at all. The claim would therefore be refuted if, for instance,
there were a sentence in some language meaning 'The black cat
and the white dog were fighting.' where the adjective corresponding to 'black' agreed with the nominal corresponding to 'dog;'
since in this case non-correferential constituents would be involved in agreement; or if there were a sentence in some language where the conjunction agreed with the locative adverbial,
since in this case a constituent would agree that has no reference
at all. There are of course many logically possible principles
according to which the choice of agreeing constituents could in
principle be defined in languages and which are distinct from the
one proposed: such as that all sentence-initial and sentence-final
words would be in some agreement relation with each other; or all
constituents within a sentence, or within a phrase, would be; non-
theless, none of these conceivable patterns have been found to
exist and all evidence I know of is compatible with the validity of
the proposed principle. [17] The actual list of agreeing constituents
includes the following: definite article, indefinite article, demonstrative adjective, possessive adjective, quantifiers, numerals,
descriptive adjectives, appositive adjectives, relative pronoun
(all of these with their head noun); verb (with its subject and

---

[17]Evidence that is consistent with this claim includes data from
so-called "agreement by attraction." Such instances of agreement
are provided by ANCIENT GREEK, for instance, such as when,
given a head noun and a relative pronoun, and given the fact that
the intrasentential case-function of the head noun in the main clause
is different from the intrasentential case-function of the relative
pronoun in the subordinated clause, the head and the relative pronoun have nonetheless the same case inflection, by either the head
noun taking on the case inflection that corresponds to the case function of the relative pronoun but not to that of the head noun phrase,
or vice versa; or when the verb agrees in number with the predicate
complement rather than with the subject (e.g. "The world are many
nations."). Although these kinds of agreement differ from the usual
pattern, they do not violate the "coreferentiality principle" since
the head and the relative pronoun that agree in the first type of example in case are coreferential; and so is the verb and the predicate
nominal.

complements); anaphoric pronoun, reflexive pronoun, reciprocal pronoun (with their antecedents); possessed noun (with its posses- sor).

The second question raised above was which of the total set of possibly agreeing constituents occur as agreeing within the sen- tences of the same language. Although it does not appear to fol- low from any basic assumption about what kind of a system a human language is that there should be any general restrictions in this respect, it appears that there are some generalizations that can be made; in particular, of two different types. First, there are some regularities across languages with respect to the agreement of con- stituents in one particular feature class; and second, there are regularities in respect to the agreement of a constituent as opposed to the lack of its agreement. In the first class belongs, for in- stance, Greenberg's observation (Greenberg 1963: 112, Universal #31) that if the verb agrees with the subject or the object in gender, then the adjective also agrees with its head noun in gender; or the observation I proposed above that if any noun-phrase-internal con- stituent agrees with the head of the noun phrase in terms of a se- mantically interpretable gender or number property, then, (if there is noun phrase external agreement in the language at all), all noun phrase external constituents, too, would agree in terms of that semantically interpretable gender or number property. The other type of generalization distinguishing between constituents of a language that agree in any property and those that do not agree at all I can examplify from the realm of verb agreement. The fol- lowing is a set of such generalizations. Since some of the criteria that are used in them to define crucial constituent classes are se- mantic and others are form-related and also because the terms used will remain undefined, it is possible that the constituent clas- ses to which individual statements make reference overlap with each other and thus the agreement or non-agreement with some specific constituent of a given sentence will be multiply predicted.

1. There is no language which includes sentences where the verb agrees with a constituent distinct from the intransitive subject and which would not also include sentences where the verb agrees with the intransitive subject.

2. There is no language which includes sentences where the verb agrees with the dative complement but which includes no sentences where the verbs agrees with the direct object com- plement.

3. There is no language which includes sentences where the verb agrees with an adverbial constituent and which would not

also include sentences where the verb agrees with a non-adverbial constituent.

4. There is no language where, given a constituent class including both definite and indefinite members, the verb would agree with some or all of the indefinite members but with none of the definite members.

5. There is no language where, given a constituent class including both animate and inanimate members, the verb would agree with some or all of the inanimate members but with none of the animate ones.

6. There is no language where, given a constituent class including both topical and non-topical members, the verb would agree with some or all of the non-topical members but with none of the topical ones.

7. There is no language where, given a constituent class including both members that precede the verb and also members that follow the verb, the verb would agree with some or all of those members following it but with none of those preceding.

8. There is no language where, given the class of direct objects so that it includes both members that are case-marked and also members that are not case-marked, the verb agrees with some or all of those not case-marked but with none of those case-marked.

9. There is no language where, given a constituent class some members of which are immediate constituents of the sentence at the point in a grammatical derivation where verb-agreement rules apply and some others members are non-immediate constituents of the sentence at that point, the verb agrees with some or all non-immediate constituents but with no immediate constituents.

This precedential ranking of constituent subclasses that is being claimed above to determine some of the constituents that agree with the verb in some sentences of a language, does not, however, necessarily apply to defining those constituents that may agree with the verb in the same sentence. This brings us to the consideration of the third question asked above: which are the intra-sententially cooccurring agreeing constituents? Thus, for instance, whereas the first generalization about the precedential agreement properties of datives over direct objects holds true for all languages that I

know of, it does not hold, as pointed out in Givón 1975, for all
sentences of languages: whereas to my knowledge there are no
languages where if the verb agrees in some sentences with the
dative it would not agree in some sentences with the direct object,
there are sentences of languages with both dative and object agreement where the verb agrees with the dative but not with the object.
Languages with both dative and object agreement, in fact, may
belong to almost any of the logically conceivable types from the
point of view of the cooccurrence of dative and object agreement
within sentences in that there are some, such as SWAHILI, where
if the sentence does include a dative, the verb must agree with it
rather than with the direct object; there are also others, such as
LEBANESE, where the verb in such sentences may agree, depending on some conditions, with either the object or with the dative
but not with both at the same time; and also again others such as
MODERN GREEK where the verb in such sentences may agree with
both. The only type not represented is that of a language where dative agreement is restricted to those sentences that do not include
a direct object and thus, in sentences that include both a direct
object and a dative, the verb would invariably agree with the direct
object and not with the dative.

3. Conclusions

Facing the various kinds of crosslinguistically valid generalizations that have been proposed above, one wonders if there is some
single general hypothesis about the nature of agreement from which
all of our observations could be derived. In closing, therefore, I
would like to informally consider one such frequently proposed
general hypothesis, according to which in a phonetically directed
grammatical derivation the derivational source of agreement markers is the same as the derivational source of anaphoric pronouns.[18]
This hypothesis, in its most restrictive form, would say that all
agreement markers are derived by the same rules as some anaphoric
pronouns in the language. If this were true, then one of the facts
that would follow from it is that all agreement markers would have
to have the same phonological form as some anaphoric pronouns in

---

[18]The hypothesis has been proposed by Cowell, Koutsoudas, and
Anshen and Schreiber in relation to ARABIC (Cowell 1964:401,
Koutsoudas 1967:48, Anshen and Schreiber 1968), Hutchinson in
relation to TEMNE (Hutchinson 1969:15, 118 and passim), by Hale
for WALBIRI (Hale 1973) and by Sanders and Givón as a universal
hypothesis (Sanders 1967, Givon 1969).

the language. Verb agreement in ENGLISH, for instance, would
be compatible with this hypothesis only if the present tense singular
third person forms of a verb such as play were play-he, play-she
play-it. I have not seen any language for which this test implication of this most restrictive version of the theory would be true in
respect to all of its agreement markers. Although historically
some agreement markers do arise from anaphoric pronouns as
pointed out, for instance, for verb-agreement markers in Givón
1975, and they often bear synchronically, too, some phonological
resemblance to anaphoric pronouns even beyond their shortness
and stresslessness, total formal identity of all agreement markers
with some anaphoric pronouns is a characteristic of no language in
my sample. The hypothesis thus in this most restrictive form has
to be considered false.

A somewhat more relaxed but still empirically very significant
hypothesis would be that even though the lexically assigned phonological shape of agreement markers is not the same as the lexically
assigned phonological shape of any anaphoric pronoun in the language, the non-phonological lexical representation of agreement
markers would be the same as the non-phonological lexical representations of some anaphoric pronouns. [19] Agreement markers and
some anaphoric pronouns of the language, that is, would be identical
except for their phonological shape. Since what characterizes non-
phonological lexical representations of anaphoric pronouns is at
least two kinds of properties: a property indicating referential
sameness with the antecedent noun phrase and a property set including some generic features of that noun phrase such as number
or gender, in order for this hypothesis to be true it would have to
be the case that all agreement markers can also be shown to have
these two types of properties: a referential sameness marker with
the noun phrase that they express agreement with and a set of generic properties identical with those of that noun phrase. Furthermore, it would also have to be true that all agreement markers
include exactly the same gender and number features of the agreed-
with noun phrase that an anaphoric pronoun of the language would.
But, as the data surveyed in the course of this paper have amply
illustrated, this version of the pronominal hypothesis, too, is false.
It is false, first of all, because, as we have seen, different constituents and differently ordered constituents in a language may agree

-----

[19]Except, possibly, for one property included either in the non-
phonological lexical representations of agreement markers or in
that of the pronouns, in order to condition differential phonological
shape assignment.

in different features with a noun phrase and thus they could not all
have the same gender-number properties as some one anaphoric
pronoun in the language. Second, it is false even if we allow that
each agreement marker should have the same gender and number
properties as <u>some</u> anaphoric pronoun in the language; since there
are some examples of languages where the categories distinguished
in agreement markers are apparently never distinguished for any
anaphoric pronoun in the language. In AKKADIAN, for instance,
the dual is a nominal but not a pronominal category; SIERRA PO-
POLUCA has no exclusive-inclusive distinction in the first person
independent pronoun although it has this distinction in the verbal
affix (Forchheimer 1953: 92-93); and, as was pointed out, the
obviative-non-obviative distinction is in no language a pronominal
category. A further reason why the hypothesis according to which
all agreement markers are derived, except for their lexicalization,
by the same rule(s) as some anaphoric pronouns in the language is
that the syntactic constituency and ordering restrictions that hold
between antecedents and their anaphors will I believe be different
from similar restrictions that hold between agreed-with and agreeing constituents.

But if agreement markers are not identical with any anaphoric
pronoun in a given language either in their phonological shape, or
in their gender, number, and person properties, or in their syntactic and linear relations that they bear to their presumed antecedents, then agreement markers cannot be said to be derivable by
the same syntactic and lexical rules as anaphoric pronouns. The
only possible version of the pronominal theory of agreement whose
universal validity still remains to be assessed is its very weakest
version: the claim that agreement markers and anaphoric pronouns
are derived by the same <u>type</u> of rules. What this would mean is
that if anaphoric pronouns are derived by a rule of reduction, or
partial deletion, whereby some but not all semantic and syntactic
properties of a noun phrase are deleted by identity with the same
features in the antecedent noun phrase, agreement markers, too,
would be derived by such a rule, where the identity condition would
be satisfied by the presence of the agreed-with noun phrase.

There is no evidence that I know of that would contradict this
hypothesis at least in its informally stated form. The test implications of this theory are these two:

1. Agreement markers must include some semantic and/or
syntactic properties of the agreed-with constituent.

2. Agreement markers must involve reference to the agreed-
with noun phrase.

The first text implication is true for all cases surveyed above--
it must be true, in fact, since it was included in our initial working
definition of agreement and thus all cases surveyed in the paper
under the term "agreement" had to conform to this condition. The
second test implication is similarly true even though it does not
follow from the working definition of agreement. As was pointed
out in the section on agreeing constituents, all constituents that
agree with a noun phrase "say something about it," so to speak;
i. e. they include reference to it. In a number of languages, in
fact, agreement markers themselves may have a pronominal function in that they themselves can substitute for a full mention of a
noun phrase; such as in HUNGARIAN, AKKADIAN, AMHARIC,
COPTIC, MAASAI, or BAKI.

Even though the pronominal theory of agreement is thus seen to
be consistent with all the data that we have in this weakest form
and it turns out to be explanatory in that two distinct observations
— that agreeing constituents involve reference to the agreed-with
noun phrase and that the semantic and syntactic properties of agreement markers are some of those of the agreed-with noun phrase --
it is nonetheless still not a really satisfactory theory of agreement.
This is not because there are some additional facts that would not
be consistent with it but because there are more facts consistent
with it than what we have encountered; in other words, it is not
restrictive enough. If we simply hypothesize that agreement markers are derived by the same type of syntactic rule as anaphoric
pronoun, this just means that agreement markers will have to include reference to the agreed-with noun phrase and that they should
include some of its features; but this hypothesis imposes no restrictions on how different the features can be that anaphoric pronouns,
on the one hand, and agreement markers, on the other, include.
It would in fact be possible that the agreement markers of a language and its anaphoric pronouns have no properties in common;
thus, for instance, that in a language with gender agreement no
anaphoric pronoun would have gender distinctions. There are,
however, some restrictions on how different anaphoric pronominal
features and agreement features can be in a language in that if
agreement markers make a particular <u>type</u> of distinction -- where
"type" means gender, number, person -- then that type of distinction will also be present in the pronominal system.[20]   If, for

---

[20] This statement is true even for languages such as AKKADIAN,

instance, a language has agreement in any kind of gender, there will be some kind of gender distinction in the pronominal paradigm.[21] This suggests that there is some relationship between agreement and anaphoric pronominalization that goes beyond the simple fact that both involve the process of identity deletion.

BIBLIOGRAPHY

Alexandre, P. 1967. Note sur la réduction du système des classes dans les langue véhiculaires à fonds bantu. La classification nominale dans les langues Négro-Africaines, 237-54.

Anshen, F. and P.A. Schreiber. 1968. A focus transformation of Modern Standard Arabic. Language 44. 792-97.

Austerlitz, R. 1959. Semantic components of pronoun systems: Gilyak. Word 15. 102-9.

Barnwell, K. 1969. The noun class system in Mbembe. Journal of West African Languages 6. 1. 51-8.

(ftnt. 20 cont.)
SIERRA POPOLUCA, and languages with obviative such as POTA-WATOMI. In these languages, as pointed out above, there is a specific distinction that is made in agreement markers but not in anaphoric pronouns. It is true for each of them, however, that the corresponding type of distinction is made in pronouns: in AKKA-DIAN, for instance, even though the dual is an agreement category which anaphoric pronouns do not have, anaphoric pronouns do have some number distinctions. Similarly, in SIERRA POPOLUCA, anaphoric pronouns have some person distinctions, even if they do not make the exclusive-inclusive distinction; and in obviative languages there are some definiteness distinctions in the pronoun.

[21] That this should be so would naturally follow with respect to person and number from Greenberg's observation according to which "All languages have pronominal categories involving at least three persons and two numbers" (Greenberg 1963: Universal #42). What is most interesting, however, is that it also holds for gender (compare Greenberg: "If a language has gender categories in the noun, it has gender categories in the pronoun." (Greenberg 1963: Universal #43)).

Blinkenberg, A. 1950. La problème de l'accord en français moderne. København.

Bloomfield, L. 1946. Algonquian. In Osgood 1946: 85-129.

Canu, G. 1967. Les classes nominales en Mo:re. La classification nominale dans les langues Négro-Africaines. Paris.

Chomsky, N. 1965. Aspects of the theory of syntax. Cambridge.

Churchward, C.M. 1964 (rev. ed., 1941). A New Fijian grammar. Fiji.

Comrie, B. 1975. Polite plurals and predicate agreement. Language 51.2. 406-419.

Cowell, M.W. 1964. A reference grammar of Syrian Arabic. Washington.

Doneux, J.L. 1967. Le Manjaku, classes nominales et questions sur l'alternance consonantique. La classification nominale dans les langues Négro-Africaines. Paris.

Dunstan, M.E. 1966. Tone and concord systems in Ngwe nominals. Ibadan.

Ferguson, C.A. and F.A. Rice. 1951. Concord classes of Arabic nouns. Handout of a paper delivered in LSA meeting, December.

Forchheimer, P. 1953. The category of person in language. Berlin.

Fraser, R.M. 1891. A grammar of the Baki language. South Sea Languages II, 73-97. Melbourne.

Givón, T. 1969. Studies in ChiBemba and Bantu grammar. Doctoral dissertation, University of California, Los Angeles.

_____. 1970. The resolution of gender conflicts in Bantu conjunction: when syntax and semantic clash. Papers from the Sixth Regional Meeting of the Chicago Linguistic Society, 250-61.

_____. 1975. Topic, pronoun, and grammatical agreement. Manuscript.

Gorgoniyev, Y.A. 1966. The Khmer language. Moskow.

Greenberg, J.H. 1963. Some universals of grammar with particular reference to the order of meaningful elements. Universals of language, ed. by J.H. Greenberg, 73-113. Cambridge.

_____. 1966. Language universals. Current trends in linguistics, III, ed. by T. Sebeok, 6-112. The Hague.

Gumperz, J. 1964. Linguistic and social interaction in two communities. American Anthropologist 66. 2. 137-54.

Hale, K. 1973. Person marking in Walbiri. A festschrift for Morris Halle, ed. by S.R. Anderson and P. Kiparsky, 308-44. Chicago: Holt, Rinehart, and Winston.

Hockett, C.F. 1948. Potawatomi I: phonemics, morphophonemics, and morphological survey. IJAL 14. 1. 1-10. Potawatomi II: derivation, personal prefixes and nouns. IJAL 14.2. 63-73.

Hoijer, H. 1945. The Apachean verb, part I: verb structure and pronominal prefixes. IJAL 11.3. 193-203.

_____. 1946a. Chiricahua Apache. In Osgood 1946: 55-84.

_____. 1946b. Tonkawa. In Osgood 1946: 289-311.

_____. 1949. The Apachean verb, part V: the theme and prefix complex. IJAL 15. 1. 12-22.

Horton, A.E. 1949. A grammar of Luvale. Johannesburg.

Hutchinson, L. 1969. Pronouns and agreement in Temne. Doctoral dissertation, Indiana University.

Jespersen, O. 1924. The philosophy of grammar. New York.

Koutsoudas, A. 1967. Double nominals in Lebanese Arabic. Glossa 1. 1. 33-48.

Li, F-K. 1946. Chipewyan. In Osgood 1946: 398-423.

Li, Ch. and S.A. Thompson. 1975. Subject and topic: a new typology of language. Manuscript.

La classification nominale dans les langues Négro-Africaines. Paris. 1967.

Lyons, J. 1968. Introduction to theoretical linguistics. Cambridge.

Mallon, A. 1956. Grammaire copte. Beirut.

McCawley, J.D. 1968. The role of semantics in a grammar. Universals in linguistic theory, ed. by E. Bach and R. Harms, 125-69. New York.

Mey, J.L. 1960. Le catégorie du nombre en finnois moderne. Copenhague.

Mould, M. 1971. The agreement of nominal predicates in Luganda. Studies in African Linguistics 2.1. 25-36.

Mullie, J. 1937. The structural principles of the Chinese language I - III. Pei-p'ing.

Obolensky, S., D. Zelelie, and M. Andualem. 1964. Amharic. Basic course. Washington.

Osgood, C. (ed.) 1946. Linguistic structures of native America. Viking Fund Publications in Anthropology 6. New York.

Postal, P. 1966. On the so-called "pronouns" in English. The Seventeenth Annual Round Table, Georgetown University Monographs on Languages and Linguistics 19. 177-206.

Robins, R.H. 1958. The Yurok language. University of California Publications in Linguistics Vol. 15. Berkeley, Los Angeles.

Robinson, G.H. 1930. Hausa grammar. London.

Sanders, G.A. 1967. Some general grammatical process in English. Doctoral dissertation, Indiana University.

_____. 1974. Precedence relations in language. Foundations of Language.

_____ and J. Tai. 1972. Immediate dominance and identity deletion. Foundations of Language 8. 161-198.

Sauvageot, S. 1967. Note sur la classification nominale en bainouk. La classification nominals dans les langues Négro-Africaines. Paris.

Smyth, H.W. 1956. Greek grammar. Cambridge.

Swadesh, M. 1946a. South Greenlandic (Eskimo). In Osgood 1946: 30-54.

_____. 1946b. Chitimacha. In Osgood 1946: 312-36.

Tayoumo, J. 1969. Notes sur le possessif en bamendjou. Camelang i. 58-72.

Till, W.C. 1961. Koptische Grammatik. Leipzig.

Tripathi, K.B. 1957. Western Oriya dialect. Indian Linguistics, Bagchi memorial volume, ed. by Sukumar Sen, 76-85.

Tucker, A.N. and J. Tompo Ole Mpaayei. 1955. A Maasai grammar with vocabulary. London.

von Soden, W. 1952. Grundriss der akkadischen Grammatik. Rome.

Voorhoeve, F. 1967. Personal pronouns in Bamileke. Lingua 17. 4. 421-30.

Whorf, B.L. 1946. The Hopi language, Toreva dialect. In Osgood 1946: 158-83.

Wolf, P.F. 1907. Grammatik des Kogboriko (Togo). Anthropos 2. 422-37.

Wonderly, W.L. 1952. Semantic components in Quechua person morphemes. Language 28. 3. 1. 366-76.

Yegerlehner, J. 1959. Arizona Tewa II: person markers. IJAL 25.2. 75-80.

Yokoyama, M. 1951. Outline of Quechua structure I: morphology. Language 27. 1. 38-67.

Some Universals
of Relative Clause Structure

BRUCE T. DOWNING

ABSTRACT

All languages use clauses to modify nouns, but the syntactic
form and positioning of these restrictive relative clauses (RC's)
fall into a wide range of types. Postnominal RC's are most common in SVO and verb-initial languages. In SVO languages relativization commonly involves one or more of three processes:
deletion of the relative NP (Rel NP), insertion of a clause-initial
relative pronoun, or insertion of an initial particle. In verb-initial
languages deletion of Rel NP and distinctive verb marking are most
common. Verb-final languages usually make use of prenominal
relative clauses, with Rel NP deletion, and sometimes verb-marking, but never any relative pronouns or movement of Rel NP. Some
permit deletion of the head NP rather than Rel NP. A number of
verb-final languages use correlative relative constructions in which
the RC precedes the entire clause containing the modified noun.
In other verb-final languages, preceding or following clauses modify a main-clause NP but may or may not be linked to it by specific
relativization processes. A number of implicational universals
may be stated on the basis of these observations. These are not
explanatory in themselves, but may be considered hypotheses to
be tested against additional data of relative clause structure, and
ultimately, if they stand, to be explained by universal linguistic
principles.

The present study was supported in part by a Summer Stipend
from the National Endowment for the Humanities. This paper incorporates material from three earlier papers: Downing 1973, 1974,
forthcoming. Among those to whom I am grateful for supplying data
and criticism at various times are Avery Andrews, Indira Junghare,
Carol Justus, Miriam Klaiman, Harvey Rosenbaum, and Guillermo
Villegas. None of them are responsible for the form their contributions have taken in the present paper. Specific acknowledgements
for sources of language data and description are listed at the end
of the paper.

CONTENTS

1. Preliminaries

1.1 Syntactic non-universals

Linguists tend to use the term 'relative clause' as if it referred to a universal grammatical entity. They ask, for example, "what are the syntactic properties of relative clauses in language X," or "do relative clauses in X precede or follow the head of the construction?" Before questions such as these can be answered, we need to know how a construction in some language can be identified as a relative clause. Are there syntactic properties common to all the units we wish to call relative clauses?

Let us consider syntactic properties of relative clause (RC) constructions found in various languages:

a. A RC contains a finite verb.
b. The verb of a RC assumes a distinctive nonfinite form.
c. A RC contains a pronoun coreferential with a noun that immediately precedes (or follows) the RC.
d. No nominal in the RC is coreferential with a preceding (or following) noun.
e. A RC together with a nominal expression forms a noun phrase (NP) constituent.
f. A RC is the sole constituent of a NP.
g. A RC is not a constituent of a NP.
h. A RC begins (or ends) with a distinctive marker.
i. A RC contains a marker that is linked by cooccurrence with a nominal marker outside the clause.
j. The internal structure of a RC is indistinguishable from that of (some) nonrelative clauses.

Obviously none of these syntactic properties is universal, since as universals they are inconsistent with one another. If, as will be illustrated below, RC's in various languages do exhibit these diverse syntactic properties (and if there are no others that they share), then we must seek on some other level a commonality in terms of which the various syntactic manifestations of what we call relative clauses can be described.

We may first consider the possibility of defining relative clauses as having shared properties at a more abstract syntactic level. Transformational grammars provide a means of characterizing the basic oneness of a variety of syntactic forms having a common meaning in a single language. This is done by positing a single

basic abstract syntactic form (a class of 'deep structures') from
which the various syntactic manifestations ('surface structures')
can be derived by general rules. All surface forms sharing a derivation from deep structures with certain common properties can
be described as syntactically of the same type, e.g., as being
'relative clauses.'

But the deep structures posited in order to account for surface
forms in various languages differ from language to language at
least with respect to the positioning of relative clauses in larger
structures. Attempts to justify a common deep syntactic representation for relative clauses in all languages (e.g. Bach 1965)
have not escaped arbitrariness, at least with respect to ordering
of elements. Not only do relative clauses precede other elements
within a single NP in some languages and follow in others; in some
languages, as we shall see, relative clauses do not enter into nominal constituents at all at the surface level, so that there is no
motivation for deriving them from an embedded position in deep
structures in those languages.

These facts suggest that a universal characterization of the
notion 'relative clause' can only be given in semantic terms.

1.2 A semantic characterization

A relative clause never stands alone as a complete sentence:
it is always linked, semantically at least, to a noun phrase that
is part of another clause. This linking is achieved through a semantic property of all constructions called relative clauses that
has already been alluded to: a relative clause incorporates, as
one of its terms, a nominal which is coreferential with a nominal
outside of the clause. Neither nominal need be expressed overtly,
although presumably one or the other must. Sentences 1.- 3. illustrate various possibilities with regard to omission of the coreferential NP's in ENGLISH. (Brackets are used in all examples to
indicate the boundaries of the relative clause; in the present examples, coreferential nominals are underlined.)

1.   The car [I saw ∅] was green.
2.   I haven't found ∅ [what I was looking for].
3.   The girl chose the ring [which cost the most].

We may refer to the coreferential nominal in the relative clause
(whether expressed or not) as the relative NP (Rel NP) and the coreferential nominal outside the relative clause as the antecedent

NP (Ant NP). In some cases, however, Rel NP may be coreferential with an entire clause, as in 4., in which case we may speak of an antecedent clause.

    4.   They locked up all the children, which pleased their parents.

    A second semantic property of relative clauses, noted by Gundel (1974) and emphasized by Kuno (1973, 1976: 420), is that "a relative clause must be a statement about" the Rel NP and thus about its antecedent. Kuno has supported this "Thematic Constraint" with evidence that in JAPANESE a clause can be a relative clause just in case Ant NP represents its theme; furthermore, relative clauses have the form of clauses from which Rel NP as theme has been deleted. Various constraints concerning which terms can serve as Rel NP, such as Ross's Coordinate Structure Constraint and Complex NP Constraint (Ross 1967) and the Keenan-Comrie Accessibility Hierarchy (Keenan and Comrie 1972) are then, according to Kuno, constraints on what can serve as theme. Parallels between relativization and thematization in a number of languages seem to bear out this hypothesis, and I know of no counter-examples.

    A third essential semantic property of RC's is the functional property of modification. This is a property of only some RC's, those referred to as adjectival or restrictive as opposed to nonrestrictive or appositive relative clauses. This is the property that distinguishes example 5. (restrictive) from 6. (nonrestrictive).

    5.   The children who have green tickets will be admitted free.
    6.   The children, who have green tickets, will be admitted free.

This is not the place for a detailed account of the distinction between restrictive and nonrestrictive clauses (for which see Thompson 1971 and Martin 1972), nor for any attempt to explicate the semantic notion of modification. (In addition to the extensive philosophical literature, one may refer to Keenan 1972a.) For present purposes it is sufficient to state that restrictive relative clauses express an assertion about some individual or class, with the function not of conveying new information but of restricting the reference of Ant NP to those possible referents of which that assertion is believed to be true.   Thus in 5. the reference of children, which by itself denotes any two or more preadolescent humans, is restricted to those of whom the proposition they have green tickets is true, whereas in 6. it is stated that any and all children will be admitted free (the only restriction being that imposed by the, which limits the reference to a previously identified class of all or some children);

the nonrestrictive clause <u>who have green tickets</u> in 6. expresses
an independent (though downgraded) assertion concerning the same
unrestricted set of children.

The properties of nonrestrictive RC's are quite different from
those of restrictive RC's across languages. Some languages apparently have no nonrestrictive RC's; in others they are syntactically quite distinct; in others restrictive and nonrestrictive RC's
are syntactically indistinguishable. To put reasonable limits on
the scope of the present survey, nonrestrictive relatives will be
ignored in the remainder of this paper, as will all those nominal
modifiers which may be thought of as reduced forms of relative
clauses.

I have avoided referring to the semantic <u>inclusion</u> of the relative
clause in the modified NP because it is a matter of dispute whether
syntactic subordination appropriately represents the deep structure
of restrictive relative clauses even for ENGLISH (see Thompson
1971) and because, as we shall see below, in some languages RRC's
are never incorporated syntactically into the clause containing the
antecedent.[1] Thus, we have just three universal defining properties
of RC's, all semantic: <u>coreference</u> between terms inside and outside the clause (Rel NP and Ant NP); the notion that the RC is an
<u>assertion</u> about Rel NP (that Rel NP is its theme); and the relation
of <u>modification</u> which holds between a restrictive relative clause
(RRC) and its antecedent.

1.3 An approach to syntactic universals

1.3.1 <u>Some questions and some types of answers</u> So far it has
been claimed that while a universal semantic definition can be provided for the notion 'relative clause,' there is no single set of syntactic properties by which RC's can be identified as a universal
syntactic category. But this is not to say that there are no true
universal generalizations to be made concerning the surface syntactic form of RC's. We can still ask questions such as these:

a. Do all languages have relative clauses?
b. If there are no formal syntactic properties common to all
   relative clauses (or the sentence structures in which they

---

[1] Thus we will avoid using the term <u>head</u> (of the relative clause)
except in those cases where a relative clause and its antecedent do
form a single phrase. <u>Head</u> being thus unavailable as a neutral
term, I see no practical alternative to using Ant NP to refer to a
modified NP even when it follows the Rel NP.

occur), are there clearly definable language types, within
which relative clauses have common syntactic properties?

c.   Can the form of relative clauses in a given language be
predicted on the basis of other formal properties of that
language?

d.   Are there, in the absence of strictly universal properties,
structural tendencies which may still be of interest in our
attempts to understand how languages are structured?

Answers to the questions just posed may be expressed as universal statements classified into four major statement types (cf.
Ferguson 1971).

a.   Absolute universals (AU):
All languages have property X.
b.   Implicational universals (IU):
If a language has property Y, it has property X.
c.   General tendencies (GT):
Most languages have property X.
d.   Implicational tendencies (IT):
If a language has property Y, it is likely to have/usually
has property X.

While universals of types a. and b. are clearly the most interesting,
strong tendencies in language structure are also of interest to the
linguist in that they demand explanation and they may suggest the
possibility of discovering conditioning factors in terms of which
they may be restated as true implicational universals. Furthermore, typologies can be constructed on the basis of generalizations
of these sorts: a language type is a class of languages of which a
set of implicational universals and implicational tendencies (restated in absolute form) are true; the larger the set of statements,
the more interesting is the type.

1.3.2 One universal and a positional typology   There seems to
be but one absolute generalization that is justified with respect to
relative clauses:

A.   All languages make use of restrictive relative clauses (as
semantically defined). (AU)

Present evidence suggests, however, that a number of implicational
generalizations can be formulated in terms of correlations between
the position of the RRC in its sentence and its internal structure,
on the one hand, and between its position and the dominant word-
order type of the language in question, on the other.   We will

therefore need to define the following terms to be used in describing positions:

> prenominal -- occurring in the position of S in the configuration $[...S...NP]_{NP}$, where S is the relative clause and the included NP is the head or modified nominal (Ant NP).

> postnominal – occurring in the position of S in the configuration $[NP...S...]_{NP}$.[2]

Together, these two types in which S is adjoined to the head NP may be referred to as <u>ad-relatives</u> (following Andrews 1971).

> replacive -- occurring in place of Ant NP with no surface manifestiation of Ant NP.

> left-extraposed -- occurring outside of and preceding the clause containing the modified nominal.

> right-extraposed -- occurring at the end of or following the clause containing the modified nominal.

Together, these latter two types will be referred to (again following Andrews 1971) as <u>co-relatives</u>. This latter term is to be distinguished from the term <u>correlative</u> (<u>relative clause</u>) which refers to a particular syntactic marking of some left-extraposed co-relative clauses, to be discussed below.[3]

We will now consider, in turn, postnominal RRC's (Section 2); prenominal RRC's (Sec. 3); replacive RC's (Sec. 4); correlative RRC's (Sec. 5); and finally other left-extraposed and right-extraposed RRC's (Sec. 6). For each type the procedure will be to illustrate representative constructions from various languages, and to make statements concerning their form in the most general terms consistent with the known facts. A summary will be provided in Sec. 7.

---

[2] Schwartz (1971) refers to these types as <u>prospective</u> and <u>retrospective</u>.

[3] There is unfortunately further potential terminological confusion which the reader should be warned against. Hale (1974 et passim) refers to our extraposed (co-relative) clauses as <u>adjoined</u> (to the main clause) and our ad-relative clauses as <u>embedded</u> relatives.

Assuming that there are significant types of RRC's distinguished by their position within the sentence, we will attempt to answer the following question: to what extent can the internal form of RRC's be predicted on the basis of other formal properties of a given language? Only when these correlations are well-understood can we hope to proceed to functional explanation in terms of psychological processing of sentences.

2. Postnominal Relative Clauses

2.1 Correlation with word-order type

The strong correlation between verb-object (VO) word order and the use of postnominal RRC's is well-known. I am not aware of any exceptional cases among VSO languages. There are, however, some exceptions among SVO languages. MANDARIN CHINESE is a basically SVO language in which RRC's are preposed, and PERSIAN, an SOV language, has postposed RRC's. According to Andrews (1975), CLASSICAL TIBETAN, HOTTENTOT, QUECHUA, PAPAGO and TURKISH all have both preposed and postposed relative clauses, although not all of these languages have finite clauses in both positions. The tendency, however, is strong enough to be worth including among our generalizations concerning relative clause formation:

B. With few exceptions, a language has postnominal restrictive relative clauses if and only if in the basic word order of the language verbs precede their objects. (IT)

2.2 Internal RC structure in SVO languages

Since I have discussed and illustrated the internal structure of postnominal RRC's in some detail elsewhere (Downing, forthcoming) and since most forms of postnominal RRC's are quite familiar to the speaker of ENGLISH, this type will be dealt with rather sketchily here.

Schwartz (1971: 142) has provided the following classification of postnominal RRC's on the basis of a) presence versus absence of an introductory particle (complementizer), symbolized below by that;[4] b) presence versus absence of a clause-initial relative

---

[4]Schwartz intends 'that' to symbolize a connective particle or a demonstrative pronoun, including pronouns "oriented toward the head," while 'WH' symbolizes an interrogative pronoun used as a

pronoun, symbolized by WH; and c) presence or absence of a (non-relative) pronoun (PRO) within the clause. (The list of languages cited here as exemplifying each type is not coextensive with that provided by Schwartz.)

i.	N [$_S$...∅...]	DYIRBAL
ii.	N that [$_S$...∅...]	VIETNAMESE, HAUSA
iii.	N that [$_S$...PRO...]	HEBREW, ARABIC, AKAN
iv.	N [$_S$ WH....]	LATIN and derivatives
v.	N that [$_S$ WH....]	INDONESIAN, HUNGARIAN

To these should be added two additional types. The first is attested in both OLD and MIDDLE ENGLISH (with different morphological forms) and, according to Givón (1973), in SPOKEN HEBREW, where the interrogative morpheme <u>me</u>/<u>ma</u> may precede the particle šɛ- in relative clauses.

      vi.   N WH that [$_S$...∅...]

The last type (vii) is found in RUMANIAN where, according to Keenan (1974), Rel NP is retained as a clitic pronoun even though the clause is introduced by a relative pronoun marked for the case function of Rel NP in its clause.

      vii.   N [$_S$ WH...PRO...]

In many languages, of course, more than one of these types is found. Modern ENGLISH uses both ii. and iv. alternatively, but also uses i. just in case Rel NP is not the subject. BLACK ENGLISH uses iii. and allows i. even when Rel NP is the subject, as in examples 7. and 8., from Tyson 1976.

     7.   Now and I have one nephew that he stays with us. (type iii.)
     8.   Porky is the little bitty one look almost like Florrie. (type i.)

     2.2.1   <u>Initial relative particles</u>   In all types of postnominal RRC's other than type i., a marker of some kind is present at the beginning

---

(ftnt. 4 cont.)
relative pronoun. For present purposes, I will rather take 'that' to refer to connective particles (possibly functioning more generally as complementizers) only, and take 'WH' to represent any relative pronoun, whether or not it has interrogative form. This interpretation does not affect Schwartz's set of formulae, but does produce a different typology.

of the clause. In types ii. and iii. this is an invariant particle
(often, historically at least, a demonstrative form). Examples
are AKAN àà, DANISH som, ENGLISH that, HAUSA da, HEBREW
šɛ-, MALAY yang, RUSSIAN čto, TUNISIAN ARABIC illi, VIET-
NAMESE má. The same kind of particle is found in combination
with a relative pronoun in types v. and vi.

2.2.2 Relative pronouns In type iv. as well as in types v. and
vi., a special pronominal form of Rel NP appears in clause-initial
position. This relative pronoun is commonly either identical with
interrogative pronouns or a demonstrative form. Examples of the
former are ALBANIAN ku, cil-, ENGLISH which, who, FRENCH
qui, où, GERMAN welchen, RUSSIAN kotorij-, TUNISIAN ARABIC
wi.n. Demonstrative forms other than those which have become
unstressed particles are, for example, EWE si, GERMAN denen,
UMBUNDU una. In some cases the relative pronoun is distinct
from both the interrogative and the demonstrative; e.g. GREEK
hós, FRENCH dont, SPANISH el cual.

2.2.3 Pronoun retention When there is no initial relative pronoun (and even, in rare cases, when there is) Rel NP may either
be deleted or retained in a non-initial position. However, a pro-
form of Rel NP in non-initial position always has a nondistinctive
weak pronominal form and is positioned where such a pronoun
would appear in a simple declarative sentence, i.e., there is no
movement assignable to relativization. Many languages delete
Rel NP in some positions and retain a proform in other positions,
obligatorily or optionally.

In some SVO languages postnominal RRC's are also marked in
some additional way (a verbal affix in HAUSA, tone changes in
AKAN), but these markers are in most cases applicable to other
subordinate clauses as well.

2.2.4 No connective Postnominal RRC's of type i. are the
least common. They are used in standard ENGLISH, DANISH and
VIETNAMESE, but only if Rel NP is not the subject, and only as
an alternative to type ii. or iv. We have seen already (example 8.
above), however, that in the BLACK ENGLISH dialect type i.
clauses are possible even with deletion of a Rel NP which is the
subject of the clause.

The use of type i. in DYIRBAL is quite different (Dixon 1969:37).
Although there is no clause-initial relative marker in DYIRBAL,
the verb of the relative clause is obligatorily marked by deletion
of the tense inflection and substitution of the relative marker -ŋu

followed by a copy of the case inflection of the antecedent. In addition, Rel NP, which is obligatorily omitted, is always reconstructable as a NP in the nominative case. (DYIRBAL is an ergative language.) An example, from Dixon 1969, is 9.

9.   yibi-∅   yaṛa-ŋgu [njalŋga-ŋgu djilwal-ŋa-ŋu-ru]
      "woman-Nom man-ERG child-ERG kick-ŋaj-REL-ERG
      buṛa-n
      see-PRES/PAST"
      'The man who had kicked the child saw the woman.'

This may be compared with the simple sentences in 10.

10.a. njalaŋga-∅   yaṛa-ŋgu djilwa-n
      "child-Nom man-ERG kick-PRES/PAST"
      'The man kicked the child.'

  = b. yaṛa-∅   njalaŋga-ŋgu djilwal-ŋa-nju
      "man-NOM child-ERG   kick-ŋaj-PRES/PAST"

Relativization by marking the verb seems to be the exception for postnominal RRC's in SVO languages but is found commonly in other RRC types. I am aware of two additional cases in which postnominal RRC's in SVO languages are regularly marked by means of Rel NP deletion plus verb marking. In both cases the facts are not entirely clear, so only a brief sketch will be given here.

In OJIBWE, according to Kenneth Truitner (personal communication), either the subject or a focussed NP precedes the verb in main clauses, but in RC's the verb is initial. Pronominal forms in all subordinate clauses are distinct from those used in independent clauses. In RC's the initial past tense marker -gī appears as gā, so that the vowel change signals the subordination in past tense clauses. There is at least one dialect in which gā has been generalized as a present and past tense relative marker.

The examples in 11. illustrate a simple declarative sentence (a.) and the same clause embedded as a relative clause (b.).

11.a. Ikwe   ogī wābamān ininiwan bijīnāgō
      "woman did   see   man   yesterday"
      'The woman saw the man yesterday.'

  b. ikwe [gā   wābamād ininiwan bijīnāgō]
      "woman did (rel) see   man   yesterday"
      'the woman who saw the man yesterday'

If it is assumed that in OJIBWE Rel NP must be in focus, and thus
sentence initial, and given that deletion of Rel NP is obligatory,
then the verb-initial order of OJIBWE RC's follows. In any case,
OJIBWE is similar to DYIRBAL in marking relatives by verb
form, but it is different in that the marker is clause-initial, like
other relative markers in SVO languages.

A somewhat similar case is that of GUARANÍ, as described in
Pederson 1974. GUARANÍ, a widely spoken language of South
America, has changed typologically from SOV to SVO over the
past 350 years, perhaps as a result of SPANISH influence. Despite the change in basic word order, GUARANÍ still maintains
postpositions, auxiliaries following the verb, and the SOV characteristic of marking relative clauses by a suffix -va on the verb,
along with deletion of Rel NP. An example of object relativization
is given in 12.

12. Pe   karaí [rehayhúva]   iñañkuhina
     "that man you-love-PRT (is) bad"
     'The man you love is bad.'

In cases of object relativization the subject prefix on the verb prevents ambiguity. But if Rel NP is the subject, then only the suffix
particle would prevent the verb from being interpreted as the main
verb when the head is subject of its clause. Perhaps for this reason, there is no relativization on subjects of transitive clauses in
GUARANÍ. Instead the clause is always passivized so that object
relativization can take place, as in 13.

13. koa   ko jagua [še suʔuvakwe]
     "this the dog   me bite-PRT-PAST"
     'This is the dog I was bitten by.'

Notice that the constraint against type i. relativization of subjects
is similar to that found in ENGLISH, DANISH and VIETNAMESE,
mentioned above. However, since GUARANÍ has only type i. relativization, there is a problem when the clause is intransitive, since
passivization is of course impossible. In this case relativization
is allowed with the active verb, as in 14.

14. Reheša   pe kwimbaʔe [oikevakwe]
     "you-saw the man   he-enter-PRT-PAST"
     'You saw the man who entered.'

There is some indication, however, that relativization on intransitive subjects is avoided; texts contain few examples.

2.2.5 <u>Transformational processes and permitted combinations</u>
The common properties of postnominal RRC's in SOV languages
can be described in transformational terms as the result of the
application or nonapplication of three largely independent processes of relativization:

  a.   insertion of an initial relative particle,
  b.   copying of Rel NP in a relative pronoun form (sometimes as
       part of an NP that contains it) in clause-initial position,
  c.   deletion of Rel NP.

It can be assumed that the assignment of an unstressed anaphoric
form to Rel NP, and in some languages, its deletion, follow from
general principles of pronominalization which are not part of the
relativization process. The seven types of postnominal RRC's
listed above result, then, from the application of the following combinations of the rules just given.

  i.   c only (accompanied by verb marking in languages that
           exhibit no other type)
  ii.   a and c
  iii.   a only
  iv.   b and c
  v.   b > a, c
  vi.   a > b, c
  vii.   b only

Thus, of the logically possible combinations of these three processes, only two are not found: there are no SVO languages which use
none of these relativization processes, and there are none (in our
sample) of the form

  viii. *NP that WH ... PRO ...
  (or)   NP WH that ... PRO ...

The least common type, i., is the one which uses neither of the
devices that serve to separate the relative clause from the immediately preceding antecedent, but even in type i. there is a tendency
to use distinctive verb marking and to position the verb at the beginning of its clause.

2.3 <u>Internal relative clause structure in verb-initial languages</u>

In a <u>strict</u> verb-initial language there can be no initial nonverbal
relative marker; a verb-initial language nevertheless may allow
particles and even pronouns to precede the verb.

In JACALTEC, a rigid VSO language with ergative case marking, the verb is inflected for both subject and object. Relative
clauses are marked by deletion of both Rel NP and the corresponding verbal affix. Oblique cases are relativized simply by deletion
of Rel NP. There is no verb-marking except that an intransitive
marker is added when the object of a transitive verb is deleted.
The deletion processes in JACALTEC serve the function of identifying the case of Rel NP. Keenan (1972b) has described similar
"verb-coding" processes in MALAGASY (a VOS language) and
other languages.

OLD IRISH had deletion of Rel NP but special verb forms or
other marking, except in some persons of the present tense where
a relative absolute was used and in some person forms where a
particle no was added.

In ZAPOTEC, on the other hand, RC's are introduced by a relative marker ni, which Rosenbaum (1971) interprets as a pronoun
on the grounds that when the antecedent is plural, ni may be accompanied by a plural marker. ZAPOTEC also has preverbal question-
words in questions, which supports Schwartz's (1971) hypothesis
that relative pronouns will be found, outside of correlative constructions, only in languages that have question-word movement --
that relative-fronting is "parasitic on" question-word fronting.

It thus appears that type i. relatives are most common in verb-
initial languages, with at least one other type, vi., possible,
whereas i. is least common in SVO languages. This difference
can perhaps be explained on the basis of perceptual ambiguity: in
SVO languages a verb in an unmarked RRC modifying the subject
could be misinterpreted as the predicate of the main clause, but
not in a VSO language, where initial position clearly identifies the
main verb. (Compare The man [∅ robbed the bank] escaped with
Escaped the man [robbed ∅ the bank].)

2.4 Postnominal relative clauses in verb-final languages

Postnominal RRC's are rare in verb-final languages. In PER-
SIAN, which is SOV and uses postnominal as well as correlative
and extraposed RC's, there is an initial particle ke, with deletion
of Rel NP when it is subject or object but retention in oblique cases.
The clause boundary is further marked by a suffix -i on the antecedent. In addition, relativization of a direct object may involve
placement of the specific direct object marker as a proclitic to the
particle ke, as shown in 15.

15. (an) märd-i   [(ra)-ke   did-i]
     "the man-REL OBJ-PART saw-you"
     'the man whom you saw'

The facts of PERSIAN show that when RRC's are postnominal,
all of the relativization processes of SVO languages may be used,
even if the basic word order is SOV. TURKISH, a rather strict
SOV language with prenominal RC's formed by quite distinct processes (see below), has borrowed the type ii. postnominal clause
from PERSIAN, including the relative particle (ki in TURKISH).

2.5 Generalizations

On the basis of the data reviewed thus far, a number of implicational universals may be stated, along with noteworthy universal
tendencies.

C. With few exceptions, in tense-marked (finite) postnominal
    relative clauses, either a) a relative particle or relative
    pronoun or both or b) the subject of the clause precedes
    the verb, in SVO languages. (IT)

D. The relative NP in a postnominal restrictive relative clause
    may not be a full lexical NP. It may be retained as a rela-
    tive pronoun (of interrogative, demonstrative, or distinc-
    tive relative form) or as an unstressed personal pronoun
    or both, or it may be omitted. (IU)

E. With few exceptions, if a relative clause contains an initial
    relative pronoun, it does not contain a personal pronoun
    form of the same NP. (IT)

F. A relative pronoun in a postnominal relative clause is always
    placed in clause-initial position (sometimes as part of a
    NP which contains it), either preceding or following the
    relative particle, if any. (IU)

G. A nonpronominal relative marker in postnominal relative
    clauses is either a clause-initial particle or an affix on the
    verb. (IU)

H. A noninitial relative NP in a postnominal relative clause
    either is deleted or assumes a weak pronominal form,
    independently of whether a copy appears in initial position
    as a relative pronoun. (IU)

I. Postnominal relative clauses contain relative pronouns only if the language allows (other) initial nonverbal elements in subordinate clauses. (IU)

J. With few exceptions, postnominal relative clauses in VSO languages contain either a) an initial relative particle or pronoun or b) a special marker on the main verb of the clause. (IT)

K. With few exceptions, if postnominal relative clauses contain a distinctive verbal affix, the verb appears in clause-initial position. (IT)

Although correlations between question formation and relativization have not been illustrated here, there is considerable corroboration of the following generalizations (see Bach 1971, Schwartz 1971).

L. If a language uses relative pronouns of interrogative form in ad-relative clauses, then in that language interrogative pronouns are placed in initial position in questions. (IU)

M. If a language places relative pronouns that are not interrogative in form in initial position in postnominal relative clauses, then either that language has initial interrogative pronouns in questions or it has a general topicalization process that places thematic material in initial position. (IU)

Schwartz (1971) suggests that demonstrative relative pronouns in GERMAN and personal relative pronouns in DUTCH can be fronted just because these languages also have a Question Word Movement rule that fronts interrogative pronouns. The relative pronouns in effect get a free ride on the question-forming rule.

3. Prenominal Relative Clauses

3.1 Correlation with word-order type   The well-known correlation between verb-final word order and pre-positioning of relative clauses and other modifiers will be illustrated below from NAVAJO, BASQUE, AMHARIC, JAPANESE and TURKISH. We have noted one verb-final language, PERSIAN, which has postnominal RC's; CHINESE is exceptional in the other direction. However, although in nearly all verb-final languages relative clauses precede Ant NP, many such languages use correlative constructions or other extraposed RC's instead of ad-relatives with either order. The generalizations to be stated are therefore as follows:

N. With few exceptions, RRC's are not postnominal if in the
basic word order of the language verbs precede their
objects. (IT)

O. With few exceptions, RRC's are prenominal only if in the
basic word order of the language verbs follow their objects.
(IT)

Prenominal RC's in SOV languages will be discussed in Sec. 3.2;
prenominal participles in TURKISH in Sec. 3.3; and the case of
CHINESE, which has prenominal clauses but SVO word-order, in
Sec. 3.4.

3.2 Internal structure of prenominal clauses

In general, the processes of relativization in prenominal RRC's
in verb-final languages are similar to those most common in postnominal RRC's in verb-initial languages. These include 1) deletion
of Rel NP (at least from some positions), and 2) distinctive marking of the verb of the RC, usually with an affix that separates the
clause from its head. Nonverbal markers of the clause boundary
seem rare. Most strikingly, there are no relative pronouns in
prenominal clauses as previously defined.

3.2.1 Verb marking

In NAVAHO, an SOV language, a "relative
complementizer" (Platero 1974) is suffixed to the verb of a relative
clause: -ígíí for nonpast and -yéé for past tense. Either Rel NP
or Ant NP (the head) is deleted, presumably by general principles
of pronominalization, obligatory in relativization. Deletion of the
head will be discussed in Sec. 4. An illustration of relativization
with deletion of Rel NP is the example in 16.

16. [Ø ałhosh   -ígíí] ashkii ałhą́ą́'
     "Ø IMPERF-3-sleep-REL boy   IMPERF-3-snore"
     'The boy who is sleeping is snoring.'

Platero describes an interesting set of constraints in NAVAHO
which have the effect of reducing ambiguity regarding the case-role
played by the deleted NP when Rel NP is deleted. But the principles involved are not specifically processes of relativization.

According to de Rijk (1972), BASQUE has fairly free word order
in main clauses, but relative clauses are prenominal with verb-
final word order. Relativization involves deletion of Rel NP and
any accompanying postposition, and the addition of a final suffix -n
to the verb. An example is 17.

17. Aitak irakurri nai du [amak erre du-en]   liburua.
    "father read   want   mother burned-has-REL book"
    'Father wants to read the book that mother has burned.'

The head of a BASQUE RC may be the indefinite determiner bat 'one' or the definite determiner -a 'the.' De Rijk (1972:127) treats these constructions as equivalent to headless or 'free' relative in ENGLISH. The BASQUE free relative is frequently used in apposition to a specific NP, either immediately following it or extraposed to the end of the main clause.

Modern AMHARIC is a somewhat inconsistent SOV language with prenominal RRC's which, until fairly recently, apparently had VSO word-order and postnominal relatives (see Hudson 1972). There is evidence that the relative marker yä-, which is prefixed to the (clause-final) verb in modern AMHARIC, as shown in 18., was originally in initial position following the head; when the word order changed, it "migrated" toward the new head position as far as its prefixal status would permit. Givón (1972) cites this as diachronic evidence for a universal pronoun/complementizer attraction principle. In its present-day form AMHARIC has typical prenominal RC structure. Rel NP, but not the corresponding agreement marker on the verb, is deleted, and a relative marker is attached to the verb, but as a prefix rather than the expected suffix.

18. [gäbäre tinäntina yä-säbbärä-t] wämbär
    "farmer yesterday REL-broke-it chair"
    'the chair that a farmer broke yesterday'

3.2.2 No marking JAPANESE formerly used a verbal suffix to mark RC's, but in modern JAPANESE there is no marking other than the deletion of Rel NP, except when the RC contains a copula, which takes a special dependent form. (When Rel NP is a genitive form, a pronoun is retained.) As Kuno (1976) observes, RC's in JAPANESE are identical to the remainder of a sentence from which a topic NP has been extracted. The examples in 19., from McCawley 1976:302, illustrate the parallel between topicalization (a.) and relativization (b.), with optional retention of the genitive NP in both cases.

19.a. Ano doobutu wa (sono) mawari ni kodomo ga atumátte ita.
     "   animal   its surrounding children   gathered"
     'An animal, the children were gathered around.'

   b. [(sono) mawari ni kodomo ga atumátte ita] doobutu
      " its surrounding children   gathered   animal"
      'an animal around which there were children gathered'

These few examples demonstrate that in prenominal RRC's in
SOV languages the clause may be finite or nonfinite, the verb
specially marked or not, but Rel NP is omitted in all cases except
in some oblique positions. In no case is there a relative pronoun,
a movement rule, or even a connective particle other than the
verbal affixes.

3.3 Prenominal relative participles

In TURKISH also, relative clauses are marked by the addition
of a suffix to the verb and deletion of Rel NP, but two distinct processes are used, one for subjects and the other for objects and
other NP's. In both cases the verb of the RC becomes nonfinite,
i.e. participial. When Rel NP is the subject, it is simply omitted
and the tense ending of the verb replaced by a special participial
suffix (-en in most instances). This is illustrated in 20.

> 20. Bu [Ankara'ya gid-en] tren ol-muş.
>   "this Ankara-to go-PART train be-suppositive"
>   'This must be the train that goes to Ankara.'

When an oblique NP is relativized, the verb receives a usually distinct substantivizing suffix, and the subject and verb of the RC are
both marked by suffixation for a possessor-possessed relation.
Since the case marking of Rel NP is lost with it and is not marked
on the verb, the role of Rel NP in the clause is sometimes not
easy to reconstruct. Example 21. shows relativization on an indirect object.

> 21. [Adam-ın yüzüğ-ü sat - tığ - ı] kadın on-u
>   "man-POSS ring-OBJ sell-PART-POSS'D woman it-OBJ
>   kaybet-ti.
>   loose-PAST"
>   'The woman that the man sold the ring [to] lost it.'

TURKISH is similar to DYIRBAL, despite the difference in pre-
versus postnominal RC position, in the following respects. Both
use a process involving deletion of Rel NP and replacement of the
tense inflection of the verb by a special relative marker (a participial morpheme), used only when Rel NP is the subject of its clause.
DYIRBAL does not allow relativization of oblique NP's at all, but
provides means by which any NP can become subject. TURKISH,
which allows only objects to become subjects, provides a distinct
process by which oblique cases can be relativized. Nevertheless,
neither language has any relative construction in which the RC

contains a finite verb form (ignoring for the moment the borrowed postnominal RC in TURKISH).

Dixon (1969) has observed that the constraint that in nonfinite, participial constructions Rel NP can only be the surface subject extends also to ENGLISH. The following examples are given by Schwartz (1971: 142).

22. a. people paying money
    b. people being paid money
    c. *money people paying

This constraint holds for prenominal participles in ENGLISH as well:

23. a. damage-causing winds
    b. *wind-causing damage

These observations suggest that nonsubject relativization in TURK-ISH should not be considered to produce true participial constructions. If there is independent evidence for such an analysis, then the general correlation can be stated as follows: in nonfinite, participial RC's, Rel NP can only be the subject.

3.4 Prenominal RC's in a VO language

MANDARIN CHINESE is the only language in the present sample with VO word order but prenominal RC's. In the verb-final languages generally, we have seen a tendency to mark the subordinate status of the clause with a verbal suffix which regularly falls between the verb and its head. In MANDARIN, where the verb will not regularly be clause final (and there is in any case no suffixation on verbs), we find a subordinating particle de in clause-final position. Deletion of Rel NP applies only to subjects (obligatorily) and objects (optionally), as in 24.

24. [wo dale (ta) de] neige ren laile
     "I   hit   him REL that man came"
     'The man that I hit came.'

3.5 Generalizations

In the languages surveyed here relativization processes in prenominal RRC's include only the following: deletion of Rel NP (in some languages not permitted in oblique positions), and marking

the end of the clause with a verbal affix in verb-final languages,
but with a nonverbal particle in the one SVO language, MANDARIN
CHINESE. In TURKISH we found that all prenominal relatives are
nonfinite. As in the postnominal relative in DYIRBAL, the simple
participle construction is used only when Rel NP is subject; unlike
DYIRBAL, TURKISH also relativizes on oblique cases, using Rel
NP deletion plus a special substantival genitive construction.

The forms of prenominal relative clauses vary slightly among
the languages described here:

viii.	$[_S \ldots \emptyset \ldots V\text{-}REL]\ N$	NAVAJO, BASQUE
ix.	$[_S \ldots \emptyset \ldots REL\text{-}V]\ N$	AMHARIC
x.	$[_S \ldots (PRO) \ldots V]\ N$	JAPANESE
xi.	$[_S \ldots (PRO) \ldots] \underline{that}\ N$	CHINESE
xii.	$[_S \ldots \emptyset \ldots V\text{-}PART]\ N$	TURKISH

The following generalizations can be stated on the basis of the
data discussed in this section:

P. In prenominal relative clauses there is no movement of the
relative NP to either the beginning or end of the clause;
initial or final relative markers (if any) are not pronouns.
(IU)

Q. In prenominal relative clauses if the relative NP is retained,
it has a weak pronominal form; there are no (strong) relative pronouns in prenominal relative clauses. (IU)

R. With few exceptions in prenominal relative clauses, the
relative NP is obligatorily deleted in at least some positions. (IT)

S. In prenominal relative clauses, either the verb is placed
in final position or there is a clause-final relative marker,
or both. (IU)

T. With few exceptions, if relativization involves a nonpersonal
marker on the verb of a prenominal relative clause, the
verb is clause final and the marker is suffixed. (IT)

The participial relative constructions of DYIRBAL and TURKISH
suggest the following generalization.

U. The verb of a relative clause may assume a nonfinite, participial form if the relative NP is the subject of its clause.

If the relative NP is not the subject, then either reletivi-
zation is impossible or a distinct process is used. (IU)

In a number of SOV languages it is possible to retain Rel NP in
its full lexical form rather than to pronominalize or delete it. In
such cases the head (Ant NP) is deleted instead. Such cases will
be discussed in the following section.

4. Replacive Relative Clauses

In all the cases surveyed thus far, Ant NP is essentially unaffected by relativization, while Rel NP is obligatorily either pronominalized or deleted.

Many languages allow the head of an ad-relative clause to be
omitted when it has no specific semantic content (e.g. such heads
as that and something in ENGLISH). In ENGLISH the headless
relative clause is fully grammatical only with an inanimate subject
or object Rel NP and only with the special relative pronoun form
what(ever):

Something that John said annoyed her.
That which John said annoyed her.
*That John said annoyed her.
*Which John said annoyed her.
What John said annoyed her.
What goes up must come down.
*Who borrowed my pen didn't bring it back.
?I don't like who you meet there.
*Where we met was beautiful.
?I don't like when the class starts.

There are no languages with postnominal RRC's that allow the head
to be deleted or pronominalized while Rel NP is retained as a full
lexical NP. There are also, to my knowledge, no SVO languages
that exhibit such constructions.

Some verb-final languages, however, allow Ant NP to be omitted
while Rel NP in a preceding RC is retained in its full lexical form.
The possibility of head-deletion of this kind in NAVAJO has already
been mentioned. While either a preceding Rel NP or the following
Ant NP may be deleted, there are constraints in the former case,
and the deletion of Ant NP is preferred, even though it may result
in serious ambiguity (out of context) when more than one NP is present. These two constructions are illustrated in 25. and 26., with
examples from Platero 1974.

25. Yádooɬtih   [tl'éédą́ą́'   Ø aɬhą́ą́'   -ą́ą] ashkii
    "FUT-3-speak last-night   IMPERF-3-snore-REL boy"
    'The boy who was snoring last night will speak.'

26. Yádooɬtih   [tl'éédą́ą́' ashkii aɬhą́ą́'   -ą́ą] Ø
    "FUT-3-speak last-night boy IMPERF-3-snore-REL
    'The boy who was snoring last night will speak.'

In cases such as 26. the RC cannot be classed as either prenominal
or postnominal. The essential form is

xiii. $[_{NP} [_{S} \ldots \text{Rel NP} \ldots \text{V}]]$

Although Platero (1974) argues that Ant NP is deleted by a general
left-to-right pronominalization rule in NAVAJO, there are other
languages in which it is difficult to establish the position of the
deleted head as preceding or following the clause. I therefore label headless RC's replacive relative clauses when the clause stands
in the place of the nominal it is used to modify.

   BAMBARA is another language which exhibits replacive RC's.
Keenan (class lecture, 1974 Linguistic Institute, University of
Massachusetts) classifies BAMBARA as having SOVX word-order,
so that it might be expected to have either pre- or postnominal RC's.
Instead the structure is as shown in 27., with the clause standing
in second or object position in place of the object NP it modifies,
and with the Rel NP within the clause marked by a relative marker
mîn.

27. tyὲ   bὲ   [n ye so   mîn ye] dyɔ
    "man the-C I-C house REL see erect" (C= nominal classifier)
    'The man is building the house that I saw.'

Except on the basis of analogy with adjectives which follow the noun
they modify, there is no way of deciding whether the RC in BAM-
BARA precedes or follows the deleted head, since the head is never
actually expressed. The failure of the strong pro-form mîn to be
moved to initial position seems to reflect the typological ambivalence
of this language.

   Replacive relative clauses are also found in other languages,
often, as in NAVAJO and BAMBARA, as alternatives to other RC
construction types in the same language.

   On the basis of the limited data reviewed here, we may venture
the following generalizations concerning replacive relative clauses:

V. If a language has replacive relative clauses, then in the
basic word order of the language verbs follow their objects,
and there is a general rule of left-to-right deletion of anaphora. (IU)

W. Replacive relative clauses contain clause-final relative
markers only if relative clauses of the same form occur
as prenominal clauses with an overt head. (IU)

X. If a relative marker is attached to Rel NP in a replacive
relative clause, Rel NP is not moved to the beginning or
the end of the clause by any process of relativization.

5. Correlative Relative Constructions

Except for the arguably interrogative pronoun mîn in BAMBARA
(see Schwartz 1971), the data so far have supported the generalization that relative pronouns, and in particular pronouns of interrogative form, are found only in postnominal RC's. It is also the case
that in the three types of relativization discussed so far, the relative
clause has preceded or followed or replaced Ant NP within a NP
constituent.

In the so-called correlative relative structure, the RC precedes
the entire clause containing the modified NP. In the typical case
neither Rel NP nor Ant NP is deleted; rather they are both marked
by correlative morphemes. These are typically an interrogative
pronoun or adjective attached to Rel NP and a demonstrative attached to Ant NP. Schwartz (1971) represents this arrangement in
his classification of RC types as follows:

xiv. $[_S \ldots WH \ldots]$ TH (N) ...

It is possible for the nominal head in one clause or the other (or
both if nonspecific) to be omitted, and some languages permit deletion of the entire Ant NP under some circumstances, giving the
form shown as xv.

xv. $[\ldots WH \ldots] \ldots \emptyset \ldots$

Many languages permit a correlative structure to be used when
the reference of the coreferential NP's is nonspecific, i.e., in
just those cases where most languages seem to allow replacive
RC's. ENGLISH, for example, has sentences such as those in 28.
and 29., where the b. and c. cases are derivable from the a. cases
by general principles of topicalization.

28. a. She gets whatever she asks for.
    b. Whatever she asks for she gets.   (type xv.)
    c. Whatever she asks for, that she gets. (type xiv.)

29. a. We liked what we saw.
    b. What we saw we liked.
    c. ?What we saw, that we liked.

Indefinites with lexical heads also seem to be generally tolerated in ENGLISH (30.).

30. a. She gets whatever toy she asks for.
    b. Whatever toy she asks for she gets.
    c. Whatever toy she asks for, that she gets.

But the construction with a definite lexical head is not permitted in many languages, including ENGLISH (31.).

31. a. *We liked what movie we saw.
    b. *What movie we saw, we liked.
    c. *What movie we saw, that we liked.

5.1 Correlation with word-order type

As far as can be determined from available descriptions of languages that utilize definite correlative constructions, all have basic SOV word-order. Surprisingly perhaps, none of these languages appears to use prenominal ad-relative clauses. Instead, some allow replacive or postnominal RC's or right-extraposed RC's as alternatives to the correlative construction. These facts suggest the following generalizations:

Y. Correlative relative constructions with a definite Rel NP and unreduced nominal heads are found only in languages in which verbs follow their objects in the basic word-order. (IU)

Z. If a language has correlative relative constructions, it does not have prenominal ad-relative clauses. (IU)

5.2 Some examples

To illustrate the correlative construction we may begin with HITTITE, whose relativization processes have been described in Berman 1972, Raman 1972, 1973 and Justus 1976.

In OLD HITTITE texts there are virtually no embedded, ad-relative clauses. The co-relative sentence generally consists of two clauses indistinguishable from the corresponding independent sentences, except for the form of the coreferential NP in each clause. Rel NP consists of a proform with the root ku- or contains a noun with a form of ku- attached as a determiner.[5] The various forms of ku- are also used in HITTITE as interrogative and indefinite forms, translating which, someone, etc. The modified NP in the second clause may take any of the following forms: demonstrative + head noun, demonstrative alone, pronominal clitic on the verb, or zero. Examples of HITTITE relative sentences, taken from Raman (1973), are given as 32. and 33.

32. [kuiš-   an āppa-ma uwatezzi] n-za apāš-   at
    "rel-nom-s-him back-ptc bring-3s ptc-ptc dem-nom-s-him
    dāi
    take-3s"[6]
    'The one who brings him back takes him for himself.'

33. [kušata-ma   kuit   piddait]   n-aš-kan šamenzi
    "brideprice-ptc rel-nom/acc brought-3s ptc-he-ptc give up-3s"
    'He shall give up the brideprice which he brought.'

The position of the relative ku- in its clause depends on the definiteness of the modified NP in ways that need not concern us here. In a small number of cases (about one or two in forty, according to Berman (1972)), the relative clause is extraposed to the right of the main clause, without any change in the internal structure of the two clauses.[7]

---

[5] Perlmutter and Orešnik (1973) argue that relative 'pronouns' are universally determiners whose heads may or may not be omitted. So far as I know, the facts of HITTITE are consistent with this claim.

[6] The various particles (ptc) are generally untranslated here.

[7] Justus (1976) argues the view that HITTITE is a topic-prominent (rather than subject-prominent) language (Li and Thompson 1974) and that the original and central function of ku- is attached to Rel NP when the modified NP serves as a focus, while Rel NP is unmarked when the clause modifies the theme of a segment of discourse. Justus further suggests (1976: 238) that "the semantic feature definite . . . tends to correlate with theme, indefinite with focus," which would explain the alternative interpretation of the ku- forms as indefinite. This

Sentence 34. illustrates the possibility of retaining the noun of Rel NP, with the order question-word + noun.

34. [[k]uiš   šagaiš   kīšari]   ta   LUGALi
    "rel-nom-s sign-nom-s occur-3s-med ptc king-dat-s
    SAL.LUGAL-ja tarueni
    queen   -ptc report-1p"
    'We will report any sign which occurs to the king and queen.'

In SANSKRIT and early GREEK a very similar construction is found, but with a morpheme yo (in GREEK ho) instead of the HIT-TITE relative indefinite ku-. Lehmann (1975:157) states that "even as late as Sanskrit and Homeric Greek, relative clauses are re-stricted in use; in Sanskrit for example they occurred only at the beginning or end of the principal clause according to Jacobi." Examples of SANSKRIT correlative RC's, taken from Lehmann (1974: 32), are given as 35. and 36.

35. [yás   tákr̥ṇoḥ   prathamám] sásy   ukthyàḥ
    "who these things you-did-first ptc-you-are to-be-praised"
    'You who did these things first are to be praised.'

36. [ye 'ṅgārā āsaṅs] te   'ṅgiraso 'bhavan
    "who coals were   these Angiras became"
    'Those who were coals became Angiras.'

Masica (1972) describes reflexes of the SANSKRIT correlative construction in the modern INDIC languages. The general form is shown in the following diagram:

$$[[\ldots J- (N_i) \ldots], \ldots DEM \; \emptyset_i \ldots]$$

In these languages the interrogative and indefinite have an initial k- (or s-), while the conditional, like the relative, has a j- stem (cf. Cardona 1965: 96). An example is 37., from GUJARATI (Ma-sica 1972:199).

(ftnt. 7 cont.)
suggests that the use of the correlative construction in HITTITE is quite similar to the situation illustrated above for ENGLISH. It would be interesting to know whether other languages that have correlative relative constructions exhibit this kind of theme/focus, definite/indefinite contrast, but published information on the point is lacking.

37. [JE   dhobii maarii saathe aavyo] TE ∅ DaakTarno bhaaii che
"which washerman my-with came that ∅ doctor's brother is"
'The washerman who came with me is the doctor's brother.'

In HINDI and GUJARATI the j-marked Rel NP is commonly moved
to the front of its clause (as here), and the correlative NP in the
second clause may also be fronted. In both GUJARATI and MARA-
THI it is possible to delete the j-marked NP, leaving the NP in the
second clause intact.

In these languages there is also, according to Masica, a postnominal relative construction of the type generally associated with
VO structure, with the demonstrative still attached to the modified
noun, and the j-morpheme functioning as an initial relative pronoun
within the subordinate clause.

We have already noted PERSIAN as an example of this group of
languages, SOV with postnominal RC's. Although not frequent, the
correlative construction is found in PERSIAN also, as in this example which Klaiman (n.d.) cites from Elwell-Sutton 1963: 114:

38. [be mard-i   ki   hadiye dodid] injo'st
"to man-Rel that gift   gave-(3) he here-is-he"
'The man to whom she gave the gift is here.'

In ad-relative clauses the suffix -i attaches to the head noun and
the following ki (the general complementizer) introduces the RC.
But here the preposition be marks mard-i as belonging to the RC.
Mard-i ki thus appears to be in a correlative relation with the
Ant NP, appearing here in the anaphoric form in 'he.'

Kuno (1974) has shown that SOV word-order with postnominal
RC's maximizes center-embedding, which seriously interferes with
sentence processing beyond two degrees of embedding. It is not
surprising then to find that SOV languages with post- rather than
prenominal relatives are the ones that provide correlative structures as an alternative.

Another language that exhibits correlative relative constructions
is BAMBARA. We have already noted that BAMBARA has replacive
RC's, as in example 27. above. As example 39., from Bird 1968,
shows, the relative marker mìn is used in correlative constructions
to link Rel NP with the demonstrative Ant NP in the following clause.

39. [n ye tyὲ mìn ye] ò   be fìni   fère
"I C man WH- see that C cloth-the sell" C=nom. classifier
'The man that I saw, he sells the cloth.'

Schwartz (1971) points out that although relative clauses may be
embedded, there is never any head noun + relative clause constituent in BAMBARA -- either the relative clause is preposed or the
head noun is omitted.

There is considerable evidence in support of the generalization
that relative pronouns of interrogative form precede the modified
noun only in correlative clauses. Since in BAMBARA the modified
noun is omitted whenever the relative clause is embedded, there
is no reason to consider this to be underlyingly a prenominal embedded clause. Rather, on the basis of overt noun-adjective order
in BAMBARA, Schwartz (1971:150) chooses to view the replacive
clause in 27. as representing a postnominal type from which the
head has been deleted.

The replacive construction does not permit recursion. But, as
Bird (1968) demonstrates, the left-branching correlative construction in BAMBARA permits unlimited recursion. This is illustrated
for two degrees of embedding in 40.

40. [[fìni mìn ka di   n ye], mùso mìn be ò fère],
    "cloth WH- is nice to me woman WH- C that sell
    à ye ò   fùru
    he C that-one marry" (literally: what cloth I like, what
    woman sells that, he married that one)
    'He married the woman that sells the cloth I like.'

We may ask under what conditions an SOV language will use
correlative constructions rather than prenominal RC's. So far as
I can see, the choice depends on the chance development of nominal
inflections instead of a verb suffix which would be appropriate to
prenominal RC structure. Klaiman (n.d.), who has addressed this
question points out that postnominal positioning of the RC in an
SOV language, as in the PERSIAN ad-relative, violates the functional principles cited by Kuno (1974). Right-extraposition of the
relative clause not only violates strict verb-final order but also
tends to place the clause far from Ant NP. The correlative construction, which places the clause in front of the matrix clause and
links Rel NP to the modified NP by the correlative morphemes,
avoids all these problems. (We will see in the next section that
PERSIAN also uses a type of right-extraposed correlative as an
alternative to the postnominal ad-relative.)

5.3 Generalizations

To summarize, the following additional generalizations concerning correlative relative constructions may be stated here:

AA. Relative markers of the same form as interrogative pronouns are found only in postnominal ad-relatives (and
their right-extraposed counterparts) and in correlative
relative clauses. (IU)

BB. In a correlative relative construction, Rel NP is marked
by a morpheme which serves also as an interrogative or
indefinite morpheme or by a unique relative morpheme,
and Ant NP, in the following clause, is marked by a
demonstrative or is reduced or deleted by general anaphoric processes. Demonstrative morphemes are not
attached to Ant NP if there is no relative marker in Rel
NP. (IU)

Among the languages cited above, the demonstratives are HITTITE
apā-, SANSKRIT and modern INDIC te, and BAMBARA ò.

6. Other Extraposed Relative Clauses

6.1 Optional extraposition

Many if not most languages appear to make some use of what I
have referred to as co-relative or extraposed RC constructions as
alternatives to the ad-relative or embedded clause types. The
correlative relative clause is just a distinctive type of left-extraposed RC, one with special markings that serve to link Rel NP
with the modified nominal.

Extraposition serves the function of preventing a long interruption between main sentence elements (the matrix verb and its
arguments) by a modifier. In many cases in a language that has
both ad-relative and co-relative clauses, the extraposed RC has
the same internal structure as its ad-relative counterpart.

In ENGLISH, for example, a RRC may be extraposed (to the
right only); acceptability of this construction depends on the length
of the material intervening between Ant NP and the clause, the
length of the clause, and the possibility of ambiguity in the identification of Ant NP, as illustrated in 41. The form is the same
whether the clause is embedded or extraposed.

41.a. The man came back who you said had been trying to see
you about helping him find a home for his cat.
 b. ?I gave the man a dollar who helped me change the tire.
 c. *The girl has a dog who lives across the street.

NAVAJO which as we have seen has both prenominal and replacive RC's, also permits right-extraposition. The internal form
of extraposed clauses is the same except that the anaphoric process
always operates from left to right, deleting Rel NP. Compare 42.
with 25. and 26. above.

42. Ashkii yádooɬtih   [tl'éédą́ą́' Ø athą́ą́   -ą́ą]
    "boy   FUT-3-speak last-night IMPERF-3-snore-REL"
    'The boy will speak who was snoring last night.'

In PERSIAN, ambiguity with extraposed RC's is reduced by the
presence of a relative suffix -i on Ant NP and by the fact that verb-
final word order makes sentences like 41.c impossible. Colarusso
(1975) points out that, although both the rule that attaches an object-
suffix to the verb and the process of right-extraposition are normally
optional in PERSIAN, either one or the other or both must be applied
as the length of the RC increases.

6.2 Obligatory extraposition

It was noted in footnote 7 above that initial RC's in HITTITE were
sometimes not marked with the correlative marker. According to
Justus 1975, this was generally the case in the earliest texts. In
later texts the presence of correlative marking depended on the
focus/theme distinction. If ad-relative clauses occurred at all in
HITTITE, they were quite rare.

Another language with both correlative and unmarked left-extraposed RC's is MABUIAG, a verb-final Australian language described
by Klokeid (1970), as reported in Andrews 1975.

MABUIAG has a correlative structure in which an indefinite
morpheme ngadh is used as a relative pronoun or determiner in
Rel NP and the modified NP is either omitted or pronominalized,
as illustrated in 43.

43. ⌈ ngadh   mabaigna-n os guudthapam-dhin] Ø uzaraidin
    "WH-ERG man-ERG horse kiss-PAST   went
    Bessaika
    Bessai-DAT"
    'The man who kissed a horse went to Bessai.'

This construction can also be used with no relativization of Rel NP,
as shown in 44. Note the three readings that this sentence can
receive.

44. [moegikazi -n gulaig gasamdhih], nui uzaraidhin Panaika
    "child-ERG captain touched   he went   Panai -DAT"
    'The child who touched the captain went to Panai.'
    'The captain who the child touched went to Panai.'
    'Because the child touched the captain, he went to Panai.'

The first ambiguity in sentence 44. arises because Rel NP is unmarked and the pronoun <u>nui</u> could refer either to the child or to
the captain. The pronoun could also be deleted. Sentence 44.,
but not 43., has an additional ambiguity in that the first clause
may be interpreted as expressing the <u>cause</u> of the event in the
second.

In addition to these constructions, MABUIAG also allows right-
extraposed RC's, but only with Rel NP marked by the relativizer
<u>ngadh</u>. In this construction, however, the modified NP is not
pronominalized, indicating that the pronominalization process
works from left to right only.

Hale 1974 provides considerable information concerning RC
constructions in WALBIRI and KAITITJ, both of which are also
languages of Australia. I will conclude this survey with a brief
summary of the WALBIRI data and some reference to Hale's interesting observations concerning problems of syntactic and semantic analysis.

In WALBIRI the word-order is typically S Aux O V in main
clauses, although a great deal of scrambling of constituents is permitted. The RC can either precede or follow the clause containing
the modified NP. In either case the RC contains a "referential
complementizer" <u>kutja</u>- (<u>ŋula</u> in some dialects). When the RC is
postposed, the usual case, Rel NP is deleted. When the clause is
preposed, Rel NP is retained, followed by <u>kutja</u>-, while the modified NP is either deleted or represented by the "anaphoric element"
(demonstrative) <u>ŋula</u>. In all cases the subordinate clause can alternatively receive a time-adverbial ("T-relative") interpretation,
provided that the two clauses make identical time reference. When
the modal and tense inflections of both clauses signify "uninstan-
tiated predications," the complementizer is <u>katji</u>- and the subordinate clause can also be interpreted as conditional. Examples (from
Hale 1974) are given in 45.

45.a. ŋatjulu-ḷu Ø-ṇa yankiri pantu-ṇu, kutja-lpa   ŋapa ŋa-ṇu
      "I-ERG AUX emu spear-PAST COMP-AUX water drink-PAST"
      'I speared the emu which/while it was drinking water.'

45. b. yankiri-ḷi kutja-lpa   ŋapa   ŋa- ṇu,   ŋatjulu-ḷu
       "emu-ERG COMP-AUX water drink-PAST I-ERG
       Ø-ṇa pantu-ṇu
       AUX spear-PAST"
       'The emu (which was) drinking water, I speared it.'
       'While the emu was drinking water, I speared it.'

     c. yankiri-ḷi kutja-lpa ŋapa ŋa-ṇu ŋula Ø-ṇa panta-ṇu
                                   "..., that AUX spear-PAST
       ŋatjulu-ḷu
       I-ERG"
       '...that one I speared/then I speared it.'

Hale points out that "it is universally true in Walbiri surface
and shallow structures that a NP-relative clause and its would-be
head never form a syntactic unit for the purposes of any well established rule of Walbiri syntax" (p. 23). There is no syntactic
evidence that Rel NP forms a constituent with the modified NP at
any level. Hale suggests that if the RC is generated outside of the
main clause, its meaning could be associated with a coreferential
NP in an adjacent (main) clause by a semantic rule. But he also
feels that there is a good possibility that

> apart from the strictly formal morphological and syntactic
> conditions on well-formedness **within** clauses, the overall
> well-formedness of a complex sentence containing a relative
> clause is not determined by the grammar, but rather by a sub-
> set of the system of maxims which are presumably observed
> in the construction of felicitous discourse .... (p. 23)

This possibility receives support from Hale's observation that the
semantic relations between the two clauses are not limited to the
NP-relative and T-relative interpretations.

Hale finds that there is no special rule of relativization of the
coreferential NP's in WALBIRI relative constructions; pronominalization and deletion operate generally from left to right and in the
same way as in other complex sentences. Thus there appear not
to be either rules or structures in WALBIRI that are uniquely associated with relativization.

Hale argues (p. 43) that if the postposed RC is taken as basic
and the preposed clause derived by a movement transformation,
the anaphoric element ŋula can be accounted for as a "trace" of
the clause, left behind by the copying rule. This would explain

why ŋula appears only when the modifying clause is preposed and
why it occurs even when there is no NP-relative interpretation (so
that it cannot in all cases be considered a remnant of a modified
NP). This is apparently the only argument for deriving one construction from another by a movement rule. There is no evidence
for a rule of extraposition of RC's from an NP-internal position.

6.3 Generalizations

In languages that have ad-relative or replacive RC's, extraposed
RC's may also be allowed. Optional extraposition is favored when
embedding would cause serious interruption of the matrix clause;
it is facilitated by correlative markings on both Ant NP and Rel NP,
but both left- and right-extraposed RC's are found without such
markings. Right-extraposition is found in both OV and VO languages and in languages having either prenominal or postnominal
RC's. We may note especially the following correlations:

CC. If a language has both postnominal and right-extraposed
     RRC's, the internal structure of the RC is the same in
     both positions. (IU)

DD. The most consistent OV languages (e.g. JAPANESE and
     TURKISH) have prenominal relatives and no right-extra-
     posed RC's. Languages with extraposed clauses (including
     correlative RC's) are not rigidly OV in structure in other
     respects. (IU)

EE. In OV languages pronominalization and deletion of refer-
     entially identical NP's may operate either from left to
     right or from right to left in both co-relative and ad-
     relative clauses. (IU)

There are some verb-final languages that have no embedded,
ad-relative clauses. Furthermore, in some cases the extraposed
clauses interpreted as relatives have no marking that results from
processes of relativization; the only properties that distinguish
such clauses from independent clauses are the result of general
anaphoric processes and perhaps general subordination marking.
In some languages the interpretation of an initial clause as relative
rather than adverbial is an entirely semantic or pragmatic matter.

There is thus no evidence for a transformational derivation of
such co-relative clauses from an embedded position by a rule of
extraposition. Although it would appear considerably easier to

state rules that depend on coreference in terms of a single NP
constituent containing both Ant NP and Rel NP, as has always been
done for ENGLISH (but see Schulz 1974), there is no empirical
basis for such an analysis in some languages.

Perlmutter and Ross (1970) have pointed out that even in ENGLISH
extraposed RC's cannot always be derived from an embedded position in which the condition of referential identity is met. The difficulty arises in sentences such as 46. containing extraposed clauses
with "split antecedents."

46. A man entered the room and a woman went out who were
quite similar.

In such cases there is no embedded source for the RC that meets
the condition of referential identity, since the who of the RC is not
coreferential with either a man or a woman, and the sentence has
no grammatical form in which the clause is not extraposed. This
appears to be strong evidence that either there is no transformational rule of extraposition or it applies in the opposite direction,
to embed postposed clauses.

In other languages, as we have seen, co-relative clauses may
be structurally identical with adverbial clauses rather than being
associated with ad-relative clauses in the same language. This
situation suggests again that co-relative clauses should not be
looked upon in general as merely relocated variants of embedded
clauses.

The following additional generalizations are suggested by the
data of co-relative clauses examined here.

FF. Extraposed relative clauses may be unmarked by any syntactic process of relativization and may be formally identical
with adverbial clauses of the same language. (IU)

GG. In a language in which verbs normally follow their objects,
the existence of extraposed relative clauses does not imply
the existence of embedded RC's in that language. (IU)

HH. If in a language the verb normally precedes its objects,
there are no left-extraposed RC's, and if there are right-
extraposed RC's, then there are postposed RC's. (IU)

II. If a language has right-extraposed RC's, then it also has
either embedded or left-extraposed RC's. (IU)

7. Summary

In all languages some clauses (not always finite) function to restrict the reference of a nominal in another clause. In some cases the modifying (restrictive relative) clause is positioned before or after the clause containing the modified nominal and may be syntactically indistinguishable from other semantically subordinate clauses in the same position. If the relative clause precedes, the coreferential NP's in the two clauses are frequently marked by correlative morphemes. Languages that use correlative constructions of this sort have OV word-order and may also have relative clauses that replace or follow the modified nominal. Other OV languages, expecially those of consistent OV typology, usually have prenominal relative clauses, typically marked by a relative suffix on the verb and by deletion of Rel NP, but Ant NP may be deleted instead of Rel NP, so that the relative clause in effect replaces the head nominal.

In VO languages relative clauses usually follow Ant NP in an embedded position or are extraposed to the right. Relativization involves pronominalization or deletion of Rel NP and, especially in SVO languages, a clause-initial connective particle or relative pronoun. If no relative marker appears in initial position in the clause, then either the subject or the verb is in initial position; if the verb is initial it usually bears a relative marker.

The generalizations which have been stated in this paper are supported by the data of relativization in a number of languages, but are subject, of course, to modification or refutation on the basis of additional language data. In their present form they may serve as a summary of observations on the nature of relative clauses across languages, with which the data of additional languages may be compared. As such generalizations are refined, they afford an increasingly solid empirical basis for the formulation of explanatory principles in functional and psychological terms.

BIBLIOGRAPHY

Sources of information (data and analysis) on the languages mentioned in this paper are indicated below, with reference to items in the bibliography which follows.

AKAN   Schachter 1973
ALBANIAN   Morgan 1972

AMHARIC	Givón 1972, Hudson 1972
ARABIC	Schwartz 1971
ARABIC, TUNISIAN	Craig 1971
BAMBARA	Bird 1968, Schwartz 1971, Keenan (class lecture, 1974, Linguistic Institute, Univ. of Massachusetts)
BASQUE	de Rijk 1972
CHINESE, MANDARIN	Tai 1973, Hou 1974
DANISH	Sadock 1972
DUTCH	Schwartz 1971
DYIRBAL	Dixon 1969, Schwartz 1971
ENGLISH, MIDDLE and OLD	Personal knowledge, Schulz 1974
ENGLISH, BLACK	Tyson 1976
EWE	Benveniste 1957-8
FRENCH	Personal knowledge
GERMAN	Loetscher 1972
GREEK, ANCIENT	Adams 1972, Lehmann 1975
GUARANÍ	Pederson 1974
GUJARATI	Cardona 1965, Masica 1972
HAUSA	Schachter 1973
HEBREW	Schwartz 1971
HEBREW, COLLOQUIAL	Givón 1973
HINDI	Masica 1972, Klaiman n.d.
HITTITE	Berman 1972; Raman 1972, 1973; Justus 1976
HOTTENTOT	Andrews 1975
HUNGARIAN	Schwartz 1971
INDONESIAN	Schwartz 1971
IRISH, OLD	Lehmann and Lehmann 1975
JACALTEC	Craig 1973
JAPANESE	Kuno 1976, McCawley 1976, de Rijk 1972
KAITITJ	Hale 1974
LATIN	Schwartz 1971
MABUIAG	Andrews 1975
MALAGASY	Keenan 1972b
MALAY (BAHASA MALAYSIA)	Omar 1973, Frommer 1974
MARATHI	Masica 1972
NAVAJO	Hale and Platero 1974, Platero 1974
OJIBWE	Kenneth Truitner (personal com.)
PAPAGO	Andrews 1975
PERSIAN	Colarusso 1975, Tabaian 1975, Elwell-Sutton 1963 (cited in Klaiman n.d.)
QUECHUA	Andrews 1975
RUMANIAN	Keenan 1974

RUSSIAN   Loop 1974, Anatole Liberman (personal
                              com.)
SANSKRIT   Lehmann 1974, 1975
SPANISH   Richart Barrutia, Helena Pereyra,
                              Guillermo Villegas (personal com.)
TAMIL   de Rijk 1972
TIBETAN, CLASSICAL   Andrews 1975
TURKISH   de Rijk 1972, Andrews 1975, Şeyda Balkan
                              (personal com.)
UMBUNDU   Wald 1970
VIETNAMESE   Payne 1974, Kenneth Truitner (personal
                              com.)
WALBIRI   Hale 1974
ZAPOTEC   Rosenbaum 1971

BIBLIOGRAPHY

Adams, Douglas Q. 1972. Relative clauses in Ancient Greek. The
  Chicago which hunt, ed. by P.M. Peranteau, J.N. Levi and
  G.C. Phares, 9-22. Chicago: Chicago Linguistic Society.

Andrews, Avery. 1971. A typological survey of relative clauses.
  Ms., M.I.T.

_____. 1975. The grammar of relative clauses. (Draft of Part
  II of doctoral dissertation, M.I.T.)

Bach, Emmon. 1965. On some recurrent types of transformations.
  Report of the annual round table meeting on linguistics and language studies, 3-18. (Georgetown University Monograph Series
  on Language and Linguistics 18) Washington: Georgetown Univ.
  Press.

_____. 1971. Questions. Linguistic Inquiry 2. 153-166.

Benveniste, Émile. 1957-58. La phrase relative: problème de
  syntaxe générale. Bulletin de la Société de Linguistique 53,
  fasc. 1.

Berman, Howard. 1972. Relative clauses in Hittite. The Chicago
  which hunt, ed. by P.M. Peranteau, J.N. Levi and G.C. Phares,
  1-8. Chicago: Chicago Linguistic Society.

Bird, Charles S. 1968. Relative clauses in Bambara. Journal of West African Languages 5. 35-47.

Cardona, George. 1965. A Gujarati reference grammar. Philadelphia: University of Pennsylvania Press.

Colarusso, John. 1975. Syntactic rule ordering in Modern Persian. Wiener Linguistische Geschichte 9. 3-10.

Craig, Colette G. 1971. Notes on the formation of complex sentences in Tunisian Arabic, with emphasis on the relative clause. Unpublished paper, Harvard University.

_____. 1973. General characteristics of Jacaltec relative clauses. (Draft of a chapter of doctoral dissertation, Harvard University.)

de Rijk, Rudolf P.G. 1972. Relative clauses in Basque: a guided tour. The Chicago which hunt, ed. by P.M. Peranteau, J.N. Levi and G.C. Phares, 115-135. Chicago: Chicago Linguistic Society.

Dixon, R.M.W. 1969. Relative clauses and possessive phrases in two Australian languages. Language 45. 35-44.

Downing, Bruce T. 1973. Toward a typology of adjective clauses. Paper presented at the Linguistic Society of America Annual Meeting, San Diego, December 28-30.

_____. 1974. Correlative relative clauses in universal grammar. Minnesota Working Papers in Linguistics and Philosophy of Language 2. 1-17.

_____. (forthcoming) Typological regularities in postnominal relative clauses. Current issues in linguistics: language typology, bilingualism, and experimental linguistics, ed. by Fred Eckman. Washington, D.C.: Hemisphere.

Elwell-Sutton, L.P. 1963. Elementary Persian grammar. Cambridge: Cambridge University Press.

Ferguson, Charles. 1971. A sample research strategy in language universals. Working Papers on Language Universals [WPLU] 6. 1-22. Stanford University.

Frommer, Paul R. 1974. Some notes on relativization in Bahasa Malaysia. Unpublished paper, University of Southern California.

Givón, Talmy. 1972. Pronoun attraction and subject postposing in Bantu. The Chicago which hunt, ed. by P.M. Peranteau, J.N. Levi and G.C. Phares, 190-197. Chicago: Chicago Linguistic Society.

_____. 1973. Some trends in spoken Hebrew relativization. Unpublished paper, Department of Linguistics, U.C.L.A.

Gundel, Jeannette Marie. 1974. The role of topic and comment in linguistic theory. Doctoral dissertation, University of Texas at Austin.

Hale, Ken. 1974. The adjoined relative clause in Australia. Unpublished paper, M.I.T.

Hale, Kenneth and Paul R. Platero. 1974. Aspects of Navajo anaphora: pronominalization and relativization. Diné Bizaad Nánilįįh/Navajo Language Review 1. 9-28.

Hou, John Y. 1974. Relative clause formation in Chinese. Unpublished paper, University of Southern California.

Hudson, Grover. 1972. Why Amharic is not a VSO language. Studies in African Linguistics 3.1. 127-165.

Justus, Carol. 1976. Relativization and topicalization in Hittite. Subject and topic, ed. by Charles N. Li, 213-245. New York: Academic Press.

Keenan, Edward L. 1972a. On semantically based grammar. Linguistic Inquiry 3. 413-462.

_____. 1972b. Relative clause formation in Malagasy (and some related and some not so related languages). The Chicago which hunt, ed. by P.M. Peranteau, J.N. Levi and G.C. Phares, 169-189. Chicago: Chicago Linguistic Society.

_____. 1974. The logical status of deep structures (logical constraints on syntactic processes). Proceedings of the Eleventh International Congress of Linguistics, 477-490, discussion 490-495. Bologna: Societa editrice il Mulino.

Keenan, Edward L. and Bernard Comrie. 1972. Noun phrase accessibility and universal grammar. Paper presented at the Annual Meeting of the Linguistic Society of America, Atlanta, December 27-29.

Klaiman, M.H. 1976. A functional view of some syntactic movement typologies. Master's essay, Department of Linguistics, University of Chicago.

_____. (no date) Another look at the position of relative clauses and complementizers (with particular reference to SOV languages). Unpublished paper, University of Chicago.

Klokeid, T.J. 1970. Research on Mabuiag. Ditto, M.I.T. (Reported in Andrews 1971.)

Kuno, Susumu. 1973. The structure of the Japanese language. Cambridge, Mass.: M.I.T. Press.

_____. 1974. The position of relative clauses and conjunctions. Linguistic Inquiry 5. 117-136.

_____. 1976. Subject, theme, and the speaker's empathy -- a reexamination of relativization phenomena. Subject and topic, ed. by Charles N. Li, 417-444. New York: Academic Press.

Lehmann, R.P. and W.P. Lehmann. 1975. An introduction to Old Irish. New York: Modern Language Association of America.

Lehmann, Winfred P. 1974. Proto-Indo-European syntax. Austin, Texas: University of Texas Press.

_____. 1975. A discussion of compound and word order. Word order and word order change, ed. by Charles N. Li, 149-162. Austin, Texas: University of Texas Press.

Li, Charles N. and Sandra A. Thompson. 1974. Subject and topic: a new typology of language. Paper presented at the Annual Meeting of the Linguistic Society of America, New York, December 27-30.

Loetscher, Andreas. 1972. Some problems concerning Standard German relative clauses. The Chicago which hunt, ed. by P.M. Peranteau, J.N. Levi and G.C. Phares. Chicago: Chicago Linguistic Society.

Loop, Terry. 1974. Russian relative clauses. Unpublished paper, University of Southern California.

Martin, Larry Walter. 1972. Appositive and restrictive relative clauses in English. Doctoral dissertation, University of Texas at Austin.

Masica, Colin. 1972. Relative clauses in South Asia. The Chicago which hunt, ed. by P.M. Peranteau, J.N. Levi and G.C. Phares, 198-204. Chicago: Chicago Linguistic Society.

McCawley, James. 1976. Japanese relative clauses. Japanese generative grammar, ed. by Masayoshi Shibatani, 295-306 (Syntax and Semantics, 5). New York: Academic Press.

Morgan, J.L. 1972. Some aspects of relative clauses in English and Albanian. Th Chicago which hunt, ed. by P.M. Peranteau, J.N. Levi and G. C. Phares, 63-72. Chicago: Chicago Linguistic Society.

Omar, Asmah Haji. 1973. Noun phrases in Malay. Language Sciences 26. 12-17.

Payne, John. 1974. Vietnamese — typological check. Unpublished ditto, University of Cambridge.

Pederson, Donald. 1974. An investigation of relative clauses in Guaraní. Unpublished paper, University of Southern California.

Perlmutter, David M. and Janez Orešnik. 1973. Language-particular rules and explanation in syntax. A festschrift for Morris Halle, ed. by Stephen R. Anderson and Paul Kiparsky, 419-459. New York: Holt.

Perlmutter, David M. and J.R. Ross. 1970. Relative clauses with split antecedents. Linguistic Inquiry 1. 350.

Platero, Paul R. 1974. The Navajo relative clause. International Journal of American Linguistics 40. 202-246.

Raman, Carol Justus. 1972. The Hittite relative construction. Paper presented at the Annual Meeting of the Linguistic Society of America, Atlanta, December 27-29.

_____. 1973. The Old Hittite relative construction. Doctoral dissertation, University of Texas at Austin.

418 Bruce T. Downing

Rosenbaum, Harvey. 1971. Constraints in Zapotec questions and relative clauses. On the theory of transformational grammar, 191-216 (Report to NSF GS-2468). Austin, Texas: Department of Linguistics, University of Texas at Austin.

Ross, John Robert. 1967. Constraints on variables in syntax. Doctoral dissertation, M.I.T.

Sadock, Jerrold. 1972. A conspiracy in Danish relative clause formation. The Chicago which hunt, ed. by P.M. Peranteau, J.N. Levi and G.C. Phares, 59-62. Chicago: Chicago Linguistic Society.

Schachter, Paul. 1973. Focus and relativization. Language 49. 19-46.

Schulz, Muriel R. 1974. Relativization in Old English. Unpublished paper, California State University, Fullerton.

Schwartz, Arthur. 1971. General aspects of relative clause formation. WPLU 6.139-171.

Tabaian, Hessam. 1975. Conjunction, relativization, and complementation in Persian. Colorado Research in Linguistics 5. 1-182.

Tai, James H-Y. 1973. Chinese as an SOV language. Papers from the ninth regional meeting of the Chicago Linguistic Society, ed. by Claudia Corum, T. Cedric Smith-Stark, and Ann Weiser, 659-671. Chicago: Chicago Linguistic Society.

Thompson, Sandra Annear. 1971. The deep structure of relative clauses. Studies in linguistic semantics, ed. by Charles Fillmore and D.T. Langendoen, 79-94. New York: Holt.

Tyson, Adele. 1976. Pleonastic pronouns in Black English. Journal of English Linguistics 10. 54-59.

Wald, Benji. 1970. Relativization in Umbundu. Studies in African Linguistics 1.131-156.

Contrastive Emphasis and Cleft Sentences

HELGA HARRIES-DELISLE

ABSTRACT

The purpose of this paper is to investigate how languages express contrastive emphasis. It is argued that all contrastively-emphasized constructions have underlying cleft sentences, independent of whether the surface structure is an equational or a non-equational one. It is furthermore argued that emphatic word orders are systematic and predictable given a certain language type, and that the position of the object plays an essential role both in cleft and non-cleft emphatic constructions.

This is a somewhat modified version of the paper published in Working Papers on Language Universals, No. 12, November 1973, pp. 85-144.

CONTENTS

1. Introduction

Contrastive emphasis is used by a speaker to mark a constituent as being in contrast with another structurally identical constituent.[1] The contrast made can be syntactically explicit as in 1. or 2.:[2]

1. a. John bought a camel.
   b. No, John didn't buy a camel, John bought a donkey.

2. a. John bought a camel.
   b. No, John bought a donkey.

Languages use syntactic as well as phonological means to express contrastive emphasis: the phonological means are increased loudness (stress) and a concomitant rise in pitch, and tonal changes, while the syntactic means comprise emphatic word orders, emphatic morphemes, and an emphatic sentence type, i.e. cleft sentences. It appears that phonological means are secondary, that is there are no languages that solely make use of phonological means to express contrastive emphasis. On the other hand, there are languages that solely use syntactic means to express emphasis. In this paper I will argue for the hypothesis that all sentences that contain a contrastively-stressed constituent are derived from an underlying cleft construction. To these cleft sentences rules apply -- optionally or obligatorily -- reducing the cleft construction to a greater or lesser degree. The ultimate reduction is that of a complex cleft sentence, e.g., 1.b. to a surface simplex, e.g., 2.b. The degree of reduction possible differs from language to language.

The above hypothesis is supported by semantic as well as by syntactic evidence. The semantic evidence is the same for all languages, i.e. a cleft sentence and the corresponding simplex contain identical presuppositions and make identical assertions.

---

[1] In this paper I will limit myself to the discussion of the contrastive emphasis of noun phrases. It is obvious that not only noun phrases but practically any element can be contrastively emphasized. One of the reasons for the above limitation is that grammars hardly ever provide any information about emphasis on non-nominal constituents. Another reason is that contrastive emphasis of other constituent types, for instance of verbs, seems to involve a slightly different mechanism.

[2] Underlining of a constituent indicates that it carries contrastive emphasis.

For instance, in 3. below the presupposition is that someone bought the camel, while it is asserted that Bill was the buyer.

3. a. The one who bought the camel was <u>Bill</u>.
     b. <u>Bill</u> was the one who bought the camel.
     c. It was <u>Bill</u> who bought the camel.
     d. <u>Bill</u> bought the camel.

On the other hand, the syntactic support for the above hypothesis is extremely diverse, including case marking, negation, and subject-verb agreement. However, before considering this evidence, I will briefly investigate the nature of a cleft sentence so that we have certain criteria which will help us to decide whether or not a given sentence can be classified as a cleft.

2. Manifestation of Cleft Sentences

2.1 Elements of a cleft sentence

The term <u>cleft</u> sentences is used in this paper to refer to sentences like 4.a. to 4.c. below.

4. a. The one who helped us was <u>Frank</u>.
     b. <u>Frank</u> was the one who helped us.
     c. It was <u>Frank</u> who helped us.

In recent linguistic writings[3] on the subject, sentences like 4.a. and 4.b. are referred to as pseudo-cleft sentences, while sentences like 4.c. are generally called cleft sentences. In my opinion this distinction is not a deep structure distinction, but is due to a movement rule. Evidence for this hypothesis will be presented later. Cleft sentences as in 4. are equational sentences which establish an identity between a known or presupposed entity and a focused entity which represents the new information. The presupposed information is contained in the subject, the new information in the predicate. The subject of a cleft sentence consists of a head noun like <u>the one</u>[4] which is modified by a restrictive relative clause. The head noun is always a neutral noun like <u>the one</u>, <u>the man</u>, <u>the person</u>, <u>the he</u>, which is more closely defined by the relative clause.[5]

---

[3] Jespersen 1949, Lees 1963, Akmajian 1970, and Schachter 1973.

[4] This head noun is only present in 4.a. and 4.b. It was deleted in 4.c.

[5] I will not investigate here what forms restrictive relative clauses can take. For some discussion see Schwartz 1971, and for a typology of restrictive relative clauses see Keenan 1972.

The predicate contains the focus constituent which in the above example is <u>Frank</u>.

   The subject-head and modifying relative clause on the one hand and the focus constituent on the other stand in an X = Y identity relation to each other. In some languages this relation is expressed by a copula morpheme, in others by simple juxtaposition. In languages that distinguish between a 'be' verb of existence and the copula, it is the latter that will show up in a cleft construction as for instance in MANDARIN CHINESE.

5. <u>copula:</u>   mao shìh dùng-wù
             "cat be animal"
             'The cat is an animal.'

6. <u>'be' of existence:</u> ta dzài wu lǐ
             "he be room in"
             'He is in the room.'

7. dzuó-tien méi lái de rén $\begin{Bmatrix} *dz\grave{a}i \\ sh\grave{i}h \end{Bmatrix}$ Yohàn
   "yesterday not came RM[6] person be John"
   'The one who didn't come yesterday was John.'

In some languages cleft constructions can contain all of the above-specified features, as for instance in ENGLISH, GERMAN, MANDARIN CHINESE, JAPANESE, HUNGARIAN, KIHUNG'AN and SWAHILI.

8. GERMAN:
   Derjenige, der segelt, ist <u>mein Bruder</u>.
   'The one who is sailing is my brother.'

9. MANDARIN CHINESE:
   wǒ kàn-jìen de rén shìh <u>Yohàn</u>.
   "I   saw RM person be John"
   'The one who I saw is John.'

10. JAPANESE:
    Mary   ō   butta hito   wa   <u>Bill</u> da.
    "Mary obj. mk. hit person subj. mk. Bill is"
    'The one who hit Mary is <u>Bill</u>.'

---

[6]RM stands for relative marker, which may be a relative pronoun, an invariable linker-subordinator, a nominalizer, etc.

11.   HUNGARIAN:
      <u>John</u> volt az, aki New York-ba repült.
      "John was that, who New York-to flew"
      '<u>John</u> was the one who flew to New York.'

12.   KIHUNG'AN:
      kiim   ki   a-swiim-in Kipes zoon   kwe k<u>i</u>t
      "thing pron. PA-buy-past Kipes yesterday is chair"
      'What Kipes bought yesterday is a chair.'

13.   SWAHILI:
      <u>mtu   huyu</u> ndiye   ninayem   taka
      "man this is-he I-am-who-him wanting"
      '<u>This man</u> is the one I wanted.'

In other languages the surface structure of an underlying clefted
construction is more reduced.   That is, the copula as well as the
neutral head noun and/or the relative clause marker can be absent.

2.2 <u>Absence of the copula</u>

It is a well-known fact[7] that many languages do not make use
of a copula morpheme to establish an identity between two constituents.   In general these languages simply juxtapose the two constituents,[8] e.g.:

14.   TAGALOG:
      mataas ang babae
      "tall   the woman"
      'The woman is tall.'

15.   ARABIC:
      Ali mu? alimun.
      "Ali teacher"
      'Ali is a teacher.'

16.   JAVANESE:
      aku muréd
      "I student"
      'I am a student.'

---

[7]See Benveniste 1960, Bach 1967.

[8]The identity relation may be signaled by a pause between the
two constituents.

It is therefore not surprising that in these languages the copula is also absent from cleft sentences which, though more complex, are basically identical to equational sentences as in 14. to 16.

17. TAGALOG:
si   Rosa ang   siyang maganda
"construct. m. Rosa nomin. he-RM pretty"
'Rosa is the one who is pretty. '

18. ARABIC (colloquial):
Ali huwa-lli jā
"Ali he-RM came"
'Ali is the one who came. '

19. INDONESIAN:
orang yang kepada siapa saya memberihan buku ini
"man RM to   resp. pron. I   give   book this"
'The man is the one to whom I gave this book. '

2.3 Absence of the neutral head noun

An optional variation found in many languages is the absence of the neutral head noun.

20. GERMAN:[9]
Der segelt, das ist mein Bruder.
"who is sailing that is my brother"
'The one who is sailing is my brother. '

21. ENGLISH:
What Frank lost was his watch.

22. MANDARIN CHINESE:
Yohàn kàn-jièn de shìh   ge   nán rén
"John saw   RM be classifier male person"
'The one who John saw is a man. ' (as opposed to a woman)

23. AMHARIC:
əssu naw yamattaw
"he is RM-came"
'He is the one who came. '

---

[9]In GERMAN head-deletion is for most speakers more acceptable if dislocation of the subject NP has taken place as in the sentence above where das 'that' is the neutral demonstrative pronoun.

24. INDONESIAN:
bukan saya yang beladjar bahasa Indónésia
"not   I   RM studying language Indonesian"
'I am not the one who studies Indonesian. '

2.4 Absence of relative clause marker

Another constituent that may or may not occur is the morpheme
that marks relative clauses. In ENGLISH its occurrence is optional
in some environments.

25. It is John I saw yesterday.

In DERA, a CHADIC language, and in RUSSIAN both the copula
and the relative clause marker can be absent.

26. RUSSIAN:
Eto   ego ja vstretil včera.
"{it   } he I met yesterday"
 {this}
'It is he whom I met yesterday. '

27. DERA:
wuni wun kapa kurei
"they ones plant corn"
'They are the ones who plant corn. '

2.5 Identical constraints on relative clause   and emphatic
     sentences

It has been shown above   that in some languages one or two of
the three features that mark the presence of an underlying cleft
sentence are optionally or obligatorily absent in the surface structure. In other languages, all three of the features, i.e. the neutral
head noun, the copula, and the relative clause marker, are absent.
However, the presence of an underlying cleft construction is revealed by the fact that in these languages relative clauses and emphatic constructions are subject to identical constraints. These
constraints can be accounted for if we assume that emphatic constructions are derived from underlying cleft sentences that contain
a relative clause. For instance, a number of languages have a
special tense form that occurs in relative clauses, emphatic constructions, and usually also in word questions. Sapir (1965) reports
for DIOLA-FOGNY, a language of the Senegal, that the verbal of a
relative clause is marked by the suffix -ɛ .

28. balba:b   bagi   lɛnɛ
"sun-the classifier-rel. linker-is cool-ɛ"
'the cool sun' (i. e. the sun which is cool)

The same marker also shows up in emphatic constructions, where it emphasizes the constituent that precedes the verb.

29. <u>kukila</u> kujɛ dakar
"they went-ɛ Dakar"
'<u>They</u> are the ones who went to Dakar.'

30. <u>dakar</u> kujɛ
"Dakar they-went-ɛ"
'It is to <u>Dakar</u> that they went.'

In TELUGU, a DRAVIDIAN language, the verb form of an emphatic construction is the relative participle plus the suffix <u>di</u>:

31. a. <u>neutral</u>:
raamaa raawu jarmaniininci kotta kaaru teppincEEDu
"Rama Rao Germany-from new car get"
'Rama Rao got a new car from Germany.'

   b. <u>emphatic</u>:
<u>jarmaniininci</u> kotta kaaru teppineindi raama raawu
"Germany-from new car get   Rama Rao"
'It is from <u>Germany</u> that Rama Rao got a new car.'

In KIKUYU, the copula nĩ occurs sentence initially in an emphatic construction and the form of the verb is that of a verb of a dependent clause:

32. a. <u>neutral</u>:
nĩn gahaica kĩrĩma kĩu rũciũ
"I shall-climb that hill tomorrow"
'I shall climb that hill tomorrow.'

   b. <u>emphatic</u>:
nĩ <u>kĩrĩma kĩu</u> ngahaica rũciũ
"is that hill I-shall-climb tomorrow"
'It is <u>that hill</u> that I shall climb tomorrow.'

MALAGASY, according to Malzac, has a relative verb form for which he does not explicitly state that it also occurs in emphatic statements. However, with one or two exceptions, all of his examples of the relative verb form involve emphatic constructions containing the emphatic marker <u>no</u> instead of the relative marker <u>izay</u>:

33. <u>ela</u>   no tsy nahitako anao
   "long-time EM not see-I   you"
   'It is a <u>long time</u> that I didn't see you.'

In KANURI, a SAHARAN language, subject emphasis is expressed by a construction in which the verb, if positive and past tense, is identical with the verb form of the relative past, i.e. the past tense form used in relative clauses. The same relative past also occurs in information questions. In HAUSA, according to Schachter (1973), certain person and aspect markers have to occur, e.g. 35., 36. Furthermore, certain pronominalization and deletion processes that are involved in the formation of emphasized constructions are identical to the pronominalization and deletion processes in relative clauses.

34. HAUSA:
   sun gaya wa yaron
   "they told to child"

35. yaron da suka gaya $\begin{Bmatrix} \text{masa} \\ \text{wa} \end{Bmatrix}$
   "child that they told to"

36. <u>yaron</u> ne suka gaya $\begin{Bmatrix} \text{masa} \\ \text{wa} \end{Bmatrix}$
   "child is they told   to"
   'It's the <u>child</u> that they told.'

According to Newman (1970), it is very common in CHADIC languages that relative clauses share syntactic characteristics with emphatic constructions and also with information questions. For instance, in TERA the verb of a neutral declarative is marked by the affix <u>wa</u> in the perfective tense. This affix is absent in relative clauses, emphatic constructions and information questions.

Constraints shared by relative clauses and emphatic constructions are not only restricted to tense and aspect but can also involve negation, agreement, constraints on deletion, and nominalization. Takizala states that in KIHUNG'AN, a BANTU language, relative clauses, emphatic constructions and information questions all use a negative particle which differs from the negative particle of neutral, unembedded declaratives:

37. <u>lo</u> i-mween kit
"neg I-saw chair"
'I didn't see the chair.'

38. kit ki a-<u>khoon</u>-in Kipes ku-suum
"chair pron. PA-fail-past Kipes to-buy"
'The chair that Kipes didn't buy.'

*kit ki lo a-swiim-in Kipes

39. Kipes ka-<u>khoon</u>-in ku-suum <u>kit</u> zoono
"Kipes Pa-fail-past to-buy chair yesterday"
'Kipes did not buy <u>a chair</u> yesterday.' / 'What Kipes did
not buy yesterday is <u>a chair</u>.'

*Kipes <u>lo</u> ka-swiim-in <u>kit</u> zoono

A further constraint on embedded sentences in KIHUNG'AN is that
the object pronoun -- which may be used as a definitizer or as a
pronoun in unembedded sentences -- cannot occur in relative clauses
and cannot occur in emphatic constructions.

Schachter and Schachter/Fromkin discuss a tonal change in
AKAN which occurs in relative clauses and also in emphatic constructions. In these sentence types certain underlying low tones
are replaced by high tones.

40. a. <u>neutral</u>: ɔ́wɔ̀ Éngìrésì
"he-in England"
'He is in England.'

b. <u>emphatic</u>: Kɔ̀fí nà ɔ́wɔ̀ Engìrési!
"Kofi RM he-in England"
'It's <u>Kofi</u> who's in England.'

In SOMALI, on the other hand, a certain agreement pattern links
the emphatic constructions to the relative clause. If in SOMALI
the subject of a sentence is emphasized, the verb is always in the
3rd person singular, independent of the number of the subject. In
other words, agreement does not take place. And this is also true
for relative clauses, i.e. in relative clauses the verb is always in
the 3rd person singular.

41. a. <u>neutral</u>: ma?allimíín-tìì wáà yì-máàdd-àà̀n
"the teachers (nom) are come (pl)"
'The teachers came.'

    b. <u>emphatic</u>: maʔallimíín-tìì báà ti-maadd-a
                    "the teachers (acc) is come (sgl)"
                    'It is the teachers who came.'

All of the above examples clearly show that relative clauses and
emphatic constructions are closely related. It has been hypothesized above that the similarities between the two structures are
due to the fact that all emphatic constructions are derived from
underlying cleft sentences which contain a relative clause. This
claim will be investigated in more detail later. Before, however,
some data will be presented which supports the claim that emphatic
sentences are underlying copula constructions in which an equational relation is established. Even in sentences which superficially
look like a non-copulative declarative, traces of an underlying copulative construction are still detectable.

2.6 Signs of an underlying equational structure

    Frequently we will find that languages make use of a special
marker to indicate emphasis, i.e. in emphatic constructions a
morpheme, either bound or free, appears in the immediate neigh-
borhood of the emphasized constituent. In some instances the
relation of the emphatic morpheme to other grammatical morphemes, especially to a copula, can be easily established, while
in other cases such a relation cannot be readily isolated. The
position of the emphatic marker (EM) is generally between the
emphasized constituent (C_ε) and the remaining sentence (X). Thus
we get the following two combinations:

    a. C_ε EM X

    b. X EM C_ε

Examples are found in many AFRICAN languages, in the MALAYO-
POLYNESIAN language group, and in INDIAN languages like BEN-
GALI, HINDI and MARATHI.

    42. MALAGASY:[10]
        a. <u>neutral</u>:   tia anao izahay
                    "love you we"
                    'We love you.'

---

[10] Where available both the neutral and the emphatic versions
are provided.

b. emphatic: izahay no tia anao
"we   EM love you"
'It is <u>we</u> who love you. '

43. TAGALOG:[11]
   a. <u>neutral</u>:   maganda ang bata
"beautiful the child"
'The child is beautiful. '

   b. <u>emphatic</u>:   <u>ang bata</u> ay maganda
"the child EM beautiful"
'It is the <u>child</u> that is beautiful. '

44. INDONESIAN:
   a. <u>emphatic</u>:   menteri lah tuan itu
"minister EM man that"
'That man is a minister. '

45. AKAN:
   a. <u>neutral</u>:   ɔwɔ Éngìrésì
"he-in England"
'He is in England. '

   b. <u>emphatic</u>:   <u>Kòfí</u> nà ɔ́wɔ́ Éngìrési
"Kofi EM he-in England"
'It is <u>Kofi</u> who is in England. '

46. KAREKARE:
   a. <u>neutral</u>:   tamakən   ranho
"sheep enter"
'The sheep entered. '

   b. <u>emphatic</u>:   ran na <u>tamakən</u>
"enter EM sheep"
'It is the <u>sheep</u> that entered. '

47. NGIZIM:
   a. <u>neutral</u>:   kadlam papiya
"you lied"
'You lied. '

---

[11]Schachter and Otanes (1972) state that the <u>ay</u> inversion forms
are not necessarily more emphatic, but rather that 43.b. can be
used as a more formal version of 43. a.

b. emphatic: kadlam papiya-n ei
"you   liod   EM you"
'It is you who lied.'

48. BADE:
a. neutral: Dlaagəna d'aaguraa-gi
"Dlaagena called-you"
'Dlaagena called you.'

b. emphatic: d'aaguraa-gi-k Dlaagəna
"called-you-EM Dlaagena"
'It is Dlaagena who called you.'

While in the above examples the emphatic constituent is either
sentence final or sentence initial, there are also languages where
the emphatic morpheme emphasizes a preceding constituent that
is not sentence final or sentence initial. Two of these languages
are LUGBARA, a NILO-SAHARAN language, and MARATHI.

49. LUGBARA:
a. emphatic: bǎ   ma á-dríi nĩ   aŋgǒ dĩmà ópi-ǒrö
"they-set-up my brother EM country their
chief"
'They set up my brother as chief of their
country.'

50. MARATHI:
a. neutral: mi tyana pəyse dein
"I them money give"
'I give them money.'

b. emphatic: mi tyanats pəyse dein
"I them money give"
'I give them money.'

Apparently this is also true for BENGALI and HINDI, though all
of the examples available to me show subject emphasis and therefore initial position of the emphasized constituent.

51. HINDI:
a. neutral: ami jabo
"I go"
'I am going.'

b. emphatic: ami-i jabo
"I EM go"
'It is I who am going.'

In some languages it is fairly easy to establish that the emphatic morpheme is either a copula, acts as a copula, is an old form of the copula, or is a contraction of the copula and the relative clause marker. In HAUSA, for instance, the emphatic nē particle also occurs in construction which indicate equivalence:

52. Audu nē malami
     "Audu is teacher"
     'Audi is a teacher.'

In INDONESIAN, the lah particle is sometimes used as a copulative element, and in LUGBARA ni occurs after nominal and adjectival predicates without emphatic function.

53. LUGBARA:
     ágú ʔdàri ɔ́pí (-mvá)-nï
     "man this chief's son is"
     'This man is a chief('s son).'

A language where the emphatic morpheme appears to be the result of a merger between the copula and the relative pronoun is AKAN. In AKAN the so-called emphatic particle is na which emphasizes a preceding constituent. According to Balmer, Grant (1929) na is a merger of ne, an older form of the copula, and of the relative clause introducer a. While in the above-discussed languages it can be shown that the emphatic marker is identical with the copula, such a relationship is not as easily established in other languages. One of the reasons is that most of the languages that use an emphatic marker in a cleft construction do not have a copula in other equational sentences. In some languages, for instance in some of the CHADIC and CUSHITIC languages, the constraints on the verb form of the emphatic sentence reveal that the emphatic sentence has an underlying cleft construction even though the nature of the emphatic marker cannot be clearly established. Further research will show whether or not all emphatic morphemes can be related in some form or other to a copula. If not, this will not invalidate the hypothesis argued for in this paper. All it will say is that some languages mark the focus constituent by using a special morpheme, comparable to the way some languages mark the focus constituent by using phonological means like increased loudness or a change in tone.

Another sign of an underlying equational structure is case assignment, as for instance in SOMALI. In SOMALI the emphasized constituent is always in the accusative which according to Tucker and Bryan is the unmarked case of SOMALI.

54. a. Subject emphasis:
       nin-kíí   báà lị̀bạ̀ạ̀h-íí arka
       "man-acc. is lion-acc. sees"
       'It is the man who sees the lion. '

    b. Object emphasis:
       nín-kíí báà lị̀bạ́ạ̀h-ị́ị́ àrkàà
       "man-acc. is lion-nom. sees"
       'It is the man that the lion sees.'

This fact can be explained if we assume that emphatic sentences
are derived from underlying equational sentences because in SO-
MALI the predicate nominal of an equational sentence is always in
the accusative case. On the other hand, if we do not make the above
assumption, then we need an ad hoc constraint which insures that
the emphasized constituent is always marked for accusative.

Another indication of an underlying equational construction is
the presence of a pause between the known information and the
focused constituent. In the examples below a pause is indicated
by a comma.

55. TSWANA:
    a. neutral:
       rrê   orêkilê   dikgômo maabane
       "my-father he-bought cattle yesterday"
       'My father bought cattle yesterday. '

    b. emphatic:
       orêkilê   dikgômo maabane, rrê
       "he-bought cattle yesterday my-father"
       'It is my father who bought the cattle yesterday. '

56. TELUGU:
    a. neutral:
       raamaaraawu jarmaniininci kotta kaaru teppincEEDu
       "Rama Rao   Germany-from new car   got"
       'Rama Rao got a new car from Germany. '

    b. emphatic:
       raamaaraawu jarmaniininci teppincindi, kotta kaaru
       "Rama Rao   Germany-from got   new car"
       'It is a new car that Rama Rao got from Germany. '

It is fairly common to use a pause instead of a copula element to
indicate an equational relation, e.g. in RUSSIAN, VIETNAMESE

and TATAR. The pause demarcates the line between the subject or known information and the predicate which contains the new information. This pause becomes especially important in longer sentences where the demarcation line is not immediately obvious from the structure of the sentence.

The claim that 55. b. and 56. b. are equational structures is further supported by the position of the emphasized constituent in sentence final position. The position of the emphasized constituent in a cleft sentence is discussed in more detail in section 4.

3. The Underlying Structure of a Cleft Sentence

Earlier in this paper it was hypothesized that all emphatic constructions are derived from underlying cleft sentences and evidence from many languages was presented to show that the underlying cleft structure is still traceable in the surface structure, even though cleft constructions can undergo considerable reductions in certain languages. In the following I will discuss the underlying structure of cleft sentences and the rule component required to generate the various surface manifestations of emphatic constructions.

In recent linguistic writings cleft sentences have been fairly widely investigated. [12] Jespersen (1949) suggested for instance that cleft sentences are derived from underlying simplex sentences by the insertion of it is -->WH:

57. The man called. --> It is the man who called.

As Lees (1963) points out, such a derivation of a complex structure from a simplex one does not account for the fact that we can have different tense and aspect markings in the two verbs of the cleft and also that we can get negation in one or the other or in both of the sentences.

58. It must have been my mother who flew to New York.
59. It is not my mother who flew to New York.
60. It is my mother who didn't fly to New York.
61. It is not my mother who didn't fly to New York.

---

[12]See Jespersen 1949, 1969; Lees 1963; Chomsky 1970; Bach/Peters 1968; Akmajian 1970; Schachter 1973. For a discussion of Bach/Peters, Chomsky, and Akmajian, see Harries 1972. For a discussion of Schachter's proposal, see below.

On the basis of the above data it has therefore been generally
assumed that cleft sentences are derived from underlying complex
structures. Less agreement is found, however, when we look at
the kinds of underlying structures proposed. Lees suggested that
clefts are derived from it + AUX + be + complement structures.
Chomsky and Akmajian assumed a structure in which the head noun
of the subject relative clause is the it morpheme which shows up
in sentences like 58. to 61.,[13] while Bach/Peters assume a head
noun the thing, thus excluding cleft constructions with the one.
That the it morpheme plays such a prominent role in nearly all
of the above analyses seems to be mainly due to the fact that all
of these linguists based their analyses on data from ENGLISH. In
ENGLISH cleft constructions with it are very common, but they
do not exist in most other languages. That is, even though as far
as I could determine all languages do have cleft constructions of
the form a) the one who ... is X, only relatively few languages
have a corresponding form like b) it is X who .... And whenever
a language has b), it also has a).

It will be argued in this paper that the it pronoun is a pro-subject
which is introduced transformationally. The exact conditions under
which the pro-subject has to be introduced will be discussed in more
detail in the following section. I will argue that certain languages
require the insertion of a pro-subject whenever the underlying subject noun phrase has been extraposed. This analysis has the advantage of accounting for the paraphrase relationship between sentences
like 62. and 63. below:

62. John was the one who helped us.
63. It was John who helped us.

62. and 63. are paraphrases because they contain identical presuppositions and make an identical assertion and consequently should
be derived from the same underlying form. However, no analysis
which assumes a structure as in 64. will be able to relate 62. and
63. in a non-ad hoc way.

---

[13] The major difference between Akmajian and Chomsky is that
the former assumes that the underlying predicate dominates the
focus constituent, while the latter assumes that the predicate dominates a dummy symbol which is replaced by one of the noun phrases
of the subject relative clause with the help of an extraction rule.

64.

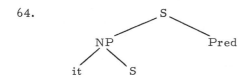

Based on the above evidence I will therefore assume that in all languages the underlying structure of cleft sentences contains a head noun of the form <u>the one</u>, <u>the person</u>, <u>the he</u>, <u>the thing</u> [14] (<u>the place</u>, <u>the time</u> -- not discussed here). I am not sure about the exact feature specification of the neutral head noun. It will always be third person; furthermore, in some languages it will be marked for number (ENGLISH, GERMAN, FRENCH), humanness (ENGLISH, MANDARIN CHINESE), gender (GERMAN, FRENCH) and possibly a few other features. However, given that it is a neutral noun, it will not contain any unique semantic features, that is features that would differentiate it from every other noun in the language.

Problematic for setting up a universal underlying structure is the linear order in which the constituents occur. In other words, the question is whether there is one universal linear order, whether there are different underlying orders which in turn are reflected in the different surface orders or whether there is no underlying syntactic order at all and surface orders are imposed by a set of language specific ordering rules. I tend to favor the latter position. However, this paper is not the place to argue these questions. All I will therefore say at this point is that the underlying structure of all cleft constructions contains a subject and a predicate. The subject is composed of a neutral head and a relative clause which restricts the large set specified by the head noun. The subject contains the known information, while the predicate contains the focus constituent which is the new information. [15] Whether or not a copula

---

[14] In VIETNAMESE the neutral head noun is identical with the classifier of the focus constituent.

ong Ba ông   ây hay di Dalat lắm.

"Mr. Ba nr. cl. that often go Dalat very"

'Mr. Ba is the one who very often goes to Dalat. '

[15] 'New information' here is meant in the sense used by Halliday (1967): "The focus of the message, it is suggested, is that which is presented by the speaker as being new, textually (and situationally) non-derivable information... But the non-predictability of the new does not necessarily imply factually new information; the newness may lie in the speech function, or it may be a matter of contrast with what has been said before or what might be expected " (pp. 205-6).

is a part of the underlying form is an open question. Bach (1967)
argued that the copula should be inserted by a transformation for
the following reasons:

    a. The copula is predictable.
    b. It complicates the grammar if the copula is in the deep
        structure.
    c. There are languages that do not have a copula.

a. seems to hold for ENGLISH but will have to be tested for other
languages. b. is difficult to verify as it subsumes the existence of
a complete grammar for a given language and of an evaluation mea-
sure. c. is true for a few languages like TAGALOG and BLACK-
FOOT. More common is it to find languages in which the copula
can be absent under certain condition. Most commonly it can be
absent in the present tense but not in the other tenses (e.g. DRAVI-
DIAN languages, RUSSIAN, HEBREW, JAPANESE, BANTU languages). In BENGALI it can be absent in the present tense if the
sentence is affirmative.

The opposite stand from that of Bach was taken by Ross (1969a,
1969b). In the first paper Ross claims that 'be' is a true verb
which is present in the deep structure and is marked for the feature
$\begin{bmatrix} +V \\ -Adj \end{bmatrix}$. [16] No evidence is presented in support of this claim. In
the second paper Ross argues that auxiliaries are underlying
main verbs and he assumes that have and be belong into this class.
There is, however, evidence from negation that even though modals
like can and must appear to be underlying main verbs, this claim
cannot be extended to auxiliaries like have and be. [17] The claim
that be is a main verb is also weakened if we look at other languages
besides ENGLISH. Outside of the INDO-EUROPEAN family we
rarely find copulas that behave like true verbs. That is, very often
the copula is an invariant morpheme which does not undergo the
inflectional processes that true verbs undergo. And frequently the
copula will have a unique negative form, i.e. negation of the copula
and of true verbs does not take the same form. Furthermore, the
copula is not always found in the position of the verb. Ferguson
(1972) notes that in languages that develop a pro-copula, [18] this form

---

[16] For a discussion see Darden 1969.

[17] For a discussion see Harries 1973a.

[18] Pro-copula is defined as "an expression whose primary function is non-copulative, used in place of zero in a copulative sentence."
(Ferguson 1972:95).

will tend to occur between the subject and the complement, even in SOV languages like BENGALI or in VSO languages like the SEMI-TIC ones.

65. BENGALI:
    a. cheliṭi chatro
        "boy   student"
        'The boy is a student.'

    b. cheliṭi $\begin{Bmatrix} \text{hɔě} \\ \text{holo} \\ \text{hocce} \end{Bmatrix}$ chatro
        "boy   is   student"
        'The boy is a student.'

    c. cheliṭi chatro nɔě
        "boy   student not-is"
        'The boy is not a student.'

In 65.b. the pro-copula occurs in medial position while in 65.e. the negative copula occurs in the final verb position.

66. ARABIC (Classical)
    a. Aliyun mu?alimun
        "Ali   a-teacher"
        'Ali is a teacher.'

    b. Aliyun huwa mu? alimun
        "Ali   he   a-teacher"
        'Ali is $\begin{Bmatrix} \text{a} \\ \text{the} \end{Bmatrix}$ teacher.'

    c. Aliyun huwa laisa mu? aliman
        "Ali   he   not-be a-teacher"
        'Ali is not a teacher.'

SEMITIC languages like ARABIC can optionally use a third person pronoun or a demonstrative as pro-copula which will occur in medial position even though ARABIC is a VSO language, and the negative verb follows the pro-copula.

All of the above outlined facts indicate that within a universal framework the copula cannot be considered a true verb as Ross proposes. On the other hand, if the copula is inserted by rule, there is no node to attach it to. I therefore assume that a pro-node is present in the underlying form of equational sentences. This node is marked for being <u>stative</u> and it is directly dominated by S. The vagueness of the node allows for the great variation in its

surface realization across languages. Some languages will not
realize it at all; others will realize it before nouns but not before
adjectives, or in the past tense but not in the present tense. In
ENGLISH it behaves in many respects like a verb, in other languages it is a grammatically unique element that does not share
any feature with the verb or any other constituent type.

4. The Surface Order of Cleft Sentences

Above I said that no underlying linear order will be assumed for
cleft sentences. However, cleft sentences do have a surface order
and I want to argue that this order depends on the language type.
That is, we can make the following prediction where S = subject NP,
Cop = copula, and F = focus NP.[19]

	Language type	Basic cleft construction		
a.	SVO	S	Cop	F
b.	SOV	S	F	Cop
c.	VSO	Cop	S	F

While examples of a. and b. are readily available, this is not true
for c. I was not able to find data of a VSO language with a copula
in initial position. As mentioned earlier, ARABIC uses a third
person pronoun as pro-copula in medial position. MAASAI, another
VSO language, has zero copula and so does TAGALOG. Unfortunately, I was not able to get any data for LOTUHO, an EAST AFRI-
CAN language with VSO order and an overt copula. It is essential,
however, that in all three language types the position of the focus
nominal corresponds to the position of the object in a non-cleft
sentence, i.e. in SVO and VSO languages the focus nominal occurs
in final position while in SOV languages it occurs in medial position. The underlined constituents are the object and the focus constituent respectively.

67. SVO -- S Cop F
     a. John bought a book.
     b. What John bought is a book.

68. SOV -- S F Cop
     JAPANESE:
     a. John   wa   Mary   o   butta
         "John subj. m. Mary obj. m. hit"
         'John hit Mary. '

---

[19]VOS languages like MALAGASY were not included in this discussion for lack of information about this language type. It appears,
however, that VOS languages should have a basic Cop F S cleft order.

b. Mary o butta no wa <u>John</u> da
"Mary obj. m. hit RM subj. m. John is"
'The one who hit Mary is <u>John</u>.'

69. VSO -- (Cop) S F
ARABIC (Colloquial):
a. kataba Ali ar-risāla
"wrote Ali the-letter"
'Ali wrote <u>the letter</u>.'

b. elli kataba ar-risāla huwa Ali
"RM wrote the-letter he Ali"
'The one who wrote the letter is <u>Ali</u>.'

Above it has been argued that if we know the position of the object
in a neutral sentence, we can predict the basic position of the focus
constituent in a cleft sentence. Later on it will be shown that the
position of the object is also the basic position of an emphatic constituent in a non-equational sentence,[20] even if the emphatic constituent is the surface subject of that sentence. However, before
investigating non-neutral emphatic word orders in surface simplexes,
I will discuss the rule component required to transform underlying
cleft constructions into emphatic surface forms, which may or may
not be clefts.

5. The Rule Component

The rules discussed below are assumed to be part of the universal
grammar though not all of the languages will have all of the rules.
Constraints on the individual rules are assumed to be language specific. The five major rules involved are: 1) deletion of the neutral
head noun, 2) deletion of the relative clause introducer, 3) deletion
of the copula element,[21] 4) extraposition, and 5) predicate lowering.

5.1 Deletion rules
5.1.1 Deletion of neutral head noun Given that the head noun
in a cleft construction does not carry any information which is not

---

[20] I shall refer to these non-equational sentences as <u>simplex</u>
<u>sentences</u> even though they could obviously also contain embedded
clauses.
[21] The rule that deletes the [static] node in certain languages
under certain conditions will not be discussed. Some of the conditions under which the copula node is deleted were mentioned above.

also present elsewhere in the sentence,[22] it is not surprising that in most languages the head noun is optionally deletable at least in some environments (see examples below). Whether there are languages in which the head noun is obligatorily deleted in all environments I was not able to establish. In some languages like ENGLISH and FRENCH, the head noun is obligatorily deleted if subject extraposition applies, while in languages like HUNGARIAN and KIHUNG'AN head deletion is optional even after subject extraposition.

70. a. ? It's <u>my friend</u>, the one who came.
    b. It's <u>my friend</u> who came.

71. FRENCH:
    a. ? C'est <u>mon ami</u> celui qui est venu.
       ? 'It's <u>my friend</u> the one who came. '

    b. C'est <u>mon ami</u> qui est venu.
       'It's <u>my friend</u> who came. '

72. HUNGARIAN:
    a. Nem <u>John</u> volt az aki New York-ba repűlt.
       "Not John was that who New York-to flew"
       'It was not <u>John</u> who few to New York. '

    b. Nem John volt aki New York-ba repűlt.
       "Not John was who New York-to flew"
       '<u>John</u> was not the one who flew to New York. '

73. KIHUNG'AN:
    a. (kwe) <u>kít</u> kiim ki a-swiim-in Kipes zoon
       "(is) chair thing that bought Kipes yesterday"
       '<u>The chair</u> is the thing that Kipes bought yesterday. '

    b. (kwe) <u>kít</u> ki a-swiim-in Kipes zoon
       "(is) chair that bought   Kipes yesterday"
       'It is <u>the chair</u> that Kipes bought yesterday.

---

[22] That is, all of the information on number, gender, humanness, etc. which can be present in the head noun can be predicted from the focus constituent, as there exist cooccurrence restriction between the head noun and the focus constituent to the effect that all of the features of the head noun must also be found in the focus constituent. For instance, a head noun marked for <u>masculine</u> can only be placed into an equivalence relation with another masculine noun.

While some languages require the obligatory deletion of the neutral head noun in some environments, others do not permit the deletion of the head noun under certain conditions. In MANDARIN CHINESE, for instance, head deletion is constrained in long sentences. The presence of the head helps to delineate the subject and to establish the equational relation. In ENGLISH the deletion of the head noun is not possible if it is human, e.g.:

74. a. The one who sang was Caruso.
    b. *Who sang was Caruso.

However, as will be seen later, a structure like 74.b. above is required to generate surface simplexes from underlying cleft sentences (see predicate lowering). It therefore appears that even in ENGLISH head deletion can take place in any environment but that either subject extraposition or predicate lowering have to apply if the head noun has been deleted.

5.1.2 <u>Deletion of the relative clause marker</u> The deletability of a relative clause marker does not seem to depend on the nature of the marker itself. That is, there is no evidence that the marker is more often deletable if it is invariant than if it is a pronoun. For instance, in ENGLISH the relative pronoun can be deleted if certain conditions are met (e.g. if the relativized constituent is not the subject of the relative clause).

75. a. The one (who) I met is <u>John's brother</u>.
    b. The one (who is) studying in the library is <u>a friend of mine</u>.

Deletion of the relative pronoun is also possible in BANTU languages like KIHUNG'AN:

76. a. (kwe) <u>kít</u> ki a-swiim-in Kipes zoono
       "(is) chair that bought   Kipes yesterday"
       'It is <u>a chair</u> that Kipes bought yesterday.'

    b. (kwe) <u>kít</u> Kipes a-swiim-in zoono
       "(is) chair Kipes bought   yesterday"
       'It's <u>a chair</u> that Kipes bought yesterday.'

77. a. (kwe) <u>Kìpés</u> wu a-swiim-in kit zoono
       "(is) Kipes who bought   chair yesterday"
       'It's <u>Kipes</u> who bought a chair yesterday.'

    b. (kwe) <u>Kìpés</u> a-swiim-in kit zoono
       "(is) <u>Kipes</u> bought   chair yesterday"
       'It's <u>Kipes</u> who bought a chair yesterday.'

In GERMAN, on the other hand, relative pronouns are not deletable.

78. a. Derjenige, den du trafst, ist Peters Bruder.
        'The one whom you met is Peter's brother.'

     b. *Derjenige du trafst ist Peters Bruder.

Among the languages with an invariant relative clause marker,
MANDARIN CHINESE does not allow the deletion of the marker
de. In MALAGASY, on the other hand, the relative marker izay
does not show up in emphatic constructions. Both head and relative marker deletion can apply in some languages.

79. TAGALOG:
     a. si   Rosa ang siyāng nakita niya
         "constr. m. Rosa nom. he-RM saw he"
         'Rosa is the one whom he saw.'

     b. si   Rosa ang nakita niya
         "constr. m. Rosa nom. saw he"
         'Rosa is the one whom he saw.'

80. KIHUNG'AN:
     a. (kwe) kit kiim ki a-swiim-in Kipes zoono
         "(is) chair thing that bought Kipes yesterday"
         'It's a chair that Kipes bought yesterday.'

     b. (kwe) kit Kipes a-swiim-in zoono
         "(is) chair Kipes bought yesterday"
         'It's a chair that Kipes bought yesterday.'

5.2 Reordering rules
5.2.1 Extraposition or fronting   Up to now we have discussed
those rules that delete certain elements from an underlying cleft
construction. Another type of change that cleft sentences can undergo is that constituents can be moved around and reordered resulting in sentences like 82. and 83.

81. The one who stole the cheese is Frank.
82. Frank is the one who stole the cheese.
83. It is Frank who stole the cheese.

Both 82. and 83. are derived from 81. by movement rules. The
effect in both 82. and 83. is that the focus constituent is brought
closer to the front of the sentence. It is a well-known fact that

frontal position is a position of emphasis in most languages. The question is: how does the focus constituent get into that position and how do we account for the difference between 82. and 83? Logically, there are two possible alternatives that will convert 81. into 82. and 83., i.e. either the focus constituent is fronted, or the known information is placed at the end of the sentence. The first rule I will call <u>focus fronting</u>, the second, <u>extraposition</u>. It is possible that either both of these rules exist in natural language or that only one or the other one does. If we assume the existence of both rules, we can account for the difference between 82. and 83. above.

84. a. Basic order: The one who stole the cheese is <u>Frank</u>.
      b. Fronting: <u>Frank</u> the one who stole the cheese is.
      c. Copula placement: <u>Frank</u> is the one who stole the cheese.

85. a. Basic order: The one who stole the cheese is <u>Frank</u>.
      b. Extraposition: is <u>Frank</u> (the one) who stole the cheese.
      c. Pro-subj. insertion: It is <u>Frank</u> who stole the cheese.

If, on the other hand, we assume that focus fronting is the only reordering rule that applies to cleft sentences, then the derivation of 83. above requires one additional rule, namely <u>copula fronting</u>.

86. a. Basic order: The one who stole the cheese is <u>Frank</u>.
      b. Focus fronting: <u>Frank</u> (the one) who stole the cheese is.
      c. Copula fronting: is <u>Frank</u> (the one) who stole the cheese.
      d. Pro-subj. insertion: It is <u>Frank</u> who stole the cheese.

On the other hand, one might want to say that focus fronting can optionally move both the focus constituent and the copula simultaneously, converting 86. a. directly to 86. c. The existence of such an optional constraint on fronting -- though technically feasable -- appears nevertheless ad hoc and is not corroborated by any additional evidence. But even if we assumed such a constraint, the copula placement rule in derivation 84. would still be required, though not the copula fronting rule assumed in derivation 86. If, on the other hand, we assume that extraposition is the only movement rule that applied to cleft sentences, no copula placement or fronting rule is required.

87. a. Basic order: The one who stole the cheese is <u>Frank</u>.
      b. Extrap. (subj. NP): is <u>Frank</u> (the one) who stole the cheese.
      c. Pro-subj. insertion: It is <u>Frank</u> who stole the cheese.

88. a. Basic order: The one who stole the cheese is <u>Frank</u>.

b. Extrap. (copula):   The one who stole the cheese <u>Frank</u> is.
c. Extrap. (subj. NP): <u>Frank</u> is the one who stole the cheese.

The difference between derivation 87. and 88. is that in 87. extraposition first applied to the subject NP, while in 88. it first applied
to the copula. This means that extraposition can apply either to the
constituent that is sentence initial as in 87., or to the constituent
that precedes the focus constituent (pre-focus constituent) as in 88.,
the common condition being that the extraposed elements contain
known information. The assumption that extraposition can apply at
two different points of the string will appear ad hoc at this point of
the analysis. It will, however, be shown later during the discussion of marked word orders in emphatic simplex sentences that we
can only account for the many and seemingly unsystematic variations
found in emphatic word order if we make the above assumptions
about extraposition. That is, we have to assume that: 1) extraposition is the only reordering rule that changes the linear order of
constituents in an emphatic sentence; 2) extraposition applies to
old or presuppositional material only; 3) extraposition can apply
to the constituent which is in sentence initial position, <u>or</u> to the
constituent that precedes the focus constituent.

5.2.2 <u>Extraposition</u>   For the moment I will not present any
further support for the above assumptions but will rather show how
extraposition accounts for cleft sentences in various languages. In
some of the above derivations a rule called <u>pro-subject insertion</u>
placed the neutral pronoun <u>it</u> into the position of the subject NP
after the latter had been extraposed. This rule is not restricted
to ENGLISH. It also applies in RUSSIAN (éto 'this'), FINNISH
(<u>se</u> 'this'), FRENCH (<u>ce</u> 'this'), HEBREW (<u>ze</u> 'this') and GERMAN
(<u>es/das</u> 'it/that').

89. HEBREW:
    a. Basic order:
        ze she pagash et axiv   haya <u>Yonatan</u>
        "this RM met DOM brother-his was John"
        'The one who met his brother was <u>John</u>.'

    b. Extraposition (subject NP):
        haya <u>Yonatan</u> (ze) she pagash et axiv
        "was <u>John</u> (this) who met DOM brother-his"

    c. Pro-subject insertion:
        ze haya <u>Yonatan</u> she pagash et axiv
        "this was John who met DOM brother-his"
        'It was <u>John</u> who met his brother.'

90. FRENCH:
   a. Basic order: Celui qui est venu est <u>François</u>.
                          'The one who arrived is <u>François</u>.'

   b. Extraposition: est <u>François</u> (celui) qui est venu
                          "is <u>François</u> (one) who arrived"

   c. Pro-subj. insertion: C'est <u>François</u> qui est venu.
                              'It is <u>François</u> who arrived.'

As far as I could establish, pro-subject insertion is restricted to SVO languages, where it takes place if the subject NP is extraposed.

91. a. Basic order: S - Cop - F
     b. Extraposition: Cop - F - S
     c. Pro-subj. insertion: PS - Cop - F - S

A probable explanation for the pro-subject insertion rule is that a surface order as in 91.b., where the verbal element is sentence initial, signals a yes-no question in many languages. In order to avoid ambiguity, a pro-subject is inserted. This hypothesis is supported by the fact that no pro-subject insertion takes place in SVO languages in which initial position of the verb does not signal a question.[23] This is for instance true for BANTU languages like SWAHILI and KIKUYU, and for MANDARIN CHINESE. In all three of these languages, 91.b. above is a possible surface construction.

92. SWAHILI:
   a. mtu aliye fika ni <u>mwalimu</u>
       "man who arrived is teacher"
       'The one who arrived is <u>a teacher</u>.'

   b. ni <u>mwalimu</u> mtu aliye fika
       "is teacher man who arrived"
       'It is <u>a teacher</u> who arrived.'

93. KIKUYU:
   a. nĩn gahaica kĩrĩma kiu nĩ <u>rũciũ</u>
       "I shall-climb that hill is tomorrow"
       '(The time) when I shall climb that hill is <u>tomorrow</u>.'

---

[23] The hypothesis that only those languages have pro-subject insertion in which initial position of a verb signals a question is also supported by the fact that VSO languages have no pro-subject insertion. Obviously, verb initial position cannot signal a question in VSO languages.

    b. nĭ <u>rŭciŭ</u> ngahaica   kĭrĭma kĭu
        "is tomorrow I shall-climb that hill"
        'It is <u>tomorrow</u> that I shall climb that hill.'

94. MANDARIN CHINESE:
    a. kàn-jièn nà-ge nán-rén   de (rén) shìh <u>Yohàn</u>
        "saw   that-cl. male-person RM (person) is John"
        'The one who saw that man is John.'

    b. shìh <u>Yohàn</u> kàn-jièn nà-ge nán-rén
        "is John   saw   that-cl. male-person"
        'It is <u>John</u> who saw that man.'

That SOV languages do not have pro-subject insertion is due to the
fact that subject extraposition will not result in a sentence initial
position of the copula.

  95. a. Basic order: S F Cop
       b. Extraposition: F Cop S

Examples of 95. are:

  96. HUNGARIAN:
    a. Basic order: Az aki New York-ba repült <u>János</u> volt.
                         "that who New York-to flew John was"
                         'The one who flew to New York was John.'

    b. Extraposition: <u>János</u> volt az aki New York-ba repült.
                         "John was that who New York-to flew"
                         '<u>John</u> was the one who flew to New York.'

  97. AMHARIC:
    a. Basic order: ya maṭṭaw saw əssu naw
                         "RM came man he is"
                         'The one who came is <u>he</u>.'

    b. Extraposition: əssu naw ya maṭṭaw
                         "he is RM came"
                         '<u>He</u> is the one who came.'

    It was argued earlier that extraposition can apply to the sentence
initial constituent or to the pre-focus constituent, provided, of course,
that these constituents represent old information. Thus, given an SVO
language, we would expect that the following variations occur:

  98. a. Basic order: S Cop F
       b. Extraposition sentence initial: Cop F S
       c. Extraposition: ?F S Cop

99. a. Basic order: S Cop F
      b. Extraposition pre-focus   ?S F   Cop
      c. Extraposition: F Cop S

The question marks indicate that I did not find any languages that have either 98. c. or 99. b. as a variation of the basic order. I can only speculate why this should be so. 98. c. and 99. b. are identical in that in both orders the copula occurs in final position, an order which S Cop F (or SVO) languages seem to avoid. However, it is conceivable that a "free" word order language would also have 98. c. and/or 99. b. as alternate orders of the basic one. While a basic S Cop F order allows for four variations, S F Cop orders (SOV languages) are much more restricted, given that the focus constituent is in second position.

100. a. Basic order: S F Cop
       b. Extraposition: F Cop S

100. b. is the only variation found in SOV languages (see the HUNGARIAN and the AMHARIC examples above).

VSO languages, on the other hand, should allow as wide a range as SVO languages:

101. a. Basic order: Cop S F
      b. Extraposition sentence initial: S F   Cop
      c. Extraposition: F Cop S

102. a. Basic order: Cop S F
      b. Extraposition pre-focus: Cop F S
      c. Extraposition: F S Cop

Unfortunately, I have very limited data from VSO languages. In ARABIC, as mentioned earlier, a. does not occur but rather S Cop F, if we want to assume that the third person pronoun functions as a copula. As a variation, c. is found in ARABIC. But further research is definitely needed before any substantive claims can be made.

As pointed out earlier, not all of the forms occur in all languages. Furthermore, there are languages that apparently do not have the extraposition rule, at least not for nominals. Thus in JAPANESE, an SOV language, the expected alternative with the focus constituent in initial position is not grammatical, nor is any other word order variation.

103. a. Mary   ō   butta hito   wa   <u>Bill</u> da
          "Mary obj.mk. hit person subj.mk. Bill is"
          'The one who hit Mary is <u>Bill</u>.'

      b. *<u>Bill</u> da Mary   ō   butta hito   wa
          "Bill is Mary obj.mk. hit person subj.mk."

In MANDARIN CHINESE, extraposition can only apply to the sentence initial and not to the pre-focus constituent and furthermore, the focus constituent has to correspond to the subject of the relative clause. Thus both 104.b. and 105.b. are ungrammatical.

104. a. kàn-jièn nà-ge nán - rén   de shìh <u>Yohàn</u>
          " saw   that-cl. male-person RM is   John"
          '<u>John</u> is the one who saw that man.'

      b. *<u>Yohàn</u> shìh kàn-jièn nà-ge nán - rén   de
          "John is   saw   that-cl. male-person RM"

105. a. dzúo-tien wǒ mǎi de shìh <u>shu</u>
          "yesterday I bought RM is book"
          'What I bought yesterday is a book.'

      b. *shìh <u>shu</u> dzúo-tien wǒ mǎi   de
          "is book yesterday I bought RM"

In HEBREW, too, extraposition can only apply to the sentence initial constituent, as an F Cop S order is ungrammatical.

106. a. zeh sheshuh pagash etmol haya <u>axiv</u>
          "this RM   met   yesterday was brother-his"
          'The one he met yesterday was <u>his brother</u>.'

      b. *<u>axiv</u>   haya zeh sheshuh pagash etmol
          "brother-his was this RM   met   yesterday"

      c. ze   haya <u>axiv</u>   sheshuh pagash etmol
          "this/it was brother-his RM   met   yesterday"
          'It was <u>his brother</u> whom he met yesterday.'

The above data suggests that if a language constrains the extraposition rule, it will exclude first the pre-focus application. In other words, sentence initial application is the more basic one. I did not find any language in which extraposition can apply to the pre-focus constituent and not to the sentence initial one. In some languages it is difficult, however, to decide which kind of extraposition took place. This is true for all those languages that have a zero copula like in the following example from DIOLA-FOGNY.[24]

107. a.   nijuk-ɛ ebe
            "I-saw-ɛ cow"
            'What I saw is a cow. '

      b.   ebe nijuk-ɛ
            "cow ⊥-saw- "
            'A cow is what I saw. '

5. 3   Predicate lowering

All of the surface manifestations of emphatic constructions dis-cussed so far involve complex equational sentences which are com-posed of a minimum of two S-nodes, the matrix S and the relative clause S. It is however, a fact that some languages have emphatic constructions that are clearly non-equational and non-complex, e. g. :

108. John saw $\begin{Bmatrix} \text{Frank} \\ \text{him} \\ \text{*he} \end{Bmatrix}$ yesterday (but not Bill).

109. GERMAN:
      Ich habe nicht $\begin{Bmatrix} \text{den Tisch} \\ \text{*der Tisch} \end{Bmatrix}$ gekauft (sondern den Stuhl).
      'I didn't buy the table, (but rather the chair). '

I will therefore argue that in many languages underlying cleft sen-tences can be reduced to surface simplex sentences. Support for the claim that John saw Frank and Ich habe nicht den Tisch gekauft are simplexes comes from case assignment. Both in ENGLISH and in GERMAN the emphasized constituent is marked for accusative case in the reduced sentence. In a cleft sentence, on the other hand, the predicate noun phrase is marked for nominative.

110. $\begin{Bmatrix} \text{He} \\ \text{Frank} \\ \text{*Him} \end{Bmatrix}$ is the one John saw.

_____

[24] I expect, however, that additional data from DIOLA-FOGNY would allow us to decide one way or the other.

$\left\{\begin{array}{l} \underline{\text{Der Tisch}} \\ *\underline{\text{Den Tisch}} \end{array}\right\}$ is nicht das, was ich gekauft habe.

'The table is not that, what I bought. '

Consequently, if the emphasized constituents in 108. and 109. were the predicates of a higher S, they should display the case marking that would be assigned to them in that S, i. e. nominative, but they don't.[25] Another sign that a complex cleft sentence has been reduced to a simplex is the order in which the constituents occur. That is, in a cleft construction the focus constituent is either to the left or to the right of the known information, but never surrounded by it. In other words, there are two possible orders (not considering the copula), one in which the focus constituent follows the known information, e. g. 112., and one in which it precedes the known information, e. g. 113., but not 114. in which the focus constituent is surrounded by old information. 114. cannot be a cleft, i. e. an equational construction.

112.   The one John watched yesterday is <u>my friend</u>.
113.   My <u>friend</u> is the one John watched yesterday.
114.   John watched <u>my friend</u> yesterday.

However, even though 114. is not a cleft, I want to argue that it was derived from a cleft like 112. What is the evidence for this claim? First, there is the semantic paraphrase relation.

115.   a.   What I bought is <u>the book</u>.
          b.   I bought <u>the book</u>.

115. a. and 115. b. are semantically equivalent, i. e. both sentences presuppose that <u>I bought something</u> and also assert that the thing bought is <u>a book</u>. Besides the semantic evidence there is also considerable syntactic evidence which supports that 115. b. is derived from 115. a. This evidence comes from negation and question formation. For instance, in an emphatic construction in languages like HUNGARIAN, GERMAN, NAVAHO, and RUSSIAN, the negative particle may occur before the emphasized constituent instead of in the regular sentence negation position before or after the verb.[26]

---

[25]SOMALI, on the other hand, is a language in which the case marking of the emphasized constituent is retained in the simplex. For a discussion see below.

[26]In languages like ENGLISH and MANDARIN CHINESE, on the other hand, reduction to a simplex is not possible if the highest S of the cleft sentence is negated. That is, both ENGLISH and

116. GERMAN:
- a. <u>neutral</u>: Mein Vater ist nicht gekommen.
  'My father didn't come.'

- b. <u>subj. emph.</u> : Nicht mein Vater ist gekommen, (sondern mein Bruder).
  'My father didn't come, (but my brother did).'

117. RUSSIAN:
- a. <u>neutral</u>: Ja ne edu v London.
  "I not going to London"
  'I am not going to London.'

- b. <u>subj. emph.</u> : Ne ja edu v London.
  "not I going to London"
  'It is not <u>I</u> who is going to London.'

118. HUNGARIAN:
- a. <u>neutral</u>: János nem vett könyvet.
  "John not bought book"
  'John didn't buy a book.'

- b. <u>subj. emph.</u>: Nem János hanem Mary vett egy könyvet.
  "not John but Mary bought a book"
  'It is not <u>John</u> but Mary who bought a book.'

119. NAVAHO:
- a. <u>neutral</u>: John adadā ado niyada
  "John yesterday not arrive-neg."
  'John didn't arrive yesterday.'

- b. <u>subj. emph.</u> : do <u>adadā</u> John niyada, hadashi
  "not yesterday John arrive-neg, but some other time "
  'John didn't arrive <u>yesterday</u>, but (he arrived) some other time.'

(ftnt. 26 cont.)
MANDARIN CHINESE cannot reduce a sentence like a. to a sentence like b.:
- a. The one who bought the oranges is not <u>Bill</u>.
- b. *Not <u>Bill</u> bought the oranges.

It has been claimed, at least for GERMAN[27] that the position of
the negative particles in sentences like 116.b. is due to 'constituent'
negation. Presumably, this means that not the sentence but a
single constituent is negated. However, in that case we have to
ask why constituent negation of this kind can only occur before a
constrastively-emphasized constituent. That is, a sentence like
116.b. is ungrammatical if the speaker does not intend to contrastively emphasize the subject. On the other hand, true word
or constituent negation as in unmöglich 'impossible,' mistrauen
'mistrust,' Nichtraucher 'non-smoker,' etc. can occur without
any such constraint.

> 120. Der Nichtraucher ist gekommen.
>   'The non-smoker came.'

> 121. *Der Nichtraucher ist gekommen, sondern der Abstinenzler.
>   'The non-smoker came,   but rather the teetotaller.'

In 120. Nichtraucher is clearly word or constituent negation. It
cannot occur in an emphatic environment, e.g. 121. Furthermore,
the position of nicht, 'not/non' in 120. differs from the position of
nicht in 116.b. in that in 120. nicht is part of the noun and therefore follows the article, while in 116.b. it is outside of the noun
and has to precede the article.

> 122. *Mein nicht Vater ist gekommen.
>   'My non/not father came.'

Consequently, given that the negative particle in sentences like
116.b. cannot be constituent negation, we have to assume that it
is sentence negation. How, then, do we account for the position
of the negative particle in these sentences? We might claim that
languages that allow this particle to occur before the emphasized
constituent have a rule which simply says: place the negative particle before the emphasized constituent. Such a rule would convert
a sentence like 116.a. into a sentence like 116.b. if the subject is
somehow marked for emphasis. However, such an analysis will
not account for the fact that contrastively-stressed sentences can
contain two negative particles, e.g.:

> 123. Nicht mein Vater ist nicht angekommen, (sondern mein
>   Bruder ist nicht angekommen).
>   "not my father is not arrived, (but my brother is not arrived)."

---

[27] See Ibañez 1970.

'It is not <u>my father</u> who didn't arrive, (but it is <u>my brother</u>
who didn't arrive).'

124.   Nem <u>John</u> nem repült New York-ba, hanem <u>Bill</u> nem repült
       New York-ba.
       "not John not flew New York-to, but Bill not flew
       New York-to"
       'It is not <u>John</u> who didn't fly to New York, but it is <u>Bill</u>
       who didn't fly to New York.'

If both occurrences of <u>nicht</u> in the surface simplex <u>Nicht mein Vater</u>
<u>ist nicht angekommen</u> constitute sentence negation, then we have to
assume that this sentence is derived from an underlying complex
structure as in 125. below:

125.

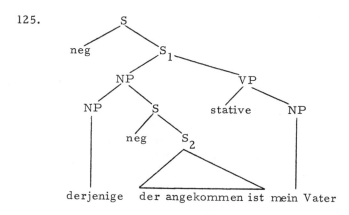

In a cleft sentence, negation of S_1 always implies that the equivalence relation between the subject NP and the predicate NP is
rejected.   This implication does not exist if S_2 is negated.   125.
undergoes negative lowering which will result in a surface form
like 126. below.

126.   Derjenige, der nicht angekommen ist, ist nicht mein Vater,
       (sondern...).
       'The one who didn't arrive ist not my father, (but...).'

126. can be further reduced to 123.   Thus the assumption that 125.
underlies a sentence like 123. allows us to account -- without any
new rules -- for the occurrence of two sentence negations in 123.
and for the position of the negative particles before the emphasized
constituent.   As 126. shows, sentence negation in an equational
structure is always placed before the predicate constituent, e.g.:

127. Hans ist kein Lehrer.
      "Hans is not-a teacher"
      'Hans is not a teacher.'

128. Marika ist nicht dumm.
      'Marika is not stupid.'

Above we have seen that evidence from negation indicates that
surface simplexes with an emphatic constituent are derived from
underlying complex sentences. Further evidence of the same kind
is provided by some languages in which the question particle can
be associated with the emphatic constituent. In FINNISH, for
instance, the question marker ko/kö is generally attached to the
verb, e.g. 129. In an emphatic question, speakers of FINNISH
have two choices. They can either retain the structure of the neutral question and stress the emphasized constituent, or they can
place the question particle on the emphasized constituent.

129. a. neutral: Näkikö äiti   Billin?
                       "saw-Q mother Bill-acc."
                       'Did mother see Bill?'

      b. subj. emph.: Näkikö äiti   Billin?
                       "saw-Q mother Bill-acc."
                       'Did mother see Bill?

      c. subj. emph.: Äitikö Billin naki?
                       "mother-Q Bill-acc. saw"
                       'Did mother see Bill?'

A similar pattern is found in TURKISH, where the question marker
mi, which generally precedes the verb, can optionally precede the
emphatic constituent.

130. a. neutral: Sen yarın oraya gidecek misin?
                       "are you tomorrow there Q-going"
                       'Are you going there tomorrow?'

      b. emphatic: Sen yarın mi oraya gidecek sin?
                       "are you Q tomorrow there going"
                       'Are you going there tomorrow?'

      c. subj. emph.: Sen mi yarın oraya gidecek sin?
                       "are Q you tomorrow there going"
                       'Are you going there tomorrow?'

Above it was established on the basis of semantic and syntactic evidence that sentences like 131. and 132. below are derived
from the same complex underlying form which is close to 131.:

131. Frantz is the one who helped us.
132. Frantz helped us.

The question which has not yet been answered is: how do we get
from 131. to 132.? As 132. contains fewer elements than 131, we
have to assume that certain elements are deleted, namely the neutral head, the relative clause marker and the copula. Even if all
of these deletions occur it does not necessarily imply that the resulting sentence is a simplex. An example of this is TSWANA, a
BANTU language. In TSWANA, an SVO language, the position of
emphasis is sentence final which corresponds to the position of the
focus constituent in a clefted sentence.

133. a. neutral: rrê   orêkilê dikgômo maabane
                        "my-father he-bought cattle yesterday"
                        'My father bought cattle yesterday.'

      b. subj. emph.: orêkilê dikgômo maabane, rrê
                        "he-bought cattle yesterday, my father"
                        'It is my father who bought cattle yesterday.'

Even though the neutral simplex sentence, e.g. 133.a. differs from
the emphatic one only by its word order and by the pause before the
emphasized constituent, we cannot consider 133.b. a simplex. The
reason is that if 133.b. was a simplex with emphatic word order,
we would not be able to account for the pause which is not present
in 133.a. The pause signals that 133.b. is an equational sentence.

While in a language like TSWANA the presence or absence of a
pause reveals the status of the sentence, it is case assignment that helps
us determine in languages like ENGLISH and GERMAN whether a
given sentence is an equational one or not. This is also true for the
NILO-SAHARAN language MURLE where an emphatic subject, if
part of a cleft, is in the absolute case, while the same emphatic subject is in the nominative if in a non-equational sentence.

134. a. alaan   ak   tu-a
          "chief (abs.) goes back"
          'The chief is the one who goes back.'

      b. ak   tu-a   alaan-i
          "goes back chief (nom.)"
          'The chief goes back.'

In SOMALI, on the other hand, the situation seems to be quite
different. As mentioned earlier, in SOMALI the form and number
of the verb plus the case assignment pattern signal the existence
of an underlying cleft construction. However, while in languages
like ENGLISH, GERMAN, and MURLE there exist case alternations which can be explained if we assume the reduction of a cleft
sentence to a non-equational one, this case alternation does not
occur in SOMALI, even though there are other signs that reduction
to a simplex has taken place. Consider the following: in SOMALI,
an SOV language, extraposition appears to be obligatory in a cleft
construction, converting a basic S F Cop order to a F Cop S order,
e.g.:

135. <u>nimán-kíí</u> báà hịlị   ʿun-ay?
      "man-acc. EM meat(acc.) ate (sgl.)"
      'The men are the ones who ate the meat.'

An alternative form of 135. is 136. below:

136. hịlịb   <u>nimán-kíí</u> báà   ʿun-ay?
      "meat(acc.) men-acc. EM ate (sgl.)"
      'The <u>men</u> ate the meat.'

The only difference between 135. and 136. is that in 135. the emphasized constituent is sentence initial, in 136. it is not.[28] The
singular marking on ʿun-ay? 'ate' signals an equational structure
with a relative clause as subject. However, while the order of
constituents in 135. is that of a cleft structure, the order in 136.
does not allow for a cleft interpretation as the emphatic constituent
is surrounded by the constituents of the relative clause, which
contains the old information. It appears, therefore, that 136. is
a simplex, but that in SOMALI, contrary to ENGLISH, GERMAN,
and MURLE, case assignment and subject-verb agreement do not
apply even if reduction to a simplex has taken place. That is, if
we assume that the focus constituent of an equational structure is
in the unmarked case (nominative in GERMAN and ENGLISH, accusative or absolute case in MURLE and SOMALI), and if we
assume that in a relative clause in SOMALI no subject-verb agreement takes place and the verb therefore is in the unmarked finite
verb form (third person singular) then we can say that SOMALI
marks an emphatic subject by blocking case assignment and subject-
verb agreement in any kind of emphatic structure, whether cleft or

---

[28]Notice that the focus constituent in 136. is in the typical position of emphasis for SOV languages, namely before the verb. For
a discussion see below.

simplex. The above analysis of SOMALI is not as ad hoc as it may seem. Kachru (1968) shows that in ergative constructions in HINDI the verb remains in the unmarked masculine singular form, i. e. agreement does not take place, thus signaling certain underlying relations. In SOMALI, absence of case assignment and subject-verb agreement appears to signal that the surface subject is not identical with the underlying subject.[29]

SOMALI is not the only language in which we can observe that features of the underlying equational structure are preserved in a non-equational surface form. For instance, it was mentioned earlier that KIHUNG'AN uses a special form of negation in relative clauses and in reduced emphatic constructions. That is, the features of the relative clause are retained even if the relative clause as such does not exist any longer :

137. a. kiim ki a-khoon-in Kipes ku-suum zoon kwe kít
"thing pro PA-fail-past Kipes to-buy yesterday is chair"
'What Kipes didn't buy yesterday is a chair.'

b. Kipes ka-khoon-in ku-suum kít zoono
"Kipes PA-fail-past to-buy chair yesterday"
'Kipes didn't buy a chair yesterday.'

The order of constituents in 137.b. indicates that the complex underlying form has been reduced to a simplex, but the features of the underlying cleft structure are retained as in SOMALI. While in the languages discussed so far either the order of constituents or the presence of a pause or a difference in case assignment indicate the status of the sentence, this is not true for some emphatic constructions in RUSSIAN. In RUSSIAN, an SVO language, the focus constituent is in final position in the basic cleft order, e. g. 138. :

138. Tot, kto priexal, eto Vanja.
"that who arrived this Vanja"
'The one who arrived is Vanja.'

Two other emphatic versions of 138. are 139. and 140. below. 139. appears to retain the cleft order with the focus constituent

---

[29] It seems that SOMALI is one of those languages which marks certain underlying relations by the non-application of otherwise obligatory agreement rules. For a discussion of additional SOMALI data and of the marking hypothesis see Delisle, 1973.

in final position, while 140. has a neutral word order in which the
focus constituent is solely marked by loudness.

139. Priexal Vanja.
      "arrived Vanya"
      'Vanya arrived.'

140. Vanja priexal.
      'Vanya arrived.'

The question is: is 139. a simplex or is it a cleft structure in
which all 'superfluous' constituents were deleted. Case assignment
will not help us, as Vanja is in the nominative in both 138. and
139. The only indication that 139. is a simplex is the sentence
intonation and the absence of a break between the verb and the
subject. That 139. is a non-equational structure is also supported
by the fact that if the focus constituent corresponds to the object
of the relative clause, it is in the nominative in the cleft construction but in the accusative in the reduced construction.

It appears, therefore, that the process of reduction from a
complex cleft construction to a surface simplex involves three
steps:

1) deletion of all non-essential constituents like the neutral
   head noun, the relative clause linker, and the copula;
2) reduction to a non-equational string and pruning of superfluous structure;
3) reordering of constituents.

Step 1) by itself does not bring about the formation of a surface
simplex as we have seen in the example from TSWANA. Another
example is TELUGU which, similar to TSWANA, requires an
intonation break between the known information and the focus constituent in final position. For the TELUGU data, see examples
125. a. and 125. b. in section 2. The mechanism involved in step
2) can be characterized as predicate lowering in which the predicate
is lowered into the relative clause. The question is: what position
is the predicate lowered into? It appears that there are two reasonable alternatives:

a. The predicate is lowered into the neutral position which is
    appropriate to the function the focus constituent will fulfil
    in the reduced sentence. For instance, if the focus con-
    stituent corresponds to the subject of the simplex, it will

be placed into initial position in an SVO language, and into medial position in a VSO language. After predicate lowering has taken place, reordering rules apply to generate marked emphatic word orders.

b. The predicate is lowered retaining the same position it had before lowering took place, i.e. the object position. Subsequent reordering generates alternative emphatic orders.

Hypothesis a. claims that the basic order of a reduced emphatic structure is identical to the neutral order of a sentence, while hypothesis b. claims that in the basic order of a reduced emphatic structure the focus constituent is in the position of the object, independent of the function of the focus constituent in the simplex. The difference between hypothesis a. and hypothesis b. can be illustrated with the RUSSIAN example. Hypothesis a. claims that a cleft structure like 138. is converted into 140. by deletions and predicate lowering and subsequently converted to 139. by a reordering rule. Hypothesis b. claims that 138. is converted to 139. by deletions and predicate lowering and then reordered to 140.

Given the two alternatives, we now have to look for evidence that will substantiate one or the other of these hypotheses. Before we can do that, however, we have to look at the data that we have to account for. That is, what kinds of emphatic word orders occur in simplex sentences. A first look convinces us that it is much more varied and complex than word order variations in cleft sentences. Though initial position is favored by many languages, there also exist final position for subject emphasis in RUSSIAN, SWAHILI and some CHADIC languages like DERA, the second position, after the verb, in MALAGASY, a VOS language, and BADE, an SVO language; and the position before the verb in SOV languages and in ZAPOTEC, an SVO language.

In all the following variations emerge. In SOV languages the contrastive emphasis of a subject results in either O$\underline{S}$V or $\underline{S}$VO surface orders. Object emphasis is expressed by an $\underline{O}$VS surface order. Examples of the above emphasis patterns are found in HUNGARIAN.

141. HUNGARIAN:
    a. <u>neutral</u>   SOV: Péter a levelet írja meg.
                      "Peter the letter is writing"
                      'Peter is writing the letter.'

    b. <u>subj. emph.</u> O<u>S</u>V: A levelet <u>Péter</u> írja meg.
                       "the letter Peter is writing"
                       '<u>Peter</u> is writing the letter.'

    c. <u>subj. emph.</u> S<u>O</u>V: <u>Péter</u> írja meg a levelet.
                       '<u>Peter</u> is writing the letter.'

    d. <u>obj. emph.</u> <u>O</u>VS: A <u>levelet</u> írja meg Péter.
                       'Peter is writing <u>the letter</u>.'

In SVO languages object emphasis is expressed by an O<u>S</u>V order in ENGLISH and RUSSIAN and an <u>O</u>VS order in GERMAN. RUSSIAN also allows S<u>O</u>V orders.

   142. a. <u>neutral</u>   SVO: I sent the letter yesterday.

         b. <u>obj. emph.</u> O<u>S</u>V: <u>The letter</u> I sent yesterday.

   143. GERMAN:
         a. <u>neutral</u>:   SVO: Ich habe den Brief gestern abgeschickt.
                            "I have the letter yesterday sent"
                            'I sent the letter yesterday.'

         b. <u>obj. emph.</u> <u>O</u>VS: <u>Den Brief</u> habe ich gestern abgeschickt.
                            "the letter have I yesterday sent"
                            '<u>The letter</u> I sent yesterday.'

   144. RUSSIAN:
         a. <u>neutral</u>   SVO: Boris vzjal knigu.
                            "Boris took book"
                            'Boris took the book.'

         b. <u>obj. emph.</u> <u>O</u>SV: <u>knigu</u> Boris vzjal.
                            "book Boris took"
                            'Boris took the <u>book</u>.'

In both GERMAN and ENGLISH there is no marked word order to express subject emphasis, while RUSSIAN and SWAHILI and some CHADIC languages have an VO<u>S</u> order or an V<u>SO</u> order (BADE-CHADIC).

   145. SWAHILI: SVO: manafunzi wadoga wanafungua vitabu.
         a. <u>neutral</u>   "students small open   books"
                            'The small students open the books.'

    b. <u>subj. emph.</u> VO<u>S</u>: wanafungua vitabu <u>wanafunzi wadogo</u>.
                  "open   books   students small"
                  'The <u>small students</u> open the books.'

In VSO languages the emphasized constituent is generally found in sentence initial position. Thus, subject emphasis is expressed by an S̲VO order while object emphasis results in an O̲VS order. In ZAPOTEC[30] we can get the following variations:

146. ZAPOTEC:
    a. <u>neutral</u>   VSO: gudo xwain biza.
                       "ate Juan beans"
                       'Juan ate beans.'

    b. <u>subj. emph.</u> SVO: xwain we ldua? ati <u>abel</u>
                       "Juan went Oaxaca not Abel"
                       '<u>Juan</u> went to Oaxaca and not <u>Abel</u>.'

    c. <u>obj. emph.</u> O̲VS: <u>biza</u> gudo xwain ati <u>bel</u>
                       "beans ate Juan not meat"
                       'Juan ate <u>beans</u> and not <u>meat.</u>'

148. MALAGASY:
    a. <u>neutral</u>   VOS: nividy vary ny vehivavy
                       "bought rice the woman"
                       'The woman bought rice.'

    b. <u>subj. emph.</u> VS̲O: nividy <u>ny vehivavy</u> vary
                       "bought the woman rice"
                       '<u>The woman</u> bought rice.'

Summarizing[31] we can make the following statements which in some cases are incomplete due to lack of information. [32]

---

[30] The ZAPOTEC data was provided by H. Rosenbaum in a talk given during the California Linguistic Conference, 1973. The title of the talk was: "Conditions on extraction rules: the case from Zapotec."

[31] Even though this section is mainly concerned with marked word orders, sequences in which the neutral word order is retained and emphasis is solely marked by phonological means were included in the above list as these sequences often round off the picture.

[32] For instance I do not know what word order marks object emphasis in MALAGASY, a VOS language.

	Neutral	Emphatic Variations: Non-neutral word order	Phonological means only
149.	S O V	a. O S V b. S V O c. O V S	d. S O V e. S O V
150.	S V O	a. V O S b. V S O c. O S V d. O V S e. S O V	f. S V O g. S V O
151.	V S O	a. S V O b. V O S c. O V S d. V O S	e. V S O f. V S O
152.	V O S	a. V S O	b. V O S c. V O S

If we want to account for all of the emphatic word orders listed above by assuming hypothesis a., where predicate lowering places the focus constituent into the neutral position, we will need many reordering rules which have in common nothing but the fact that they reorder constituents. There will be no way to predict in which direction reordering will move the emphasized constituent. Hypothesis a., therefore implies that reordering for emphatic purposes in reduced emphatic sentences differs from the reordering processes in cleft sentences, as in the latter the whole purpose of reordering is to bring the focus constituent closer to the sentence initial position. On the other hand, if we assume hypothesis b., where predicate lowering places the focus constituent into the object position, we can establish a parallel between cleft sentences and reduced emphatic sentences. In both sentence types the basic position for the focused or emphasized constituent is that position which is filled by the object in a neutral sentence. Furthermore, the only reordering rule that applies to both cleft sentences and their reduced counterparts is the extraposition rule which — by moving constituents that contain presuppositional material to the end of the sentence — places the emphasized constituent closer to the beginning of the sentence.

The assumption that the object position is the basic position of emphasis allows us to account for a number of facts for which we

have otherwise no explanation. For instance, final position of an
emphasized subject is only found in SVO and in VSO languages,
e.g. in RUSSIAN and DERA, and in ARABIC and MURLE respectively, but not in SOV and VOS languages. Given hypothesis b.,
this fact can be explained since the basic position of emphasis in
SVO and VSO languages is the final position, i.e. the position of
the object, while in SOV and VOS languages, the basic position
of emphasis is the one before and after the verb, respectively.
Thus, hypothesis b. actually predicts that VO_S orders should
occur in some SVO and VSO languages. That VO_S is not found
as an emphatic order in all SVO and VSO languages is due to
language-specific constraints, which do not permit final position
of a subject. Another fact which is explained by hypothesis b.
involves SOV languages. Dezső (1968) observed that there exists
a hierarchy in SOV languages among the possible emphatic word
order alternations. The most basic order, or the order highest
in the hierarchy, is the one in which the emphasized constituent
is immediately to the left of the verb, e.g. OS_V. Only if a language has this order can it also have an additional S_VO order.
And the highest ranking OS_V order corresponds to the basic emphatic order proposed in hypothesis b., as in OS_V the emphasized
subject is in the position of the neutral object, i.e. the position
before the verb. Thus, TURKIC languages in general have OS_V
orders as the only emphatic order. The same holds true for
GALLA, a CUSHITIC language, while HUNGARIAN also allows
an S_VO order, (see example 141. above).

154. TURKISH:
    a. <u>neutral</u>   SOV: Kim sana bunu söyledï?
                        "who you this told"
                        'Who told you this?'

    b. <u>subj. emph.</u> OS_V: Sana bunu <u>kim</u> söyledi?
                        "you this who told"
                        '<u>Who</u> told you this?'

155. GALLA:
    a. <u>neutral</u>   SOV: niiti-n ilm sāl-te
                        "woman son she-bore"
                        'The woman bore a son.'

    b. <u>subj. emph.</u> OS_V: ilm <u>niiti-n</u> sāl-te
                        "son woman she-bore"
                        'The <u>woman</u> bore a son.'

In MALAGASY the position of emphasis is after the verb, i. e.
V<u>S</u>O, (see example 148. above). Apparently, no other variations
are possible. Given hypothesis a., we will need a special rule for
MALAGASY which says: convert a VO<u>S</u> structure to a V<u>S</u>O structure. However, given hypothesis b., the MALAGASY data becomes
perfectly regular. Since MALAGASY is a VOS language, the basic
position of emphasis is the position after the verb.

It has been shown above that hypothesis b. has to be preferred
over hypothesis a. because it simplifies[33] the description and establishes a parallelism between cleft sentences and their simplex
counterparts, and because it explains certain data involving specific language types for which hypothesis a. cannot account. Given
hypothesis b., we arrive at the following set of basic emphatic
positions.

| | Basic | Emphatic | Positions: |
156. Language type	Subject emphasis	Object emphasis
S V O	V O <u>S</u>	S V <u>O</u>
S O V	O <u>S</u> V	S <u>O</u> V
V S O	V <u>O</u> <u>S</u>	V S <u>O</u>
V O S	V <u>S</u> O	V <u>O</u> S

If we compare this list with that of 149. to 152. above which
contains all or at least most of the variations found in languages,
it is clear that many marked word orders do not correspond to the
basic emphatic positions for subjects and objects. Below I will
therefore investigate how we can account for the remaining forms.
A consequence of assuming that there exists one basic word order
for emphatic simplexes is that all other word orders are derived
from the basic one by reordering. This reordering takes place by
movement rules. During the discussion of alternate word orders
in cleft sentences it was argued that the only reordering rule that
applies to cleft sentences is an extraposition rule that moves constituents which contain old information to the right of the focus constituent. It was furthermore argued that this rule can apply either
to the sentence initial constituent or the pre-focus one. Given that
extraposition functions to place the focus constituent into a position

---

[33]The fact that hypothesis b. allows for a simpler description
will become especially clear later on where it will be shown that
only one reordering rule is needed if we assume hypothesis b.

of prominence at the beginning of the sentence, there is no reason to expect that the application of this rule is restricted to complex sentences. As a matter of fact, by assuming that extraposition applies to simplexes as well, we can generate all of the marked word orders listed in 149. to 152. as the following derivations show.

157. Language type: S O V

    a. Subject emphasis:
        1. basic emphatic order: O S̲ V (TURKISH. HUNGA-
                                             RIAN, GALLA)
        2. extraposition: S V O (HUNGARIAN, VOGUL)

    b. Object emphasis:
        1. basic emphatic order: S O V̲
        2. extraposition: O̲ V S (HUNGARIAN)

158. Language type: S V O

    a. Subject emphasis:
        1. basic emphatic order: V O S̲ (RUSSIAN, BANTU,
                                             CHADIC)
          extraposition S-initial: O S̲ V
                                      S̲ V O (GERMAN)
        2. basic emphatic order: V O S̲
          extraposition pre-foc.: V   S̲ O (BADE)
                                      S̲ O V (BULGARIAN,
                                             FINNISH)

    b. Object emphasis:
        1. basic emphatic order: S V O̲
          extraposition S-initial: V O̲ S (BULGARIAN)
          extraposition: O̲ S V (ENGLISH,
                                           FINNISH)
        2. basic emphatic order: S V O̲
          extraposition pre-foc.: S   O̲ V (RUSSIAN)
          extraposition: O̲ V S (GERMAN, SWA-
                                          HILI, BULGARIAN)

159. Language type: V S O

    a. Subject emphasis:
        1. basic emphatic order: V O S̲ (MURLE, ARABIC)
          extraposition S-initial: O S̲ V
          extraposition: S̲ V O (ARABIC, ZAPOTEC)

2. basic emphatic order: V O S̲
   extraposition pre-foc.: V   S̲ O (ARABIC)
   extraposition: S̲ O V (ARABIC,
                                        ZAPOTEC)

   b. Object emphasis:
      1. basic emphatic order: V S O̲
         extraposition S-initial: V   O̲ S
         extraposition: O̲ S V

160. Language type: V O S

   a. Subject emphasis:
      1. basic emphatic order: V S̲ O (MALAGASY)
         extraposition: S̲ O V

   b. Object emphasis:
      1. basic emphatic order: V O̲ S
         extraposition: O̲ S V

The above list shows that in some instances the emphatic word
order corresponds to the neutral one.[34] Given hypothesis b. this
is always the case for object emphasis since hypothesis b. claims
that the neutral word order and the basic position of emphasis for
objects are identical. However, this is not true for subject emphasis. Given the basic emphatic order and extraposition, only
SVO and VSO languages should allow an S̲VO and a VS̲O order
respectively. Examples of those orders are found in ENGLISH
and ARABIC.

   161. Bill̲ didn't see John, but Mary saw him.

   162. ARABIC:
        kataba Ali̲ ar-risāla
        "wrote Ali the-letter"
        'Ali̲ wrote the letter.'

In SOV and VOS languages, on the other hand, no S̲OV and VOS̲
order is generated by the rules proposed so far. Consequently,
if there are SOV and VOS languages that do have an S̲OV or a VOS̲

---

[34] It appears that identity between the neutral word order and an
emphatic one is only possible if the emphatic constituent is marked
by some other means for instance by phonological ones.

order respectively, the rule component has to be modified to the effect that in addition to extraposition there exists a regrouping process which generates the neutral word order, converting, for example, an OSV order into an SOV one. Evidence from HUNGA- RIAN indicates that such a regrouping process which generates neutral word orders does not exist, as in HUNGARIAN the neutral word order cannot be used to express subject emphasis, e. g. (164. b.):

163. neutral : János könyvet vett.
"John book bought"
'John bought a book. '

164. subj. emph. : a. János vett egy könyvet.
'John bought a book.'

b. *János könyvet vett.

The ungrammaticality of 164. b. indicates that the neutral order is an alternative emphatic order only if it happens to be one of the orders generated by predicate lowering (e. g. an SVO order in ENGLISH), and by the extraposition rule (e. g. an SVO order in GERMAN), but not if it has to be generated by a special ordering convention that establishes the neutral order (e. g. an SOV order in HUNGARIAN).

During the discussion of the extraposition rule in cleft sentences it was mentioned that data from marked word orders in non-equa- tional sentences supports the claim that extraposition and not focus fronting is the rule that is responsible for the regrouping of con- stituents. The failing of the fronting rule as a possible alternative to extraposition was not that obvious in cleft sentences, mainly because a cleft sentence can be more easily divided into two parts, the subject NP and the predicate, which may or may not contain the copula. But as soon as more than two elements are involved, fronting can be shown to be totally inadequate. A fronting rule predicts: 1) that the focus constituent is placed into sentence-initial position, and 2) that the order of the remaining constituents is not affected. Both of these predictions are violated by many of the above examples. Consequently, if we assume the fronting rule, we will need a number of highly idiosyncratic and ad hoc rules which would have to apply after the fronting rule to generate marked sur- face orders. Let us look at a few examples. In RUSSIAN object emphasis can result in an SOV order. To derive this order from an underlying SVO order by fronting, we have two alternatives:

1) front the object and have an additional rule that moves the object back before the verb, 2) have an alternative rule for RUS-SIAN that places an emphatic object before the verb. In ZAPOTEC, a VSO language, SOV signals object emphasis. The reader can see for himself that a conversion of VSO to SOV by fronting would lead over a very tortuous road. BADE, a CUSHITIC SVO language, would again require a very specific rule to generate VSO subject emphasis, namely a rule that places an emphatic subject behind the verb. Extraposition, on the other hand, can generate all of the attested marked emphatic word orders without the need for any additional rules. All that is required are language-specific con-straints on the rule that state which orders are possible in a given language. The fact that I did not find examples for some of the predicted word orders is not especially disturbing. The most likely reason is that not enough languages were investigated,[35] but it is also possible that certain orders will never occur because of the existence of a still undiscovered principle.

Summarizing this section on predicate lowering and marked word orders we can say that there is ample evidence in support of a rule that reduces complex cleft sentences to surface simplexes, and that there is furthermore considerable evidence that during this reduc-tion the focus constituent is placed into the position which is held by the object in a neutral statement. This position I have called the basic emphatic position. Subsequent to the reduction and placing of the focus constituent, extraposition can apply with the effect that the focus constituent moves closer to the front of the sentence. Whether or not the focus constituent will be moved all the way to the front or only 'half-way' depends on language-specific constraints. Also language-specific is whether the extraposition rule will apply to the sentence-initial constituent, or to the pre-focus one. Pre-focus application is only possible in those languages in which the basic position of emphasis is clause final, i.e. in SVO and VSO languages. This accounts for the fact that SVO and VSO languages have more alternative word orders than SOV and VOS languages, in which the basic emphatic position is medial.

The question which has not been mentioned at all in this paper and which will have to be investigated thoroughly is: what happens

---

[35]One of the greatest problems in working with grammars is that if they discuss word order at all, they hardly ever mention which of the constituents in a marked word order is the emphasized one. Thus, if it is said that an SVO language also has an alternative OSV order, it can mean either OSV or OSV, or possibly even OSV.

if more than the basic subject, object, verb constituents are present? Does extraposition influence the order of those additional constituents and if yes, how? Or are those constituents left outside of the regrouping process? The very limited sample from GERMAN and ENGLISH I looked at suggests the latter, but considerable research in this area is still required before we can come to any definite conclusions.

6. Phonological Manifestations of Emphasis

Above it was briefly mentioned that if the marked word order is identical with the neutral one, heavy stress on the emphasized constituent is often used to mark it. However, emphatic or contrastive stress is not only used in the above cases, but can also occur on the emphasized constituent in cleft sentences and in non-neutral word orders, depending on how much a speaker wants to underline a certain contrast. Phonological manifestations of emphasis appear to be secondary, that is, all languages that use increased loudness or a tonal change to indicate emphasis also have syntactic means like cleft constructions and marked word orders to express emphasis. Though most of the languages I investigated can make use of contrastive stress — INDO-EUROPEAN languages, FINNO-UGRIC languages, most BANTU languages, and CHINESE — some languages do not use it. For instance, VEI, a MANDAN language of West Africa, AMHARIC and MOHAWK do not use loudness or any other phonological mechanism to signal emphasis. In KIHUNG'AN, on the other hand, the emphasized constituent undergoes a change in tone, i.e. a low tone becomes a high one.[36]

165. <u>neutral:</u>   Kìpès ká-swíím-ín kìt zòòn
                    "Kipies buy-past chair yesterday"
                    'Kipes bought a chair yesterday.'

166. <u>obj. emph.</u>:   Kìpès ká-swíím-ín kít zóónó
                    "Kipes buy-past chair yesterday"
                    'Kipes bought <u>a chair</u> yesterday.'

167. <u>subj. emph.</u>: Kìpés ká-swíím-ín kìt zóónó
                    "Kipes buy-past chair yesterday"
                    '<u>Kipes</u> bought a chair yesterday.'

---

[36] From the limited data available it appears that if an emphasized word has more than one low tone, it is the last tone that will be changed.

While supra-segmentals play an important role in marking the emphatic character of a constituent, other phonological alternations were not observed. That is, no language was found in which phonological segments were systematically converted into other phonological segments to signal emphatic contrast, though increased loudness is usually coupled with a slowing down of the speed of the utterance which in turn results in a lengthening of the stressed vowel.

It would go beyond the framework of this paper to investigate in detail where and how contrastive stress is assigned. I will therefore only make a few remarks which might lead to further investigations. As the term already indicates, contrastive emphasis contrasts, implicitly or explicitly, two or more elements which are members of parallel sentences in the deep structure. Contrastive emphasis is assigned on the basis of syntactic parallelism, that is, in two parallel sentences the non-identical constituents are stressed. One of the parallel structures can be implied as in 168.

168. a. Bill helped to repair the car.
      b. No, it was <u>John</u> who helped to repair the car.

In 168. b. a full sentence is deleted except for the <u>no</u>, namely the sentence: [37]

168. c. No, it was not Bill who helped to repair the car.

While 168. c. is deleted anaphorically with 168. a. as the antecedent, deletion of a parallel sentence can also take place if the contrasted constituent in that sentence is left vague as in 169. a.

169. a. No, it was not <u>John</u> who helped, it was <u>somebody else</u>.
      b. No, it was not <u>John</u> who helped.

169. a. and 169. b. are semantically identical, i. e. no information is lost by the deletion.

Given that the parallel structure can be destroyed by deletion of one of its members, and assuming that contrastive stress is assigned on the basis of this parallel structure, it appears that stress

---

[37] For further discussion and evidence for the existence of 168. in the underlying form of 168. b., see Harries 1972.

has to be assigned before deletion takes place. [38] Both members of the parallel structure have to be present in some languages if the first member is negated.

170. GERMAN:
    a. Nicht <u>Jürgen</u> ist gekommen, sondern <u>Hans</u>.
       '<u>Jürgen</u> didn't come, but <u>Hans</u>.'

    b. ?Nicht <u>Jürgen</u> ist gekommen.

171. HUNGARIAN:
    a. Nem János repült New York-ba hanem <u>Imre</u>.
       "Not John flew New York-to but Imre"
       'John didn't fly to New York, but <u>Imre</u>.'

    b. ? Nem <u>János</u> New York-ba repült.

7. Schachter's Promotion Analysis

The analysis on which this paper has been based is generally called the 'pseudo-cleft analysis,' as it assumes that the underlying form of cleft sentences is a so-called pseudo-cleft as below:

172. The one who left early was Frank.

The pseudo-cleft analysis was rejected by Schachter (1973) for the following reason: there exists a set of cleft sentences for which there exists no corresponding set of pseudo-clefts. For instance, if we want to claim that all cleft sentences are derived from underlying pseudo-clefts, then we have to assume that 173.d. below is derived from an ungrammatical form, namely 173.f.

173. a. John bought the book for Bill.
      b. It was Bill that <u>John</u> bought the book for.
      c. It was Bill <u>for whom</u> John bought the book.
      d. It was for Bill that John bought the book.
      e. The one that John bought the book for was Bill.
      f. *The one that John bought the book was for Bill.

---

[38] For a discussion as to where stress is assigned, see Bresnan, 1971 and 1972, and Berman & Szamosi, 1972. Bresnan claims that "intonation depends systematically on underlying syntactic structure" (1972:326).

By rejecting the pseudo-cleft analysis on the basis of the ungrammaticality of 173.f., Schachter takes the position that a grammatical surface form should not be generated from an ungrammatical underlying form. However, the same problem is encountered with some adjectives which can occur in attributive but not in a predicate position. That is, for these adjectives relative clause reduction and front moving is obligatory.

> 174.   a. *My hand which is left is hurt.
>   b. My left hand is hurt.

But even if we reject the derivation of a grammatical surface form from an ungrammatical underlying form, this does not necessarily imply that clefts are not derived from pseudo-clefts. There are certain properties about sentences like 173.d. which show that they are not equivalent to sentences like 173.c. The most striking difference is that the <u>that</u> in 173.d. is not a relative pronoun as in 173.b., but rather a complementizer. That this is so is more obvious in GERMAN and FRENCH where the complementizer and the relative pronoun have different forms. In the sentences below, the a. versions contain a relative pronoun, while the b. versions contain a complementizer.

> 175.   a. Das ist <u>Hans</u>, für den ich das Buch gekauft habe.
>   'It is <u>Hans</u> for whom I bought the book.'
>
>   b. Das ist für <u>Hans</u> $\left\{ \begin{array}{l} \text{daß} \\ \text{*für den} \\ \text{*dem} \end{array} \right\}$ ich das Buch gekauft habe.
>   'It is for <u>Hans</u> that I bought the book.'

> 176.   a. C'est <u>Jean</u> pour qui j'ai acheté le livre.
>   'It is <u>John</u> for whom I bought the book.'
>
>   b. C'est pour <u>Jean</u> $\left\{ \begin{array}{l} \text{que} \\ \text{*pour qui} \\ \text{*qui} \end{array} \right\}$ j'ai acheté le livre.
>   'It is for <u>John</u> that I bought the book.'

And even in ENGLISH, <u>that</u> in 2.d. cannot be replaced by a wh-pronoun.

> 173.   g. *It was for Bill $\left\{ \begin{array}{l} \text{for whom} \\ \text{whom} \\ \text{who} \end{array} \right\}$ John bought the book.

The above data suggests that sentences like 173.c. have a different underlying form from sentences like 173.d. and the latter sentence type therefore does not necessarily constitute counter-

evidence to an analysis which claims that all so-called pseudo-
clefts underly all other cleft constructions.

However, Schachter considers sentences like 173.d. counterevidence and therefore proposes the <u>promotion theory</u>. This theory
claims that we can account for the fact that relative clauses and
cleft sentences show so many similarities on the basis that both
undergo the same rule, namely the promotion rule. This rule
copies noun phrases out of an embedded S into a dummy △ in a
higher S. That is, relative clauses have an underlying form as
in 177. while cleft sentences have as underlying form as in 178.

177.

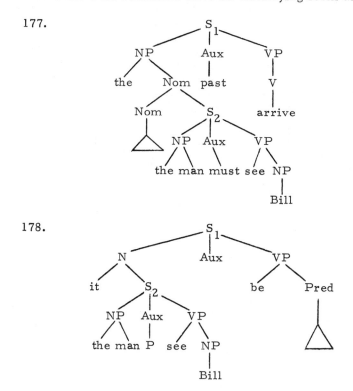

178.

Let us first look at the rule or rules needed to replace the dummy
symbols with a constituent. In order to convert 177. into a surface form, one [39] of the NP's of S_2 has to be copied onto the dummy

---

[39]Schachter himself points out that the fact that the promotion
rule can choose any one of the noun phrases in the embedded S
violates the assumption held by most linguists today, namely that

symbol to lexicalize the head of the relative clause. In 178. on
the other hand, a noun phrase is copied onto the dummy node in the
predicate. Thus, the structural descriptions of the two rules are
quite different. What they have in common is that they copy a constituent of a lower S onto a dummy symbol in a higher S. Another
difference between the two rules is the kind of constituents they
can raise. While the head of a relative clause can only be a noun
phrase, the predicate of a cleft sentence is much less restricted.
It can be a noun phrase, an adjective, or an adverb. Furthermore,
the noun phrases that are raisable are more restricted in a relative
clause than in a cleft sentence. For instance, if we want to derive
surface forms like 173. d. from an underlying form like 180, the
promotion rule has to copy the noun phrase and the preposition,
and subsequent rules that effect the original constituent in the embedded S have to be made sensitive to whether a noun phrase was
copied with a preposition or without it. If it was copied without a
preposition, the original constituent is relativized (e. g. 173. b. and
173. c.). However, if the original constituent was copied with a preposition, then the original has to be deleted and a that-complementizer
has to be introduced (e. g. 173. d.). Consequently, even in Schachter's
framework the derivation of a sentence like 173. d. is quite different
from the derivation of a sentence like 173. b. and requires special
constraints. Besides the constraints listed above, Schachter also
has to stipulate that the rule of extraposition from it is obligatory,
even though this kind of rule is usually considered optional.

Another drawback of the promotion hypothesis is that it cannot
relate clefts and pseudo-clefts; that is, it makes the claim that sentences like 179. and 180. below are completely unrelated.[40]

179. The one who arrived is John.

180. It is John who arrived.

(ftnt. 39 cont.)
the underlying syntactic structure of a sentence must have a unique
semantic interpretation. Schachter's proposal therefore requires
a change in the theory to the effect that the semantic interpretation
of a sentence takes place somewhere between the deep structure
and the surface structure representation. A similar change in the
theory is needed to accommodate co-occurrence constraints.

[40]Schachter does not attempt to relate 179. or 180. above to
the emphatic simplex, i. e. John arrived.

Given that 179. and 180. are unrelated in Schachter's analysis, he also fails to account for the facts discussed by Akmajian, which support the hypothesis that clefts are derived from pseudo-clefts. The data presented by Akmajian involves the occurrence of certain pronouns in the relative clause of the cleft sentence. These pronouns cannot be accounted for if we assume an underlying it-cleft, but are perfectly regular if we assume an underlying pseudo-cleft with a third person head. There exist similar evidence in GERMAN involving the relative pronoun. Consider the following data:

181.   a.   Es ist bloßer Neid, was aus ihm spricht.
            "it is pure envy, what out him speaks"
            'It is pure envy, what motivates him.'

The relative pronoun was [neuter] cannot have Neid [masculine] 'envy' as antecedent, as GERMAN has obligatory gender agreement between the head and the relative pronoun. However, if we assume that 180.a. is derived from 181.b., then we can account for the occurrence of was in 181.a.

181.   b.   Dasjenige (Ding), was aus ihm spricht, ist bloßer Neid.
            "that   (thing), what out him speaks is pure envy"
            'That (thing), what motivates him, is pure envy.'

Further evidence that was cannot have Neid as antecedent is that was as a relative pronoun only occurs in certain environments, i.e. if the head has been deleted or is somehow undetermined or vague, e.g. 182. Otherwise the neuter relative pronoun is das 'that.'

182.   Alles, was er tut, ist sinnlos.
        'All what he does is senseless.'

Finally, I will discuss a more general problem that Schachter's analysis faces. It has been shown by Sanders and Tai (1972) that in languages like MANDARIN CHINESE, BENGALI, SYRIAN ARABIC, etc., an object cannot be removed from the VP, i.e. it cannot be deleted or topicalized.[41] This constraint would have to be violated by Schachter's analysis as 183.a. below would be generated from an underlying form like 183.b., where the future focus constituent shu 'book' is the object of the relative clause.

---

[41] For a discussion of this data and its analysis see Sanders and Tai 1972 and Harries 1973b.

183. a. dzúo-tien wǒ mǎi de shǐh běn shu
         "yesterday I buy RM is clas. book"
         'What I bought yesterday is a book. '

b.

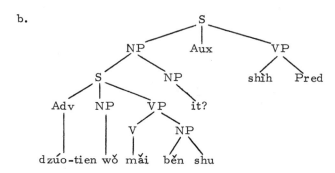

Summarizing this brief discussion of Schachter's proposal we
have to say that as it stands the promotion hypothesis proves to be
inadequate in too many respects to be considered a viable alternative to the pseudo-cleft analysis. Schachter's whole argument
against the pseudo-cleft analysis is that there exist certain cleft
sentences which do not have any pseudo-cleft counterparts in ENG-
LISH, e.g. example 173.d. It has, however, been shown above
that those sentences are not only problematic for the pseudo-cleft
analysis, but also for the promotion analysis. Schachter claims
that his analysis explains why cleft sentences and relative clauses
are very similar in many languages. But all that this relationship
is built on, according to Schachter, is that two different underlying
structures undergo a similar, though by no means identical, rule.
This appears to be a rather weak link to account for such obvious
similarities, especially as the similarities between relative clauses
and clefts are not brought about by the promotion rule. In other
words, the similarities — for instance the constraints on the embedded verb — are not a result of the application of the promotion
rule, and consequently the promotion rule cannot be the reason for
these similarities. The pseudo-cleft analysis, on the other hand,
has been shown to be adequate not only for ENGLISH, but on a
universal basis. It accounts for all the varied data presented in
this paper and does not require any rules that are not needed elsewhere in the grammar.

8. Conclusion

In conclusion I will summarize the major claims made in this
paper and will briefly discuss an area not touched on so far, namely
the relation of cleft sentences to word questions and their answers.

8.1 Summary

The basic claim of this paper is that all sentences that contain a contrastively emphasized noun phrase are derived from underlying equational sentences. In these equational sentences the known information is represented by the subject, while the new and focused information is represented by the predicate noun phrase. To the underlying cleft sentence rules can apply to generate different surface structures. In most languages the full cleft structure is grammatical, but in some languages deletion and/or reordering rules must apply obligatorily. The two sets of rules that account for the variations in the surface form of emphatic structures are deletion rules, i.e. head deletion, copula deletion, and relative marker deletion, and reordering rules, i.e. extraposition, and predicate lowering. It was argued that extraposition of the subject and not fronting of the focus constituent accounts for the reordering of constituents in a cleft sentence. While extraposition does not effect the underlying equational structure, predicate lowering reduces the original equational structure to a surface form which is no longer equational, thus relating sentences like 184.a. and 184.b.

184. a. The one who fell from his bike is <u>a friend of John's</u>.
       b. <u>A friend of John's</u> fell from his bike.

It is argued that the focus constituent is lowered into the unmarked position of emphasis which is the position of the object or complement. This is also true for cleft sentences, i.e. both in an equational and in a non-equational emphatic structure the basic position of emphasis corresponds to the position of the object in a neutral sentence. Only if we make this assumption, can we account in a principled way and without any ad hoc rules and constraints for all of the emphatic word order variations that can occur.

Finally, in a discussion of Schachter's promotion hypothesis it is shown that Schachter's approach not only fails to account for all of the data, but it also requires major adjustments in the theory which are not otherwise justified.

8.2 Word questions and their answers

I have argued elsewhere[42] that all word questions and their answers closely resemble contrastively emphasized structures and are in fact derived from underlying cleft sentences. Functionally,

---

[42]Harries 1972.

questions and their answers and contrastively emphasized structures are very similar. A contrastively emphasized structure
contrasts one or several members of a related set, while a word
question requests the identification of one or several members of
a set. This identification is provided in an appropriate answer,
which names those members of the set which fit the description
provided in the question and contrasts it with all other members
of the set which do not fit the description. For instance, in 184.
below, it is requested that the answering person only names that
member of the specified set who is sick and contrasts him with
all the other members of the set who did not get sick.

185. a. Who flew to the moon and got sick on the way?
     b. Frank Miller (but not Bill Johson, John Smith, etc.).

The same parallelism that exists in contrastively emphasized
structures between the equational version and its non-equational
counterpart also exists for questions and for their answers. That
is, 186 below is a paraphrase of 185. a. in that it contains the same
presuppositions.

186. Who is the one who flew to the moon and got sick on the way?

The hypothesis that emphatic constructions and word questions
are related has been put forward before for a number of languages.
Takizala (1972) points out that in KIHUNG'AN word questions are
subject to the same constraints on negation and object pronoun
infixation as relative clauses and emphatic constructions, and he
therefore concludes that word questions have an underlying cleft
structure. In CHIPPEWA, word questions behave like sentences
with embedded relative clauses, that is word questions always
contain a subordinate verb form. In CHADIC languages, word
questions generally share characteristics with emphatic constructions, i. e. the same constraints hold for both sentence types.
While in the above-discussed cases word questions reveal their
cleft origin, there are some languages in which this is also true
for the answer. For instance, Hutchinson (1969) observes that in
TEMNE both a question and its answer have to be clefts, e. g.
187. a. and 187. b. 187. c., the non-cleft counterpart to 187. b.,
is not an acceptable answer to 187. a.

187. a. kanɛ n nəŋk a?
        'Who was it that you saw? '

     b. ɔbại kɔnɛ i nəŋk.
        'It was the chief whom I saw. '

187. c. ɔ i nəŋk ɔbą̇i
'I saw the chief.'

It is claimed, then, that word questions and their appropriate
answers have an underlying equational structure in which the focus
constituent of the question, i. e. the question word, is only partially specified. This partial specification is filled in by the focus
constituent of the answer. The only other difference between a
question and its answer is the performative involved. The subject
noun phrases are identical as they contain the presuppositions.[43]
Thus word questions have an underlying structure like 188. a.,
answers like 188. b.

188. a.

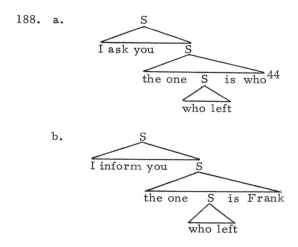

b.

Both word questions and their answers can be the input to the rules
discussed in this paper. For instance, in some languages like
ENGLISH and GERMAN, extraposition has to apply to 188. a. while
in other languages, like the BANTU ones, this is not necessarily
so. Thus, the rules that are needed to generate word questions
are the same rules that apply to non-interrogative equational structures, and no specific 'question rules' are required.

---

[43] In my thesis I argued that an answer to a given question is
appropriate only if the two share the same presuppositions.

[44] Truitner, Dunnigan (1972) mention that the question word in
CHIPPEWA appears to be complex. There is also some evidence
from GERMAN involving negation which suggests that the predicate
nominal is part of a complex structure of the form: the one who is
Frank. See Harries 1972.

Given the above hypothesis the next step will be to determine what kinds of language specific constraints are found in word questions. In other words, we will have to investigate what is and what is not a possible constraint on a word question.

BIBLIOGRAPHY

Akmajian, A. 1970. On deriving cleft sentences from pseudo-cleft sentences. Linguistic Inquiry 1.2. 149-68.

Ashton, E.O. 1944-1970. Swahili grammar. London.

Bach, E. 1967. Have and be in English syntax. Language 43.3. 562-85.

_____ and S. Peters. 1968. Pseudo-cleft sentences, preliminary version. University of Texas, Austin.

Balmer, W.T. and F.C. Grant. 1929. A grammar of the Fante-Akan language. London.

Bell, C.R. 1968. The Somali language. New York.

Benveniste, E. 1960. "Etre" et "avoir" dans leurs fonctions linguistiques. BSL 55. 113-34.

Berman, A. and M. Szamosi. 1972. Observations on sentential stress. Language 48.2. 304-25.

Beythan, H. 1943. Praktische Grammatik der Tamilsprache. Leipzig: Vlg. O. Harrassowitz.

Borras, M. and R.F. Christian. 1961. Russian syntax. Oxford.

Bresnan, J. 1971. Sentence stress and syntactic transformations. Language 47.2. 257-81.

_____. 1972. Stress and syntax: a reply. Language 48.2. 326-42.

Chomsky, N. 1970. Remarks on nominalization. Readings in English transformational grammar, ed. by R. Jacobs and P. Rosenbaum. Waltham, Mass, 184-221.

Cohen, M. 1970. Traité de langue amharique. Paris.

Cole, D. T. 1955. An introduction to Tswana grammar. London.

Cowell, M. W. 1964. A reference grammar of Syrian Arabic.
Arabic Series, No. 7, ed. by R.S. Harrell. Institute of Languages and Linguistics, Georgetown University.

Crazzolara, J. P. 1960. A study of the Logbara (Ma'di) language.
Oxford University Press.

Darden, B. 1969. On the question of the copula. Papers of the
Fifth Regional Meeting of the Chicago Linguistic Society, 30-35.

Delisle, G. 1973. Non-standard concord and the marking hypothesis. WPLU 11. 85-138.

Dezsö, L. 1968. Einige typologische Besonderheiten der ungari-
schen Wortfolge. In Acta Linguistica Academiae Scientiarum
Hungaricae Tomus 18 (1-2), 125-59.

Ellis, J. and L. Boadi. 1969. 'To be' in Twi. The verb 'be' and
its synonyms, ed. by J. Verhaar, Part 4, V. 9, 1-65.

Ferguson, C. 1972. Verbs of 'being' in Bengali, with a note on Amharic.
The verb 'be' and its synonyms, ed. by J. Verhaar, Part 5,
V. 4, 74-114.

Halliday, J. 1967. Grammar, society, and the noun. Inaugural
lecture 1966, University College, London.

Harries, H. 1972. Cleft sentences, questions, and presupposition sharing. Doctoral dissertation, University of Minnesota.

_____. 1973a. A note on double negation and modals as main
verbs. WPLU 11. 211-17.

_____. 1973b. Coordination reduction. WPLU 11. 139-209.

Horne, E. C. 1961. Beginning Javanese. Yale Linguistic Series 3.
New Haven.

Hutchinson, L. 1969. Pronouns and agreement in Temne. Doctoral dissertation, University of Indiana.

Ibañez, T. 1970. Emphase und der Bereich der Negation: Satz -
vs Satzgliednegation. Arbeitspapier, Nr. 9, Institut für Sprachwissenschaft, Universität zu Köln.

Jespersen, O. 1949. A Modern English Grammar, Vol. VII, part
4. Heidelberg, (originally published in 1909).

_____. 1969. Analytic syntax. Transatlantic Series in Lin-
guistics. New York.

Kachru, Y. 1965. A transformational grammar of Hindi verbal
syntax. Unpublished Ph. D. dissertation, University of London.

Kähler, H. 1965. Grammatik der Bahasa Indonésia. Wiesbaden.

Keenan, E. L. 1972. Relative clause formation in Malagasy (and
some related and not so related languages). In Chicago Which
Hunt Papers from the Relative Clause Festival. Chicago Linguistics Society, 169-89.

Koelle, S. W. 1884. Outlines of a grammar of the Vei language.
London (1968 edition).

Krishnamurti, B.H. and P. Sivananda Sarma. 1968. A basic
course in Modern Telugu. Hyderabad.

Kuno, S. 1972. Functional sentence perspective: a case study
from Japanese and English. Linguistic Inquiry III. 3. 269-320.

Lakoff, G. 1965. On the nature of syntactic irregularity. Doctoral dissertation, Indiana University.

Lehtinen, M. 1963. Basic course in Finnish. Uralic and Altaic
Series, V. 27, Indiana University Publications.

Lees, R.B. 1963. Analysis of the "cleft sentence" in English.
Zeitschrift für Phonetik, Sprachwissenschaft und Kommunika-
tionsforschung, Bd. 16, Heft 4, 371-88.

Lukas, J. 1937. A study of the Kanuri language. Oxford University
Press.

Malzac, R. P. 1960. Grammaire malgache. Paris.

McQuown, N. A. and S. Koylass. 1945. Spoken Turkish. New York.

Meskill, R.H. 1970. A transformational analysis of Turkish syntax. The Hague: Mouton.

Myers, Amy. 1970. A grammar of Tera. University of California Press.

Ross, J.R. 1969. Adjectives as noun phrases. In Modern Studies in English, ed. by D. Reibel and S. Schane, 352-60.

_____. 1969b. Auxiliaries as main verbs. Studies in philosophical Linguistics, Series I, ed. by W. Todd. Evanston, Ill.: Great Expectations Book Sellers and Publishers, 77-102.

Sapir, J.D. 1965. A grammar of Diola-Fogny. West-African Language Monograph, No. 3. Cambridge.

Sanders, G. and J. Tai. 1972. Immediate dominance and identity deletion. Foundations of Language 8.2. 161-97.

Schachter, P. 1973. Focus and relativization. Language 49.1. 19-46.

_____ and V. Fromkin. 1968. A phonology of Akan. Working Papers in Phonetics 9, UCLA phonetics laboratory.

_____ and F.T. Otanes. 1972. Tagalog reference grammar. University of California Press.

Schuh, R.C. 1971. Reconstructions of the syntax of subject emphasis in certain Chadic languages. Studies in African Linguistics, Supplement 2. 67-78.

Schwartz, A. 1971. General aspects of relative clause formation. WPLU 6. 139-71.

Takizala, A. 1972. Focus and relativization in Kihung'an. Studies in African Linguistics 3.2. 259-87.

Thank Bĭhn, D. 1971. A tagmemic comparison of the structure of English and Vietnamese sentences. The Hague: Mouton.

Thompson, L.C. 1969. A vietnamese grammar. Seattle: University of Washington Press.

Tompa, J. 1968. Ungarische Grammatik. The Hague: Mouton.

Truitner, K. and T. Dunnigan. 1972. Wh-questions in Ojibwe.
Papers from the 8th Regional Meeting of the Chicago Linguistics
Society, 359-67.

Tucker, A.N. and M.A. Bryan. 1956. The non-Bantu languages
of north-eastern Africa. London.

Ultan, R. 1969. Some general characteristics of interrogative
systems. WPLU 1. 41-63a.

Van Chiuh, T. 1970. Structure de la langue vietnamienne. Paris.

Welmers, W.E. 1964. The syntax of emphasis in Kpelle. The
Journal of West African Languages 1.1. 13-26.

Westermann, D. 1967. Grammatik der Ewe-Sprache. Berlin.

Relations Between
Subordination and Coordination

LEONARD TALMY

ABSTRACT

In relation to complex sentences like <u>We stayed home because it was raining</u>, the paper investigates compound sentences like <u>It was raining, (and) so we stayed home</u>, calling them 'copy-cleft' sentences. Copy-clefting, in applying also to clauses, is a generalization over the 'left-dislocation' (or 'topicalization') process for nominals. Some languages, like JAPANESE, virtually lack copy-cleft forms, while others, like ENGLISH, abound in them. Copy-clefting is the source of all clause-coordinationg conjunctions (accordingly lacking in JAPANESE), of some gerundive, infinitival, and relative constructions, and of (all?) manner adverbs. A number of further semantic and syntactic characteristics of copy-clefting are investigated.

This work is a moderately revised version of a paper titled "Copy-Clefting" as it appeared in Working Papers on Language Universals, no. 17, June 1975, Stanford University; © 1975 by the Board of Trustees of the Leland Stanford Junior University.

CONTENTS

1. Overview[1]

1.1 Introduction

The realm of semantic/syntactic linguistic phenomena treated in this presentation is perhaps best introduced by pointing out the close relationship between such sentences as those in the following pairs:

1. a.   We stayed home because it was raining.
         It was raining, so we stayed home.

    b.   We went out even though it was raining.
         It was raining, but we went out anyway.

    c.   She went home after stopping at the store.
         She stopped at the store, and then went home.

    d.   He works at a sideline in addition to holding down a regular job.
         He holds down a regular job, and also works at a sideline.

---

[1] This paper is conceived as the third in a tetrad on complex sentences. The first, "Figure and ground in complex sentences" is in this volume. The second, still in draft stage, will be titled "Subordinating prepositions and conjunctions." The fourth, whose title in isolation would be "Clause-conflation," now appears as the last section of Talmy (1975a: 222-38). Presupposed in this paper are the following notions:

The underlying form of a complex sentence is: two clauses embedded as nominals in a 4-constituent matrix, as in (a). Deriving from this are forms with a subordinate clause, considered equally so whether consisting of a prepositional+nominalized clause, as in (b), or of a conjunction+finite clause, as in (c):

(a) [we went out] BE DESPITE [the rain was pouring down]
(b) We went out despite the rain's pouring down.
(c) We went out although the rain was pouring down.

The propositions specified by the first and second clauses are considered to be respectively 'asserted' and 'presupposed.'

A 'deep morpheme' is one which is inferred to exist in deeper structures but which is always involved in transformations that remove overt trace of it before it can reach the surface; it is written here with capital letters.

'Conflation' is any derivational process whereby a simpler substring comes to stand in the place of a more complex one.

In this paper, a superscript eks, ^{x}, is placed before a sentence of questionable acceptability.

My thanks go to Prof. Haruo Aoki for help with the JAPANESE forms in this paper.

By traditional grammar, the upper form in each pair is a complex
sentence with subordinate clause introduced by a subordinating
conjunction or preposition(al). And the lower form is a compound
sentence with coordinating conjunction. This latter form will, however, be referred to hereafter as a "copy-cleft" sentence for reasons developed below.

While the semantic relation between the two forms is evident,
an immediate illustration of the possibility of a syntactic relation
is provided by a pair like

2. a. I'll scream if you come any closer.
   b. (You) come any closer and I'll scream.

Here, the initial clause in 2.b. cannot be taken as an independent
imperative form because of the <u>any</u> it contains:

3. *Come any closer!

It is, rather, identical with the final clause of 2.a., where the <u>any</u>
is wholly appropriate.

The most noteworthy cross-linguistic observation in the present
matter is that some languages, e.g. JAPANESE and JÍVARO, almost entirely lack any copy-cleft forms like those preceding. True,
undoubtedly every language has the precursor of copy-clefted forms,
consisting of two closely linked, but separate, statements with what
I call a 'zero' or 'semi-colon' connective in between, as exemplified for JAPANESE by:

4. a. <u>complex sentence</u>:

   hongyoo   o motte ite,   John wa   hukugyoo o motte iru.
   "main work obj. (on top of) holding, John subj. side work obj. holds"
   'John holds down a side job on top of holding down a main job.'

   b. <u>copy-cleft precursor</u> with 'semi-colon connective':

   John wa hongyoo   o motte iru; sono ue ni   hukugyoo
   "John subj. main work obj. holds   on top of that side work
   o   motte iru
   obj. holds"
   'John holds down a main job; he holds down a side job on top
   of that.'

But for a more closely knit, single-statement form, languages like

JAPANESE, lacking a copy-clefting process, have available only the complex sentence construction. Thus, of the sentences in 1., JAPANESE has equivalents only for the upper pair-members, as indicated in 5. (the subordinate clauses here have been preposed to match JAPANESE clause order):

5. a. <u>Because</u> it was raining, we stayed home.

$$\cdots \begin{cases} \text{tame ni} \\ \underline{\text{kara}} \end{cases}, \cdots$$

b. <u>Although</u> it was raining, we went out.

$$\cdots \begin{cases} \text{ga} \\ \text{keredomo} \end{cases}, \cdots$$

c. <u>After</u> she stopped at the store, she went home.

$$\cdots \begin{cases} \underline{-te} \\ \underline{\text{a\underline{to} ni}} \\ \underline{\text{kara}} \end{cases}, \cdots$$

d. <u>In addition to</u> holding down a regular job, he works at a sideline.

$$\cdots \begin{cases} \underline{-te}/ \underline{-i} \\ \underline{\text{si}} \\ \underline{\text{hoka ni}} \\ \underline{\text{ue ni}} \end{cases}, \cdots$$

This is to say that such languages lack -- among other structures which arise in the copy-clefting process -- all clausal coordinating conjunctions, the equivalents of our <u>and, but, nor,</u> etc.

There seem to be just four structural types of connection between the parts of a copy-cleft sentence: "zero," a coordinating conjunction, a nonfinite formation (e.g., gerundival and/or infinitival), and a relative formation. The first two types have been seen above. The full range can be illustrated in ENGLISH, e.g., by the copy-cleft counterparts of the complex sentence <u>Mays provided some excitement for the viewers by batting in three runs:</u>

6. a. Mays batted in three runs; he provided some excitement for the viewers thereby.

b. Mays batted in three runs, and provided some excitement for the viewers thereby.

c. Mays batted in three runs, providing some excitement for the viewers thereby.

    c'. Mays batted in three runs, to provide some excitement
        for the viewers thereby.

    d. Mays batted in three runs, whereby he provided some
        excitement for the viewers.

1.2 <u>The syntactic relation between a complex and a copy-cleft
sentence</u>

The clue to the syntactic relation between a complex sentence
and a copy-cleft sentence, e.g. such as between

7. a. We went out even though the rain was pouring down.
    b. The rain was pouring down, but we went out anyway.

emerges in comparing a wider set of a.-like forms with a wider set
of b.-like forms. Comparable to 7.a., with its subordinating conjunction (whether <u>even though</u>, <u>though</u>, or <u>although</u>) and its embedded
finite clause, are forms (reflecting a derivationally prior structure,
as noted in footnote 1) with a 'subordinating preposition(-al phrase)'
and an embedded nominalized clause:

8.
    We went out $\left\{\begin{array}{l}\text{despite}\\\text{in spite of}\\\text{regardless of}\\\text{notwithstanding}\end{array}\right\}$ the rain's pouring down.

Beside 7.b. are not only forms with expressions similar to <u>anyway</u>:

9.
    The rain was pouring down, but we went out $\left\{\begin{array}{l}\text{regardless}\\\text{nevertheless}\\\text{even so}\\\text{all the same}\end{array}\right\}$.

but, crucially, also ones with expressions containing a pronoun:

10.
    The rain was pouring down, but we went out $\left\{\begin{array}{l}\text{despite}\\\text{in spite of}\\\text{regardless of}\\\text{notwithstanding}\end{array}\right\}$
    that.

In this last copy-cleft sentence set, the portion after <u>but</u> can be seen
to be identical to the whole of one or another complex sentence in 8.
except for the appearance of the pronoun <u>that</u> in place of the embedded clause. Since a duplicate of this clause (in the finite form)

appears before the <u>but</u> in 10.'s copy-cleft sentence, we may suppose
that it has pronominalized what in deeper structure was its double
embedded on the right. The supposition is strengthened by the existence of a copy-cleft form like

    11. The rain was pouring down, but we went out despite the rain's
         pouring down.

(pronounced with a heavy stress on <u>despite</u> and a low pitch on the
remainder), which, though reserved for special effect, is within such
usage virtually synonymous with the form in 10. Hence, we may
conclude that the original identity of the post-conjunctional portion
of a copy-cleft sentence is, simply, a complex sentence.

    Within that portion, when the complex sentence's subordinate
clause is pronominalized -- yielding, e.g., <u>despite that</u> in 10. --
the term 'pro-clause' will here be applied to it. Expressions like
<u>anyway</u> and the other pronounless forms bracketed in 9., may then
be considered further derived forms of the pro-clause, in which all
overt trace of the contained pronoun has disappeared. An expression like <u>anyway</u> is essentially a pro-form for the whole of an original subordinate clause.

    The origin of the duplicate clause appearing initially in a copy-
cleft sentence is a matter of some consideration. On the one hand,
sentences like 2.b. seem to indicate that it is a transformationally
preposed replica of an original clause, the one embedded in the
complex sentence. On the other hand, a copy-cleft sentence like
12.b. could not be derived by any meaning-preserving transformation from any complex source, e.g., from 12.a.:

    12. a. Go home after you stop at the store!
         b. Stop at the store, and go home after that!

This suggests that the initial clause in a copy-cleft sentence is present at the deepest syntactic level as an independent entity, one that
is identical (enough for pronominalization) to a clause rightward in
the structure. I favor the latter interpretation for reasons which
will be given shortly below in a discussion of the semantics of the
copy-cleft construction. As to the name given to the construction,
by the former interpretation it would be more accurately called
'replica-and-original clefting;' by the latter it would be more accurately called 'antecedent-and-anaphor clefting;' but in order to
leave open the interpretation settled on as to the initial clause's
origin, the word 'copy' has been chosen because of its range of
meaning from 'replica' to 'identical counterpart.'

1.3 Grammatical characteristics of the pro-clause

Each particular pro-clause, whether less or more derived in form, has its own pattern of syntactic characteristics. These include: which connectives it co-occurs with, where in the copy-cleft sentence it must/may/cannot appear, what its prosody and juncturing must be, and what it permits/requires of the clausal subject as to equi-NP deletion.

We can illustrate with the concessive pro-clauses seen in 9. and 10., to which can be added still, yet, however, and though. Of these however and though can occur only with a "zero" connective, yet cannot occur with but, and only yet can occur gracefully with and:

13. a. It was raining; (*but/*and) $\begin{Bmatrix} \text{however we went out.} \\ \text{we went out, however/though.} \end{Bmatrix}$

    b. It was raining, $\begin{Bmatrix} \text{*but/and yet} \\ \text{but/}^x\text{and despite that} \end{Bmatrix}$ we went out.

Anyway and though cannot move out of final position, while still and yet must do so; only still and nevertheless can appear after the subject:

14. a. It was raining, but $\begin{Bmatrix} \text{even so} \\ \text{*anyway} \\ \text{still} \end{Bmatrix}$ we went out $\begin{Bmatrix} \text{even so} \\ \text{anyway} \\ \text{*still} \end{Bmatrix}$.

    b. It was raining, but we $\begin{Bmatrix} \text{still/nevertheless} \\ \text{*even so/*despite that} \end{Bmatrix}$ went out.

However and though, appearing finally, must occur after a junctural pause and with a special low intonation:

15. It was raining; we went out, however/though.

1.4 Transformations and surface forms

The sentences treated in the foregoing discussion have differed from each other in a certain set of formal respects, which can be abstracted and codified: They either lacked or had an initial duplicate clause (the factor distinguishing complex from copy-cleft sentences); and, among the latter, they either lacked or had a connective; lacked or had pronominalization of the embedded clause; had or lacked an overt pronoun in the resulting pro-clause; and had or lacked the pro-clause in (its original) sentence-final location. The relations between these different forms can be represented, perhaps with the least redundancy, by an ordered set of process-specifying transformations something like the following (including one additional one discussed later):

16. (0. copy-preposing)
    1. connective-introduction
    2. pronominalization = pro-clause formation
    3. pro-clause derivation
    4. pro-clause movement
    5. conflation of connective and pro-clause

(the order of 1 and 2 here is irrelevant, and that of 3 and 4 can be reversed with a slight change as to what each transformation would involve).

The derivation that these transformations make up can be illustrated symbolically for the concessive ("despite") form discussed above:

17. a. S_1 BE DESPITE S_2 [=basic complex S]

   b. $(\Rightarrow)S_2; S_1$ BE DESPITE S_2 [by "0"][=basic copy-cleft S]

   c. $\Rightarrow S_2,$ AND S_1 DESPITE S_2 [by "1"]

        (It was raining, but we went out despite its raining.)

   d. $\Rightarrow S_2,$ AND S_1 DESPITE THAT [by "2"][and, by lexical-insertion:]

        [$\Rightarrow$...despite/in spite of/regardless of/notwithstanding/...that]

        (It was raining, but we went out despite that.)

   e. $\Rightarrow S_2,$ AND S_1 DESPITE-THAT [by "3"][and, by lexical-insertion:]

        [$\Rightarrow$...anyway/regardless/nevertheless/even so/all the same/
        still/yet/however/though/$\emptyset$]

        (It was raining, but we went out anyway.)

   f. $\Rightarrow S_2,$ AND DESPITE-THAT S_1 [by "4;" shown here is only one
                       of the possible movements]

        (It was raining, but even so we went out.)

   g. $\Rightarrow S_2,$ AND-DESPITE-THAT S_1 [by "5"]

        (-- no examples for "despite" forms; see section 3)

The connective-introducing transformation at c. can be skipped with the succeeding operations still taking place:

   f'.   It was raining; even so we went out.

On the model of stages d. and e. of the preceding, we can present the surface pro-clauses for sentence-types involving other interclausal relations than that of concession. Corresponding to a complex sentence of "reason" -- S_1 BE BECAUSE-OF S_2 -- are the copy-cleft forms:

18. d. S_2, AND S_1 BECAUSE-OF THAT

   ⇒... <u>because of</u>/<u>on account of</u>/<u>by reason of</u>/<u>due to</u>/...<u>that</u>
   <u>for that reason</u>/ <u>on that account</u>
   <u>therefore</u>/<u>therefor</u>

   e. S_2, AND S_1 BECAUSE-OF-THAT

   ⇒...<u>hence</u>/<u>so</u>

Corresponding to a complex sentence of "temporal succession" --
S_1 BE AFTER S_2 -- are the copy-cleft forms:

19. d. S_2, AND S_1 AFTER THAT

   ⇒ ... <u>after</u>/<u>subsequent to</u>/...<u>that</u>

   e. S_2, AND S_1 AFTER-THAT

   ⇒ ... <u>afterwards</u>/<u>subsequently</u>/<u>then</u>/∅

Corresponding to a complex sentence of "additionality" -- S_1 BE IN-ADDITION-TO S_2 -- are the copy-cleft forms:

20. d. S_2, AND S_1 IN-ADDITION-TO THAT

   ⇒ ...<u>in addition to</u>/<u>besides</u>/<u>on top of</u>/...<u>that</u>

   e. S_2, AND S_1 IN-ADDITION-TO-THAT

   ⇒...<u>in addition</u>/<u>besides</u>/<u>as well</u>/<u>to boot</u>/<u>also</u>/<u>too</u>/∅

1.5 Copy-clefting of nominals

Copy-clefting is a more general process, with a wider domain of application, than that so far seen. First of all, an initial clausal copy needn't be of the clause following the subordinator in a complex sentence, but, really, can be of any clause, including, e.g., one in the subject position:

21. The rain's pouring down was why we stayed home.
   The rain was pouring down, and that's why we stayed home.

Secondly, it is not only clauses which can be involved in copy-clefting, but also nominals. Known by the term 'left-dislocation' (or 'topicalization'), the nominal process can now be seen as completely subsumed under the more general copy-clefting process. Thus, beside a FRENCH simplex sentence like

22. a. J'ai vu ma mère.
       'I saw my mother.'

a form like

    b. Ma mère, je l'ai vue.
       'My mother, I saw her.'

parallels a clausal copy-cleft form in having (in process terminology) a preposed copy, a pronominalized original, and a similar constructional meaning, as discussed below. (Alternatively, of course, copy-cleft forms like those in 1. can be considered to involve a generalization of "left-dislocation" or "topicalization" from nominals to clauses.)

JAPANESE, which virtually lacks any copy-cleft construction for clauses, has it highly developed for nominals. The preposed nominal copy receives the special marker wa; the original nominal with its postposition may be presumed first to pronominalize -- yielding the counterpart of the pro-clause -- and then to delete. E.g., beside what may be considered a more basic dative-containing form like

23. a. Mary ga   John ni mieru
       "Mary subj. John to is-visible"
       'John can see Mary.'

is the copy cleft form

    b. John wa   Mary ga   mieru
       "John copy Mary subj. is-visible"

which may be taken to derive via pronominalization and deletion from the form

    c. John wa,   Mary ga   John ni   mieru
       "John copy Mary subj. him   to   is-visible"
                              ∅

Sign-language can copy-cleft at one time two nominals of different function in a sentence. Thus, beside a presumably more basic form (each sign that would be made is indicated by an underlined ENGLISH word)

24. a. <u>Hank</u> <u>went-to</u> <u>Fresno</u>.

is a doubly-cleft form suggestively renderable as

    b. You know <u>Hank</u>? You know <u>Fresno</u>? Well, <u>he-went-there</u>.

Nominal copy-clefting can take place not only across the scope
of a whole sentence, but also within a constituent. E.g., in GER-
MAN, beside a presumably more basic possessor-possessed construction like that in

25. a. Ich habe <u>den Bleistift</u>   <u>des Jungen</u> gesehen.
      " I have the pencil(acc.) the boy(gen.) seen"
      'I saw the boy's pencil.'

is the regularly used copy-cleft formation in

    b. Ich habe <u>dem Jungen</u> <u>seinen Bleistift</u> gesehen.
      "I have the boy(dat.) his pencil(acc.) seen"

(the formation can also be used in most functions besides that of direct
object). This can be taken to derive from the a. form via these steps:

26. a.   [ACC- der Bleistift] [GEN- der Junge]

    b. ⇒ [DAT- der Junge] [ACC- der Bleistift] [GEN- der Junge]

    c. ⇒ [DAT- der Junge] [ACC- der Bleistift] [GEN- er ('he')]

    d. ⇒ [DAT- der Junge] [ACC- seiner Bleistift]

    e. ⇒ [dem Jungen] [seinen Bleistift]

    where b: copy-preposing (with <u>DAT</u> as the marker for "copy");
    c: pronominalization (of original by copy); d: possessive ad-
    jective formation; e: lexicalization of case-marker.

ENGLISH, too, has nominal copy-clefting within a constituent, as
seen by comparing the straightforward construction underlined in

27. a. Now we'll investigate <u>the more general process of popu-
      lation stabilization</u>.

with the copy-cleft one in

    b. Now we'll investigate <u>a more general process, that of
      population stabilization</u>.

1.6 Semantics and pragmatics of the copy-cleft construction

The main semantic property of the copy-cleft construction for clauses is that it provides for the independent assertion of a proposition that would otherwise be expressed solely presuppositionally. Both illocutionary forms are often necessary for a proposition: first, an assertion of it because it is new information, and then, once it is established in the domain of the known, the presuppositional use of it as a reference-ground against which to assert a further proposition. Thus, for the copy-cleft sentence of l.c., 'her stopping at the store' is needed as a known reference event in relation to which the event of 'her going home' can be temporally located; but it must also be asserted for the listener who is now finding out about it for the first time. For, e.g., to the complex sentence form, which does not additionally assert the reference event:

28. a. She went home after stopping at the store.

a listener could well respond to the presumption of certain prior knowledge on his part:

   b. Oh, I didn't even know she'd stopped at the store in the first place.

whereas to the copy-cleft sentence form, which does assert the event:

   c. She stopped at the store and then went home.

he could not. It is mainly this semantic difference between the two constructions -- the extra propositional assertion made by a copy-cleft form as against the complex sentence form -- which earlier in this paper prompted the favoring of two distinct underlying structures rather than deriving one form from the other.

The second main property of the copy-cleft construction is that it breaks up a certain type of complexity into more handleable parts. The type is where a complicated constituent requiring much linguistic processing is embedded within a complicated construction that also requires much processing. For a non-cleft construction, the former's processing must take place amid the latter's in what may be too cumbersome a performance task. But the copy-cleft construction provides for the constituent's processing independently and beforehand. And it leaves a place-holding token of

the gestalted result (viz., a pronoun) in the larger construction for
the processing, now simplified, next to occur there. The easing
of the performance load provided by copy-clefting is particularly
evident in 24. and 27. of the examples above.

2. The Connectives

The 'connective-introduction' process, listed as transformation 1
in 16., is understood to apply to a basic copy-cleft structure with a
'zero' or 'semi-colon' connective, such as is indicated in 29.a. It
here introduces a 'connective' morpheme under a node 'C' (for "Connective") before the embedded complex sentence, and forms of these
two a new constituent, whose node can be labeled 'CS' (with a letter
donated from each dominated node), as indicated in 29.b.

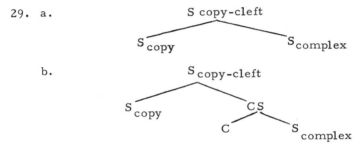

29. a.   S copy-cleft

             S copy   S complex

    b.   S copy-cleft

          S copy   C S

                          C   S complex

The 'C' node is conceived as labeling a new syntactic category, one
to which belong 'coordinating conjunctions' and other forms next
shown to be related thereto (the category is virtually unrepresented
in some languages, e.g. JAPANESE). Pending the noticing of any
new types, all the connective formations in the languages looked at
so far seem to fall into three main categories: a coordinating conjunction that takes a finite form of the embedded complex sentence,
a gerundivizing or comparable element with the (accordingly non-
finite) embedded sentence, and a relativizing element again with a
finite form of the embedded sentence. These three types can be
represented syntactically by having the C node able to dominate
only three deep connective morphemes, such as can be represented
(for any language) as

30.   C
                                 |
                           ⎧ AND   ⎫
                           ⎨ WITH   ⎬
                           ⎩ SUCHTHAT ⎭

Each of these in turn gives rise (by lexical insertion) to various of the surface forms present in a particular language. The three formations will now be considered one by one.

2.1 — AND —

For each of the deep connectives, the types of embedded complex sentences with which it can occur must be determined. In ENGLISH, AND can occur before all the types I've looked at except that of anteriority (before), as indicated in

31.   :
                                       .

$$S_2, \text{ AND } S_1 \left\{ \begin{array}{l} \text{BECAUSE OF} \\ \text{AFTER} \\ \text{IN-ADDITION-TO} \\ \text{IN-THE-EVENT-OF} \\ \text{BY} \\ *\text{BEFORE} \\ \text{DESPITE} \\ \text{IN-PLACE-OF} \end{array} \right\} \text{ THAT } (=S_2).$$

                                       :
                                       .

The occurrence in ENGLISH of surface and in construction with each of the first five subordinator types listed here has already been seen in the examples of 1., 2., and 6 (an and can be inserted before the so in 1.a. to make it a suitable illustration here). Its inappropriateness in construction with BEFORE can be seen in

32. a. *She went home, and she (had) stopped at the store
         before that.

in contrast with the gerundive connective which can occur in such a construction:

b. She went home $\left\{ \begin{array}{l} \text{having stopped at the store before that} \\ \text{having first stopped at the store} \end{array} \right\}$.

AND in construction with the last two subordinators in 31. lexicalizes in ENGLISH as surface but, as seen already for DESPITE in 1.b. and as shown for IN-PLACE-OF in

33. a. We stayed home instead of going to the movies.
                                   (complex)
     b. We didn't go to the movies, but stayed home instead.
                                   (copy-cleft)

Investigation will be required to determine the semantic differential between those complex sentence types which construct in a
copy-cleft form with surface <u>and</u>, those which do so with surface
<u>but</u>, and those with neither. However, it is a concomitant of the
notions in this study that, in the first instance, a connective like
<u>and</u> has no meaning of its own beyond that involved in its selection
over others, e.g., over <u>but</u>, and that signaling the constructional
meaning of copy-clefting. Thus, the usual notion that there is a
basic meaning to clause-conjunctional <u>and</u> of 'coordinative addition'
(the 'and also' meaning) -- or, secondarily, of 'temporal sequence'
(the 'and then' meaning) — is disputed here. It is held, rather,
that the pro-clause is basically the constituent which specifies the
inter-clausal relation; that its deletion from the surface, as of

34. a. <u>also</u> or <u>in addition to that</u> from
         He holds down a regular job and works at a sideline.

     b. <u>then</u> or <u>after that</u> from
         She stopped at the store and went home.

     c. <u>in that event</u> from
         Come any closer and I'll scream.

can make the connective, now left alone, appear to be the original
bearer of such specifications; and that the usual notion is in any
case faulted by observation of the range of meanings, outside of
'additionality,' which solo <u>and</u> is involved in, as in the sentences
of 34.

2.2 — <u>WITH</u> --

Beside a complex sentence form like the following, referring,
e.g., to a man siphoning out a gas tank:

35. a. He spilled gas all over in the process of draining the tank.

is not only a copy-cleft form with <u>and</u> and a finite clause:

     b. He drained the tank, and spilled gas all over in the process.

but also one with a gerundivized clause:

     c. He drained the tank, spilling gas all over in the process.

In addition to this, there are certain related copy-cleft forms with
a preposition-like element before the gerundivized clause -- one
where the S_1 clause has a negative:

36. a. He didn't spill any gas in the process of draining the tank.
    b. He drained the tank without spilling any gas in the process.

and one where the two clauses have different subjects:

37. a. The gas spilled all over in the process of his draining
        the tank.
    b. He drained the tank, with the gas spilling all over in
        the process.

This suggests that 35.c. in a deeper structural form also has such
a prepositional element, perhaps with, which then disappears along
with the equi-deleted subject nominal. It further suggests that
gerundivization in a copy-cleft sentence is the concomitant of a
particular deep prepositional connective form, aptly representable
as WITH. Or, indeed, it may be the consequence of it, if that form
is understood to give rise to the gerundivizing morphemes themselves:

38. a. ..., WITH [he spilled gas all over in the process (of that)]
        with... (-'s)... -ing

   ⇒b. ..., with his spilling gas all over in the process.
              ∅

The deep connective WITH differs from AND as to the types of
embedded complex sentence before which it can occur in ENGLISH,
as indicated in

39.

$$S_2, \ \text{WITH} \ S_1 \left\{ \begin{array}{l} \vdots \\ \text{ALL-DURING} \\ \text{IN-the PROCESS-OF} \\ \text{BY} \\ \text{AFTER} \\ \text{BEFORE} \\ *\text{BECAUSE-OF} \\ *\text{DESPITE} \\ *\text{IN-the EVENT-OF} \\ \text{IN-the DOING-OF} \\ \vdots \end{array} \right\} \ \text{THAT} \ (=S_2).$$

The following sentences, some of which have been seen in a comparable form earlier, illustrate the first listed acceptable usages.

40. a. He slept, dreaming $\begin{Bmatrix} \text{the whole time} \\ \text{the while} \end{Bmatrix}$. [2]

 b. He drained the tank, spilling gas all over in the process.

 c. Mays batted in three runs, thereby providing some excitement for the viewers.

 d. The fawn rose for a second to its feet, then immediately falling back down.

 e. She went home, having first stopped at the store.

The unacceptable usages listed can be illustrated by:

41. a. *We were tired, therefore staying home.

 b. *We were tired, nevertheless going out.

 c. *Come any closer, with me screaming (if you do/in that event).

The complex sentence type characterized in 39. by the deep subordinator IN-the DOING-OF may well come to be seen as the source for ordinary manner adverbs, which would then be understood to arise only after copy-clefting. Thus beside a complex sentence form like

42. a. I $\begin{Bmatrix} \text{was careful} \\ \text{had care} \end{Bmatrix}$ in drying the cups.

are copy-cleft forms like

 b. I dried the cups, $\begin{Bmatrix} \text{being careful} \\ \text{with care} \end{Bmatrix}$ $\begin{Bmatrix} \text{in the doing} \\ \text{at it} \\ \text{about it} \\ \text{-}\emptyset \end{Bmatrix}$

(the with of with care is taken not as the connective, but as a component of having, as in the boy [who has >] with the dog).

---

[2] Although gerundive-cleft forms (especially when containing an overt with or without) may at first seem like ordinary complex sentences with a main and a subordinate clause, sentences like that in 40.a. militate against such an interpretation. For, as discussed in Talmy (1975b), certain event-relations can be expressed in only one direction, e.g., that of 'contingent contemporaneity' only with the contingent event in the S_1 clause:
He dreamt while he slept.
*He slept while he dreamt.
The arguments of such irreversible relations can be used as 'tracers' to show, in such transformed structures as 40.a., which clause has gone where.

Here, the first-bracketed expressions may be considered able to derive further into a manner adverb that would have to be followed by the zero pro-clause option:

c. I dried the cups carefully.

If taken as such, this manifestation of copy-clefting -- as the route by which adverbial manner expressions arise -- may well be universal among languages.

The copy-cleft type listed at top in 39. and exemplified in 40.a. -- i.e., a gerundival form expressing 'temporal concomitance' -- may be another copy-cleft type that is universal. Even JAPANESE, in what may well be its only breach (except for adverbs) of copy-cleftlessness, uses its gerundive verb form in the service of a copy-cleft version of this interclausal relation:

43.   (^{x}sono aida ni   ) yume   o   mite ite, nemutta
      "\in the course of that/ dreams 'obj.' seeing   slept"
      'He slept, dreaming (the while.'

JAPANESE seems to have no other copy-cleft use of the gerundive form.[3]   E.g., it cannot be used to express '...-ing...after that,' as in:

44.   *Sono ato de uti e kaette,   mise ni yotta.
      "after that home to returning store at stopped"
      'He stopped at the store, returning home after that.'

Some languages have two different gerundival forms for use in copy-cleft constructions, that between them divide up the expression of the different semantic types listed in 39. Thus, SWAHILI, in addition to having a gerundive form — marked by a -ki- prefix in the verb -- that expresses at least temporal concomitance and,

---

[3] The gerundive otherwise acts to mark the subordinate clause in an ordinary complex sentence, where it has such meanings as 'while...-ing,' as in (i), and 'after having...-ed,' as in (ii):
  (i) Nemutte ite, yume o   mita.
      "sleeping   dreams 'obj.' saw"
      'He dreamt as he slept.
  (ii) Mise ni yotte,   uti e kaetta.
      "store at stopping/having stopped home to returned"
      'He returned home, (after) having stopped at the store.'

I think, several other notions, has a further gerundive form --
marked by a -ka-prefix -- which specifically expresses temporal
succession, i.e., '...-ing,...after that' or 'then...-ing':

45. ni-li -kwenda soko-ni, ni-ka   -rudi
    "I past go   market-to I then...-ing return"
    'I went to the market, then returning.'

The ka-containing verb is understood not to be a finite verb form --
which, e.g., in 45. would then merit a gloss like 'and then I returned' -- because it lacks the overt tense markers of such a form;
rather, it always follows a finite form, drawing its tense sense
therefrom.

Though the gerundive construction in a copy-cleft form is non-
finite, often some relative tense indication can be made. In ENG-
LISH, some degree of 'prior' versus 'contemporaneous' relative
temporal placement is possible with the '...having...-ed' versus
'...-ing' inflections, as in 40.e. and 40.b. There is in addition
the somewhat marginal 'relatively future' form '...being to...,'
of which the being deletes along with the with and the equi-deleted
subject, as in

46. a. They were never again to meet after they parted. (complex)
    b. They parted, never again to meet.   (copy-cleft)
         (<..., with their being never again to meet [after that])
                        Ø

If WITH is taken as the deep connective for the surface appearance of any non-finite clause in a copy-cleft sentence, then another
surface form to which it gives rise aside from the specifically gerundive -- for languages which, like ENGLISH, have the distinction
and the option -- is the infinitival, as in

47. a. Mays batted in three runs,
              WITH [he provided some excitement for the
                                    viewers thereby]
              for...to

    b. ⇒..., for him to provide some excitement for the
                  Ø   viewers thereby

    c. ⇒..., to provide some excitement for the viewers thereby.

In YIDDISH, the infinitive form in cu in certain copy-cleft constructions specifically has the 'temporal concomitance' meaning
seen for the gerundive in 40.a.:

48. a. Es iz gekumen cu geyn/forn in štot a soyxer.
         "it came   to walk/ride to town a merchant"
         'A merchant came walking/riding into town.'
         (i.e., '...came into town, walking/riding thereduring')

     b. Er hot gebraxt cu trogn/firn sxeyre
         "he brought   to carry/cart wares"
         'He carried/carted in wares.'
         (i.e., '...brought wares, carrying/carting them
         thereduring')

2.3 — SUCHTHAT —

The third main category of copy-cleft sentence types, as noted
earlier, consists of those with a relative formation for the embedded
complex-sentence, as in

49. a. She stopped at the store, after which she went home.
     b. He holds down a regular job, in addition to which he
         works at a sideline.
     c. Mays batted in three runs, whereby he provided some
         excitement for the viewers.
     d. The door swung open, whereupon I entered.

The kinds of complex sentences which can appear thus in a relative
formation seem generally to be the same as can construct with AND.
In fact, a rough surface version of the general syntactic structure
of relative-clefted forms can be provided by the one given in 31. for
AND-clefted forms with the AND removed and the that replaced by which.

As for the deeper basis of relative clefting, either of two different structures might be involved. One would be a zero-cleft structure, where the relativizing element (wh-, or whatever) appears
beside the nominal that it affects, as in 50.a. The other is a con-
nective-cleft structure, where the connective introduced is the
relativizing element itself as in 50.b.:

50. a. S_2; S_1 AFTER   wh- THAT (=S_2)

     b. S_2, SUCHTHAT S_1 AFTER THAT (=S_2)

The latter alternative seems preferable for the following reasons.

First, with this interpretation, the various types of copy-cleft
formations receive a unified syntactic account.

A second reason for introducing relativization as a connective on a par with the others, as done under the C-node in 30., is that it cannot co-occur with them. Thus, while each of the connectives SUCHTHAT, WITH, AND singly yields a grammatical copy-cleft form, e.g., in

51. a. Mays batted in three runs, $\begin{cases}\text{whereby he provided} \\ \text{thereby providing} \\ \text{and thereby provided}\end{cases}$ some

   excitement for the viewers.

the combination of SUCHTHAT with WITH or with AND does not:

b. *Mays batted in three runs, $\begin{cases}\text{whereby providing} \\ \text{and whereby he provided}\end{cases}$

   some excitement for the viewers.

Thirdly, there are arguments why a relative construction of any type should be underlain by a structure comparable to 50.b., i.e., where the relativizing element is outside the relative clause and the relativized nominal is a pronoun within it. First, a number of languages have just such a structure at the surface, e.g. YIDDISH with its vos succeeded by a pronoun in any grammatical function:

52.   Der boxer vos   ix gib em   esn š̌teyt   dortn.
      "the boy 'suchthat' I give him(dat.) food is standing there"
      'The boy I give food to is standing there.'

as well as OLD ENGLISH with its þe, HEBREW with š̌e and SWA-HILI with its interfixed -cho-/-vyo-/...(in agreement with the antecedent).

Secondly, the surface relative construction in ENGLISH and many other languages derives quite directly from such a structure: simply by the pronoun's moving to where the relativizing element already is, and conflating with it to form a relative wh- word, e.g.:

53. a. the boy SUCHTHAT I give food to him is standing there.

     b. ⇒the boy SUCHTHAT-him I give food to -- is standing there.

     c. ⇒The boy whom I give food to is standing there.

Thirdly, the localization, in a deep morpheme like SUCHTHAT, of the syntactic 'relative' relation between two clauses permits also the explicit representation there of that relation's meaning (still to be investigated)· In other treatments, where, e.g., the 'relative' relation is represented by the location of clause within determiner, its meaning is nowhere explicitly represented.

3. Conflation of Connective and Pro-clause

In some cases, a pro-clause which has moved to beside the connective then conflates with it to give rise to a wholly (phonologically) distinct form.

3.1 Involving AND

With AND as the connective, a certain pair of forms which can newly arise are also what traditional grammar would classify as coordinating conjunctions. One of these is or (else), which arises in a copy-cleft form whose embedded complex sentence expresses the notion 'if not for':

54. a. S_2, but S_1 EXCEPTFOR(-)THAT (=S_2)

  ⇒... except for/but for/other(wise) than for/...that
  if not for/if it were not for/...that
  otherwise/else

  e.g.: I didn't have the time, but I would have joined if
    not for that.

 b. ⇒S_2, but else S_1
    or (else)

  e.g.: I didn't have the time, or I would have joined.

Additional evidence for a different derivational origin for this clausal or is that it cannot be paired with either:

55. *Either I didn't have the time, or I would have joined.

The other one is nor, which arises in a copy-cleft sentence of 'negative additionality' (i.e., one deficiency augmented by another). The symbolic formulation in 20. for the '(positive) additionality' copy-clefts serves as well here, with the S_1 and S_2 understood as both containing negatives. The list of pro-clauses in 20. e. now must additionally contain either and neither, the use of which is exemplified by sentences like:

56. a. He doesn't hold down a regular job, and he doesn't
   take any odd jobs either.
 b. He doesn't hold down a regular job, and neither does
   he take any odd jobs.

The and and neither juxtaposed, as in 56. b., can be taken to undergo optionally the further step of conflating into <u>nor</u>, as in

> c. He doesn't hold down a regular job, no r does he take
>   any odd jobs.

3.2 <u>Involving a relative</u>

There is a class of sentences which contain what at first glance
look like subordinating conjunctions, but which nevertheless somehow strike this writer's semantic sensibilities as copy-cleft forms,
e.g.:

> 57. a. Her real name is Catherine, <u>although</u> she calls herself
>   'Jackie.'
>   b. Wood is flammable, <u>while</u> our new plastic is fire-proof.
>   c. Everyone already knows that the earth is a sphere,
>   <u>whereas</u> I now know that it's a hollow sphere. (said
>   by a mad scientist)
>   d. He was lecturing to his class <u>when</u> suddenly the door
>   burst open.
>   e. The cherry trees were in bloom <u>when</u> I first fell in love.

The main reason for such an interpretation no doubt is that, in
these constructions, relatively background information is asserted
independently and before the newer information, the same 'S_2, S_1 $(+S_2)$'
set-up seen for unmistakably copy-cleft forms. In these constructions, the second clause seems, in particular, to be based on a
relative formation, by semantic effect as well as in having neither
conjunction nor gerundive. If the copy-cleft interpretation is accepted, then the conjunction-resembling clause-introducers,
underlined above, may be taken as arising by the conflation of
SUCHTHAT ($\rightarrow\rightarrow$ <u>which</u>) and the pro-clause, something like:

> 58. a. ..., <u>notwithstanding which</u> or ..., <u>in the face of which</u>
>   although   although
>   b. ..., <u>in distinction to which</u> or..., <u>in comparison with which</u>
>   while   while
>   c. ..., <u>in contrast with which</u> or..., <u>above and beyond which</u>
>   whereas   whereas
>   d. ..., <u>in the midst of which</u>
>   when
>   e. ..., <u>(a period) during which</u>
>   when

Conclusive demonstration of the copy-cleft interpretation is not yet forthcoming, but a couple of indications in that direction can be shown.   First, the putative conflates are in some cases grammatically distinct from the unmistakable subordinating conjunctions to which they are lexically kin.   E.g., while true subordinating although can be replaced by even though, or by despite and gerundivization, without substantial meaning change for the sentence:

59. a. She calls herself 'Jackie' $\left\{ \begin{matrix} \text{although} \\ \text{even though} \end{matrix} \right\}$ her mother asked her not to. $\Big\}$
despite her mother's asking her not to.

the putatively copy-cleft although, e.g., that seen in 57.a., cannot be so replaced without changing the meaning, or in fact in some cases, as here, rendering the sentence slightly absurd:

b. ˣHer real name is Catherine $\left\{ \begin{matrix} \text{even though she calls herself 'Jackie.'} \\ \text{despite her calling herself 'Jackie.'} \end{matrix} \right\}$

(the implication here seeming to be that reality has willfully thwarted someone's practice).   The copy-cleft although clause, as in 57.a., furthermore, seems to have a special prosody, something like that of a low-intoned aside.   And, while a true subordinate clause introduced by when can prepose:

60. a. The projector was turned off when he finished lecturing
         to his class.
   =   When he finished lecturing to his class, the projector
         was turned off.

the when clause in 57.d., putatively a distinct copy-cleft form, cannot:

b. *When suddenly the door burst open, he was lecturing
      to his class.

Secondly, the sentences that can be found which are basically equivalent in meaning to those of 57. (except for the independent S_2 assertion), but which have the reverse clause order, are true complex sentences whose subordinators are the same as or like those suggested in 58.   E.g., clearly related to 57.c. is the complex sentence

61. a. I now know that the earth is a hollow sphere, above and
         beyond everyone's already knowing that it's a sphere.

and related to 57.d. is

61. b. The door suddenly burst open in the midst of his
    lecturing to his class.

4. Neo-subordination

While the right-hand clauses in sentences like those of 40. and
57. have been seen as the post-connective clauses -- following,
respectively, a gerundivizer and a conflated relativizer -- in copy-
cleft sentences, they nevertheless look like and to a certain extent
act like the subordinate clauses in complex sentences. For this,
they can be said to be instances of 'neo-subordination.' E.g.,
whereas a copy-cleft sentence with <u>AND</u> or unconflated <u>SUCHTHAT</u>
cannot prepose the connective-clause:

62. a. *And then she went home, she stopped at the store.
       *So we stayed home, it was raining.
       *But we still went out, it was raining.
    b. *After which she went home, she stopped at the store.
       *Whereupon I entered, the door swung open.

the copy-cleft sentences with neo-subordination, like regular complex sentences, all (except 57.d.) <u>can</u> do so:

67. a. Dreaming the while, he slept.
       Without spilling any gas in the process, he drained the
       tank.
    b. Although she calls herself 'Jackie,' her real name is
       Catherine.
       When I first fell in love, the cherry trees were in bloom.

And, to a very small degree, a copy-cleft form with neo-subordination can in turn constitute the complex-sentence-like model on
the basis of which a new copy-cleft form takes shape, suggesting
that, if copy-clefting is taken as a transformational process, it
must also be considered cyclic. Thus, beside an already gerundive-
cleft:

63. a. He drained the tank without spilling any gas in the
       process (of it).

is the further gerundive-clefting

    b. He didn't spill any gas in the process of draining the
       tank, draining it without doing so.

(here, the pronominalization <u>doing so</u> reads better than <u>that</u>.)

BIBLIOGRAPHY

Kuno, Susumu. 1973. The structure of the Japanese language. M.I.T. Press.

Talmy, Leonard. 1975a. Semantics and syntax of motion. Syntax and semantics, vol. IV, ed. by J. Kimball. New York: Academic Press.

_____. 1975b. Figure and Ground in complex sentences. This volume.

_____. 1976. Semantic causative types. Syntax and semantics, vol. VI, ed. by M. Shibatani. New York: Academic Press.

Coordination Reduction

HELGA HARRIES-DELISLE

ABSTRACT

The purpose of this paper is to investigate the process of coordination reduction in various languages and to propose a universal
set of rules that will account for all types of coordination reduction.
In a brief discussion of some of the more recent proposals on coordination reduction it will be shown that these proposals fail to
account for the data in a principled way, mostly because they assume the directionality constraint. It will be argued that coordination reduction consist of a deletion rule that only operates forward,
and of a regrouping rule that functions to restore the scope relations
within the reduced sentence. Finally, it will be suggested that many
of the constraints on deletion and regrouping can be accounted for
if we assume the principle of scope.

This is a modified version of a paper published in Working Papers
on Language Universals, No. 11, April 1973, 139-209. I would like
to thank the following consultants for their cooperation: Salisu Abu-
bakar, Steven Begay, Dina Crockett, Maria Erdi, Arnold Ertan,
Pamela Frydman, Amil Joglekar, Hysatoyo Kato, Susan Lenkey,
Mohamed Redjeb, Vicky Shu.

CONTENTS

1. The Rule Component

1. 1 The deletion rule

The subject of coordination reduction has been extensively dis-cussed in recent linguistic writings. Nevertheless, many relevant questions still remain unanswered, and this paper is an attempt to answer at least some of them. Before presenting and justifying my own proposal, I will briefly discuss three analyses of coordination reduction, namely those of J. Ross, A. Koutsoudas, and G. Sanders. These three analyses were chosen because the coordination reduction processes proposed in them are assumed to be universal. Ross (1967a, 1967b) argued that two rules are needed to reduce coordinate structures, namely a rule -- called 'gapping' -- which applies to verbs only, and a conjunction reduction rule that applies to other kinds of constituents. Ross had observed that "the order in which Gapping operates depends on the order of elements at the time that the rule applies; if the identical elements are on left branches, Gapping operates forward; if they are on right branches, it operates backward" (1967b: 5). This dependency of the direction of deletion on the branching structure of the identical constituents has been called the directionality constraint. Right or left branching also plays a role in Ross' conjunction reduction rule which Chomsky-adjoins "to the right or left of the coordinate node a copy of some constituent which occurs in all conjuncts on a right or left branch, respectively, and then deletes the original nodes" (1967a: 175). According to Ross, therefore, the deletion of verbs differs from the deletion of other constituent types and consequently two different rules are needed. Ross' position was first attacked by G. Sanders (1970), who claimed that not only verbal reductions but all other reductions as well are subject to the directionality condition, and that consequently there is no need for two reduction rules.

Sanders' claim that all instances of coordinate reduction can be accounted for by one single reduction rule was substantiated by Koutsoudas (1971), who proposed the following coordination reduc-tion rule:

"Coordination Deletion (Optional)

Given a coordination in which each conjunct includes a consti-tuent which is identical to the corresponding constituent of each other conjunct, all but one of the identical constituents may be deleted, the undeleted constituent being that of the first conjunct if it is a left-branching constituent, and that of the last conjunct if it is a right-branching constituent." (p. 347)

In other words, if the identical constituents are on right branches, deletion operates backward, if they are on left branches, it operates forward. An example of both forward and backward reduction is provided by verbal deletion in ENGLISH. In sentences with intransitive verbs, the verbs are on right branches and deletion operates backward, e.g., 1.

    1. a. John laughed and Mary laughed.
        b. John and Mary laughed.

In sentences with transitive verbs, on the other hand, the verbs are on left branches and deletion operates forward, e.g., 2.

    2. a. John bought a book and Mary bought a magazine.
        b. John bought a book and Mary a magazine.

Ross' and Koutsoudas' approaches therefore have in common that they attempt to restrict their respective reduction rule(s) in such a way that it will only generate grammatical surface forms, i.e. the reduction rule not only deletes constituents, it also attempts to generate correct surface orders. This is implicit in the directionality constraint and more explicit in Ross' conjunction reduction rule which regroups constituents before it deletes some of them. Furthermore the reduction rules are constrained in such a way that they will only generate surface orders which are identical to the orders permitted in unreduced sentences; that is, both Ross' rules and Koutsoudas' predict that if in a given language the object precedes the verb in an unreduced structure, it will also do so in a reduced structure. For example, the reduction rules predict that an unreduced $\underline{SOV + SOV}$ order will always reduce to an $\underline{SO + OV}$ order. [1]   However, in many languages $\underline{SOV + O}$ reductions are also grammatical surface reductions of an unreduced $\underline{SOV + SOV}$ structure; that is, these languages allow split object coordination as the two objects do not have to be adjacent in the reduced surface structure. As Ross' and Koutsoudas' reduction rules do not generate any reduced structures with split coordination, ad hoc movement rules are needed which move one of the non-identical constituents. For instance, in the above case, an object movement rule would convert the $\underline{SO + OV}$ output order of the reduction rule into a $\underline{SOV +}$ $\underline{O}$ order. A specific example discussed by both Ross and Koutsoudas

---

[1] In this paper the following abbreviations are used:
S = subject of a sentence (except if used in a phrase marker, where S represents the sentence node); V = verb of a sentence; O = object of a sentence; ADV = adverb of a sentence; P= participle of a sentence.

is split object coordination in HINDI. In HINDI the surface order of constituents is SOV. However, if we have a coordinate structure like 3.a. below and if the verb is deleted, we not only get a surface order as in 3.b., but also an alternate order as in 3.c.

3. a. SOV + SOV
    b. SO + OV
    c. SOV + O

Examples of 3.b. and 3.c. are 4.a. and 4.b. respectively.

4. a. Jon-ne kela aur safarchand bech lia.
        "John banana and apple bought"
        'John bought a banana and an apple.'

    b. Jon-ne kela bech lia aur safarchand bhi.
        "John banana bought and apple also"
        'John bought a banana and also an apple.'[2]

3.b. is the reduced order predicted by Ross' and Koutsoudas' analyses, thus claiming that in HINDI the object precedes the verb, independent of whether it is a conjoined object or not. In 3.c., however, one of the objects follows the verb, which is not permitted in an unreduced sentence, e.g. 5.:

5.   *Jon-ne bech lia kela.
        'John bought a banana.'

In order to account for 3.c. both Ross and Koutsoudas assumed that HINDI has an underlying SVO order and a movement rule which in Ross' analysis obligatorily postposes the verb. This verb postposing rule applies to unreduced as well as to reduced structures, and it is unordered with respect to gapping; that is, it can apply before gapping, i.e. 6.b., or after gapping, i.e. 6.a.:

6. a.   SVO + SVO   b. SVO + SVO

    gapping, opt.   SVO + S O   ----------
    verb postposing, obl.   SOV + S O   SOV + SOV
    gapping, opt.   ----------   SO + SOV

Split coordination of objects is not only found in HINDI, but also in languages like RUSSIAN and HUNGARIAN.

---

[2] The occurrence of <u>also</u> will be discussed later.

7. RUSSIAN
    a. Vanja vodu pil, a Maša vino pila.
        "John water drank and Mary wine drank"
        'John drank water, and Mary drank wine. '

    b. Vanja vodu, a Maša vino pila.
        "John water and Mary wine drank"
        'John drank water and Mary wine. '

    c. Vanja vodu pil, a Maša vino.
        "John water drank and Mary wine"
        'John drank water and Mary wine. '

8. HUNGARIAN:
    a. János egy almát vett és János egy banánt vett.
        "John an apple bought and John a banana bought"
        'John bought an apple and John bought a banana. '

    b. János egy almát és egy banánt vett.
        "John an apple and a banana bought"
        'John bought an apple and a banana. '

    c. János egy almát vett és egy banánt.
        "John an apple bought and a banana"
        'John bought an apple and a banana. '

Ross does not discuss the HUNGARIAN data, but presumably he
would account for it in the same way as he does for the RUSSIAN
data. In order to generate sentences like 7.c., Ross claims that
languages like RUSSIAN have a rule called 'scrambling' which
places the verb after the object. He furthermore claims that gapping is an 'anywhere' rule that can either apply before or after
scrambling, allowing for the following derivations:

9. a.   SVO + SVO   b. SVO + SVO

        gapping, opt.   SVO + S O   ----------
        scrambling, opt.   SVO + S O   SOV + SOV
        gapping, opt.   ---------   SO + SOV

Thus, both orders are generated. [3]

---

[3]For a detailed discussion of Ross' approach see Sanders 1970
and Koutsoudas 1971.

Contrary to Ross who needs one movement rule -- called verb-postposing -- for HINDI and another movement rule -- called scrambling -- for languages like RUSSIAN, Koutsoudas argues that only one movement rule is needed to account for object coordination in HINDI, RUSSIAN, and HUNGARIAN, namely a rule that preposes the object after coordination reduction has taken place, resulting in the following derivation.

10.		SVO + SVO
	coord. red., opt.	SVO + S O
	obj. prep., opt.	SOV + S O

Object preposing is optional. If it does not apply, sentences like 7.b. and 8.b. are generated, if it does apply, 7.c. and 8.c. are generated.

The above data shows that Koutsoudas' analysis is more general than that of Ross'. Furthermore Koutsoudas' analysis is independently motivated for RUSSIAN and HUNGARIAN if we assume that their underlying form has an SVO order as there has to be a rule that converts SVO orders to SOV ones. However, Koutsoudas' rule has one major drawback -- it allows for the generation of ungrammatical surface forms. That is, if RUSSIAN has an object preposing rule that follows coordination reduction, this rule will not only generate all of those reduced structures which are grammatical in RUSSIAN but cannot be directly generated by Koutsoudas' coordination deletion rule, but it will also generate SV+SOV surface structures, which can be derived from an underlying SVO conjunction.

11.		SVO + SVO
	coord. red., opt.	SV + SVO
	obj. prep., opt.	SV + SOV

A derivation like 11, however, results in RUSSIAN as well as in HUNGARIAN in ungrammatical surface forms, e.g. 12. and 13.

12. RUSSIAN
    *Vanja kupil, a Maša jabloko s"ela
    "John bought, and Mary the apple ate"

13. HUNGARIAN:
    *János vett és Vili egy almát evett.
    "John bought and Bill an apple ate"

Consequently, in order to block the generation of sentences like 12. and 13., Koutsoudas has to constrain his object preposing rule so that it does not apply if the object is in the second conjunct.

Of the three analyses mentioned at the beginning of this paper, only those proposed by Ross and Koutsoudas have been discussed so far. Sanders' analysis was left aside, because its premises differ considerably from those of Ross' and Koutsoudas'. While these assume that constituents are ordered in their underlying syntactic representation, Sanders assumes that underlying structures are order free and that surface order is imposed by a set of ordering rules. He furthermore assumes that coordination reduction precedes the application of these ordering rules, i.e. the same set of rules will impose a surface order on unreduced and on reduced sets of constituents. From this follows that the surface order of reduced sentences does not differ from the surface order of unreduced sentences. However, as we have seen above, the surface order of reduced sentences is not always identical to that of unreduced sentences. We have also seen that Ross and Koutsoudas try to account for this fact by assuming the existence of movement rules that apply after coordination reduction. However, Sanders cannot make use of special movement rules which would apply after coordination reduction, as such rules would violate one of the constraints he imposes on his grammar, i.e. the Invariant Order Constraint. [4] He therefore has to formulate his ordering rules in such a way that they will generate all of the surface forms that occur in reduced sentences. The two ordering rules that Sanders proposes for languages like RUSSIAN are 14. and 15. below (Sanders' 43.i. and 43.ii., p. 21).

14.   (-O, O) → (-O & O) (a non-object precedes an object)

15.   (-V, V) → (-V & V) (a non-verb precedes a verb)

We can infer from the way Sanders applies these rules that they are ordered with respect to each other, i.e. 14. always precedes 15, and that the reapplication of the rules is optional. [5] The latter

---

[4]The Invariant Order Constraint "requires that if an element A is ordered to the left of an element B in any line of any derivation, there is no line in that derivation in which A is ordered to the right of B" (Sanders 1970: 1). In other words, constituents cannot be moved around by rules after ordering has taken place.

[5] As all constituents have to be ordered with respect to each other, this means that if an ordering rule A does optionally not

assumption is made use of to derive reduced $\underline{SO + SOV}$ surface orders, e.g. 16. (Sanders' 45. right hand column, p. 21).

16. a. $\underline{(S, \, (V, \, O), \quad (S, \, O)}$
          $-O \qquad O \quad -O \quad O$
          ‾‾‾‾‾‾‾‾‾‾‾‾‾‾‾‾‾‾‾‾
          $O \quad -O$

          RULE $\downarrow$ 14

     b. $(\underline{S} \, \& \, \underline{O}) \, \& \, (\underline{S} \, \& \, (V, \, O))$
          $-O \quad O \quad -O \qquad O$
          ‾‾‾‾‾‾‾‾‾‾‾‾‾‾‾‾‾‾‾‾‾‾‾‾‾‾
          $-O \qquad\qquad\qquad O$

     c. $(S \, \& \, O) \, \& \, (S \, \& \, (\underline{V}, \, \underline{O})$
          $\qquad\qquad\qquad\qquad\quad | \quad V - V$
          RULE 15 $\downarrow$

     d. $(S \, \& \, O) \, \& \, (\underline{S} \, \& \, (O \, \& \, V))$

In 16.d. all the constituents are ordered with respect to each other. As the rules are optional, rule 14. does not have to reapply to 16.c., but it could reapply, and if it does, the result is an ungrammatical surface form, e.g. 17.d.

17. a. $\underline{(S, \, (V, \, O)), \quad (S, \, O)}$
          $-O \qquad O \quad -O \quad O$
          ‾‾‾‾‾‾‾‾‾‾‾‾‾‾‾‾‾‾‾‾‾‾
          $O \quad -O$

          RULE 14 $\downarrow$

     b. $(\underline{S} \, \& \, \underline{O}) \, \& \, (\underline{S} \, \& \, (\underline{V}, \, \underline{O}))$
          $-O \quad O \quad -O \qquad O$
          ‾‾‾‾‾‾‾‾‾‾‾‾‾‾‾‾‾‾‾‾‾‾‾‾‾‾‾
          $-O \qquad\qquad\qquad O$

     c. $(S \, \& \, O) \, \& \, (S \, \& \, (V, \, O))$
          $\qquad\qquad\qquad\qquad | \quad -O \quad O$
          RULE 14 $\downarrow$

     *d. $(S \, \& \, O) \, \& \, (S \, \& \, (V \, \& \, O))$

(ftnt. 5 cont.)
apply, a later rule B has to order the constituents that were left un-ordered by rule A. This implies that rules have to overlap, which is the case for the RUSSIAN rules, as both a non-object and a non-verb can refer to subjects. Thus the concept of optionality used by Sanders differs from what is generally understood by optionality in transformational grammar, i.e."rule A can or cannot apply," but not "rule A can or cannot apply and if it does not apply, the structure that could have been effected by rule A has to be effected by rule B."

If, instead of rule 15., rule 14 reapplies to 17.c., 17.d. is
generated as a surface order. But 17.d. is not only ungrammatical in RUSSIAN, it is according to Ross' and also according to my
analysis a surface order which is expected to be ungrammatical
in all languages.

Aside from generating ungrammatical surface forms, Sanders'
analysis faces another problem, namely the fact that it allows conjunct switching as lines a. and b. in 16. show. That is, as the
reapplication of the two ordering rules is optional, an unordered
(S (V, O)), (S, O) structure can be converted either into an ordered
(S & (V & O)) & (S & O) structure or into an ordered (S & O) &
(S & (V & O)) structure by switching the order of the two conjuncts.
However, in certain instances the order of two or more conjuncts
cannot be switched without changing the semantic content. This
is true for all those cases where and has an and then interpretation. For instance, the order of 18. cannot be changed to that
of 19., as the two sentences do not have the same meaning.

18. I bought and cooked some mushrooms.
19. I cooked and bought some mushrooms.

18. does not have the same meaning as 19. While 18. is derived
from a structure like 20., 19. is derived from a structure like
21. or 22.

20. I bought some mushrooms and I cooked some mushrooms.
21. I cooked and I bought some mushrooms.
22. I cooked some mushrooms and I bought some mushrooms.

In Sanders' approach, however, a set of constituents with the
semantic content of 20. could be converted into a surface form
like 18. or 19.

Summarizing the brief discussion of Ross', Koutsoudas', and
Sanders' treatment of coordination reduction we can say that they
all generate the data, but that they contain serious flaws. One of
the major flaws is, of course, that not only grammatical but also
ungrammatical surface forms are generated. A second major flaw
is the lack of generality, and the need for ad hoc movement rules.
Though according to Koutsoudas only one reordering rule is needed
which furthermore is independently motivated, this is not true any
longer if we look at a wider range of coordination reductions and

at more languages. Since Ross, as well as Koutsoudas and Sanders, restrict their data nearly exclusively to verb and object reductions, they overlook that split coordination is also encountered in the coordination of other constituent types like adjectives, adverbs, and possessive constructions. And for every case of split coordination, Ross and Koutsoudas have to assume the existence of an additional and not otherwise motivated movement rule. In RUSSIAN, for instance, split coordination is not only found in reduced sentences with a structure as in 23.b., but is also found in a number of other constructions, e.g. 24.b. to 27.b.

23. a.	SOV + SOV	25. a.	SOV + SOV	27. a.	SVO + SVO
b.	SOV + O	b.	SOV + SO	b.	SVO + SV
c.	SO + OV	c.	SO + SOV	c.	SV + SVO

24. a.	S V + S V	26. a.	AN + AN
b.	S V + S	b.	AN + A
c.	S + S V	c.	A + AN

That split coordination is not only found with objects is obvious in examples 24.b. and 26.b., for which Ross and Koutsoudas, and probably also Sanders, would need specific movement rules, namely a verb preposing rule for 24.b. and a noun preposing rule for 26.b. A closer investigation of 23. to 27. reveals that an alternate order is found in all those cases where the directionality constraint operated from right to left, i.e. backward, and it is characteristic of the alternate order that it could be derived by left to right or forward reduction. We can therefore say that whenever split coordination occurs as an alternate order, the directionality constraint is neutralized and that it is the function of movement rules like Koutsoudas' object preposing rule to optionally create the alternate order which is excluded by the directionality constraint.

Split coordination is not only found in RUSSIAN but also in many other languages. Let us take ENGLISH, for example. In ENGLISH possessive constructions like my sister's garden, the possessor precedes the possessed. Thus we would expect that the conjoined noun phrases in 28.a. are reduced to 28.b.; that is, we would expect that reduction operates backward as the identical constituents are on right branches.

28. a. Both my sister's garden and my friend's garden are overgrown.
    b. Both my sister's and my friend's garden are overgrown.

However, 28.b. is not the only way in which 28.a. can be reduced.
Consider 28.c.:

28. c. Both my sister's garden and my friend's are overgrown.

In 28.b. and 28.c. the same pattern is revealed that we encountered in RUSSIAN, i.e. if the two identical constituents are on
right branches, deletion can go both ways. Split coordination is
also found in ENGLISH in sentences like 29., though they might
be marginal for some speakers of ENGLISH.

29.   John bought a book for my birthday, and (also) a record.

Both 28.c. and 29. represent instances where the surface order of
a reduced sentence is <u>less restricted</u> than that of an unreduced
sentence, e.g.:

30.   *My garden sister's is overgrown.
31.   *John bought for my birthday a record.

Below we will now consider some structures which show that in
some languages the surface order of reduced sentences can be
<u>more restricted</u> than that of unreduced ones. That is, certain
constituent orders found in unreduced sentences are not found in
reduced sentences. One of these languages appears to be QUE-
CHUA, cf. Pulte 1971.[6] QUECHUA is a so-called free word
order language, that is, according to Pulte, it has a scrambling
rule. We therefore would expect the following pattern for verb
reduction.

32.   <u>SVO + SVO</u>   <u>SVO + SVO</u>

gapping, opt.   SVO + S O   ----------
scrambling, opt.   SOV + S O   SOV + SOV
gapping, opt.   ---------   SO + SOV

However, <u>SO + SOV</u> is not an acceptable surface order in QUECHUA.
Pulte therefore suggests a constraint which is specific to QUECHUA
and which has the following wording. "In any sentence which has
undergone identity deletion of the subject, object, or verb, the unreduced conjunct must be left-most" (p. 195). In effect Pulte is

----

[6] More specifically, Pulte discusses the COCHABAMBA dialect
of BOLIVIAN QUECHUA.

saying that one part of the directionality constraint does not hold
for QUECHUA, namely there is no backward reduction. Which
means that in order to account for QUECHUA, both Ross and
Koutsoudas will have to place a specific constraint on their coordination reduction rule, while Sanders will have to constrain his
ordering rules. All of the above-listed analyses therefore have
to use a constraint for QUECHUA, which is quite different in nature
from the machinery needed to account for split coordination. Below it will be shown, however, that the QUECHUA data can be
accounted for if we assume that the grammar of QUECHUA does
not contain a rule found in the grammar of all of the other languages
investigated so far. An isolated instance of the pattern displayed
by QUECHUA is found in ARABIC. In CLASSICAL ARABIC a
coordinate structure like 33. a. can be reduced to 33. b. but not
to 33. c.

33.   a.   VS + VS
      b.   VS + V
      c. *V   + VS

34.   a.   akala Ahmed wa shariba Ahmed
           "ate Ahmed and drank Ahmed"
           'Ahmed ate and Ahmed drank. '

      b.   akala Ahmed wa shariba.
           "ate Ahmed and drank"
           'Ahmed ate and drank. '

      c. *akala wa shariba Ahmed
           "ate and drank Ahmed"

That is, in CLASSICAL ARABIC verbal conjunction will always
result in split coordination. However, if we assume the directionality constraint, it is 33. c. that is generated and not 33. b. , and
an obligatory subject-preposing rule will be needed to generate
sentences with a structure like 33. b.

   Summarizing the above discussion we can say that if we want to
maintain the claim that the deletion process in coordinate structures
is subject to the directionality constraint, we not only need one or
two language-specific rules and constraints but a great many of
them, which will increase as the investigation of coordination reduction proceeds. These rules are necessary to counteract the
effect of the directionality constraint. In the following I will show
that the constraints on the surface order of constituents in reduced

sentences are not due to constraints on the deletion rule but rather
are the result of constraints on a regrouping process that applies
after coordination deletion. That is, I will argue that the process
of coordination reduction is not effected by one rule as in the above-
discussed analyses, but by two rules: a deletion rule and a regrouping rule. The deletion rule only operates forward, i. e. of a number
of identical constituents only the left-most is retained, and the output of the deletion rule undergoes reordering by a regrouping rule.
It will be shown that all of the above-discussed examples which
seem to deviate from the expected pattern are cases in which regrouping did optionally or obligatorily not apply.

The above claims are justified in that they allow us to explain,
without any ad hoc machinery, all of the cases which violated the
directionality constraint and in that they will allow us to account for
a much wider range of data than any other analysis of coordination
reduction (see section 3.). Further support is provided if we compare the pattern found for deletion with that found for pronominalization in coordinate structures. If it is true that pronominalization
and deletion are very closely related processes, [7] we would expect
that similar constraints hold for both of them. But as was shown
by Langacker (1969), pronominalization can only operate forward
in conjoined structures, e. g. :

35.   a.   John built a boat and John sailed the boat to Hawaii.
      b.   John built a boat and he sailed it to Hawaii.
      c.   *He built it and John sailed the boat to Hawaii.

35. b. but not 35. c. can be derived from 35. a. Below, I will first
investigate the deletion rule and the kind of structures it predicts.
Specific constraints on deletion like the ones discussed by Sanders
and Tai (1972) will be dealt with later. The deletion rule proposed
here, i. e. 36., is a universal rule. This claim does not necessarily imply that this rule is included in the grammar of all languages. [8] But it does imply that if a language has coordination
reduction, it will have rule 36, and no other rule.

---

[7]For a detailed discussion see Hankamer 1971. Hankamer argues
that pronominalization rules are a special kind of deletion rules.

[8]It seems likely, however, that all languages allow at least some
kind of coordination reduction, even though it may be very restricted
as it appears to be the case in HAUSA.

36. Deletion rule (optional)

In a coordinate structure in which each conjunct contains a constituent which is identical[9] to a corresponding constituent in all other conjuncts, delete all but the leftmost of these identical constituents.

Given rule 36., we can now generate directly, that is, without the help of additional movement rules, all of those forms which proved to be problematic for analyses that impose the directionality constraint, namely all forms with split coordination. Thus, rule 36. will generate the forms with split coordination found in RUSSIAN (see 23. to 27.).

23'.		a.	SOV + SOV	26'.		a.	AN + AN
delet. r.	b.	SOV + O		delet. r.	b.	AN + A

24'.		a.	S V + S V	27'.		a.	SVO + SVO
delet. r.	b.	S V + S		delet. r.	b.	SVO + SV

25'.		a.	SOV + SOV
delet. r.	b.	SOV + SO

It is therefore claimed that reduced sentences with split coordination represent the output order of the deletion rule, i.e. they are the more basic forms which did not undergo regrouping.[10] In a given language, the output order of the deletion rule can be grammatical in all cases, in some cases, or in no cases. HINDI and RUSSIAN seem to belong to the first category, i.e. all output

---

[9]I am not concerned in this paper with the definition of <u>identical</u>. It appears that contrary to pronominalization, deletion demands lexical and structural identity as in the example below. However, no crosslinguistic study of the subject was undertaken.
 a. John fell down the stairs and everybody laughed about $\begin{Bmatrix} \text{John} \\ \text{him} \end{Bmatrix}$.
 b. *John fell down the stairs and everybody laughed about.

[10]Not all output orders of the deletion rule will display so-called split coordination, e.g., a. below is reduced to b. by rule 36.
 a. John ate and John drank.
 b. John ate and drank.
While discussing the output order of the deletion rule and the optionality of regrouping I will, however, generally use examples with split coordination because it is only in these examples that regrouping brings about a change in the surface order of the constituents.

orders of the deletion rule are grammatical. Like RUSSIAN,
HINDI not only allows split coordination for objects and subjects
but also for adjectives, e.g. 37.:

37. HINDI:
　　a. khubswrat bachhe aur hoshiyar bacche
　　　　"pretty children and clever children"
　　　　'the pretty children and the clever children'

　　b. khubswrat bacche aur hoshiyar
　　　　"pretty children and clever"
　　　　'the pretty and clever children'

　　c. khubswrat aur hoshiyar bacche
　　　　"pretty and clever children"
　　　　'the pretty and clever children'

I will call those languages in which the output order of the deletion
rule is grammatical for all reduced structures RUSSIAN-type languages. [11]   As far as I was able to determine, HUNGARIAN comes
very close to being a RUSSIAN-type language with one exception.
That is, HUNGARIAN does allow split coordination for most reductions, including adjectives, e.g. 38., but it does not allow
SVO + SV reductions, e.g., 39.b.

38. HUNGARIAN:
　　a. a helyes gyerekek és az okos gyerekek
　　　　"the pretty children and the clever children"

　　b. a helyes gyerekek és az okosak
　　　　"the pretty children and the clever"
　　　　'the pretty and clever children'

　　c. a helyes és az okos gyerekek
　　　　"the pretty and the clever children"

---

[11]All of the above claims that make an all or nothing statement
may ultimately be proven false. Thus, it may turn out that there
exist instances in HINDI or RUSSIAN where regrouping is not optional, and there may be structures in JAPANESE for which it is.
Though I used a fairly large corpus, I did not cover all possible
conjunction reduction patterns. Especially in the area of conjunction reduction in other than and-coordinated structures my data is
very sketchy.

39. a. János vett egy almát és Vili evett egy almát.
     "John bought an apple and Bill ate an apple "

   b.*?János vett egy almát és Vili evett.
     "John bought an apple and Bill ate "

   c. János vett és Vili evett egy almát.
     "John bought and Bill ate an apple "

On the basis of the ungrammaticality of 39.b. HUNGARIAN there-fore has to be classified as a language in which some but not all of the output orders of the reduction rule are grammatical. Languages like ENGLISH and GERMAN fall into the same class as HUNGA-RIAN. Thus the above-mentioned reduction for possessive con-structions in ENGLISH can be accounted for by assuming that 40.b. is the output order of the deletion rule, which -- by application of regrouping -- can be optionally transformed into 40.c.[12]

40. a. My mother's house and my sister's house were sold
       by an agent.
   b. My mother's house and my sister's were sold by an agent.
   c. My mother's and my sister's house were sold by an agent.

The output order of rule 36. is also acceptable in ENGLISH if a locative or a temporal adverb has been deleted in the second con-junct, i.e. 41.b. is an acceptable surface form.[13]

---

[12]Whether or not regrouping can be truly optional, that is, whether or not the speaker can freely choose between the regrouped and the non-regrouped version of a reduced sentence, seems to vary from language to language. In RUSSIAN there appears to be no semantic difference between an SVO +SV order and its regrouped SV +SVO version. This is, however, not true for ENGLISH, where the non-regrouped sentence usually conotates an afterthought. This phen-omenon will be treated in more detail in the discussion of constraints on regrouping.

[13]It is interesting that in the case of temporal adverbs the output order for the deletion rule is more acceptable than the order achieved by regrouping, i.e. 41.c. below (see next page for 41.a. and 41.b.).
   41. c. John left and Mary arrived yesterday.
A possible reason is that by regrouping the adverb is too far re-moved from the constituents it modifies. Support for this assump-tion is that if the conjuncts are lengthened, a final position of the adverb becomes even less acceptable.
   ?Mary sold all of her books and John gave his records away today.

41. a. John left yesterday and Mary arrived yesterday.
     b. John left yesterday and Mary arrived.

Similarly, if we assume rule 36. and optionality for the regrouping
process, we can account for the fact -- pointed out by Ross in his
thesis -- that in GERMAN subordinate clauses the identical verb
can occur in the first or in the second conjunct. Thus 42. a. below
is converted to 42. b. by rule 36. and can subsequently be rear-
ranged to 42. c. by regrouping.

42. a. Weil Hans keine Zeit hat und weil Peter kein Geld hat,
         können wir nicht ins Kino gehen.
         "because Hans no time has and because Peter no money
         has can we not to-the movies go"
         'We cannot go to the movies because Hans has no time
         and because Peter has no money.'

     b. Weil Hans keine Zeit hat und Peter kein Geld, können
         wir nicht ins Kino gehen.
         "because Hans no time has and Peter no money can
         we not to-the movies go"
         'We cannot go to the movies because Hans has no time
         and Peter no money.'

     c. Weil Hans keine Zeit und Peter kein Geld hat, können
         wir nicht ins Kino gehen.
         "because Hans no time and Peter no money has can
         we not to-the movies go"
         'We cannot go to the movies because Hans has no time
         and Peter no money.'

While in languages like ENGLISH, HUNGARIAN, and GERMAN
the output order of the deletion rule is an acceptable surface order
for some of their and-conjoined structures, regrouping is never
optional[14] in languages like JAPANESE and MANDARIN CHINESE.
In these languages split coordination does not occur; that is, regrouping has to apply whenever its structural description is met,
e. g. 43. b. always has to be converted to 43. c.

---

[14] The above statement is not quite correct as JAPANESE at
least does allow non-regrouped surface forms if an afterthought is
to be expressed. However, a special morpheme has to occur to
mark the non-regrouped constituent as an afterthought. For the
discussion of this phenomenon see section 2.

43. a. Toyo wa ringo o katta, Toyo wa banana o katta.
          "Toyo subj.- marker apple obj - marker bought   Toyo
          subj - marker banana obj.-marker bought"
          'Toyo bought an apple and Toyo bought a banana. '

     b. *Toyo wa ringo o katta to banana.
          "Toyo subj-marker apple obj-marker bought and banana"

     c. Toyo wa ringo to banana o katta.
          'Toyo bought an apple and a banana. '

Up to now it has been shown that there are languages in which
the output order of the deletion rule always corresponds to an
acceptable surface form, while there are other languages in which
the output order of the deletion rule only sometimes or never corresponds to an acceptable surface form. It was also pointed out
that if the output order of rule 36. is an acceptable surface form,
there always exists an alternate order which is brought about by
the application of regrouping. There are, however, also languages
in which the output order of the deletion rule is the only acceptable
surface order, i. e. regrouping cannot apply. This seems to be the
case in QUECHUA. As mentioned above, QUECHUA in Pulte's
analysis does not allow that the reduced conjunct is left-most after
subject, object, or verb deletion. [15] In other words, the unreduced
conjunct cannot be right-most. According to my analysis, the output of the deletion rule will always be such that the unreduced conjunct is left-most while the right-most is reduced. Only regrouping
can, given certain conditions, make the right-most conjunct appear
to be the unreduced one. QUECHUA therefore seems to be a language that does not allow regrouping in and-conjunctions. Thus,
in the derivation below, 44. a. can be reduced to 44. b. by the
application of rule 36, but 44. b. cannot undergo regrouping as
44. c. is not an acceptable surface form in QUECHUA.

44.   a. SOV + SOV
     delet. r.   b. SOV + SO
     regroup.   c. *SO + SOV

Other instances where regrouping cannot apply are the previously-
mentioned example from ARABIC where finite verbs cannot be

---

[15]Pulte only discusses subjects, objects, and verbs. This might
imply that the constraint does not hold for adverbs and adjectives, or
it might imply that these constituents were not investigated, and that
the constraint holds for all constituent types. I will assume the latter.

regrouped, and an example found in CHIPPEWA where regrouping
cannot take place for objects if one of them is animate and the other
one inanimate. This later example will be discussed more thoroughly in the section on constraints. The following chart provides
a tentative classification of the languages investigated. The 'rarely'
category includes those languages which only allow the output order
of the deletion rule as an alternate surface order if a special morpheme is present to mark an afterthought or in disjunctions.

Output Order of the Deletion Rule

Languages	As an alternative surface order			As the only surface order	
	always or nearly always	sometimes	rarely	sometimes	rarely
Arabic			x	x	
Bengali			x		
Chippewa			x	x	
English		x			
German		x			
Hausa			x		
Hindi	x				
Hungarian	x				
Japanese			x		
Mandarin			x		
Navaho			x		
Quechua					x?
Russian	x				
Turkish*		x			

*According to Ross, TURKISH is a language that has SO + SOV
and SOV + SO verbal reductions, which in may analysis implies that
in TURKISH regrouping is optional after verbal reduction. The
TURKISH dialect I worked with only allows optionality for regrouping if an intransitive verb has been deleted, but not after the deletion of a transitive verb, e.g.:

1. a. Jon ve Mary ulaştı.
      "John and Mary arrived"
   b. Jon ulaştı ve Mary de.
      "John arrived and Mary also"
2. a. Jon muz ve Bill balık satın aldı.
      "John banana and Bill fish bought"
      'John bought a banana and Bill a fish.'
   b. *Jon muz satın aldı ve Bill balık.
      "John banana bought and Bill fish"

Concluding the discussion of the deletion rule we can say that by assuming an exclusive left to right or forward application of the rule, we can account for all of those cases which are problematic for a coordination reduction rule that is subject to the direction-ality constraint. In all of the problematic cases the directionality constraint predicts that of two or more identical constituents the right-most is retained while in fact it is the left-most that is re-tained. In order to account for these deviations from the predic-tions of their rules, both Ross and Koutsoudas need movement rules that are not independently motivated. On the other hand, the analysis proposed in this paper provides a principled and general account for all cases of split coordination by arguing that deletion only operates from left to right and that the output order of the deletion rule can be -- and in some cases must be -- a surface order.

1.2 The regrouping rule

Up to now we discussed those reduced structures that correspond to the output order of the deletion rule. However, not all reduced sentences correspond to such an output order and I therefore pro-pose an additional regrouping rule that applies after deletion and that generates all of those structures which are not directly gen-erated by the deletion rule. In working with regrouping and con-straints on regrouping and deletion it became obvious that regrouping as defined in this paper functions to reestablish the scope relations that existed before deletion applied. For instance, in 45. a. below both verbs are modified by the same adverb.

45.   a.   John ate greedily and John drank greedily.

After deletion, however, only the verb in the first conjunct member is modified by the adverb, i.e. 45.b. is not a paraphrase of 45.a.:

45.   b.   John ate greedily and drank.

Regrouping therefore has to apply to move the adverb into a position where it can modify both verbs as in 44.c. below:

45.   c.   John ate and drank greedily.

In order to convert the above b. sentence into the c. sentence, I propose the following universal regrouping schema, which will rearrange constituents after deletion has taken place.

46. Regrouping

Chomsky-adjoin the lowest constituent that exhaustively
dominates all lexical nodes in the reduced conjunct to
the corresponding node in the unreduced conjunct.

Rule 46. will change 47.a. which represents 45.b. to 47.b. below.[16]

47. a.

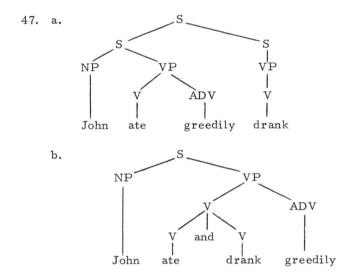

b.

Rule 46. will also apply to structures like 48.a. below, converting
them to structures like 48.b.

48. a.

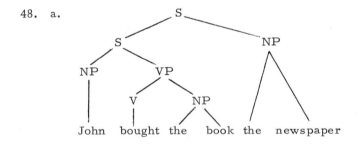

---

[16] I am not concerned in this paper about when, where and how
morphemes like and and or are inserted.

48. b.

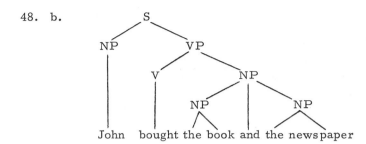

48. b. is an example where regrouping did not change the linear order of constituents but only their dominance relations. That the linear order is not changed is due to the fact that after coordination reduction the two non-identical constituents happen to be adjacent. If for instance the VP in 48. a. contained an adverb as in 49 below, regrouping would change the order of constituents to that in 49. c.

49. a. John bought the book last night and John bought the newspaper last night.
b. John bought the book last night and the newspaper.
c. John bought the book and the newspaper last night.

Most analyses of coordination reduction assume some kind of regrouping, either before or after anaphoric deletion. Koutsoudas is, to my knowledge, the only one who assumed that no form of regrouping takes place. In two of his papers (1968, 1971) he tries to establish that regrouping is not only a superfluous rule but that its presence in the grammar actually complicates the derivation of certain sentences, for instance sentences with split object coordination in HUNGARIAN. Within the framework of his approach this was a possible assumption, given that the only function of a regrouping process would have been to create A-over-A structures.[17] In other words, in Koutsoudas' analysis no rearrangement of the linear order of constituents has to take place as his deletion rule is formulated in such a way that the conjoinable constituents are always adjacent after the application of the rule. All Koutsoudas has to show, therefore, is that the formation of an A-over-A

---

[17] Below is an example of an A-over-A structure, i.e. the dominating node is identical to the nodes that are dominated.

structure is superfluous as there are no rules to refer to such a
structure. He attempts to do this by arguing that all movement
rules like passivization and topicalization precede coordination
reduction, and that agreement and pronominalization rules do not
necessarily have to refer to an A-over-A structure. There exists,
however, considerable evidence that the presence of a common
node is essential both for agreement and pronominalization; that
is, regrouping must at least be able to optionally apply, even if
the conjoinable constituents are adjacent after the application of
the reduction rule. Consider the following data from RUSSIAN.

50. a. Vanja priexal i Maša.
              [sing.]
         "John arrived and Mary"

     b. Vanja i Maša priexali.
                   [plur.]
         "John and Mary arrived"

     c.*Vanja priexali i Maša.
              [plur.]
         "John arrived and Mary"

     d.*Vanja i Maša priexal.
              [sing.]
         "John and Mary arrived"

51. a. Priexal Vanja i Maša.
         [sing.]
         "arrived John and Mary"
         'John arrived and Mary. '

     b. Priexali Vanja i Maša.
         [plur.]
         'John and Mary arrived. '

The reason why a singular verb cannot follow a conjoined subject,
i.e. 50.d., but can precede a conjoined subject becomes obvious
when we look at the derivation of these sentences. [18]

---

[18] The derivation given above does not detail all states of the
derivation as it assumes the application of the agreement rule,
either after coordination reduction or after regrouping.

50'.   Vanja priexal i Maša priexala.
              "John arrived and Mary arrived"
del.   Vanja priexal i Maša.
(opt.)   "John arrived and Mary"
regr.   Vanja i Maša priexali.
(opt.)   "John and Mary arrived"

51'.   Priexal Vanja i priexala Maša.
              'John arrived and Mary arrived.'
del.   Priexal Vanja i Maša.
(opt.)   'John and Mary arrived.'
regr.   Priexali Vanja i Maša.
(opt.)   'John and Mary arrived.'

50'. and 51'. show that the application of the regrouping rule
accounts for the plural marking of the verb. If regrouping does
not apply, that is, if the output order of the deletion rule is the
surface order as in 50.a. and 51.a., then the verb is in the singular as its subject is in the singular. However, if regrouping
applies, then the subject is converted into a conjoined one and the
verb receives a plural marking as in 50.b. and 51.b. This becomes
very clear if we look at the tree structures below, where 52.a.
corresponds to 50.a., 52.b. to 50.b., 53.a. to 51.a., and 53.b.
to 51.b.

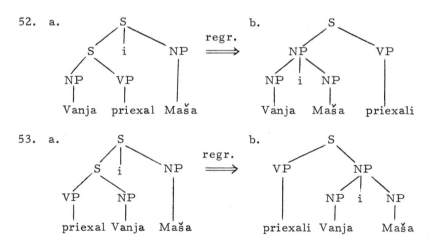

The generation of 50.d. is excluded because a conjoined subject to
the left of the verb can only be created by the regrouping process,
which always results in an A-over-A structure and subsequent
plural verb marking. Koutsoudas, on the other hand, has no way

to exclude the generation of 50.d. except by some <u>ad hoc</u> constraint. Furthermore, his approach will generate identical derived structures for 51.a. and 51.b., i.e. structures like 53.a., which precludes an explanation of the difference between the two sentences. Concluding we can therefore say that any analysis that attempts to account for the properties of reduced sentences will need a regrouping process in order to account for facts like the RUSSIAN ones. The claim that regrouping is part of the grammar of most languages -- though probably not of all -- also frees us from having to order all movement rules before coordination reduction. Though a rule like topicalization may apply before coordination reduction and regrouping, it can also apply after to a structure like 54.a., which would be converted to 54.b. given the Coordinate Structure Constraint.[19]

> 54. a. John bought the book and the newspaper.
>   b. The book and the newspaper John bought.

Above we have considered some evidence which supports the assumption that there is a universal regrouping process. However, we have not yet investigated in any detail the kind of changes that are brought about by regrouping. The question is: does the rule simply form A-over-A structures as assumed by Tai (1971) and also in rule 46. above, or does it have additional functions! Below I will show that regrouping is a process that operates in two steps, i.e. it brings about the formation of A-over-A structures and, under certain circumstances, raises the constituent that acted as antecedent to the deletion. The need for the latter process becomes evident if we consider the following derivation.

> 55. a. <u>Input to the deletion rule</u>

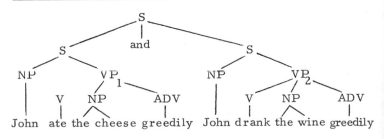

---

[19]The Coordinate Structure Constraint was proposed by Ross (1967a). It has the following wording: "In a coordinate structure, no conjunct may be moved, nor may any element contained in a conjunct be moved out of that conjunct" (p. 161).

55. b. <u>Output of the deletion rule and input to the regrouping rule</u>

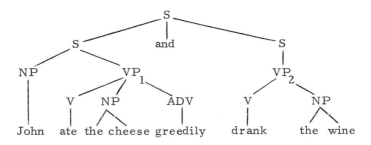

c. <u>Output of the regrouping rule</u>

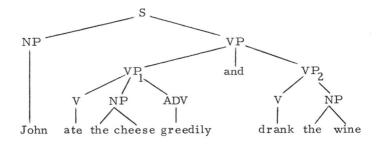

When rule 46. applies to 55.b., it will choose VP_2 for regrouping as that is the highest node that exhaustively dominates the remaining constituents of the reduced conjunct and will Chomsky-adjoin it to VP_1, converting 55.b. to 55.c. However, 55.c. is not a paraphrase of 55.a. Consequently, regrouping as specified in 46. cannot bring about the desired surface order which in the case of 55.a. above would be 55.d. below.

55. d. John ate the cheese and drank the wine greedily.

In order to generate 55.d., rule 46. has to have the power to move the adverb to the right of both conjuncts.[20] That is, whenever the node that acted as antecedent for the deletion is dominated by one of the conjunct nodes after the formation of the A-over-A structure, that node has to be moved out and raised. In 55.c., for example, the adverb is dominated by one of the conjoined verb phrases and

---

[20] In an A-over-A structure I will refer to the whole structure as a coordinate structure, to the node that dominates it as coordinate node, to the members of the coordinate structure as conjuncts, and to the nodes that dominate the conjuncts as conjunct nodes.

consequently has to be raised and Chomsky-adjoined to the coordinate node. And as the adverb in 55.b. is phrase-final, it will
have to be adjoined to the right of the conjunct node, converting
55.c. to 55.d'.

55.d'.

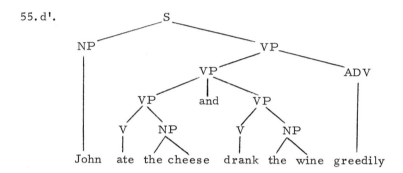

I therefore propose the following addition to rule 46.

    46'. If after the formation of the A-over-A structure one of
        the conjunct nodes dominates a constituent which acted
        as antecedent[21] to the deletion of an identical constituent,
        and if this node is conjunct initial or conjunct final, that
        node is raised and Chomsky-adjoined[22] to the right or
        to the left of the coordinate node. The raised constituent
        is adjoined to the left if it is conjunct-initial, it is ad-
        joined to the right if it is conjunct final.

46'. claims that the antecedent constituent is not only moved but
also raised. Some justification for this claim will be provided
during the discussion of constraints on deletion and regrouping.
Further support comes from facts involving intonation. Thus,
56.a. below has a different intonation pattern than 57.a., which
is reflected in the respective tree structures 57.a. and 57.b.

    56. a. John sat down and read a book.
        b. John quickly bought and read the book.

---

[21] The notion of antecedent will be discussed in some detail later.

[22] Chomsky-adjunction was chosen over sister-adjunction as the
structure created by the former seems to be required to account
for certain constraints on movement transformations (cf. ftnt. 20).
It is, however, possible that a reinterpretation of the data will remove the need for Chomsky-adjunction.

57. a.

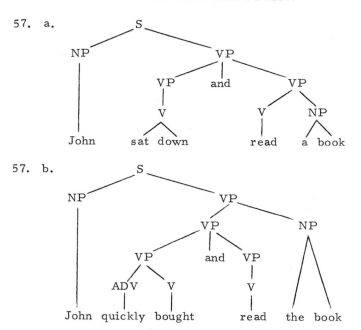

57. b.

A slowed-down utterance of 56.a. and 56.b. reveals that in 56.a. a break can be made before <u>and</u> but not before the object NP, while in 56.b. the most natural break is before the object NP and not before the <u>and</u>. This difference is reflected in 57.a. and 57.b. Another example is 58.a. below which is ambiguous in writing but which is disambiguated by intonation to either 58.b. or 58.c.

58. a. John quickly ran home and closed the door.

     b. John [[quickly ran home] and [closed the door]].
              VP VP   VP

     c. John [quickly [[ran home] and [closed the door]]].
              VP   VP VP   VP

If a speaker wants to say 58.b., he can make a break before the <u>and</u>, while no such break is possible in 58.c. where both verbs are modified by the same adverb.

Besides claiming that the antecedent constituent is raised, rule 46'. also makes certain claims about <u>where</u> the raised constituent is Chomsky-adjoined. The rule states that the direction of the raising depends on the position of the antecedent constituent. 59. below shows that the direction of the raising is essential, as a

non-adherence to the constraint as stated in rule 46'. will result
in ungrammatical surface forms.

59.   a.   <u>After deletion</u>

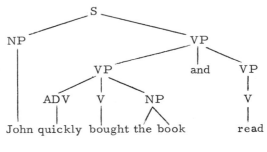

*b.

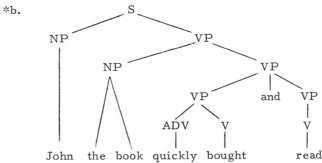

Rule 46. also insures that if two or more antecedent constituents
are in conjunct-initial or conjunct-final position, the original order
of constituents is retained as in the following derivation.

60.   a.

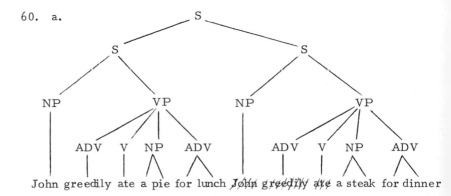

60. b. <u>Rule 46., formation of A-over-A structure</u>

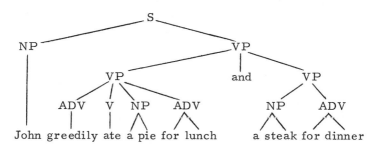

c. <u>First application of rule 46'., raising of antecedent constituent</u>

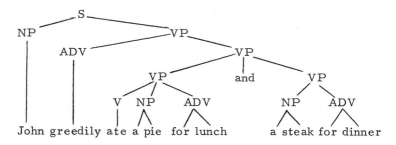

d. <u>Second application of rule 46'.</u>

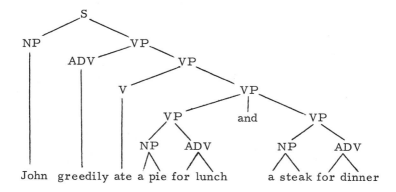

In the above derivations, 46'. raises what has been referred to as the 'antecedent constituent,' namely that constituent which acted as antecedent to the deletion of an identical constituent in another conjunct. However, the question arises: how does the rule know

what is and what is not an antecedent constituent?   And the answer
is: it doesn't. Nothing in 56. b. above indicates that the manner
adverb acted as antecedent. But this information is essential.
Consider the following data, where 61. is the input to the regrouping rule.

61.   Yesterday John bought some food and cooked.

If 61. is derived from 62. a. below, regrouping has to apply to
generate 62.b. , but if 61. is derived from 63. , regrouping cannot apply.

62.   a.   Yesterday John bought some food and yesterday John
           cooked some food.

      b.   Yesterday John bought and cooked some food.

63.   Yesterday John bought some food and yesterday John
         cooked.

The way the regrouping rule has been formulated, it could change
an input like 61. to a surface form like 62.b., independent of the
underlying structure of 61. This means that the reduction process
can be instrumental in changing the meaning of a sentence, i. e.
the output sentence of the reduction process is not necessarily a
paraphrase of the input sentence. It is therefore of crucial importance that the regrouping rule has access to an earlier presentation of the structures it is operating on. This information has to
be present independent of the formulation of the reduction and regrouping rules. Consider, for instance, the regrouping process
proposed by James Tai, who, as far as I know, is the only one to
discuss the process of regrouping in any detail. His rule[23] Chomsky-
adjoins the constituents of the reduced conjunct – which in his analysis might be either the right or the left conjunct depending on the
branching -- to the corresponding constituent in the unreduced
conjunct. Tai's rule is supposed to not only account for regrouping in sentences as discussed above, but also for _respectively_ and
each other regroupings. In order to generate _respectively_ sentences, Tai must allow -- and his examples show that he does --
for the individual constituents of the reduced conjunct to be Chomsky-
adjoined to the corresponding constituents in the unreduced conjunct.
This process can, however, bring about a meaning change. Consider
the following example.

---

[23]See Tai 1971:269.

64. Bill ate and John bought some apples.

64. is two-ways ambiguous. It can either have the meaning of 65. or the meaning of 66.

65. Bill ate some apples and John bought some apples.
66. Bill ate something and John bought some apples.

If 64. is a paraphrase of 66., it cannot undergo regrouping. However, at the point where regrouping applies in Tai's analysis, we do not know whether 64. has the meaning of 65. or of 66. In either case 64. can be regrouped to 67.

67. Bill and John ate and bought some apples, respectively.

Thus, even if 64. has the meaning of 66., it can be converted to 67., which constitutes a meaning change. In the following I will therefore investigate how the regrouping rule can be provided with the necessary information about the constituent structure that a given string had before coordination reduction applied. One possibility is to assume that a global constraint[24] holds between the coordination rule and the regrouping rule to the effect that regrouping can only apply if coordination reduction did. However, such a constraint would be of no use in the above example as 61., even if derived from 63., underwent reduction of the subject NP and the time adverb. What the regrouping rule requires is the exact information as to which constituents have been deleted or will be deleted. The information as to which constituents will be deleted can be extracted from a conjoined structure <u>before</u> coordination reduction takes place. It is probably for this reason that Ross incorporates into his conjunction reduction rule a regrouping process that precedes anaphoric deletion. This regrouping process "Chomsky-adjoins to the right or the left of the coordinate node a copy of some constituent which occurs in all conjuncts, on a right or left branch, respectively," (1967a: 175). Subsequently, the original node is deleted. If we apply Ross' rule to 62., only the subject <u>John</u> and the adverb are copied and Chomsky-adjoined, while if we applied it to 62. a., the subject, the adverb, and the object are copied. Ross' approach therefore avoids the above-discussed problem but it encounters some others. First, it seems intuitively wrong to order regrouping before coordination reduction as the reason for the existence of regrouping appears to be that it restores a constituent order which was interfered with by the application of

---

[24] For a discussion of global constraints see Lakoff 1970.

coordination reduction. Furthermore, from a more formal point
of view, the order regrouping -- coordination reduction demands
that we place certain constraints on the relation between these
two rules. That is, deletion has to apply if regrouping did, and
deletion cannot apply if regrouping did not apply. From this follows that we would not be able to account for the difference between
sentences like 68. a. and 68. b.:

> 68. a. My father's house and my sister's were sold.
>   b. My father's and my sister's house were sold.

by assuming that 68. a. was derived by the application of deletion
but not of regrouping, while 68. b. was derived by the application
of both rules. If we assume that regrouping applies before deletion,
only one of the above sentences will be the output of the regrouping
and deletion process, while the other sentence has to be generated
by an additional movement rule. Enough evidence has, however,
been presented earlier to reject such an approach to coordination
reduction.

Another way of retaining information from an earlier stage of
the derivation is the use of derivational constraints as proposed by
Lakoff (1969). [25] Such constraints preserve information that would
otherwise be lost in form of a feature. I therefore propose that
the deletion rule marks the constituent that acted as antecedent by
a special feature, i. e. [ant] and that the regrouping rule refers to
this feature. Thus 61. above can be represented by two different
phrase markers, namely 69. a. and 70. a. below, where 69. a. corresponds to 62. and 70. a. to 63.

---

[25] Postal (1970) shows that such a constraint is required in the
deletion of NP's by the Equi-NP deletion rule. That is, at the point
where deletion has to apply the complement subject is no longer in
the required configuration. Postal therefore suggests to mark the
NP that is to be deleted by the feature [+doom]. The feature [doom]
is, however, not suited for the problem under discussion as its use
would greatly complicate the reduction process. It would, for instance, require that deletion applies in two steps, before regrouping
to mark the deletable constituent, and after regrouping to eliminate
the doomed constituent. Besides, regrouping would have to be formulated such that the rule checks for each constituent whether it
has an identical counterpart marked [doom] in the other conjuncts
before raising can take place.

69. a.

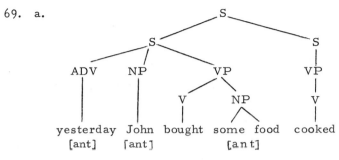

70. a.

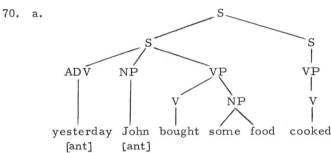

69. a. can be regrouped to 69. b. below, while 70. a. can only be regrouped to 70. b.

69. b.

70. b.

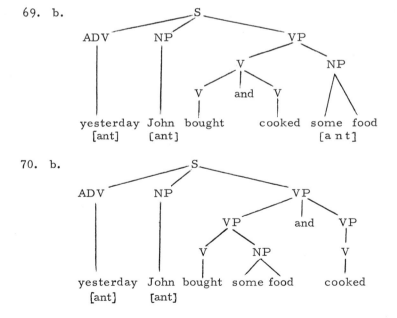

On the basis of the above discussion rule 46'. is therefore revised
to rule 46''.

46''. <u>Revised version</u>

If after the formation of an A-over-A structure one of
the constituents in the conjunct is marked [ant] and if
this node is conjunct initial or conjunct final, raise that
node and Chomsky-adjoin it to the coordinate node immediately to the right or the left of the conjunct nodes.
The constituent is adjoined to the left if it is conjunct-
initial, it is adjoined to the right if it is conjunct-final.

After having discussed in some detail the process of regrouping
which involves the formation of an A-over-A structure and the
raising of the antecedent constituent, I will now examine a slightly
different reordering process, namely the one needed to generate
<u>respectively</u> constructions.   Thus, 71. a. below can be regrouped
to 71. b. or to 71. c.

71. a.

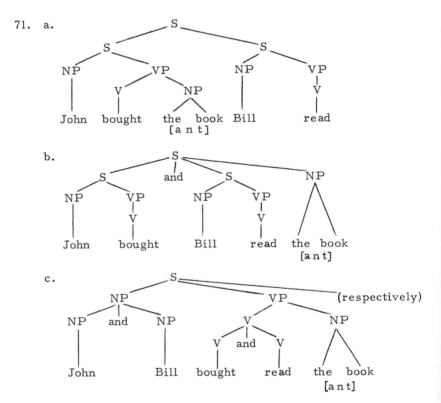

71.c. shows that <u>respectively</u> constructions violate one of the conditions stated in 46., namely that regrouping can only apply to the
lowest constituent that <u>exhaustively</u> dominates <u>all</u> lexical nodes in
the reduced conjunct. Thus, for regroupings that result in <u>respec-</u>
<u>tively</u> sentences, the first part of the regrouping rule is less
specific, i.e. 72.

72.	Chomsky-adjoin the constituent(s) of the reduced conjunct
to the corresponding constituent in the unreduced conjunct.

Even though 72. is the less specific rule, it can result in more
complex surface structures, which is probably the reason why
some languages do not have a rule like 72. and why those which
do have 72. reserve its use nearly exclusively for the written
language. Among those languages that do not allow regrouping
as specified in 72. are ARABIC, HAUSA and NAVAHO, while 72.
is found in written HUNGARIAN, RUSSIAN (restricted), BENGALI
(restricted), JAPANESE, FRENCH (very restricted), GERMAN
and ENGLISH. As pointed out by Tai, <u>respectively</u> construction
can occur in ENGLISH even if reduction has not taken place, e.g.
73.

73.	John and Bill sailed and dived respectively.

This indicates that, at least for ENGLISH, 72. can be formulated
even more generally, i.e. 72'.

72'.	Chomsky-adjoin the constituent(s) of a conjunct to the
corresponding constituent of another conjunct.

A closer look at 72'. reveals that it will generate sentences like
73. as well as sentences like 71.b. and 71.c., as no specific constraints are placed on the rule as to which constituent(s) may be
Chomsky-adjoined. Thus, for languages with <u>respectively</u> constructions, we can stipulate a regrouping process that is subject
to fewer constraints than the regrouping process in languages that
do not have <u>respectively</u> constructions. However, if we want to
characterize the difference between the spoken and the written
language, then we have to assume that languages like ENGLISH
have two regrouping processes, one for the spoken language which
requires exhaustive dominance (rule A below), and one for the
written language, which does not have such a requirement (rule B
below).

Rule A: Regrouping (spoken language)

Chomsky-adjoin the constituent that exhaustively dominates all
remaining constituents in the reduced conjunct to the corresponding node in the unreduced conjunct. If after the formation of the
A-over-A structure, one of the constituents in the conjunct is
marked [ant] and if this node is conjunct-initial or conjunct-
final, raise that node and Chomsky-adjoin it to the coordinate
node immediately to the right or the left of the conjunct nodes.
The constituent is adjoined to the left if it is conjunct-initial,
it is adjoined to the right if it is conjunct-final.

Rule B: Regrouping (written language)

Chomsky-adjoin the constituent(s) of a conjunct to the corresponding constituents of another conjunct. If after the formation of the A-over-A structure, one of the constituents in the
conjunct is marked [ant] and if this node is conjunct-initial or
conjunct-final, raise that node and Chomsky-adjoin it to the
coordinate node immediately to the right or the left of the conjunct nodes. The constituent is adjoined to the left if it is
conjunct-initial, it is adjoined to the right if it is conjunct-final.

Concluding the discussion on regrouping, we can therefore say
that regrouping is a reordering process that restores the order of
constituents which was interfered with by the application of the
deletion rule. In some languages the order which results from
the application of the deletion rule is an acceptable surface order,
in others it is not or only for certain structures and regrouping
has to apply. This fact is accounted for by assuming that for the
former languages regrouping is optional while for the latter it is
only sometimes or never optional. By claiming that the reduction
process only involves two rules, deletion and regrouping, and no
additional movement rules, we can predict for all languages all of
the surface orders of reduced coordinate structures, as there are
only two choices:

i.   the surface order is identical with the output order of the
     deletion rule;
ii. the surface order is identical with the output order of the
     regrouping rule.

The list below shows various input orders to the deletion rule
which, given specific reductions, e.g. object reduction, can be
converted into two possible output orders corresponding to i. and
ii. above. Sometimes the order of constituents will be identical

before and after regrouping, e. g., d. subject reduction, as the list
only reflects linear order and not dominance relations. None of
the input orders below should have an output order not mentioned
on the list.

Reduction Patterns

a. Verbal reduction (trans.)

input to delet. r.	VSO + VSO	SVO + SVO	SOV + SOV
output of delet. r.	VSO + SO	SVO + S O	SOV + SO
output of regrpg. r.	---------	---------	SO + SOV

b. Verbal reduction (intrans.)

input to delet. r.	VS + VS	SV + SV
output of delet. r.	VS + V	SV + S
output of regrpg. r.	V + VS	S + SV

c. Object reduction

input to delet. r.	VSO + VSO	SVO + SVO	SOV + SOV
output of delet. r.	VSO + VS	SVO + SV	SOV + S V
output of regrpg. r.	VS + VSO	SV + SVO	---------

d. Subject reduction

input to delet. r.	VSO + VSO	SVO + SVO	SOV + SOV
output of delet. r.	VSO + V O	SVO + VO	SOV + OV
output of regrpg. r.	---------	SVO + VO	SOV + OV

e. Subject-verb reduction

input to delet. r.	VSO + VSO	SVO + SVO	SOV + SOV
output of delet. r.	VSO + O	SVO + O	SOV + O
output of regrpg. r.	VSO + O	SVO + O	SO + OV

f. Object-verb reduction

input to delet. r.	VSO + VSO	SVO + SVO	SOV + SOV
output of delet. r.	VSO + S	SVO + S	SOV + S
output to regrpg. r.	VS + SO	SVO + O	S + SOV

g. Subject-object reduction

input to delet. r.	VSO + VSO	SVO + SVO	SOV + SOV
output of delet. r.	VSO + V	SVO + V	SOV + V
output of regrpg. r.	VS + SO	S + SVO	S + SOV

h. Adjective reduction

	AN + AN	NA + NA
input to delet. r.	AN + AN	NA + NA
output to delet r.	AN + N	NA + A
output to regrpg. r.	AN + N	N + NA

i. Noun reduction

	AN + AN	NA + NA
input to delet. r.	AN + AN	NA + NA
output to delet r.	AN + A	NA + A
output to regrpg. r.	A + AN	NA + A

It was said above that a reduction form that does not appear on the chart is predicted not to exist in a natural language. However, there is one reduced structure which I found in HINDI and which is not on the list, namely object reduction resulting in a SV + SOV surface order. In HINDI object reduction can take two forms, namely the one above and the one in the chart, i.e. SOV + SV.

74. a. Jon-ne safarchand kharida aur Bill-ne safarchand khaya.
       "John apple bought and Bill apple ate"
       'John bought an apple and Bill ate the apple.'

    b. Jon-ne safarchand kharida aur Bill-ne khaya.
       "John apple bought and Bill ate"
       'John bought and Bill Ate an apple.'

    c. Jon-ne kharida aur Bill-ne safarchand khaya.
       "John bought and Bill apple ate"
       'John bought and Bill ate an apple. '

Reduced structures as in 74. c. are not generated by the rules as proposed in this paper, while 74. b. is the output of the deletion rule. One way of generating 74. c. is to assume that HINDI has an object-movement rule which optionally moves the object from the first, the unreduced conjunct, to the second, the reduced conjunct. Such a rule would, however, be totally ad hoc and therefore must be rejected. Another way to account for the HINDI data is to assume that HINDI is an underlying SVO language and that it has an obligatory object preposing rule, resulting in the following two derivations for object-reduced sentences in HINDI.

75.

	SVO + SVO	SVO + SVO
	SVO + SVO	SVO + SVO
deletion (opt.)	SVO + SV	SVO + SV
regrouping (opt.)	SV + SVO	-----------
object preposing (obl.)	SV + SVO	SOV + SV

The claim that HINDI is an underlying SVO language was made by Ross as well as by Koutsoudas. They had to make this assumption to account within their framework for the occurrence of split co-ordination in HINDI. Some evidence to support the claim that HINDI is an underlying SVO language is provided by typological facts observed by Koutsoudas.

"It was found that a definite generalization seems to exist regarding the above two properties of objects, namely a language allows split coordination of objects if and only if it allows both SVO type sentences and SOV type sentences. GERMAN, MODERN GREEK, RUSSIAN, and TURKISH are examples of languages that behave exactly like HUNGARIAN with regard to the two properties in question; ENGLISH, JAPANESE, NORWEGIAN, and INDONESIAN are, on the other hand, examples of languages in which there is no split coordination of objects and in which there are either SVO type sentences or SOV type sentences but not both." (1971: 371, capitals according to WPLU conventions.)

HINDI is an exception to this generalization as it allows split object coordination but no SVO surface order.

2. Constraints on Coordination Reduction

After having discussed the process of regrouping, we will now investigate certain constraints that have to be placed on the coordination reduction process. These constraints are not expected to be universal, but are assumed to be based on universal principles. Constraints on coordination reduction can be either syntactic or semantic. In the former case, constraints have to be imposed to prevent the generation of ungrammatical surface forms, while in the latter case constraints are imposed to prevent that the reduction process brings about a change in meaning. A clear example of a syntactic constraint is found in CHIPPEWA[26] where regrouping cannot take place under certain conditions. In CHIPPEWA the object and the verb agree with respect to animacy and number, e.g. 76., and regrouping appears to be obligatory for most types of constituent.

76. jīman indayān
    "a-boat (inan., sing.) I-have (inan., sing.)"
    'I have a boat.'

---

[26]The same constraint holds for MICMAC and apparently also for other ALGONQUIAN languages.

If two inanimate or two animate objects are conjoined, regrouping takes place, i. e. 77. a. can be reduced to 77. b. and is regrouped to 77. c.

77. a. jīman indayān mīnawā abwi indayān.
        "a-boat (inan., sing.) I-have (inan., sing.) and a-paddle
        (inan., sing.) I have (inan., sing.)"
        'I have a boat and I have a paddle. '

      b. jīman indayān mīnawā abwi.
          "a-boat I have and a-paddle"
          'I have a boat and a paddle. '

      c. jīmān mīnawā abwi indayānan.
          "a-boat and a-paddle I-have (inan., pl.)"
          'I have a boat and a paddle. '

A similar paradigm can be put together for two animate objects. However, regrouping as in 78. c. is blocked if the two objects differ in animacy, as neither the animate nor the inanimate marking can be neutralized and regrouping would result in conflicting markings on the verb. Thus 78. a. below can be reduced to 78. b. but 78. b. cannot be regrouped to 78. c. nor 78. d.

78. a. jīmān indayān mīnawā akik indayāwa.
        "a-boat (inan., sing.) I-have (inan., sing.) and a-pail
        (an. sing.) I-have (an., sing.)"
        'I have a boat and a pail. '

      b. jīmān indayān mīnawā akik.
          "a-boat I-have and a-pail"
          'I have a boat and a pail. '

      c. *jīmān mīnawā akik inayānan.
          "a-boat and a-pail I-have (inan., pl.)"

      d. *jīmān mīnawā akik inadāyawāg.
          "a-boat and a-pail I-have (an., pl.)"

Based on the universal principle of ranking, Delisle (1972) explains the above data by demonstrating that in CHIPPEWA animate and inanimate are equally ranked, i. e. neither of these features can neutralize in a conjunction and regrouping therefore has to be avoided. Contrary to CHIPPEWA, FRENCH allows the neutralization of features and regrouping is obligatory in the following example.

79.   a. La petite fille est belle et le petit garçon est beau.
                " the little girl is pretty (fem., sing.) and the
                little boy is pretty (masc.,sing.)"

delet.   b. *La petit fille est belle et le petit garçon.
                " the little girl is pretty and the little boy. "

regr.   c. La petite fille et le petit garçon sont beau.
                " the little girl and the little boy are pretty
                (masc., pl.)"

In 79. c. a [fem] and a [masc] noun are grouped together and marking on the predicate adjective is [masc]. This implies that in
FRENCH the feature [fem] is neutralized if brought into conjunction with a [masc] marking.

Another instance where regrouping cannot apply is found in
CLASSICAL ARABIC where finite verbs cannot be conjoined. In
CLASSICAL ARABIC a verb that precedes the subject is always
marked for singular, while a verb that follows the subject agrees
with it in number, e. g. 80.

80. akala al-awlād   wa   sharibū.
       "ate (masc., sing.) the-boys (masc., pl.) and drank (masc., pl.)"
       'The boys ate and drank. '

80. cannot undergo regrouping, possibly because of the different
specifications on the verbs. That the verb specifications play a
role in blocking the application of regrouping is supported by COL-
LOQUIAL ARABIC where both verbs agree in number with the
subject and where regrouping can take place, e. g. 81.

81. l-wulād akalū wu sheribū mudda ṭawīla.
       "the-boys ate (masc., pl.) and drank (masc., pl.) period long"
       'The boys ate and drank for a long time. '

Above we have examined some syntactic constraints on regrouping. In the following, we will investigate some semantic constraints
that either block or require regrouping. Given two sentences with
identical lexical items and different word orders, there are two
logical possibilities: either the difference in word order signals
a difference in meaning or it doesn't. Thus in 82. below, there
appears to be no difference in meaning between the a. and the b.
version, while there definitely is a difference between 83. a. and
83. b.

82. a. Joe picked up the telephone.
     b. Joe picked the telephone up.

83. a. Mary loves Bill.
     b. Bill loves Mary.

Consequently, if a language has two surface orders for a given
reduced sentence, we would expect that in some languages the difference in word order corresponds to a difference in meaning while
in others it doesn't. We should furthermore expect that if the difference in word order reflects a meaning difference, this meaning
difference does not necessarily have to be the same from language
to language. An example where regrouping does not change the
meaning is found in GERMAN sondern 'but rather' conjunctions.
84. below which has not been regrouped is a paraphrase of the
regrouped 84. b.

84. a. Nicht Hans ist angekommen sondern Mary.
         "Not Hans is arrived but Mary"
         'It wasn't Hans who arrived but Mary. '

     b. Nicht Hans sondern Mary ist angekommen.
         "Not Hans but Mary is arrived"
         'Not Hans but Mary arrived. '

However, in and conjunctions in GERMAN the non-regrouped sentence often has a slightly different interpretation than the regrouped
sentence. This is also true for ENGLISH as the following example
shows.

85. a. John bought a book at the store, and a newspaper.
     b. John bought a book and a newspaper at the store.

In 85. a. and a newspaper is added as an afterthought, it is somehow
ranked lower, considered less important information. The idea of
afterthought is even more stressed if we insert an also.

85. c. John bought a book at the store, and also a newspaper.

In some languages the use of a morpheme denoting also is required
if regrouping did not take place, e. g. JAPANESE:

86. a. Toyo wa ringo o katta, banana mo.
         "Toyo subj-marker apple obj-marker bought, banana also"
         'Toyo bought an apple, and a banana. '

86. b. *Toyo wa ringo o katta, to banana.
"Toyo subj-marker apple obj-marker bought, and banana"

While in languages like JAPANESE an afterthought is always clearly marked, this is not true in languages like ENGLISH. We cannot say, for instance, that whenever regrouping did not apply, all constituents that follow the conjunction are part of an afterthought. In both of the examples below regrouping did not apply, but neither 87. b. nor 88.b. necessarily imply that the reduced conjunct is meant as an afterthought.

87.   a. John bought a record and Bill bought a guitar.
delet. b. John bought a record and Bill a guitar.

88.   a. Hans hat einen Apfel gekauft, und Peter hat eine Banane gekauft.
"Hans has an apple bought, and Peter has a banana bought"
'Hans has bought an apple and Peter has bought a banana. '

delet. b. Hans hat einen Apfel gekauft und Peter eine Banane.
"Hans has an apple bought and Peter a banana"
'Hans has bought an apple and Peter a banana.'

However, both 87. b. and 88.b. differ from sentences like 85.a. in that the former cannot be regrouped while the latter can be regrouped to 85.b. A tentative hypothesis therefore is that if in an <u>and</u> conjunction the structural description of the regrouping rule is met and the rule does not apply, then the resulting sentence contains an afterthought. This seems to be true for ENGLISH and for GERMAN, but it is probably not true for a language like HAUSA where the distinction between a regrouped and a non-regrouped sentence is used to signal a different kind of distinction.

89. a. Audu ya zo dà Bella.
"Audu he came with Bill"
'Audu and Bill came. '

b. Audu dà Bella sun zo.
"Audu with Bill they came"
'Audu and Bill came. '

89. a. means that Audu came and he brought Bill, while 89. b. means that Audu and Bill came together.

Similar to HAUSA, an **and** conjoined subject in NAVAHO always
implies togetherness. Thus 90. can only mean 'John and Mary arrived together. '

90.   John do Mary niaz.
'John and Mary arrived. '

If the speaker intends to indicate that they did not arrive together,
he will not reduce the second occurrence of the verb.

Above we briefly discussed some conditions under which regrouping has to be blocked for syntactic or semantic reasons. In the
following we will investigate why regrouping is so often obligatory
and why deletion cannot take place under certain circumstances.
It will be argued that regrouping is a restructuring process that
affects the linear order of constituents and their dominance structure in order to restore the functional relations that existed within
a given sentence before deletion applied. It will furthermore be
argued that if the output order of the deletion rule is such that regrouping cannot bring about the required structure, deletion has to
be blocked.

When deletion applies as specified in rule 36, it deletes a constituent which has a certain material and relational content. However, as deletion can only take place under identity, this content
is still preserved in the antecedent constituent which now has to
extend its function to also encompass that of the deleted constituent.
For instance, if in 91. a. below the second adverb is deleted, the
remaining adverb in 91. b. has to extend its range over both verbs.

91.   a.   John quickly walked home and John quickly ran upstairs.
      delet.   b.   John quickly walked home and ran upstairs.

In 91. b. the adverb is in such a position that it does not have to be
moved in order to be in relation with both verbs. However, this is
not the case if the adverb is in verbphrase-final position as in 92. b.
In that case the adverb has to be moved into such a position that its
range extends over both verbs as in 92. c.

92.   a.   John ate greedily and John drank greedily.
      delet.   b.   *John ate greedily and drank.
      regr.   c.   John ate and drank greedily.

Thus it appears that in ENGLISH a manner adverb which is dominated by a verb phrase can range over one or several verbs that

either precede or follow the adverb, but it cannot range over a
preceding and a following verb at the same time as 92.b. is not a
paraphrase of 92.a. Similar constraints hold for objects in ENG-
LISH. 93.a. has to be reordered to 93.c., as a noun can only be
the direct object of a verb if it is placed to the right of that verb. [27]

93.   a. Fred borrowed a book and Fred read the book.
    delet. b. *Fred borrowed the book and read.
    regr.   c. Fred borrowed and read the book.

While ENGLISH nouns can only be in a direct object relation
with a verb if that verb precedes, RUSSIAN nouns have no such
constraint. In RUSSIAN an object can either precede or follow a
verb which allows for <u>SVO</u> and <u>SOV</u> surface orders. Thus 94.a.
can either be reduced to 94.b. or to 93.c. In both cases the object
is within the range of both verbs.

94. a. Vanja kupil jabloko, a Masa s"ela jabloko.
         "John bought apple   and Mary ate apple "
         'John bought an apple and Mary ate an apple. '

     b. Vanja kupil jabloko a Masa s"ela.
         "John bought apple and Mary ate"
         'John bought and Mary ate the apple. '

     c. Vanja kupil, a Masa s"ela.
         "John bought and Mary ate apple"
         'John bought and Mary ate an apple. '

That RUSSIAN relies less on word order to specify relations between constituents than ENGLISH is reflected in the fact that in
RUSSIAN regrouping is optional. In a language like ENGLISH, on
the other hand, where order is the main method for relating constituents, regrouping plays a much more important role.

Up to now I have presented data to justify the claim that the
regrouping rule moves constituents under certain conditions. These
conditions can vary from language to language and from constituent
type to constituent type. It was argued that the regrouping rule
changes the linear order of constituents to restore functional relations which existed before the application of deletion. However, the

---

[27] I am disregarding the fact that direct objects can occur to the
left of verbs in some instances, for instance after topicalization.

regrouping rule as specified in this paper not only influences the
linear order of constituents, it can also rearrange the existing
dominance relations by raising the antecedent constituent to the
coordinate node. It is claimed that raising is a necessary process
to account for certain syntactic facts. Consider the following argument. In GERMAN adverbs that follow the verb have the same
constraints as their ENGLISH counterparts; that is, their range is
restricted to one or several preceding verbs. Thus 94. b. has to
undergo regrouping if a paraphrase of 95. a. is to be generated.

> 95. a. Hans aβ gierig und Hans trank gierig.
>   "Hans ate greedily and Hans drank greedily"
>
> b. *Hans aβ gierig und trank.
>   "Hans ate greedily and drank"
>
> c. Hans aβ und trank gierig.
>   "Hans ate and drank greedily"

In 95. c. the adverb ranges over two preceding verbs. This is,
however, not true in a sentence like 96. b. below; that is, 96.b. is not
a possible reduction of 96. a., even though both verbs precede the
adverb.

> 96. a. Hans aβ gierig den Apfel und Hans trank gierig den Wein.
>   "Hans ate greedily the apple and Hans drank greedily the wine"
>   'Hans greedily ate the apple and Hans greedily drank the
>   wine. '
>
> b. *Hans aβ den Apfel und trank gierig den Wein.
>   "Hans ate the apple and drank greedily the wine"

One possible hypothesis is that the adverb cannot range over the
verb in the first conjunct because of the intervening object. But
this is not so, as in 97. below the range of the adverb extends over
the object to the verb.

> 97.   Hans aβ das Fleisch gierig.
>   "Hans ate the meet greedily"

It therefore appears that not only the linear order may influence the
scope of a constituent, i. e. in ENGLISH an adverb in verb-phrase-
final position may only range over preceding but not over following
verbs, but that the range of an adverb and of any other constituent
type is influenced by its dominance structure. In GERMAN the

scope of manner adverbs is limited by the constituent that immediately dominantes it. In other words, manner adverbs can only
range over those constituents which are dominated -- though not
necessarily immediately -- by the same constituent that immediately dominates the adverb. In 96.b. the adverb is immediately
dominated by a conjunct VP node which does not dominate the other
conjunct VP as the P-marker below shows, and consequently the
adverb in VP$_3$ cannot range over the verb in VP$_2$.

96. b'.

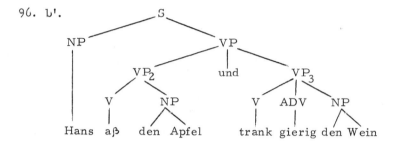

In order for the adverb to extend its scope to the verb in VP$_2$ above,
it would have to be immediately dominated by the coordinate node,
i.e. VP$_1$, as in 98 below, where 98. represents a paraphrase of 96.a.

98.

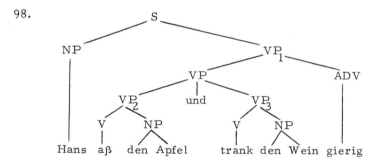

Thus we can say that in GERMAN the scope of a manner adverb is
upward-bounded by the node that immediately dominates it. The
same constraint also holds for ENGLISH manner adverbs.[28]

---

[28]While a manner adverb is upward-bounded by the constituent
that immediately dominates it, this is not true for a time adverb,
which can extend its scope to the S-node even if that node does not
immediately dominate it. For instance, b. below is a possible reduction of the a. sentence.
   a. John read a book last night and Barbara played a record last night.
   b. John read a book last night and Barbara played a record.
See also discussion below.

99. a. below cannot be reduced to 99. b. as the adverb is immediately dominated by a VP that does not dominate the VP in the second conjunct. However, if the adverb is sentence-initial and is Chomsky-adjoined to the coordinate node as in 100., then the adverb ranges over both verbs.

 99. a. John quickly ran upstairs and Bill quickly closed the doors.
    b.*John quickly ran upstairs and Bill closed the doors.

 100. a. Quickly John ran upstairs and quickly Bill closed the doors.
    b. Quickly John ran upstairs and Bill closed the doors.

The P-marker that corresponds to 100. b. is 101.

101.

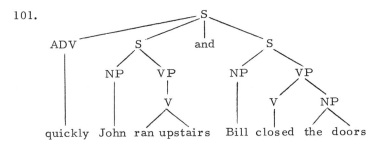

The constraints that were established for ENGLISH and GERMAN manner adverbs also seem to hold for manner adverbs in MANDARIN CHINESE.

 102. a. Yohàn hěn-hsung-de dǎ-le nà nán-hái-tze, Bill hěn-
     hsung-de dǎ-le nà nyu-hái-tze.
     "John furiously hit-past part. that boy Bill furiously
     hit-past part. that girl"
     'John furiously hit that boy, Bill furiously hit that girl.'

    b.*Yohàn hěn-hsung-de dǎ-le nà nán-hái-tze, Bill dǎ-le
     nà nyu-hái-tze.
     "John furiously hit-past part. that boy Bill hit-past part.
     that girl"

In RUSSIAN, on the other hand, the scope of manner adverbs is less restricted; i.e. the scope of the adverb is not upward-bounded by the constituent that immediately dominates it but seems to be identical to the scope of time adverbs which are upward-bounded by the S node. 102. a. below can be reduced to 103. b.

103.   a. Ivan žadno el pirog, a Boris žadno pil vino.
                   "Ivan greedily ate the pie, and Boris greedily
                   drank the wine"
     delet. b. Ivan žadno el pirog, a Boris pil vino.
                   "Ivan greedily ate the pie, and Boris drank the wine"

Thus, while in RUSSIAN a manner adverb can be deleted independent
of its position in the sentence, this is not true for ENGLISH, GER-
MAN and MANDARIN CHINESE. These languages consequently
need a constraint which prevents the anaphoric deletion of manner
adverbs in sentences like 95. a., 99. a., and 102. a., respectively.
The constraint has to take into account the constituent type that is
to be deleted and the position of the constituent within the sentence
before deletion. The constituent type has to be taken into account
because each type has its own scope; for instance in ENGLISH time
adverbials have a scope that differs from that of manner adverbials.
The position, on the other hand, is essential because it determines
whether or not regrouping can take place. Thus if the input to the
deletion rule is not 100. a. but 104. a. below, regrouping can raise
the adverb and place it into a position where both verbs are within
its scope.

104.   a. $[_S[_S$ John $[_{VP}$ quickly ran down the stairs$]]$ and
                                     $[_{VP}$ quickly closed the door$]]$

     delet. b. $[_S[_S$ John $[_{VP}$ quickly ran down the stairs$]]$ and
                                     $[_{VP}$ closed the door$]]$

     regr. c. $_S[$ John $[_{VP}$ quickly $[_{VP}[_{VP}$ ran down the stairs$]$ and
                                     $[_{VP}$ closed the door$]]]$

The following data from GERMAN provides further support for
the claim that constraints on deletion are tied in with whether or
not regrouping can apply to the output of the deletion rule and can
rearrange the sentence in such a way that it is identical to the input sentence.

105.   a. Hans kaufte den Apfel und Peter aβ den Apfel.
                   "Hans bought the apple and Peter ate the apple"

     delet. b. *Hans kaufte den Apfel und Peter aβ.
                   "Hans bought the apple and Peter ate"

     regr. c. Hans kaufte und Peter aβ den Apfel.
                   "Hans bought and Peter ate the apple"

106.   a. Hans hat den Apfel gekauft und Peter hat den Apfel
           gegessen.
           "Hans has the apple bought and Peter has the apple
           eaten"
           'Hans has bought the apple and Peter has eaten the apple.'

delet. b. *Hans hat den Apfel gekauft und Peter hat gegessen.
           "Hans has the apple bought and Peter has eaten"

105.a. and 106.a. differ in two aspects, namely in their tense and
in the position of the constituents. It appears rather unlikely that
a constraint on deletion can be directly correlated with a tense
difference, but indirectly the tense difference is responsible for
the constraint, as in GERMAN the tense difference happens to involve a difference in word order. While in 105. the object is in
sentence-final position, this position is taken in 106. by the past
participle. From this follows that regrouping cannot apply to 106.b.
and the object cannot be brought within the scope of both verbs.
Even if we reformulate the regrouping rule so that it would apply
to 106.b. and would raise the object, the resulting sentence would
be ungrammatical, as there is no position which would fulfill the
following two requirements: a) to be a position which objects can
occur, and b) to be a position which allows the object to be within
the scope of both verbs.[29]

Up to now it has been argued that if we assume the principle of
scope, we can account for certain constraints on deletion, and it
has also been argued that scope has a horizontal or linear, and a
vertical or dominance dimension. In the following it will be shown
that the assumption that scope is upward-bounded allows us to
account for the fact that in a language like CHINESE certain reductions are ungrammatical, while the corresponding reductions in a
language like ENGLISH result in acceptable surface forms. The
first to investigate these constraints were Sanders and Tai (1972)
who assumed that certain languages are subject to the Immediate
Dominance Condition on deletion while other languages are not.
Sanders and Tai had observed that all languages seem to allow the

---

[29]This statement is oversimplified as the object could be topicalized resulting in:
    Den Apfel hat Hans gekauft und Peter gegessen.
    "the apple has Hans bought and Peter eaten"
    'The apple Hans has bought and Peter eaten. '
Whether or not topicalized sentences like the above can be related
to constraints on regrouping will have to be further investigated.

deletion of an identical subject or predicate in a coordinate structure, but that languages like ENGLISH and languages like CHINESE
differ in that the former allow the deletion of objects and verbs
while the latter do not. Thus, in CHINESE 107. a. and 108. a. cannot be reduced to 107. b. and 108. b. respectively, while the ENG-
LISH glosses are grammatical.

107. a. Yohàn dǎ-le nán-hái-tze, Bill dǎ-le nyǔ-hái-tze.
         "John hit-past part. boy Bill hit-past part. girl"
         'John hit the boy, and Bill hit the girl.'

    b. *Yohàn dǎ-le nán-hái-tze, Bill nyǔ-hái-tze.
        "John hit-past part. boy Bill girl"

108. a. Yohàn dǎ-le nán-hái-tze, Bill tǐ-le nán-hái-tze.
         "John hit-past part. boy Bill kick-past part. boy"
         'John hit the boy, and Bill kicked the boy.'

    b. *Yohan dǎ-le, Bill tǐ-le nán-hái-tze.
        "John hit-past part. Bill kick-past part. boy"

In order to account for the ungrammaticality of sentences like 107. b.
and 108. b. Sanders and Tai propose the non-universal Immediate
Dominance Condition (henceforth IDC) which says that there exists
a "restriction against the deletion of any constituent which is not
immediately dominated by a conjunct sentence" (p. 165). This condition is part of the grammar of languages like CHINESE, HAUSA,
LEBANESE ARABIC, etc. while it is not found in the grammar of
languages like ENGLISH, JAPANESE, GERMAN and RUSSIAN.
Thus, by setting up a condition like the IDC, Sanders and Tai aim
to achieve two objectives, namely to account for constraints on deletion in languages like MANDARIN CHINESE, and to provide a
"systematic explanation of various differences between languages
like MANDARIN CHINESE and languages like ENGLISH" (p. 161).
Below it will be argued that even though the IDC seems to account
for most of the data, it fails to account for some crucial cases. It
will also be argued that by claiming that constraints on deletion
are governed by language-specific conditions, we draw a dividing
line between languages like ENGLISH and languages like CHINESE
which is not empirically justified and which prevents us from discovering a more general principle. The sets of sentences below
contain data from ENGLISH and MANDARIN CHINESE. A comparison reveals that constraints on object and verb deletion are
nearly identical for both languages, the only exception being 110. b.
and 114. b. where the CHINESE counterpart of the ENGLISH sentence is ungrammatical.

109. a. John bought the book and John read the book.
     b. John bought and read the book.

110. a. John bought the book and Bill read the book.
     b. John bought and Bill read the book.

111. a. I gave my mother a book and John gave my mother a
         record.
     b. *I gave my mother a book and John a record. [30]
     c. I gave my mother a book and John gave a record.

112. a. John gave a book to my mother, and I gave a book to
         my father.
     b. *John gave a book to my mother, and I gave to my father.

CHINESE:
113. a. Yohǎn mǎi-le nài běn shū, Yohǎn kàn-le nài běn shū.
         "John buy-past that clas. book, John read-past that
         clas. book"
         'John bought that book, John read that book.'

---

[30] It has been claimed (cf. Hankamer 1971), that a sentence like
111.b. is ungrammatical because it is ambiguous as to whether it
was derived from (1) or from (2) below:
   (1) I gave my mother a book and John gave my mother a record.
   (2) I gave my mother a book and I gave John a record.
But, even in GERMAN where case markings disambiguate the sentence, a reduction as in 111.b. is ungrammatical.
   (3) *Ich gab meiner Mutter ein Buch und mein Vater eine Schall-
       platte.
   "I gave my mother a book and my father a record"
However, I am not sure at present on the basis of which principle
the generation of a sentence like 111.b. can be excluded. It does
not seem to be scope, as in ENGLISH a verb can extend its scope
into another sentence, e.g.:
   (4) Bill bought an apple and John a banana.
That the principle is not avoidance of ambiguity is supported by the
above data from GERMAN, and also by the fact that if we remove
the ambiguity in the ENGLISH sentence, the resulting sentence is
still ungrammatical.
   (5) *I have my mother a book and Bill my mother a record.
However, if the indirect object in the first conjunct is constrasted
with another indirect object, then the resulting sentence is acceptable:
   (6) I gave my mother a book and Bill my father a record.

113. b. Yohàn mǎi-le, yǐeh kàn-le nài běn shū.[31]
    "John buy-past   also read-past that clas. book"
    'John bought and read that book. "

114. a. Yohàn mǎi-le nài běn shū, Bill kàn-le nài běn shū.
    "John buy-past that clas. book Bill read-past that clas. book"
    'John bought that book, and Bill read that book. '

    b.*Yohàn mǎi-le, Bill kàn-le nài běn shū.
    "John buy-past, Bill read-past that clas. book"

115. a. Wǒ gěi-le wǒ mama yì běn shū, Yohàn gěi-le wǒ
    mama yì chang ch'àng-pìen.
    "I give-past my mother one clas. book John give-past my
    mother one clas. record"
    'I gave my mother a book, and John gave my mother a record.'

    b.*Wǒ gěi-le wǒ mama yì běn shū, Yohàn yì chang ch'àng-pìen.
    "I give-past my mother one clas. book John one clas.
    record"

    c. Wǒ gěi-le wǒ mama yì běn shū, Yohàn gěi-le yì
    chang ch'àng-pìen.
    "I give-past my mother one clas. book John give-past one
    clas. record"
    'I gave my mother a book, and John gave a record. '

---

[31] Sanders and Tai claimed that verbal conjunction as in 113.b.
above is not possible in CHINESE, which presented a problem for
their analysis as the IDC could not account for this constraint.
However, verbal conjunction is grammatical in MANDARIN if yǐeh
'also' is inserted. What MANDARIN does not allow is the direct
juxtaposition of two finite verbs which occurs if yǐeh is not inserted
since MANDARIN does not have a conjunction corresponding to the
ENGLISH and.
    (1) a. Yohàn hsìao-le, yǐeh wǔ-le.
        "John laugh-past   also dance-past"
        'John laughed and danced. '

       b.*Yohan hsìao-le, wǔ-le.
       "John laughed-past dance-past"

    (2) a. Yohan dǎ-le, yǐeh tǐ-le nán-hái-tze.
        "John hit-past   also kick-past boy"
        'John hit and kicked the boy. '

       b.*Yohàn dǎ-le, tǐ-le nán-hái-tze.
       "John hit-past kick-past boy"

116. a. Yohằn gĕi-le wŏ māma yĩ bĕn shū, wŏ gĕi-le
       wŏ baba yĩ bĕn shū.
       "John give-past my mother one clas. book I give-past
       my father one clas. book"
       'John gave my mother a book, I gave my father a book.'

    b. *Yohằn gĕi-le wŏ māma, wŏ geĩ-le wŏ bằba yĩ bĕn shū.
       "John give-past my mother, I give-past my father one clas.book"

Problematic for Sanders' and Tai's analysis is the grammaticality
of 115. c; which, according to the IDC, should be ungrammatical.
It should be ungrammatical because at no time during the derivation is the indirect object immediately dominated by a conjunct node,
which is the condition for deletion stipulated by the IDC. A similar
problem is found in BENGALI. While spoken BENGALI seems to
stay within the constraints imposed by the IDC, written BENGALI
allows the deletion of a verb even if that verb is not immediately
dominated by a conjunct node.

117. a. John ekta kola kinlo ar Bill ekta aapel kinlo.
       "John a banana bought and Bill an apple bought"
       'John bought a banana and Bill bought an apple. '

    b. John ekta kola ar Bill ekta appel kinlo.
       "John a banana and Bill an apple bought"
       'John bought a banana and Bill an apple. '

The fact that sentences like 117. b. are found in written but not in
spoken BENGALI indicates that it is a performance or functional
constraint rather than a formal one like the IDC which excludes
sentences like 117. b. from spoken BENGALI.

    On the basis of the data presented above we can say that Sanders
and Tai fail to accomplish their two objectives, namely to account
for <u>all</u> of the constraints on deletion in languages like CHINESE,
and <u>to</u> systematically explain the differences between languages
like CHINESE and languages like ENGLISH. The former objective is not achieved because Sanders' and Tai's hypothesis cannot
account for the grammaticality of sentences like 115. c. and 117. b.,
which the IDC predicts to be ungrammatical. The latter objective
is not achieved, because even though Sanders' and Tai's hypothesis
accounts for the fact that a sentence like 110. b. is grammatical in
ENGLISH but not in MANDARIN (i.e. 114. b.), their hypothesis
does not account for the similarities between languages like ENG-
LISH and languages like CHINESE. For instance, Sanders'
and Tai's approach forces us to assume that the ungrammaticality
of 112. b. and of the corresponding 116. b. is due to unrelated

principles, even though the environments in which the deletion of
the object is constrained seem to be identical. Below I will show
that we can account for these similarities by assuming that ENG-
LISH and CHINESE, like all other languages, are subject to the
universal principle of scope, and I will also show that we can
account for the differences by assuming that the scope of a given
constituent type is upward-bound and that the boundaries may differ from language to language.

If an object is deleted in a SVO language and if regrouping takes
place, the object is raised to a higher node. This implies that if
the object is to be within the scope of the verb, this scope cannot
be upward-bound by the node that immediately dominates the verb,
i. e. if 118. below represents a grammatical surface form, both
verbs have to have the raised object NP within their scope.

118.

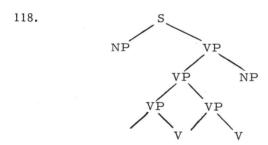

Structures like 118. are grammatical in all languages investigated
by me. However, there is some evidence that there are languages
in which a reduction as in 118. is ungrammatical. According to
Sanders and Tai MANDARIN CHINESE is one of these languages,
but sentences like 113. b. contradict their statement. Other languages that do not allow a structure like 118. are listed by Koutsoudas (1971:346). Assuming that this list is correct, we can then
state that in these languages the scope of a verb is upward-bound
by the node that immediately dominates the verb. This constraint
excludes sentences with a structure like 118. but permits sentences
with a structure like 119. and 120.

119.

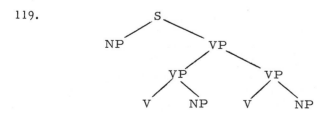

120.

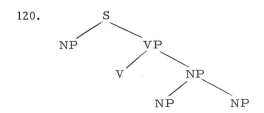

If an object has been deleted but not a subject, that is, if the conjunct nodes are S nodes, regrouping has to raise the antecedent constituent to the coordinate S node, which results in a structure like 121 below.

121.

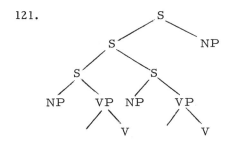

121. implies that the verbs have to extend their scope beyond the S nodes that dominate them into a higher S. This is not possible in languages like MANDARIN CHINESE, NAVAHO, and spoken BENGALI, while sentences with a structure like 121. are accepted in ENGLISH, GERMAN and written BENGALI. However, even in these languages sentences like the ones below are considered marginal by many speakers and are mostly used in writing, if at all.

122.   John bought and Bill read the book.
123.   ? John bought his mother and Bill bought his father a book.
124.   ? John hastily bought and Bill cooked some food.
125.   Hans kaufte und Bill verspeiste den Aal.
        "Hans bought and Bill ate the eel"
126.   ? Hans kaufte seiner Mutter und Fritz kaufte seinem Vater
        ein Klavier.
        "Hans bought his mother and Fritz bought his father
        a piano"
127.   ? Hans kaufte gestern vormittag und Fritz las gestern
        nachmittag die Zeitung.
        "Hans bought yesterday morning and Fritz read yesterday
        afternoon the newspaper"
        'Yesterday morning Hans bought and yesterday afternoon
        Fritz read the newspaper. '

Given the questionable status of some the above sentences, we can say that ENGLISH and GERMAN sometimes allow the scope of the verb to reach into the highest S, but that the acceptability of these sentences decreases with the number of constituents that intervene between the verbs and the raised object.

The assumption that in languages like CHINESE and BENGALI the scope of a verb is restricted by the VP that dominates it also accounts for the fact that these languages do not allow the deletion of verbs under certain conditions.

128. a. Yohàn mǎi-le yì běn shu, Bill mǎi-le yì chang ch'àng-pièn.
"John bought one clas. book Bill bought one clas. record"
'John bought a book, and Bill bought a record.'

b. *Yohàn mǎi-le yì běn shu, Bill yì chang ch'àng-pièn.
"John bought one clas. book Bill one clas. record"
'John bought a book, and Bill a record.'

129. a. Yohàn mǎi-le yì běn shu, Yohan mǎi-le yì chang ch'àng-pièn.
"John bought one clas. book John bought one clas. record"
'John bought a book, and John bought a record.'

b. Yohàn mǎi-le yì běn shu gen yì chang ch'àng-pièn.
"John bought one clas. book and one clas. record"
'John bought a book and a record.'

P-markers 130. and 131. below represent 128. and 129. respectively.

130.

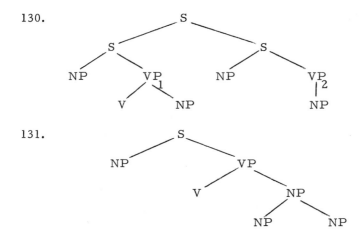

131.

In 130. the scope of the verb in VP_1 has to extend into another S to range over the object noun phrase in VP_2. However, as we have seen earlier, CHINESE restricts the scope of the verb to the VP that dominates it in this case to VP_1 and 130. can consequently not be a grammatical structure in CHINESE. In 131., on the other hand, the verb and the conjoined objects are dominated by the same VP and our hypothesis predicts that sentences with a structure like 131. are grammatical in MANDARIN CHINESE.

The above hypothesis, that constraints on object deletion depend on the scope of the verb, also predicts that a language like CHINESE or BENGALI in which the scope of the verb is upward-bound by the VP node will not have topicalization of the object as in 132 below.

132. a. John bought the book.
b. The book John bought.

This seems to be true for CHINESE[32] and is definitely true for BENGALI, LEBANESE ARABIC and NAVAHO, i. e. precisely those languages where we would expect topicalization not to occur. Sanders and Tai accounted for the non-occurrence of object topicalization in languages like CHINESE and LEBANESE ARABIC by claiming that topicalization is a process of copying and deletion and not a movement transformation. Thus they can say that topicalization is ungrammatical in CHINESE because the copied object NP cannot delete the original under the conditions imposed by the IDC. The hypothesis presented in this paper, on the other hand, makes no claims about the steps involved in topicalization. All it says is that the topicalization of an object NP will be ungrammatical in languages in which the scope of the verb is upward-bounded by the VP. Topicalization will be ungrammatical because it 'moves' the object NP beyond the scope of the verb by placing it into S-initial position.

Another example which supports the hypothesis that language-specific constraints on deletion can be accounted for by assuming that the scope boundaries of constituent types are language-specific is time-adverbs. While manner adverbs in both ENGLISH and CHINESE are upward-bounded by the constituent that immediately dominates the adverb, ENGLISH and CHINESE differ with respect to the upper boundary of time adverbs. It appears that in ENGLISH

---

[32] For a discussion of some data on topicalization and especially of the CHINESE data see Sanders & Tai 1972: 170-75.

time adverbs can extend their scope beyond the constituent that immediately dominates the adverb, e.g. 133., while CHINESE time adverbs seem to have the same constraints as manner adverbs, e.g. 134.

133. a. John saw his girlfriend yesterday, and Mary saw her mother yesterday.
   b. John saw his girlfriend yesterday and Mary saw her mother.
   c. Yesterday John saw his girl friend and Mary saw her mother.

134. a. Yohàn tzúo-tien tǐ-le nán-hái-tze, Bill tzúo-tien dǎ-le nyǔ-hái-tze.
   "John yesterday kicked boy   Bill yesterday hit girl"
   'Yesterday John kicked the boy, and yesterday Bill hit the girl.'

   b. *Yohàn tzúo-tien tǐ-le nán-hái-tze, Bill dǎ-le nyǔ-hái-tze.
   "John yesterday kicked boy   Bill hit girl"

   c. Tzúo-tien Yohàn tǐ-le nán-hái-tze, Bill dǎ-le nyǔ-hái-tze.
   "yesterday John kicked boy   Bill hit girl"
   'Yesterday John kicked the boy, and Bill hit the girl.'

In 133.b. the adverb is immediately dominated by a VP, but it is not upward-bounded by this node as it can extend its scope into the VP of another coordinated sentence, i.e. 133.b. can be a paraphrase of 133.a. In CHINESE, however, 134.b. is not a possible reduction of 134.a., because 134.b. does not imply that 'Bill hit the girl yesterday.' On the other hand, if the adverb is dominated by the S node as in 134.c., it can extend its scope over both verbs and 134.c. can be a paraphrase of 134.a.

We have seen so far that the principle of scope seems to account for many of the constraints found in coordination reduction. However, we have not yet considered which of the two rules -- deletion or regrouping — should be constrained. The most likely place appears to be the deletion rule which will be prevented from applying if regrouping cannot place the antecedent constituent into a position in which the scope constraints of a given language are met. Failure to place the antecedent constituent into an appropriate position can either be due to the fact that regrouping cannot apply because the structural description of the rule is not met, or it can be due to the fact that regrouping would raise the antecedent constituent beyond the scope boundaries of the constituent(s) the former is in construction

with. For example, one constraint on the deletion rule in ENGLISH
as well as in GERMAN is that deletion of a direct object can only
take place if the object is in verb-phrase-final position, a position
which permits the reordering and raising of the object.

135. a. John bought the book and Bill read the book.
      b. John bought and Bill read the book.

136. a. John bought the book for Christmas and Bill read the
          book.
      b. *John bought the book for Christmas and Bill read.

RUSSIAN, on the other hand, does not have this constraint, as
137. a. can be reduced to 137. b.

137. a. Vanja kupil jabloko, a Masa s"ela jabloko.
          "John bought apple   and Mary ate apple"
          'John bought an apple and Mary ate an apple. '

      b. Vanja kupil jabloko, a Masa s"ela.
          "John bought apple   and Mary ate"
          'John bought and Mary ate the apple. '

Concluding this discussion of the hypothesis that constraints on
coordination reduction depend on the scope of individual constituent
types, we can say that even though many questions still remain
unanswered, enough justification has been put forward in support
of the above hypothesis that it merits further investigation.

3. Coordination Reduction in Disjunctions, Questions etc.

Analyses like those proposed by Ross, Sanders, and Koutsoudas
attempt to account for coordination reduction in conjoined affirmative declaratives, but they exclude coordination reduction involving
disjunctive and adversative coordination, negated conjuncts, or
coordination of other sentence types, e.g. of questions. Although
no extensive research of the above types of data was undertaken,
all of the data investigated so far substantiates the hypotheses presented in this paper, i.e. all of the reduction patterns stay within
the framework predicted by the deletion rule and the regrouping
rule. In disjunctions and adversatives split coordination is more
common than in and conjunctions. For example, in GERMAN 138. a.
is a doubtful surface form, while 139. a. is perfectly acceptable
because in 139. a. the meaning of und is adversative.

138.　a.　? Hans ist gekommen und Monika.
　　　　　"Hans is come and Monika"
　　　　　'Hans arrived and Monika. '

139.　a.　Hans ist gekommen und nicht Monika.
　　　　　"Hans is come and not Monika"
　　　　　'Hans arrived and not Monika. '

138. a. is doubtful because regrouping is obligatory in GERMAN
for sentences like 138. a. unless und Monika has the meaning of
an afterthought, while regrouping is optional for sentences like
139. a.

138.　b.　Hans und Monika sind gekommen.
　　　　　"Hans and Monika are come"
　　　　　'Hans and Monika arrived. '

139.　b.　Hans und nicht Monika ist gekommen.
　　　　　"Hans and not Monika is come"
　　　　　'Hans and not Monika arrived. '

Among the languages investigated split coordination in disjunctions
occurs in BENGALI, HEBREW, ARABIC, RUSSIAN, HUNGARIAN,
GERMAN, HINDI, HAUSA(?), and ENGLISH.

140.　BENGALI:
　　　a.　John ekta aapel kinlo kimba John ekta kola kinlo.
　　　　　"John one apple bought or John one banana bought"
　　　　　'John bought an apple or John bought a banana. '

　　　b.　John ekta aapel kinlo kimba ekta kola.
　　　　　"John one apple bought or one banana"
　　　　　'John bought one apple or one banana. '

　　　c.　John ekta aapel kimba ekta kola kinlo.
　　　　　"John one apple or one banana bought"
　　　　　'John bought an apple or a banana. '

141.　CLASSICAL ARABIC:
　　　a.　akala Faruk mousan au akala Medhat mousan.
　　　　　"ate Faruk banana or ate Medhat banana"
　　　　　'Faruk ate a banana or Medhat ate a banana. '

　　　b.　akala Faruk mousan, au Medhat.
　　　　　"ate Faruk banana or Medhat"
　　　　　'Faruk ate the banana, or Medhat. '

An example of an adversary conjunction in which regrouping is
optional are the GERMAN <u>sondern</u> 'but rather' construction.

142.   a.   Nicht Hans ist gestern angekommen sondern Klaus
             ist gestern angekommen.
             "not Hans is yesterday arrived but-rather Klaus
             is yesterday arrived"
             'It isn't Hans who arrived yesterday but rather it is
             Klaus who arrived yesterday. '

         b.   Nicht Hans ist gestern angekommen sondern Klaus.
             " not Hans is yesterday arrived but-rather Klaus"
             'It is not Hans who arrived yesterday but Klaus. '

         c.   Nicht Hans sondern Klaus ist gestern angekommen.
             " not Hans but-rather Klaus is yesterday arrived"
             'It is not Hans but Klaus who arrived yesterday. '

Coordination reduction in negated conjuncts obeys the same
principles as reduction in non-negated conjuncts though in some
respects reduction involving negation is more restricted because
of the presence of the negative particle. Below it is shown that
all of the paraphrases of 143. a. can be generated if we assume
the existence of rules 36. and 46. [33]

143.   a.   John arrived but Mary didn't arrive.
         b.   John arrived but Mary didn't.
         c.   John did but Mary didn't arrive.
         d.   *John but Mary didn't arrive.

Below are the respective derivations where the i. forms are not
claimed to be the underlying forms.

---

[33]There are two other sentences which are closely related to
143. a. , namely (1) and (2) below.
   (1)   John arrived but not Mary.
   (2)   John but not Mary arrived.
Whether or not (1) and (2) are paraphrases of 143. a. in that all
three of these sentences are derived from the same underlying
form cannot be decided here. It is very likely that (1) and (2)
and possibly also 143. a. are derived from underlying clefted sentences. Such a derivation accounts for the position of <u>not</u> in (1)
and (2). For a discussion of the derivation of the GERMAN counterparts of (1) and (2) see Harries 1972.

143'. b. i. John past arrive but neg. Mary past arrive.

                                        <u>neg. -lowering</u>

    ii. John past arrive but Mary past neg. arrive.

                                          <u>deletion</u>

    iii. John past arrive but Mary past neg.

                                          <u>do-insertion and</u>
                                          <u>affix-movement</u>

    iv. John arrived but Mary didn't.

143'. c. i. John past arrive but neg. Mary past arrive.

                                          <u>neg. -lowering</u>

    ii. John past arrive but Mary past neg. arrive.

                                          <u>deletion</u>

    iii. John past arrive but Mary past neg.

                                          <u>regrouping</u>

    iv. John past but Mary past neg. arrive.

                                          <u>do-insertion and</u>
                                          <u>affix-movement</u>

    v. John did but Mary didn't arrive.

Thus, while the rules will generate 143.b. and 143.c., they will not generate 143.d., as a form like i. in 143'.b. or in 143'.c. could only be converted into 143.d. if coordination reduction applied backwards, which is excluded in the present analysis.

Coordination reduction in conjoined questions is subject to the same constraints as coordination reduction in declarative as the following data from ENGLISH and HUNGARIAN shows.

144. a. Did John read a book or did John write a book?

                                          <u>deletion</u>

    b. Did John read a book or write?

                                          <u>regrouping</u>

    c. Did John read or write a book?

145. a. Vett Bill banánokat és evett John banánokat?
        "bought Bill the banana and ate John the banana"
        'Did Bill buy the banana and did John eat the banana?'

                                          <u>deletion</u>

    b. Vett Bill banánokat és evett John?
        "bought Bill the banana and ate John"
        'Did Bill buy and John eat the banana?'

                                          <u>regrouping</u>

    c. Vett Bill és evett John banánokat?
        "bought Bill and ate John the banana"
        'Did Bill buy and John eat the banana?'

In HUNGARIAN regrouping is not only optional in most declaratives but also in questions and both 145.b. and 145.c. are grammatical surface orders, while regrouping is obligatory in ENGLISH, i.e. 144.b. is not an acceptable surface order.

4. Conclusion

It has been shown in this paper that the analyses of coordination reduction as proposed by Ross, Koutsoudas, and Sanders fail to account for the facts in a principled way. In order to generate all possible surface forms they have to take refuge to ad hoc measures like otherwise unmotivated movement rules and constraints. Special movement rules are needed in all those cases where coordination reduction can result in two alternate orders, and it was shown that these cases are far more numerous than Ross' and Koutsoudas' writings indicate. Special constraints are required for languages like QUECHUA where the directionality relation predicts an order which does not occur, while an order that is not predicted does occur. In the treatment of coordination reduction presented in this paper, on the other hand, the above problems are avoided. By assuming a reduction rule that only operates forward and subsequent regrouping, all of the data can be accounted for in a very general and principled way. The rules proposed make strong predictions about the surface orders of reduced coordinate structures that can occur in natural languages. They predict that if a language allows alternate ordering for a given reduced structure, these fall into the two categories below.

i.   The order of the reduced structure is identical to the output order of the deletion rule.

ii.   The order of the reduced structure is identical to the output order of the regrouping rule.

It is those structures characterized in ii. that are considered 'normal' or 'basic' in Ross' as well as in Sanders' and Koutsoudas' approaches, while structures that fall under i. are problematic for them if they result in split coordination.

The rules proposed here furthermore predict that if a language only allows one surface order for reduced sentences, this surface order must either fall under i. above -- no regrouping -- or under ii. -- regrouping obligatory. As pointed out before, object-reduction in HINDI constitutes to my knowledge the only potential counterexample to the above predictions. The HINDI data can, however, be accounted for if we assume that HINDI is an underlying SVO language.

In the section on constraints it was argued that if we assume a universal principle of scope, i. e. if we assume that every constituent type has a certain scope which has a linear and a dominance dimension, and if we assume that this scope is language specific, then we can account for many of the constraints on deletion and for the differences that exist between languages. Deletion has to be prevented in all those cases where in a given language after coordination reduction the constituents would be in a linear and/or dominance configuration that does not have the same relational content as the input sentence to the coordination reduction process. In other words deletion has to be prevented where neither the output order of the deletion rule nor the output order of the regrouping rule meet the scope constraints of a given language. The assumption that the scope of a given constituent type is language specific accounts for the differences between languages. Note, however, that the choices open to a language are rather restricted. For instance, we found three types of upper boundaries for the scope of a finite verb, namely the scope is either restricted by the node that immediately dominates the verb, by a VP node that dominates the verb, or by an S-node that dominates the verb (see 118.b. and 121. above). For an adverb, there seem to exist two choices, namely it is either upward-bounded by the node that immediately dominates it, or by an S node that dominates it. In ENGLISH manner adverbs belong to the first category, while time adverbs belong to the second. In CHINESE both adverb types belong to the first category, while in RUSSIAN both seem to belong to the second category. The choices open to other constituent types as well as the language specific constraints will have to be determined by further research.

Finally, in section 3. it was shown that the proposed analysis not only accounts for coordination reduction in and conjunctions but seems to account for all other kinds of coordination reductions as well. Whether or not it will also account for reductions in non-coordinate structures will have to be established by further research.

BIBLIOGRAPHY

Crockett, D. 1972. More on coordination reduction. Papers from the Eighth Regional Meeting, Chicago Linguistic Society. 52-61.

Delisle, G. 1972. Universals and person pronouns in Southwestern Chippewa. Doctoral dissertation, University of Minnesota.

Hankamer, J. 1971. Constraints on deletion in syntax. Doctoral dissertation, Yale University.

Harries, H. 1972. Cleft sentences, questions, and presupposition sharing. Doctoral dissertation, University of Minnesota.

Jackendoff, R. 1971. Gapping and related rules. Linguistic Inquiry 2.1. 21-35.

Koutsoudas, A. 1968. The A over A convention. Linguistics 46. 11-20.

_____. 1971. Gapping, conjunction reduction, and coordinate deletion. Foundation of Language 7.3. 337-386.

Lakoff, G. 1969. On derivational constraints. Papers from the Fifth Regional Meeting, Chicago Linguistic Society. 117-39.

_____. 1970. Global rules. Language 46.3. 627-40.

Langacker, R. 1969. On pronominalization and the chain of command. Modern studies in English, ed. by Reibel and Schane. Englewood Cliffs : Prentice Hall. 160-86.

Postal, P. 1970. On coreferential complement subject deletion. Linguistic Inquiry 1.4. 439-500.

Pulte, W. 1971. Gapping and word order in Quechua. Papers from the Seventh Regional Meeting, Chicago Linguistics Society. 193-97.

Ross, J. 1967a. Constraints on variables in syntax. Doctoral dissertation, M.I.T.

_____. 1967b. Gapping and the order of constituents (manuscript). Appeared in Actes du Xe Congres Internationale de Linguistes, II, Bucarest, 1970.

Sanders, G. 1970. Invariant ordering. Mimeographed paper, Indiana University Linguistic Club.

_____ and J. Tai. 1972. Immediate dominance and identity deletion. Foundation of Language 8.2. 161-97.

Tai, J. 1969. Coordination reduction. Doctoral dissertation, Indiana University.

_____. 1971. Identity deletion and regrouping in coordinate structure. Papers from the Seventh Regional Meeting, Chicago Linguistics Society. 264-74.

Word Order Variation:
A Typological Study

SUSAN STEELE

ABSTRACT

Many languages allow variations on the basic order of noun subject, noun object and verb. This paper establishes which re-orderings are likely and which are less so. The pattern to the difference between the two suggests two constraints on word order variation, one of which refers crucially to the position of the verb in the sentence and the other of which refers crucially to the position of the subject and the object relative to the verb. Within this framework, a classification distinguishing between free, rigid and mixed word order languages can be established.

This paper was written under the auspices of the Stanford Language Universals Project. It has benefited considerably from the suggestions of the members of the Project and of the participants in a class I taught at the 1976 Summer Linguistic Institute in Oswego, New York.

CONTENTS

1. Introduction

   All languages have a dominant word order, a surface ordering
of subject, object and verb relative to one another that is at least
more common than other possible orders.[1] Typological studies of
the order of elements in language, such as, e.g. Greenberg 1966
and Lehmann 1972 and 1973 have depended on and assumed this fact.
Most languages allow variations on their basic word order. This,
too, has been noted by those who do typologies of word order, but
in the main only as it bears on the question of deciding what is a
dominant word order. Whether there is a typology of word order
variation remains an unasked question. Such a typology is the subject of this paper.

   1.1 A typological investigation, most fundamentally, must
establish which of the logically possible language states are actually
attested. Once this is established it is necessary to set up a classification whereby a language can be pigeonholed; that is, the criteria by which a language can be assigned to a particular type must
be stated with precision. A more ambitious -- and truly successful
-- typology will attempt two even more elusive goals. First, it will
attempt to explain why only certain of the logically possible language
states exist. Second, and equally difficult, it will provide some
method of predicting where a language will be pigeonholed; that is,
it will look for correlations between the particular typological feature
under consideration and other typological facts.

   With an examination of the possible word orders in 63 languages,
section 3 of this paper meets the most fundamental requirement for
establishing a typology on word order variation. This examination
reveals that certain variations on a basic word order are universal
or nearly so -- and others are almost nonexistent. The section concludes with a series of constraints on word order variation, constraints which allow the common variations and proscribe the less
common; the section thus meets the third requirement suggested
above. Section 4 takes up the second requirement of typological
studies. Given that certain constraints on word order variation can
be established, we can classify languages according to whether they
conform to or break these constraints. Section 4 thus confronts an
issue that has been discussed with massive imprecision -- the

---

[1] This is an assumption, of course, but one which is justified.
Even grammars which talk about the absolute freedom of position
for the elements of the sentence will note that certain orders are
more common than others.

question of what is meant by freedom or rigidity of word order.
Section 5 takes up the fourth requirement of typological studies;
it investigates whether those languages which exhibit the rarer
word order variations have any common typological features.
Hypotheses about what allows word order variability have concentrated on the presence or absence of case inflection. Section 5
will show these hypotheses to be unwarranted.

1. 2   The discussion of word order variation to follow is based
on data from 63 languages. The languages in the language sample
are listed in Table 1 by genetic affiliation.[2] The languages were
selected with an eye to both genetic and typological diversity. The
purpose was to make the sample as representative as possible.[3] The
genetic diversity is apparent in Table 1 (next page). Not all language
families are represented nor do all language families have equal
representation, but the coverage is quite broad. Typologically, I
was primarily concerned to get a fair sampling of languages within
each of the basic word order types. A language can be characterized as having one of six basic word orders: SOV, SVO, VSO, VOS,
OVS, OSV. (As will be seen, part of the examination of word order
variation will consider the order of constituents in intransitive
sentences, so characterizing a language by one of these six labels
should be viewed as a mnemonic device.) The first two types are
relatively common; the third and fourth slightly less common; the
fifth and sixth almost nonexistent. The number of languages of
each type in the sample corresponds roughly to the frequency of
occurrence of each basic type. SOV and SVO are heavily represented, VSO and VOS less so, and OVS and OSV not at all. Table
2 presents the division of the languages of the language sample in
terms of their basic word order.

---

[2] The most comprehensive genetic groups are listed in Table 1;
agreement on the validity of these genetic groups ranges from near
universal to chaotic disagreement. By the labels in Table 1 I do
not indicate either commitment to or rejection of any particular
genetic group.

[3] A problem for any cross-linguistic study is how to make a
sample representative, that is, how to ensure that a different set
of languages might not yield a different set of conclusions. I had
thought about word order at some length before I began the research
for this paper; I could find no reason to suspect that some consideration other than the two I used here -- genetic and word order typology -- is germane. Therefore, I am relatively confident that the
conclusions which result from this sample are fully representative
of any other (equally carefully chosen) sample.

Table 1. Language Sample

I. INDO-EUROPEAN
   English
   Albanian
   Czech
   Faroese

II. DRAVIDIAN
   Kolami
   Koya

III. URAL-ALTAIC
   Turkish
   Yakut
   Vogul
   Yurak

IV. JAPANESE
   Japanese

V. AFRO-ASIATIC
   Somali

VI. CONGO-KORDOFANIAN
   Diola-Fogny
   Ibibio
   Gbeya

VII. NILO-SAHARAN
   Fur
   Bari

VIII. SINO-TIBETAN
   Lahu
   Mandarin
   Burmese
   Thai

IX. VIETNAMESE
   Vietnamese

X. AUSTRONESIAN
   Tagalog
   Kapampangan
   Sonsoral-Tobi
   Indonesian

XI. AUSTRO-ASIATIC
   Kharia

XII. OCEANIC
   Ulithian
   Tongan
   Pukapukan
   Iai
   Tahitian

XIII. AUSTRALIAN
   Gunwingju
   Walbiri
   Dalabon
   Jiwadja
   Narinjari
   Maranungku
   Garadjari

XIV. NADENE
   Navajo

XV. ALGONKIAN-MOSAN
   Wiyot
   Yurok
   Maleceet-Passamoquoddy
   Squamish
   Puget Salish

XVI. INDO-PACIFIC
   Kapau

XVII. AZTECO-TANOAN
   Hopi
   Classical Aztec
   Luiseño

XVIII. ANDEAN-EQUATORIAL
   Piro
   Inga
   Cacua

(continued next page)

XIX. HOKAN-SIOUAN   XXI. MACRO-OTOMANGUEAN
      Mojave   Trique
      Karok
      Tuscarora   XXII. MACRO-CHIBCHAN
                                          Ica

XX. PENUTIAN   XXIII. TARASCAN
      Achi
      Sahaptin   Unrepresented groups:
      Jacaltec   I.   CAUCASIAN
      Chinook   II.   PALEOSIBERIAN
      Chorti   III. ESKIMO-ALEUT
                                   IV.   GE-PANO-CARIB

Table 2. Word Order Classification

SOV (30)	SVO (20)	VSO (10)	VOS (3)
Kolami	English	Tahitian	Tagalog
Koya	Albanian	Pukapukan	Kapampangan
Turkish	Czech	Narinjari	Tongan
Yakut	Faroese	Squamish	
Yurak	Diola-Fogny	Puget Salish	
Vogul	Ibibio	Achi	
Japanese	Gbeya	Sahaptin	
Somali	Bari	Jacaltec	
Fur	Mandarin	Chinook	
Lahu	Thai	Trique	
Burmese	Vietnamese		
Kharia	Sonsoral-Tobi		
Gunwingju	Indonesian		
Walbiri	Ulithian		
Dalaban	Iai		
Jiwadja	Maleceet-		
Maranungku	Passamoquoddy		
Garadjari	Classical Aztec		
Navajo	Tuscarora		
Wiyot	Chorti		
Yurok	Tarascan		
Kapau			
Hopi			
Luiseño			
Piro			
Inga			
Cacua			
Mojave			
Karok			
Ica			

Obviously, with such a broad language sample the analysis of
any one language is relatively superficial. A language was assigned
a basic word order on the statement of the person who described it
or, if I was familiar with the language, by my own analysis.[4] Similarly, although some of the data is drawn from my own work with
native speakers, most of the information about word order variation
is culled from explicit statements -- and examples — to that effect
in grammatical descriptions. Since the paper is concerned with
the variations in the <u>surface</u> word order of certain constituents of
the clause, I do not take the necessary superficiality of the analyses
to be a detriment.

2. Preliminaries

2.1 This paper is by no means an exhaustive study of word
order variation. It is concerned exclusively with the relative
order of nominal subjects, nominal objects and verbs in declarative main clauses.[5] Although the decision to narrow the scope of
the investigation along these lines is in some sense arbitrary, it
is an important and necessary delimitation.

Let me first make the exclusions explicit. By focusing on clauses
I exclude from consideration the order of constituents in a phrase
and the order of morphemes in a word. By focusing on main clauses
I exclude from consideration the order of the constituents in subordinate clauses. By focusing on declarative main clauses I exclude

---

[4] Data on most of these languages was gleaned from published
sources. Data on TRIQUE, INGA, ICA and CACUA was supplied
by members of the Instituto Lingüistico de Verano. I have personally worked on LUISEÑO, KAPAMPANGAN, CLASSICAL AZTEC,
HOPI, ALBANIAN and SAHAPTIN.

[5] This statement presupposes that subjects and objects are not
only identifiable cross-linguistically, but also that it should be
possible to state how they can be identified. Keenan's work has
made clear that, although <u>subject</u> is a term linguists use regularly
and with confidence, a precise characterization of the notion eludes
us. A similar situation may pertain as regards the notion <u>object</u>.
I am not going to agonize over the problem. In languages where I
am dependent on someone else's description I simply accepted their
decision as to what was a subject and what was an object. In languages with which I was familiar I didn't use any formal criteria to
identify subject and object, but rather assumed the validity of such
concepts and, with no obvious evidence to the contrary, expected
that they would correspond roughly to ENGLISH.

from consideration all non-declarative sentences, i.e. questions
and imperatives. By focusing on the relative order of subject,
object and verb in declarative main clauses I exclude from consideration the order of other constituents of the main clause, as e.g.
adverbial elements. By focusing on the relative order of nominal
subjects, nominal objects and verbs in declarative main clauses
I exclude from consideration the position of pronominal subjects
and pronominal objects.

With these exclusions the corpus to be examined has a coherence
it otherwise wouldn't. Each constituent type excluded has restrictions on order that do not pertain to the type under consideration.
The constituents of a clause have more potential for reordering than
the constituents of a phrase or the morphemes which make up a
word. Subordinate clauses not uncommonly exhibit more rigid word
order than main clauses. Questions and imperatives in many languages have certain word order requirements which are not found
in declarative sentences. Constituents of the clause other than
subject, object and verb tend cross-linguistically to occur in certain
sentential positions in the clause. For example, sentential adverbs
occur clause initially, clause finally or in sentential second position.
Finally, the position of pronominal subjects and pronominal objects
often do not reflect the positions of nominal subjects and nominal
objects. It is certainly important that possibilities for reordering
in each of these constituent types be examined in some detail. But,
in support of my delimitation, it is enough to note that there are
differences.

2.2   I have defined what types of constructions will be examined
in this consideration of word order variation; I have yet to say
what is to be included under the term variation. Stating what should
be excluded — and hence what should be included — is easy; making
the exclusions in a regular fashion is slightly less so. Basically,
in the tabulation of variations on a basic word order any highly
marked word order will be excluded. ENGLISH sentences with a
topicalized object noun are a case in point.

1.   That man I dislike.

I would not want to say on the basis of such sentences that ENGLISH,
an SVO language, has an OSV variation; my intuitions as a native
speaker of ENGLISH identify these as a very special word order.
I obviously cannot appeal to native intuition for the other languages
examined, but there are certain criteria which can be adduced to
remove such highly marked variations on a basic word order from

consideration. First, and most importantly, such highly marked variations are usually either not mentioned in descriptive studies or are identified as such. Second, and slightly more problematic, such highly marked word orders often are to be distinguished from the corresponding basic word order in other than the order of their elements. They may have a distinctive intonation contour. For example, consider the intonation contour for ENGLISH sentences with a dislocated noun as in 1. or a dislocated noun as in 2.

2. That man, I dislike him.

Sentences like 1. and 2. can have two intonation contours, one on the dislocated or topicalized noun, the second on the rest of the sentence. The corresponding sentences without a topicalized or dislocated noun do not. There may be syntactic differences as well as, or rather than, phonological differences between sentences with the basic word order and sentences with a variation of that word order. For example, the marking of the noun may be different in the variation than it is in the basic word order, or some element may be necessary in the variation. As an illustration of the first, consider KAPAMPANGAN. KAPAMPANGAN regularly has verb initial surface word order.

3. Salwan ne ing mangga ning lalaki king Sabadu
   "buy he:it the mango the boy on Saturday"
   'The mango will be bought by the boy on Satuday.'
   (Mirikitani 1972: 147)

Nouns in a KAPAMPANGAN sentence are preceded by a particle which, among other things, indicates case. In the above sentence lalaki is marked by ning as both agentive and non-subject; in the sentence below lalaki is marked by ing as both agentive and subject.

4. Sinali ya ng mangga ing lalaki king tindahan
   "bought he a mango the boy at store"
   'The boy bought a mango at the store.' (Mirikitani 1972: 147)

If lalaki is moved to the front of the clause, that is, is topicalized, in a sentence like 3., it is no longer marked by ning but rather by ing.[6]

---

[6] There is also an intonation break between ing lalaki in 5. and the remainder of the sentence.

5. Ing lalaki seli   ne   ing mangga
    "the boy bought he:it the mango"
    'The boy, he bought a mango.'   (Mirikitani 1972: 151)

    As an example of the second, the appearance of some element
in a sentence with a variation on the basic word order, consider
CLASSICAL AZTEC. CLASSICAL AZTEC allows SVO, SOV, VSO
and VOS surface word orders.[7]

6. in nota?tzin oquitzonhuilan in nonantzin
        (S)   (V)   (O)
    "article my:father he:dragged:her:around article my:mother
    by:the:hair"
    'My father dragged my mother around by the hair.'
                                         (Anderson 1973: 107)

7. auh   in   mextli yohual tequitl quitlaza
              (S)   (O)   (V)
    "and article moon night duty he:takes:it"
    'And the moon does the night's work.'   (Garibay 1970: 135)

8. niman oncan caltia in   ticitl   in   piltzintli
          (V)   (S)   (O)
    "then there she:bathed:him article midwife article baby"
    'Then the midwife bathed the baby there.'
                                    (Dibble and Anderson 1969: 201)

9. quinotza in cozulli in ticitl
        (V)   (O)   (S)
    "she:addressed:it article cradle article midwife"
    'The midwife addressed the cradle.'
                                    (Dibble and Anderson 1969: 206)

However, if the object precedes the verb and the subject, that is,
if the word order is OVS or OSV, the object is followed by a particle,
usually ca.

10. in cocoliztli ca oconpolo
        (O)   (V)
    "article sickness ca it:destroyed it"
    'It destroyed the sickness.'   (Garibay 1970: 54)

---

[7] There are, however, obvious differences in the frequency with
which each type appears in the textual material which forms the
CLASSICAL AZTEC corpus. SOV is the least common, by far;
VSO is somewhat more common; SVO and VOS are the most common word orders.

I have excluded from the discussion to follow any variations on
a basic word order which include some phonological or syntactic
feature that is not required in the basic word order, the assumption
being that such features indicate the marked nature of the word
order for that particular language. Any variation on a basic word
order, on the other hand, which neither was described as marked
nor is distinguished by some feature from the basic word order is
included in the discussion to follow.

This definition of variations on a basic word order allows the
possibility that the basic word order and any of the variations
thereon will not be semantically identical. That is, it is not required that a variation on a basic word order, to be considered a
variation, be an exact semantic equivalent of the basic word order.
Variations on a basic word order commonly indicate some change
in topic and/or focus.[8] For example, "in CZECH [Topic Comment
Articulation] (together with certain phenomena of emphasis) is the
prevailing factor determining the word order, whereas the grammatical factor [i.e. grammaticized word order] is decisive in some
cases only, e.g. as to the position of some types of adnominal ad-
juncts..." (Sgall et al. 1973:15). Other semantic effects of variation
on a basic word order are at least possible. It is possible that an
order of subject, object and verb relative to one another would indicate something about the completion of the action of the verb on the
object. For example, in ENGLISH one of the distinctions between
the two possible orders of direct and indirect objects is roughly this.

11. Mary threw John the ball.

12. Mary threw the ball to John.

In the first John has to be actively participating in the act; in the
second he needn't.

13. *Mary threw John the ball, but he wasn't looking.

14. Mary threw the ball to John, but he wasn't looking.

---

[8] The problem is to distinguish between those languages where
topicalization and/or focus isn't achieved by some highly marked
word order and those where it is, rather than to distinguish between orders that mark differences in topicalization and those that
don't. Hence the discussion above of how to identify a marked
word order.

It is also possible that the relative order of verb and object would indicate the definiteness or indefiniteness of the object. For example, in CHINESE the object is definite in OV order and indefinite in VO order.

15. Zhāng-sān dǎ-può zhuānghu le
    (S)   (V)   (O)
    "Zhang-san hit-broken window aspect"
    'Zhang-san broke (a) window.'

16. Zhāng-sān bǎ zhuānghu dǎ-può le
    (S)   (O)   (V)
    "Zhang-san ba window hit-broken aspect"
    'Zhang-san broke the window.'   (Li and Thompson 1975:1)

There were no examples in the language sample of a difference like the former possibility pertaining to the relative order of subject, object and verb; the latter difference involves not only word order but the presence in OV and the absence in VO of ba. However, it is certainly possible that some word order variations will have the effect of the former and that some word order variations can effect the latter without the presence or absence of some grammatical element.

I allow, then, the possibility that variations on a basic word order will have certain semantic effects. It is not obviously the case that all variations on a basic word order involve (possibly very slight) semantic shifts. For example, Schachter and Otanes report that the orders VOS and VSO in TAGALOG are equally possible and involve no clear semantic distinction. It doesn't matter for the purposes of this paper whether the variations on the basic word order have semantic effects or what those effects are; it only matters that there not be something about the sentence which distinguishes it either phonologically or syntactically from a sentence with the basic word order.

2.3 A final caution. Although I have assumed that languages have a basic word order and although I will discuss variations on that basic word order, I do not necessarily assume that the variations involve reordering of the basic word order, that is, that the base rules produce a certain word order which the reordering processes apply to. Nothing in this paper hinges on whether we assume that the alternate word orders are actually reorderings of the base or whether each of the possible word orders in any one language, including the most common one, are produced independently.

3. Variations

  As promised above, this section establishes which variations
on each of the four word order types are attested and offers some
hypotheses in explanation of the data. The first task, upon which
the second hinges, is not as straightforward as it would appear.
With a few exceptions all of the possible variations on the word
order types are attested. Once we examine the frequency of each
variation cross-linguistically, however, certain patterns of word
order variation emerge.

  3.1 All of the possible orders are attested for both intransitive
and transitive sentences in SOV, SVO and VSO language types.[9]
That is, for each variation on the basic word order that is logically
possible in each of these types, we find at least one language that
attests it. For the VOS language type only two of the possible
variations on transitive sentences are found.

  Consider intransitive sentences first. In the SOV and the SVO
types we expect the order SV_i; the order V_iS is also found.

  17. LUISEÑO:
       qalwun=pum ?iyixwun ?ataaxum kiikatum
        (V)   (S)
       "are=aux   also   people   little"
       'There are little people.'   (Steele, n.d.)

  18. CLASSICAL AZTEC:
       nican ompenhua in zazanillatolli
          (V)   (S)
       "here it:begins article fable"
       'Here begins the fable.'   (Hunt 1895:116)

  ----

  [9] I began this paper with the assumption that there would be
significant differences between transitive and intransitive sentences
in the relative order of subject and verb. In fact, there are a
number of SVO languages where the subject of an intransitive verb
can follow the verb, but the subject of a transitive verb cannot (see
Appendix). But the difference isn't as obvious in the other language types. The ordering possibilities for transitive and intransitive sentences are, however, kept distinct in the tabulation to
follow.

In the VSO and the VOS type we expect the order $V_i S$; the order
SV_i is also found.[10]

19. SAHAPTIN
ku?anat?caxi naxc wincka at?łiyawiya
        (S)   (V)
"and:again:also one male:now died"
'And then one male died as well.'   (Jacobs 1931: 282)

Transitive sentences involving more constituents have more
potential word order variations. Again, in each of the SOV, SVO
and VSO types, all of the possible word order variations on the
basic word order are found. That is, taking the SOV languages
together we find not only the basic SOV word order but also OSV,
SVO, OVS, VSO and VOS. The following are all examples from
WALBIRI (Hale 1973: 312).

20. wawiritjara palaŋu ŋarkaŋku pantunu kuladalu
        (O)   (S)   (V)
"two:kangaroos aux man speared with:a:spear"
'The man speared two kangaroos with a spear.'

21. ŋarkaŋku palaŋu pantunu wawiritjara kuladalu
        (S)   (V)   (O)

22. wawiritjara palaŋu kuladalu pantunu ŋarkaŋku
        (O)   (V)   (S)

23. pantunu palaŋu kuladalu ŋarkaŋku wawiritjara
        (V)   (S)   (O)

24. pantunu palaŋu kuladalu wawiritjara ŋarkaŋku
        (V)   (O)   (S)

Similarly, taking the SVO languages together we find not only the
basic SVO word order but also VOS, VSO, VOS, SOV and OSV.
MALECEET-PASSAMOQUODDY is described as having all these
possibilities, but no examples are given. CLASSICAL AZTEC
allows all but OVS and OSV; examples of each of the remaining
possibilities were given above in 7. to 9.

---

[10] That SV_i order is found in VSO languages is an extrapolation
from the ordering possibility in transitive sentences, the regularity
with which some nominal can precede the verb, and from the fact
that the grammars do not proscribe against it.

Finally, taking all the VSO languages together we find not only the basic word order VSO but also VOS, SVO, OVS, SOV and OSV. CHINOOK is described as allowing all word order possibilities (Sapir 1921: 63), but no examples are given. Boas agrees, but gives only a few examples of which the following are representative (Boas 1969: 647).

25. tgigE'nxautē ikanā'tē tEmēwā'lEma
      (V)   (O)   (S)
    "they:watch:it soul ghosts"
    'The ghosts watch a soul.'

26. aqui'nEmikc tkalā'mukc atqā'qcx ō'lExkul
      (S)   (V)   (O)
    "five:men they:hold:her in:their:mouths dried:salmon"
    'Five men hold dried salmon in their mouths.'

27. ē'ō'k aLgē'lElōtx kLtōplEnā'n tê'lx·Em
     (O)   (V)
    "blanket he:gives:it:to:them"
    'He gives a blanket to those who named the people.'

In contrast only the basic word order and VSO and SVO alternates are attested for the group of VOS languages -- although the sample is admittedly small. The first is an example from TAGALOG; the second, one from KAPAMPANGAN.

28. Nakita si Ben ni Pedro
     (V)   (O)   (S)
    "saw Ben Peter"
    'Peter saw Ben.'   (Schachter and Otanes 1972: 183)

29. ing lalaki sinali yang mannga king tindahan
       (S)   (V)   (O)
    "the boy bought he:a mango at store"
    'The boy bought a mango at the store.' (Mirikitani 1972: 151)

Few restrictions on the variations on a basic word order are evident from the above; however, if we consider the frequency of a particular variation for a particular word order, certain patterns are immediately obvious. All VOS languages allow a VSO and an SVO alternate; the other possibilities for transitive sentences are unattested; the situation for intransitive sentences was discussed in footnote 10.

I. VOS: 3 languages

VOS	3	OSV	0
SVO	3	OVS	0
SOV	0	$S V_i$	?

Over half of the VSO languages allow a VOS alternate and half allow an SVO alternate; fewer have an OVS alternate and still fewer allow an SOV or an OSV alternate. $S V_i$ is as uncommon as the first of the three uncommon possibilities for transitive sentences.

II. VSO: 10 languages

VOS	6	OSV	2
SVO	5	SOV	1
OVS	3	$S V_i$	3

The majority of SOV languages allow an OSV alternate, half allow an SVO alternate word order and very few allow any of the three other possibilities; the order $V_i S$ is about as uncommon as the orders OVS, VOS and VSO.

III. SOV: 30 languages

OSV	23	VOS	5
SVO	15	VSO	4
OVS	6	$V_i S$	7

No alternation on the basic SVO word order type for transitive sentences is attested with any regularity; however, the order $V_i S$, while found in fewer than half of the SOV languages, is still more common than any of the possible reorderings for transitive sentences.[11]

IV. SVO: 20 languages

VOS	5	VSO	4
OSV	4	OVS	3
SOV	4	$V_i S$	8

---

[11] Among those languages which are counted as allowing $V_i S$ order is FAROESE. FAROESE allows this word order as long as the verb is preceded by some other element in the sentence. That is, the verb is necessarily the second element in the sentence, regardless of whether the subject noun precedes or follows it.

Table 3 presents the distribution for all four language types. For a word order variation to be considered very common, it must occur in over half of the languages in a particular type; to be considered common, in at least half; to be considered uncommon, in substantially less than half.[12] The one variation labeled not uncommon occurs in slightly less than half of the languages for the particular type.

Table 3

	VOS	VSO	SOV	SVO
Very common	VSO	VOS	OSV	
	SVO			
Common		SVO	SVO	
Not uncommon				V_i S
Uncommon		OVS	OVS	VOS
		OSV	VOS	VSO
		SOV	V SO	SOV
		SV_i	V_i S	OSV
				OVS
Nonexistent	SOV			
	OSV			
	OSV			

3.2 A comparison of the most common variations (i.e. very common and common) with the rest of the variations suggests two constraints on word order variation. First, let me sum up the patterns revealed in the common word order variations. The only word order variations which are attested with any frequency involve one of two types of differences from the respective basic word

---

[12] The terms very common and uncommon have slightly different meanings for each of the language types. In VOS languages all the languages in the sample allow VOS and SVO alternates, while in SOV languages approximately three quarters allow OSV, and in VSO languages 60% allow VOS. The variations labeled uncommon in SVO languages occur in a quarter or less of the languages in the language sample; those so labeled in SOV languages occur in a fifth or less of the languages in the language sample; those so labeled in VSO languages occur in a third or less of the languages in the language sample. That the use of the label is relative to a particular language type should be kept in mind in the examination of Table 3.

orders. First, and most commonly, the relative order of subject
and object will be reversed. So, VOS has a VSO (or an SVO) alternate; SOV, an OSV alternate; and VSO, a VOS alternate. Second,
and less common both within a particular word order type and across
the types, a noun will occur on one side of the verb in the basic word
order and on the other in the variation on the basic word order, but
in the variations only the subject will occur to the left of the verb
and only the object will occur to the right of the verb. So, VOS and
VSO have SVO variations; SOV has an SVO variation.

The first constraint on word order variation has to do with the
possible positions for the verb in these variations, and it has a
strong and a weak form. The strong constraint on the position of
the verb is revealed when we compare the position of the verb in
the basic word orders and the most common variations thereon to
the position of the verb in the uncommon and nonexistent word orders.
In the most common variations -- with one exception -- the verb has
the same position in the clause that it has in the basic word order;
in the uncommon and nonexistent variations — with one exception —
the verb has some other position in the clause. The principle of
word order variation suggested by this distribution is formulated
as A below.

A. A variation on the basic word order in which the verb
    occurs in other than its position in the basic word order
    is to be avoided.

However, the constraint must be weakened since in fact there are
common variations in VSO and SOV languages and a very common
variation in VOS languages which do exactly what A proscribes.
Consider, then, another comparison, this time between both the
very common and the common variations in these three language
types and the uncommon ones. None of the common variations on
these basic word orders allow the verb to occur either initially or
finally if the verb does not occur there in the basic word order;
the verb is initial or medial in the common variations on VSO and
final or medial in the common variations on SOV. All the uncommon variations on the basic word order in the former type position
the verb finally; all but one of the uncommon variations on the latter
position the verb initially. The principle of word order variation
suggested by this distribution is formulated as A' below.

A'. A variation on the basic word order in which the verb
    occurs either initial or final to the clause is to be

avoided, if the verb was neither initial nor final respectively in the basic order.[13]

I have concentrated in this discussion on the order of subject, object and verb in transitive sentences. Note that in VSO and SOV languages the orders SV_i and V_iS respectively violate A and A', but are uncommon. In SVO languages the order V_iS violates both A and A' and is the most common variation. However, in intransitive sentences in such languages, the position of the verb will necessarily violate A'; that is, in the expected SV_i order, the verb is final to the clause.[14]

Although individual languages may be constrained by either A or A' — and if they are constrained by A, they are constrained by A' — the different language types will be characterized as being subject to either the stronger or the weaker form of the constraint. The SVO language type, by allowing no common variations, is subject to Constraint A; each of the other three types are to be characterized as subject to Constraint A', since in all three there is at least a common variation which violates Constraint A.

The second constraint on word order variation has to do with the position of subject and object relative to the verb. Constraint A and its weaker counterpart Constraint A' proscribe only certain positions of the verb in variations on the basic word order. Constraint A would allow, in SVO languages, the variation OVS; the verb remains in the position it has in the basic word order. Constraint A' would allow, in VSO, VOS and SOV languages, the variation OVS; the verb is neither final (which would violate the constraint in VSO and VOS languages) nor initial (which would violate the constraint in SOV languages). Yet in none of the four language types is the order OVS a common variation on the basic word order. In Greenberg 1963: 110 is stated the following universal:

---

[13] The term _initial_ here can only mean before the subject and object nouns; the term _final_, after the subject and object nouns. Whether the verb is absolutely initial or absolutely final, that is, unpreceded or unfollowed by some adverbial, for instance, isn't important to the purposes of this paper.

[14] Sgall _et al_. argue that a verb may precede its subject in an existential sentence because the verb in such sentences contains the old information.

In declarative sentences with nominal subject and object, the
dominant order is almost always one in which the subject
precedes the object.

But we would not want to ascribe the non-occurrence of the order
OVS to the relative order of subject and object. The most common
variations on VSO and SOV have the object preceding the subject.
The constraint on word order variation which the non-occurrence
of the variation OVS suggests, then, appears to be as stated in B.

B. A variation on the basic word order in which the object
     precedes and the subject follows the verb is to be avoided.

3.3 I have suggested two constraints on possible variations on
a basic word order. These constraints predict that certain variations on a basic word order will be less common than others cross-
linguistically; they also explain why. Constraints other than those
suggested in the preceding section are logically possible. For
example, it is logically possible that languages would constrain
variation on the relative order of subject and object or that constraints on the variations for a basic word order would refer crucially to the position of only the object noun or only the subject
noun. That such logically possible constraints are not suggested
by the cross-linguistic data is, therefore, worthy of note. Rather,
one of the constraints on word order variation (in both of its formulations) refers crucially to the position of the verb and the second
refers crucially to the position of the subject and the object relative
to the verb. These constraints, then, support the growing body of
evidence confirming the intuitively obvious hypothesis that the verb
is central to the sentence. There is apparently a strong tendency
to anchor the verb in one position in the sentence; failing that, the
verb can be medial preceded by the subject noun and followed by
the object noun.[15]

---

[15] Explanation is a tricky term. I am claiming that the constraints
themselves are explanations; I am not offering explanations for the
constraints. Even with the evidence that the verb is central to the
sentence, it is not obvious why it should anchor in a particular position, except that where the verb is anchored is one of the basic
distinctions between verb initial, verb medial and verb final languages. But at this point the argument becomes circular. In short,
reasons for the constraints will probably be difficult to get at.

4. Classification

I stated at the beginning of this paper that once the types of
variations on a basic word order had been established, it would
be possible to classify languages according to which of those they
allowed. It is this classification to which I now turn. The classification is based on whether a language conforms to or breaks
Constraints A and B.

In the preceding section I proposed two constraints, one with
two formulations, on word order variation. These constraints predict the common variations cross-linguistically, but they are not,
as noted above, equally applicable to each language type. For the
purpose now of classification, let me restate which constraints
apply to which language type. All the common variations in the
VSO and VOS language types conform to Constraint A' and Constraint
B; that is, in all the common variations the verb either retains the
position it has in the basic word order or is preceded by the subject
noun. All the common variations in the SOV language type conform
to Constraint A' and Constraint B; that is, in all the common variations the verb either retains the position it has in the basic word
order or is followed by the object noun. There are no common
variations in SVO languages; Constraint A and Constraint B predict
this.

Any language in which the variations conform to whichever constraints are applicable for the particular language type will be
called a rigid word order language. For example, a VOS language
which has those variations allowed by Constraint A is a rigid word
order language. Any language in which the variations break whichever constraints are applicable for the particular language type
will be called a free word order language. For example, a SOV
language which has variations on the basic word order breaking
both Constraint A' and Constraint B is a free word order language.
Any language which breaks only some of the constraints for the
particular language type will be called neither rigid nor free, but
rather mixed. For example, an SVO language which has only an
OVS alternate is a mixed word order language.

The terms rigid word order and free word order are commonly
employed in descriptive sketches and typological studies. Not only
do the terms mean different things depending on who uses them,
but the identification of a language as one or the other is usually
done outside the perspective of what is a possible or likely variation

on a basic word order. As an example of the former, JAPANESE,
an SOV language with OSV and SVO alternates, has been said to
have relatively free word order and PAPAGO, an SOV language
with VSO, SVO, OSV, VOS and OVS alternates, has been said to
have relatively rigid word order. As an example of the latter it
has occasionally been assumed that a rigid word order language is
one in which no variations on the basic word order are allowed or,
conversely, that any variation on the basic word order argues for
calling the language a free word order language. If the definition
suggested above is valid, the terms rigid word order and free word
order are made precise. We would expect a language to exhibit
certain variations on its basic word order and not to exhibit others.
Languages which conform to all those expectations would be considered rigid word order languages; languages which confound all
those expectations would be considered free word order languages.

There are three facts implicit in the data presented up to this
point which support distinguishing between languages on the basis
of their conformity to certain constraints. First, an examination
of charts I to IV upon which the discussion of the previous section
was based will reveal that almost all non-SVO languages allow
some variation upon their basic word order. Hence, it is seldom
the case that a language will have absolutely rigid word order.
Second, an implicational hierarchy of word order variation for
each individual language follows directly from the distribution in
Table 3 and Constraints A, A' and B. Although the constraints
predict which variations will not be possible in the majority of
languages in the language sample, a number of languages allow
variations which do not conform to the constraints. Any language
which has one of the uncommon variations listed in Table 3 breaks
one of the constraints. However, in no language is it the case that
a variation which doesn't conform to the constraints will be allowed
while one which does will not. That is, any language which has one
of the uncommon variations in Table 3 will also have the more
common variations. For example, there is no SOV language which
has a VSO variation but which does not have either OSV or SVO as
well. Hence, any language which breaks any of the constraints
will necessarily have more possible variations than a language
which does not. And it follows that one which breaks all the constraints will necessarily have more possible variations than one
which breaks only one.[16]

---

[16] An interesting question is whether the more common cross-
linguistic variants will be more common within a particular language
than the less common cross-linguistic variants.

Finally, and in support of the category of mixed word order languages, it is clear that we want to distinguish between languages which break all the constraints applicable to a particular language type and languages which break only one. SVO languages usually allow no variation on their basic word order; Constraints A and B were drafted to reflect this fact. If it were the case that those SVO languages which allowed any variation (that is, which broke either Constraint A or Constraint B) also allowed a number of variations, we could simply distinguish between rigid and free word order languages. However, four SVO languages in the language sample (DIOLA-FOGNY, ULITHIAN, TARASCAN and FAROESE) have only one variation each on their basic SVO word order in transitive sentences -- SOV for DIOLA-FOGNY, OSV for ULITHIAN, VOS for TARASCAN and OVS for FAROESE. Even though the first three of these variations break Constraint A and the last breaks Constraint B, there is not a variety of word orders in any of the languages and it is not satisfactory to call them free word order languages. On the other hand, there is no obvious pattern to the variations and it is, therefore, not satisfactory to call them rigid word order languages.

The constraints established in Sec. 3, then, allow us to distinguish between three types of word order variation patterns. Table 4 below divides the languages of the language sample among the three.

Table 4. Classification by Word Order Variation

Rigid	SOV	Koya, Turkish, Yakut, Yurak, Vogul, Japanese, Somali, Fur, Lahu, Burmese, Kharia, Gunwingju, Dalaban, Jiwadja, Maranungku, Navajo, Kapau, Hopi, Piro, Mojave, Ica
	SVO	English, Albanian, Ibibio, Bari, Gbeya, Thai, Vietnamese, Indonesian
	VSO	Tahitian, Pukapukan, Narinjari, Squamish, Puget Salish, Sahaptin, Jacaltec
	VOS	Tagalog, Kapampangan, Tongan
Free	SOV	Wiyot, Walbiri, Garadjari, Luiseño, Cacua, Karok
	SVO	Czech, Maleceet-Passamoquoddy, Classical Aztec, Tuscarora

(Table 4 continued)

Free	VSO	Achi, Chinook
	VOS	None
Mixed	SOV	Kolami, Inga, Yurok
	SVO	Faroese, Diola-Fogny, Mandarin, Sonsoral-Tobi, Ulithian, Iai, Chorti, Tarascan[17]
	VSO	Trique
	VOS	None

5. Typology

All but one of the goals of a successful typological study as suggested in the introduction to this paper have been met. The data on word order variation has been presented, explanations offered for its distribution, and a classification of languages has been proposed according to the word order variation each allows. What remains to be done is to establish whether the classification of languages proposed in Sec. 4 correlates with some other typological fact(s) about the languages in question.

If certain variations on a basic word order are to be expected, it follows that we would not expect those languages which exhibit only these to have some other typological feature in common. Rather, it is the languages which exhibit other than the expected word orders that are potentially interesting from a typological point of view. In these remarks I will concentrate on those languages that were classified in the preceding section as free word order languages.[18] As noted in the introduction, hypotheses about what allows freedom of word order have concentrated on the presence of case marking. For example, it has been suggested that ENGLISH word order became rigid as case inflections were lost (see, e.g., Vennemann 1974).

---

[17]MANDARIN, SONSORAL-TOBI, IAI, and CHORTI are classed as mixed word order languages on the basis of the order allowed in intransitive sentences. All allow V_iS, a word order which breaks Constraint A.

[18] Whether mixed word order languages are typologically distinct is left an open question.

The first part of this section examines that claim -- and explodes it. The second part of this section suggests that freedom of word order as defined in Sec. 4 correlates rather with a certain type of agreement.

Case marking is some morphological indication on a noun (or a pronoun) of its grammatical role in a sentence. So, in LUISEÑO (animate) nouns are marked for object:

30. xwann hunwut-i ?ariq
    "John bear-OBJ. is:kicking"
    'John is kicking the bear.'   (Steele, n.d.)

and in MOJAVE nouns are marked for subject.

31. hatčoq-č masdeek
    "dog-SUBJ. is:afraid"
    'The dog is afraid.'   (Munro 1974:19)

The specification of morphological indication is supposed to exclude prepositions and postpositions as indications of case, but the distinction between the latter and the former is not always as clear as we would like.[19] In any case in what follows I have endeavored to remove these from consideration.

It is clearly not true that those languages which have free word order necessarily have case-marked subjects and/or objects. Of the twelve languages which have free word order, seven -- over half -- have no case marking (CLASSICAL AZTEC, KAROK, ACHI, WIYOT, TUSCARORA, GARADJARI and MALECEET-PASSAMO-QUODDY). Both sentences below are from CLASSICAL AZTEC. The noun which is the subject of the first sentence is the object of the second. Note that there is no distinction in form between them.

32. ahuellaticpacquiza   in   piltzintli
    "could:not:come:forth:on:earth article baby-SUBJ."
    ' The baby could not come forth on earth.'
                                 (Dibble and Anderson 1969:157)

33. niman oncan   caltia   in   ticitl   in piltzintli
    "then there she:bathed:him article midwife article baby-OBJ."
    ' Then the midwife bathed the baby there.'
                                 (Dibble and Anderson 1969:201)

---

[19] The distinction is blurred in at least some of the AUSTRONE-SIAN languages where every noun is preceded by an element which indicates its case function. Some of these correspond to what are called determiners in ENGLISH; some, to what are called prepositions.

If objections to the definition of case suggested above are raised, if some other definition of case is suggested, it will not change the conclusion that the presence or absence of case marking has nothing to do with freedom of word order. Nouns in these seven languages with free word order have nothing which marks them as either subject or object.

There is one typological feature, however, which these languages with free word order hold in common. All of them exhibit a particular type of agreement phenomenon — person agreement with the subject of the sentence. Moreover, in at least a third of the free word order languages, the markers of person agreement are transparently related to the independent pronominal forms of the language and in most of the others there is substantial resemblance between the two.

The term _agreement_ commonly refers to some systematic covariance between a semantic or formal property of one element and a formal property of another. For example, adjectives may take some formal indication of the number and gender of the noun they modify.

33. Ich trinke kaltes Wasser gern.

I am concerned here with a subset of agreement phenomena, the formal indication somewhere in the sentence of the person of the subject of the clause. For example, in CLASSICAL AZTEC first person singular subject is indicated by the prefix ni-:

34. ni-ctepo?polhuia
    "I-forgive:someone:it"
    'I forgive someone it.'   (Anderson 1973: 22)[20]

Not all the languages in the language sample have person agreement with the subject of the sentence. These are listed below in Table 5. Of the languages in Table 5 one has only number agreement

---

[20] The phenomenon commonly referred to as concord would be a second subtype of this type of agreement. In languages which exhibit concord agreement the class of the noun subject is indicated on the verb. The form of this marker usually matches the class marker on the noun.

(HOPI); the rest have no agreement with the subject of the sentence at all.[21]

Table 5. Languages without Person Agreement

English	Indonesian
Hopi	Lahu
Vietnamese	Gbeya
Burmese	Bari
Mandarin	Tahitian
Japanese	Tongan
Thai	Pukapukan

Now, if we examine the set of languages in Table 5, we find that none of the languages with free word order are contained therein. Hence, all the languages with free word order have person agreement. It is not the case, however, that the class of languages with person agreement is coterminous with the class of languages that have free word order. The first is larger than the second. So, although we cannot say that if a language has person agreement, it will have free word order, we can say that if a language has free word order, it will have person agreement. Conversely, if a language has no person agreement, it will not have free word order.

With an examination of person agreement we can sharpen the statement above. The remainder of the languages in the language sample, the majority of languages in the language sample, have person agreement with the subject of the clause, but it is not of a single type. In one type the agreement elements show an obvious resemblance to the independent pronouns of the language. Consider CLASSICAL AZTEC. The morphemes which mark person are listed in 35. and the independent pronouns in 36.

35. ni   ti
    ti   an
    ∅   ∅

---

[21] ENGLISH is included in Table 5 even though the present form of a verb or auxiliary verb will agree with a third person singular subject. In all other persons and with a past form of the verb or auxiliary verb, there is no person agreement with the subject (except for the verb be). ENGLISH is, therefore, much closer to the set of languages in Table 5 than it is to the rest of the languages in the language sample.

36. ne?waatl   te?waan
     te?waatl   am?waan
     ye?waatl   ye?waan

In another type the agreement elements show no obvious resemblances
to the independent pronouns. Consider TURKISH. In 37. is the verb
paradigm for the past tense of 'to write' and in 38. are the independent subject pronouns.

37. yazdím   'I wrote'   yazdík   'we wrote'
     yazdín   'you wrote'   yazdıníz 'you wrote'
     yazdí   'he, she, it wrote' yazdılár 'they wrote'
                                            (Swift 1963: 156)

38. ben   biz
     sen   siz

     bu(n)   this
     su(n)   that (close)
     o(n)   that (far)   (Swift 1963: 199)

I will call the first type, the type exemplified by CLASSICAL AZTEC,
copy agreement and the second type, the type exemplified by TURK-
ISH, inflectional agreement. The term copy agreement is not meant
to refer necessarily to a syntactic process, but rather to the phonological (and morphological) similarity between the agreement elements and the independent pronouns.

The languages with person agreement for the subject of the sentence do not divide neatly into these two types. There are some
languages where the agreement elements are more different from
the independent pronouns than they are in CLASSICAL AZTEC, but
not as different as they are in TURKISH. Consider ACHI. The
independent pronouns of ACHI are listed in 39. and the person
agreement elements in 40.

39. in   oj
     at   ix
     a/Ø   e

40   in/w   ka/k
     a/aw   i/iw
     u/r   qui/c   (Shaw and Neuenswander 1966: 38)

I will call this type of agreement semi-copy.

Listed in Table 6 is the type of person agreement exhibited by each language in the language sample that has person agreement.[22]

Table 6. Types of Person Agreement
(free word order languages are underlined)

Inflectional	Copy	Semi-Copy	?
Turkish	Luiseño	Somali	Chorti
Faroese	Walbiri	Navajo	Puget Salish
Albanian	Classical Aztec	Gunwingju	Ibibio
Kolami	Maleceet-	Achi	Maranungku
Dalabon	Passamoquoddy	Mojave	Cacua
Squamish	Tagalog	Karok	Fur
Diola-Fogny	Kapampangan	Wiyot	Inga
Yurak	Narinjari	Sonsoral-Tobi	Iai
Yakut	Kharia	Tuscarora	
Trique	Sahaptin		
Ica	Jacaltec		
Yurok	Chinook		
Ulithian	Garadjari		
Tarascan			
Kapau			
Vogul			
Koya			
Piro			
Jiwadja			
Czech			

Now, if we examine Table 6, we find that the majority of languages with free word order exhibit either copy or semi-copy agreement. Again, the set of languages with either of these two types of agreement is larger than the set of free word order languages. So, although we cannot say that if a language has copy or semi-copy agreement, it will have free word order, we can say that if a language has free word order, in all likelihood it will have copy or semi-copy person agreement.

The question, of course, is why such a correlation exists. With person agreement, the person and number of the subject of the

---

[22]Note that not all languages are classified as one of the three types. In a few languages I was unable to determine, due to lack of adequate data, what type of person agreement was exhibited.

sentence is indexed. It might be argued, then, that the subject
(and the object) are, therefore, free to occur in any position in the
sentence. This argument would assume, like the assumption upon
which were based the claims about the relationship between case
marking and freedom of word order, that it is possible to have
freedom of word order only when the grammatical function of the
nouns in the sentence is explicit. The assumption is as ill-conceived
in regard to person agreement as it was shown to be in regard to
case marking. If both noun subject and noun object are third person
singular or third person plural, it will still be impossible to distinguish which noun is subject and which noun is object. And, of
course, such a hypothesis does not explain at all why languages
with free word order should in general have a specific kind of person agreement.

An explanation of the correlation would require a complete study
of person agreement. I am not prepared to launch such a study. I
will tentatively suggest, however, the possibility that copy agreement and free word order are both manifestations of the fact that
in languages which exhibit either the sentence is composed of a
verb and the grammatical elements which pertain to the sentence.[23]
The noun subject and the noun object are in some undefined sense
appositives to the sentence (or perhaps sentences in their own right).
Hence, almost all the languages which have copy or semi-copy
agreement for the subject also have person agreement for the object
of the sentence. Hence, in free word order languages the nouns
are often unmarked for case. The question then becomes: why are
there languages with copy person agreement for subject (and agreement for object) which have rigid word order?

6. Conclusion

This paper has considered word order variation. We know that
there are certain general patterns to word order variation and that
there are principles which explain these patterns. We know that
languages can be classified according to whether they violate the
principles or not and that those languages that do have a certain
typological characteristic — person agreement, specifically copy
or semi-copy agreement. While the reason for this last correlation
remains to be fully elucidated, this paper has otherwise fulfilled the
objectives of a successful typological study suggested at the beginning.

---

[23] In some languages these are attached, sometimes loosely, to
the verb. In others they are independent of the verb, occurring in
certain sentential positions.

APPENDIX

Data on Word Order Variation

In the charts below an x in a column indicates that the language exhibits that word order.

A. SOV languages, transitive sentences

	VOS	VSO	SVO	OVS	SOV	OSV
Kolami			x		x	x
Koya					x	x
Turkish			x		x	x
Yakut					x	x
Yurak					x	x
Vogul					x	x
Japanese			x		x	x
Somali					x	x
Fur					x	?
Lahu					x	x
Burmese					x	x
Kharia					x	x
Gunwingju			x			
Walbiri	x	x	x	x	x	x
Dalaban			x		x	
Jiwadja			x		x	
Maranungku			x		x	x
Garadjari	x	x	x	x	x	x
Navajo					x	
Wiyot			x	x	x	x
Yurok					x	x
Kapau					x	x
Hopi					x	
Luiseño	x	x	x	x	x	x
Piro			x		x	x
Inga			x	x	x	x
Cacua	x	x	x	x	x	x
Mojave					x	
Karok	x		x		x	x
Ica					x	x

B. SVO languages, transitive sentences

	VOS	VSO	SVO	OVS	SOV	OSV
English			x			
Albanian			x			

B. SVO languages, transitive sentences (continued)

	VOS	VOS	SVO	OVS	SOV	OSV
Czech	x	x	x	x	x	x
Faroese			x	x		
Diola-Fogny			x		x	
Ibibio			x			
Gbeya			x			
Bari			x			
Mandarin			x			
Thai			x			
Vietnamese			x			
Sonsoral-Tobi			x			
Indonesian			x			
Ulithian			x			x
Iai			x			
Maleceet-Passamoquoddy	x	x	x	x	x	x
Classical Aztec	x	x	x		x	
Tuscarora	x	x	x	?	?	x
Chorti			x			
Tarascan	x		x			

C. VSO languages, transitive sentences

	VOS	VSO	SVO	OVS	SOV	OSV
Tahitian		x				
Pukapukan	x	x				
Narinjari	x	x				
Squamish	x	x				
Puget Salish	x	x				
Achi		x	x	x		x
Sahaptin	x	x	x			
Jacaltec		x	x			
Chinook	x	x	x	x	x	x
Trique		x	x	x		

D. VOS languages, transitive sentences

	VOS	VSO	SVO	OVS	SOV	OSV
Tagalog	x	x	x			
Kapampangan	x	x	x			
Tongan	x	x	x			

Charts A' to D' contain data on the order of subject and verb in intransitive sentences. Where there are blanks for both possible word orders in intransitive sentences it simply means that the description had no explicit information on the order of subject and verb in intransitive sentences. It may be safe to assume that the lack of information indicates that the order of subject and verb in intransitive sentences is not to be distinguished from the order of subject and verb in transitive sentences, but it is also likely that the person writing the description never questioned that there might be a difference in the first place.

A'. SOV languages, intransitive sentences

	$V_i S$	$S V_i$
Kolami	x	x
Koya		
Turkish		
Yakut		
Yurak		
Vogul		
Japanese		x
Somali		
Fur		
Lahu		
Burmese		
Kharia		
Gunwingju		
Walbiri	x	x
Dalaban		
Jiwadja		
Maranungku		
Garadjari	x	x
Navajo		x
Wiyot	x	x
Yurok	x	x
Kapau		
Hopi		x
Luiseño	x	x
Piro		
Inga		
Cacua		
Mojave		
Karok	x	x
Ica		

B'. SVO languages, intransitive sentences

	$V_i S$	$S V_i$
English		x
Albanian		
Czech	x	x
Faroese	(x)	x
Diola-Fogny		x
Ibibio		
Gbeya		
Bari		x
Mandarin	x	x
Thai		x
Vietnamese		x
Sonsoral-Tobi	x	x
Indonesian		
Ulithian	x	x
Iai	x	x
Maleceet- Passamoquoddy	x	x
Classical Aztec	x	x
Tuscarora		
Chorti	x	x
Tarascan		

C'. VSO languages, intransitive sentences

	$V_i S$	$S V_i$
Tahitian		
Pukapukan		
Narinjari		
Squamish		
Puget Salish		
Achi	x	x
Sahaptin	x	x
Jacaltec		
Chinook	x	x
Trique		

D'. VOS languages, intransitive sentences

	$V_i S$	$S V_i$
Tagalog		
Kapampangan		
Tongan		

BIBLIOGRAPHY

Anderson, Arthur J.O. 1973. Rules of the Aztec language. Salt Lake City: University of Utah Press.

Beaton, A.C. 1968. A grammar of the Fur language. Linguistic Monograph Series No. 1. Khartoum: Sudan Research Unit, University of Khartoum.

Biligiri, Hemmige S. 1965. Kharia: phonology, grammar and vocabulary. Poona: Deccan College.

Boas, Franz. 1969. Chinook. The handbook of American Indian languages, Vol. I. The Netherlands: Anthropological Publications, Oosterhout N.B.

Bright, William. 1957. The Karok language. University of California Publication in Linguistics [UCPL] 13. Berkeley and Los Angeles: University of California Press.

Capell, A. 1962a. Dalabon grammar. Some linguistic types in Australia: Handbook of Australian languages, Part 2. Oceania Linguistic Monograph No. 7. 90-126. University of Sydney.

_____. 1962b. Garadjari grammar. Some linguistic types in Australia: Handbook of Australian languages, Part 2. Oceania Linguistic Monograph No. 7. 51-89. University of Sydney.

_____. 1962c. Jiwadja grammar. Some linguistic types in Australia: Handbook of Australian languages, Part 2. Oceania Linguistic Monograph No. 7. 127-170. University of Sydney.

_____. 1969. Grammar and vocabulary of the language of Sonsoral-Tobi. Oceania Linguistics Monograph No. 12. University of Sydney.

Chung, Sandra. 1976. On the gradual nature of syntactic change. Manuscript.

Craig, Colette. 1975. Jacaltec syntax: a study of complex sentences. Doctoral dissertation, Harvard University.

Decsy, Gyula. 1966. Yurak chrestomathy. Uralic and Altaic Series, Vol. 50. Indiana University Publications. Bloomington: Indiana University.

Dibble, C.E. and Arthur J.O. Anderson. 1969. Florentine codex, book 6: rhetoric and moral philosophy. Santa Fe: School of American Research and the University of Utah.

Emeneau, M.B. 1955. Kolami, a Dravidian language. UCPL 12.

_____. 1951. Studies in Vietnamese (Annamese) grammar. UCPL 8.

Foster, Mary LeCron. 1973. Tarascan. Studies in American Indian languages, ed. by Jesse Sawyer. UCPL 65. 77-112.

_____. 1969. The Tarascan language. UCPL 56.

Garibay, Angel Maria. 1970. Llave del Nahuatl. Mexico City: Editorial Porrua.

Greenberg, Joseph. 1963. Some universals of grammar with particular reference to the order of meaningful elements. Universals of language, ed. by Joseph Greenberg. Cambridge: M.I.T. Press.

Haile, Berard. 1926. A manual of Navaho grammar. Sante Fe: Santa Fe New Mexican Publishing Corp.

Hale, Kenneth. 1973. Subject marking in Walbiri. A Festschrift for Morris Halle, ed. by Stephen Anderson and Paul Kiparsky, 308-344. Cambridge: M.I.T. Press.

Heine, Bernd. 1975. The study of word order in African languages. Proceedings of the Sixth Conference on African Linguistics. Ohio State University Working Papers in Linguistics 20. 161-183.

Hess, Thomas. 1973. Agent in a Coast Salish language. IJAL 39. 89-94.

Hunt, A. 1895. (trans.) Fabulas de Esopo. Proceedings of the XI Congreso Internacional de Americanistas. 100-116. Mexico.

Jacobs, Melville. 1931. Northern Sahaptin grammar. University of Washington Publications in Anthropology Vol. 4. 87-291.

Jeanne, LaVerne Masayesva and Kenneth Hale. 1974. Hopi data. Manuscript.

Kalman, Bela. 1965. Vogul chrestomathy. Uralic and Altaic Series, Vol. 46. Indiana University Publications.

Kaufman, Elaine Marlowe. 1968. Ibibio grammar. Doctoral dissertation, University of California, Berkeley.

Keenan, Edward. 1976. Subject in universal grammar. Subject and topic, ed. by Charles Li. New York: Academic Press.

Kirk, J.W.V. 1905. A grammar of the Somali language. Cambridge University Press.

Krueger, John R. 1962. Yakut manual. Uralic and Altaic Series, Vol. 21. Indiana University Publications.

Kuipers, Aert. 1967. The Squamish language. Janua Linguarum series practica LXXIII. The Hague: Mouton.

Kuno, Susumu. 1973. The structure of the Japanese language. Cambridge: M.I.T. Press.

Lehmann, W.P. 1973. A structural principle of language and its implications. Language 49.1. 47-66.

_____. 1972. Converging theories in linguistics. Language 48.2. 266-275.

Li, Charles and Sandra Thompson. 1975. The semantic function of word order: a case study in Mandarin. Word order and word order change, ed. by Charles Li, 165-195. Austin: University of Texas Press.

Liem, Nguyen Dang. 1969. Vietnamese grammar. Pacific Linguistics, Series C. No. 4. Canberra: The Australian National University.

Lockwood, W.B. 1955. An introduction to Modern Faroese. København: Ejnar Munksgaard.

Matteson, Esther. 1965. The Piro (Arawakan) language. UCPL 42.

Matisoff, James Alan. 1967. A grammar of the Lahu language. Doctoral dissertation, University of California, Berkeley.

Mirikitani, Leatrice. 1972. Kapampangan syntax. Oceanic Linguistics Special Publication 10. Honolulu: University of Hawaii Press.

Munro, Pamela. 1974. Topics in Mojave syntax. Doctoral dissertation, University of California, San Diego.

Newmark, Leonard. 1957. Structural grammar of Albanian. Indiana University Research Center in Anthropology, Folklore and Linguistics 4. Bloomington: Indiana University Press.

Oakley, Helen. 1966. Chorti. Language of Guatemala, ed. by Marvin K. Mayers. Janua Linguarum, studia memoriae, series practica XXIII. 235-250. The Hague: Mouton.

Oates, Lynette Francis. 1964. A tentative description of the Gunwinggu language [of Western Arnheim Land]. Oceania Linguistic Monograph No. 10. University of Sydney.

Oates, W. and L. Oates. 1968. Kapau pedagogical grammar. Pacific Linguistics, Series C. No. 10. Canberra: Australian National University.

Robins, R.H. 1958. The Yurok language. UCPL 15.

Samarin, William J. 1966. The Gbeya language. UCPL 44.

Sapir, Edward. 1921. Language. New York: Harcourt, Brace and World, Inc.

Sapir, J. David. 1965. A grammar of Diola-Fogny. West African Language Monograph 3. Cambridge University Press.

Schachter, Paul and Fe T. Otanes. 1972. Tagalog reference grammar. Berkeley and Los Angeles: University of California Press.

Sgall, Petr, Eva Hajicova and Eva Benesova. 1973. Topic, focus and generative semantics. Kronberg: Scriptor Verag GmbH.

Shaw, Mary and Helen Neuenswander. 1966. Achi. Languages of Guatemala, ed. by Marvin K. Mayers. Janua Linguarum, studia memoriae, series practica XXIII. 15-48. The Hague: Mouton.

Silverstein, Michael. 1972. Chinook jargon: language contact and the problem of multi-level generative systems, I and II. Language 48. 378-406, 596-625.

Snyder, Warren A. 1968. So. Puget Sound Salish: phonology and morphology. Sacramento Anthropological Society Paper 8.

Sohn, Ho-Min and B.W. Bender. 1973. A Ulithian grammar. Pacific Linguistics, Series C. No. 27. Canberra: Australian National University.

Spagnola, L.M. 1933. Bari grammar. Verona: Missoni Africane.

Steele, Susan. 1975. A law of order: word order change in Classical Aztec. IJAL 42.1. 31-45.

_____. n.d. Luiseño field notes.

Stewart, J.A. 1955. Manual of colloquial Burmese. London: Luzac and Co., Ltd.

Swift, Lloyd B. 1963. A reference grammar of Modern Turkish. Uralic and Altaic Series Vol. 19. Indiana University Publications.

Teeter, Karl. 1973. The main features of Malecite-Passamaquoddy grammar. Studies in American Indiana languages, ed. by Jesse Sawyer. UCPL 65.

_____. 1964. The Wiyot language. UCPL 37.

Tryon, D.T. 1968. Iai grammar. Pacific Linguistics, Series B. No. 8. Canberra: Australian National University.

_____. 1970. An introduction to Maranungku (Northern Australia). Pacific Linguistics, Series B. No. 15. Canberra: Australian National University.

Tyler, Stephen A. 1969. Koya: an outline grammar. UCPL 54.

Vennemann, Theo. 1974. Topics, subject and word order: from SXV to SVX via TVX. Historical linguistics, ed. by J.M. Anderson and C. Jones, 339-376. Amsterdam: North Holland Pub.

Williams, Marianne Mithun. 1973. A case of unmarked subordination in Tuscarora. You take the high node and I'll take the low node, 89-95.

Yallop, Colin. 1975. The Narinjari language 1864-1964. Narinjari: an outline of the language studied by George Taplin. Oceania Linguistics Monograph No. 17, Part 1. 1-109. Sydney.

Figure and Ground
in Complex Sentences

LEONARD TALMY

ABSTRACT

The asymmetry of a sentence like <u>The bike is near the house</u> is shown by its meaning-difference from [?]<u>The house is near the bike</u> and can be ascribed to its nominals' having different semantic roles, here called Figure and Ground. These roles -- in embodying special semantic notions and applying to nominals in many sentence-types -- overcome certain differences in Fillmore's case system. In addition to nominals, the roles pertain as well to the clauses in a complex sentence, where their significance seems to be the same as that of 'asserted' and 'presupposed,' and so constitute a generalization over these notions. In a complex sentence in general, it appears that every asymmetric relation between two propositions can be expressed (or expressed more simply) in only one direction. The particular directional bias in each case is probably universal. Thus, probably no language has, beside a form like <u>We went out although it was raining</u>, expression for any inverse form like *<u>It was raining in-noneffective-counteractance-to our going out.</u> Universal principles seem to determine the direction of bias for the various relations, e.g.: an earlier/causing event tends to be treated as Ground (presupposed) in the subordinate clause, with respect to a later/resulting event as Figure (asserted) in the main clause.

This is a revised and amplified version of a paper by the same title appearing in Working Papers on Language Universals, issue No. 17, June 1975; © 1975 by the Board of Trustees of the Leland Stanford Junior University.

CONTENTS

Figure and Ground

We begin by noticing a certain pair of cognitive-semantic categories. Their relevance shows up, in the first instance, in relation
to a semantic event of motion or location (as treated in Talmy 1975b),
i.e. one considered to signify

one physical object moving or located with respect to another.

Here, each object is taken as bearing to the whole event a significant and distinct relation, termed respectively that of "Figure"
and that of "Ground."   The following sentences can serve for
immediate exemplification of these categories:

The pen lay on the table.
The pen fell off the table.

In both, the pen specifies the object which functions as Figure,
and the table the object which functions as Ground.   The terms
have been taken from Gestalt psychology, but are here given the
following particular characterization for use in linguistic semantics:

The Figure object is a moving or conceptually movable
point whose path or site is conceived as a variable the particular value of which is the salient issue.

The Ground object is a reference-point, having a stationary
setting within a reference-frame, with respect to which the
Figure's path or site receives characterization.[1]

---

[1] One can see with the aid of the diagram below -- schematizing,
as an example, a pen falling off a table -- that for there to be any
notion of the motion of an object (i.e. the Figure), there must also
be present both a reference-point (the Ground) and a reference-
frame.

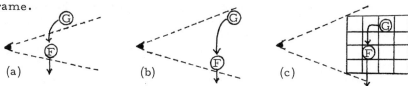

(a)   (b)   (c)

For, as illustrated in (a), if an observer (or conceiver) has in sight
(or mind) only the Figure object, he can know only that the object
exists, but nothing of change of position. Even when, as in (b), the
observer sees both Figure and Ground objects -- still without any
reference-frame, however -- he can additionally know only that there

While these categories are clearly assignable within a motion
event where one object is moving and the other is stationary, they
might there be thought to be merely a restatement of the fact of
movement vs. locatedness rather than independent notions in their
own right. The existence of these categories in semantics can be
demonstrated, therefore, in a locational event where both objects
are stationary. Thus, whereas one might expect two sentences
like

    a. The bike is near the house.
    b. The house is near the bike.

to be synonymous on the grounds that they simply represent the two
inverse forms of a symmetric relation, they in fact do not mean
the same thing. They <u>would</u> be synonymous if they specified <u>only</u>
this symmetric relation -- i.e., here, the quantity of distance between two objects. But in addition to this a. makes the non-symmetric specifications that, of the two objects, one (the house) has
a set location within a framework (here, implicitly, the neighbor-
hood, world, etc.) and is to be used as a reference-point by which
to characterize the other object's (the bike's) location, understood
as a variable (realistically so in this instance, since the bike will
be in different locations on different occasions) whose particular
value is the salient issue. On the other hand, b. makes all the
reverse specifications -- ones which do not happen to conform with
the exigencies of the familiar world, and hence more clearly flag
the sentence as different from a. The non-synonymy of the two
sentences is thus due to the differentiality with which their nominals
specify the semantic functions of variable-point and reference-point,

----

(ftnt. 1 cont.)
is a change from the two objects' being together to their being apart,
but could not know which object (or if both) moved nor whether there
is any further motion once the two objects are apart, since there is
no way to determine (change of) distance. Only when the observer
sees both objects within a framework, as in c., can he know which
object is stationary, which object moves, by how much, and along
what path. The notion of the motion of an object also crucially depends on the correlation of the spatial points of its path with points
of the temporal continuum, but this will be taken up in detail in a
subsequent study on space and time in language.
    I am not committed to the terms "Figure" and "Ground" for
the concepts involved. Other terms, e.g. "variable element"
and "reference element" may be preferable to some.

i.e. of Figure and Ground, as can be indicated by parenthesized function markings abbreviatedly symbolized as F and G:

    a. The bike (F) is near the house (G).
    b. The house (F) is near the bike (G).[2]

Even where a speaker does not want to assert anything about relative referencing, language inescapably <u>imposes</u> that semantic addition upon a basic proposition in formulations like the preceding. It might at first be thought that certain grammatical constructions, e.g. the reciprocal, are specific means available in a language with which to avoid expressing the referencing notion. But in fact, the reciprocal does not abstract the symmetric relation common to two inverse asymmetric forms, but rather <u>adds</u> the two together. This is shown by the fact that the reciprocal for the present example is odd in the same way that the second sentence above is odd:

[?]The bike and the house (F_1 & F_2) are near each other (G_2 & G_1).

---

[2]In this example the nominals' semantic roles vary in correlation with their surface grammatical relation (subject or nonsubject). In other cases the nominals keep the same semantic role, even through changes in surface relation:
    a. Smoke (F) slowly filled the room (G).
    b. The room (G) slowly filled with smoke (F).
-- as we know by virtue of the fact that the same nominal (the room) retains its reference-point function with respect to the other's (the smoke's) motion.
    There is clearly a semantic difference between such inverse forms, but it seems to involve other factors than variable-point vs. reference-point. One such factor may be "perspectival viewpoint": where one places one's mental eyes to look out over the rest of the scene (see Talmy 1976b). Thus, for a., the author feels himself riding the crest of an advancing smoke wave, while for b., he is positioned at the room's rear watching the wave approach. (Viewpoint difference is lexicalized in ENGLISH's two generic pronouns <u>you</u>/<u>they</u>. Witness the difference in a. and b. between the perspective of a smoker and of a potential tobacconist in talking to a neighborhood resident:
    a. Where can you buy cigarettes around here?
        or: Where do they sell cigarettes around here?
    b. Where do they buy cigarettes around here?
        or: Where can you sell cigarettes around here?)

Consideration now of some non-physical situations that behave
homologously with the preceding physical ones will help develop
further the Figure / Ground notion.   Thus, though some might
at first claim an invertible symmetry for it, the locative-like
sentence

   a. She resembles him.

-- which can be taken to derive from something like

      She is near him in appearance.
   or Her appearance is near his appearance. --

is not understood in the same sense as

   b. He resembles her.

for all the reasons given above: that not merely quantity of resemblance is being specified, but, additionally, that one of the objects
is taken as a reference-point and the other object is taken to have
a variability whose particular value is at issue.   These additional
understandings are brought into relief when, beside the above
locative-like sentences, we place the motion-like sentence

   a. She grew to resemble him.

which would never be claimed to be equivalent to

   b. He grew to resemble her.

An 'equational' sentence, whose very name implies an assumption of its invertible equivalence, actually shows the same difference
between its nominals as to variable vs. reference-point functions as
was seen above for the spatial sentences.   This can be seen upon
semantic inspection of an inverse-pair of sentences like that below
in an example drawn from comicdom, where it is known that the
'real' identity of the man from Krypton is 'Superman' and his identity of disguise is 'Clark Kent.' It is thus appropriate to treat the
former identity as a fixed reference point and the latter identity as
displaced therefrom, and inappropriate to treat them in the reverse
way, hence the difference in acceptability between the otherwise
equivalent inverse sentences:

   Clark Kent is Superman.
   ?Superman is Clark Kent. [3]   (ftnt. next page)

So far from any aptness in characterizing 'equational' sentences like the preceding on the model of mathematics, quite the reverse is the case. For, in the standard form of equations, like

$$y = 3x^2 + 1,$$

y, Figure-like, is considered a 'dependent variable' and appears alone on the left, while x, Ground-like, is considered an

---

(ftnt. 3 from previous page)

So semantically parallel are 'equational' sentences to locative sentences that I would even propose including in their underlying structures a deep preposition homologous with at, as if one could say at the surface, e. g.

Clark Kent is at Superman.

There is in fact syntactic evidence for something of this sort in ENGLISH with the preposition as, at least for copula sentences where the second nominal expresses the role or function of the first:

Jim is on the throne in the play. ⇒ The play has Jim on the throne (in it).
Jim is [as] the king in the play. ⇒ The play has Jim as the king (in it).

Some languages do have a pre-/postposition at the surface beside the 'predicate nominal' of a copula sentence, SAMOAN overtly so with its 'o preposition as in

'o   se atua ia
"(as) a god he"   'He was a god. '

'o le agasala 'ea   le tulafono
"(as) the sin (interrogative) the law"   'Is the law sin? '

and JAPANESE, somewhat disguisedly, in its desu verb, as in

kore   wa   pen desu
"this (topic-marker) pen is"   'This is a pen. '

This latter in some of its paradigmatic forms clearly breaks up into a postpositional particle de plus the verb aru (otherwise the 'be-located' verb for inanimate objects); the coalesced form desu follows the only postpositionless nouns in JAPANESE. The de coalesced in desu may be identified with the elsewhere-appearing postposition de, having instrumental 'with' meaning, making the whole JAPANESE copula construction with desu parallel to that of RUSSIAN, where the 'predicate nominal' is in the instrumental case, as in

On byl doktorom (instr).
"he was (as) a doctor!"   'He was a doctor. '

'independent variable,' appears on the right, and is there grouped
together with all operators and modifiers. This arrangement has
no purely mathematical significance but rather derives from the
same cognitive-semantic processes which determine the form of
sentences like

> The bike is to the left of the house.
> Clark Kent is really Superman in disguise.

Complex Sentences

   Now, what the categories Figure and Ground pertain to can
be generalized from the relative location of objects in space to the
relative location of events in time -- spatio-temporal homologies
such as are illustrated by the following sentence pairs:

> The fly was located (at a point) along the branch.
> The explosion took place (at a point) during the performance.

> Flies were located all along the branch.
> Explosions took place all during the performance.

> This road goes (extends) for three miles/to the next town.
> The performance went on (lasted) for three hours/until 11 o'clock.

Paralleling that given earlier for spatial objects, the categories can
be given the following more precise characterization for temporal
events:

> The temporal site of the Figure event is considered as a
> variable whose particular value receives characterization
> with respect to a Ground event, considered as a reference-
> point set in a temporal reference-frame (usually, the one-
> dimensional time-line).

Figure and Ground, applied to events, are very near, if not
the same as, 'assertion' and 'presupposition' for propositions, and
constitute a generalization of these notions because of their applying
as well to object referents.

   The applicability of these semantic categories to temporal structures can be seen in a complex sentence like

> He exploded after he touched the button.

which seems to assign a Ground interpretation to the button-touching event— setting it up as a fixed, known reference-point -- and seems to assign a Figure interpretation to the explosion event— establishing the location in time of this more salient occurrence with respect to the other. That such assignments have really taken place is perhaps demonstrated simply by noting that the inverse sentence

He touched the button before he exploded.

is different in meaning: to this speaker, in fact, it sounds comical, acquiring a becoming seriousness only after the imagining of such special circumstances as an official search into the possible causes of a known death. [4]

Since either asymmetric relation in an 'inverse-pair' equally well specifies the same relational information, the advantage to a language in having lexification for both -- as ENGLISH has in before/after -- is precisely that either of the related events can be specified as functioning as the Figure. In any language, however, there are inverse-pairs for which simple means of expression exist for only one of the relations (and it may be deemed that the language's expressive range suffers for the lack of the other). Such is the case in ENGLISH, e.g. for the inverse-pair expressing 'temporal-inclusion' between a 'point event' and an 'extent event.' When it is the point event that is relatively less known and is to be temporally located -- as 'included within' -- with respect to the better known extent event, the relation has simple lexical representation, as in

Shāh Mat of Persia was assassinated during Caesar's reign.

---

[4] The form of the complex sentences cited here -- i.e. consisting of a main and a dependent clause with subordinating conjunction -- derives, as I will develop the matter in a subsequent paper, from a syntactically deeper structure of a different form. This form is more closely reflected in a surface sentence that consists of two nominalized clauses, a relational verb, and a 'subordinating preposition,' as in the following analogs of the cited sentences

His exploding occurred after his touching the button.
His touching the button occurred before his exploding.

This form is homologous with that of a locative sentence. In all three sentence-types -- the simple locative, the complex with preposition, and the complex with conjunction -- the subject(-like) constituent functions as Figure and the object(-like) one as Ground.

But when it is the extent event that is relatively less known and is
to be temporally located -- as 'including' -- with respect to the better
known point event, there is no simple apt lexical representation,
as seen in

$^?$Shāh Rūkh ruled Persia $\begin{cases} \text{around} \\ \text{through} \\ \text{before and after} \end{cases}$ Christ's crucifixion.

Although this inverse-pair is exemplified for ENGLISH, one
might expect to find all languages having the same bias toward the
'included within' pair-member. In fact, probably for every inverse-
relation-pair, there holds one of two universal statements, an implicational one:

  a. Only where a language has some, or simple, or simpler
     lexical means for the specification of an asymmetric rela-
     tion R (of a complex situation) does it also have means for
     the specification of the inverse relation R^{-1}.

or an absolute one:

  b. Whereas a language may have lexical means for the speci-
     fication of the asymmetric relation R (of a complex situa-
     tion), it never has such for the inverse relation R^{-1}.

Besides 'during,' an example of a relation to which the first
universal statement seems to apply is 'after.'[5] ENGLISH, of course,
has the presence of lexical means, and equally simple such, for the
specification both of this relation and of its inverse in the words
after and before. A TSUGEWI for one, however, expresses the notion 'after' simply and directly with a verb suffix (akin in function
to RUSSIAN's 'past gerundive' ending), as in

  Having-eaten, we left.

whereas it expresses the notion 'before' in a more complex and
indirect way (by the addition of two independent words to the 'after'
verb form), as in the inverse counterpart of the preceding:

  Still not having-left, we ate.

---

[5] The remarks made here about particular relations that exemplify
the universals are not based on a survey of many languages but
rather on a spot check, and are accordingly to be considered heu-
ristic, pointing out a direction for investigation.

Universal a., if it is true for 'after' vs. 'before,' thus implies that
a language may, like ENGLISH, have means for expressing 'before'
equally simple as for 'after,' or may, like ATSUGEWI, have less
direct means for expressing 'before' than 'after,' but that no language will have simpler and more direct means for expressing
'before' than 'after.'

An example of a relation to which the second universal statement seems to apply is 'all-during,' as expressed at the surface,
e.g. in ENGLISH, by all during, the whole time that, while, etc.
Since this relation may at first seem symmetric (aside from issues
of Figure and Ground), it first behooves us to show that it is
not. This can be done by demonstrating that there is a difference
in the characteristics required of the first and of the second events
which may comprise the terms of the relation, and that therefore
the terms cannot always be acceptably reversed. The sentences
below reveal that for the second event in the relation, the extent
of time occupied is necessarily bounded at both ends, for a second-
position clause which specifies an inherently unbounded (at either
end) event, such as the state of being dead, creates an unacceptable
sentence:

She was studying in an American college the whole time
that $\begin{cases} \text{her father in Iran was ill.} \\ \text{*her father in Iran was dead.} \end{cases}$

On the other hand, the first event in the relation is not necessarily
bounded at both ends, as is shown by putting into first-position the
same clause specifying an inherently unbounded event and this time
getting an acceptable sentence:

Her father in Iran was dead the whole time that she was
studying in an American college (but she didn't know it).

The difference between the first and second events as to the necessity of the temporal boundedness is schematized in the following
diagram:

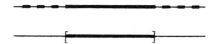

With the asymmetry of 'all-during' thus receiving a first demonstration, the second universal's holding for this relation would
mean that while many languages may have a direct means for
expressing the equivalent of

Her father in Iran was dead
   while she was studying in an American college
   (but she didn't know it).

none will have the means for expressing

*She was studying in an American college
   while^{-1} her father in Iran was dead.

For a second demonstration of the asymmetry of 'all-during,' it is
to be noticed of the two events comprising the terms of this relation that if the possibility of occurrence of one event is contingent
on the occurrence of the other, it is only the former which can
function as the relation's first term. For example, since the act
of dreaming is contingent on the state of being asleep, a clause
specifying the former can acceptably appear only in first-position
in a sentence which specifies the occurrence, extensionality, and
contemporaneousness of the two events:

He dreamt while he slept.
*He slept while he dreamt.

The second universal's holding for this redemonstratedly asymmetric relation 'all-during' would mean that no language has a
lexical equivalent for while^{-1} such that it can express the equivalent of

*He slept while^{-1} he dreamt. [6]

and indeed, in at least the several languages I have asked for such
a form in, none exists.

   It can be clear only after an extensive survey of languages
whether there exists any universal bias toward one as against the
other relation of asymmetric inverse-pairs like those above as
well as of other pair-types. And it would have to be determined
whether such bias is total or is proportional, involving relative
simplicity of expression. But it is tentatively suggested that such

––––––––––––––––––––––––––––––

[6] Not to be confused with this apparently universally lacking
form is a form present in many languages, including ENGLISH,
which arises secondarily by a process I have called 'copy-clefting'
(Talmy, 1975a, this volume):

He slept $\begin{Bmatrix} \text{and he dreamt the while} \\ \Longrightarrow \text{dreaming (the while)} \end{Bmatrix}$.

a survey will reveal that sentences like the upper ones of the following pairs (merely an illustrative selection) represent the favored,
or unmarked, relations of inverse-pairs, and that sentences like
the lower ones represent relations — the corresponding inverses —
which either are never or are not more simply expressed -- and
which in most cases here can in fact be indicated only by devised
ENGLISH phrases:[7]

   a. She departed <u>after</u> his arrival. (... <u>after</u> he arrived.)
      He arrived <u>before</u> her departure.

   b. He had two affairs <u>during</u> his marriage. (... <u>while</u> he was married.)
      He was married <u>through-a-period-containing</u> two affairs of his.

   c. He dreamt <u>(all)</u> <u>during</u> his sleep. (...<u>while</u>/<u>the whole time</u> he slept.)
      He slept <u>(all)</u> <u>during</u>$^{-1}$ his dreaming. (... <u>while</u>$^{-1}$ he dreamt.)

   d. He's playing <u>instead of</u>/<u>rather than</u> working.
      He's not working <u>in-replacement-by</u> playing.

   e. She awoke <u>upon</u> his arrival. (...<u>when</u> he arrived.)
      He arrived <u>immediately-(and-causally)-before</u> her awakening.

   f. She slept <u>until</u> his arrival. (...<u>until</u> he arrived.)
      He arrived <u>immediately-(and-causally)-before-the-end-of</u>
                             her sleeping.

   g. We stayed home <u>because of</u> his arrival. (...<u>because</u> he had
                                         arrived.)
      He arrived <u>to-the-occasioning-of-(the-decision-of)</u> our staying
                                         home.)

---

[7] This investigation, it should be reemphasized, only involves
the expression of relationships by a subordinator in a complex sentence. There do exist coordinate sentences that express the related
propositions in the same order as in the lower pair-members. Thus,
there are, for example, the following counterpart sentences:
   d'. He's not working, but playing instead.
   g'. He arrived, (and) so we stayed home.
   h'. He arrived, but we went out anyway.
But even these forms are not countercases to the bias observation.
For in such coordinate sentences, the right-hand clause is equivalent
to the whole of one of the complex sentences, and always one of the
favored ones. (We conclude thus on the basis that <u>instead</u> = <u>instead</u>
<u>of that,</u> <u>so</u> = <u>because of that,</u> and <u>anyway</u> = <u>despite that,</u> as argued
in Talmy 1975a, this volume).

h. We went out <u>despite</u> his arrival. (...<u>even though</u> he had arrived.)
He arrived <u>in-ineffective-counteracting-of- (the-decision-of)</u>
                                                                our going out.

i. We'll stay home <u>in the event of</u> his arrival. (...<u>if</u> he arrives.)
He will arrive <u>as-a-potential-event-effectively-occasioning</u>
                                                        our staying home.

j. We'll go out <u>except in the event of</u> his arrival. (... <u>unless</u> he
                                                                    arrives.)
He will arrive <u>as-the-sole-potential-effective-counteractant</u> to
                                                        our going out.

k. The door slammed shut <u>from</u> the wind blowing on it.
The wind blew on the door <u>to</u> its slamming shut.

l. I broke the window <u>by</u> leaning against it.
I leaned against the window <u>to</u> breaking it.

An inspection of the biases in this array reveals that each is not
simply peculiar to its own relation-pair, but that they generally
follow a pattern. Consider those pairs for which the two related
events are temporally sequential with respect to each other -- viz.
a. and e.-l. -- rather than overlapping or substitutional, as in b., c.
and d. With the exception of the <u>until</u>-type in f. (though see below),
the favored relation has the earlier-occurring event in the subordinate clause and the later-occurring event in the main clause, where
they function, respectively, as Ground and Figure. This observation suggests that there may exist for language the following possibly
universal tendency.

The unmarked (or only possible) linguistic expression for
any particular relation between two events that are in temporal
sequence treats the earlier event as a reference-point, or
Ground, and the later event as requiring referencing, i.e. as
the Figure.

Where the complete surface form is that of a whole complex
sentence, the two events are accordingly expressed in the
subordinate clause and in the main clause, respectively.[8]

---

[8]The reason for putting it this way -- with semantic roles given
precedence over syntactic forms -- is that there <u>are</u> certain variant
syntactic forms which nevertheless basically conform to the semantic bias. These include surface forms in which what would

All the above relation-types with sequential events can, and
some chiefly do, express causality between the events. A pattern
can be discerned here, too. The favored pair-member has the
causing event in its subordinate clause and the resulting event in the
main clause. Now, in the physical world, cause and result correlate
with earlier and later, and if cognition and language always followed
suit with physics, this linguistic finding about causality could have
been predicted from the previous one about sequentiality. They do
not, however, and so the observation about causality (demonstrated
more detailedly in Talmy 1976a: 55-58) prompts an independent
statement of suggested universal tendency:

> The unmarked (or only possible) linguistic expression for a
> causal relation between two events treats the causing event
> as Ground and the resulting event as Figure. Where the com-
> plete surface form is a full complex sentence, the two events
> are in the subordinate and the main clause, respectively.

The problem of <u>until</u>'s apparently exceptional sequential properties may find resolution by observation of its causal properties.
For when the relation has a causal implication -- as it can in the
top sentence of f. -- this follows the general pattern at least to this
extent: the causing event -- 'his arrival' in f. -- is expressed in the
subordinate clause. Now, semantically, what this event causes is
<u>not</u> the event expressed in the surface main clause -- 'her sleeping'
in f. -- but rather the <u>end</u> of that event. And temporally, that end
is indeed after the causing event. From this, we may infer a deeper
precursor for the <u>until</u> forms, one for which both the clauses conform to both the universal tendencies. Such a deeper form, if exemplified for f., would look like:

[THE END OF [she slept]] BE AT [he arrived].

This form would then be taken to derive into either alternative of:

[she slept] $\begin{Bmatrix} \text{HAVE-ITS-END AT} \\ \text{EXTEND UNTIL} \end{Bmatrix}$ [he arrived],

---

(ftnt. 8 cont.)
otherwise be the subordinate clause appears as a pronoun, as in
(i), is implicit or deleted, as in (ii), or is conflated into the main
clause (see Talmy 1975b: 222-38 for this), as in (iii):
   (i)   He arrived; she left despite that [= his arriving].
   (ii) She broke the window [by ACTing ON it with SOMETHING].
   (iii) I kicked the ball over the fence.
       [< I MOVEd the ball over the fence by kicking it.]

which would give rise to the roughly equivalent surface sentences:

She stopped sleeping when he arrived.
She slept until he arrived.

Of the list above, we have not yet dealt with three relation-pairs, each with a bias toward one pair-member -- the 'at-times-during' type, the 'all-during' type, and the 'instead-of' type in b., c. and d. Each of these involves a relational property that is unique in the list and is, of course, instantiated only for ENGLISH. In future research, accordingly, we should look for relation-types considered that might share the property -- and should check all these types in other languages -- to see if there is the same bias. But the bias in the cases at hand is so strong that we tentatively put forward already the following possible universal tendencies:

A larger, temporally-containing event acts as Ground (in the subordinate clause) with respect to a contained event as Figure (in the main clause).

A necessary (i.e. ontologically prior) event acts as Ground (in the subordinate clause) with respect to a contingent event as Figure (in the main clause).

A non-occurrent event acts as Ground (in the subordinate clause) with respect to an occurrent event as Figure (in the main clause).

If these universal tendencies prove to be the case, we can speculate on deeper reasons for them. Assuming that linguistic universals reflect innate organizational and functional characteristics of the language-related portions of the brain, we may suppose that some of these characteristics are continuous with those of more general cognition-related areas. Let us consider here only the first universal about sequential events from this perspective.

At times a newly cognized item will illuminate or necessitate the rearrangement of items already in memory. But generally it seems that items in memory constitute the basis, afford the analytic categories, and function as the reference-points by which a newly cognized item is assessed, characterized, and analyzed. In particular, of two non-concurrent events, both cognized, the earlier one will, of course, already be in memory when the later one is newly occurrent, and so is generally to be used as part basis for the latter's assessment. The parallelism between this cognitive

characteristic -- the earlier used as basis for assessing the later --
and the linguistic characteristic -- earlier and later treated seman-
tically/syntactically as Ground/subordinate-clause and Figure/
main-clause -- suggests the following: this feature of cognitive functioning may well have become incorporated in the innate structuring
for conceptual/grammatical organization of the brain's speech area,
as this evolved.[9]

There is another tendential feature of language organization for
which deeper reasons should be sought: in a simplex or complex
sentence, the Figure constituent appears as the subject or main
clause, and the Ground constituent appears as some form of object
or in the subordinate clause. But this must remain a matter for
future speculation.

APPENDIX

A few further notes on the characteristics of Figure and Ground
are presented here in amplification of the text. At the end, this
paper's system is compared with Fillmore's case system and applied to some child language data from Bowerman.

1. The two-role system presented in this paper has been abstracted
from a more extensive system that has been observed for language
and described elsewhere. In this, Figure and Ground -- insofar as
they pertain to moving or located objects -- are two components out
of four that make up the next more complex unit, an event of motion
or location. The other two components are the "Path" -- the particular course followed or site occupied by the Figure with respect
to the Ground -- and the "State-of-Motion" -- which can be either
'moving' or 'stationary.' Outside the motion/location event proper,
the Figure can concurrently be in some independent activity or
state; this bears a relation -- one that I term "Manner" -- to the
first event. These elements can be illustrated with our original
example sentences:

_____

[9] There is still this problem, though: hearing a sequential-type
complex sentence involves the cognizing not of two actually occurring separate events, but of adjacent descriptions thereof. And so,
it is not completely obvious why a connection should have arisen
here between cognition and language.

The pen rolled off / lay on the table.

Here, the Path is specified by off and on (as being, respectively:
'away from any point of the surface of' and 'at a point of the surface
of'), the State-of-Motion is specified by rolled and lay (as: 'moved'
and 'was located'), and a Manner is simultaneously specified by
these same words (as: 'spinning about the axis [the while]' and 'in
horizontal contact along its length [the while]').

For any understanding of syntax that distinguishes a "rationalized"
level from an "observable" level,[10] all the above elements seem --
from much evidence within and across languages -- to be universally
associated, at the rationalized level, with particular syntactic categories and relations.   E.g. in terms of generative underlying structure, a motion/location event would be represented by a four-constituent
phrase-marker; the Figure object by the subject nominal; the Ground
object by the (oblique-) object nominal; the Path by an adposition;
and the State-of-Motion by the verb: in particular by either of two
deep verbs representable as MOVE and BE-Located -- as diagrammed
below. Not shown below, the Manner would be represented by a subordinate clause. Where in fact these elements characteristically
show up in the surface structures of various languages is the basis
for a three-way universal typology, as detailed in Talmy (1973).

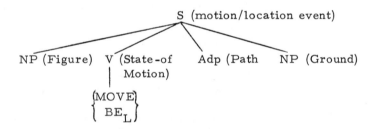

S (motion/location event)

NP (Figure)   V (State-of   Adp (Path   NP (Ground)
                  Motion)

                  $\begin{Bmatrix} \text{MOVE} \\ \text{BE}_L \end{Bmatrix}$

2. A sentence like:

The pen rolled off the table onto the floor.

is not taken to specify two Paths and two Grounds. Rather, it refers
to an event in which the Figure object follows a single path with respect to a single reference-background. These, however, happen

---

[10] Generative grammar does so, with its "underlying" structure
and "surface" structure; and dual-hierarchy grammar does so,
with its "logical" level and "pragmatic" level.

to be of a (complex) kind that is not simply characterizable in surface structure. Some Path and Ground cases of this kind can be
referred to at the surface both in simple and in compound form.
In such cases, the underlying comparability of the two types of
surface form can be more easily recognized:

I swam from one to the other side of the river in one minute.
I swam across the river in one minute.

3. The Path component in general is not a simplex element at
the underlying level, but has much regular internal structure. It
would, e.g. represent the ENGLISH surface preposition series
on/onto/off(of) and in/into/out of roughly as in a. and b.:

a. AT/TO/FROM a POINT of the SURFACE of
b. AT/TO/FROM a POINT of the INSIDE of

and thereby abstract the topological feature common to each series
as well as the directional differentiæ therein. The elements of the
internal Path structure generally refer to such abstract directional
notions as 'at,' 'to,' 'from,' 'via,' 'along,' 'alength,' 'from...to' and
such abstract topological notions as 'point,' 'bounded extent,' and
'unbounded extent.' Details appear in Talmy 1975b: 198-206.

4. For simplicity of statement, the original definitions of Figure
and Ground used the word "point" ("...moving or conceptually movable point," "...reference-point"). For their basic definitional
roles to be fulfilled, however, neither element need be topologically
idealizable as a point, but can as well be a multiplicity of points,
a linear extent, an area, or a volume, as illustrated by:

Rocks filled the box.
The river flowed alongside the mountain range.

5. It is possible for a sentence that refers to an event of motion
to leave indeterminate which of two involved objects is the Figure
and which the Ground:

He sheathed his sword.

6. A particular type of motion/location event is one that is
"self-referencing." It involves either a set of objects moving or
positioned with respect to each other, as in a., or a single object
moving or disposed with respect to itself, as in b.:

    a.   The pens rolled apart (away from each other).
         The pens lay in a circle.

    b.   The balloon swelled out (expanded).
         The balloon was round.

The objects in a. are taken as "multiple Figures" moving or located
with respect to each other as their own Grounds. Now, from an
analytic perspective, the object in b. is not really a Figure. Rather,
it is the minute <u>parts</u> of the object that function as multiple Figures,
moving/located with respect to each other as their own Grounds.
The role performed by the object obtains only at a higher level of
semantic/cognitive organization. As a whole, the object functions
as a "meta-Figure" moving/located with respect to itself as its own
"meta-Ground." (See Talmy 1972: 217-34 for details.)

    7.   The language pattern sketched in note 1 is part of a still more
extensive system, one that includes the matter of causation. A causative situation of the most basic sort consists of one motion event
causing another. As argued in the text (e.g. for the basic causative
sentence in k.), the resulting event functions as the Figure in the
whole situation, and the causing event as Ground. These semantic
categories and relations can be represented in underlying structure
as diagrammed below:

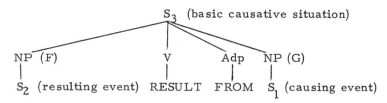

$$S_3 \text{ (basic causative situation)}$$

NP (F)   V   Adp   NP (G)

S_2 (resulting event)   RESULT   FROM S_1 (causing event)

    Now, included in this system is the concept of the derivation of
semantic functions -- i.e., where certain non-basic, higher-level
role notions are construed in a hierarchical structure containing
only basic roles. In particular here, the object that functions as
the Figure in a causing event is understood to function as the "Instrument" with respect to the whole causative situation, as suggested in c. below:

    c. S_1:   A baseball (F_1) sailed into the aerial (G_1)

        S_2:   The aerial (F_2) toppled off the roof (G_2).

        S_3:   The aerial $(F_2 \Rightarrow F_3)$ toppled off the roof $(G_2 \Rightarrow G_3)$
             from a baseball $(F_1 \Rightarrow I_3)$ sailing into it $(G_1 = F_3)$.

In more extensive structures yet, the role of "Agent" is comparably understood as a higher-level notion emerging in a certain
constellation of lower-level roles. These matters are detailed in
Talmy 1976a.

8. Within certain sets of semantically equivalent surface-
structure types, there is a universally observable preponderance
of one of the types over the others. This has led to the present
theory's concept of basicness for such a type and for the particular
association therein of each semantic role with some specific grammatical relation -- and to the notion that the alternative types are
non-basic or derived. Thus, -- though there are some doublets like
The perfume slowly suffused through the room. / The room slowly
suffused with perfume. -- the preponderant occurrence of forms like
The ball rolled into the box. over any forms like *The box rolled
(in) with the ball. has led to the conclusion, as asserted in 1, that
the Figure and the Ground are basically associated, within their
own clause, with the subject and the oblique object, respectively.
Accordingly here, moreover, the Figure preponderantly appears
before the Ground. When the motion/location clause is embedded
within an agentive matrix, the Figure generally appears at the surface as the direct object -- but still before the Ground. Thus it is
that, where we find cases allowing both of the surface-structure
types for both the nonagentive and the agentive -- as with the verbs
suffuse and drain -- we consider half of the four forms to be in basic
order and half in non-basic, or "inverted," order:

    basic: Perfume (F) suffused through the room (G).
    inverted: The room (G) suffused with perfume (F).
    basic: I (A) suffused perfume (F) through the room (G).
    inverted: I (A) suffused the room (G) with perfume (F).

    basic: The blood (F) drained from his veins (G).
    inverted: His veins (G) drained of their blood (F).
    basic: I (A) drained the blood (F) from his veins (G).
    inverted: I (A) drained his veins (G) of their blood (F).

It is to be noted that in any language, certain notions involving
motion/location have surface expression only in an inverted form.
E.g., while the Path notion 'TO ALL POINTs of the SURFACE of'
can be expressed in a basic-order agentive sentence in ENGLISH
with the preposition all over:

    I (A) poured water (F) all over the table (G).

the parallel Path notion 'TO ALL POINTs of the INSIDE of' has
only inverted-order expression:

*I (A) poured water (F) all/full into the glass (G).
  I (A) poured the glass (G) full of water (F).

*I (A) filled water (F) (all) into the glass (G).
  I (A) filled the glass (G) with water (F).

Comparably, the Path notion 'INTO COLLISION WITH,' associated
with the action of 'throwing,' has no basic-order preposition to represent it, but must be expressed in inverted order with the here
suppletively used verb hit:

*I (A) threw/hit the ball (F) into/against the man (G).
  I (A) hit the man (G) with the ball (F).

All these matters are detailed in Talmy 1972: 301-75.

   9. We set out now to compare Fillmore's (1968) case system
with the system outlined in this paper, and to point out certain dif-
ficulties with the former that are overcome by the latter.

   In Fillmore's system, several problems arise out of the fact
that all the cases are ranged together on a single level without
subgrouping or some other index of abstracted commonality. Thus,
firstly, there is nothing explicit in the system to show that six of
the cases:

Source, Goal, Path, Locative, Patient, Instrument

have in common the property of pertaining to objects moving or
located with respect to one another — as distinguished, e.g., from
Agent. By contrast, the present system abstracts that property
out into its integral and embeddable unit, the motion/location
event, in which appear only those case roles that together are
equivalent to the above set of six.

   Secondly, there is nothing in Fillmore's system to show that
the first four of the above cases, Source, Goal, Path, and Locative,
have in common a property -- viz. their function as reference-point
-- not shared by any other case, such as Patient, Instrument, or
for that matter, Agent. By contrast, the present system abstracts
out precisely what is common to these cases, their reference-point
function, and sets that up in its own right as the pertinent role notion, Ground.

   Thirdly, there is nothing in Fillmore's system to show that of
the preceding four related cases, the first three, Source, Goal,

Path, have in common a property that is counterposed by a property
of the fourth case, Locative -- viz. pertaining to motion as against
stationariness. In the present system, the pair of properties as a
set is abstracted out as a category in its own right, State-of-Motion.
Each property is individually designated by a deep verb, MOVE or
BE$_L$. And the properties' counterposed complementarity is captured by the condition that one and only one of the two verbs must
appear in underlying structure.

There is also a set of problems in Fillmore's system associated
with its incorporating certain dimensional/spatiodirectional specifics
in its very case-role notions. Such problems do not arise in the
present system, where all such specifics are abstracted out into
an independent component, Path. Thus, firstly, because of the
distribution among the cases of certain directional characteristics,
there is no way within the Fillmore system to capture in one place
certain other characteristics held in common -- e.g. to abstract
out the topological 'SURFACE' feature possessed in common by
the referents of on N (Loc), onto N (Goal), and off of N (Source) --
as does take place within the present system's Path component.

Secondly, using directional features as the basis for setting
up distinct cases entails the problem as to which features of what
degree of fineness should be used and, correlatively, how many
cases of what sort there should be. E.g. the directional features
'from,' 'to,' and 'along' seem to be the differential bases for having
set up the cases Source, Goal, and Path, which, accordingly, well
suit such nominals as the final ones in:

                    The ball rolled --
    Source: out of the bathroom/ off the table / away from the sofa.
    Goal: into the kitchen / onto the carpet / up to the wall.
    Path: along the hallway.

But to what cases -- the preceding ones or some new ones -- are we
to assign the final nominals in:

                    The ball rolled
                    across the crack / past the TV / around the lamp. ?

Likewise, the same issue is raised by the very applicability, as
just seen, of a case like Goal to many distinct forms like into N,
onto N, and up to N. Should there not be as many cases here as
distinct expressions? The issue here of how fine to set the case-
distinguishing features causes special problems in the context of
the remainder of Fillmore's case system. For other cases are

associated with only a single meaning-preserving surface marker,
as Instrument is with <u>with</u>, whereas the cases here are associated
with many different surface markers that add distinctions of meaning. The present system's Path component must face comparable
issues -- i.e., where and how to represent all the distinctions and
capture all the generalizations relevant to spatiotemporal characteristics -- but it has more, and more flexible, internal machinery
to do so, not the single dimension of noun cases that must also suit
other, quite distinct functions.

10. Melissa Bowerman (personal communication) has found the
linguistic Figure-Ground notions relevant to interpreting certain
data from her daughter Christy from 3;6 to 4;6 years of age.
When Christy at 3;6 first started using verbs like <u>hit</u>, <u>bump</u>, and
<u>touch</u> with explicit nominals for both Figure and Ground, she nor-
malized their expression to the predominant pattern. I.e., instead
of the rarer pattern required by these verbs: "I hit/bumped/touched
G with F," as discussed in note 8, she produced forms of the type:
"I hit/bumped/touched F to G." Sometimes this involved undoing
certain one-object forms of the type: "I hit/bumped/touched G,"
which she had earlier produced correctly. There was no problem
of difficulty in introducing a <u>with</u> phrase, for she had been correctly
producing instrumental <u>with</u>s from age 2. Bowerman hypothesizes
that the child at the later age pieces together the notions of Figure
and Ground and the main pattern for their order and grammatical
relations, and then overgeneralizes this. Some examples of utterances (C = Christy, M = mother):

I hitted this into my neck. (After bumping self with toy.)
Feel your hand to that. (= Feel that with your hand.
   C instructing M to put her hand over one end of a hose,
   then C blows through other end.)

Her other daughter, Eva, made the same reformulations, including
ones for <u>fill</u>:

My other hand's not yukky. See? 'Cause I'm gonna
   touch it on your pants.
This is something we can fill some stuff up in. (Bringing
                                             basket to C.)
M: You can get a baggie out of the drawer.
E: Then fill some marshmellows up in it?

BIBLIOGRAPHY

Fillmore, C.J. 1968. The case for case. Universals in linguistic theory, ed. by E. Bach and R.T. Harms. New York: Holt, Rinehart and Winston.

Talmy, L. 1972. Semantic structures in English and Atsugewi. Doctoral dissertation, University of California, Berkeley.

_____. 1973. The basis for a crosslinguistic typology of motion/location, Parts 1 and 2. Working Papers on Language Universals 9 and 11. Stanford University.

_____. 1975a. Relations between subordination and coordination (this volume).

_____. 1975b. Semantics and syntax of motion. Syntax and semantics, Vol. 4. New York: Academic Press.

_____. 1976a. Semantic causative types. Syntax and semantics, Vol. 6. New York: Academic Press.

_____. 1976b. Communicative aims and means. Working Papers on Language Universals 20. Stanford University.

_____. 1977. Rubber-sheet cognition in language. Proceedings of the Chicago Linguistic Society, Vol. 13. University of Chicago.

Indexes

Index of Languages

Index of Authors Cited